The Encyclopedia of

GARDENING
TECHNIQUES

EDITOR IN CHIEF: CHRISTOPHER BRICKELL, DIRECTOR OF THE R.H.S. GARDEN

Exeter Books*New York

The Encyclopedia of Gardening Techniques

Editor-in-chief Christopher Brickell
Technical editor Kenneth A. Beckett

The Royal Horticultural Society's Encyclopedia of
Practical Gardening
© Mitchell Beazley Publishers 1981
The Royal Horticultural Society's Concise
Encyclopedia of Gardening Techniques
© Mitchell Beazley Publishers 1983

First published in USA 1984
by Exeter Books
Distributed by Bookthrift
Exeter is a trademark of Simon & Schuster, Inc.
Bookthrift is a registered trademark of Simon & Schuster, Inc.
New York, New York
ISBN 0-671-07047-9

The Royal Horticultural Society's Concise
Encyclopedia of Gardening Techniques was
edited and designed by Mitchell Beazley

Phototypesetting by Tradespools Ltd, Frome, Somerset
Origination by Culver Graphics Ltd,
High Wycombe, Buckinghamshire
Printed in Italy by New Interlitho Spa, Milan

Contributors

Tony Biggs, who wrote the section on vegetables, is a former
lecturer in horticulture at Wye College, University of London. He
now lectures in Australia.

Kenneth A Beckett, Technical Editor of the Encyclopaedia and
contributor of the section on growing under glass, is a full-time
gardening writer and consultant.

Christopher Brickell, Editor-in-Chief of the Encyclopaedia and
author of the chapter on pruning, is Director of the Royal
Horticultural Society's Garden at Wisley, Surrey.

Harry Baker, who writes on fruit, is Fruit Officer at the Royal
Horticultural Society's Garden at Wisley.

David Pycraft, who contributed the sections on lawns and ground
cover, is on the staff of the Royal Horticultural Society's Garden at
Wisley.

Phillip McMillan Browse, who writes on propagation, has been a
lecturer on the subject for 20 years.

Alan Titchmarsh, author of the basic techniques section, trained as
a gardener, then lectured at Kew, then built up a reputation as a TV
and radio gardening expert.

Contents

Introduction 4—5

WEATHER AND CLIMATE 6—7

BASIC TECHNIQUES
Soil 8—9
Drainage 10—11
Improving the soil 12—13
Garden compost 14—15
Digging 16—17
Watering 18—19
Basic tools 20—21
Cultivation techniques 22—25
Protecting plants 26
Moving and storing plants 27
Placing plants 28—29
Rock gardens 30—31
Hedges 32—33

VEGETABLES
Crop rotation 34
Lettuces 35—37
Growing brassicas 38
Cabbages 39—41
Brussels sprouts 42—43
Cauliflowers 44—45
Broccoli 46
Kale 47
Spinach/New Zealand spinach 48
Spinach/Swiss Chard 49
Asparagus 50—51
Celery 52
Rhubarb 53
Bush beans 54—55
Runner beans 56—57
Broad beans 58—59
Garden peas 60
Garden peas/Asparagus peas 61
Corn 62

Onions 63—65
Shallots/Garlic 66
Leeks 67
Carrots 68
Parsnips 69
Turnips and Rutabagas 70—71
Beets 72
Radishes 73
Potatoes 74—76
Cucumber 77
Tomatoes 78—79
Squashes 80—82
Sweet potatoes/Southern peas 83
Peppers 84
Eggplants 85
Herbs 86—89

FRUIT
Planning 90—91
Soft fruits 92
Strawberries 93—95
Raspberries 96—98
Blackberries 99—100
Black currants 101—102
Red and white currants 103—104
Gooseberries 105—106
Heathland fruits 107—108
Grapes 109—111
Melons 112
Tree fruits 113
Pollination 114
Planting fruit trees 115
Apples and pears 116—129
Plums 130—132
Sweet and Duke cherries 133—134
Sour cherries 135
Peaches and almonds 136—139
Apricots 140
Passion fruit 141
Citrus fruits 142—143
Pecans 144
Physalis 145

LAWNS
Preparing the site 146—149
Lawn grasses 150—151
Seed or sod? 152
Growing lawns from sod 153—155
Growing lawns from seed 156
Weed control in new lawns 157
Month-by-month guide 158
Mowing 159—160
Weed control in lawns 161
Moss control in lawns 162

GROUND COVER
Preparing the site 163
Planting and spacing 164
Maintenance 165
Problem sites 166—170

WEED CONTROL 171

PROPAGATION
Tools and equipment 172
Environmental control 173
Composts 174
Rooting hormones/Wounding 175
Fertilizers 176
Sowing in containers 177
The developing seed 178—179
Root cuttings 180—182
Tuberous roots 183
Tubers 184
Rhizomes 185
Corms 186
Bulblets and bulbils 187
Division 188—189
Offset/Runners 190
Layering/Simple layering 191
Simple layering 192
Tip layering 193
Making a stem cutting 194—195
Soft woods 196—197
Green woods 198

Semiripe woods 199
Leaf petiole cuttings 200
Foliar embryos 201
Grafting/Whip-and-tongue 202—203

PRUNING
Roses: introduction 204
Time of Pruning 205
Hybrid Teas and Hybrid Perpetuals 206
Floribundas 207
Climbers and Ramblers 208—211
Species and Shrub roses 212—214
Standard Roses 215
Shrubs: introduction 216—217
Deciduous Shrubs 218—225
Evergreen Shrubs 226—227
Climbing and wall plants: introduction 228
Clematis 229—231
Wisteria 232—233
Caenothus and Honeysuckle 234
Chaenomeles and Pyracantha 235

GROWING UNDER GLASS
Introduction/Hygiene 236—237
The year in a cold greenhouse 238—239
Ornamentals 240—242
Fruits 243
Tomatoes 244—245
Vegetables and salads 246—247
The year in a cold greenhouse 248—249
Bedding plants 250—251
Ornamentals 252—253
Fruits and vegetables 254—255
Using frames 256—258
Using cloches 259

PESTS AND DISEASES 260—265

GLOSSARY 266—265
ACKNOWLEDGEMENTS 268
INDEX 269—272

Introduction 1

Gardening can be a relaxing, absorbing hobby, or it can become a chore. Once you have a garden, it is impossible to ignore it: some basic tasks must be undertaken if it is to stay a garden and not become a jungle.

The key to happy gardening is mastery of the central techniques. Over many years and in every season, soil and climate, gardeners have built up a store of ways of doing things: ways of digging without undue fatigue, ways of combatting pests, of pruning a tree so that it gives fruit, of coaxing crops out of difficult ground.

The Royal Horticultural Society's famous and beautiful garden at Wisley is admired by thousands each year, but it is more than a showplace: it is a centre for research into plants and techniques. This *Encyclopedia* draws upon the RHS resource of practical, common-place expertise. Because it is concerned with methods, with techniques, *The Encyclopedia of Gardening Techniques* is designed around sequences of step-by-step illustrations with detailed captions. These sequences amplify the accompanying text and provide the gardener with the keys he or she needs to complete – and enjoy – gardening tasks.

The Encyclopedia of Gardening Tech-niques is a book for the practical gardener. It has been researched, written and edited by experts, specialists in their fields, under the overall supervision of the Royal Horticultural Society.

Using the Concise Encyclopedia
This book is divided into eight sections – Basic Techniques; Vegetables; Fruits; Lawns; Ground Cover and Weed Control; Propagation; Pruning; Growing under Glass; and Pests and Diseases. Each section contains illustrations for identification as well as the sequences of step-by-step drawings. In this respect the resources of the Royal Horticultural Society's Garden at Wisley were invaluable in obtaining information for illustrating each operation.

The first section of *The Encyclopedia* is arranged to be of particular help to the gardener who is tackling a new plot or one which is overgrown or neglected. Advice is given on drainage, soil cultivation, modification and enrichment so that the ground can be brought into a fertile and workable state before planting and basic construction begins.

The rewards of vegetable gardening have been justifiably proclaimed many times before. Ecologists, gourmets and health enthusiasts agree, from their different viewpoints, that growing vegetables is a worthwhile pursuit; it can also be extremely enjoyable.

The chapter on growing vegetables assumes no prior knowledge and cuts no corners. It reveals what the experts do and why they do it. Each vegetable is dealt with in clear detail from the moment you step outside with a spade to the day, weeks or months later, when you return with a basket of succulent produce.

Few gardeners will deny that one of the most rewarding aspects of gardening is growing and tasting freshly picked sun-warmed fruits. The first pages of this section deals with the practical aspects of fruit growing. The second part concerns soft fruit and the third tree fruit.

A well-maintained lawn is a valuable feature of many gardens, and, as such, it is not only important to tend to the lawn to keep it healthy, its shape should also be considered. The lawns section begins with the preparation of the site then continues with creating a lawn, from seed or from sod, and maintaining it once it has been established.

In recent years gardeners have learned to imitate nature by utilizing the ground covering properties of suitable plants for dealing with those problem areas where little except weeds will normally grow. Not only do ground cover plants keep the ground free of weeds, they also make the area attractive and have the added advantage that once established they require little maintenance. Here we explain how to prepare the site, plant and maintain. Suitable plants are recommended for problem sites; those, for example, that are shady, hot and dry or damp.

Plant propagation, making several new plants from one, has been practised ever since early man abandoned itinerant life and settled down on the land. The techniques of vegetative propagation developed in such ancient civilizations as those of the Babylonians and the Chinese are still relevant and in use in the twentieth century.

In this section is listed the basic tools and equipment you will require. We then discuss environmental control, composts, rooting hormones and fertilizers. Propagation from seeds in containers and the germination and the development of the young plant is examined. The rest of the section then presents a wide range of ways to propagate vegetatively. It starts with a chapter on roots and

Introduction 2

progresses through to sections on stems and leaves. Lastly, there is an explanation on grafting using whip-and-tongue techniques.

Pruning is a skill that is crucial to maintaining an attractive and healthy garden. Yet this basic technique causes much worry to gardeners who are nervous about taking secateurs and saw to their precious plants. This section is carefully written and designed to explain the subtleties of this key gardening art in a practical way. Each stage of pruning is shown, indicating which branch or stem should be removed and how the plant will look after the operation.

When using the step-by-step diagrams remember that your own plant of the species concerned will not be exactly like the one shown. The diagrams are designed to show the basic principles and methods. Different tones of green have been used to designate each year of growth. This enables the gardener to see how the framework of the plant is built up and to identify easily the parts of the plant that should be pruned.

The essential difference between growing outside and under glass is total control of the environment. This element of control is a large part of the appeal of greenhouse and frame gardening, for the plants are completely dependent on the care and skill of the cultivator. Maintaining a temperature regime to meet the needs of a range of plants is the heart of climate control under glass. Many greenhouse owners grow a motley assortment of plants from different countries and climates. Striking a balance might seem impossible, but many plants have wide tolerances and it is surprising how plants from diverse habitats will co-exist satisfactorily—if not to perfection—under the same set of conditions in a greenhouse.

In this section we describe the running of a greenhouse beginning with the importance of hygiene. The growing of plants is covered in the sections on cold and cool greenhouses. Each section begins with an outline of key sowing, flowering and cropping times and routine tasks and then goes on to the cultivation of various types of plants. Finally, there is a section on frames and cloches with detailed step-by-step sequences.

The final chapter of *The Encyclopedia* is concerned with the identification, prevention and treatment of pests and diseases, particularly those that infect and attack fruit and vegetables.

A glossary of common terms and an index complete the *Concise Encyclopedia*.

Safety

Accident reports constantly show that the most dangerous place on earth is the home. More accidents occur there than anywhere else. Although this state of affairs is brought about as a result of spending much of the time in and about the house, it is as well to remember that carelessness is the cause of most domestic disasters. It is also the major cause of those that occur in the garden.

There is certainly no need to be frightened of using power tools and chemicals in the garden provided that sensible precautions are taken, but so often familiarity breeds contempt and the gardener takes unnecessary (and foolish) risks.

It is vital to follow the instructions on packages when using garden chemicals.

Remember to wear stout shoes, boots or wellingtons when digging or using soil cultivating equipment. Take special care when using electrical apparatus and make sure that the cables are sound and properly connected. Wear rubber gloves when mixing and applying chemicals and store all such preparations out of the reach of children and animals—under lock and key if necessary. Precautions only seem excessive before an accident.

Common-sense gardening

The soil is rather like a bran-tub—you only get out of it what you put in. It is quite unreasonable to expect an undernourished soil to produce healthy, vigorous plants which are capable of withstanding drought and pest and disease attack. Plants extract nearly all their food from the soil, and on cultivated ground the gardener is responsible for stocking the larder. All manner of living organisms are necessary to keep soil fertile, and it is the addition of organic matter in particular that ensures their wellbeing.

Fertilizers, too, are essential if plants are to be quickly supplied with vital chemical elements, and the sensible gardener will rely both on organic matter and fertilizers to keep his soil "in good heart". Neglect the soil, and all other cultivation techniques and expert knowledge will be of little value.

No-one has ever learned all there is to know about gardening, and that is probably why the craft remains fresh and fascinating. A knowledge of the principles involved and a mastery of the basic skills needed to grow plants will provide anyone with "green thumbs". *The Encyclopedia of Gardening Techniques* sets out to do just that.

Weather and climate 1

Weather is what happens day by day, climate is the set of conditions prevailing at a given spot over a period. The climate of a garden depends first upon major factors such as latitude, distance from the sea and prevailing winds, and second on the local topography. The local climate, which can vary quite widely from the norm of the district, is called the microclimate.

Hardiness

Plants which will grow in a given climate are said to be hardy in that area. Hardiness depends upon resistance to frost and upon adaptation to the cycle of seasons prevailing. Thus plants hardy in sub-tropical areas are not hardy, and must be given protection, in more northern zones. Conversely, sub-Arctic plants used to short growing seasons and long periods of dormancy may not thrive in temperate places.

Zones of hardiness The map, right, divides N. America into ten zones according to the length of the growing season. The growing season is defined as the number of days in the year when the temperature rises above 6°C/43°F, the temperature at which grass begins to grow. The zones vary from 1, which has only 100 growing days a year, to 10, where growth is continuous.

In the lower zones, speed of growth is the key factor in hardiness. Plants must be able to complete their cycle of growth within the number of days when growing temperatures prevail. Thus in low zones fast-maturing, late-flowering and early-cropping varieties of fruit and vegetables are grown.

Some plants, such as deciduous fruits, require a period of dormancy during winter. In higher zones they are provoked into year-long growth, with consequent loss of quality.

Major climate factors

As can be seen from the map, proximity to the coast is a major factor in moderating climate. Coastal areas are warmer in winter, and cooler in summer, than those inland. Large regions have their own weather patterns, governed by the movements of air masses and by physical features such as mountain chains. Air masses are formed over land (continental) or over the sea (maritime).

They can be polar (P) or tropical (T). Mountainous areas experience lower temperatures and heavier precipitation. There is usually an area of low rainfall in the lee, or rain shadow, of high ground. This lee is usually to the east, reflecting the prevailing westerly winds.

Microclimate

As well as being affected by the area climate, each garden has its own microclimate which is governed by more local factors. The secret of coping successfully with a particular microclimate is either to modify it or to grow plants capable of surviving in the conditions it provides.

Sun and shade The aspect of a garden will influence greatly the types of plant that can be grown. A south-facing slope will receive the maximum amount of light and heat, for the ground is presented to the sun at a direct angle. Growth will start earlier in the spring and continue until later in the autumn. Flat ground, or land sloping in directions other than south, is presented to the sun at a more acute angle and therefore the light and heat it receives are less intense and spread over a

Types of windbreak

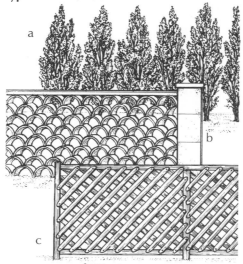

The best windbreaks are pervious, letting through some wind. They can be of wood (a), concrete blocks (b) or screens of trees (c).

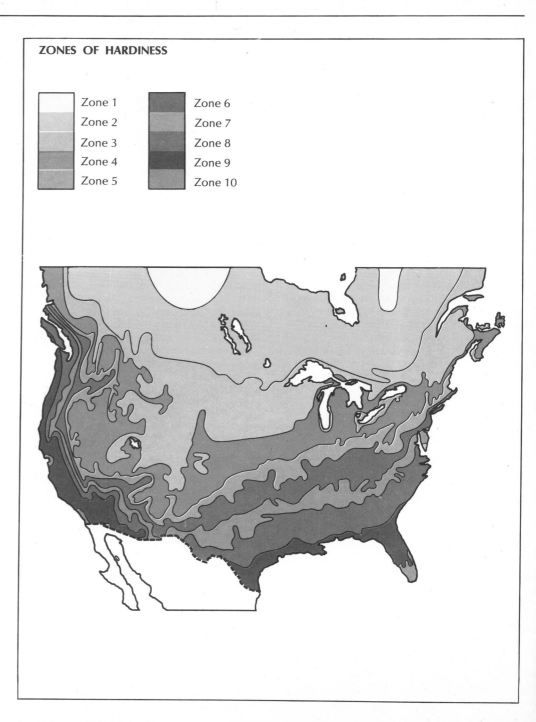

ZONES OF HARDINESS

Zone 1
Zone 2
Zone 3
Zone 4
Zone 5
Zone 6
Zone 7
Zone 8
Zone 9
Zone 10

Weather and climate 2

SUN ANGLES

	Latitude	Summer	Winter
Miami	26°N	87°	41°
Los Angeles	34°N	79°	33°
New York	40°N	74°	28°

The table above shows the noon angle of the sun to the horizon at various latitudes and in representative places. The sun is at its lowest on December 21, and at its highest on June 21. Simple scales, similar to a slide rule, are available, allowing the sun angle at a given date and place to be calculated. When the angle has been calculated, draw a sectional plan of the garden and house, showing shade trees, windows and walls. Using the angle, it will be possible to draw in shade areas. It is thus easy to calculate the areas of sun blinds, to work out which areas will be in shade and which in sun, and otherwise to plan the garden to make best use of the sun. Take care that fences, screens and evergreen hedges do not cut out too much sun, especially in winter.

shorter part of the year. Light is naturally less intense during the winter when the sun is lower in the sky, and sites which are reasonably well lit in the summer may be shady right through the winter. The table in the box above lists the angles of the sun at various latitudes. Ground overshadowed by trees and buildings will be cooler and less hospitable to plants requiring good light, but it will provide an ideal situation for plants native to woodlands. Walls facing north receive less light than south-facing walls, while east- and west-facing walls get full sun for about half the day.

Soil During the day the soil absorbs sun heat and then, under normal conditions, gives off this heat at night when the air above it cools. In this way the soil acts as a heat store, and the heat it radiates protects the plants above it from frost. However, if the soil is mulched it cannot absorb heat so effectively during the day and therefore has less to give off at night. For this reason mulches are laid on the soil in spring and dug in during autumn to allow the soil to absorb more heat in winter. Weeds prevent the absorption of heat in the same way as a mulch and so should be kept under control at all times.

Soils vary in the rate they give off heat absorbed during the day. Clay soils are slow to warm up, and also store heat for longer. Sandy soils absorb and give off heat quickly. Compacted ground is a more effective radiator of heat than soil which has a finely-tilled surface that acts as a blanket, keeping in the heat and allowing the plants above to become frosted. Walls absorb and give off heat in the same way as soil, which is one reason why tender plants thrive grown against them. Plants listed as tender in a given zone can be grown in the shelter a wall provides.

Frost Cold air, like water, seeks the lowest level, and areas at the foot of sloping ground will be far more susceptible to frosts than land higher up the slope. Do not position tender plants, especially fruit trees with susceptible blossoms, in frost pockets, and avoid creating pockets by erecting solid fences or hedges across a slope. Cold air flowing down the slope will pond up behind such obstacles, leading to frost and damage to plants. Permeable barriers such as open fences allow cold air to seep through, and are therefore to be preferred.

Wind Frost may be the main problem in low-lying gardens, but strong winds are a constant hazard in exposed or hilltop places where they will physically damage trees and shrubs and cause water to be lost from soil and foliage more rapidly. The answer is not to erect a solid wind break, for wind cannot simply be halted—its energy has to be dissipated. A solid wall or fence presented to the wind will cause the air currents to rise up and then fall directly behind the wall, creating damaging down-draughts and turbulence. The way to cut down damage from strong winds is to erect a relatively permeable barrier such as a hedge or open screen. This will reduce the force of the wind to a level which plants can tolerate, and it will not create eddies or turbulence. A permeable barrier will effectively reduce the wind speed for a distance equal to ten times its height. Thus a 50 ft barrier of poplar or leyland cypress trees will protect up to 500 ft of ground on its leeward side. The prevailing wind usually comes from the west or south-west, so wind breaks are best erected to run from north-west round through west to south-east. Rows of plants running in the same direction as the wind can create a funneling effect, and should, if possible, be planted across its path to diffuse the force. Wind tunnels created by buildings and walls should have their entrances sheltered by shrubs, trees or open screens.

Rainfall The wind plays an important part in the distribution of rainfall, and frequently ground at the base of walls or trees to the leeward side of the wind will remain dry—most of the rain being blown over the top. Soil below north- and east-facing walls will dry out due to a shortage of rain; and that below south- and west-facing walls will also become dry due to the increased amount of sunlight it receives. Irrigation is essential if plant growth is not to be checked.

Altitude The higher the ground, the colder it will be. For every rise of 250 ft above sea level, the average temperature drops by about one degree. This factor may be of little consequence in summer, but it can make for a later start to the growing season in spring and an earlier cessation in winter.

Urban heat

The heat generated by a large town or city will greatly influence the minimum winter temperature. Large conurbations give off quantities of heat day and night which can artificially lift temperatures and allow a wider range of plants to be grown. The atmosphere in such areas is often charged with pollutants, however, and in some places smoke or haze can cut the amount of sunshine received.

Weather records

The use of simple instruments such as thermometers and barometers allows a picture of the local microclimate to be built up. Keep records of rainfall, wind and temperature. After a few years the records will allow optimum planting dates to be chosen.

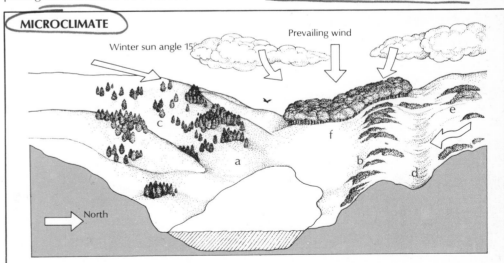

MICROCLIMATE

The lake shore (a) has a moderate climate due to the water's influence. The south-facing slope (b) gets more sun than slope (c) which faces north. Cold air flows down hill at night to form a frost pocket (d). The hilltop (e) is about one degree colder than (b) due to the effect of altitude. The woodland shelters the field (f), reducing wind.

Soil 1

Soil is the result of organic forces working on the inorganic rock. In a ceaseless process rocks are broken down and living creatures colonize the resulting debris. The nature of the parent rock decides much of the character of the resulting soil.

Soil formation

Several factors are responsible for the development of soil; the most important of these is climate. Rainwater passing over and through the parent rock breaks it down, and repeated freezing and thawing shatters the rock into smaller particles. Organic matter, such as leaves and dead animals, lodges in this rock waste, allowing bacteria and fungi to go into action. Seeds germinate in the resulting mixture. Once plants are established they will contribute organic matter to the soil, so making it capable of supporting other life in the form of more bacteria and fungi, insects, worms and animals.

Soil profile

A cross-section of the soil (known as a soil profile), can often be seen in the side of a ditch or trench. In most temperate climates there will be five layers or "horizons" (see diagram right). The shallow, topmost layer (a) will consist of humus unless the ground has recently been cultivated, in which case this layer will have been incorporated in the top-soil. The most important layer as far as the gardener is concerned is the top-soil (b). Ideally this should be 2–3 ft deep to sustain a wide range of crops. It should contain adequate supplies of plant nutrients and organic matter, and should be well-drained and aerated. Below the top-soil is the sub-soil layer (c), consisting of partially broken-down rock. It is infertile but can contain useful nutrients. A layer of fragmented rock (d) may occur between the sub-soil and the solid parent rock or bedrock (e). Soil profiles will tend to vary from area to area depending upon the geology, the climate, the history of cultivation and the vegetation cover.

Types of soil

From the gardener's point of view soils are classified according to the amount of sand or clay particles they contain, and according to their acidity or alkalinity.

Clay Clay particles are very small and tend to adhere to one another, making drainage and air penetration slow and cultivation difficult. Clay soils are sticky when wet, hard when dry, slow to warm up in spring and described by the gardener as heavy. They are usually rich in nutrients and, unlike sands, chemically active. To test a soil for clay, squeeze a sample between finger and thumb. If the particles slide readily and the soil looks shiny it has a high clay content. A squeezed handful will readily bind together.

The addition of organic matter greatly improves clay soils, for it causes the particles to clump together in larger groups, so allowing water and air to pass between them. Lime, when added to clay soils, also causes particles to bind together by the process of flocculation (forming into compound masses or clumps).

Sand Sandy soils consist of large particles surrounded by air spaces. Water drains through them rapidly and there is ample air for plant roots. They are easy to cultivate and quick to warm up in spring, but they dry out very easily and, due to their rapid drainage, nutrients are quickly washed away. To test a soil for sand, squeeze the particles between finger and thumb. If the sand content is high the particles will both look and feel rough. A squeezed handful will not bind together well.

Soil profile

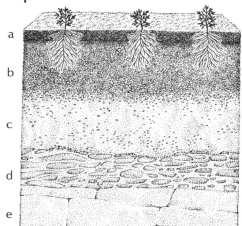

a

b

c

d

e

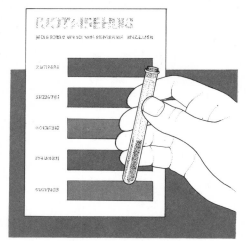

Improve sandy soils by adding organic matter such as garden compost.

Silt Silty soils have particles intermediate in size between sand and clay. They are sticky and fairly heavy, and can be difficult to cultivate because they are not flocculated and liming is of little help. Improve the texture of silt soils by applying large amounts of humus-producing material.

Loam This is the ideal soil, containing a mixture of clay and sand, or silt, particles, plus an adequate supply of organic matter and plant nutrients. It is easy to cultivate, retains moisture and nutrients, yet is well-drained. Loam varies and may be classified as light, medium or heavy, depending on the clay-to-sand ratio.

Peat Made up of partially decomposed organic matter, peaty soils are inclined to be acid and poorly drained. The addition of lime, nutrients, coarse sand, grit or weathered ashes, and the construction of artificial drainage systems improves their quality.

Acidity and alkalinity

The amount of lime a soil contains governs its acidity. A soil rich in lime or chalk is said to be alkaline. One which lacks lime is described as acid or sour. The degree of acidity or alkalinity is measured on the pH scale, which runs from 0 to 14. A soil with a pH above 7.0 is called alkaline, and one with a pH of below 6.5 is said to be acid. Soils with pH readings above 8.5 and below 4.5 are rare. Most plants prefer a soil with a pH in the range 6.5 to 7.0.

Humus

The dark brown crumbly organic matter within the soil is humus. It consists of plant and animal remains in various stages of decay and ensures the continued survival of bacteria, which are essential if a soil is to be fertile. Humus also retains moisture, keeps the soil well aerated and is a source of plant nutrients. On cultivated ground humus breaks down more quickly than it would if left undisturbed, so it is important that the soil is amply replenished with well-rotted manure, compost, leaf-mold or other humus-forming material whenever possible.

Soil life

Earthworms, insects, burrowing animals, slugs, snails, bacteria and many other forms of life all contribute to the organic content of the soil and, unless their presence is a severe nuisance they should be encouraged.

SOIL TESTING

Simple soil testing kits can be bought which allow a rough check to be made on the soil's pH level. Take small random samples of soil from different parts of the garden and shake them up in the solution included with the kit. Allow soil to settle then check the color of the liquid against the range of colors on the chart in the kit. The pH value is indicated by the depth of the color of the solution in the tube.

Testing kits are also available which measure mineral levels in the soil and allow deficiencies to be corrected. Alternatively, send a soil sample to the state agricultural extension service which will test it.

Check the pH level regularly, especially if attempts are being made to modify the soil's pH level.

Soil 2

Plant nutrients

A good soil will contain all the nutrient elements necessary for plant growth. The major ones, required in relatively large quantities, are nitrogen, potassium and phosphorus plus lesser amounts of magnesium, calcium, sulfur, carbon, hydrogen and oxygen. The minor, or trace elements are iron, manganese, boron, molybdenum, zinc and copper.

A plant lacking any of these elements shows certain symptoms. The more common ones are: nitrogen deficiency—slow, stunted growth and pale leaves; phosphate deficiency —stunted growth with red or purple leaves; potassium deficiency—pale yellow or brown leaves; magnesium deficiency—yellowing of older leaves; and iron deficiency—yellowing of young leaves. For details see the Pests and Diseases section (pages 260–262).

Drainage

Both water and air are necessary in the soil if plants and soil organisms are to thrive. In poorly drained soils, the roots of plants are restricted to the top few inches of ground where they cannot anchor the plant firmly or search very far for nutrients. Lack of air inhibits the uptake of minerals from the soil.

Causes of bad drainage The structure of the soil may be responsible for poor drainage. Small, tightly packed particles of clay or silt may make the escape of water difficult, or problems may be produced by a sub-soil pan (see Box right) or a high water table. The water table is the level in the soil below which the ground is saturated with water. The level is higher in winter than in summer. In bogs and marshes the water table may be level with the surface of the ground; but normally it is to be found within 6–8 ft of the surface. In soils where a high water table inhibits cultivation, some artificial means of drainage must be constructed to move water to a lower level (see pages 10–11).

Natural drainage Under natural conditions, rainwater which lands on the soil is distributed in several ways. Some of it runs off the surface; some is taken up by plant roots and later transpired by the foliage; some evaporates, and the rest drains through the soil.

Artificial drainage This is vital where the incorporation of organic matter, coarse sand and grit fails to improve the natural drainage sufficiently. Very heavy clay soils, ground where the water table is inconveniently high and land with impenetrable sub-soil all have to be provided with artificial drainage to make healthy plant growth possible. See pages 10–11 for details of drainage systems.

Water retention If all rainwater were carried too rapidly down to the level of free drainage in the soil, plant roots would have little time to absorb water. In most soils, however, the humus content acts like a sponge, absorbing adequate moisture for the plant's needs and allowing excess water to drain away naturally.

Light soils lacking in humus, such as those with a high sand or chalk content, dry out quickly. Frequent applications of well-rotted organic matter—leaf-mold, peat and compost—improve moisture retention without causing waterlogging by creating humus, which acts as a sponge.

Adding organics

Dig in organic material to improve soil condition, especially on clay, where organics will encourage particles to stick together.

PANNING

Soil particles rich in elements such as iron and aluminum sometimes form a hard layer, or pan, often only 1 ft or 18 in below the surface. This impairs drainage, makes digging difficult, prevents root penetration and inhibits plant growth.

Continuous plowing or tilling at the same level, and compaction caused by vehicles, can also form pans. On small plots, use a sledge hammer and a heavy steel bar to break up the pan. Deep digging will also break up pans formed by cultivation. Over large areas, traverse the land with a tractor fitted with a mole plow. This will break the pan and leave a gully below it into which water can drain. After dealing with a pan, cultivate at different levels to avoid a recurrence of the problem.

The water cycle

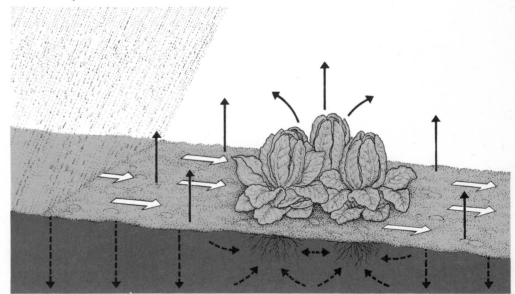

Water in the form of rain or snow percolates through the soil and runs off into streams and ditches, is retained in the soil, sinks down to the water table, or is lost through evaporation into the atmosphere. Plants tap the water retained in the soil. This can be up to two-thirds of the rain that falls.

9

Drainage 1

If a piece of land must be provided with a drainage system, the gardener can choose from a number of alternatives.

Ditches The cheapest way of draining land is to dig ditches to carry the excess water from the cultivated soil to a drywell, stream or river. Ditches are of particular value on flat, low-lying land where the necessary slope or "fall" needed for tile drains is difficult to obtain. A system of ditches will allow drainage of the water from the soil. Once in the ditches, it will disperse by evaporation or by flowing into a watercourse.

On slightly sloping ground, dig a cut-off ditch at the top of the plot to intercept water from higher ground before it has a chance to saturate the soil further down. Dig another ditch parallel to the first at the foot of the slope to disperse the water received by the slope itself. The top ditch should be connected to the bottom one either by another ditch or by a system of tile drains. The water discharges from the bottom ditch into a drywell or stream.

Open ditches must be excavated properly at the outset, either by mechanical digger or with a spade. Make them 3–4 ft deep and slope the sides outwards at a 20–30 degree angle to make them stable. The banks of ditches in clay soils will be more stable than those in sand, so they can be steeper.

Clear all ditches of weeds and undergrowth at least once a year and check that there are no blockages which will restrict the flow of water. For safety and efficiency it is a good idea to erect a fence along the ditchside.

Land drains Land or tile drains are short sections of earthenware or longer sections of plastic pipe which are laid end to end, usually in a herringbone system of filled trenches, to collect drainage water and discharge it at a chosen point. The plastic pipes are perforated, flexible and can be bent to avoid obstacles. Concrete drains are a relatively inexpensive alternative.

Dig trenches 2–3 ft deep and about 1 ft wide, taking care to keep top-soil and sub-soil separate. Give the trenches an overall slope of about 1 in 40 to ensure that they can take away water efficiently. The spacing of the side drains (which run into the central main drain) will depend on the nature of the soil—on heavy clay they will need to be closer together than on lighter soils. As a rough guide, space them 15 ft apart on clay, 25 ft apart on loam, and 40 ft apart on sandy soil.

The central drain should consist of 4 in pipes and the subsidiary or side drains of 3 in pipes. Lay the pipes at the bottom of the trench on a 2 in layer of coarse gravel or pebbles and cover them with more rubble or gravel before replacing the top-soil. Discard the sub-soil. The pipes are simply butted together to allow water to percolate between them and the side drains should meet the main drain at an angle of 60 degrees. Cover these junctions with a piece of flat tile to prevent blockages.

Rubble drains On small sites where ditches and tile drains would be impractical, use rubble drains. Take out a single trench across the plot and lead it to a drywell in an out-of-the-way corner. Make the trench the same dimensions as a tile drain trench and give it a similar fall. Fill it with broken bricks and rubble to half its depth, cap this layer with gravel, then with turf placed upside down and replace the top-soil. Such a system will drain a modest-sized plot adequately and unobtrusively.

Drywells Tile drains, rubble drains and ditches can all be connected to a drywell if there is no convenient watercourse into which their water can be discharged.

Dig a hole approximately 6 ft in diameter and at least 6 ft deep (the overall size of the drywell will be governed by the size of the plot being drained). For best results line the sides with concrete blocks to support the wall of soil and to prevent silting of the dry-well, yet allow the water to seep through. Fill the drywell with rubble or coarse clinker and top with turf, again to prevent silting.

Mole drains These are constructed by a tractor attachment which pulls a torpedo-shaped steel head through the sub-soil at a chosen depth. The "mole" makes a continuous drain in the sub-soil which allows excess water to disperse. This system of drainage is really effective only when used on land which

Laying a tile drain system

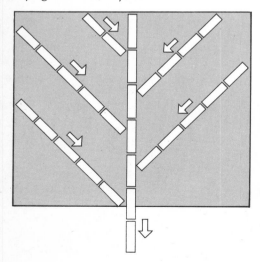

1 Plan ditches in a herringbone pattern, with the main pipe leading to a watercourse or drywell. Space ditches 15 ft apart on clay, 25 ft on loam and 40 ft on sandy soils.

2 Dig trenches 2–3 ft deep with an overall slope of at least 1 in 40. The side trenches should meet the main drain at an angle of 60 degrees.

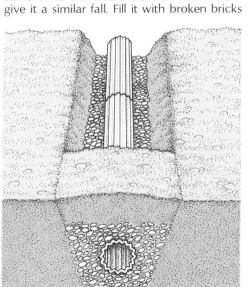

3 Lay the plastic or clay pipes on a 2 in layer of gravel and add more gravel before replacing the soil. The pipe sections are butted together, not joined.

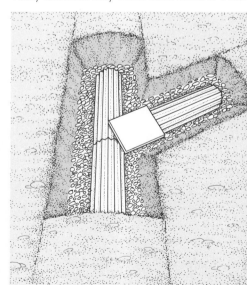

4 Cover pipe junctions with a piece of flat tile to prevent blockages before replacing first sub-soil, then top-soil.

Drainage 2

has clay sub-soil, where it will last for several years. Mole drains should be excavated to the same pattern, depth and fall as tile drains.
Cultivation It is important to keep a careful check on the depth of soil cultivation where underground drains have been constructed. Deep digging or plowing may break them and create boggy patches.

Draining hard surfaces

Patios and paths can be made impassable by every shower of rain if they are not constructed so that they shed water. When making a paved or concrete area, build in a slight slope so that water is shed and does not stand about in pools. A fall of about 1 in 40 will move water quite quickly either onto border soil (where it can be used by plants), or into a shallow gully which can be led to a drywell or drain. Construct the gully from half-round ceramic pipes bedded in cement, or from cement which has been troweled into a similar shape.

If a hidden gully is desirable on a patio or path, lay half-round ceramic pipes down the center of the area and slope the paving or concrete very gently towards the gully, overlapping the edges. A $\frac{1}{2}$ in gap in the center will let water run into the channel.

Retaining walls

A reservoir of water will often build up behind a retaining wall if no provision is made for drainage. Not only does the water make the soil inhospitable to plants but it also causes the brick or stonework to become discolored. To overcome this problem, lay a single row of tile drains, with a suitable fall, immediately behind the wall at its base. Surround the tiles with coarse gravel and lead them to a drywell or drain. "Weepholes" are made in the face of the wall to allow more water to escape. Leave one vertical joint unmortared every 5–6 ft along the wall in every second or third course of bricks or stones. Alternatively, insert short lengths of pipe, sloping forwards, at similar intervals to do the same job. Lay a gully of half-round pipes at the foot of the wall if the soil is likely to shed large amounts of water.

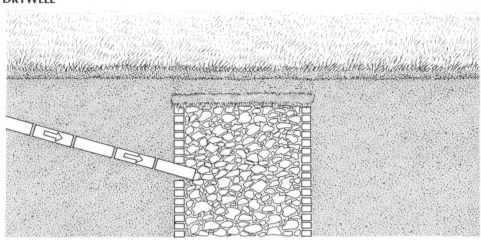

DRYWELL

A drywell must be constructed if there is no suitable watercourse for a drainage system to run to. Dig a hole up to 6 ft deep and across. Line it with uncemented concrete blocks, then fill the drywell with rubble or coarse clinker. Top with turf.

Ditches

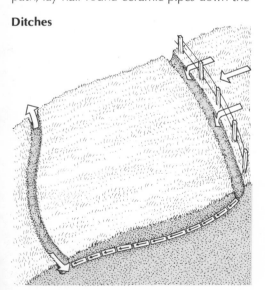

If the land slopes, dig a cut-off ditch across the top of the plot to intercept water from higher ground. Connect it to another at the bottom of the slope by ditches or tile drains.

Rubble drains

Half fill a 2–3 ft trench, dug at the same spacings as tile drain ditches, with broken concrete blocks or rubble. Cap with a layer of gravel then replace the top-soil.

Mole drains

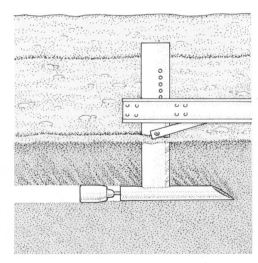

Mole drains are effective in clay soils. They are made by an attachment fitted to a tractor, and can thus only be used on large, open plots.

Retaining walls

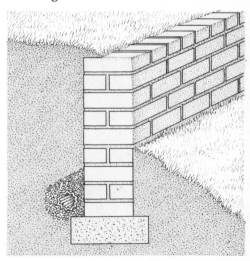

Lay a row of tile drains in gravel at the base of the wall. Leave vertical joints unmortared in every third course, 6 ft apart, to allow water to pass through.

Improving the soil 1

As soon as a piece of land is tilled or dug, the process of humus breakdown is speeded up. Added to this, the gardener may discover that the soil is not ideally suited to the crop he wants to grow. This means the soil structure and the organic and chemical content may have to be altered to provide a more satisfactory medium. There are many materials, bulky or granular, organic or inorganic, that can be used to improve soil and turn it into the best possible growing medium for a wide range of plants.

Organic enrichment

Humus is essential in the soil. It helps to retain water and hence nutrients dissolved in it, while at the same time improving drainage (especially in clay). It also helps keep the soil well aerated, maintains soil structure, and it supports the bacteria which break down organic matter into humus. A soil may be rich in chemical fertilizers but if no organic matter is present, most bacteria will not be able to survive. In such impoverished soils plant growth is poor. Humus-rich soils are dark in color and thus absorb heat more readily than pale soils.

Bulky organic manures have other advantages over fertilizers than the obvious one of improving soil texture and structure by virtue of their consistency. They are often rich in trace elements which may be lacking in fertilizers, and they release their nutrients relatively slowly.

Although each plant has its own particular preferences, it is usually possible to compromise and provide a soil which will suit a number of crops. (See rotation, page 34.)

Most plants thrive in soil that has been dressed with well-rotted manure or compost in the autumn before planting. Fresh manure should not be added to the soil before it has had a chance to decay, because in its fresh state it gives off harmful ammonia. Also, until bacterial decay occurs, nitrogen in the soil is not available to plants.

The nitrogen cycle The nitrogen cycle, by which nitrogen passes from the air to soil to plants and animals and back to the air, involves five basic processes: fixation of nitrogen from the air by micro-organisms and by lightning to form nitrates in the soil; use by plants of these nitrates to make proteins; conversion of proteins into ammonia compounds in decaying plant and animal matter; and finally the recycling of ammonia compounds either into nitrates or into nitrogen gas, which is released into the atmosphere.

Organic materials

A wide variety of organic materials can be used to improve soil. The choice is often governed by what is available, but some substances, such as pulverized bark, are easier to store and apply than are manure and garden compost.

Leaf-mold The leaves of deciduous trees, collected in autumn and stacked (in an open position) can be returned to the soil the next year, after they have broken down to a crumbly dark brown mold. Leaf-mold is valued more for its ability to improve soil texture and structure than for the small amounts of plant food it contains. It has the disadvantages of breaking down rather quickly in the soil and may contain weed seeds if weeds have been allowed to grow and seed on the leaf heap. Leaves of the plane, poplar, sycamore and horse chestnut take longest to decompose while those of the oak take a relatively short time. Leaf-mold can be dug into the soil or applied as a mulch. Application rate: 5 lb per square yard.

Animal manures Manure consists of animal droppings, urine and variable amounts of litter such as straw, peat, sawdust, or wood shavings. It must always be stacked before being used so that the litter can be allowed to decompose. Animal manures contain a good proportion of nutrients and many trace elements and are among the best soil conditioners. Horses produce the richest manure, followed by pigs, cows and poultry. Horse manure is quick acting; pig and cow manure break down more slowly. Pig and chicken manure are particularly caustic to plant roots and should not be applied fresh. All are best dug into the soil in autumn or applied as a mulch in spring, where decomposition has occurred during stacking. Application rate: 10–15 lb per square yard.

Peat Peat consists of partially decayed plant remains in which decomposition has been slowed down by the presence of water. Sedge peat comes from lowland marshes in which sedges and reeds predominate and is usually darker in color than sphagnum peat (also known as moss peat or peat moss) which is from peat bogs in moorland areas. The main ingredient of sphagnum peat is sphagnum moss. Sphagnum is spongier than sedge peat

and therefore more absorbent. Because it darkens the soil, and so helps to absorb heat, peat is valued as a soil conditioner rather than as a fertilizer. Most peats are of an acid nature but when applied at reasonable rates they will not increase the acidity of soil. They are sterile and slow to break down and can be applied as a mulch or dug in. Most commercial peats are blends of different types. Application rate: 10 lb of moist peat per square yard.

Garden compost Garden compost is a valuable alternative to animal manures, which may be difficult to obtain. It may consist of a wide variety of garden and kitchen waste which has been rotted down over a period of several months. (See pages 14–15.) Garden compost is relatively rich in nutrients and a good soil conditioner. It may be applied as a mulch or dug into the soil. Application rate: 10 lb per square yard.

Spent hops A by-product of the brewing industry, spent hops may be available in certain areas. They contain relatively few nutrients but are a good soil conditioner and can be dug in during autumn and winter. Spent hops make a useful mulch. Application rate: 10 lb per square yard.

Sawdust Sawdust helps raise acidity; use 10 lb per square yard. If the soil lacks lime add 1 lb of ground limestone to a bucket of sawdust. Also add 1 lb of nitrate of soda per bucket. Apply half the nitrogen and the balance during the growing season.

Spent mushroom compost Although they vary considerably in their nutrient value, the spent composts sold off by mushroom growers are well worth using to boost the organic content of soils. They usually contain animal manure, loam and chalk in varying quantities and can be used in all soils except those being used to grow rhododendrons and other lime-hating plants. Application rate: 5–10 lb per square yard.

Seaweed Gardeners in coastal areas may have the opportunity of using seaweed as an organic manure. Spring tides and storms often deposit large amounts of it on beaches. Seaweed contains reasonable amounts of plant nutrients, particularly potash, and it decomposes quickly. It may be dug straight into the ground while wet, or else composted

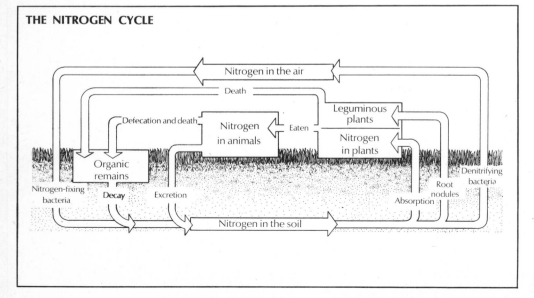

THE NITROGEN CYCLE

Nitrogen in the air

Death

Defecation and death

Nitrogen in animals

Eaten

Leguminous plants

Nitrogen in plants

Organic remains

Nitrogen-fixing bacteria

Decay

Excretion

Absorption

Root nodules

Denitrifying bacteria

Nitrogen in the soil

Improving the soil 2

with garden waste and applied when partially broken down. Dried seaweed meal can be bought from garden suppliers. Application rate of wet seaweed: 10–12 lb per square yard.

Pulverized bark This product is now widely available with or without the addition of fertilizers. The ordinary kind, which does not contain fertilizers, needs nitrogen to break down the bark so it is mainly used as a mulch. Pulverized bark is slow to break down. Use it as a 2–3 in thick mulch.

Sewage sludge Dried sludges described as "digested" or "activated" are the safest way to use sewage. Raw sludge, which is sometimes available, may transmit human diseases if applied to ground where salad ("raw") crops are being grown. Sludge-treated land should not be used for "raw" crops for 12 months. Sewage sludge is not particularly high in organic matter, but contains a good supply of nitrogen and some phosphates. It is best dug into the ground in autumn and winter. Application rate: 1½–2½ lb per square yard.

Green manure This is a method of improving soil with organic material by sowing certain crops and then digging them into the ground to enrich the soil. (See pages 14–15.)

Many organic materials can be used to condition soil, such as; bagasse (ground sugarcane), coffee grounds, buckwheat hulls, ground corncobs, peanut hulls, pecan hulls, tobacco stems and rice hulls (although they are not so widely available). First, apply as a mulch, then dig in as they decompose.

Inorganic soil conditioners

On heavy soils the incorporation of inorganic soil conditioners such as weathered wood and fuel ashes, coarse sand, grit, sawdust, wood shavings and pine needles may be of considerable help in making cultivation easier. These materials will open up the soil to some degree, allowing in air, but are best applied in combination with organic matter rather than on their own.

Modifying pH

Although ground limestone will improve the structure of a clay soil by encouraging the soil particles to combine into larger groups, so allowing water to drain away more freely, it is as a means of adjusting the acidity, or

sourness, of a soil that it is of greatest value. This is especially so on light, sandy soils which drain freely and lose lime rapidly by leaching. Some bacteria also will not increase or thrive in acid soils and liming improves the breaking down of organic material.

Some plants find it easier to extract nutrients from an acid soil, others prefer to grow on limed soil. While it is generally advisable to grow plants which are suitable to the soil, sometimes this is neither desirable nor practicable. Then the pH, or acid/alkali balance, of the soil has to be adjusted.

A soil with a pH of between 6.5 and 7.0, or neutral, will grow a wide range of crops, and 6.8 is the figure to aim for when correcting acidity. Soil with a pH balance below 6.5 affects the uptake of major and minor plant nutrients. Hydrated lime (calcium hydroxide) is the most effective type to use for pH adjustment as relatively small amounts of it will be needed. It is also more stable than the more expensive quicklime. Ordinary ground limestone or chalk (calcium carbonate), often cheaper, can also be used. An advantage is that it can be used before planting or sowing without damage to the crop.

More lime will have to be applied to acid clay soils, and those containing large quantities of organic matter, than to acid sandy soils. The list on this page (above) shows some plants that respond to lime. Acid soils should be tested annually and suitable amounts of lime added to replace that lost by the soil in the previous season.

Applications of lime are usually made in autumn or early winter. Lime should not be allowed to come into contact with manure or it will react with it, releasing valuable nitrogen into the air. Apply lime and manure in different years, or allow several weeks to elapse between the digging in of the manure and the dusting of the lime. Left on the surface of the soil the lime will gradually be washed in. If necessary, a vegetable plot may be limed in autumn and manured in winter with no ill effects.

Alkaline soils

It is much more difficult to alter the pH of an alkaline soil than that of an acid one. Start by enriching the soil with peat and

other acidic organic matter which will lower the alkalinity to some degree. Then apply flowers of sulfur at the rate of 4 oz per square yard on sandy soils and 8 oz per square yard on heavy soils. Test the soil at monthly intervals to monitor the pH. At below pH 6.5 the availability of nitrogen, phosphorus, potassium and molybdenum decreases while that of iron and manganese increases. On soils with a high pH calcium decreases the uptake of potassium. If the soil is very alkaline, apply flowers of sulfur each year, but also try to grow plants which will tolerate some degree of alkalinity. An efficient drainage system will help to leach some of the chalk out of the soil.

Where iron deficiency is a problem on chalky soils, iron chelates or sequestrene can be watered on to make this nutrient more readily available. Three or four applications a year at the manufacturer's recommended rate should be sufficient for most gardens.

Fertilizers such as sulfate of ammonia are acid-reacting and should be used on chalky ground in preference to fertilizers of an alkaline nature.

Types of fertilizer

There are two basic kinds of fertilizer: organic and inorganic, and both are equally valuable in the garden.

All organic fertilizers contain carbon and have been derived from living organisms. Before organic fertilizers can be absorbed by the plant they must be broken down in the soil by bacteria and fungi into inorganic chemicals. It will be seen from this that organic fertilizers actually encourage soil bacteria and so increase fertility. They are released for plant use relatively slowly.

Inorganic fertilizers do not contain carbon. They cannot improve soil texture and do not add any humus, but they are often very quick-acting and, pound for pound, richer in nutrients and are cheaper than organic fertilizers.

The conscientious gardener will use a combination of organic and inorganic fertilizers together with bulky organic soil conditioners to improve his land and keep it in good condition.

All fertilizers are labeled to show their nutrient content in terms of nitrogen (N), phosphoric acid (P_2O_5) and potash (K_2O). Some fertilizers are described as "straight", meaning that they supply just one of these nutrients; others are called "compound" and supply varying quantities of all three nutrients.

Application

Fertilizers may be applied to the ground before sowing or planting (in which case they are known as base dressings) or while the crop is growing, as top dressings.

Apply base dressings to the soil a few days before sowing crops or at the time of planting, working the fertilizer into the top few inches of soil with a fork or rake.

Dust top dressings of fertilizers around growing plants or crops while the soil is moist and hoe them lightly into the top few inches. Where large areas are being fertilized, wheeled fertilizer distributors may be used. These can be adjusted to spread a given quantity of fertilizer evenly over the surface of the soil.

Certain fertilizers are sold in soluble powder or liquid form and can be watered onto the soil or sprayed over plant foliage. These foliar feeds are generally quick-acting and should be applied when the soil is moist. Foliar feeds are best given in dull weather rather than in bright sunshine.

Assessing plant needs

Most plants will be adequately supplied with nutrients if given a base dressing of a compound fertilizer before being sown or planted and one or two top dressings of a similar material during the growing season. Fertilizers containing a large amount of nitrogen can be used to induce rapid leaf and shoot growth where this is lacking. Those containing phosphates will encourage root activity where trees and shrubs are being planted; and fertilizers rich in potash will improve the fruiting ability of a range of crops from tomatoes and beans to apples and pears. The most important requirement, however, is to balance the soil with a mixture of nutrients necessary for a particular crop. Over-application of one nutrient may cancel the effect of others.

13

Garden compost 1

Animal manure may be difficult to obtain, and proprietary organic soil conditioners are expensive. An alternative source of bulky organic matter is garden compost. A compost heap will cheaply and quickly turn garden and kitchen waste into valuable soil-enriching material.

Principles of compost making

To make good, crumbly compost the heap must be properly constructed so that the organic material can decompose rapidly and not turn into a pile of stagnant vegetation.

Air, moisture and nitrogen are all necessary if bacteria and fungi are to break down the raw material efficiently. Air is allowed in through the base and sides of the heap. Water should be applied with a can or hose if the heap shows signs of drying out, and moisture can be kept in by covering the heap with burlap, old carpet or polyethylene sheeting. Nitrogen must be provided in the form of

manure, compost activator or a nitrogenous fertilizer. It will aid bacteria and fungi in the breaking-down process.

The heap will be able to function best if it is sited in a sheltered and shady place but not under trees or where tree roots may move into the compost. It must be protected from becoming dried out by the sun and wind. Allow ample time for decomposition.

Compost bins

It is possible to rot down compost satisfactorily by simply stacking it in a spare corner of the garden, but in this way the heap may become untidy and the material on the outside will dry out. Decomposition will take place more rapidly in a home-made or proprietary compost bin which allows air in and retains moisture. For best results, compost bins should not be more than 4 ft high. They can be much longer than wide, for example, 4 × 4 × 8–10 ft is a useful size.

There are many ways of making a compost bin. One of the simplest is to erect a square cage of wire netting, supported by four stout posts driven into the ground. Make the front removable to allow the rotted compost to be easily extracted. For large bins, make a false floor by placing a layer of twiggy branches or brushwood in the base, or support a few short planks on bricks. This will allow air to permeate the compost. Line the inside of the cage with newspaper to prevent excessive drying out. A piece of burlap or polyethylene can be weighted down with bricks on the top of the heap to keep the moisture in.

A more solid structure can be made from angle-iron posts and wooden boards which are fashioned with gaps to allow in a certain amount of air. The internal structure of the heap is the same as with a wire cage. Brick or concrete block structures may be used provided that occasional vertical joints are

left unmortared to allow in air. The front of such bays can be equipped with removable wooden slats.

A series of two or three compost bins is very useful, particularly in large gardens. When one bin is full the compost can be left to decompose and another bin brought into use. In this way a cycle of compost production can be kept going.

There are many proprietary compost bins available. Some are equipped with sliding sides to allow the compost to be shoveled out, and with lids to keep in moisture. Check that the bin is strong and large enough for the garden's compost needs, bearing in mind the length of time it takes to decompose.

Compostable materials

Garden and kitchen waste in great variety can be turned into good compost if it is properly mixed. One of the secrets of ensuring rapid decomposition is not to allow large quantities

Building a compost heap

1 Choose a suitable site for the heap, and, if preferred, erect a wire or rigid-sided bin.

2 Spread a 6–9 in layer of compostable material over the base of the heap and firm lightly.

3 Scatter sulfate of ammonia at ½ oz per square yard over the heap, then add more compost material. Water the heap.

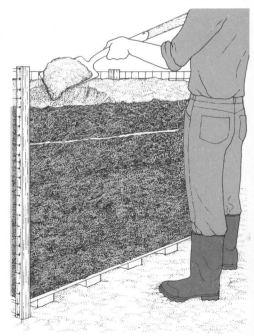

4 Continue until the bin is full or the heap is 4 ft tall. Cover finally with a 2 in layer of soil.

Garden compost 2

of one particular material to build up in the heap. All the following materials may be composted if properly mixed together: annual weeds, grass clippings (unless the lawn has been treated with hormone weedkillers), potato peelings, tea leaves, crushed eggshells, animal manure and urine, torn-up newspapers (but not glossy magazines), soft hedge clippings, dead flowerheads, pea pods, vegetable leaves and stems, tree and shrub leaves. Do not use woody material or any vegetation which has been sprayed with herbicides or is affected by diseases and pests.

Constructing the heap

When the bin has been erected the composting can start in earnest. On top of the false floor, if used, place a 6–9 in layer of compost material and lightly firm it down with the head of a rake or the back of a fork. Scatter sulfate of ammonia over this layer at the rate of $\frac{1}{2}$ oz to the square yard and then add

another layer of compost material. Continue in this fashion until the bin is full. Keep a cover over the top of the heap at all times, and if the compost becomes dry, remove the cover and water it to encourage the rotting process.

The layer of sulfate of ammonia may be alternated with one of lime to counteract acidity encouraged by sulfate of ammonia. Never add lime and sulfate of ammonia at the same time. Alternatively, proprietary compost activator may be used between each layer. Animal manure may also be added between the layers of vegetation but it should not come into contact with the fertilizer or lime. If it does, a chemical reaction will be triggered which will result in valuable nitrogen being given off into the atmosphere. When the bin is full a 2 in layer of soil may be spread over the top instead of burlap or polyethylene. Leave the bin and if possible start to construct a second bin.

Using the compost

In a well-made bin which has been sensibly filled the compost will not need turning, for virtually all the material will decompose sufficiently. Decomposition will be more rapid in spring and summer than in autumn and winter, but a good heap should be ready to use within six months of being completed, sooner in warm weather. Check the heap at intervals and, if possible, shovel out the usable compost from the bottom. The compost should be brown and crumbly, though some of the material may still be recognizable. Unrotted material may be left behind as the basis of the new heap.

Use only very well-rotted compost as a mulch, for partially decomposed material may contain weed seeds that will soon germinate and become a nuisance. Alternatively, dig in the compost during soil cultivations in autumn and winter at the rate of 10 lb per square yard.

Leaf-mold

The leaves of deciduous trees and shrubs may be rotted down on their own to make soil-enriching leaf-mold. A wire bin (similar to that made for compost) makes a suitable container, and 6–9 in layers of leaves can be sprinkled with sulfate of ammonia. A fast space-saving alternative is to pack the layers of leaves and fertilizer in black polyethylene sacks that have been perforated to allow in air. Filled, tied at the top and stood in an out-of-the-way corner, the sacks of leaves, will form good leaf-mold which can be used in the spring following autumn collection. Leaves in outdoor bins may take rather longer to decay. All leaves of deciduous trees and shrubs can be composted, but plane, poplar, and sycamore take longer to decompose than oak and beech. Leaves of evergreens are not suitable for leaf-mold production. Leaf-mold can be dug into the soil or used as a mulch. See page 12.

Leaf-mold

Fill perforated polyethylene sacks with dead leaves. Tie the tops and allow the sacks to stand until the leaf-mold is formed.

GREEN MANURE

Seed	Sowing time	Rate/sq yd
Rape	March–June	$\frac{1}{12}$ oz
Mustard	March–August	$\frac{1}{8}$ oz
Vetches	March–May	$\frac{3}{4}$ oz
Annual lupin	March–July	$\frac{1}{2}$ oz

The practice of sowing certain crops and digging the resulting plants into the ground to enrich the soil, provide a source of nitrogen and improve texture is known as green manuring. Rape, annual lupins, vetches, mustard and perennial rye grass may all be used. Broadcast the seed quite thickly over the ground in spring or early summer and then rake it in. The plants will grow quickly; dig them in just before they flower. Apply a dusting of sulfate of ammonia at the rate of 2 oz per square yard when the crop is dug in to prevent any temporary deficit of nitrogen. If there are no plants in the area, the sulfate of ammonia will assist bacteria in the breakdown process by providing nitrogen. Green manure plants are also often sown after a crop has just been cleared from the ground, for example in early spring or early autumn.

TYPES OF COMPOST BIN

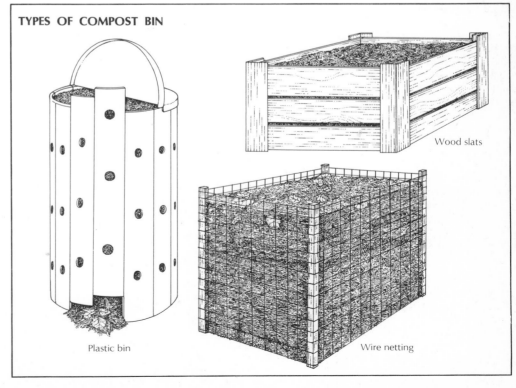

Wood slats

Plastic bin

Wire netting

Digging 1

Single digging

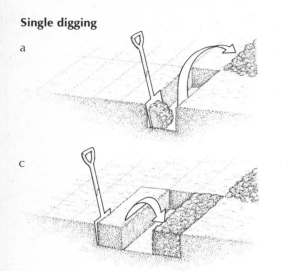

Double digging

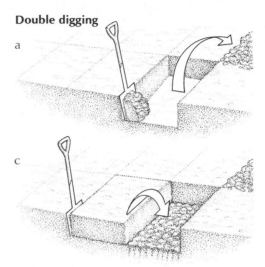

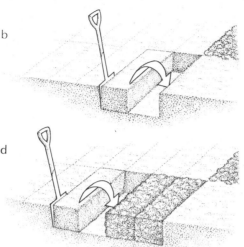

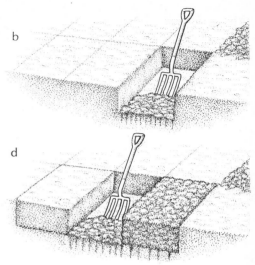

Although in nature the soil is seldom disturbed, except by worms and other underground life, man usually finds it necessary to cultivate the ground in which he grows plants for several reasons. These are: to control the growth of weeds; to incorporate manures, composts and fertilizers; to relieve compaction and improve soil texture, so allowing seeds to germinate and young roots to penetrate the soil; and to allow in air, so speeding up the process of humus decomposition and making nutrients available.

Digging

Digging is the most thorough of all soil cultivations because it disturbs the ground to the greatest depth. It is usually carried out annually on the vegetable plot, or on any ground being brought under cultivation for the first time.

As a general rule, digging is best done in the autumn and winter to allow the frost, wind, snow and rain to work on the rough-turned clods of earth and gradually break them down. This action is particularly valuable on heavy soils containing a high proportion of clay. However, never work on any soil when it is frozen or very wet. Digging is difficult in such circumstances and the soil's structure may become temporarily damaged through compaction by feet and tools.

On lighter soils, exposure to frost is not essential, for the clods will be naturally friable. For this reason, light soils can be cultivated at any time during winter and early spring, provided that they are allowed to settle for two or three weeks before the crop is sown or planted.

There are three main methods of digging, which involve cultivating the soil to different depths. See the illustrations above.

Single digging This is the most widely practised form of digging. It is adequate for most ordinary soils of reasonable depth which do not overlay an intractable sub-soil. During single digging the soil is cultivated to the depth of one spade blade (about one foot).

Begin single digging by taking out a trench one spade deep and about 12–15 in wide across one end of the plot to be dug (a). Pile the soil removed from this trench at the opposite end of the plot (it will eventually be used to fill the final trench). If the soil is to be manured as it is dug, throw the organic matter into the bottom of the trench at this point and mix it well in. Now take up the spade, starting behind the trench, lift up a comfortable spadeful of soil and throw it forward into the trench, turning it upside-down as you do so (b). This action ensures that any annual weeds are buried. Perennial weeds such as couch grass, dandelions, dock,

bindweed and ground elder should be painstakingly removed. If a portion of root is left, the weed will multiply. If grassland is being dug, the mat of grass can be skimmed off with the spade and thrown into the trench where it should be chopped up.

Work along the first trench throwing the soil over and forwards until another trench has been created (c). More manure may then be added and the operation repeated (d). When the end of the plot is reached, the soil from the first trench is used to fill the last.

If the plot is very wide, divide it in two lengthways and take out the first trench on one half of the plot, depositing the soil at the same end of the other half. Now work down the first strip of land and back up the second, throwing the soil from the first trench into the last one. By dividing the plot into two the chore of wheeling all the soil from one end to the other is avoided.

Double digging or bastard trenching With double digging the soil is cultivated to a depth of two feet. The technique is especially useful on land which has not been cultivated before or where a hard sub-soil layer is impeding drainage and the penetration of plant roots.

To double-dig a piece of land, first take out a trench 2 ft wide and one spade deep at one end of the plot (a). The soil removed is again

positioned alongside the spot to be occupied by the final trench. The plot may be divided in two, as for single digging, if it is very large.

When all the soil has been removed from the first trench, fork over the base to the full depth of the garden fork's tines (b). Compost or manure may be forked into the lower layer of soil or scattered on top of it after cultivation.

When the base of the trench has been cultivated, start to dig and throw forward the soil adjacent to it in the same way as for single digging (c). Make sure that the soil is turned over and perennial weeds are removed. When 2 ft of soil has been thrown forward into the first trench, the second trench will have been created and the base is forked over (d). The cycle continues until the entire plot has been dug to a depth of about 20 in. This method of digging improves the friability of the sub-soil without bringing it nearer the surface, so the richer layer of top-soil is always closest to the young roots of cultivated plants.

Trenching By far the most labor-intensive way of cultivating soil, trenching should only be practiced where a deep sub-soil pan is causing problems. During trenching the ground is cultivated to a depth of about 30 in —three spades deep—and manure can be forked into the broken-up sub-soil.

Digging 2

Trenching

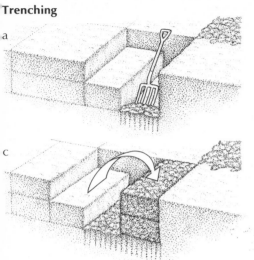

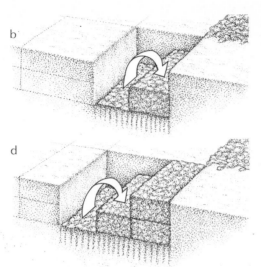

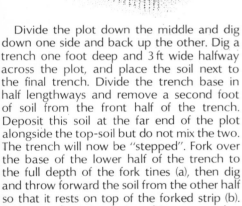

Ridging

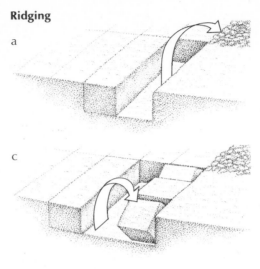

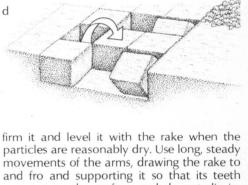

Divide the plot down the middle and dig down one side and back up the other. Dig a trench one foot deep and 3 ft wide halfway across the plot, and place the soil next to the final trench. Divide the trench base in half lengthways and remove a second foot of soil from the front half of the trench. Deposit this soil at the far end of the plot alongside the top-soil but do not mix the two. The trench will now be "stepped". Fork over the base of the lower half of the trench to the full depth of the fork tines (a), then dig and throw forward the soil from the other half so that it rests on top of the forked strip (b). Fork over the strip of ground just exposed.

Mark out the next 18 in wide strip of top-soil on the plot using a garden line, and throw this soil forward onto the step of second-foot soil in the front of the first trench, inverting it and removing perennial weeds (c). Now transfer the second foot of newly exposed soil to the forked strip alongside it (d), and cultivate the base of the newly created trench with a fork. This cycle of cultivation continues right down the plot—the two piles of soil taken from the first trench being used to fill the second foot and first foot trenches that are left.

Ridging On very heavy soils the type of digging known as ridging may be beneficial, for it exposes a greater surface area of soil to

the elements. Divide the plot in two as described in Trenching above. Then mark out a 3 ft wide strip at one end of the plot to be dug and remove a 1 ft wide trench at one end of this strip. Pile the soil by the final trench (a). Now work backwards along the marked-out strip, throwing the central spadeful of soil forwards and turning it upside down (b). The spadefuls of soil at either side of this are also inverted, but are turned inwards so that they lie against the first spadeful (c). In this way a ridge will be built up. Repeat the process (d), working along the first strip, then mark out a second and work backwards along that and so on until the plot is ridged.

Digging sensibly The craft of digging is something that can only be learned by practice, but there are some rules that will prevent it from becoming a back-breaking chore. First, remember to keep the spade vertical; a slanting cut achieves less depth. Drive the spade in at right angles across the trench to free the clod of earth and allow it to be lifted away cleanly. Lift up small spadefuls of soil that are easy to handle. It is possible to dig land faster by taking a greater number of small spadefuls rather than a lesser number of very heavy spadefuls which will tire the gardener rapidly.

Second, dig a little ground at a time on a regular basis. Cultivate a yard strip every

day rather than attempting to dig the entire plot at once.

Finally, only dig the soil when it is easily workable, not when it is snow-covered, frozen or very wet.

Forking On very stony or heavy ground which is difficult to penetrate with a spade, a fork may be used instead, and for cultivating the bottom of trenches during double digging and trenching, it is an invaluable tool. The disadvantages of using the fork for the entire digging operation are that it is unable to slice cleanly through surface weed growth, and that light soils may fall through its tines. However, the fork may be used to good effect as a cultivating tool between established plants, and in spring to break down rough-dug land that has been weathered through the winter.

Raking This is an important task but one which is often overdone. The main reason for raking should be to level a piece of ground, either for seed sowing, planting or laying paving materials. Certainly the rake is also used to break down clods of soil to a reasonably fine tilth, but if used to excess it will create a dusty surface that will cake in the first shower of rain. Over-raking will also expose an abundance of stones. As a general rule, it is best to break down the clods of soil with the back of a fork. Then trample the ground to

firm it and level it with the rake when the particles are reasonably dry. Use long, steady movements of the arms, drawing the rake to and fro and supporting it so that its teeth sweep over the surface and do not dig in. The rake can also be used to lightly cover seeds after broadcast sowing, to replace the soil in drills, and to collect leaves and other garden debris.

No-dig gardening

Some gardeners believe that digging is harmful to the soil as it disturbs the activity of bacteria and earthworms and so upsets the natural balance. Non-diggers prefer to apply thick mulches of well-rotted compost, manure or peat to the surface of the soil and let earthworms and other organisms incorporate this enrichment. Seeds are sown in the compost and subsequent mulches are applied while the plants are growing.

There is no doubt that this technique works and saves labor, but it does require very large quantities of compost or manure so that organic matter may have to be brought in. Digging may be more laborious but it is certainly cheaper and the yield and quality of some crops has been shown in experiments to be markedly improved in land dug to 3 ft. To dig or not to dig is thus more a philosophical than a horticultural question.

Watering 1

If plants are to grow healthily without check, they must have access to a constant supply of water (see water cycle, page 9). For most of the year in temperate climates, the soil contains sufficient moisture to satisfy the plants' needs. But during very dry spells in spring and summer the plants may find it impossible to extract sufficient water to keep them turgid; they will wilt and growth is temporarily halted. If water is not made available to them soon after wilting, their leaves will turn crisp and brown and they will eventually die.

For this reason the gardener must be able to provide "artificial" supplies of water, or irrigate, before the plants wilt.

Timing of applications

The timing of irrigation is particularly important with vegetable crops if they are to develop steadily and produce the maximum yield. Care must also be taken to give plants sufficient water. There must be enough to reach the roots, not just to wet the soil surface.

As a general rule, an inch of water will travel to a depth of 9 in in the soil. To water an acre of land to this depth, a total of 22,650 gallons must be applied. Continuous light applications of water during periods of prolonged drought are not to the plants' best advantage. They will not reach the majority of roots; they will harden the surface of the soil, and they will encourage the plants to produce surface roots, which will suffer in future droughts.

Sandy soils will dry out much more quickly than those containing clay, and will have to be watered sooner during spells of drought. The surface is seldom a good guide as to the state of the rest of the soil, so dig down for 9–12 in with a trowel to see if the soil is moist. If it is dry or only just moist, water.

With vegetable crops in particular the water can best be utilized while the plants are growing rapidly—usually during late spring and early to mid-summer. Shortages of water at this time cause the greatest check and may even result in some crops bolting (prematurely running to seed).

Food crops Later in the summer excessive quantities of water may do real harm to certain vegetables. Melons, for instance, should be kept on the dry side once their fruits are beginning to ripen, otherwise the fruits will split and be spoiled. Late summer rains or irrigation can impair the storage qualities of onions, just when they should be drying off prior to being strung. Beans and peas should be watered at 1–2 gal per square yard per week when the flowers and pods appear. Too much water during early growth encourages leaves at the expense of flowers and crops.

However, for most green crops such as lettuces and brassicas, good supplies of water will keep them cropping, both prolonging and increasing their yields. A rate of 2–3 gal per square yard per week is adequate.

Ornamentals Less research has been done on the water needs of ornamental plants. However, ornamental plants have much the same water needs as food crops. Pot-grown flowers and shrubs are at greater risk than those in open ground. Do not let them dry out.

Planting

Most applications of water to growing plants will be given in spring and summer, rather than in autumn and winter. Spring is the prime planting season for deciduous trees and shrubs, and it is a good idea to water them in well unless the ground is extremely moist at planting time. Such watering-in is not necessary so much to keep the plant growing, as to settle the soil particles around the roots in readiness for summer growth.

Susceptible sites

Plants growing in open ground may certainly dry out due to exposure to sun in summer, but they will also receive their full quota of winter rains. Other sites in the garden may not be so well catered for and the gardener should see that they are given extra attention. Beds and borders against walls are particularly prone to drying out and should be enriched with organic matter to make them absorbent. This means that they can readily soak up any rainfall they receive, and also supplies of irrigation water given during dry spells. Soil close to walls is often poor and low in organic matter and can be very difficult to wet once it is dry. The same goes for soil under trees and alongside hedges.

Plants in tubs, pots and particularly hanging baskets will need regular applications of water through the summer because they can dry out very quickly. When filling the container with compost, leave a gap between the surface of the soil and the rim of the container to allow a sufficient amount of water to be applied. Water when the top inch of the container soil dries out. Aim to keep the top inch damp but not sodden. Both over- and under-watering can harm container-grown plants.

Techniques of watering

Water may be applied to the soil or to plants in containers by several different means.

Watering can The simplest method of transporting water to plants is by the use of a watering can. There are several designs and sizes, but a two-gallon can will be found the most useful for general garden needs. Cans larger than this are difficult to lift when full, and smaller ones involve too many journeys to and from the faucet. Choose a can with a long spout, good balance when full and a long reach. Steel and plastic cans are available and both have their good and bad points. Steel cans tend to develop leaks after a while, but they can usually be repaired. If handled carefully, plastic cans last many years, but once they start to leak they are

Irrigation and root systems

1 If water is applied in small amounts, the soil surface will harden, and plants will develop surface roots in an effort to reach the moist top layer of soil.

2 Check the moisture content of the soil by digging a hole with a trowel. The state of the soil 9–12 in down is the best guide to watering needs.

3 If the soil is dry, water well to make sure that the moisture reaches the roots of the plants.

Watering 2

useless. Spray heads or "roses" are supplied with most cans. These vary from fine to coarse. Use a fine rose on seeds and seedlings.

When using a can fitted with a rose to water flats of seedlings, begin pouring to one side of the plants then pass the can over them, maintaining a steady flow. Move the can away from the plants before stopping the flow of water. This technique avoids sudden surges of water which can damage tender plants and displace soil.

Hoses If a faucet is situated in or near the garden, a hose will avoid tiresome journeys with the watering can. It may be left running on a patch of soil and moved around at intervals, or it may be held over a particular plant or group of plants if the gardener has the patience and time to spare. Take care not to allow strong flows of water to wash away soil and expose the roots of plants. On the vegetable garden water can be allowed to run from the hose along furrows made between crop rows. Water applied in this way will quickly get to the roots. Buy a strong hose which will not kink when bent and which will retain its suppleness over the years. Cheap hoses will crack and leak, especially if used in cold weather. Hoses reinforced with

nylon thread are especially strong. A wide range of clip-on connectors and nozzles is available for use with hoses.

Perforated hoses Large expanses of ground are time-consuming to irrigate unless some kind of semi-automatic system is used. Sprinklers are useful because they can be turned on and left to apply large quantities of water to the ground in a fine spray which is easily absorbed. This type of application is to be preferred to flooding because it ensures that the water is more evenly distributed in the soil. The perforated lay-flat hose type of sprinkler is attached to a faucet and laid across the land to be irrigated. When the water is turned on, it is discharged at many different angles from the pin-prick holes in the hose. Move the pipe from time to time to provide an even distribution of water.

Sprinklers There are three main types of sprinkler, both of which can be attached to a hose. The oscillating type consists of a perforated tube which rocks backwards and forwards, distributing its water over a square or rectangular area. It can usually be adjusted to cover a chosen part of the garden. The rotating sprinkler ejects water from one or more nozzles which are forced around by the

water pressure. This type of sprinkler covers a circular area. The fixed type simply sprays water out over one rather restricted area. All sprinklers are controlled by the water pressure.

Pop-up sprinklers which oscillate or rotate can be laid in lawns or vegetable gardens and supplied with water by underground pipes. The nozzles sit just below the surface of the soil when out of action (useful on the lawn where mowers can then be used safely) and spring up when the water is turned on.

The evenness of distribution of any sprinkler can be tested by placing jam jars at intervals over the soil being watered. The quantities the jars contain after an hour or so can be compared. The jars will also give an approximate indication of when an inch of water has been applied.

Sprinklers may be less effective on ornamental plants than on vegetables, especially in summer. The foliage of some ornamentals will deflect much of the spray, and heavy blooms and foliage can be weighed down and damaged by the water. Sprinklers are best used on ornamentals not in bloom.

Drip irrigation Lengths of pipe fitted with short drip nozzles, or with longer "spaghetti"

tubes that can be directed to individual plants, are particularly useful where water has to be kept off plant foliage. In flower beds, borders and garden frames, and among pots and hanging baskets, such hoses can be fitted to dispense water slowly when the faucet is turned on. They keep soil disturbance to a minimum and supply the water slowly enough to ensure instant absorption into the soil and fast take-up by plants.

Soaker hoses Canvas hoses pierced with small holes are called soaker hoses. They allow water to ooze onto the soil. Ideal for vegetable gardens, soaker hoses supply water so that it reaches the roots rapidly.

Use of natural water sources

The diversion of streams and ditches is practised infrequently in temperate climates, but it can be used to advantage, particularly at the start of the growing season. If a stream runs through or past the garden, it is a simple task to pump water from it at any time and apply it to crops. If taking water from a source that is bordered by several properties, make sure that other property owners are left with their fair share of water. Check with river authorities for abstraction laws.

Planting

After planting trees and shrubs, water them in well to settle the soil around the roots. This speeds growth.

Containers

When planting in containers, leave a gap between the compost and the rim of the pot to allow for watering. When watering, carefully fill this space.

Watering seedlings

1 Begin pouring to one side of the flat or pot to allow the water to flow steadily.

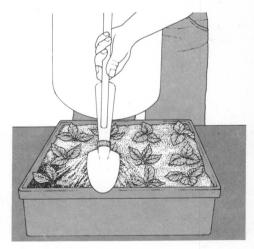

2 Pass the can across the seedlings, keeping the angle constant, moving it clear of the pot or flat before halting the flow of water.

Basic tools 1

Every gardener should aquire a few basic tools of good quality, rather than a large selection of cheap implements that will be uncomfortable to use, short-lived and of little practical value. Although a good spade or fork is not cheap, with care it will probably have as long a life as its owner.

Shafts and handles

The shafts of tools can be made from several different materials, including wood, metal and plastic. Wood is traditional and long lasting. Make sure that the wood of the shaft is close grained and that the grain runs down the length of the shaft. Check that it is smooth and not likely to splinter.

Shafts made from polypropylene are light-weight yet strong, and lighter tools such as hoes and rakes are often equipped with tubular aluminum alloy shafts which are coated with plastic. All these materials will offer good service if they are not ill-treated.

Spades and forks are fitted with handles in two shapes: "D", and "YD". If possible try both when choosing a tool so that the more comfortable is selected.

Spade

Spades are available with shafts of different lengths and blades of different sizes. The standard spade blade measures about $11\frac{1}{2}$ in by $7\frac{1}{2}$ in; that of the ladies' spade 10 in by $6\frac{1}{2}$ in, and that of the border spade 9 in by $5\frac{1}{2}$ in. Choose whichever is most comfortable to use and bear in mind that heavy digging will probably be easier with the middle size. Choose a shaft length to suit the height of the user.

The shaft of the spade should have a gentle bend to allow maximum leverage, and the strapped or tubular socket should be securely attached to the shaft. Metal treads welded to the upper edge of the blade make digging heavy soil less painful to the foot.

Spades with stainless steel blades are far more expensive than those equipped with blades of forged steel, but they are exceptionally long lasting and penetrate the soil more easily than ordinary steel spades.

Uses An essential tool for digging and trenching, the spade is also efficient for skimming weed growth off the soil before cultivation

begins. Always hold the spade upright when cutting into the soil prior to lifting it, so that the ground is cultivated to the full depth of the blade. The spade is also useful for planting trees and shrubs, and for mixing compost.

Fork

The fork is just as useful as the spade and is similarly manufactured. The four tines may be square in cross-section, as in the general purpose or digging fork, or flat as in the potato fork which is designed to avoid tuber damage at harvesting time. The head of the digging fork measures 12 in by $7\frac{1}{2}$ in, and that of the smaller border fork 9 in by $5\frac{1}{2}$ in. Stainless and forged steel types are available.

Uses A fork is easier to use than a spade for digging heavy soil, though it cannot be used to skim off weeds. It is essential for breaking down rough-dug soil and for lightly cultivating well-worked ground before seed sowing and planting. The smaller border fork can be used to cultivate the soil among herbaceous plants and shrubs, and the larger fork for moving compost and manure. Both can be used to aerate lawns.

Hand fork

Of the same size as a trowel, the three- or four-pronged hand fork is similarly made.

Uses For transplanting seedlings, for working among tightly packed plants such as alpines in the rock garden, and for intricate planting and weeding, the hand fork is unsurpassed.

Rake

The most popular type of garden rake has a steel head 12 in wide which is fitted with teeth 2 in long. The shaft should be approximately 5 ft long and smooth to allow a good back-wards and forwards motion. Larger wooden rakes are useful for raking up leaves, grass and debris, which clog in steel rake teeth. However, wooden rakes wear out faster.

Uses The main use of the rake should be to level soil which has been previously broken down to a reasonable tilth with a fork. Although the rake will make the soil texture even finer, it should not be over-used or the soil will be inclined to pack. Move the rake backwards and forwards over the soil in a sweeping motion, first in one direction and then at right angles to ensure an even finish.

Hoe

There are many different types of hoe but the two most important are the Dutch hoe and the draw hoe. Both are equipped with 5 ft handles and forged or stainless steel blades. The head of the Dutch hoe consists of a horseshoe-shaped piece of metal, across the open end of which is attached a flat 4–5 in blade designed to cut almost horizontally through the soil. The rectangular or semi-circular head of the draw hoe is of a similar width but is attached at right angles to the handle and is used with a chopping or scraping motion.

Uses The Dutch hoe is perhaps the best tool for general weeding, for the operator skims it backwards and forwards just below the surface of the soil while walking backwards. In this way the cultivated ground is not walked over and the weeds (severed from their roots) are left to dry out in the loose soil. The Dutch hoe is also used for breaking up packed surface soil.

With the draw hoe the operator must move forwards, chopping the soil and pulling it towards him slightly, or scraping the weeds

---

HANDLE SHAPES

D-shape

YD-shape

Using a spade

Keep the blade of the spade vertical when cutting into the soil. This ensures that the ground is dug to the full depth of the spade.

Using a hand fork

Aerate the soil around rock garden plants by the careful use of a hand fork. Hold plants back with one hand.

Basic tools 2

off the surface. The draw hoe (despite its disadvantage of forcing the operator to walk over the cultivated soil) is safer to use among closely spaced plants than a Dutch hoe.

Both types of hoe can be used to draw seed drills against a taut garden line, and the draw hoe is used to hill up vegetables such as potatoes, leeks and celery.

Trowel

An invaluable planting tool, the trowel may have a wood, steel or polypropylene handle 4–6 in long. Longer-handled versions are available but may be less comfortable to use. If possible buy a trowel with a stainless steel rather than a forged steel blade for it will be much easier to use and less likely to bend.
Uses The trowel may either be used like a shovel or flour scoop and also as if it were a digging claw. Either method may be used depending on the preference of the gardener. Scoop the soil out of the hole. Insert the plant in the hole and refirm the soil around the roots with the hands. Use the trowel for planting bedding and vegetable plants, herbaceous plants and bulbs.

Wheelbarrow

In larger gardens and on the vegetable plot a wheelbarrow can save a lot of time and energy. Always check the weight distribution of a barrow before buying it—as much of the load as possible should be placed over the wheel so that the barrow, and not the operator, takes most of the weight. Barrows are available with large, inflated, ball-shaped wheels, and these are especially useful if the land to be traversed is soft. Small, two-wheeled barrows can be easier to load, unload and push than single-wheeled types. Solid tire models are adequate where sinkage will not be a problem. Make sure that the chosen barrow is large enough without being too heavy. Two-wheeled trailers can be obtained which can be towed by cultivators or garden tractors. Before purchasing a trailer check the widths of garden paths and gates.
Uses Compost, manure, soil, sacks of fertilizer and all manner of tools and equipment can be moved around the garden with the aid of a barrow. Stand the barrow upright against a wall or under cover when it is not in use to prolong its life.

TYPES OF BARROW

Ball-wheeled

Traditional

Two-wheeled

Using a rake

Level previously dug soil by moving the rake backwards and forwards across the soil surface.

Using a Dutch hoe

Skim the blade of the hoe just below the soil surface while walking backwards. Keep the blade horizontal to cut cleanly.

Using a draw hoe

Use a chopping motion, moving forward and drawing the soil towards the feet.

Use a trowel to make a planting hole

Scoop soil out of the hole, insert the plant and firm the soil with the hands.

Cultivation techniques 1

Once the ground has been prepared, the fundamental techniques of cultivation help to keep the soil in the correct state and maximize plant growth.

Hoeing

No gardener can afford to be without at least one kind of hoe to cultivate the soil around his ornamental plants and fruit and vegetable crops. Hoeing serves two useful purposes: it keeps down weeds and so reduces competition for light and nutrients; and it relieves compaction and allows vital air into the soil. It is also claimed that a layer of fine soil on the surface of the ground acts like a mulch and prevents excessive water loss.

There are many designs of hoe to choose from (see pages 20–21). One of the best is the Dutch hoe. It has a flat blade held at the end of two metal arms which allow soil to pass between them. The tool is pushed and pulled back and forth just below the surface of the soil so that it severs the stems of weeds from their roots. If used too deeply the Dutch hoe is less effective at controlling weeds. Pronged cultivators may be used in a similar manner. They are more valuable for breaking down the soil than for weeding.

The three-pronged cultivator looks like a fork fixed at right angles to the end of a stout shaft. It is used with a chopping and pulling motion and the operator works forwards (instead of backwards as with the Dutch hoe).

Hoes of a similar design but with a solid blade are very common. The draw hoe or swan-necked hoe is a long-handled version. It is the best tool for drawing seed drills and is also very useful for hilling up. The onion hoe is a much smaller version of the draw hoe and can be used effectively with one hand to thin out many crops in the seedling stage—the chosen seedlings are held firm and the rest chopped out with its blade.

Hilling up

The gardener may draw up soil around the stems of plants, or "hill them up", for one of several reasons. Young and tender shoots may emerge too early in spring and a covering of soil will be needed to protect them from frost. This is often the case with potatoes and some herbaceous plants. Pull a little fine soil over the shoots with a draw hoe or a rake.

Brassicas such as cauliflowers, kale and Brussels sprouts will often become top-heavy when nearing maturity. A mound of soil pulled around the base of the stems will give them extra stability. A draw hoe is the best tool to use.

Vegetables grown especially for their crisp, white stems or leaf stalks are surrounded by soil both to keep out the light (a process known as blanching) and to encourage them to extend. With leeks this process can be carried out gradually through the growing season. Celery is hilled up at the end of summer when the plants are almost mature. Hold the leaf stalks together by a tube of paper or cardboard and bank soil up against them with a spade. The paper helps to keep the celery hearts clean.

With potatoes hilling up prevents the tubers from being exposed to the light, which will cause them to become green and unpalatable. A draw hoe or pronged cultivator will be found useful for this task, which should be carried out at ten-day intervals in the early stages of growth.

Blanching

Blanching aims to prevent light reaching certain vegetable crops so that their leaves, leaf stalks or stems become white instead of

Earthing up

To protect new shoots of herbaceous perennials from frost in spring, pull a little fine soil over them with a draw hoe or rake.

Support tall brassica plants such as Brussels sprouts by forming mounds of soil around their stalks with a draw hoe, helping to prevent wind damage.

Hill up celery every three weeks as the plants grow. Draw soil gently up around the stems with a spade or hoe. Do not let soil fall into the hearts.

Hill up potatoes, using a draw hoe, at ten-day intervals during the early stages of growth.

Cultivation techniques 2

green. In such a state certain vegetables have a better flavor and are crisper. The blocking of light prevents the production of chlorophyll—the green coloring in plants. Hilling up, a method of blanching celery and leeks, is described above.

The hearts of endives are blanched to improve their flavor. Place a plastic pot over the plant. Cover the pot's holes to exclude light. The pot will prevent light from reaching the leaves and in a few weeks the endive can be harvested with a crisp, white heart.

Forcing

A number of plants can be coaxed into early growth if they are provided with the necessary conditions. In this way the gardener can produce flowers and food when they are out of season and consequently expensive to buy in the shops.

Most plants that are to be forced require

some heat, but a low temperature of 10°–15°C/50°–60°F will suffice. Greenhouses, frames or propagating cases may be used.

Potatoes and green beans can be potted up in 12 in pots or tubs in December and January and grown on to maturity in their containers. Rhubarb, chicory and seakale require different conditions. To produce the best crops of these three vegetables light must be excluded. When the roots or crowns have been potted or boxed up in soil, put them under the greenhouse staging or in a frost-free place and cover them with a sheet of black polyethylene supported by wire hoops, or, in the case of pots, place a second inverted, pot on top of the first. Should light enter, the shoots will become yellow and, in the case of chicory and seakale, bitter.

Strawberries potted up in summer may be moved into the greenhouse in January to provide early crops, and container-grown

flowering shrubs may be similarly treated.

Flowering bulbs can be given eight weeks or so in cool conditions to encourage root production and then moved into a greenhouse to bring them into flower early.

Most vegetable plants are best discarded after one forcing, but if necessary they can be planted in the garden and allowed to recover—no crop being taken the following year. Bulbs, too, can be planted outdoors after forcing. Flowering shrubs should only be forced every other year, and forced strawberries should be discarded after use.

Ring culture

Where greenhouse border soil is poor or infected with disease, ring culture offers an alternative means of growing healthy tomato plants. Erect 8 in high boards down either side of the border, flatten the soil and lay a sheet of polyethylene over it. Pierce the

polyethylene sheet at intervals with a garden fork to make drainage holes.

On top of the sheet place a 6 in deep layer of coarse gravel or weathered ashes. Tomatoes are best grown in 9 in diameter whale-hide or aluminum rings or in 9 in plastic pots with their bases removed. Before planting, space the rings 18 in apart on the bed of gravel and fill them with potting mix or good soil. Put them in position a few days before planting to allow the soil to warm up.

Water the soil after planting to settle the tomatoes in, but apply all subsequent waterings to the gravel. Apply diluted liquid feeds to the soil. This encourages two distinct root systems to develop: feeding roots in the ring and water-absorbent roots in the gravel. Flood the gravel at the end of each season to remove any impurities and disease organisms. Use fresh soil or potting mix every year.

Blanching

Blanch endive hearts by placing an inverted plastic pot on crocks over the plant. Cover the hole to exclude light.

Forcing

Pot up rhubarb, chicory or seakale in soil. Cover the pots with black polyethylene and put in a frost-free place.

Alternatively, force rhubarb by covering the plants with a bucket or trash can in mid-January–February. Insulate with straw. Pick 5–6 weeks later.

Ring culture

Place rings on a bed of gravel or ashes and fill with soil. Water should be applied to the gravel to encourage root growth.

Cultivation techniques 3

There are many gardening techniques which are specifically designed to improve plant performance and yield. They modify the growth and habit of a plant, changing its natural growth pattern in order to satisfy the gardener's requirements.

Thinning

Thinning is practiced on the fruits of such crops as grapes and peaches which the plant produces in large numbers. Some fruits are cut out while they are still small to allow a lighter crop to develop more fully. Such action also saves the plants' energy, so increasing the likelihood of their cropping well the following year. Gooseberries can be thinned from late May, when the fruits are large enough for cooking. Remove every second fruit, leaving the remainder to develop into large dessert fruits. Grapes under glass are thinned in June over a 10–14 day period, removing the interior berries first and then the smallest, leaving a pencil thickness between the developing berries. Thin developing fruit and flowers from melons, leaving one fruit per shoot of frame-grown plants.

Apples and pears should be thinned to one or two fruits per cluster, with the clusters 6 in apart. Thin in mid-June and again a month later. Thin plums similarly, leaving them 2–3 in apart. It is essential to thin peaches if very large fruits are to be produced. Thin over a period, aiming for fruits 9 in apart.

Pinching

Many plants are naturally bushy and form a well-spaced framework of shoots or branches. The stems of others possess what is known as apical dominance—the shoot at the tip of the main stem will grow vigorously and the growth of all other shoots is retarded. Some plants with this habit tend to become tall, spindly and ugly if not encouraged to bush out. Ornamentals such as fuchsias benefit from pinching and develop an attractive bushy habit. The way to reduce apical dominance is to pinch out the terminal shoot. Other shoots will then develop and the plant will become more shapely. Successive pinching of these shoots may be needed on some plants to maintain a bushy habit.

Vines, cucumbers and melons are pinched at certain stages to encourage fruit development, and chrysanthemums grown for show are "stopped," or pinched back, to obtain a definite number of shoots per plant if large flowers are required.

Disbudding

On plants such as roses, chrysanthemums, dahlias and carnations, the gardener can choose whether he wants a cluster of small blooms or one large one. Exhibitors will invariably attempt to produce the largest bloom possible, allowing only the terminal flower bud to remain on each stem—all the others being pinched out as soon as they are large enough to handle.

Pollination

The transference of pollen from the male stamen to the female stigma of a flower is the first step in seed production and is known as pollination (see page 114). It is essential that most plants grown for fruit are pollinated, and occasionally the gardener must give nature some help—particularly in the greenhouse where natural pollinators such as bees may not be present at flowering time. Spray the blooms of peaches and grapes with a fine mist of water or dust them with a soft paintbrush or rabbit's tail to transfer the pollen grains. Some flowers may simply be shaken; on those such as melons, which produce separate male and female flowers, detach the male blooms and dust them over the female blooms.

Feeding

Plants both in open ground and in containers must be kept supplied with nutrients to maintain healthy, vigorous growth. Outdoors the rain will leach plant foods from the soil, and the nutrients in container soil are quickly used up by the developing plant.

From March to September all actively growing plants in containers will benefit from being given a fortnightly feed diluted at the recommended rate in water. Only apply fertilizer when the soil around the roots is already moist so that the nutrients can be quickly absorbed. There are many proprietary brands, but certain straight fertilizers can be diluted in water and used as liquids (see

Thinning fruit

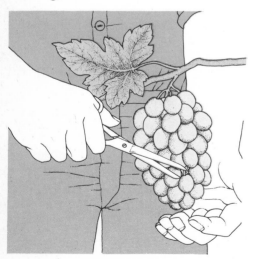

Thin dessert grapes with scissors, carefully removing interior berries in order to leave a pencil thickness between berries.

Thin wine grapes by bunches, removing surplus bunches to leave the required number per spur.

Thin gooseberries in May, picking every second fruit and using them for cooking. The remainder will be dessert fruits.

Thin apples and pears to one or two fruits per cluster. Thin in mid-June and again a month later.

Cultivation techniques 4

page 13). Plants such as tomatoes grown for their fruits will benefit from being given high potash fertilizer at an early stage of fruit development. Leafy crops will benefit from fertilizers with a high nitrogen content and root crops from those containing a high proportion of phosphates. Different crops have different nutritional needs and therefore these generalized recommendations should be treated with care. See **Fruit** (pages 90–145) and **Vegetables** (pages 34–89).

Liquid fertilizers may be applied with a watering can or through a special dilutor which can be attached to a hose. This acts as a reservoir for the liquid fertilizer and controls the amount mixed with the water.

Certain liquid fertilizers may be applied to the foliage of plants where they will be quickly absorbed into the sap-stream. Foliar feeds are useful for giving plants a quick boost but they should be used with caution on species with hairy leaves.

Mulching

A 2–3 in thick layer of organic matter spread around plants growing in beds and borders will serve several useful purposes. It will slowly decompose and help to enrich the soil; it will suppress weed growth, and it will conserve soil moisture. Suitable materials for mulching are described on page 12. Mulches are best applied in spring. Remaining material can be forked into the soil in autumn. The soil can then be allowed to weather and absorb the winter rains. It is important to ensure that the soil is moist before applying a mulch. If the soil is dry the mulch slows down the passage of rainwater.

A mulch of black polyethylene can be used with crops such as strawberries and potatoes. Stretch yard-wide strips across the prepared soil, anchor the edges in shallow trenches and make planting holes with a knife or a bulb planter. The strawberries are planted after the polyethylene has been laid. Potatoes grown under a plastic mulch do not have to be hilled up, as although they develop on the surface of the soil they are protected from light by the plastic. Although such a mulch will not enrich the soil, it does suppress weeds and retain moisture. It is especially useful where organic matter is scarce.

THINNING SEEDLINGS

Seeds sown where the plants are to grow to maturity will frequently produce dense clusters of seedlings which, if they are not reduced in number, will compete and become weak and spindly. For this reason they are usually thinned out as soon as they are large enough to handle to the distance apart required by the mature crop, or by the growing plants if they are to be further transplanted. Thin seedlings while the soil is damp, pressing firmly on the ground around seedlings to be retained and pulling up and discarding those which are not wanted. Alternatively thin with an onion hoe, which is a tool similar to a draw hoe only small enough to be used with one hand. Hold the seedlings to be retained with one hand and chop away surplus seedlings using the onion hoe. Carefully remove thinnings and put them on the compost heap. Thinnings left lying on the ground may harbor pests and diseases. Water seedlings after thinning.

Pinching

Pinch out the growing tip of plants such as fuchsias to encourage the growth of side-shoots and a bushy habit.

Pollination

Pollinate melons by detaching the male flowers and brushing them against the female flowers.

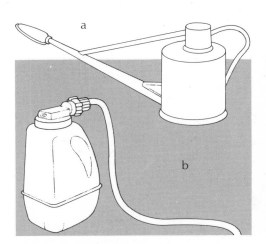

Transfer pollen from the male stamen to the female stigma using a camel-hair brush.

Feeding

Apply liquid fertilizers with a watering can (a) or with a reservoir attached to a hose (b).

Mulching

Black polyethylene can be laid on ground where vegetable crops are to be grown and the plants grown through slits cut in it.

Protecting plants

Staking and supporting

Newly planted trees will be able to support themselves as soon as the roots are established, but require staking initially, particularly in windy places. Other garden plants such as chrysanthemums produce large heavy blooms and need constant support.

Trees Dig the planting hole and check that it is large enough for the tree's roots. Then pound a stake into the soil until one third of its length is buried. The stake should be either a length of 2 in by 2 in timber, treated with a preservative other than creosote, or a larch pole similarly protected. Position the stake to windward of the tree. The top should be just below the lowest branch.

With the stake firmly in place, plant the tree. Then fix one tree tie 2 in from the top of the stake and another 1 ft above soil level. Check the ties regularly and loosen them as necessary.

Another method of staking, used in orchards, is carried out immediately after the tree has been planted rather than before. Hammer a stake into the soil at an angle of 45 degrees so that it crosses the tree trunk

2–3 ft above soil level. The top of the stake should point to windward. Bind the tree to the stake with strong twine.

Alternatively, hold the tree firm with three guy ropes. Fasten these around the trunk and lower branches of the tree and cushion them either with short lengths of rubber hose through which the rope is led, or with burlap. Space the guy ropes equally around the tree and peg their lower ends to the soil.

Flowers Support dahlias, delphiniums and other plants which have top-heavy stems either with stout bamboo canes or 1 in wooden stakes pushed into the ground alongside them. Fasten the stems to the supports with soft twine or raffia. Make sure that the support does not touch the flower or damage may result.

Support bushy herbaceous plants by pushing twiggy branches among them while they are small. As the plants grow they mask the branches but are held steady by them. More permanent herbaceous plant supports include wire hoops on legs. These are available in various sizes and can be adjusted as the plants grow.

Vegetables Among vegetables only beans and peas normally need support. Pole beans can be grown up wigwams of 8 ft canes pushed into the ground in 4 ft circles held together at the top with wire or stout twine. Alternatively, grow the plants up canes or poles spaced 18 in apart. Tie opposite poles together near the top to leave a V-shaped gap. Lay further poles or canes along these gaps and then bind the whole structure together. Support peas with twiggy branches in the same way as herbaceous plants, or with plastic netting on canes.

Wind protection

Wind can cause great damage in the garden, particularly to newly planted trees and shrubs. The plants may be blown over and they may become desiccated, which causes their foliage to wilt and turn brown.

Anti-desiccant sprays These chemicals seal the pores through which the plant loses moisture, and so help it to remain turgid. Spray with diluted mixture at planting time.

Screens may be used to shelter trees or shrubs. For example, a plastic fertilizer sack,

slit at the base to make a sleeve, can be held around a shrub with three or four canes. Alternatively nail a sheet of burlap to two posts pounded into the ground on the windward side of the plant.

Frost protection

The crowns of tender perennial garden plants such as globe artichokes, agapanthus, eremurus and gunnera are susceptible to frost. Protect them by laying a piece of wire netting over each crown. Cover this with dry straw or bracken and fasten another layer or netting over the top to make a warm blanket. Protect larger plants and shrubs by surrounding them with a cylinder of wire netting filled with straw or bracken.

Protection from wet

Some alpines are particularly sensitive to excess moisture in winter. In their natural habitat, they are covered with a layer of dry snow which protects them. To prevent them from rotting off, cover each with a pane of glass supported on wooden or wire pegs. Tie the glass down with wire.

Staking

Pound a stake into the planting hole on the windward side of the tree. Ensure one third of its length is below the ground.

Secure the tree to the stake with two tree ties, placed 2 in from the top and 1 ft above soil level.

Supporting flowers

Support top-heavy flowering plants with bamboo canes. Tie the stems to the canes with soft twine or raffia.

Support herbaceous plants by inserting bushy twigs among them. The plants will grow through the branches.

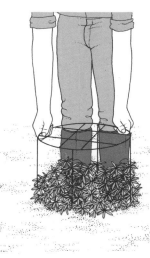

Wire plant supports can also be used to support herbaceous plants.

Wind protection

Use a plastic sack fixed to four canes to keep down the force of the wind.

Moving and storing plants

It is sometimes necessary to move plants, from alpines to large shrubs and young trees, from one part of the garden to another, or to another garden. The technique outlined here is for large plants. The same basic process, with modifications, should be used for all plants. Always insert burlap or plastic sheet under the rootball and never lift a plant by its neck or branches.

Moving trees and shrubs

The operation is best carried out in early spring or the fall. First, tie in any spreading branches or wrap the plant in burlap to prevent the stems from being damaged and to allow room for lifting. Next, using a spade, cut a vertical slit around the plant. Aim to cut at a distance equivalent to the spread of the top-growth. This cut will sever any side-spreading roots. Using this slit as the inner edge, take out a trench 1ft wide and one spade deep all around the plant, severing any roots that protrude from the ball of soil left around the plant.

Ease away any loose soil around the shoulder of the rootball and then thrust the spade underneath the rootball at an angle of 45 degrees to cut off more roots. The aim should be to retain as large a ball of soil around the roots as can be conveniently handled.

When the plant is movable, ease a sheet of burlap or polyethylene underneath it and then wrap up the entire rootball to retain the soil and prevent moisture loss. Tie the material firmly in place around the stem or trunk. Transport the plant with care to its new site and dig a hole wide and deep enough to accommodate the rootball with 1ft to spare all round.

Dig a generous helping of rotted manure, peat or leaf-mold into the base of the new planting hole, together with a few handfuls of bonemeal to promote fresh root growth. Carefully position the plant. Replace and refirm the soil all round and water it in thoroughly. Spread a 3–4 in mulch of organic matter such as peat, leaf-mold or pulverized bark around the plant.

Considerable amounts of water may be lost by evergreen shrubs and conifers during the move, and an anti-desiccant spray may be applied to the foliage immediately before transplanting to reduce transpiration.

On exposed sites some protection from wind after transplanting will cut down water loss and reduce the likelihood of "wind rock", which will dislodge the roots from the soil and cause them to dry out. Three or four wooden posts can be hammered into the ground around the plant and a screen of burlap or close-weave plastic netting nailed to them. Remove the screen when the plant is established.

Storing plants

Smaller plants can be easily stored in a temporary trench dug in a spare corner of the garden. This technique, called heeling in, should also be used for bare-root shrubs and container-grown plants which are not to be planted immediately. Using a spade, cut a V-shaped furrow at the chosen site. Do this by thrusting the spade vertically into the ground and pulling it back, while still in the earth, to form a trench or slot. Lay the plants against the upright side of the trench and replace the soil loosely.

HEELING IN

Lay bare-root plants in a shallow trench at an angle of 45 degrees. Cover the roots with loose, friable soil.

Moving trees and shrubs

1 Tie in any spreading branches to protect the plant during the move. Wrap smaller shrubs in burlap.

2 Cut a vertical slit in the soil around the plant with a spade. Make the slit 1–2 ft away from the stem, depending on size.

3 Take out a trench 1ft wide and 1 spade deep starting from the slit. Sever any roots that protrude into the trench.

4 Thrust the spade under the rootball at a 45-degree angle, cutting the roots. When it will move, ease the rootball on to a sheet.

5 Dig a hole at the new site 1ft wider all round than the rootball. Add leaf-mold or peat and two handfuls of bonemeal.

6 Carefully place the plant in the hole. Firm the soil and mulch well. Support with guy-lines if necessary.

Placing plants 1

Having decided on the layout of the garden, it is time to consider exactly which plants will be grown where. It makes sense to start with trees. These will be the largest and most permanent specimens, acting as focal points to which other plantings can lead.

Trees

Site garden trees where their form can be appreciated and where they will have room to develop unhindered. Avoid planting specimens that will outgrow available space. Consider the habit of the tree as well as its flower, foliage and berry color. In confined spaces fastigiate (columnar) trees are best; where space needs to be filled, those with spreading branches can be chosen. For small gardens choose trees which have several attractive features and which can be enjoyed for much of the year, rather than those which only have a spectacular but brief blossoming period. Evergreen trees provide form and interest all the year round, though many deciduous trees are attractive even when bare. Trees can affect nearby buildings, causing shade and extracting water from the sub-soil, creating the risk of subsidence. Plant large trees away from buildings if possible.

The ground under deciduous trees will have to be cleared of leaves in autumn. For this reason do not position pools or sandpits under their canopy. Evergreens will also lose a proportion of their leaves during the year and these too can be a nuisance.

Shrubs

Once garden trees have been chosen and plotted on a plan, shrubs can be used to build up the framework of the planting scheme. Distribute those which have evergreen leaves over the whole of the garden. This is advisable for two reasons: first, it will give a certain amount of form to the entire plot, and second, it will prevent one particular corner from becoming heavy and unchanging, which might be the case if the evergreens were all planted together. In very small gardens where trees cannot be fitted in, shrubs must take their place, acting as focal points as well as a framework.

When designing shrub and mixed borders, plot in the plants on a plan and number them from one to twelve according to the month in which they are at their best. In this way it is possible to see exactly what will be of interest in the garden at any time of year. Obvious gaps can be filled, or plants repositioned to distribute color and form more evenly over the garden and over the months of the year. A little careful planning at this stage will help to create a garden for all seasons.

Herbaceous perennials

Strictly speaking, herbaceous perennials are those plants which survive for many years but whose stems and leaves die down each winter and re-emerge afresh in spring. However, some of these plants possess foliage which is more persistent and may be present to a lesser degree through the winter months.

No garden would be complete without herbaceous plants. If shrubs are invaluable as framework then these plants have just as important a role to play as fillers. This is not to say that the plants lack form; some of them are majestic and bold, but their stature is enjoyed only for part of the year.

Plan the herbaceous border in the same way as one devoted to shrubs. In most gardens the two types of plant are intermingled in "mixed borders", which are the best solution where year-round form is required.

Plants for walls

House and garden walls, fences, pergolas, arches and ugly buildings can all be improved by training climbers and wall shrubs over their surfaces. All these plants will benefit from good soil preparation and manure enrichment to encourage moisture retention, for the earth at the foot of walls and fences can become very dry. Many of them will need some form of support. Ivy and Virginia creeper will cling on their own, but for the rest some horizontal wires stretched between wall nails, or sections of wooden trelliswork fastened to the wall will help them to remain upright (see page 91). Most shrubs will need tying in and may need regular pruning to keep them trim and close to the wall.

Make sure that the right plant is chosen for a wall of a particular aspect—the planting lists (page 29) offer advice on suitability.

Single-color schemes

In most gardens color schemes will involve the use of a wide range of shades, although these should be carefully toned so that they do not clash. However, it is possible to plan beds, borders and even entire gardens with plants having one particular flower or foliage color. White gardens—where gray-foliaged and white- and cream-flowered plants are grouped together—have been successfully created, as have red and silver gardens, and gardens based on variegated leaved plants.

In small gardens such schemes are best confined to individual borders if they are not to become overpowering and monotonous. However, if annual flowers are used there is no reason why such a scheme should not be changed from year to year: blues, violets and purples one year; reds, pinks and creams the next; greens and yellows to follow.

Some form of permanent skeletal planting in shades of green and gray can be used to good effect in single-color gardens. Not only will such plants set off the flowers well, they will also provide interest during the darker months of the year.

Planning

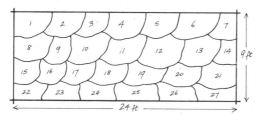

(1) 3 Aster 'Fellowship'. Soft pink, September. 4 ft.
(2) 5 Helenium 'Moerheim Beauty'. Rich crimson, July-Aug. 3 ft.
(3) 3 Echinops 'Taplow Blue'. Metallic blue, July-Aug. 5 ft.
(4) 5 Heliopsis 'Incomparabilis'. Golden orange, July-Aug. 4 ft.
(5) 4 Delphinium 'Blackmore's Glorious'. Mauve, June-July. 5-7 ft.
(6) 3 Aster 'Crimson Brocade'. Deep red, September. 3 ft.
(7) 5 Polygonum Amplexicaule 'Astrosanguin

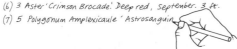

Plan a border by numbering plants on a plan according to the month they are at their best.

Tree forms

It is important to know the habit of a tree before planting it. Trees can be spreading (a), weeping (b), fastigiate (c) or conical (d).

Check the eventual height and spread of the tree and allow it adequate space when planning the garden.

Placing plants 2

KEY
E Evergreen foliage
T Texture and color of bark
B Berries
F Flowers
L Leaves
S Stems
H Habit or form

KEY

E	Evergreen foliage
T	Texture and color of bark
B	Berries
F	Flowers
L	Leaves
S	Stems
H	Habit or form

CLIMBERS AND WALL SHRUBS FOR WALLS OF VARIOUS ASPECTS

North-facing walls
Camellia species and varieties
Chaenomeles species and varieties
Cotoneaster horizontalis
Escallonia macrantha
Forsythia suspensa and varieties
Garrya elliptica
Hedera species and varieties
Jasminum nudiflorum
Parthenocissus species
Tropaeolum speciosum

South-facing walls
Actinidia kolomikta
Callistemon species
Campsis species
Ceanothus species and varieties
Clianthus puniceus
Fremontodendron species and varieties
Lonicera species and varieties
Magnolia grandiflora
Rosa species and varieties
Wisteria species

East-facing walls
Celastrus orbiculatus
Chaenomeles species and varieties
Clematis species and varieties
Garrya elliptica
Hedera species and varieties
Hydrangea petiolaris
Kerria japonica 'Pleniflora'
Parthenocissus species
Pyracantha species and varieties
Tropaeolum speciosum

West-facing walls
Abutilon vitifolium
Camellia species and varieties
Carpenteria californica
Chimonanthus praecox
Cytisus battandieri
Fremontodendron species and varieties
Magnolia grandiflora
Passiflora caerulea
Solanum crispum
Wisteria species and varieties

TREES AND SHRUBS WITH COLORED FOLIAGE

	Height	Color
Abies species and varieties	20–150 ft	Gray/silver
Acer negundo 'Variegatum'	20–50 ft	Green and white
Acer palmatum 'Atropurpureum'	10 ft	Maroon
Calluna vulgaris varieties	1 ft	Yellow/orange/gray
Catalpa bignonioides 'Aurea'	35 ft	Yellow
Cedrus atlantica 'Aurea'	30 ft	Yellow/gold
Chamaecyparis lawsoniana varieties	1–45 ft	Silver/blue/yellow
Convolvulus cneorum	2 ft	Silver-gray
Corylus maxima 'Purpurea'	10 ft	Deep maroon
Cotinus coggygria 'Royal Purple'	10 ft	Maroon
Elaeagnus pungens 'Maculata'	15 ft	Yellow and green
Gleditsia triacanthos 'Sunburst'	35 ft	Yellow
Juniperus chinensis varieties	3–25 ft	Gray/green/blue
Juniperis horizontalis 'Plumosa'	1 ft	Gray-purple
Juniperus sabina varieties	2–5 ft	Gray/blue
Juniperis virginiana	100 ft	Blue-white
Ilex × altaclarensis 'Golden King'	15 ft	Yellow and Green
Pieris formosa 'Wakehurst'	4–8 ft	Red
Picea glauca albertiana 'Conica'	6 ft	Light green
Robinia pseudoacacia 'Frisia'	30 ft	Yellow
Thuja occidentalis	50–65 ft	Yellow/gold

TREES AND SHRUBS FOR SPECIFIC LOCATIONS

Small gardens	Height	
Acer palmatum varieties	10 ft	L
Betula pendula 'Youngii'	15 ft	H
Corylus avellana 'Contorta'	10 ft	FS
Gleditsia triacanthos 'Sunburst'	35 ft	
Malus 'John Downie'	20 ft	FB
Pyrus salicifolia 'Pendula'	25 ft	LH
Robinia pseudoacacia 'Frisia'	30 ft	L
Sorbus aucuparia 'Beissneri'	25 ft	FBL

Fastigiate trees	Height	
Chamaecyparis lawsoniana varieties	20 ft +	E
Ilex aquifolium 'Green Pillar'	20 ft	EB
Juniperus virginiana 'Skyrocket'	20 ft	E
Prunus 'Amanogawa'	20 ft	F
Prunus 'Spire'	25 ft	F
Sorbus commixta	20 ft	LBF
Sorbus 'Joseph Rock'	25 ft	LBF
Taxus baccata 'Fastigiata Aureomarginata'	15 ft	E

Weeping trees	Height	
Betula pendula 'Dalecarlica'	40 ft	HL
Crataegus monogyna 'Pendula Rosea'	15 ft	F
Fagus sylvatica 'Pendula'	50 ft +	L
Laburnum watereri 'Alford's Weeping'	15 ft	F
Prunus subhirtella 'Pendula'	15 ft	F
Pyrus salicifolia 'Pendula'	15 ft	L
Salix × chrysocoma	40 ft	LS
Ulmus glabra 'Camperdownii'	15 ft	L

Acid soils	Height	
Betula pendula 'Dalecarlica'	40 ft	TL
Calluna vulgaris & varieties	1 ft	EF
Erica species & varieties	1 ft	EF
Pernettya mucronata	2–3 ft	EB
Pieris formosa & varieties	10 ft	EF
Rhododendron species & varieties	3–15 ft +	EF

Coastal gardens	Height	
Arbutus unedo	15 ft	EFB
Choisya ternata	8 ft	FE
Elaeagnus pungens 'Maculata'	15 ft	E
Fuchsia magellanica varieties	6 ft	F
Griselinia littoralis	12 ft	E

Coastal gardens cont.	Height	
Hebe species & varieties	1–6 ft	EF
Lavatera olbia	6 ft	LF
Phlomis fruticosa	3 ft	LF
Phormium tenax varieties	3–6 ft	L
Pyracantha species & varieties	10 ft	EFB
Senecio 'Sunshine'	5 ft	EF
Sorbus aucuparia varieties	20 ft +	FLSTB
Tamarix pentandra	10 ft	LF

Lime soils	Height	
Aucuba japonica & varieties	10 ft	EB
Buddleia davidii & varieties	10 ft	LF
Cistus species & varieties	3 ft	EF
Crataegus oxyacantha	15 ft	FB
Deutzia varieties	6 ft	F
Forsythia species & varieties	6–10 ft	F
Genista species & varieties	1–10 ft	F
Hebe species & varieties	1–4 ft	EF
Helianthemum varieties	1–2 ft	EF
Ilex aquifolium varieties	15 ft	EB
Mahonia aquifolium	4 ft	EF
Philadelphus varieties	8 ft	F
Rhus typhina	15 ft	L
Sorbus aria & varieties	20 ft	FLB

Shrubs for shade	Height	
Aucuba japonica	10 ft	EB
Buxus sempervirens	1–10 ft	E
Gaultheria shallon	5 ft	EFB
Hypericum calycinum	1 ft	EF
Juniperus × media 'Pfitzerana'	3 ft	E
Mahonia aquifolium	4 ft	EF
Mahonia japonica	3 ft	EF
Pachysandra terminalis	1 ft	EF
Sarcococca confusa	3 ft	EF
Vinca species & varieties	Trailing	EF

Scented flowers or leaves	Height	
Buddleia davidii & varieties	10 ft	F
Chimonanthus praecox	8 ft	F
Choisya ternata	8 ft	FL
Daphne species & varieties	2–5 ft	F
Eucalyptus species	20 ft +	L
Hamamelis mollis & varieties	12 ft	F
Lavandula species & varieties	1–2 ft	FL
Lonicera periclymenum	8 ft	F
Lippia citriodora	4 ft	L
Mahonia japonica	6 ft	F

29

Rock gardens 1

Plants from mountain and rocky regions are usually called alpines. They are plants which have adapted to very different soil and climate conditions to those found in the normal garden. If they are to thrive they must be provided with the right site and soil. For this reason the plants are usually grown in specially mixed soil among rocks, which provide shaded root-runs and also form the right background to show off these small plants to best effect. Rock gardens should be planned as garden design features as well as plant habitats and carefully integrated into the overall garden plan. Alpine plants have well-defined soil and site requirements. Many rock garden plants are not true alpines and are easily grown, but the special needs of true alpines must be catered for.

Site Nearly all alpines require an open and sunny spot. Shelter by distant fences or trees is beneficial in cutting down drying winds, but avoid heavy shade from trees,

which will shed leaves onto the plants. Roots from trees can penetrate rock gardens and inhibit growth.

Drainage and soil In their natural environment many alpines are covered in a dry blanket of snow through the winter. This protects them from severe frost, then melts away in late spring, watering the plants as it does so. Their growing medium is often less soil than rock waste or gravel. Ideally, therefore, plants should be sheltered from winter rain and grown in a freely-draining medium which can nevertheless retain some moisture. In practice, ideal conditions are not obtainable except in an alpine house. Efforts must be made to avoid the major problems of damp and summer desiccation.

Construction

The traditional rock garden aims at re-creating a natural rock outcrop, with the plants growing between carefully bedded stones.

The true rock garden is on a slope, but rock beds can also be built on level ground with rocks and dwarf conifers or shrubs adding height.

The site can be graded to provide a slope, or a depression can be dug and the sides terraced. Top-soil should be removed first and replaced evenly when the re-shaping is complete.

Improving drainage If the site is level, check the soil drainage. If it is at all poor, remove the top-soil to a depth of 12 in, then put down a 6 in layer of rubble. Top this with a 9–12 in layer of loam, sand, grit, leaf-mold and peat mixed together to form a suitable rooting medium. Ensure that the drainage of the surrounding area is adequate. Lighter, better-drained soils should be improved by the addition of grit, sand and peat, so that free drainage and adequate moisture retention are ensured. Carefully remove all weeds, and cultivate to a depth of 1 ft.

Rocks Most rock gardens are made from sand stone or limestone, and occasionally from granite. Choose local stone, which will blend with its surroundings and which may also be available more cheaply. The rock should be of a kind that will weather easily to give a natural appearance. Several large pieces of rock are to be preferred to a multitude of smaller boulders which will tend to give a "plum-pudding" effect. Rock is never cheap so use small quantities wisely. It is usually sold by the ton, which is about 14 cu ft of rock pieces. Specify the largest and smallest sizes required when ordering. Fifty pounds is the heaviest one person can comfortably handle.

Shape the ground into the required contours using a fork and a rake and tread the entire site firm before positioning the rocks. Choose the best faces of the rock and bury any newly-broken surfaces which will take a long time to weather. Move the rocks to their sites and position them with their best faces

TYPES OF ROCK GARDEN

Alpines can be grown in spaces between paving stones (a), in traditional rock gardens (b), in dry walls packed with soil (c), or in sink gardens or troughs (d).

Construction

1 After clearing and draining, if necessary, fork over and rake the bed, molding the soil into the required shape. Tread the soil.

2 Position the rocks on the site, making sure that the strata run the same way. Adjust until the desired result is achieved.

3 When all the rocks are in place, firm soil around them, taking care to avoid air pockets.

Rock gardens 2

forward and with their strata running in the right direction. Group small rocks around one large piece of stone to give the impression that they are part of it, taking care that the strata correspond. Aim to build up natural-looking terraces, with the layers running horizontally with a slight backwards slope. Rocks do not have to be buried deeply. No more than a quarter of the rock need be below the surface.

Once the rocks are in position they can be let into the soil. Have on hand sufficient mixed soil or compost to create planting pockets between the rocks. Excavate sufficient soil with a spade, maneuver the rock into position and then ram the soil firmly behind it. Leave no air pockets. When the rock is positioned it should look and feel firm.

Planting

Once the rocks are laid, lightly rake the soil around them to relieve surface compaction. Plant when the soil is moist but not too wet.

In milder areas planting is best undertaken in early autumn. In colder places and where wet winters are common early spring is a better time, but make sure that spells of early summer drought do not check the plants' root development.

Water the rock garden well before planting. Remove each plant from its pot, having first given it a good watering. Excavate a hole in the required place using a trowel or hand fork. Lower the plant in, refirming the soil so that no air pockets are left and the surface of the potting compost around the plant is level with the surface of the soil on the rootball of the plant. Consider the habit of each plant before positioning it, and allow it sufficient room for growth.

When planting is completed, a 1 in layer of coarse grit can be spread over the surface of the soil. This will ensure that the necks of the plants do not become waterlogged, will show them off well, keeps down weeds and helps to retain moisture. Label each plant.

Maintenance

A grit layer will help to keep down weeds, but any which do emerge should be removed at once. In prolonged dry spells between April and July water the rock garden. To check if watering is necessary, scrape any gravel away and probe the soil with a trowel. When the soil is dry 2 in down it is time to water. Use a sprinkler which will apply a steady and penetrating spray.

Remove all leaves that blow onto the rock garden in autumn and cover any plants that cannot tolerate winter wet with a sheet of glass supported on wire legs. Leave this protection in place from November to February. Top-dress rock garden plants with a mixture of equal parts loam, grit and leaf-mold in early spring. Work a few handfuls around and among each plant. Lightly clip over those alpines which produce untidy seedheads or straggly growth as soon as they have finished flowering. Prune plants which spread too far, using secateurs.

Planting

1 Excavate a hole large enough for the plant's roots. Fill it with water and allow it to drain away.

2 Lower the plant into the hole and firm the soil around the roots to avoid air pockets.

Maintenance

Cover plants that cannot tolerate winter wet with a sheet of glass supported on wire legs. Spread a layer of grit 1 in deep around the plants to keep down weeds.

SCREE BEDS

Rock garden plants which require extremely sharp drainage are best cultivated in scree beds, designed to simulate the naturally-occurring conditions at the foot of mountain slopes where there is a deep layer of finely broken rock and a certain amount of humus.

A scree bed is essentially a raised bed with much of the soil replaced by stone chips. Retaining walls of sandstone, brick or broken paving slabs may be used to support the sides of the bed, and these should be given an inward batter to make them stable. Lay the lowest stones on a concrete foundation; the upper courses may be dry or filled with soil to accommodate plants that enjoy growing in vertical crevices (these should be inserted as building progresses) Leave drainage holes in the base of the wall at frequent intervals. The bed should be at least 2 ft high over clay soils to provide good drainage; at least 1 ft high over sandy soil. Place a 4-to-6 in layer of broken bricks and rubble in the bottom of the bed and use the following compost to fill the rest of the space: 10 parts stone chips, 1 part loam, 1 part peat or leaf-mold and 1 part sand, plus a slow-release fertilizer. Plant in autumn or spring.

Hedges 1

Initial pruning of hedges

Group One
Blackthorn (*Prunus spinosa*), box (*Buxus sempervirens*), hawthorn (*Crataegus monogyna*), *Lonicera nitida*, Myrobalan plum, privet (*Ligustrum ovalifolium*), snowberry (*Symphoricarpos spp*), Tamarisk (*Tamarix gallica*): cut each

plant back to 6 in from ground level.

Group Two
Beech (*Fagus sylvatica*), *Corylus maxima* 'Atropurpurea', flowering currant (*Ribes sanguineum*), hazel, hornbeam (*Carpinus betulus*): cut back leading shoots and longer side-shoots by one-third.

Group Three
Conifers and evergreens such as cherry laurel (*Prunus laurocerasus*), gorse (*Ulex europaeus*), *Griselinia littoralis*, holly (*Ilex aquifolium* and vars), laurel (*Aucuba japonica*), Lawson cypress (*Chamaecyparis lawsoniana* and vars), Leyland cypress (× *Cupressocyparis leylandii*), New Zealand daisy bush (*Olearia* × *haastii*),

× *Osmanthus burkwoodii*, *Osmanthus delavayi*, *Poncirus trifoliata*, *Viburnum tinus*, Western red cedar (*Thuja plicata* especially 'Atrovirens', yew (*Taxus baccata*): cut back untidy laterals, do not prune the leader.

Hedges make excellent garden barriers where walls and fences are undesirable. They provide a natural backdrop to other garden plants and thorny hedges are effective obstacles against domestic and farm animals. The traditional garden hedge is formal, close-clipped to give it a regular outline. But there are many shrubs which will make excellent informal hedges.

Hedges do have two main disadvantages. First, they must be clipped or pruned annually, and in some cases two or three times in one year; second, they use soil nutrients which may be needed by plants growing close to them. The first problem is eased if an electric hedge trimmer is used for clipping, and the second by applying liquid fertilizer each spring to the plants growing alongside the hedge and to the hedge itself. Mulching with rotted manure is beneficial as it makes the hedge's roots less likely to spread in search of food.

Planting
The time of planting will depend on the shrub being used. Deciduous shrubs which are lifted from the open ground and supplied "bare root" should be planted in early spring. Evergreens and conifers may be planted in April and May or in September and October. If the plants arrive at an inconvenient time or when the ground is unfit for planting, heel them in (see page 27). Container-grown shrubs can be planted at any time of year provided attention is paid to watering in dry spells.
Ground preparation Hedges usually remain in place for a long time, so make sure that ground preparation is thorough. Use bamboo canes and stout twine to mark out the strip of ground to be occupied by the hedge. Excavate a trench 2–3 ft wide and one spade deep along the line that the hedge will take. Fork over the base of the trench, incorporating well-rotted compost, manure, peat or leaf-mold. Set aside more of the organic matter to mix with the soil when it is firmed back around the plants. Two or three handfuls of compound fertilizer can be forked into each running yard of the trench.
Choosing plants It is tempting to choose plants which are very large so that an instant

effect is achieved. Avoid doing this. Smaller plants, around 12–18 in high, are not only cheaper but will usually establish themselves much more quickly than older specimens. If immediate protection is needed, erect a post and wire fence alongside the young hedge.
How to plant Plant when the soil is moist and easily workable, not when it is very dry, frozen or muddy. Trim any broken or damaged roots from the plants with sharp shears and space them out in the trench at the required distance (see table right). Remove the containers from container-grown shrubs but do not disturb the rootball unless the roots are pot-bound, when they should be gently teased out.

Where hedges of 3 ft or more thickness are required, use a staggered double row of plants. Set the rows 12–15 in apart, against garden lines stretched along the trench.

Spread out the roots of bare-root plants and replace the soil, firming it around the roots with the foot. The old soil mark on the stem of each plant should rest at or just below soil level. Container-grown plants should have their rootballs just buried, so that the new soil level is about 1 in above the old. Firm the soil around the stem.

Immediately after planting neatly cut off any ungainly or damaged stems or branches with a pair of shears. Prune most deciduous hedges to one third of their height, and hawthorn and privet to 6 in from ground level. Evergreens and conifers may be sprayed with an anti-desiccant solution to reduce transpiration and encourage the rapid establishment of the young plants.

Aftercare
Spread a 2–3 in mulch of moist peat or pulverized bark over the soil at the foot of the hedge in the first spring after planting. Do so immediately in the case of spring-planted conifers and evergreens. Make sure the soil is moist before the mulch is applied.

The hedge must not be neglected after planting if it is to grow unchecked and establish itself rapidly. In dry weather frequent waterings will be necessary. In frosty weather the ground should be refirmed around the plants every day so that the roots do not dry out in the lifted earth.

Planting

Excavate a trench 2–3 ft wide and 1 ft deep where the hedge is to grow.

Fork over the base of the trench, incorporating organics. Add compound fertilizer at 4 oz per yard.

Trim any broken or damaged roots from bare-root plants with shears.

Spread out the roots of bare-root plants, place them in the trench and replace soil, firming well.

Initial pruning

Cut plants back on planting to encourage strong basal growth. See chart at top of page.

Cutting

Trim formal hedges at least twice a year. Stretch a garden line taut along the hedge to ensure straight cut.

Hedges 2

Key to hedging plants table

Site	Features	Pruning	Growth rate
A: suitable for coastal sites	1: flowers	For pruning groups see list at top of page 48	The figures give the number of years taken by the plant to grow to 5 ft.
B: suitable for windy sites	2: foliage	S: cut with shears	
C: suitable for lime soils	3: fruits	Sh: cut with secateurs	
D: suitable for heavy soils	4: thorns		

Clipping and pruning

For most formal hedges twice-yearly clipping is necessary, though privet may need three clips. May and August are the best times to carry out the operation and the shears (or electric trimmer) should be sharp and well lubricated. Aim to create a hedge which is slightly narrower at the top than at the base so that light is allowed to reach the lower portions and snow is shed more easily.

Informal hedges, which are often grown for their flowers, may be pruned to shape with a pair of shears immediately after flowering and then left untouched until the same time the following year.

Cut all formal deciduous hedges and small-leaved evergreens with hedge clippers or an electric trimmer. For informal hedges and large-leaved evergreens such as laurel and holly use shears, which will leave the foliage unmarked and produce a better shape. Clippers can be used if the hedge is very long. Remove damaged leaves and stems with shears after cutting with clippers.

Gather up and burn all the clippings as soon as the job is finished; do not allow them to lie on lawns or among border plants.

Chemical retardants are available to reduce the growth of both formal and informal hedges. They are usually applied in spray form shortly after the spring clipping or pruning. After application, the hedge will retain its shape until the following spring when a further cut and spray will be necessary. Follow the instructions on the label closely and do not apply the retardant to those species listed as being unsuitable for treatment.

Weeds have a tendency to grow unnoticed at the foot of hedges, and leaves and litter may also collect there. Clear out all this rubbish during the winter when it can easily be seen and removed and apply a weedkiller such as simazine to inhibit germination.

Screens and windbreaks

Where strong winds severely limit the types of plant that can be grown in a garden, it is a good idea to establish a row of trees to act as a windbreak. Such barriers may also be useful in hiding an ugly view. Trees make excellent windbreaks for they filter the wind, so slowing it down, rather than stopping it dead like a wall and creating turbulence and damaging eddies. Plant the screen at right angles to the wind. It will cut down the force of the wind on its leeward side for a distance up to 20 times greater than its height.

Suitable upright windbreak and screening trees include: *Chamaecyparis lawsoniana* (Lawson cypress), × *Cupressocyparis leylandii* (Leyland cypress), *Populus alba* (White poplar), *Populus nigra* 'Italica' (Lombardy poplar), *Thuja plicata* and cultivars.

HEDGING PLANTS

		Site	Features	Planting distance	Pruning	Evergreen/ deciduous	Formal/ informal	Growth Rate
Aucuba japonica 'Green hedger'	Laurel	C D	2	24 in	Group 3 S	E	F/I	5
Berberis darwinii	Barberry	C D	1 2 4	18 in	Sh	E	F/I	6
Berberis × *stenophylla*	Barberry	C D	1 2 4	18 in	Sh	E	F/I	5
Buxus sempervirens	Box	C	2	12 in	Group 1 S	E	F	8
Carpinus betulus	Hornbeam	C D	2	12 in	Group 2 Sh	D	F	6
Chamaecyparis lawsoniana and vars	Lawson cypress	D	2	24 in	Group 3 Sh	E	F	5
Corylus maxima 'Atrapurpurea'			2		S	D	F	
Cotoneaster simonsii		A C D	1 2 3	18 in	S	E	F/I	5
Crataegus monogyna	Hawthorn/Quick	A B C D	1 2 4	12 in	Group 1 Sh	D	F	7
× *Cupressocyparis leylandii*	Leyland cypress	A	2	30 in	Group 3 S	E	F	3
Escallonia macrantha		A D	1 2	18 in	S	E	F/I	4
Fagus sylvatica	European beech	B C	2	12 in	Group 2 Sh	D	F	5
Forsythia × *intermedia* 'Spectabilis'	Golden bells	C D	1 2	18 in	S/Sh	D	F/I	4
Fuchsia magellanica		A C	1 2	12 in	S	D	I	5
Ilex aquifolium and vars	Holly	A D	2 3 4	18 in	Group 3 Sh	E	F	8
Lavandula spica and vars	Lavender	A	1 2	12 in	Sh	E	I	Only 2 ft
Ligustrum ovalifolium	Privet	C	2	12 in	Group 1 Sh	E	FF	4
Lonicera nitida		C D	2	12 in	Group 1 Sh	E	F	5
Metasequoia glyptostroboides	Dawn redwood		2	24 in	Sh	D	F	5
Olearia × *haastii*	New Zealand daisy bush	A C	1 2	12 in	Group 3 S	E	I	7
Poncirus trifoliata			4		Group 3 Sh	D	F/I	
Prunus laurocerasus	Cherry laurel		1 2 3	24 in	Group 3 S/Sh	E	F/I	3
Rhododendron ponticum	Common rhododendron	B	1 2	24 in	S	E	I	5
Rosa rubiginosa	Sweet briar	A C D	1 2 4	18 in	S	D	I	3
Rosa rugosa	Ramanas rose	A C D	1 2 4	18 in	S	D	I	5
Tamarix gallica	Tamarisk	A B	1 2	12 in	Group 1 S	D	I	4
Taxus baccata	Yew	B C D	2	24 in	Group 3 Sh	E	F	8
Thuja plicata 'Atrovirens'	Western red cedar	C D	2	24 in	Group 3 Sh	E	F	5
Ulex europaeus	Gorse	A B	1 2 4	18 in	Group 3 S	E	I	6
Viburnum tinus	Laurustinus	A B C	1 2	18 in	Group 3 S/Sh	E	F/I	5

Crop rotation

Growing the same vegetables in the same piece of ground each year eventually results in a build-up of soil-borne pests or diseases. Such continuous growing of brassicas, for example, favors club-root, and successive crops of onions are likely to cause a build-up of stem eelworm.

Different types of vegetables require different ground preparation and cultivation procedures. Potatoes need a deeply cultivated soil which is continually moved during hilling up. On the other hand, root crops—such as carrots, parsnips and beets—need a firm, level soil with a fine tilth which is disturbed very little during the growing season.

Fertilizer, lime and manure requirements also vary. Potatoes respond to large applications of organic manure and fertilizer but they should not be limed. Brassica crops also respond to applications of manure and fertilizer but they require a soil between pH 6.5 and 7.5.

These are the major reasons for practicing crop rotation in the vegetable garden. It must be said that rotations are easier to effect on paper than they are on the ground.

Grouping the crops
It is useful to put vegetables together in groups which have similar crop protection, cultivation, manure, fertilizer and liming requirements. Groups are then moved sequentially around the vegetable plot so that, over a period of years, a particular piece of ground grows all the crops. In theory it is better to leave as large an interval as possible between growing a crop again on the same site, but it is rarely possible to leave more than three or four years. Thus three and four year rotations have been devised and a three year plan is considered here. A certain amount of compromise is necessary in order to simplify the rotation. Potatoes are grouped with root crops, even though they benefit from applications of organic manure and root crops do not.

Having divided the vegetables in this way, the groups are moved sequentially around the plot over a three year period. The plot is roughly divided into three equal sized units, but an area should be left at one end on which perennial vegetables, such as asparagus and artichokes are grown permanently.

In year one the potato and root crop unit receives no manure or lime but moderately heavy quantities of fertilizer. The legume and onion unit receives heavy dressings of manure and little fertilizer or lime. The brassicas receive average amounts of manure and fertilizer but heavy applications of lime. Crop rotation therefore ensures that all parts of the plot receive manure, fertilizer and lime regularly while the dangers of pest and disease build-up are minimized.

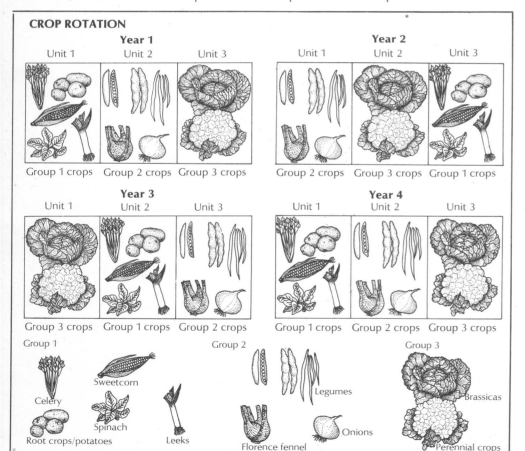

CROP ROTATION

Year 1
Unit 1 — Unit 2 — Unit 3
Group 1 crops — Group 2 crops — Group 3 crops

Year 2
Unit 1 — Unit 2 — Unit 3
Group 2 crops — Group 3 crops — Group 1 crops

Year 3
Unit 1 — Unit 2 — Unit 3
Group 3 crops — Group 1 crops — Group 2 crops

Year 4
Unit 1 — Unit 2 — Unit 3
Group 1 crops — Group 2 crops — Group 3 crops

Group 1: Celery, Sweetcorn, Spinach, Root crops/potatoes, Leeks
Group 2: Legumes, Florence fennel, Onions
Group 3: Brassicas, Perennial crops

CATCH CROPPING AND INTERCROPPING

Some vegetables grow and mature more quickly than others so there are times of the year when gaps appear in the vegetable plot. These gaps can be used to grow—or catch—a crop of rapidly maturing vegetables. Thus the ground occupied by peas in Unit 2 of the crop rotation plan may not be needed for brassicas until the following spring and can be used for crops such as radishes or endive.

Intercropping Rapidly maturing crops can also be intercropped or grown between slower maturing crops. Spinach can be grown between rows of slow-growing leeks, for example.

Lettuces 1

OUTDOOR LETTUCE
Head types (butterheads)
'Arctic King', 'Buttercrunch',
'Cobham Green', 'Fortune',
'Mildura' (mildew resistant),
'Suzan'.

Head types (crispheads)
'Avoncrisp' (resistant to mildew
and root aphids), 'Great Lakes',
'Webbs Wonderful',
'Windermere'.
 Cos types:
'Little Gem', 'Lobjoits Green Cos',
'Winter Density'.

Lettuce is the salad plant for all seasons. Although an annual that matures naturally during the early summer, the use of suitable varieties, cloches or heated frames, and the correct growing conditions make it possible to harvest lettuce throughout all but the very coldest months.

Types of lettuce

Several different types of lettuce have been bred and they vary considerably in size, form and texture. Three main groups may be recognized although there are intermediates.

Head lettuce These include the butterheads with globular soft-leaved heads, and the crispheads, also round-headed but with crinkly, crisped leaves. They will usually tolerate poorer and drier soils than the other groups.

Cos lettuce The lettuces of this group are upright in growth with more or less oblong heads of crisp leaves. They grow best in rich, moist soils. Modern varieties do not need to be tied to produce a compact head.

Leaf lettuce These non-heading lettuces produce masses of curled foliage but no true head. The leaves can be picked a few at a time and the plants will continue to grow and produce further leaves for later picking. Some varieties of cos lettuce will continue growing in the same way if closely spaced.

Cultivation

Many modern varieties of lettuce have been specially bred to mature at particular seasons and it is important to select those suitable for the crops required. Depending on the weather and the region, summer- and autumn-maturing lettuce is sown successively from late March to early August to mature from June to October. In warm regions, heat-resistant varieties should be grown during summer months because lettuce germinate and thrive best in a cool climate. Lettuce sown outdoors in August will mature in November to December if kept under cloches from just before the first frost. Mildew-resistant and forcing varieties should be used at this time of year. For eating from January to March, lettuce must be sown and raised in a heated (7°C/45°F) greenhouse from November to January. Small varieties can also be grown indoors under fluorescent lights. In mild areas, early spring lettuce is obtained from seeds sown in September or October and grown under cloches to mature in April.

Soil and situation All lettuce varieties prefer an open position in a well-drained and fairly rich soil of pH 6.5–7.5. Lettuces require considerable quantities of water during the growing period and the soil must be humus-rich so that it is able to retain and supply moisture for the rapidly growing plants. A soil well manured for a previous crop is ideal, but on poor, thin soils dig in a further dressing of well-rotted compost at a rate of 10–15 lb per square yard when the site is prepared. Apply a balanced general fertilizer at 20 oz per square yard, and before sowing rake the soil to produce a fine tilth.

Sowing To reduce the amount of thinning later, always sow lettuce seed very thinly. Sow in drills $\frac{1}{4}$ in deep at a rate of no more than 10–12 seeds for each 12 in run of drill—head lettuces will have a final spacing of 9–12 in apart in the row. Alternatively, lettuce can be sown in boxes or in a seedbed and then transplanted when the seedlings are no taller than 1 in. Extreme care is needed when handling the delicate seedlings. Take care not to sow too deeply as this inhibits germination, which should occur within 6–12 days. It is sensible to maintain a regular supply by making frequent sowings with short intervals between, because lettuces, once headed, do not stand in good condition for very long and soon "bolt", or run to seed.

Spacing

Various spacings and planting patterns are recommended for heading varieties. The most efficient is to stagger the plants in adjacent rows in a triangular pattern so that the maximum use is made of the land available. Place the plants at 12 in intervals in rows 10 in apart. For dwarf varieties and cloche-grown lettuce spacings of 9 in between the plants and 8 in between the rows may be used. This triangular pattern is particularly valuable for cloche-grown lettuces. If the familiar square pattern with plants opposite one another in adjacent rows is used, the spacings should be 12 in × 12 in, or 9 in × 9 in for dwarf varieties. With conventional leaf-

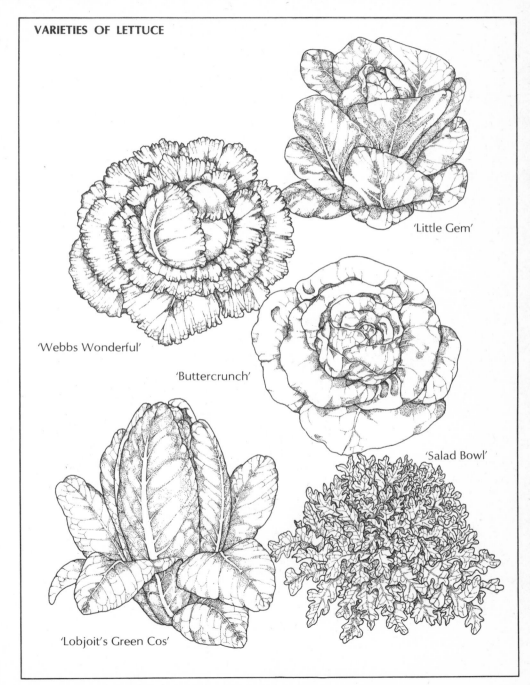

VARIETIES OF LETTUCE

'Webbs Wonderful'

'Little Gem'

'Buttercrunch'

'Salad Bowl'

'Lobjoit's Green Cos'

LEAF LETTUCE
'Salad Bowl', 'Lobjoits Green
Cos', 'Paris White' (cos),
'Vai. ...o' (cos).

PROTECTED LETTUCE
Head types
'Amanda Plus', 'Avondefiance'
(mildew resistant), 'Delta',
'Knap', 'Kwiek' (mildew resistant).

Lettuces 2

lettuce of the 'Salad Bowl' type, spacings are similar to those given for heading varieties. Some cos lettuces, however, will produce well during spring and summer with only 5–6 in between the rows and 1 in between individual plants.

Thinning and transplanting Direct-sown crops should be thinned as soon as the seedlings are large enough to handle. Never let the seedlings become overcrowded as this will check growth. There is a tendency to grow more lettuce than can be consumed and this is particularly true with sown crops. Trans-

planting allows more control. The method of plant raising is critical however, since any check to growth at transplanting may easily lead to "bolting"—premature running to flower, induced by high temperatures (over 21°C/70°F) and dry conditions. Lettuce transplants for outside should always be raised in small individual peat pots or blocks and never grown in a seedbed for bare-root planting. Sow lettuce seed in a $3\frac{1}{2}$ in pot every ten days and prick out as many seedlings as necessary into pots or blocks. Do this at the first true leaf stage.

Keep the seedlings cool to produce short, sturdy plants and transplant them when they have four or five true leaves.

Watering The best crops are produced when there has been no check to growth. The quality and size of the crop will be improved greatly by weekly applications of 3–4 gal of water per square yard in dry weather. If this is not possible, a single application at the same rate 7–10 days before they are due to mature will increase the size of the lettuce heads markedly in spring and summer. Over-wintered lettuce should not normally need additional watering.

Try to water in the morning, and on sunny, drying days if possible, so that the leaves are dry by nightfall. Lettuces that are wet over-night are vulnerable to disease.

Pests and diseases

Birds, slugs and cutworms may be trouble-some but can be controlled by the methods

Protected lettuce

described on page 265. Leaf aphids may be controlled by the use of systemic aphicides such as dimethoate or by applying derris as the plants near maturity. Some varieties are resistant to lettuce root aphids but applications of diazinon during the summer may be necessary for other varieties. Zineb or thiram sprays may be used against downy mildew, which is encouraged by overcrowding.

Botrytis cinerea or gray mold may be a problem on lettuce in damp, cool weather. Affected plants should be destroyed and a preventive spray of thiram or benomyl applied to the remaining plants.

Lettuce viruses show up either as a mosaic or pronounced vein network on the leaves. Burn infected plants because there is no really effective method of control once the symptoms appear. Remove weeds, which may harbor viruses, by completely uprooting them and control any aphids that appear. For control of aphids see page 264.

LEAF LETTUCE

'Salad Bowl', 'Grand Rapids' and 'Oak Leaf' are the conventional leaf lettuces but certain cos varieties can also be grown successfully for leafing. Closely spaced, leaf lettuces can produce good leaf in 40–50 days compared with the 60–80 days required for other lettuces. They also

have the advantage of growing again from the base to provide a second crop. Grown this way, one square yard of leaf lettuce sown each week from April to late May, and again from mid-July to the end of August, will produce lettuce leaves throughout summer and early fall.

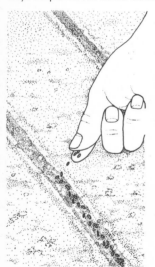

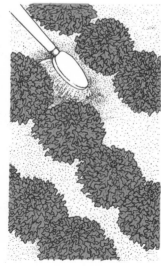

1 April to mid-May. At weekly intervals sow the seed in $\frac{1}{2}$ in drills, 4–5 in apart in the prepared seedbed, allowing 10–15 plants per 12 in of drill.

2 Early May to June. Allow the seedlings to develop unchecked without thinning. Water in dry weather. Spray aphids and diseases as required.

3 Late May to late June. Harvest the leaves by cutting them off near ground level. Leave stumps to re-grow.

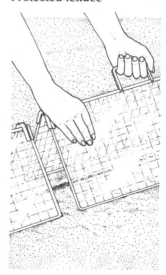

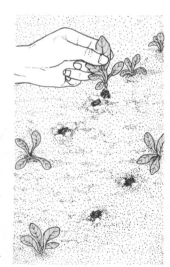

1 Sow 3–4 seeds $\frac{1}{2}$ in deep at 3 in intervals in drills 8 in apart in the prepared seedbed, and place cloches over the drills.

2 When the seedlings are $\frac{1}{2}$ in high, thin each group, leaving the strongest plant at each position. Ventilate on mild days.

3 As growth accelerates, thin to 9 in (6 in for dwarf varieties). In dry weather, water the plants 7–10 days before harvesting.

Lettuces 3

1 In the prepared seedbed take out ½ in drills 10 in apart (8 in for dwarf varieties) and sow the seed thinly. Cover the drill.

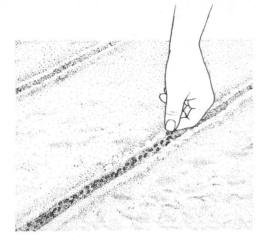

2 Sow the seed thinly in ½ in drills 10 in apart in the prepared seedbed. Cover the drills with fine soil.

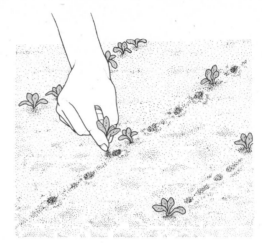

3 When the seedlings are ½–1 in high, thin to 12 in (9 in for dwarf varieties). Alternate the seedlings in adjacent rows.

4 Hoe between the rows to keep down weeds which compete with the seedlings.

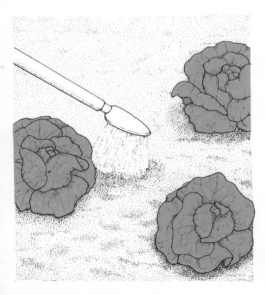

5 In dry weather apply 3–4 gal of water per square yard each week. Direct the water on to the soil and keep it away from the leaves. Damp encourages mildew.

6 Spray the developing plants with insecticides against aphids and fungicides against diseases as necessary.

7 Push heading lettuces gently with the back of the hand to test for firmness. Squeezing between the fingers damages the heads.

8 When firm, harvest by cutting the plants below the lower leaves. Alternatively, pull up whole plants and trim off roots. Harvest every second lettuce when young, allowing the remaining plants to grow larger. Place debris on the compost heap.

Growing brassicas

Admirably suited to cooler climates, the brassicas, such as cabbages, Brussels sprouts, cauliflowers, broccoli and kale, are key plants in any vegetable grower's plot. Certain general principles apply to their cultivation. Most brassicas, except some varieties of kale and Chinese cabbage, should be raised in a special brassica seedbed and then transplanted, usually 5–7 weeks later, to a permanent bed. This saves space, because the main brassica plots can be used for other vegetables while the seedlings are growing. Alternatively, buy young brassica plants ready for planting out.

Brassicas need a fertile soil and they should not be grown in the same plot more than one year in three. Move them around each year, preferably to ground where peas or beans have been grown the previous year (see page 34). Peas and beans leave nitrogen in the soil at a level which suits brassicas. The other reason for keeping brassicas on the move is the danger of previous infections of club-root lingering on in the soil. Another, resistant, vegetable can be grown in a plot which has suffered from club-root. Brassica crops must not be grown again in an affected plot for at least seven years.

Dig the ground early in winter and leave it to consolidate. All brassicas need firm ground. If the area has been dug shortly before sowing or planting, work it over with a three-pronged hand cultivator and firm it well with the feet. All brassicas need a pH of 6.5–7.5.

The seedbed

The seedbed should be in an open, sunny but sheltered position. Ideally, make a seedbed on soil manured for a previous crop. If this is not possible, in autumn apply well-rotted manure or garden compost (1 bucketful per square yard) and leave the plot to weather over the winter. Before sowing, rake in a balanced general fertilizer at a rate of 2 oz per square yard. At the same time apply diazinon to combat cabbage maggot and club-root. Firm the soil and rake to produce a fine tilth.

Sowing If the seedbed is dry, water thoroughly before sowing. Use a foot-board to avoid compacting the surface of the bed while sowing. Mark out shallow drills 6 in apart and draw out the drills $\frac{3}{4}$–1 in deep. Dust the seed with Captan or thiram before sowing to control damping-off disease. Mark each row with sticks, placing a label with sowing date

and variety, written in indelible ink. Germination takes 7–12 days. Keep the seedlings free from weeds, and water them during dry weather. Thin the seedlings to 1–2 in apart as soon as they can be handled. Firm back the soil after thinning.

The permanent (planting) bed

Double-dig the permanent brassica plot in winter and dress it with 10–15 lb per square yard of well-rotted manure or compost. Experiments have shown that a marked increase in yield can result from preparing soils deeply for brassicas. The roots of Brussels sprouts, for instance, penetrate 36 in or more into deeply dug soils. Although it is seldom practical to dig the plot to this depth, double-dig it if possible to a depth of 18–12 in. Brassicas are greedy for water, and deep digging allows their root systems to develop and extract more water from lower levels in the soil. It also reduces the uptake of water from the upper soil layers, which remain moist for longer than would be the case with shallower digging.

Transplanting

The young brassicas are ready to transplant

5–7 weeks after sowing, when they have 3–4 leaves and are 4–6 in tall. The day before transplanting, water the seedlings thoroughly so that they lift easily with minimum damage to the roots.

Lift the seedlings carefully so that the roots are disturbed as little as possible. Cover them with burlap or polyethylene so that they do not dry out before being planted. Dip the roots of the seedlings in calomel paste to control cabbage maggot and club-root. Plant the seedlings with a trowel or hand fork at the appropriate distance for the brassica concerned. The prepared plot should be watered thoroughly the day before planting takes place. Firm the soil around the roots by hand. Water the plants in, using a nozzle on the can or, if the weather is dry, prepare planting holes and "puddle" in the young plants. Make sure they are firm by tugging the upper leaf gently. Water them until they become established, placing $\frac{1}{4}$ pint of water around the base of each plant daily. In hot, sunny weather protect the transplants by covering them with newspaper during the day to cut down transpiration. Within three days of planting-out apply diazinon to the soil as a further insurance against cabbage maggot.

1 Lift the seedlings carefully, taking care not to damage the roots. Dip the roots in paste made of calomel, available at drugstores.

2 Plant the seedlings at the spacing given for each brassica and check that they are firmly planted by gently tugging a leaf.

3 In dry weather prepare planting holes and puddle in the young plants.

4 Apply diazinon to the soil at each plant's base within 3 days of planting. Water until they are established.

Cabbages 1

SPRING
'April', 'Harbinger', 'Offenham' (very hardy).

SUMMER/FALL
'Golden Acre', 'Hispi', 'May Star', 'Primo'.

Storing varieties
'Decerma', 'Langendijk', 'Winter White'.

WINTER
'Christmas Drumhead', 'January King', 'Winter Salad'.

Savoys
'Best of All', 'Ormskirk-Rearguard'.

RED CABBAGE
'Blood Red', 'Ruby Ball'.

CHINESE CABBAGE
'Nagaoka—50 days', 'Sampan'.

TYPES OF CABBAGE

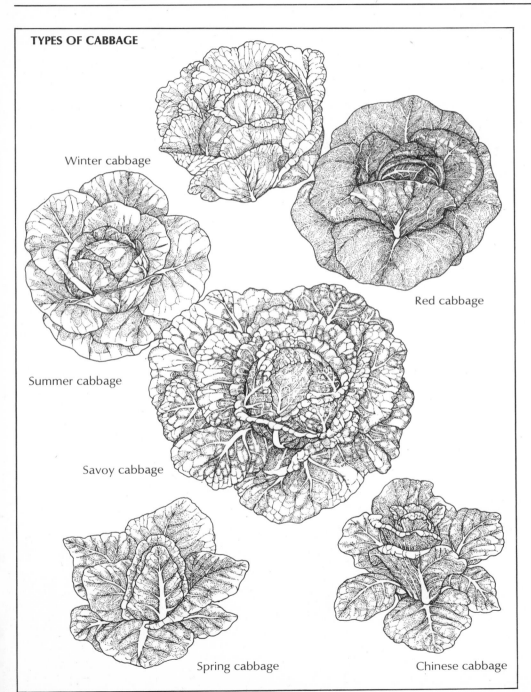

Winter cabbage

Red cabbage

Summer cabbage

Savoy cabbage

Spring cabbage

Chinese cabbage

Cabbage is a biennial plant and the most widely grown brassica. Individual tastes can be satisfied throughout the year with the four types available. Summer cabbage, both early and mid-season varieties, provides a welcome alternative to summer salads. Winter cabbage, including savoys, is easy to grow and is hardy. Apart from its pickling qualities, red cabbage is delicious as a cooked autumn vegetable. The increasingly-popular, autumn-harvested Chinese cabbage can be cooked (with little aroma) or used in salads.

Spring cabbage

Spring cabbage is grown from summer varieties that are planted in zones 8 to 10 in late October or November to mature in spring. "Spring greens" are simply closely planted spring cabbages eaten before they head up.

Sowing The seed is sown directly in the garden in rows 12 in apart and thinned to 12 in between the plants in each row if headed cabbages are required.

Spring greens If space is limited and spring greens are required thin to 4 in intervals in the rows. The plants can either be left to produce unheaded greens, or two out of every three plants can be removed and used for greens in early spring while the remaining plants, now spaced at 12 in by 12 in, will head up for use later. Wider row spacings are often recommended but these give a lesser yield.

After plants are well-established it is useful to pull a little soil around the stems to give some additional protection against winter cold. No fertilizer should be given at this stage and, apart from keeping the plot free from weeds, the only attention the plants need until growth starts in late winter is to firm back plants loosened by frost or other adverse weather.

In early March, if the weather is good, apply and water in a dressing of nitrate of soda or sulfate of ammonia at a rate of 2 oz per square yard. This encourages rapid growth as the weather becomes warmer. Alternatively, in nitrogen-rich soils, a balanced fertilizer can be used at the same rate.

Harvesting

The crop may be harvested as required. In mild seasons spring greens are ready in February while in late seasons headed cabbages stand until early June. In some cold areas cloches may be used to protect spring cabbages over winter.

Summer cabbage

Summer cabbage is sown indoors in February and March for harvesting from mid-May until August, depending on the variety. When deciding how much to grow, remember that it matures at the same time as many other vegetables. The permanent plot should be well prepared in late winter. Sowing indoors during February for planting out after last frost provides the earliest crops, but seeds can also be sown in a seedbed shortly before last frost for later crops.

Sowing On a seedbed sow the seed thinly in $\frac{3}{4}$–1 in deep drills 6 in apart. Water the drills beforehand to encourage speedy germination and if the weather is warm and dry, dust along the length of the drills with derris or HCH before the seedlings emerge as a precaution against flea beetle. Summer cabbages are very vulnerable to cabbage maggot and it is important to apply appropriate control measures against this and club-root at both the sowing and transplanting stages.

If seeds are started indoors in flats, use a prepared sterile planting soil such as Jiffy-Mix and just cover them.

Transplanting From April to May dip the seedlings in calomel paste and plant them in the permanent bed, at 18 in intervals in rows 18 in apart for large-headed varieties or at 14 in intervals in rows 14 in apart for smaller-headed varieties. Firm the seedlings into their holes and water thoroughly.

When the plants are well-established, apply and water in a balanced fertilizer, such as 10-10-10 at 2 oz per square yard. Throughout the growing season, hoe between the rows to keep down weeds and maintain a water-conserving tilth. If necessary spray or dust to control any pests or diseases that occur.

Harvesting

Headed summer cabbages are ready for cutting from late June until fall. Cut with a sharp knife just above soil level.

Cabbages 2

Spring cabbage

1 October to November. Take out $\frac{3}{4}$–1 in drills, 6 in apart in the garden. Sprinkle diazinon along the drills and water them thoroughly.

2 October to November. Sow the seed thinly and dust with derris along the drills. Cover with fine soil.

3 When seedlings are well-established, thin them to the desired spacing in the rows.

4 Pull up a little soil around the base of each plant to protect against cold. Firm any plants loosened later by adverse weather.

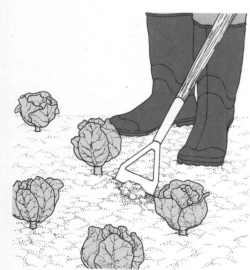

5 Throughout the growing season hoe between the rows regularly to keep them weed-free and maintain a good tilth.

6 February to March. Spread and then hoe in 2 oz of nitrate of soda or sulfate of ammonia to encourage heading.

7 March. To obtain spring greens, remove 2 plants out of 3. Those remaining will head up for later use.

8 April to June. Cut spring cabbages as required. Clear any stumps and roots away.

Cabbages 3

Winter cabbage

Winter cabbages are sown in May or June and harvested from late summer on. They include the savoys, which are easily recognized by their dark green, wrinkled leaves. All the varieties are easy to grow and hardy, succeeding better on poor soils than most other brassicas. Apart from the times of sowing, transplanting and maturing their cultivation differs little from that of summer cabbage.

Sowing In May sow the seed very thinly in $\frac{3}{4}$–1 in drills that are 6 in apart. Water the drills before sowing.

Transplanting In July transplant the seedlings to the permanent bed, which should have been enriched with fertilizer a few weeks before (see page 38). Plant the seedlings at 18 in intervals in rows 18 in apart. If the weather is very dry, pour a little water into each hole before putting the plants down. Remember also to sprinkle diazinon into the holes before setting out the seedlings and firming them in well. When the plants begin to grow apply a nitrogen-rich fertilizer and hoe it in lightly.

Water the growing plants frequently during the summer and hoe lightly between the rows to keep down the weeds.

Harvesting

From September on, cut the individual heads as they mature.

Red cabbage

Red cabbage is sown in the spring at the same time as summer cabbage but it needs a slightly longer growing season. In warm climates it can also be treated like spring cabbage. Before sowing, work out what is needed because a few plants are enough for pickling purposes. Cultivate red cabbage in the same way as summer cabbage. Sow the seed indoors in late winter or outdoors after frost and transplant when the seedlings are 4–6 in tall, and transplant 12–15 in each way.

Harvesting

Red cabbage is ready from mid-July onwards. Be sure to cut the mature heads well before there is any danger of severe frost.

Red cabbage can be stored for several months in a cool, frost-free place.

HARVESTING AND STORING CABBAGE

Some types of cabbage, especially the Danish varieties, can be stored after harvesting in the fall. They will keep until April but should be inspected for blemishes or rot two or three times during the winter.

1 Lift the whole plant up with a fork when the head is firm to the touch.

2 Cut off the roots and stem and remove the coarse outer leaves.

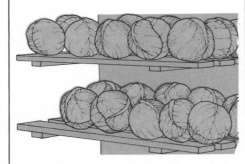

3 Store cabbages on slatted shelving, in heaps if required, in a dark, humid place.

Chinese cabbage

Chinese cabbage is a versatile vegetable that is easier to grow than other vegetables in the brassica group and has a relatively short growing season. The general principles of brassica growing (page 38) apply. It is especially important to have a moisture-retentive, rich seedbed because Chinese cabbage is not transplanted but is matured in the area where it has been sown.

Sowing About three months before first fall frost, sow 2–3 of the large seeds at 8–9 in intervals in $\frac{3}{4}$–1 in deep drills, 12 in apart. Thin the seedlings to one plant per station.

Keep them well watered because they may "bolt" in hot summer weather. Do not water, however, if the weather is wet, as this may cause "splitting" of the heads. When the plants begin to head up in August, tie the leaves together with raffia. This is not necessary with self-heading varieties.

Harvesting

From September to November cut the heads just above soil level with a knife.

1 Early July. Dribble water into the $\frac{3}{4}$–1 in deep drills, 12 in apart, and sow 2–3 seeds at 9 in intervals.

2 July. Thin each group of seedlings to leave a single plant at each station. Apply diazinon around the base of each plant.

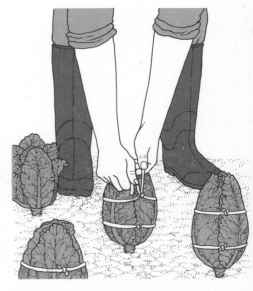

3 August. When the plants begin to head up tie the outer leaves together with raffia. Keep them well watered.

Brussels sprouts 1

F₁ hybrids
'Citadel', 'King Arthur',
'Peer Gynt'.

CONVENTIONAL VARIETIES
'Irish Elegance', 'Market
Rearguard', 'Winter Harvest'.

Brussels sprouts are popular and hardy brassicas, and for many people they are a traditional ingredient of the Christmas dinner. In recent years F₁ hybrids have been bred, mostly of compact growth, that mature all their uniform "button" sprouts at the same time. While these are ideal for the freezer, most gardeners still grow some of the open pollinated, conventional varieties. With these, the sprouts mature a few at a time on individual plants, so picking may be carried out over a period of several months. This is important for growers without freezers, who may require only a pound or two at a time.

The most useful crops are gathered from October to about December, because few other fresh vegetables are available at this time. In mild climates, they can be left standing outdoors for harvest at any time.

Cultivation

The general principles of brassica growing apply to Brussels sprouts (see page 38). An open position, in full sun but sheltered from strong winds, is most suitable although they will tolerate slight shade. A firm soil is important because Brussels sprouts may grow to 3 ft or more and good root anchorage is essential. In light soils hilling up the stems slightly about a month after transplanting helps to anchor them, but in exposed areas staking is sometimes necessary.

Soil and situation Brussels sprouts grow best on fertile soil that has been deeply dug and well manured the previous winter. Like other brassicas, Brussels sprouts need lime. A pH of between 6·5 and 6·8 is ideal. As they are not usually planted out until June or July, another crop is often taken from the same land beforehand. The site should be dug over about a week before planting and a dressing at 2 oz per square yard of a balanced general fertilizer raked in. The seed is sown in the brassica seedbed during May or June and the seedlings are transplanted in four to six weeks later to the prepared site. Nitrogenous fertilizer applied during growth produces weak plants.

Sowing Sow the seed thinly in ¾–1 in drills that are spaced 6 in apart. The seed is sown thinly to prevent overcrowding and to encourage strong plants, which are necessary for the successful growth of this tall, top-heavy vegetable. Brussels sprouts are vulnerable to club-root and cabbage maggot and the same control measures given for cabbages must be applied at both the sowing and transplanting stages. Seeds sown in cold frames in February for planting out in April will give an earlier crop. This method is useful for producing sprouts in August in addition to the main crop sown in the open to provide fall sprouts, but results are not so reliable.

F₁ hybrids If F₁ hybrids to produce button sprouts for freezing are being grown, spacings of 20 in between the rows and 20 in between plants can be used. This provides a good yield from a relatively small area for picking at one time. Remove the growing point and smaller leaves when the lower sprouts are about ½ in across to encourage most of them to mature at the same time.

For the "cut and come again" requirement of most gardeners, spacings of 36 in × 36 in are used. Grown at these distances most varieties produce an excellent crop while allowing easy access for harvesting. There

1 June. Dig over the planting site and rake in a balanced, general fertilizer, such as 10-10-10, at 2 oz per square yard.

2 Transplant the seedlings from the seedbed into rows 36 in apart with 36 in (20 in for F₁ hybrids) between plants. Plant them firmly with the lowest leaf at soil level.

3 At the same time, puddle in the young plants and check that they are firmly planted by gently tugging each top leaf.

4 June. Apply diazinon to the soil at the base of the plants to combat cabbage maggot.

5 June. Continue to water the young plants until they are well-established.

Brussels sprouts 2

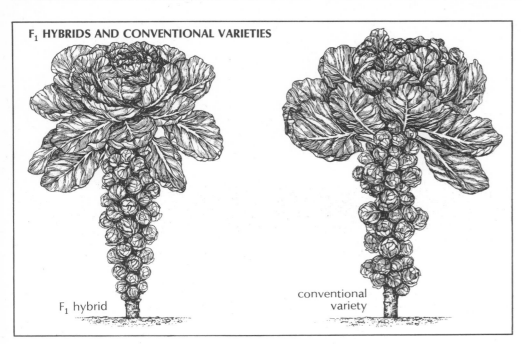

F₁ HYBRIDS AND CONVENTIONAL VARIETIES

F₁ hybrid

conventional variety

appears to be no advantage in closer spacing unless dwarf varieties are used, when spacings of $2\frac{1}{2}$ ft each way are sufficient. Firm planting is essential and the seedlings should be set with the lowest leaves at soil level to help establish a good root system. Water or puddle in the young plants. Check that they are firmly established by tugging gently at the top leaf of each plant.

Although additional watering during the growing season is often beneficial to cabbages, there appears to be no advantage in watering Brussels sprouts regularly unless the weather is very dry. Brussels sprout plants are in the ground for a long period, so regular weeding and hoeing should be carried out and any necessary pest and disease controls should be applied as necessary.

Aphids are often particularly troublesome and if left can spoil the developing sprouts. Aphids must be sprayed as soon as they are spotted, or they will penetrate the sprouts themselves. Sparrows may attack the sprouts. A system of stakes carrying netting will protect the growing crop against birds and help to support the plants. Application of a foliar feed or a high potash fertilizer in July–August is often beneficial, particularly if crops are grown on light soils.

Harvesting
As the sprouts mature, remove any yellowing leaves from the lower part of the stem to improve air circulation. Pick or cut the sprouts when they are still tight and about the size of a walnut. Start picking from the base. When all the sprouts have been picked from a stem, use the Brussels sprout tops as "winter greens".

Aftercare
Surplus leaves can go on the compost heap, but the woody stems should be pulled up with the roots, dried and burned at the end of the season.

Do not leave Brussels sprouts in the ground to flower and seed, because they will continue to draw up nutrients from the soil and leave an unnecessarily large deficit for the crop that follows them.

6 July. In light soils or exposed sites draw up a little soil round the base of each stem. Hoe regularly between the rows to keep the plants free from weeds.

7 July. Apply a foliar feed or water in a high potash fertilizer at a rate of 1oz per square yard. Spray with dimethoate to control aphid attacks.

8 September onwards. Remove yellowing leaves from the stems, and any "blown" (loose and open) sprouts.

9 As soon as the buttons are firm, gather them as required from the bottom of the stem.

Cauliflowers 1

SUMMER
'Alpha', 'Dominant',
'Predominant', 'Snowball'.

SUMMER/FALL
'All the Year Round',
'Barrier Reef'.

WINTER (HEADING BROCCOLI)
'Late Enterprise', 'Snowball',
'Thanet'.

To American gardeners the word "cauliflower" means a vegetable with a large head of tightly packed, white, immature flowers known as "curds". Broccoli has a flatter, somewhat wider head of little green buds that open into yellow flowers if not picked at the right time. Also listed in most seed catalogs is "Purple Head Cauliflower", which looks and tastes more like broccoli than cauliflower and has a dense head of purplish buds that turn green when cooked.

This understanding of the closely related cauliflower-broccoli tribe is different from the European thinking. In that part of the world, cauliflower is the same vegetable that we know. But broccoli is called calabrese. And Purple Head Cauliflower is known as sprouting broccoli. The Europeans also have a white sprouting broccoli.

Nomenclature to the contrary, the vegetables are the same. But there are fewer American varieties, and they cannot be grown in so many months of the year. Except in warm climates, ours are planted either in early spring for summer use or in mid-summer for fall use. All can be frozen for winter use.

Cauliflowers

A favorite among brassicas, the cauliflower is one of the more difficult vegetables to grow successfully because it is demanding in its soil, moisture and food requirements.

Soil and situation A deeply dug, fertile soil rich in humus is essential to obtain crops of good quality. The general principles of brassica growing apply—thorough soil preparation with heavy dressings of manure helping to provide food and retain moisture during the growing period (see page 38). The pH of the soil should be between 6.5 and 7.5 and the site should be open but not exposed. Cauliflowers are less hardy than other brassicas and cannot withstand severe weather. They require ample food during their period of growth and, in addition to the manure dug in during the winter, a dressing of 2–3 oz per square yard of a general fertilizer should be raked into the soil before planting.

Cauliflowers are particularly susceptible to deficiencies of vital elements in the soil. A deficiency of the major elements can be corrected by following the general principles of brassica fertilization. A deficiency of the trace elements will have an equally adverse effect on the crop but, unlike a disease, mineral deficiency should not be a problem once it has been identified.

Molybdenum deficiency causes whiptail (abnormally formed leaves), and the plant may lose its growing points or fail to form curds. Making the soil neutral (pH 7) should cure the deficiency. Potassium deficiency causes yellowing and poor quality curds. This may result from an incorrect ratio of nitrogen to potassium in the soil, due to too much nitrogenous fertilization. Boron deficiency causes small, bitter curds and brown coloration. Water the soil with a solution of borax—use $\frac{1}{2}$ ounce of borax in $\frac{1}{2}$ gal of water to treat 30 square yards of soil. Be careful not to exceed the dosage because too much boron makes the soil toxic.

Cauliflower seedlings need careful handling and firm planting. They should never be short of water or they will produce small, premature heads of poor quality. Applications of up to 4 gal of water per square yard during dry periods improve the quality and yield. To maintain healthy, vigorous growth a dressing of 1 oz per square yard of sulfate of ammonia should be watered in when the young plants are well established but before the curds start to form. As with other brassicas, club-root and cabbage maggot may be troublesome and the appropriate control measures should be applied as a matter of routine.

Summer cauliflowers mature from June to August and may be raised in several ways depending on the facilities available. The easiest is to sow the seed indoors in February or March for transplanting at about the time of the last spring freeze.

Maximum yield of summer cauliflower is dependent on water supply. If the crop can be watered frequently, the spacing can be as close as 18 in by 18 in. In drier conditions, spacings of 24 in by 24 in are better.

Autumn Cauliflowers

Autumn cauliflowers are in season from September to frost and are sown outdoors in seedbeds two-and-a-half to three months before first fall frost. Their cultivation is similar to that of summer cauliflowers.

Summer cauliflower

1 Winter. Dig the soil deeply and incorporate a dressing of 15–20 lb per square yard of well-rotted manure.

2 April. Rake in a dressing of 2–3 oz per square yard of a balanced fertilizer 1–2 weeks before planting.

3 Water the seedlings before lifting them. Lift them carefully and dip the roots in calomel paste to combat club-root.

4 Plant the seedlings at 24 in intervals in rows 24 in apart on the prepared site, watered on the previous day. Water or puddle in the transplanted seedlings. Check that they are firmly planted by tugging the uppermost leaf of each.

Cauliflowers 2

BLANCHING

A new variety of cauliflower is self-blanching. Other varieties, whether grown for summer or autumn use, require blanching. To do this tie the outer leaves up over the flower head when it is about the size of an egg. Tie the leaf tips together tightly to keep out sun, but do not blanch the leaves so close around the head that its growth is restricted. Harvest when it reaches 6–8 in in diameter.

Pests and Diseases of Brassicas

Brassicas can be attacked and damaged by a number of different pests and diseases.

Pests There are several pests that feed on the leaves of brassicas including mealy cabbage aphid, cabbage whitefly and some species of caterpillar. Mealy cabbage aphids are blue-gray sap-sucking insects. They turn the foliage yellow and can cause severe stunting. They usually occur on the undersides of leaves but may also infest Brussels sprout buttons and the hearts of cauliflowers and cabbages, making them inedible. If aphids are present spray with dimethoate, formothion or menazon. Burn old plants after cropping to kill the aphids' over-wintering eggs. Cabbage whitefly, a small white moth-like insect, is a much less damaging pest since it generally attacks only the outer leaves.

Caterpillars of the large and the small cabbage white butterfly and of the cabbage looper all eat holes in the foliage and often burrow into the hearts of cabbages. Remove them by hand as soon as the damage is seen. Alternatively, dust plants with carbaryl or spray with fenitrothion, trichlorphon or *Bacillus thuringiensis*.

The roots of brassicas may also be damaged by pests. Cabbage maggots eat the roots of seedlings and newly planted brassicas until the root system is reduced to a blackened, rotting stump, growth ceases and the foliage turns blue-green. Prevent attacks by treating seed rows and the soil around transplants with diazinon, chlorpyrifos, bromophos or azinphos-methyl. If symptoms of the trouble are seen, drench the soil with spray-strength trichlorphon. Turnip gall weevil causes galls on the roots which are often mistaken for club root disease. However, if cut in half, the weevil's small white grub can be seen. The plants' growth is not affected.

Diseases Club root is the most serious disease of brassicas. It causes the roots to become a distorted and swollen mass and, since they cannot function normally, the plants' growth is poor and stunted. Prevent attacks by buying only healthy plants, improving the drainage of heavy soils, liming very acid soils and by destroying all cruciferous weeds, which can act as hosts for the organism. Alternatively, apply PCNB to the seedbed before sowing brassicas and spray young plants with this pesticide when transplanting.

If brassicas are grown too soft, that is given too much nitrogenous fertilizer, they may be attacked by various fungi, particularly in wet seasons. Leaf spot fungi cause round brown spots on the leaves that sometimes fall away leaving holes. Gray mould fungi produce a gray-brown growth on the plants, and bacterial soft rot causes the affected parts to turn slimy with an unpleasant smell. If any of these diseases occur, remove and burn affected leaves, or the whole plant if necessary, and thin out plants that are growing too close together. Reduce the risk of attacks by limiting the use of nitrogenous fertilizers and by applying a dressing of sulfate of potash before planting.

Disorders The chief physiological disorders affecting cabbages are splitting and failure to heart. Prevent these by watering before the soil dries out completely and planting seedlings carefully in well prepared, humus-rich soil. Broccoli and cauliflowers may be affected by whiptail, caused by molybdenum deficiency; the leaves are reduced to the mid-rib and the heads fail to develop. Apply a solution of sodium molybdate at 1oz in 2½ gal of water to each 10 sq yd of soil.

5 Apply bromophos or diazinon to the soil around the plants to combat cabbage root fly. Continue to water the transplants daily until they are fully established. Make sure they are never short of water because otherwise they will produce small heads.

6 May (frame-raised plants) or July (plants sown outdoors in March to April). Water in a dressing of sulphate of ammonia at 1oz per square yard before the curds start to form.

7 In dry weather apply water at 4 gal per square yard each week. If this is not possible give a single application at the same rate, when the curds are forming or 2–3 weeks before the crop is due to mature, to improve quality and yield.

8 June to August/September. Cut the mature cauliflowers as needed. The curds are ready for harvesting when they are firm and well developed but not yet beginning to open.

Broccoli

Purple cauliflower

Purple cauliflower takes about a month longer to mature than standard varieties but is grown in the same way for summer or fall use. It is not blanched. After the large head is cut, small heads will continue to develop on side shoots for a couple of months. Pick them regularly to stimulate further young growth and to prevent flowering. If the shoots are allowed to flower the production of side-shoots stops.

Broccoli

Broccoli is a little hardier than cauliflower and easier to grow. The general principles of brassica growing, including pest and disease controls, apply to it although it will grow well in relatively poor soils.

Sowing The seed is sown indoors in February or March and the young seedlings are trans-planted to the vegetable plot at about the time of the last freeze. For a later crop, seed is sown where the plants are to grow shortly after the last freeze and for a fall crop, seed is sown in a seedbed or directly in the garden about 90–100 days before the first fall frost. In all cases, the seedlings should be planted in rows 18 in apart with 18 in between the plants. Closer spacings of 12 in by 12 in may be used provided that ample water is available for irrigation.

Pests and diseases

Club root and cabbage maggot may be troublesome. Cabbage maggots can devas-tate seedlings and young plants. Damaged plants stop growing and wilt in warm weather. Treat seed rows and transplanting sites with diazinon or bromophos. Check attacks on established plants by drenching the soil with spray-strength trichlorphon. Club root causes plants to become stunted. Apply PCNB to the seedbed before sowing, and spray young plants with the chemical when transplanting.

Harvesting

As the large flowerheads mature, cut them off on a slant (so water will run off the stem) and then water in a light dressing of $\frac{1}{2}$ oz per square yard of a general fertilizer around the plants. This encourages the growth of side-shoots. Pick these every few days.

Late April to May

1 Water the seedlings in the flats the day before transplanting. Lift the seedlings carefully. Dip the roots in calomel paste to combat club-root.

2 Plant the seedlings at 18 in intervals in rows 18 in apart and water them in well. Check that they are firmly planted by gently tugging the uppermost leaves.

3 Apply diazinon to the soil around the plants to combat cabbage maggot. Water the transplants daily until they are fully established.

June onward

4 Keep the plants free from weeds. In dry weather apply water at 4 gal per square yard each week or give 1 application at the same rate as the central head forms.

5 When the central heads mature cut them for use. Water in a dressing of $\frac{1}{2}$ oz of a general fertilizer.

6 Cut the side-shoots of broccoli every few days as they mature to maintain a succession of spears.

Kale

The dark green, crinkly leaves and shoots of kale can be eaten in spring and fall. As it is extremely hardy it is a most useful vegetable for winter use. Kale is often said to taste bitter, but if the small tender shoots and leaves are used instead of larger coarse foliage, the flavor is very pleasant. It often succeeds where other brassicas will not, because it is tolerant of most diseases and pests, and it will grow and crop reasonably well on poor soils. It also tolerates harsher climatic conditions than other brassicas. Whether curly or plain-leaved, all popular varieties are usually sown in the garden where they are to grow. But they can also be started in flats or seedbeds and then transplanted like other brassicas.

Some types of kale are ornamental, with colored decorative leaves. These can be grown in flower beds where they fill the dual purpose of an ornamental and food crop. Perennial kales can be grown but they are of less use as a food crop.

Cultivation

Although tolerant of poor soils, kale does best in fertile conditions. It will grow in most soils, whether acid or alkaline. The soil must however, be well-drained because waterlogged conditions cause root rot. The general rules for brassica cultivation (see page 38) should be followed and the site should be open. Less shelter is needed than for other brassicas, but in areas exposed to cold winter winds some protection will be repaid by better growth. As with Brussels sprouts, firm planting is important, particularly with the tall varieties, because the crop may have to withstand winter winds.

The seed is sown directly in the garden as soon as the soil can be worked in the spring. You should then be able to start harvesting in two months. However, the more common practice—especially in the South—is to sow seed two months before first fall frost. Pick off leaves as you want them throughout the fall and even into the winter. Light freezing improves the flavor. Kale should be planted in rows 18 in apart with 12 in between the individual plants in the rows.

As with cabbage, avoid nitrogen-rich fertilizers which encourage soft growth and thus increase the risk of frost damage. Hill up around the stems to protect the plants from wind and frost.

Harvesting

Use young leaves and shoots only, pulling off and discarding yellowing or tough old leaves. Further side-shoots will be produced, and again these should be gathered when young and succulent. Pick the side-shoots from the top downward. Some varieties produce edible flowering heads.

If the plants are given some protection, they should survive the winter in all but the coldest areas so that they can be harvested again in early spring, providing a useful gap-filler before the new season's crops mature. Protect with cloches or straw.

Collards

Collards are brassicas grown primarily in the South—although they can be grown in all climate zones—as a substitute for cabbage. They have crumpled leaves that generally form a loose cluster but sometimes form a head. When young, the entire plant is cooked. When older, the tender leaves at the top of the plant are used.

Cultivation

Collards are grown like cabbage. Seeds are usually sown directly in the garden where the plants are to grow. Sow seeds for a spring crop before the last spring freeze; for a fall crop, in August. Space plants 15 in apart in rows 2 ft wide. Harvest when stalks are young and tender. The leaves can be blanched by tying them together loosely 2–3 weeks before harvesting. 'Vates' is a popular variety, tolerant of cold and 24- to 36-inch tall. Leaves can be picked after 75 days' growth. 'Georgia' is another very adaptable variety.

1 Sow seed thinly where the plants are to be grown as soon as the soil can be worked. Make the drills ¾–1 in deep. Space the drills 18 in apart.

2 Thin the plants to 12 in apart when the seedlings are large enough to be handled.

3 Hill up each plant to the base of the first leaf as a protection against frost and wind.

4 Harvest kale by picking the young shoots from the top of the plant downward. Some varieties produce edible flowering heads. Use young shoots and leaves only.

Spinach/New Zealand spinach 1

SPINACH

SUMMER
'Long Standing Round'.

WINTER
'Green Market' (hardy),
'Long Standing Prickly',
'Sigmaleaf' (bolt resistant).

NEW ZEALAND SPINACH
No named varieties available.

Spinach (*Spinacia oleracea*) is an annual plant. Highly nutritious, it is grown for the use of its leaves which are either cooked or eaten raw in salads. New Zealand spinach (*Tetragona tetragonioides*) is not botanically related to ordinary spinach but is also grown for its leaves. The roughly triangular, blunt-tipped leaves are milder in flavor than those of ordinary spinach and are therefore preferred by many gardeners.

NEW ZEALAND SPINACH

New Zealand spinach needs a good medium to light soil and an open sunny position. It is not a hardy plant and must be sown indoors in early March for planting out in May or as soon as the danger of frost is past. The seeds are very hard and it helps germination if they are soaked in water overnight before sowing. Sow three seeds together in a $\frac{1}{2}$ in drill with 1 ft between each group of seeds. Thin the seedlings when they emerge, leaving the strongest one from each group of three. New Zealand spinach has a trailing habit and takes up a lot of ground. Unlike ordinary spinach, however, it does not bolt in hot dry weather although it should be watered well during such spells to encourage growth. Hoe regularly at first to keep down weeds, but later the plants' own thick growth will control them. Pinch out the tips of well-grown plants to produce more branching and young leaves. From June to September harvest New Zealand spinach by picking a few leaves from each plant. It is a cut-and-come-again vegetable, regular picking encourages it.

Cultivation

Ordinary spinach needs a soil rich in organic matter and therefore capable of retaining water. When winter digging, add well-rotted compost and manure.

Soil and situation Spinach will not thrive on poor, dry or extremely acid soils. It grows best at a pH of 6.5–7.5. Since it is very fast growing, summer spinach can be cultivated as a catch crop between rows of taller vegetables, such as peas or beans, which provide slight shade in the summer months.

Summer spinach

For a continual supply of fresh leaves throughout the summer, sow the seed at two or three week intervals from early spring (as soon as the soil is workable) to May. Take out $\frac{1}{2}-\frac{3}{4}$ in drills, 12 in apart, and sow the seed very thinly.

Thinning Spinach has a much better flavor if it grows without any check and for this reason both thin sowing and early thinning are important tasks. Overcrowding in the row results in weak plants that run to seed easily. As soon as the seedlings have emerged and are large enough to handle, thin them until the individual plants are 3 in apart. As soon as these plants begin to close in on each other, thin again until they are 6 in apart. These thinnings can be eaten. Hoe between the rows very regularly to keep down weeds.

Watering Spinach must be kept well watered, especially in hot dry weather when there is a risk of bolting. Give the plants up to 4 gal per square yard each week in such conditions, even if they are still very small.

Fall spinach

Late-season sowings can be disappointing. Sow the seed in the usual way 6–8 weeks before first fall frost, but at this time it is best to choose a sunnier site. In zone 7, if you cover the plants with cloches after the first frost, they should continue growing through most or all of the winter. Leave the cloches in place as long as necessary.

In areas with mild winters, a second sowing can be made later in the fall and a third sowing can be made in late January. In this way plants can be grown virtually throughout the year without protection.

SPINACH AND SWISS CHARD VARIETIES

Melody, winner of an All-America award, is hardy. It is adaptable to either early spring or late fall sowings in northern areas, and it can also be successfully grown as a winter crop in the South in zones 8–10. Melody also has the advantage of being disease-resistant and it is vigorous. Cold Resistant Savoy is a 45-day crop, useful for overwintering in the milder zones to provide a harvest of spinach in early spring. Other varieties include Long Standing Bloomsdale and America. Swiss chard varieties include Lucullus and White King.

Summer spinach

1 Winter. Incorporate well-rotted compost into the soil during winter digging.

2 March to May, every 2–3 weeks. Sow the seed thinly in $\frac{1}{2}-\frac{3}{4}$ in deep drills, 12 in apart. Thin to 3 in apart.

3 When the seedlings begin to touch each other, thin again to 6 in apart. These thinnings can be eaten.

4 In dry weather apply water at a rate of up to 4 gal per square yard each week. Hoe weeds regularly.

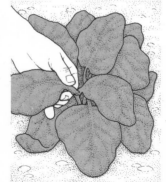

5 Six to eight weeks after sowing, cut or pick the outside leaves by breaking away their stalks.

Fall spinach

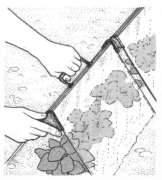

6 October onward. In cold areas cover the growing plants with cloches.

Spinach/Swiss Chard

Harvesting

Summer spinach is ready to pick 6–8 weeks after sowing. Up to half the foliage on each plant can be picked at a time.

Fall and winter spinach takes longer to mature and is not ready until about 10–12 weeks after sowing. Only a few leaves should be taken from each plant at any one time.

Pick the outside leaves while they are young and tender by breaking the stalk by hand. Do not tear the leaf stems away from the plant's base because this damages the plant. If spinach is harvested regularly in this way the plants are encouraged to produce more leaves and the cropping period is longer.

Storing Spinach is best consumed as soon as possible after harvesting, although it can be frozen successfully.

Pests and diseases

Proper thinning of the growing plants and vigilant watering should deter downy mildew. But if it does strike, spray the plants with zineb or a copper fungicide.

Swiss chard

Swiss chard is also known as seakale beet or silver beet. A very attractive vegetable, it has extra wide leaf stalks and midribs. The leaves are treated in the same way as ordinary spinach but the stalks and midribs may be used instead of asparagus. The midribs do not have the same texture as asparagus.

In April sow three seeds together at 15 in intervals in $\frac{1}{2}$–$\frac{3}{4}$ in deep drills that are 15 in apart. Thin the seedlings to the strongest in each group. Hoe regularly throughout the summer and water liberally, especially during dry weather. The plants should continue growing throughout the summer if you pick the leaves as they are ready. But you can make repeat sowings at any time up to mid-summer. With cloche protection in fall, growing should continue for a long time.

Swiss chard is ready to pick from June or about two months after sowing. As soon as the leaves are big enough a few can be picked at a time from each plant. Break the stalks off at the base, taking the outside ones first. Swiss chard does not keep well and should be eaten immediately.

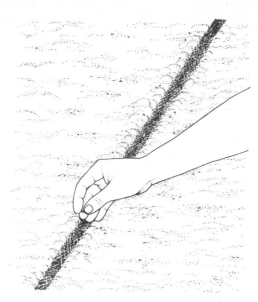

1 April to July. Sow 3–4 seeds at 9 in intervals in $\frac{1}{2}$–$\frac{3}{4}$ in deep drills, 15 in apart. Choose a soil rich in organic content and water-retentive.

2 When the seedlings are big enough to handle thin the groups, leaving 1 seedling at each station.

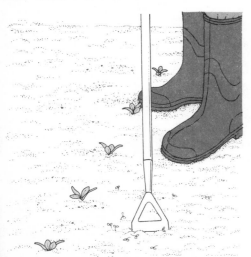

3 During the growing season hoe between the rows regularly.

4 Fall. Protect the plants with cloches as necessary to extend the growing season.

5 As they develop, water the growing plants liberally, up to 2–3 gal per week in dry weather.

6 June onwards. Harvest a few of the largest leaves from each plant regularly, picking them off as close to the ground as possible. Pick regularly to encourage production.

Asparagus 1

Asparagus is a perennial fern-like plant grown for its young shoots which are cut as fat, succulent spears soon after they come through the soil. Appreciated as a luxury vegetable, asparagus is expensive to buy but economical to grow because the same plants, when established and well-managed, will provide crops for 20 years or even longer. Asparagus is easy to grow and it is a beautiful plant, but it does require time and patience.

Cultivation

Plants may be raised from seed but there is a three-year delay between seed sowing and the first crop. The more usual way of starting an asparagus bed is with bought crowns, which can be one, two or three years old. For all ages the period between planting and harvesting is the same. The one-year-old is the best buy because it is cheaper and it establishes a good root system as quickly after planting as does a two- or three-year-old. Order the crowns from the grower well in advance and ask for delivery in April, which is the best planting time.

Soil and situation Asparagus will grow in most soils but a pH of 6.5–7.5 is preferable and good drainage and freedom from perennial weeds are essential. Dig a dressing of well-rotted manure or compost at 15 lb per square yard into the top foot of soil in the fall or early winter before planting. Asparagus roots tend to develop laterally so it is best to maintain the food supply in the top spit. Asparagus grows best in an open site.

The first year

Never let the crowns dry out; choose a damp day for planting and leave the crowns wrapped until the last minute.

Planting The traditional asparagus bed, which consists of three rows of crowns with access on either side, is more than 5 ft wide. However, if only a single row is planted in each trench, weed control and cutting are easier. In April dig a trench about 10 in deep and 15 in wide for each row. Then lightly fork in a balanced general fertilizer, such as 10-10-10, at 3 oz per square yard. In very nitrogen-rich soils dig in $1\frac{1}{2}$ oz superphosphate and 1 oz

SOWING ASPARAGUS

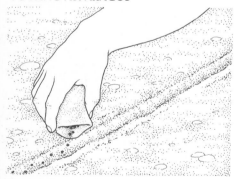

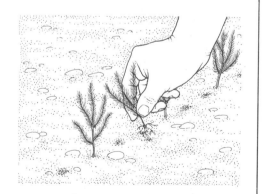

Asparagus seed can be sown outdoors in March or early April.

Sow the seed thinly in $\frac{1}{2}$–$\frac{3}{4}$ in deep drills, 18 in apart. When the seedlings emerge thin them until they are eventually 6 in apart. Keep the bed completely weed-free and water in dry weather. The seedlings can be transplanted to the permanent bed in March or April of the following year.

However, another year in the seedling row will mean that the seed-bearing female plants can be identified and removed before their seeds fall and germinate. In a permanent bed planted with male crowns only there is no seedhead production and constant weeding out of unwanted seedlings will not be necessary. Plant out and proceed as for one-year-old crowns.

The first year

1 Winter. Dig the ground to a depth of 1 spit and incorporate well-rotted manure or compost with a fork. Also remove perennial weeds.

2 April. Dig a trench 15 in wide and 10 in deep. Lightly rake in fertilizer at 3 oz per square yard. Make a 3 in deep ridge at the bottom of the trench.

3 April. Plant the crowns at 18 in intervals on the ridge with the roots sloping outwards. Cover the crowns with 2–3 in of soil.

4 October. Cut the fern when it has turned yellow. Apply a 2–3 in layer of manure or compost and mound up the soil several inches deep over the row.

Asparagus 2

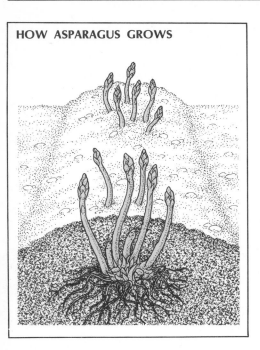

HOW ASPARAGUS GROWS

sulfate of potash. Make a ridge in the bottom of the trench and place each crown at 18 in intervals on the ridge, with the roots spread outwards over the ridge. Cover them quickly and carefully with fine soil to fill in the trench. If more than one trench is dug the rows should be 4 ft apart.

Once an asparagus bed is established its upkeep is routine. The common reasons for deterioration are lack of weeding, cutting over too long a season and disregard of the need for fern production. Hand weed regularly and never cultivate deeply or dig near a bed because asparagus roots spread out widely and are easily damaged. In the fall when the foliage turns yellow, cut it down and clear any weeds. Mound up the soil several inches deep over the row.

The second year
In late February or early March top-dress with a balanced general fertilizer, such as 10-10-10, at 3 oz per square yard.

Do not cut the foliage until it yellows in the fall. Then clear the bed and apply a 2–3 in layer of well-rotted manure or compost. Ridge up the row with soil if necessary.

Harvesting
Do not cut any spears until the third season after planting. Eventual heavy cropping depends on a slow build-up of crown size, starting with the all important first two seasons, when no cutting should be done.

The cutting season for asparagus is from the end of April to late June, and no longer. Cut all the spears when they are 5–6 in above ground, even if they vary in thickness. In the third year cut for a period of six weeks after the first shoots appear. In the fourth and subsequent years the cutting period is up to eight weeks.

A special asparagus knife is ideal for cutting, but an ordinary sharp knife used carefully will do. By the time a bed is established the crowns will be about 4 in below the soil surface.

Cut the spears obliquely about 1–2 in below the soil surface. An asparagus crown produces many small shoots at different stages of maturity and it is important to cut the spears cleanly and carefully so that the plant will continue to crop.

Aftercare
From June onwards the ferns must be allowed to grow in order to play their vital role in building up food reserves in the crown for the following year's crop. To encourage this growth apply a general, balanced fertilizer at 3 oz per square yard immediately after the last cutting.

When the ferns have turned yellow, and not before, cut them down to ground level. Burn them because they are too woody for the compost heap. Clear away any debris, such as dried leaves and stems, and tidy the bed after cutting the ferns down.

Pests and diseases
If asparagus beetle grubs damage shoots during the cutting season spray the plants with derris. If slugs are troublesome control them by the methods described in the section on pests and diseases (see page 263).

The second year

5 Late February to early March. Top-dress the bed with fertilizer at 3 oz per square yard.

6 Fall. Cut down the yellow ferns and apply manure or compost. Ridge up the row with soil if necessary.

Third and subsequent years

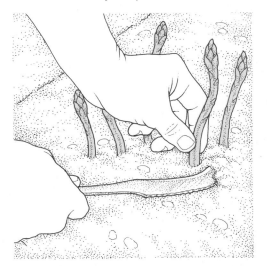

7 April to late June. Cut all the spears with a sharp knife when they are 5–6 in above soil level. Cut each spear obliquely 1–2 in below the soil surface.

8 June onward. Immediately after the last cut, apply a general, balanced fertilizer at 3 oz per square yard to the bed.

Celery

Celery is a biennial plant grown as an annual for its blanched stems which are cooked or used for salads. There are green and yellow varieties.

Cultivation

Choose an open site with rich, well-drained soil of pH 6.5–7.5. There are two methods of growing celery. By tradition it is grown in trenches which are gradually filled in to blanch the stems. Alternatively, self-blanching varieties can be used which do not require hilling up but these are less hardy (with a correspondingly shorter growing season) than the trenched varieties. They require much less work and are especially suitable for heavy soils which are laborious to trench and where the trench may become waterlogged with consequent slug damage and rotting.

Trench method Take out a trench 15 in wide and 12 in deep in March or April. If more than one trench is required the centers of each should be 4 ft apart. Fork manure into the bottom of the trench at a rate of 15 lb (1 bucketful) per square yard and return the soil to within 3 in of ground level. The trench should then be left open until planting out time in early summer.

Sowing Use treated seed if available. In February or March (10 weeks before last spring frost) sow the seed thinly in flats in a prepared sterile soil mixture at 13°–16°C/55°–60°F. Do not cover the seed but keep it moist. The seed germinates in 2–3 weeks. Prick out the seedlings when they have two true leaves into flats of soil mixture. Alternatively, place them singly in 3 in pots. Harden them off gradually for planting out in late May or June. Just before planting, rake in a balanced general fertilizer at the rate of 2–3 oz per square yard into the bottom of the trench and apply a diazinon drench to combat carrot rust fly.

Planting When danger of frost is past, plant out the seedlings at 9 in intervals in double-staggered rows 9 in apart in each trench. Water the plants thoroughly. When the plants are about 12 in high cut out any side-shoots at the base and loosely tie the stems just below the leaves, using raffia or soft string.

As with all leafy crops ample water is essential during the growing season. In dry weather apply 4 gal per square yard. Alternatively, 10–20 days before the final hilling up apply 4 gal per square yard. This improves the quality and size of the crop markedly.

Hilling up As the plants grow, hill up progressively at intervals of about three weeks, leaving plenty of leaf above the soil and taking care not to let soil fall into the hearts. Hill up after rain when the soil is damp, never when it is dry, because the foliage acts as an umbrella and keeps the soil around the roots as dry or as damp as it was when hilled up.

Harvesting

Most varieties mature in about 4 months. Lift celery carefully with a trowel as they are required. The roots may penetrate very deeply and in such cases it is best to lift with a fork. Bracken or straw placed over the trench assists lifting in frosty weather.

Pests and diseases

Celery fly larvae bore into the foliage leaving brown blisters. Pinch out affected leaves and spray with dimethoate at the first sign of damage. Slugs may be a problem, especially on heavy soils, and so put down slug pellets around the plants. Carrot rust fly may attack the roots of celery and should be combated by applying diazinon before transplanting.

Celery leaf spot can be prevented by using treated seed or spraying the plants with benomyl as soon as any spots are visible on the leaves. For early and late blight, which cause brown spots on stems and leaves, spray weekly with zineb. For later crops of celery, seed is sown in an outdoor seedbed 4–4½ months before last frost.

SELF-BLANCHING CELERY

 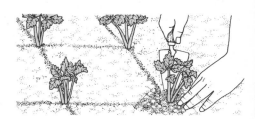

Sow the seed as for trench-grown varieties but plant out the seedlings on the flat. Prepare the bed in April by digging in well-rotted manure or compost at 15 lb per square yard. Plant out the seedlings during May in a square, not in a row, 11 in apart each way or 6 in each way for a higher yield of smaller sticks.

1 February or March. Dig a trench 15 in wide and 12 in deep. Fork manure into the bottom and return the soil to within 3 in of ground level.

2 March or April. Sow the seed thinly in seed compost at 13°–16°C/55°–60°F. Do not cover and keep moist. After 2–3 weeks prick the seedlings out in flats of potting soil.

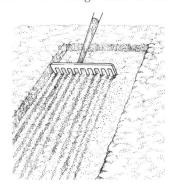

3 Just before planting, rake fertilizer into the trench bottom at 2–3 oz per square yard.

4 May. Plant out the seedlings at 9 in intervals in double-staggered rows 9 in apart. Water well.

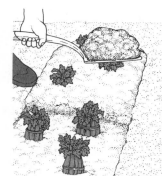

5 July. When the plants are 12 in high loosely tie the stems just below the leaves. Hill up every 3 weeks when the soil is damp to cover the leaf bases.

6 October. Lift celery by carefully loosening with a trowel or a fork.

Rhubarb

FORCING
'Timperley Early'.

MAIN CROP
'Hawke's Champagne',
'Prince Albert', 'Sutton',
'Victoria'.

Rhubarb (*Rheum rhaponticum*) is a hardy perennial grown for its delicately-flavored pink leaf-stalks, and is therefore classed as a vegetable not a fruit. The leaves contain oxalic acid and are poisonous. Rhubarb is in season from March to July, although earlier crops can be obtained in January and February by forcing plants.

Cultivation

Rhubarb grows best on a sunny site in a fairly heavy, acid soil of pH 5.0–6.0. However, it will tolerate a wide range of conditions and is likely to fail only on very waterlogged soils. The plants will stand for about 5–10 years, so the bed should be thoroughly prepared in the fall before planting.

Dig the ground deeply, removing all perennial weeds and incorporating organic manure or well-rotted garden compost at a rate of 20–30 lb per square yard. Just before planting rake in a dressing of 3–4 oz of fertilizer.

Propagation Raising rhubarb from seed is a lengthy process which often gives poor results, so either propagate it from root-cuttings or obtain offsets of a named variety from a nursery. Propagation should be from established plants at least three years old. Cut the roots into sections that have at least one eye with a sharp knife.

Planting Plant in early spring, leaving 3 ft between the plants. If more than one row is required, leave 3–4 ft between the rows. The eyes should be just below the soil surface. Firm in and water if necessary during dry weather. Cut out flowering shoots as they appear.

Harvesting

Rhubarb can be harvested from April to July. Do not pull at all in the first year after planting and only lightly in the second. Hold the stalk near the base and pull up with a twisting movement. Take a few stalks from each crown as required, but always leave 3–4 leaves on each plant to avoid weakening it.

Aftercare In autumn, when harvesting is over and the foliage has died down, clean up around the plants and apply a light top dressing of a balanced general fertilizer at 2–3 oz per square yard. In late winter mulch with well-rotted compost or manure.

Pests and diseases

Stem and bulb eelworm may attack rhubarb, causing poor growth and distorted leaves. Crown rot is the only major disease, the symptoms of which are dull foliage, small stalks and dead buds. There is no cure for either of these problems so dig up and burn affected plants. Do not replant rhubarb on the same ground.

FORCING RHUBARB

Forcing the plants during the winter produces earlier crops of pinker, more tender rhubarb. It can be harvested from February to March if forced *in situ* or as early as January if forced indoors.

Outdoors In mid-January to February cover the plants to be forced with a bucket or barrel to exclude the light. Put straw or strawy manure over and around the cover for insulation. The plants should not normally need watering and the stalks will be ready in 5–6 weeks. Do not pick from the plants for at least two years after forcing to allow them to recuperate.

Indoors In October to early November dig up strong clumps and leave them on the soil surface exposed to frosty weather for 1–2 weeks. This encourages rapid growth during forcing. Then pack the roots close together in a box, cover with a thin layer of soil and water well. Invert another box and place it on top, and exclude light with newspaper or black polyethylene. Keep in a warm greenhouse or shed at 10°–13°C/50°–55°F. Water the plants occasionally to keep them moist. Pull the stalks in 4–5 weeks. Stagger the times of boxing for a constant supply.

First year

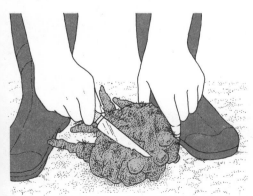

Second and subsequent years

1 Early spring. Cut the roots of an established plant into sections, ensuring each has at least 1 eye.

2 Plant the sections 3 ft apart in well-prepared ground, with the eyes just below the soil surface. Rows should be 3–4 ft apart.

3 Summer. Water the plants in dry weather and cut out any flowering shoots.

4 October. Remove old foliage. Apply 2–3 oz of fertilizer to each plant.

5 April to July. Pull stalks by grasping near the base and twisting upwards.

Bush beans 1

CLIMBING
'Blue Lake', 'Earliest of All'.

CLIMBING PURPLE
'Blue Coco', 'Purple Podded'.

DWARF
'Masterpiece' (prolific),
'The Prince', 'Sprite',
'Tendergreen'.

DWARF YELLOW
'Kinghorn Wax-pod'.

BUSH BEANS

Bush beans (also called snap beans or green beans) are tender annuals. Dwarf and climbing (pole) types are available. They grow best in warm conditions. The beans are eaten with the pods. Green podded types with either flat or cylindrical pods are most common, and there are also yellow, so-called "wax" beans and a purple bean that turns green when cooked. Two rows of dwarf beans 18 in apart should produce 10–15 lb of beans—pole beans produce 20–30 lb. Like other beans, bush beans are valuable for their vitamin and mineral content.

Cultivation

Bush beans grow best in a well-drained, fertile soil of pH 6.5–7.0. A layer of farmyard manure or compost dug in during the winter is sufficient to maintain fertility in most soils. Do not grow bush beans in shaded situations. Apply and work in a fertilizer, such as 10-10-10, at 1–2 oz per square yard a couple of weeks before sowing. Overrich soils and too much nitrogenous fertilizer encourage soft growth and excessive leaf production. No top dressing should be needed for this crop.

Sowing Do not make outdoor sowings too early. A soil temperature of at least 10°C/50°F is needed for successful and rapid germination. Be sure that all danger from frost has passed. Bush beans do not thrive in cold soils and the seeds will rot if conditions are too wet. The first dwarf bean sowings can be made outside in May in most places. Monthly sowings until July or even August give beans throughout the summer.

Pole types should be sown in mid-to-late May in cold regions.

Sow dwarf beans in rows 18 in apart. Space the seeds 2–3 in apart in 2 in drills. Water the bottom of the drill before sowing to encourage germination. Pole beans are sown in the same way but usually in hills spaced 3 ft apart.
Growing Pole beans need a support and training system because the plants grow to 6–7 ft. The usual practice is to make a tripod from three 8 ft poles lashed together at the top. Sow the beans around this in a circle and thin out to about 5 plants. Another method is to plant the beans in rows and build a tall framelike trellis of poles with 2–3 wires stretched between them. Tie strong vertical strings between the wires at about 9 in intervals. Let one or two plants climb each.

Hoe out any weeds and mulch the plants in June with peat, straw or lengths of black polyethylene. Once the seedlings are established, do not water until the flowers appear unless the weather is dry. Too much water during early growth encourages leaves to grow at the expense of the flowers.

Water the plants generously once the flowers appear; beans are particularly sensitive to moisture stress at the flower-opening and pod swelling stages and it is essential to keep them well watered at these times.

1 During winter, dig in a layer of farmyard manure or compost where the beans are to be grown.

2 Late April. Rake in general balanced fertilizer at 1–2 oz per square yard 1–2 weeks before sowing.

3 Take out a 2 in drill, spacing rows 18 in apart. Water the bottom of the drill to encourage germination.

4 May. Sow individual seeds at 2–3 in intervals in 2 in drills, 18 in apart for dwarf; 3–4 in intervals and 2 ft apart for pole.

Bush beans 2

Watering at 3–4 gal per square yard each week markedly increases pod-set, yield and quality. Syringing the flowers to "set" the pods, a traditional practice, is not effective. The organic matter dug in during the winter will help to retain moisture.

Harvesting

Regular picking is essential to maintain a continuous supply of beans. Dwarf beans produce their pods over a relatively short period (hence the successive sowings) but pole types continue to crop throughout the summer. Pick the beans while they are young and tender. Over-mature pods are stringy and show the beans bulging out the pod walls. Remove the pods carefully so as not to damage the plants; they should snap off the plants cleanly.

Pests and diseases

Aphids (green and black) may feed on the growing shoots, and red spider mites may be found on the under surfaces of leaves. These mites produce yellow dots on the upper surfaces of leaves, which eventually become bronzed and brittle. Gray mold (*Botrytis cinerea*) and mildew diseases can be problems during wet weather in the picking season. Damaged pods are soon infected and rot on the plant. Spray the plants regularly with zineb during wet or humid conditions.

Bacterial blight may attack bush beans (see page 263). It causes dark, water-soaked areas on leaves and pods, and the characteristic "halo" forms a yellow edge around the dark areas. Damp, humid conditions favor the spread of bacterial blight and fungicidal sprays are usually ineffective against it. Destroy any bush beans affected by the disease and never save seed for the next season from them. The worst insect pest is the yellow Mexican bean beetle, but this is readily controlled by dusting with rotenone.

SUPPORT SYSTEMS

Pole beans must be supported on sticks, strings or nets because the plants grow up to 6–7 ft tall. Supports can be nets attached to poles, poles arranged in tripods, tied at the top, or wires stretched between poles.

5 Throughout summer. Hoe to keep down weeds and then mulch with peat, straw or black polyethylene to preserve moisture.

6 In June, mulch the plants with peat, straw or black polyethylene to keep down weeds.

7 As flowers appear, carefully apply water at a rate of 3–4 gal per week. Avoid splashing the foliage.

8 July onward. Pick the pods when they are 5–6 in long. They should snap in half easily and show no stringiness.

Runner beans 1

Runner beans are perennials that produce small root tubers, but they are usually grown as half-hardy annuals. In temperate zones they may be damaged by frost at the beginning or at the end of the season. The plants are very attractive with different varieties having white, pink or, more usually, scarlet flowers. Their tall habit and dense foliage make them a useful screen plant. A runner bean wigwam makes an attractive centerpiece in an annual flower border.

Cultivation

Runner beans should not be growing while frost is still a danger. When they are sown or planted rapid growth is required, however, and light, well-drained, fertile soils of pH 6.0–7.0 are best suited for this crop. Wet soils cause the large seeds to rot. Careful soil preparation for runner beans is rewarded with excellent growth and yields. Prepare a 2 ft wide, single spade depth trench in early spring. Fork large quantities of farmyard manure or well-rotted garden compost into the bottom of the trench before replacing the soil. These materials retain moisture during the life of the crop and encourage good growth and setting.

Situation Choose a sheltered but open, sunny site for runner beans, because winds can damage the plants and young beans. Still conditions also encourage the insects which are essential for runner bean pollination. One or two weeks before sowing, hoe in 2–3 oz per square yard of a general fertilizer such as 10-10-10.

Plant establishment There are several possible support systems for runner beans and the method of propagation varies with the system. Beans may either be sown or planted. Plants are raised in a cool greenhouse (10°C/50°F) in individual containers. Sow the seed approximately four weeks before the expected planting date. Pre-germinate the seeds first between layers of moistened kitchen toweling kept in a warm place. A germination rate of more than 80 per cent can be expected. Keep the propagation temperature down to maintain strong, sturdy growth. Harden the plants in a cold frame or under cloches for a few days before planting. Do not plant out until all danger of frost

EARLY CROPS

Early crops can be produced from transplanted plants raised by sowing seeds in pots in a cool greenhouse. Sow the seeds about four weeks before the expected planting date, which must be after the last frost. Make a good-sized hole with a trowel and plant a single bean plant beside each cane, pole or string. Sufficiently long shoots should be twisted around their support and the plants must be thoroughly watered at the base.

has passed. Sowing should take place outside from mid-May onwards depending on the frost incidence in the area. A soil temperature of at least 10°C/50°F is needed for germination. Cloches can be used to protect sowings made during April. Use the cloches to warm up the soil for three or four weeks before sowing and sow a single row with the beans spaced 6 in apart. Runner bean seeds should be sown 2 in deep and the positioning in the row depends on the support system.

Support systems

Runner beans are usually grown up supports. They can be trained up canes, poles, strings or nets. The plants will grow 8 ft tall, but they can be stopped by pinching out the growing point when they reach the top of the support.

Single rows of beans can be grown up any of the supports mentioned. In windy areas, a wall can provide shelter for a single row of beans. Nail or screw a batten horizontally on a wall about 8 ft above the ground. Canes or poles can then be pushed into the soil and secured to the batten with string, wire or nails. If a second batten is fixed to the wall near the ground, a row of strings can be tied vertically at the desired interval. Seeds should be sown at 6 in intervals and the canes, poles or strings should be spaced 6 in apart. If nets are used they should be attached to wires stretched between vertical stakes.

Double row systems use 8 ft canes or poles which are crossed over and wired or tied together at the top to form an inverted V-shape. Sow the beans at 6 in intervals in the rows which should be 24 in apart. If poles are scarce or expensive, two plants can climb each support, but the yield will be reduced. Leave a 36 in path between double rows.

Canes or poles can also be made into wigwam support frameworks. Four to ten supports may be used. A 4-cane wigwam has canes at the corners of a 3 ft square. The canes or poles are wired or tied together at the top. In this case erect the wigwam and sow or plant the beans next to each cane or pole. Runner beans, when fully grown and cropping, are heavy and prone to wind damage. Make the support system used robust.

1 Early spring. Take out a trench one spit deep and 2 ft wide. Dig 1–2 bucketsful of farmyard manure or well-rotted garden compost into the bottom and re-fill with the original soil.

2 April. Rake in 2–3 oz per square yard of a balanced general fertilizer. Use cloches to warm the soil in cold seasons.

3 Mid-May. Sow individual seeds 6 in apart in 2 in deep drills. Two drills 24 in apart are sown for double row growing systems.

Runner beans 2

Growing Gently twist the plants counter-clockwise around their supports to encourage them to climb. Water runner beans only when they are in flower or cropping. Too much water early on encourages leaf growth at the expense of flowers and beans. If the plants become short of water, flowers will drop off and pods fail to develop. Bulky organic manures dug in during the soil preparations help to retain moisture around the roots. Mulch around the plants to eliminate weeds and minimize moisture loss.

Runner beans are insect pollinated and so care is needed when using insecticides. Use low persistence chemicals, such as malathion, and apply them in the evening when pollinating insects have finished working. Pinch out the growing points of beans at frequent intervals to keep the plants compact.

The first severe frost kills runner bean foliage, which can be cut down and composted if it is disease-free. Diseased foliage should be burned. Dig the small root tubers into the soil because they will add useful nitrogenous material. Clean and store the canes or poles for next season. Nets and strings should be burned after one season but plastic netting can be sterilized and used again for beans or other crops.

Harvesting
Picking of the cloched and pinched crops starts in July, with the supported crops coming in at the beginning of August. Careful and rigorous picking of pinched crops keeps down the number of soil-splashed and bent beans. Harvesting from these crops continues for about three or four weeks.

Supported crops produce beans until the first severe frost kills the plants. Pick them regularly to maintain a continuity of production. At the height of the season it is necessary to pick every other day.

Pests and diseases
Aphids and red spider mites are major pests, and gray mold (*Botrytis cinerea*) and bacterial blight may be problems in wet or humid weather. See page 55 for details of symptoms and treatment.

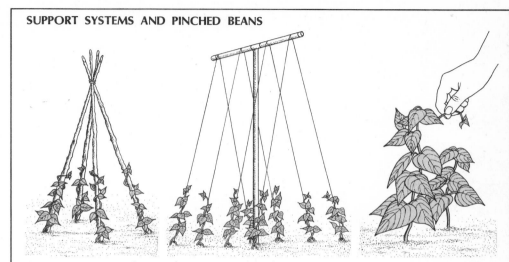

SUPPORT SYSTEMS AND PINCHED BEANS

Strings, canes or poles are the most usual supports although nets are sometimes used. Plants may be grown in single or double rows. Wigwam supports are formed by joining 4–10 canes or poles together at the top. Unsupported plants—pinched beans—have the growing point removed to produce a dwarf habit.

Supporting a double row

4 June. When the plants are 3–4 in tall erect a double row of crossed 8 ft poles. Space them 6–12 in apart, and train 1–2 plants up each. Place a horizontal pole on top for added stability.

5 June to July. Mulch around the plants once they are established. Use a 3–4 in layer of straw or peat.

6 June to July. Spray against aphids and red spider mites if necessary. Spray late in the evening to avoid harming heavy-bodied insects, such as bees.

7 Late July to early August. Pick young, tender beans with no hint of swollen seeds through the pod wall. Regular picking, every other day if possible, encourages more runner bean pods to form.

Broad beans 1

Broad beans

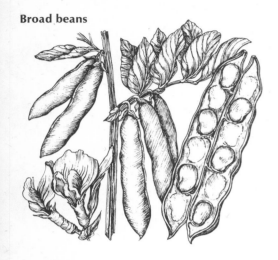

The broad bean is a hardy annual vegetable. It is a legume and is therefore grown both for its value to the soil (it enriches the soil with nitrogen which is fixed by nitrogen-fixing bacteria in the roots of the plants) and also as a rich source of protein. It can either be eaten freshly picked (like peas) or it can be dried, stored for months at a time and used in an assortment of recipes. Broad beans are slow to mature so give them as long a growing season as possible by sowing the seeds as the variety and climate will allow. The first pickings are made in July.

Cultivation
Broad beans—in common with other legumes—ideally prefer neutral or slightly alkaline soils, but grow well between pH 6.0–7.0. They tolerate relatively infertile soils but better growth and heavier yields occur on rich, fertile, well-drained soils. Cold, wet soils must be avoided especially for the over-wintered crops. However, fava broad beans can withstand cool soils and can be sown soon after last spring frost. The soil should be kept evenly moist throughout the growing season. Mulch to conserve moisture and keep down weeds. Broad beans have the largest seeds of all vegetables and they will soon rot in waterlogged soils. Soil for broad beans should be given a dressing of 2–3 oz per square yard of a balanced fertilizer, such as 10-10-10, 1–2 weeks before sowing. No more fertilizer should then be needed.

Sowing Broad bean seeds are very large and there is no need to prepare a very fine seedbed. Sowing of broad beans can begin outdoors as soon as the soil is workable.

Unlike bush beans, broad beans withstand some frost. The seeds germinate well at soil temperatures of 5°C/39°F. The germination rate should be at least 80 percent. Successive sowings at monthly intervals will produce beans through the fall.

Single and double rows
Broad beans can be grown in either single or double rows. Research has shown that dwarf varieties should be sown 9 in apart with 9 in between rows. Taller varieties should be spaced 5 in apart with 18 in between rows. The seeds may be sown in a 3 in deep drill taken out with a draw hoe. Alternatively, they can be sown at the same depth in holes made with a trowel or dibble alongside a line.

Broad beans can also be sown in pots under glass in February or March and planted out

1 March or April. Make drills 18 in apart and 3 in deep. Sow single seeds 5 in apart. For dwarf varieties make the drills 9 in apart and sow the seeds at 9 in intervals. Broad bean seeds are very large so there is no need to prepare a very fine seedbed for them.

2 April. Hammer stakes into the ground at each end of the rows, leaving 3–4 ft above the ground.

3 April onward. Hoe regularly around the plants and when they are big enough run string around the stakes at 12 in intervals to provide support as they develop.

4 When the plants are in full flower pinch out 4–6 in of shoot to reduce the danger of bean aphid attack and to encourage a uniform development of pods up the plants.

Broad beans 2

as soon as the garden soil is workable. This system is useful in cold climates if you want the earliest possible crop. Hoeing for weed control is necessary until there is a good foliage cover of beans. Taller varieties need not be supported. Stakes should be hammered in at the ends or corners of the rows. Leave 3–4 ft of stake above ground and wind successive lengths of string from the stakes all around the plants. Layers of string should be attached at 12 in intervals. Keep the plants well watered during flowering and cropping, but water only in dry spells at other times in the growing period.

Watch for bean aphids which will attack the plants in May or June. They feed on the young shoot tips and their arrival usually coincides with the flowering of the beans. Remove 4–6 in of the growing tips to dis-courage this pest and to encourage more uniform development of pods up the plant. Spray the plants with primicarb.

Harvesting

Picking begins in July and can continue, from successive spring sowings, into the fall. Broad beans are usually shelled from the pods before cooking and the stage of picking is critical. The pods should not be tough and fibrous, while the beans themselves must be young and tender. Pods can also be picked when immature (4–6 in long) and either cooked whole or sliced.

After harvesting, cut off the plant tops and dig the roots in so that the nitrogen-fixing bacteria which they contain is kept to improve the soil fertility for subsequent crops. The roots also make excellent compost, and can be dug up and composted if their fertility value is needed for another part of the garden.

Pests and diseases

Bean aphids can be sprayed with low-persistence insecticides such as malathion, pyrethrum or derris. Spray late in the evening to minimize damage to pollinating insects such as bees. It is best to spray before the infestation takes a firm hold of the crop. Repeat the spraying weekly during the most likely months of attack. Pea and bean weevils feed on leaves, producing a scalloped pattern around the edge. Nearly all broad bean crops develop dark brown spots or blotches on the leaves and stems, although the pods are attacked only in severe outbreaks. These are the symptoms of chocolate spot fungus caused by a type of gray mold (*Botrytis cinerea*). If you soak beans in water before sowing to help them germinate then be sure to spray with Maneb to check the spread of disease among the seeds. Poorly grown plants are attacked most severely, with damaged leaves, overcrowding and soft, lush growth contributing to the spread of the disease. It is rarely sufficiently severe to warrant chemical control measures and it is much better to avoid the disease by growing healthy plants.

Lima beans

The lima bean is also called the butter bean or butter pea. They are shelled from the 3–4 in pods and eaten fresh or dried. Pole or bush varieties are grown. Sow seed when the soil is warm, usually in early to mid June in cooler zones. Thin to 8–12 in apart and mulch well. Harvest when pods are full.

5 During flowering and cropping, water well to boost crop yield. Do not water before flowering unless the weather is very dry because too much watering during the early life of broad beans increases leafy growth at the expense of flowers and fruit.

6 June to July onward. Pick young broad beans before the pod walls become tough and fibrous. Shell them from the pods before cooking—the attachment scars of individual seeds should be green rather than black.

7 After harvesting. Cut down the stems to within 4 in of the soil immediately after picking has finished. Compost healthy stem material and dig in the stem bases and roots.

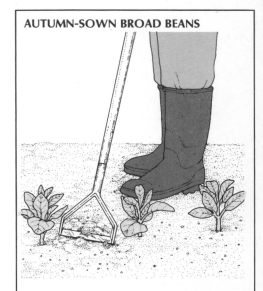

AUTUMN-SOWN BROAD BEANS

Sow broad beans in November in the usual way, using the special winter-hardy varieties available. Do not fertilize, or there will be too much growth which will suffer from winter frosts.

In February, apply a top-dressing of nitrogenous fertilizer, such as nitro-chalk, at a rate of 1–2 oz per square yard and hoe it in around the plants.

Garden peas 1

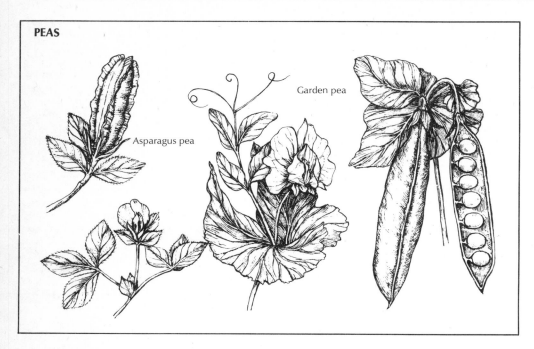

PEAS

Asparagus pea

Garden pea

Peas are treated as hardy annuals. The round-seeded types are hardier than the wrinkle-seeded types. Sugar or snow peas and the petit pois of France are closely related to garden peas. The yield depends upon the variety grown. Tall types produce two to three times as many peas as do dwarf types. Peas are usually shelled from the pods before cooking.

Cultivation

Peas must be grown on well-drained, rich, fertile soils of pH 6.0–7.0. Dig in a 2 in layer of farmyard manure or well-rotted garden compost in the winter to improve soil fertility and retain moisture. Peas grown on well-manured soils do not require any fertilizers, but crops grown on low fertility soils respond to an application of 1–2 oz per square yard of a balanced fertilizer with low nitrogen content. Incorporate the fertilizer just before sowing the peas.

Sowing Popular varieties of peas mature in 55–75 days. Successive sowings from late March to mid-May of each maturity type produce peas from about mid-June until August. A final sowing with an early variety can be made in July for picking in September or October, but don't count on success

Although pea seeds germinate at 5°C/39°F and the plants tolerate below-freezing temperatures, sowing as soon as frost is out of the ground rarely gives as much of a head-start as many gardeners think, because the plants will make slow growth if the weather continues cold and they may be killed by disease. It is better to wait for several weeks.

Peas may be sown in single rows in a V-shaped drill or broadcast in an 8–10 in wide flat-bottomed drill. Experiments have shown that the best yields can be expected from lines of three drills 5 in apart, with 18 in between each group of drills. Space the peas 5 in apart in the drill, which should be 2 in deep. If sowing in a flat-bottomed drill, first make the drill with a broad-bladed draw hoe or with a spade. The drill should also be 2 in deep. Broadcast the seeds evenly in the drill so that they are about 3 in apart each way. Rake soil back into the drill and firm it lightly

Garden peas

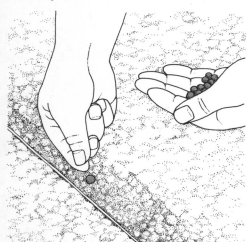

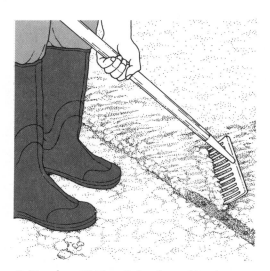

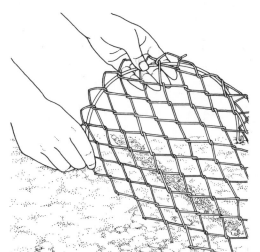

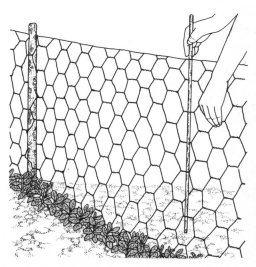

1 March until May. Use a draw hoe to make drills 2 in deep. Sow the seeds about 5 in apart in the bottom of the drill. For the distance between drills (18–48 in) check the mature height of the variety being grown.

2 March until May. Rake the soil back into the drill after sowing. Firm the soil down onto the seeds by lightly tamping with the back of the rake.

3 At the same time, put hoop-shaped, fine-meshed wire netting over the rows immediately after sowing to deter birds from digging up the seeds or eating newly emerged seedlings.

4 When the plants are 3–4 in tall erect the support system. Use a post and wire framework to support the netting up which the peas should climb.

Garden peas/Asparagus peas

with the back of the rake. The distance between rows should be the same as the eventual height of the mature crops. This varies from 18 in for the dwarf varieties to 5 ft for later varieties. These spaces can be used for catch crops of rapidly-maturing vegetables such as radishes early in the season. Birds may dig up the peas unless wire mesh guards are put over the rows immediately after sowing.

Sugar peas and petit pois are sown in the same way but they reach heights of 4 ft and 3 ft respectively.

Growing Peas can be grown without supports but growth and yields are better if the plants—especially of tall varieties— are able to climb and develop off the ground. The traditional method was to use twiggy branches pushed in alongside and within the rows. If these are difficult to find, use wire or nylon netting. Erect a post and wire framework along each row and attach an appropriate width of netting for the expected height of the peas. Put up the supports when the plants are 3–4 in tall.

Watering Never allow peas to become too dry when they are in full bloom or when the pods are swelling. Too much water before flowering reduces the yield; water only in very dry spells.

Mulching the plants with peat, straw or black polyethylene helps to reduce water loss. Mulching also keeps down weeds, and organic mulches add nutrients.

Harvesting

Picking of garden peas should begin about four weeks after full flower. Regular picking encourages more pods to develop. Pods at the base of the plant are ready first. The pods are the edible portion of sugar peas and it is vital that the peas inside them have not started to swell.

Petit pois must be harvested young or they lose their sweet, delicate flavor and become hard and unpalatable.

Cut down pea plants after harvesting and either put the roots on the compost heap or dig them into the soil in order to improve fertility.

Pests and diseases

Pea thrips attack the pods of peas. They are tiny insects up to $\frac{1}{10}$ in long which suck sap from the foliage and pods. Control thrips by spraying thoroughly with fenitrothion or malathion as soon as signs of damage are noted. Viruses such as pea mosaic virus cause stunting of plants and green or green and yellow mottling on leaves. Burn all affected plants. Aphids can infest the growing tips of pea plants. Spray with an insecticide, using primocarb, which is relatively harmless to bees, when the plants are in flower. Pea moth caterpillars can attack late pea crops. To control them, spray at dusk with fenitrothion seven days after flowering starts.

Asparagus peas

The asparagus or winged pea is quite different from other garden peas. It is half-hardy and has a bushy habit. The red flowers produce 4-winged fruits, 1–1½ in long, which are eaten whole. Asparagus peas are sometimes grown as a fodder crop.

Cultivation

Choose a light, well-drained soil in a sunny position on which to grow asparagus peas. Apply 1–2 oz per square yard of a general, balanced fertilizer two weeks before sowing.

Sowing Asparagus peas will be killed by frost, so choose a sowing date that takes this into account. Sow outside in early May when the main danger of frost is over. Space the seeds 4–6 in apart in 1 in deep drills, which should be 12 in apart. Water the bottom of the drill before sowing to encourage germination. Alternatively, the seeds can be sown in small pots indoors in early April and planted out at the end of May.

Growing Hoe weeds from around developing plants. Keep them well supplied with water from flowering time onwards. Too much water in the early stages reduces the yield. Asparagus pea plants have a tendency to sprawl and they should be supported by sticks.

Harvesting

It is important to pick the pods young, when about 1 in long, because they become tough.

Asparagus peas

5 Mid-June to August. Pick young and tender but well-filled pods. Regular harvesting encourages more pods to develop.

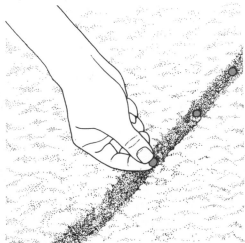

1 Early May. Sow the seed outside at 4–6 in intervals in the drill. In dry weather water the drill before sowing to aid germination. Choose a light, well-drained soil in a sunny position.

2 When 2–3 in high, add stakes to support the plants.

3 Late July to early August. Pick asparagus peas when they are 1 in long, otherwise they soon become stringy and tough.

Corn

This half-hardy annual grows most sweet and tender in northern gardens. It thrives on warmth—especially warm nights—and bright sunshine. Male and female flowers are produced in different places on the same plant. Male flowers grow at the top of the plant whereas the female flowers—which develop into the corn cobs—are found lower down. You can expect each plant to produce one or sometimes two cobs.

Cultivation

A light, well-drained and fertile soil of pH 5.5–7.0 is essential. Dig in a 2–3 in layer of bulky manure or garden compost during the winter. Avoid shaded sites but choose a sheltered position because the plants can be damaged by wind. Corn plants need plenty of food and water.

Apply 3–4 oz per square yard of balanced fertilizer a couple of weeks before sowing or planting and be prepared to topdress with an additional 1–2 oz per square yard in June or July.

Sowing Early sowings can be made under cloches at the end of April provided the cloches have been used to warm up the soil beforehand. Outdoor sowings should not take place until all danger of frost is past and soil temperature has reached 10°–13°C/50°–55°F. Sow 1 in deep. To assure that pollination takes place, you should plant either in two or more parallel rows or in hills. In rows, sow seeds 4–6 in apart and thin to 1 ft; the rows should be 24–30 in apart. If you use the hill method, sow 5–6 seeds together in a 1 ft circle, and space the hills 30 in apart in both directions. You may have to protect the seeds and plants against birds with fabric or by dipping the seeds in creosote.

Growing Hoe to keep down weeds but be careful not to damage the young plant stems. Keep the plants moist if dry spells occur. No watering is normally needed until the flowers (tassels) appear, when regular weekly applications of 3–4 gal per square yard (unless the weather is very wet) will improve the quality and yield. In windy positions stake the plants, but raising the soil around the stems is usually sufficient to keep the plants upright.

Harvesting

Pollen is produced from the male flowers from July onwards and falls on to the female flowers. These soon begin to wither, and the cobs should be ready about a month later. The cobs should be firm and well filled and are ready when the silks have turned brown but before they are completely dry. Test maturity by pushing a fingernail into one of the grains. A creamy liquid indicates that the cob is ready. Twist the cobs off the plant and cook or freeze them immediately. Corn is a vegetable which freezes well. Eat frozen corn on the cob within 6–8 weeks of freezing.

All the main ears in a single planting of one variety mature within a 5–7 day period. If the plants produce second ears, these mature together in the same way at a slightly later date. Therefore, if you want to eat corn throughout the summer, you must make more than one planting. You can either (1) use the same variety and make successive sowings at 10–14 day intervals from spring until 75–90 days before first fall frost; or (2) plant three different-maturity varieties at the same time in the spring; or (3) use a combination of both methods.

Popcorn

Popcorn ears are generally smaller and more irregular than sweetcorn ears. The kernels are usually yellow or white but may be red. All varieties take three months or more to mature. The same cultivation methods as for corn should be employed.

Popcorn is grown like sweetcorn, but both varieties are kept apart. If you plant yellow popcorn close to white sweetcorn, the sweetcorn ears will contain yellow kernels. Let the ears of popcorn remain on the stalks till the kernels are dry. Then pick, husk and store them in a dry place until the kernels fall off easily when you rub your fingers along the ears. They are then ready to be popped or bagged.

Harvesting

1 Winter. Dig a 2–3 in layer of manure or garden compost into the soil. Choose a sunny, sheltered site with a well-drained soil of pH 5.5–7.0.

2 Spring. When all danger of frost is past, sow seeds 4–6 in apart in parallel rows. Alternatively, sow in a circle on hills 30 in apart.

3 Harvesting. When the silks have withered press a fingernail into 1 of the grains underneath the protective leaves on each cob.

4 If the pressed grain exudes a creamy-white liquid harvest the cobs with a twisting, downward movement away from the plant stem.

Onions 1

ONIONS

AUTUMN-SOWN
'Express Yellow', 'Kaizuka',
'Kaizuka Extra Early', 'Yellow
Globe'.

SPRING-SOWN
'Ailsa Craig', 'Bedfordshire
Champion', 'Hygro', 'Wijbo'.

ONION SETS
'Sturon', 'Stuttgarter Giant'.

PICKLING ONIONS
'Paris Silverskin', 'The Queen'.

SALAD (SPRING) ONIONS
'White Lisbon', 'Winter Hardy'.

The onion is a biennial plant which is grown as an annual. The familiar bulbs are formed from swollen leaf bases. Salad onions (spring onions) are grown for the immature plants and should not produce bulbs.

Cultivation

Onions are easily grown from seed, and the bulb crop may also be grown from sets or transplants. Seed sowings can be made outdoors in the North in March and April, or under glass in January or February, to mature in late summer and fall. In the South, sowings made outdoors in October and over-wintered are ready the following summer. Sets planted in March to April mature in July to August. Sow salad onions in the spring for summer and fall use. For earlier salad onions, plant sets. Onion seed germinates very slowly and seedling growth is also slow.

Soil and situation The soil for onion growing should be well drained, reasonably fertile but not freshly manured. The pH should be more than 6.5. Choose a sunny but sheltered site. Soil-borne diseases can be serious, so do not grow onions on the same ground each year. This avoids most disease problems.

Double dig the land in early winter, working a 2–3 in layer of bulky organic material into the lower spit. Leave the surface rough to allow it to break down naturally during the winter. If onions are to be grown to full size, give them a fertilizer which contains about twice as much potash as nitrogen. Apply 2–3 oz per square yard of such a compound 7–10 days before sowing.

Spring-sown crops

Onion seed germinates at temperatures of 7°C/45°F and above. In cold areas it is wise to raise seedlings under glass. Sow in January or February for planting out in April or May. Sow in March under cloches, and in April in the open. The seedbed is most important. Digging in early winter should ensure that the soil is friable and breaks down easily. Work it down with a cultivator and rake it into a fine tilth, then make it firm and level. Be careful on silt or clay soils, where very fine tilths "cap" over if wet conditions are followed by drying weather (see pages 18–19). The young seedlings can find it difficult to penetrate the capped surface. Sow the seed thinly in drills 9–12 in apart and ½ in deep. Water the drill gently if the soil is dry. Thin to . 2–3 in between seedlings as soon as they have straightened up.

During the summer onions should be kept free from weeds. Additional watering is not usually required except in very dry weather in spring or early summer when applications of 2 gal per 10 ft run may be given each week. Further feeding is unnecessary. As the bulbs approach maturity in mid-to-late August or September, their leaves begin to yellow and topple over. In wet seasons this may be delayed, and the tops should be bent over by hand to assist the ripening of the bulbs. The leaves of some plants in a row may remain standing and these bulbs often have a wide neck (bull necks). Do not attempt to keep these bulbs as they soon rot in storage.

Autumn-sown crops

Onions sown in autumn mature from May to June, earlier than crops sown in spring. The seed should be sown in the same way as for spring-sown onions. Onion seed does not germinate well above 24°C/75°F, so in hot weather germination may be erratic. Pre-germination of the seeds at lower temperatures or lowering the soil temperature of the seedbed by frequent light waterings may be necessary in some seasons.

If the seed has been sown thinly the young onions should be left to over-winter and thinned to 1½–2 in (3 in for larger onions) in spring (March to April) as growth begins. A top dressing of 1–2 oz per square yard of a balanced fertilizer should be hoed in after thinning. Autumn-sown onions should not be transplanted because they tend to bolt.

Spring cultivation is then as for spring-sown onions.

Growing from sets

Growing from sets is probably the most convenient method of growing onions, especially in areas where the growing season is short. It is important to keep onion crops free from weeds but this is best done by hand because any digging near the roots is harmful to the bulbs. Mulch to discourage weeds and conserve moisture. Sun is essential to ripen the bulbs—usually from late July to August, when watering should have stopped. Bend the leaves over in wet seasons to help ripening. The crop is ready for harvesting when the leaves have turned yellow.

Spring-sown onions

1 Early March. Apply a balanced fertilizer at a rate of 2–3 oz per square yard 7–10 days before sowing. Rake it in and tread the soil down to produce a firm seedbed with a fine tilth.

2 March to April. Draw out drills 9–12 in apart and ½ in deep. Water the drills if the soil is dry. Sow the seed thinly.

3 May. As soon as the seedlings have straightened up thin them to 1–2 in apart, or 3 in apart if large onions are required. Water the rows with diazinon solution against onion maggot.

4 May to July. Keep the developing onions free from weeds. In very dry weather water at a rate of 2 gal per 10 ft run each week.

Onions 2

If onions are to be stored successfully, care should be taken to ripen them correctly. Spoiled crops can usually be avoided by seeing that the bulbs are properly dried and stored in a well-ventilated place. Only sound bulbs should be selected for storage and it is important that the leaves are not broken off, leaving the bulb exposed. Lay the bulbs on burlap or on a raised wire netting frame in a sunny part of the garden until the leaves are brittle. Store them in wooden crates, or string and hang them in a cool, frost-free place. Remove those that have gone soft during the winter.

Less common onions

A number of other *Allium* species, grown mainly for their curiosity value or in the herb garden, are also excellent for eating and easily cultivated. The tree onion is a perennial plant which forms normal clumps of bulbs at ground level but also sends up tall stems bearing clusters of small onions instead of flowers. These may be used in cooking or to increase the stock by using them as sets. Easily grown on any well-drained soil and providing crops for several years without

complications, an alternative common name might be the "lazy gardener's onion".

The potato onion, which forms a number of mild-flavored offsets just below soil level, can do duty for shallots. All are easily grown, providing useful and unusual space-fillers in a small garden.

Pests and diseases

Female onion flies lay their eggs in the base of the leaf shafts, near the ground, in the spring. They hatch into maggots which tunnel into the developing bulbs, causing the whole plant to turn yellow and die. Young plants should be protected before the eggs are laid. Water along the rows with a diazinon solution or dust the seedlings with lindane (gamma HCH). A seed disinfectant may help.

Downy mildew can be particularly bad in wet seasons. Gray patches appear on the leaves and turn purple as the disease progresses. Eventually the leaves topple over and collapse. Spray with zineb at the first sign of trouble. The best way to protect onions against other diseases, such as pink root and smudge, is to plant in well-drained soils and rotate crops on a 4-year basis.

TRANSPLANTED ONIONS

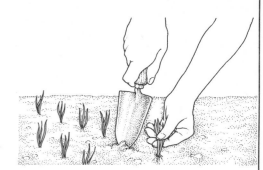

Early onions and those intended for showing should be transplanted. Sow the seed in flats during January or February in a warm, bright spot. Keep them at a temperature of 16°C/60°F. Germination is slow, but when the seedlings are large enough to handle they can be pricked out. For exhibition purposes grow each plant in a $3\frac{1}{2}$ in pot containing a proprietary potting compost. For general garden purposes prick out the onion seedlings individually into peat pots or into a seed tray, spacing them 2 in apart each way.

Gradually reduce the temperature to 10°C/50°F and harden off the plants in a cold frame or under a cloche for a few days before planting. Plant outdoors soon after the soil is workable in rows 12–15 in apart. Space the onions 2–3 in apart in the row. Plant shallowly with a trowel—deep planting hinders bulb development. Water thoroughly after planting.

5 August to September. If the leaves have not toppled over naturally, which sometimes happens in wet weather, bend them over by hand to assist ripening. Plants which remain standing may have bull necks.

6 September. Lift the bulbs for drying and storing when the fallen tops have begun to yellow and become brittle.

Autumn-sown onions

1 August to September. Prepare the ground and sow as for spring-sown onions, but do not thin the plants.

2 March to April. Thin the young plants to $1\frac{1}{2}$–2 in apart, 3 in if large onions are required. Top-dress with 1–2 oz per square yard of balanced general fertilizer or nitro-chalk after thinning.

Onions 3

Onion sets

Sets are partly developed onion bulbs. They are stored during winter and replanted in the spring, when they grow away rapidly. Sets are particularly useful for growing onions in places with short growing seasons. Consistently higher yields are possible from sets or seedling plants. As the sets have to be bought, it is more expensive to grow onions this way. This expense can be avoided by saving some onions from the previous season's crop and drying them carefully so that they become next season's sets. The best sets are $\frac{1}{2}-\frac{3}{4}$ in in diameter and firm. It is also sensible to buy small sets of this size because they are less likely to bolt than larger bulbs and are cheaper per plant.

Planting onion sets

Plant onion sets as soon as the soil is worked into a fine tilth. Mark out rows 10 in apart with a garden line and push the sets 1 in into the ground at 2–3 in intervals, or at 4 in intervals if larger bulbs are required. There is no point in using the wider spacings sometimes recommended because the yield from a given area will be much reduced. Firm the soil around the sets.

Birds may pull up the sets and prolonged frosty weather may also lift them out of the ground. In either case, they should be replanted immediately. As a precaution against birds, excess dried leaves should be cut close to the bulb but avoid exposing the inner leaves. The remaining operations are as for spring-sown or transplanted bulb onions.

SPRING ONIONS

Spring onions, or scallions, are immature onion plants. They are grown close together and eaten as a salad vegetable when the bulb is $\frac{1}{2}-1$ in across. Many of their requirements are the same as for bulb onions. The earliest spring onions are ready in the spring from sets and transplants. Continuity through the summer is then maintained from successive sowings made at two-week intervals from March until mid-June. Spring onions are grown close together in rows 4 in apart to prevent bulbs from developing. Sow the seed reasonably thinly in $\frac{1}{2}$ in drills. The drills should be watered before sowing if the soil is dry. The plants should grow $\frac{1}{2}-1$ in apart in the rows. Pull the onions before the bases swell. It helps to water them before pulling from dry soils. Pulling is easier if rows are first well watered.

1 February to June, every 2 weeks make sowings in $\frac{1}{2}$ in deep drills 4 in apart.

2 Summer. Lift the immature onions with a fork as the bases swell.

RIPENING AND STORAGE

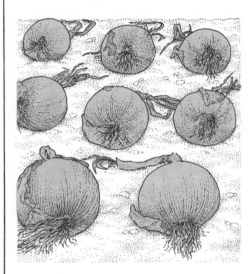

1 After digging up onions, place the bulbs outside in a shady, airy spot to dry and ripen further.

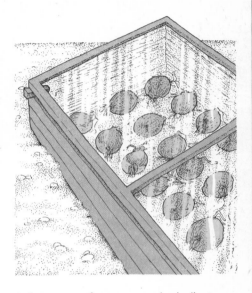

2 In wet weather arrange the bulbs in a single layer in a shed.

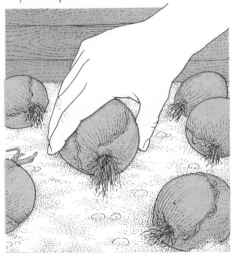

3 Turn the bulbs regularly to prevent diseases developing on the damp skins and wait 3–4 weeks for complete drying.

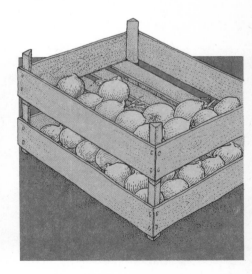

4 Store well-dried onions in trays that aid circulation and inspection, at a temperature of about 0°C/32°F.

Shallots/Garlic

Shallots have a milder flavor than bulb onions and are sometimes grown in preference to onions in smaller gardens, because they keep better and are more easily grown. They are grown from small bulbs (offsets) saved from the previous year's crop. Each newly planted bulb produces a cluster of 8–12 daughter bulbs by the end of the season.

Cultivation
Soil and fertilizer requirements are the same as for spring-sown or planted bulb onions (see page 63). Early planting is very important for shallots, so dig the land as soon as it becomes available.

Planting Save sound, firm bulbs from the previous season, or buy sets. Small bulbs of about $\frac{1}{3}$ oz weight (50 to the pound) are best to obtain maximum yield. Plant the bulbs when the soil is workable; space them 6 in apart in rows which are 8 in apart. Larger bulbs should be spaced 6 in apart with 12 in between the rows. Push the bulbs into the ground so that only the tips show above the soil surface. Alternatively, the bulbs can be planted in a shallow drill and then covered

and firmed. Shallots can also be planted outdoors in early fall and left in the ground until they are harvested in late spring.

Weeds can be a problem, especially while the crop is young. Hoe carefully around the clusters, but do not damage the developing bulbs or they will not keep. Do not water unless the weather is very dry. Shallots suffer from the same pests and diseases as do onions (see page 64).

Shallots are ready for harvesting earlier than are spring-planted onions. They should be ready in July, and the bulbs will begin to ripen about three weeks before that. Draw away the soil from around the bulbs to encourage quicker ripening.

Harvesting
Dig up the clusters of bulbs when the leaves turn yellow. Separate them into individual bulbs and, in fine weather, leave them on the soil to dry off; dry them under protection in wet weather.

Remove soil and any loose, dry leaves from the ripened bulbs before storing them in nets in a cool, but frost-free place.

Shallots

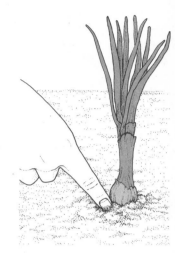

1 March. Push the bulbs into the ground so that their tops are just visible. Space them 6 in apart in rows 8 in apart.

2 April to July. Use a small onion hoe to keep the developing plants weed-free at all times. Remove any difficult weeds by hand.

3 July. Remove soil from around the clumps of onions by hand to speed up the ripening process.

GARLIC

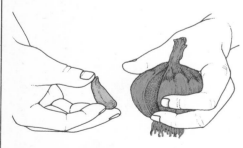

Garlic is a member of the onion family. Because of its strong flavor it is used sparingly in cooking. The plant is a perennial with long flat leaves and attractive white flowers. It can be grown in the open or in a pot or window-box. The soil must be rich, moist and well drained.

Garlic grows best in a sunny position, because high temperatures are needed to ripen the bulbs. Before planting prepare

the ground as for onion growing. Garlic seed is not readily available and so plants are usually grown from bulb segments (cloves) saved from a previous crop or bought from a food store. In the North, they are planted in March or April; in zones 8–10, in late summer or fall. Split a bulb into cloves. Plant them 1 in deep and 4 in apart with their pointed ends upward. The rows should be 6–8 in apart. Do not press the cloves into the soil because this prevents root development. Weed carefully between the bulbs with an onion hoe.

In late summer the stems and leaves begin to yellow and bend over. Loosen the bulbs gently out of the ground with a fork. Dry the bulbs in a cool, dry, shady spot. Do not handle the bulbs roughly because this may damage their necks and encourage rotting. Store garlic in string bags in a cool but frost-free shed. Cloves can be taken from bulbs as needed.

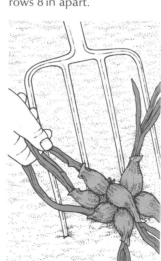

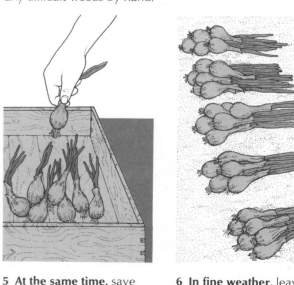

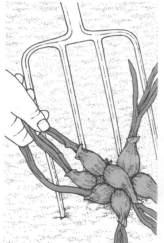

4 July onward. Lift shallots when the leaves turn yellow. Remove soil from around the roots and rub off loose leaves.

5 At the same time, save small bulbs of about $\frac{1}{3}$ oz in weight (50 to the pound) for next year's propagation material.

6 In fine weather, leave the bulbs in rows in the garden to dry out. In wet weather, dry them under protection in a well-ventilated place.

Leeks

EARLY
'Early Market', 'Lyon-Prizetaker'.

MID-SEASON
'Musselburgh',
'Walton Mammoth'.

LATE
'Royal Favorite', 'Winter
Crop' (very hardy).

Leeks are biennial plants grown as annuals. The stem-like collection of rolled leaves is eaten. Leeks have a long growing season and start to mature from late August. They are winter-hardy in mild climates and can be left in the garden for harvesting as you need them; but in cold climates, they should be dug up and stored or frozen. Leeks grow best in fertile, well-drained soils of pH 6.5–7.5. Although they will tolerate slightly more acid or alkaline conditions, they do not thrive in heavy soils which remain wet in winter. Dig the soil well because they must be planted deeply or hilled up to blanch. The ground should be dug well during the winter before planting. Incorporate a 2–3 in layer of bulky organic material or well-rotted garden compost. Do not give so much fertilizer that the plants become too lush and incapable of standing through frosty fall conditions. Apply 2–3 oz per square yard of a well-balanced fertilizer, such as 10-10-10, one or two weeks before planting.

Sowing and planting The germination and early growth of leeks are slow. The seeds need a soil temperature of at least 7°C/45°F for successful germination.

For early crops, sow in a seed tray about eight weeks before the last spring frost. Prick out into other trays when the leaves have straightened up, spacing the seedlings 2 in apart each way. Maintain a cool temperature until hardening off the plants in a cold frame during March. The plants should be planted on the mean date of the last frost.

Main crop leeks are sown outside in March to April shortly before the last frost, and can be transplanted during late May or June or left to grow where they are. Sow the seed thinly in drills ½ in deep and in rows 6 in apart.

Planting Leek plants should be planted out when pencil-thick and 6–8 in tall. Plant in rows 12 in apart. Make 2 in wide, 6 in deep holes with a dibble at 6 in intervals. After putting a seedling into the hole, do not replace the soil but fill each hole with water. This will settle sufficient soil around the roots. Alternatively, leeks can be planted on the flat or in 2 in deep trenches and blanched by progressively drawing up soil around the plants during the growing season. Hoe out any weeds. Water the plants only in very dry

conditions, when 2 gal of water per 10 ft row should be applied weekly. Mulch crops grown on dry soils. On poor soils liquid fertilizer can be used, but do not apply fertilizer to leeks late in the summer because soft growth prone to frost damage will be produced. Leeks are relatively free from pests and diseases.

Harvesting
Early varieties are ready in late August; others are ready a little later. Lift them as required using a fork. Leeks are hardy and in mild areas, they will remain usable until May.

Pests and diseases
Leeks are susceptible to the same pests and diseases that affect other members of the onion family (see page 64) but in fact they are seldom diseased.

PLANTING ON THE FLAT

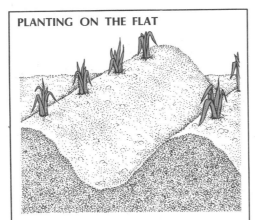

Blanched stems are produced when leeks are planted in holes, as described on the left, but longer white stems can be obtained if plants are hilled up. Plant the leeks 6 in apart in rows 12 in apart. Make holes 2–3 in deep and firm the soil around the base of each plant. Gradually draw up soil around the plants as they develop. Cardboard or paper collars may be tied around them to prevent soil getting into the plant centers.

Continue hilling up until only the tops of the leaves show above the soil. It might be necessary to add further collars to exclude earth as the leeks develop.

Sowing

1 Late March to mid-April. Prepare a seedbed. Sow the seeds thinly in ½ in deep drills 6 in apart.

2 Early May. Thin the seedlings to ½–1 in apart. Firm the soil around the bases of the remaining seedlings.

Planting

3 Late May to early June. Make 6 in deep holes, with a dibble, every 6 in in rows 12 in apart. Drop 1 plant into each. Fill with water.

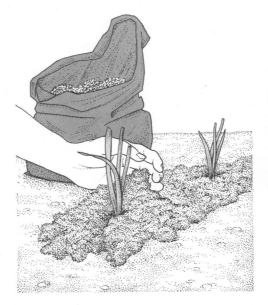

4 June until harvest. Mulch the crop with peat, black polyethylene (or similar) once the seedlings are established.

5 August onward. Lift leeks as required with a fork. Trim off the roots and tips of the leaves.

Carrots

SHORT
'Amsterdam Forcing', 'Nantes', 'Paris Forcing'.

INTERMEDIATE
'Autumn King', 'Chantenay Red-cored', 'Red Intermediate'.

LONG
'St Valery', 'Scarlet Perfection'.

Carrots are hardy biennial plants grown as annuals for their tasty roots. Depending on the variety, the roots range from $3\frac{1}{2}$ to 9 in long. A 10 ft row can yield 10–12 lb, depending on the variety. All can be eaten immediately or stored or frozen for winter use.

Cultivation

Long-rooted varieties need a deep soil but short-rooted varieties are suitable for shallow soils and will grow in heavy conditions.

Soil and situation The ideal soil has a pH between 6.5 and 7.5, is well-drained, stone-free and of medium texture. It should not have been manured for at least a year before sowing. Thorough, deep winter digging is important. An application of balanced general fertilizer at 2–3 oz per square yard about a week before sowing will maintain fertility. Choose an open situation for carrots.

Watering If deprived of water carrots become woody and coarse. In dry weather apply water at a rate of 2 gal per square yard at weekly intervals. If the plants become too wet as a result of applications of water in rainy weather, the development of foliage as opposed to roots is encouraged.

Early carrots In February or March, sow short varieties under cloches or in frames in $\frac{1}{2}$–$\frac{3}{4}$ in deep drills, 6 in apart. Always sow carrot seeds very thinly and thin the seedlings to $1\frac{1}{2}$–2 in intervals when they emerge. Young carrots mature from mid-May onward.

Alternatively, sow the seed outdoors every three to four weeks from March to August. These carrots are ready from June until November. Cover the later crops with cloches from September onward.

Main crop carrots From April to June, sow intermediate or long varieties very thinly in $\frac{1}{2}$–$\frac{3}{4}$ in deep drills, with 6 in between the rows. These mature from July to September.

Hoe between the rows, and as soon as the first rough leaves appear, thin the seedlings until the distance between the plants is 2 in for short-, medium- and long-rooted varieties. Water the plants to refirm them after thinning. The thinnings from larger varieties of carrots can be eaten. Hill up soil over roots that become exposed to keep the shoulders from turning green.

Carrot rust flies are attracted by the smell of crushed foliage. The females lay eggs around the plants and the resulting larvae eat the roots. Attacks can be minimized by thinning the carrots late in the evening, removing the thinnings and watering immediately afterward.

Harvesting

Start pulling the early sowings by hand as soon as they are big enough to eat. Young tender roots are the sweetest. Gently ease up carrots for storage, with a fork, in October. Reject any that are unhealthy or damaged.

Remove the soil and foliage from carrots before storing them.

Storing Healthy carrots will last until March or April of the following year if they are stored properly in the right conditions. In many regions, they can be left in the ground and lifted as required. Protect them from severe frost with a covering of straw or similar material, but even if they are frozen into the ground they are still good to eat.

Pests and diseases

A brown discoloration of the foliage is often a symptom of carrot rust fly attack. By the time the symptom appears the infestation has already damaged the crop, so prevention is better than cure. Apply diazinon granules at sowing time. Spray greenfly with derris or malathion.

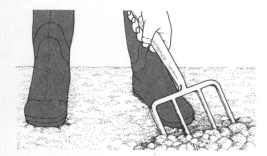

1 Winter. Dig the soil early so that a crumbly tilth develops. In spring apply fertilizer at 2–3 oz per square yard.

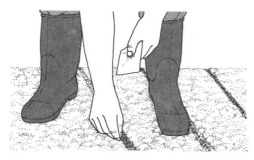

2 March onward. Prepare a fine tilth. Sow the seed in $\frac{1}{2}$–$\frac{3}{4}$ in deep drills 6 in apart. Cover the drills.

3 Thin the seedlings regularly after the first rough leaf appears to 2 in for short-, medium- and long-rooted varieties.

4 Water and firm the rows after thinning. Do not leave thinnings lying about. Hoe between the rows.

5 Throughout the summer. Pull early sowings by hand while they are young and tender.

6 October. Leave carrots in the ground where they have been grown but protect them from frost with a covering of straw.

7 Alternatively, dig up carrots required for indoor storing with a fork. Select healthy roots only and twist off the foliage.

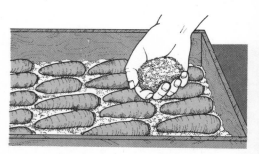

8 Pack the roots in boxes of dry sand, keeping individual roots apart, and store them in a cool frost-free place.

SHORT
'Avonresister' (canker resistant).

INTERMEDIATE
'White Gem'.

LONG
'Improved Hollow Crown',
'Leda', 'Offenham', 'Tender and
True' (canker resistant).

Parsnips

Parsnips are hardy biennial plants grown as annuals for the production of their edible roots. They have a long growing season.

Cultivation

Parsnips need a well-drained soil of medium texture which must not have been manured for at least a year before sowing. Parsnips have a low nitrogen requirement, take care not to overmanure and do not use nitrogen-rich fertilizers. As with other root crops, parsnips are likely to develop with forked roots—caused either by soil that is freshly manured or the application of too much nitrogenous fertilizer. Also, a soil that is too rich in nitrogen or is deficient in lime encourages canker. The best soil is slightly acid or neutral (pH 6.5–7.0) and the best position is open and sunny, although parsnips will tolerate a lightly shaded spot. Avoid stony soil. Deep digging in the winter is essential because parsnips often root down to a depth of 2 ft. Dig the soil one spade deep and if the layer below is too packed for the feeding roots to penetrate easily, loosen it with a fork. Such deep digging is not really necessary for short varieties, however. One to two weeks before sowing apply a balanced fertilizer, such as 10-10-10, to the soil at 2 oz per square yard.

Sowing Parsnips are best when the roots are frozen—sow the seed in summer $2-3\frac{1}{2}$ months before first fall frost. Always use fresh seed because older parsnip seed rapidly loses its viability. Even with fresh seed, the germination rate is low. Take out $\frac{1}{2}-\frac{3}{4}$ in deep drills. Keep a 12 in distance between rows for large-rooted varieties. If the soil is dry, water the drill before sowing. Sow the seeds in groups of three or four, with 6 in spacings between groups. Small-rooted varieties should be sown 3 in apart with 8 in between rows. Parsnip seeds germinate slowly, so it is advisable to mark the rows before seedlings appear by sowing quick-germinating radishes between the stations.

In warm climates, parsnip seed is sown in winter about six weeks before last spring frost, and they are harvested in the spring. But they do not have such fine flavor as those that are frozen.

When the seedlings have their first true leaves carefully remove all but the strongest plant in each group. Weed between the seedlings by hand in the early stages. Carefully hoe between the plants later. If the shoulders of young plants are damaged, parsnip canker or other diseases are likely to infest the plants.

Never allow the soil to dry out. If the soil becomes dry and is then dampened by rain or watering, the parsnips often split. Water at a rate of 2 gal per square yard per week unless the weather makes it unnecessary.

Harvesting

Lifting may begin when the foliage begins to die down, usually in late fall or early winter. Use a fork to dig along the side of the row so as to lift without breaking the roots.

Storing Leave parsnips in the ground throughout the winter and lift the roots as required. If parsnips are dug up in the fall, store them in soil in a cold garage or outdoor pit.

Pests and diseases

Young seedlings should be protected from carrot rust fly. Sprinkle diazinon along the row when the seedlings are about 2–3 in tall.

Parsnip canker develops in the crown of the plants and causes the roots to rot. There is no chemical control—prevention is the only answer. Premature sowing, lime deficient soils and damage to roots by carrot rust fly larvae or careless hoeing are all likely to encourage the disease.

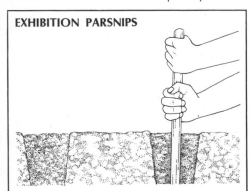

EXHIBITION PARSNIPS

For long straight roots prepare the soil well and use a crowbar to make holes 3 ft deep and 6 in in diameter. Fill these conical holes with fine soil or potting compost and sow the seed in the usual way as early as possible. Throughout the growing season weed by hand and mulch with peat or black polyethylene to retain moisture.

Water regularly, especially when dry weather is forecast, to prevent any cracking of the long roots. Lift them as near as possible to the showing date. Remove the rootlets and cut off the tops. Protect exhibition parsnips from damage by wrapping them in damp cloth.

1 June to July. Dig the soil 1 spit deep. If the layer below is compacted break it up with a fork.

2 Apply fertilizer at 2 oz per square yard 1–2 weeks before sowing. Apply diazinon against carrot rust fly.

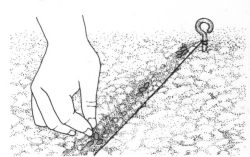

3 Sow 3–4 seeds at 6 in intervals (3 in for small varieties) in $\frac{1}{2}-\frac{3}{4}$ in deep drills 12 in (8 in) apart.

4 When the first true leaves appear thin the seedlings to leave the strongest plant at each station.

5 Throughout the summer. Water frequently and hoe weeds regularly, taking care not to damage the shoulders of young plants.

6 Late fall onward. When the foliage dies down lift parsnips as needed, using a fork to loosen the surrounding soil.

Turnips and Rutabagas 1

TURNIPS
SUMMER
'Jersey Navet', 'Snowball', 'Tokyo Cross'.

WINTER
'Golden Ball' (very hardy), 'Manchester Market'.

RUTABAGAS
'Bronze Top', 'Chignecto' (club-root resistant), 'Purple Top'.

Turnips and rutabagas are biennials grown mainly for their edible roots. Rutabagas are usually grown as a crop for winter harvesting, but turnips may be eaten all summer. Cut young leaves or "turnip greens" in May.

Cultivation

Turnips and rutabagas are brassicas and have broadly similar requirements to cabbages and Brussels sprouts.

Soil and situation They thrive in light, well-drained, firm soils of pH 6.0–7.0, rich in humus and water-retentive during the growing season. Main crop turnips and rutabagas require much the same methods of cultivation, although sowing dates and plant spacings differ. Soil preparation is identical and both crops are thinned in the seed rows to the appropriate distance and not transplanted.

The roots fork if they are grown in soil that has received dressings of fresh manure and so a site well manured for a previous crop should be used if possible. The site is dug over and prepared as a seedbed. Before sowing rake in a dressing of balanced fertilizer at 3 oz per square yard to improve fertility. Then apply calomel dust to combat club-root, and diazinon to control cabbage maggot.

Watering The size and quality of both turnips and rutabagas are improved if ample water is available. If they are allowed to become dry at any stage the roots are likely to become woody and less palatable. Experimental work has shown that applications of 2 gal per square yard of water each week in dry weather increase both yield and quality, although flavor is slightly reduced.

Pests and diseases

Turnips and rutabagas like other brassicas, are attacked by cabbage maggot, and flea beetle, turnip gall weevil and aphids (with virus as a consequence) may also be troublesome. Rutabagas are less mildew-resistant than turnips.

Turnips

Turnips are fast-growing and are ready to eat 6–12 weeks after sowing. They germinate within a few days and must never become crowded in the rows. Thinning should take place as soon as possible when the first rough, true leaves appear (at about 1 in high) or the roots will not develop satisfactorily.

In the North, the main crop is sown in July or August for fall use but earlier sowings can be made from March (under cloches) through spring and early summer. Turnips can be used in 6 or 8 weeks from sowing, so when they are 1½–2 in in diameter, they are excellent for intercropping. In the middle South, turnips are main-cropped in early spring and fall, and in the deep South, they are also planted in winter.

Rutabagas

Rutabagas, or swedes, have a sweeter taste than turnips and they are mainly grown for winter use, although immature rutabagas pulled in late summer make excellent eating. They should never be allowed to develop to the huge size of field-grown crops, which are often woody and more fitted for cattle than human consumption. They are much slower to mature than turnips, taking 90–110 days to develop fully from seed, but are hardier and can be dug as required during the winter rather than stored. Cultivation is as for main crop turnips but rutabagas are sown in late June or early July in drills 15 in apart. When the seedlings are large enough to handle, thin to 9 in apart in the rows.

PESTS AND DISEASES	
Pests	**Means of control**
Aphids (and viruses)	Systemic insecticide
Cabbage maggot	Bromophos/diazinon
Flea beetle	Derris
Gall weevil	Bromophos/diazinon
Diseases	**Means of control**
Brown heart	Boron (applied as borax)
Club-root	PCNB
Soft rot	Remove affected plants

EARLY BUNCHING TURNIPS

Bunched turnips are a good salad or early summer cooked vegetable. They must grow quickly with ample supplies of water. Dig the soil early in the autumn and cover the ground with cloches for 2–3 weeks before sowing the earliest crops which are protected. Prepare a fine seedbed and apply PCNB dust against club-root and bromophos or diazinon against cabbage maggot. Then sow short-leaved, early varieties from February onward, at two week intervals for a succession. Mark out the ground into a 5 in crossed pattern with a stick, making the marks ½ in deep. Sow 2–3 seeds where the marks cross. Alternatively, sow the seed thinly in ½ in drills 12 in apart. Thin out the squared system to leave one plant per station. Row crops should be thinned to 4 in apart. Hoe very carefully in the early stages and never allow the soil to dry out.

Harvesting The roots are pulled like radishes. The first sowings mature during May when the roots are 2 in in diameter.

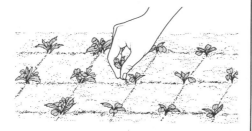

1 March. Thin grid-sown turnips to one plant per station. Thin row crops to 4 in apart at the same stage.

2 May. Pull the plants up by the leaves when the roots are 2 in in diameter.

Main crop turnips

1 July to August. Rake in 3 oz per square yard of fertilizer to the prepared seedbed and apply PCNB dust and diazinon.

2 July to August. Water the seedbed the day before sowing. Draw out drills ½–¾ in deep and 12 in apart. If the soil is dry, dribble water into the drills and allow it to drain away.

Turnips and Rutabagas 2

3 Then, sow the seed very thinly, cover, firm and gently rake over the soil.

4 Thin the seedlings to 3 in apart as soon as they produce their first rough leaves when about 1 in high. Water them if the weather is dry.

5 Dust the seedlings with derris to combat flea beetle and other pests.

6 August to September. Thin to 6 in apart as soon as the leaves of adjacent seedlings touch within the rows. Firm back the soil after thinning.

7 Keep the rows free of weeds. In dry weather water at a rate of 2 gal per square yard each week.

8 October. Lift as needed in mild areas. In cold areas lift the roots carefully in late fall when the leaves have turned yellow. Store them in boxes of sand, peat or dry soil in a frost-free shed.

RUTABAGAS SHOOTS AS GREENS

The roots of rutabagas lifted in mid-winter, if trimmed and packed closely in boxes of peat or soil and then placed in a garage or shed in semi-darkness, will sprout to produce nutritious, partly blanched growth that can be eaten like turnip tops.

TURNIP TOPS AS SPRING GREENS

In September sow the seed of winter varieties thinly in rows 3 in apart. Leave over winter without thinning. Cut the young leaves in March or April when they are 4–6 in high. If cut frequently they re-sprout several times.

Beets

GLOBULAR
'Boltardy' (bolt resistant),
'Crimson Globe', 'Detroit'.

LONG
'Cheltenham Green Top',
'Dobies Purple'.

Beets are biennial plants which are grown as annuals for their edible swollen roots. They usually have red flesh and the root shape may be round or long and tapering. Beets are good for intercropping as a useful catch crop; small beets mature in about 60 days.

Cultivation

Beets are in season from May or early June through to the fall.

Soil and situation Do not grow beets on freshly manured ground. Early crops can be grown only on well-drained, fertile soils, prepared in early spring, but fall-maturing crops will tolerate heavier conditions. Beets grow best in soil with a pH of 6.5–7.5. A balanced fertilizer applied at 2–3 oz per square yard is sufficient to maintain growth. An open, shade-free site is preferable.

Sowing Beet "seeds" are actually fruits with two or three seeds contained within a cork-like pellet. They do not germinate well below 7°C/45°F, therefore warm spring weather is needed for early crops. To improve germination, soak the seeds for an hour or place them under running water before sowing.

Early crop In March, space-sow two or three seeds of round, bolt-resistant varieties at 4 in intervals under cloches or frames in rows 7 in apart. For outdoor sowing, the seeds are sown at the same spacing but from late March to early April. The plants are thinned to one per station. Station sowing can avoid thinning while the plants are under glass.

Main crop In May and June, space-sow two or three seeds of round or long varieties outdoors at 4–6 in intervals (depending on the type of beet) in rows 12 in apart. Make successional sowings to within two months of the first fall frost to provide a supply of salad-sized beets in late fall.

Watering In hot dry weather, water the plants at the rate of 2 gal per square yard each week, to maintain succulent, juicy growth. Give no more than this, however, because an excess of water may result in too much leaf at the expense of root.

Hoe around the developing roots with a short-handled hoe. Damaged roots bleed readily and are susceptible to disease so great care is needed.

Harvesting

Round varieties can be pulled as soon as they are large enough. Early sowings are ready from May to July. The main crops mature from July onward. Late crops can be lifted for use or stored for winter use.

Lift the young roots and twist off the leaves. Store sound, disease-free roots in boxes of peat, sand or sawdust in a frost-free building. Distinct white concentric rings in the flesh when the roots are cut is a sign of old age; these beets will not keep well.

Very late-sown beets are ready from October and in favorable locations this crop can be left in the ground during winter, if protected against frost with a covering of straw or similar material.

Main crop beets

1 Early May. Apply a balanced fertilizer at 2–3 oz per square yard to the prepared seedbed.

2 May or June. Soak the seeds of round or long varieties in water for an hour before sowing to improve germination.

3 Space-sow 2–3 seeds at 4–6 in intervals (depending on variety) in 2 in deep rows, 12 in apart.

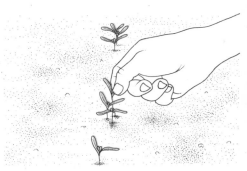

4 At the first true leaf stage thin to leave a single seedling at each station.

5 Hoe very carefully around the developing plants with a short-handled hoe and water at 2 gal per square yard in dry weather.

6 July or August. Gently lift beets with a fork when the roots are large enough to eat. Use immediately or store.

7 For storing, cut off the leaves to 3 in above each crown and remove dead or decaying leaves.

8 Arrange the beets in a box of sand. The roots should not touch. Keep the box in a cool frost-free place.

Radishes

SUMMER
'Cherry Belle', 'Wood's Early Frame',
'French Breakfast', 'Icicle',
'Red Forcing', 'Scarlet Globe'.

WINTER
'Black Spanish', 'Chinese Rose'.

Radishes are most commonly grown for use in salads but some varieties have much longer roots and these are cooked as a winter vegetable. Salad radishes have red, or red and white, skins and globular or cylindrical roots, whereas winter radishes have white, black or pink skins.

Cultivation
Both radish crops grow quickly and they are often grown as a catch crop.

Soil and situation All radishes require a fairly rich and well-drained, but not freshly manured, soil to grow well. The soil must retain enough moisture to ensure rapid uninterrupted growth but too much moisture, or fertilizer, results in excessive leaf growth. Apply 1oz per square yard of a balanced general fertilizer before each sowing.

An open situation is preferable for early and late sowings, but sowings from June to August should be made in a slight shade between other crops. Even then they may not succeed because radishes dislike hot weather.

Spring and summer radishes
The earliest salad radishes come from sowings made under cloches or frames in February and March. Successive outside sowings, without protection, can start in March and continue until August or September at two week intervals. Radishes are attacked by flea beetles and cabbage maggot. Apply diazinon to the drills before sowing as a deterrent.

Sow the seed thinly in $\frac{1}{2}-\frac{3}{4}$ in deep drills which are 4–6 in apart. Alternatively, broadcast the seed on to the prepared seedbed and rake it in lightly. When the seedlings emerge, thin, if necessary, until they are 1 in apart.

Keep the roots moist at all times. Dry, hot weather encourages hot-tasting radishes and during such periods apply water each week at the rate of 2 gal per square yard.

Winter radishes
Winter radishes are often 12 in long so a deep, friable soil is required. No fertilizer is needed when winter radishes are grown immediately after another crop, but on poor soils a general fertilizer should be raked in at a rate of 1oz per square yard before sowing. Sow winter radishes two months before first fall frost.

Take out $\frac{1}{2}-\frac{3}{4}$ in deep drills 12 in apart, and before sowing apply diazinon. Sow the seed very thinly and when the seedlings are big enough to handle thin until they are 6 in apart. Alternatively, the seed can be space-sown in groups of 3–4 at 6 in intervals and thinned to one per station.

The rapid growth of this crop means that it shades out weeds, except in the very early stages. Water in dry weather.

Harvesting
Pull spring and summer radishes when the roots are about $\frac{3}{4}$ in in diameter and they are firm and crunchy. Over-mature roots are hollow and unpalatable. The time taken to mature varies from 5 to 7 weeks at the end of the season to 3–4 weeks in midsummer.

Winter radishes are ready within about 60 days of sowing. Lift them before frost and store in boxes of dry sand for use as required. In mild areas leave them in the ground protected against frost.

EARLY SALAD RADISHES
The first sowing can be made in February. Put cloches over the ground for 3–4 weeks beforehand to dry it out. Rake the soil into a fine tilth.

Using short-topped varieties of radish broadcast the seed at $\frac{1}{4}$ oz per square yard or sow it thinly in $\frac{1}{2}-\frac{3}{4}$ in deep drills, 4–6 in apart. Water the seedbed thoroughly and keep the radishes moist throughout their life with regular applications of water.

Ventilate the crop on warm days because high temperatures under the cloche encourage leaf growth at the expense of roots.

Early salad radishes should be ready to be harvested in about eight weeks after sowing.

Spring and summer radishes

1 March. Prepare the seedbed, rake in 1oz of a balanced general fertilizer per square yard and water well.

2 March. Draw out $\frac{1}{2}-\frac{3}{4}$ in deep drills 4–6 in apart and apply diazinon. Sow the seed thinly. Cover and firm.

3 After 10–14 days. Thin the seedlings to 1 in as soon as they can be handled easily. If the weather is dry water them each week.

4 Pull the radishes as required when the roots are $\frac{3}{4}$ in in dia.

Winter radishes

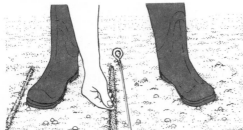

1 August or September. Space-sow the seed in groups of 3–4 at 6 in intervals in $\frac{3}{4}$ in deep drills, 12 in apart.

2 After 7–10 days. Thin the seedlings to 1 plant per station as soon as they can be handled easily. Water after thinning.

3 October. Lift the roots carefully. Twist off the leaves and store them in dry sand in a frost-free place.

Potatoes 1

FIRST EARLIES
'Arran Pilot', 'Epicure',
'Ulster Chieftain'.

SECOND EARLIES
'Craig's Royal', 'Maris Peer',
'Pentland Dell'.

MAIN CROP
'Desiree', 'King Edward',
'Majestic'.

The potato is the most widely grown vegetable in temperate zones. It is a South American perennial but it is only half-hardy in the U.S. Late frost in the spring kills the emerged leaves of a potato crop, and the first fall frosts kill the remaining foliage.

The potato is grown for its edible tubers and it is propagated from specially grown tubers ("seed") saved from the previous season. It is possible to save tubers from home-grown crops, but this is not advisable because potato plants and tubers soon become infected by debilitating virus diseases and if infected, crop yield and quality suffer. Virus-free "seed" is produced in areas where aphids that spread viruses are less of a problem. Always use certified seed.

Always use small "seed" tubers because large seed potatoes produce too many sprouts. For the maximum yield and to prevent crowded tubers being forced to the surface and "greening," small seed tubers with only two or three sprouts are ideal.

Like some other vegetables, potatoes are classified according to the time at which they mature. Earlies are ready to eat in late spring or early summer. Late varieties—the main crops—mature in the fall for winter storage. Mid-season varieties mature in October.

Cultivation

Soil and situation Potatoes tolerate a wide range of soils but they grow best in deep, fertile, well-drained soils with sufficient bulky organic manure to retain moisture in dry weather. Do not apply lime before planting potatoes because they grow best at a pH of 5.0–6.0 and alkaline conditions favor potato scab disease. Dig in 15–20 lb per square yard of well-rotted manure in the fall.

In spring, fork over the ground and rake in a general fertilizer, such as 10-10-10, at the rate of 4 oz per square yard and apply diazinon to combat wireworm and cutworm. A deep tilth is needed for hilling up. Plant in an open site but not in a frost pocket.

Planting Seed potatoes should be about 1 oz in weight, the size of a small hen's egg. Larger tubers are cut into 1½–2 oz blocks, each containing an eye. These should be planted immediately into moist soil but should be allowed to dry in a humid location if the soil is dry. Plant the tubers with the "eyes" upward in 6 in deep drills, with 12 in between early potato tubers and 16 in between mid-season and late varieties. Cover the planted drills immediately after planting. Mound up the soil 4–6 in high over each row.

Early potatoes Plant in early spring when the soil is reasonably dry and easily worked, but late enough for the plants to escape injury from frost after they appear. Plant in rows 24 in apart with 12 in between the tubers.

Mid-season and main crop Plant three to four weeks later in rows 27–30 in apart with 16 in between the tubers.

Potatoes are usually grown in ridges which are formed gradually during the season by hilling up (ridging) every two to three weeks. Cultivate and hoe between the initial mounds to provide sufficient loose soil for hilling. Use a draw hoe to pull up soil into ridges around growing plants. Cultivating and hoeing kills developing weeds.

Watering Earlies should be watered at the rate of 3–4 gal per square yard every 10–14 days to increase yield from an early stage of growth. If they are watered at the "marble" stage (when the small developing tubers are the size of a marble, approximately ½ in diameter) and not before, at the rate of 3–4 gal per square yard, they mature earlier.

Main crops should be given 4 gal per square yard at flowering time, which markedly increases yield and depresses scab.

Harvesting

Early potatoes should be ready about three months after planting, in June and July. The potatoes should be ready when the flowers are fully open. Lift as needed.

Mid-season and main crop potatoes should be lifted from August onward when the tops have died down.

Use a flat-tined fork to avoid too much damage to the tubers when lifting potatoes. Leave the tubers on the soil surface for two to three hours to dry. In wet conditions dry the tubers in a garage, a cold frame or under cloches. Make sure that all the potatoes are lifted so that no disease is carried over to the next year by overlooked tubers.

Storing Store only sound, healthy tubers.

1 Spring. Fork over the ground and rake in general balanced fertilizer at 4 oz per square yard, and apply diazinon against wireworm and cutworm.

2 March to April. Take out 6 in deep drills, 24 in apart for earlies, 27–30 in apart for later crops (according to the variety being grown).

3 At the same time, place the seed tubers in the drills at 12 in intervals for earlies, 16 in for mid-season and main crops, with the buds or "eyes" upward.

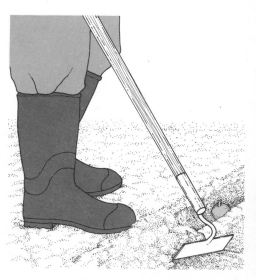

4 Use a draw hoe to cover the drills. Draw up soil from both sides to produce 4–6 in high mounds over the planted rows.

Potatoes 2

Any damaged potatoes should be used or discarded immediately. Store in a frost-free building. Boxes with raised corner posts are ideal. Keep them in the dark or cover with black polyethylene to prevent the tubers turning green. Large quantities of potatoes can be stored in pits. After lifting leave them to dry out for several hours, having removed the stems. Heap them up underneath straw to "sweat" for a couple of days before mounding up with earth.

Pests and diseases
Use virus-free seed to avoid potato virus diseases. To prevent attacks by wireworm and cutworm apply diazinon at planting. Scab is rarely a serious problem. Ample watering is a good deterrent. To control other pests, such as flea beetles and potato beetles, apply a general-purpose garden spray or dust.

Potato blight This is the worst fungal disease of the crop and it can be particularly bad in warm, humid conditions from July onward. The symptoms appear first on the leaves as yellow blotches on the upper surface. A white fungal growth may be seen underneath the leaves. The blotches turn brown and whole leaves are killed in severe attacks. Fungal spores are washed into the soil, where they can also infect the developing tubers. Regular spraying or dusting with a general-purpose garden spray (which contains fungicide such as zineb or maneb) is the only control.

5 During the summer, hoe regularly in the furrows between the ridges. Water during dry weather.

8 July. Lift early potatoes when the flowers are fully open, using a flat-tined fork to avoid excessive damage to tubers.

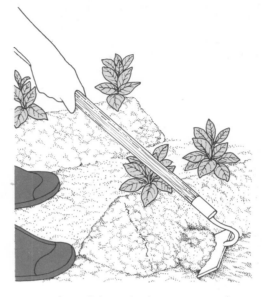

6 Hoe the soil from the furrows into ridges around the growing plants at 2–3 week intervals, until the ridges are 12–15 in high.

9 September onward. Lift mid-season and main crop potatoes when the tops have died down.

7 May onward. At 10 day intervals, in warm humid conditions, spray all the surfaces of the leaves with a general-purpose garden spray for control of insects and blight.

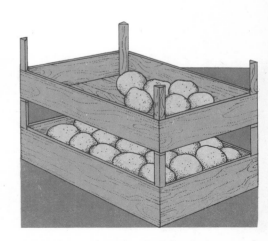

10 Store in a frost-free building in boxes with raised corner posts for easy inspection.

Potatoes 3

Place a single layer of tubers—"eyes" up-ward—in boxes or trays and keep them in a light, airy place. Begin the process in March so that sturdy shoots about ¾–1 in long will have formed prior to planting. Sprouted tubers grow quickly when planted and are particularly useful for early crops which have a relatively short growing period. It may be worth while sprouting mid-season or main crop varieties in areas where late planting is necessary because of the likelihood of frost.

Potatoes are normally grown outdoors as described on the previous pages. There are alternative systems, however, for growing out-of-season potatoes or for less intensive cultivation of this basic vegetable crop.

Out-of-season potatoes

Very early potatoes can be grown in a green-house to mature in March or April. Plant sprouted seed in a slightly heated greenhouse at a temperature of 7°–10°C/45°–50°F in Jan-uary and grow in the same way as outdoor crops. Never allow the temperature to get very high or too much foliage and few tubers will be produced. Keep the soil moist.

Growing in pots

Plant 2 or 3 sprouted tubers in large pots which are at least 12 in wide and deep, containing good garden soil.

An alternative is to grow the plants in pots. Plant 2–3 sprouted tubers in a large box or pot containing good garden soil. Keep the pots in a slightly heated greenhouse and grow as for the greenhouse crop.

Early outdoor plantings can be covered with glass cloches or polyethylene tunnels to speed development and give protection against frost. Cover the cloches with sacking when frosts are forecast.

Non-cultivation system

Potatoes can be grown without hilling up. Water the ground well before planting. In April, push sprouted tubers into the soil and

Growing under black polyethylene

1 April. Water the ground and push sprouted tubers into the soil at the same spacings as for outdoor potatoes.

cover and mound over the drills. Cover with a black polyethylene sheet to prevent greening and weed growth, to warm the soil and to conserve moisture. Make a slit above each tuber. Bury the edges of the polyethylene by pushing them into the soil with a spade.

Slugs and wireworms thrive in the con-ditions provided by polyethylene. Control them by scattering slug pellets around the mounds.

When the shoots emerge they begin to push up through the slits in the sheet toward the light. Roll back the sheet to expose the tubers for harvesting or take them out as required through the slits.

2 Cover and mound over the drills. Scatter slug pellets around the slightly mounded ridges.

3 Cover the ridges with a 36 in wide length of black polyethylene and bury the edges to leave a 24 in wide strip exposed.

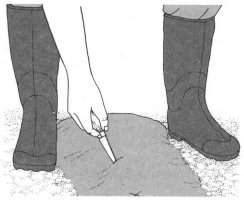

4 Make slits with a sharp knife above each tuber where the shoots have pushed against the polyethylene.

5 May. As the shoots emerge they push up through the slits in the polyethylene.

6 July. As the tubers develop, roll back the polyethylene sheeting to expose the potatoes for harvesting.

Cucumber

Cucumbers are sub-tropical plants grown for their green-skinned fruits, which are used raw in salads and made into pickles. In Great Britain, cucumbers are commonly grown in greenhouses and the varieties used produce long, cylindrical, rather slender fruits. In the US, cucumbers are almost always grown outdoors. These have shorter, thicker fruits for the most part.

American seedsmen offer two types of cucumber: slicing, or standard, varieties for use in salads and pickling varieties that are more productive and have shorter, blockier fruits. In practice, the varieties can be used interchangeably.

A recent cucumber development is the gynoecious hybrid, which produces an enormous profusion of predominantly female flowers (the female flowers are the small flowers; the large flowers are males). The result is an equally enormous profusion of fruit. In fact, there is more fruit than one family can consume, so unless it is planned to set up a small-scale pickle factory, these hybrids should either be avoided or restricted to a few plants.

Cultivation

Like most cucurbits, cucumbers grow fast and are prolific producers: therefore do not overplant. The soil should be well dug and enriched with humus and a balanced fertilizer, such as 10-10-10. If nematodes (microscopic soil insects that infest plant roots and cause a general malaise of the plants) are prevalent, the soil should be treated with a soil fumigant before cucumbers are planted; but an easier way to cope with these pests is to avoid planting cucumbers (or any other cucurbits) in the same place year after year. Growing marigolds in the vicinity of the vegetable garden also appears to discourage some nematodes.

Because of their unique flavor, cucumbers are often blamed for crossing with other cucurbits growing nearby in the same garden and altering their flavor. Actually, this happens only if seeds are saved from fruits and sown the following year. But if fresh seed from a recognized seedsman is sown every year, cucumbers can be planted alongside any other cucurbit without getting a mixture of flavors.

Planting For an extra-early crop, cucumber seeds can be sown in peat blocks indoors about four weeks before they are moved into the garden. At the time of transplanting, the seedlings should have only true leaves: larger seedlings do not transplant well. If the weather is still cold and frost threatens, cover the seedlings with cloches.

Normal practice, however, is to sow seeds directly in the garden where the plants are to grow after all danger of frost is past and the soil is warm. One or two later sowings can be made up to within about 75 days of the first fall freeze; but this is hardly necessary if the plants of the initial sowing are kept growing and producing well.

Cucumber seeds are sown $\frac{1}{2}$ in deep. They can be sown in drills 5 ft apart (if you let the plants run on the ground) or only 2 ft apart (if you train the plants up a sturdy fence of wire mesh). The alternative is to sow seeds in hills about 8 ft apart in both directions. Thin to three or four plants per hill or to 12–18 in apart in drills.

Feeding and watering About four weeks after cucumbers are thinned, side-dress them lightly with balanced fertilizer or nitrate of soda. Keep plants well watered and pull out weeds faithfully. Mulching with grass clippings, hay or black polyethylene film keeps down weeds and greatly reduces the need for watering.

Pests and diseases

Control insects, such as the spotted cucumber beetle, aphids and mites, by spraying or dusting frequently with carbaryl or rotenone after the plants are thinned. The best way to prevent attacks of mildew or mosaic is to plant cucumber varieties resistant to these diseases (if they are troublesome in the area). Diseased plants are stunted and bear puckered, yellow-mottled leaves. Destroy affected plants. Spray nonresistant varieties with a mildewcide.

Harvesting

Cucumbers can be picked when very small but have more flavor when they reach maturity. Old fruits are of poor quality and also inhibit growth and yield when left on the plant. Harvest fruits daily.

1 For early crops, sow seed indoors in peat pots about four weeks before they are to be planted out.

2 Sow outdoors in drills $\frac{1}{2}$ in deep. Space the rows 2 ft apart for supported plants, 5 ft for trailing plants.

3 Thin the seedlings to 12–18 in apart when they have produced their first true leaves.

4 Four weeks after thinning, side-dress the cucumber plants lightly with balanced fertilizer.

5 Mulch the growing plants with black polyethylene, hay or grass clippings to keep down weeds.

6 Spray against insect pests with carbaryl or rotenone after the plants are thinned.

Tomatoes 1

Tomatoes are probably the most widely grown vegetable in the United States. They can be raised in all ten climate zones, although they are not reliable in zones 1 and 2. Picked when fully ripe, they are far more delicious than tomatoes found in the supermarket. Most of the varieties grown produce large, red fruits but a few have large, yellow fruits. There are also varieties that produce tiny red or yellow fruits for cocktail use.

The varieties offered by the average seed company are technically known as indeterminate, which means that the stems continue to elongate and produce new clusters of fruit throughout the late summer and fall. Determinate varieties have terminal clusters of blossoms and fruits which prevent stem growth beyond that point. Because most of the fruits ripen at the same time, determinate tomatoes are of interest primarily to commercial growers; but they are useful to home gardeners who like to can large quantities of stewed tomatoes and juice. Large tomato crops can also be turned into tomato paste.

Raising tomato plants
Tomatoes are so easily raised from seeds that there is no reason to buy plants. Sow the seeds in flats in a prepared starting mixture six to eight weeks before the last spring frost. If possible, grow the seedlings under fluorescent light; otherwise, keep them in a warm, sunny window. The seeds germinate quickly and make rapid growth. As soon as the seedlings have two true leaves, carefully move them into individual peat pots (the ideal arrangement) or into small flats about 1–1½ in apart. Keep the soil damp but not wet. Apply a balanced nutrient solution occasionally as the time for planting out approaches.

In hot climates, two sowings can be made: one in early to mid-winter for a spring crop and another in July or August for a late crop. Seed for the late crop is best started in a seedbed and moved into the garden as a succession crop.
Planting out Tomatoes are tender and should not be planted outdoors until all danger of frost has passed. If wished, however, the season can be extended a little by planting them out a week or two earlier than this and keeping them under cloches at night. In either case, before moving them into the garden, harden them off gradually by moving the flats outdoors into a sunny spot for a longer and longer time every day for about a week. They can also be hardened off in a cold frame.
Soil and planting The garden soil must be well dug and, if possible, manured before the plants are set out. Spacing for the plants depends on how they are to be trained. If you follow the common practice of tying each plant to a tall 1-inch thick stake, plant indeterminate varieties 2 ft apart in rows 24–30 in apart. If you use wire cages or tripod supports, increase spacing between plants and rows by 6–12 in. If you let the plants trail on the ground, space them 3 ft apart in rows 6 ft apart. Determinate varieties are not staked because they form more compact plants. Space them 30 in apart in rows 3 ft apart.

Tomatoes put out roots from their stems, so they can and should be planted much deeper than other vegetables. Dig the holes with a trowel about 6 in deep so the stems are covered to a depth of 2–3 in. Spindly plants should be set even deeper. Water well at planting time.
Staking Tomatoes that are allowed to sprawl on the ground require less attention during the growing season and produce more fruit than supported varieties; but they take up a lot of space. Most gardeners prefer to provide some sort of support. If you use single stakes or a tripod of stakes, start tying the plants when they reach about 15 in. Use soft twine or strips of cloth; tie it securely to the stake and loop it loosely around the plant stems under the fruit clusters. Continue tying as the plants grow. If, instead of stakes, tall, 1 ft diameter cylinders of heavy wire mesh are used, no tying is necessary.

When tomatoes are tied to single stakes, they should be pruned to prevent them from becoming so top-heavy that they fall over in

Raising tomato plants

1 Sow the seed thinly in trays 8 weeks before planting. Cover with ⅛ in of sieved compost and water before covering with glass and newspaper. Keep at 18°C/65°F.

2 Ten to twelve days after sowing, gently remove the seedlings by inserting a small dibber beneath the roots. Plant them in 3 in peat pots of potting mix.

3 Water to firm, then water little and often. Reduce the temperature to 16°C/60°F when the plants begin to shade each other. Liquid feed before planting.

4 Plant tomatoes when they are 6–9 in tall with the flowers on the first truss just opening. Water well before and after planting.

Tomatoes 2

wind or heavy rain. Some people remove all but one main stem to facilitate handling and produce fruit of maximum size; but just as big tomatoes and more of them will be produced if two stems are kept and all suckers nipped out.

This is the only way in which tomatoes—no matter how they're trained—should be pruned. Do not thin the foliage, even though it may seem excessive, because it protects the fruits from sunburning and puts more strength into the plants.

Feeding and watering About six weeks after plants are set out, give each one a small handful of balanced fertilizer, such as 10–10–10, and repeat this treatment about a month later. Keep the plants well watered until shortly before harvest starts; then reduce the supply somewhat, otherwise the fruits may crack. Remove weeds as they appear but do not hoe deeply because the roots are shallow. Maintaining a mulch of grass clippings or other organic matter at all times helps to control weeds, prevent evaporation of the moisture and nourish the soil.

Tomatoes often drop their early blossoms if the temperature falls below 55°F. In areas that frequently experiences such low temperatures, spray the first blossom clusters when most of the flowers have opened fully (and not before) with a fruit-setting hormone such as Blossom Set. Direct the spray at the backs of the flowers and keep it off the rest of the plant as much as possible. Just dampen the flowers: don't apply enough spray to drip.

Pests and diseases

Tomatoes have several problems but the two commonest are weather-related and there is little that can be done about them. Blossom-end rot, characterized by big black, sunken spots in the base of the fruits, generally occurs when cool, wet weather during fruit development is followed by a period of hot, dry weather. Besides more careful watering during the hot, dry spell, the only thing that may prevent the rot is to spray with a dilute solution of calcium chloride.

Cracking of fruits around the stems occurs when the plants, because of warm, damp weather or an application of fertilizer, put on a sudden spurt of growth after a period of dry or cool weather. Again, the best preventive action is to keep the plants watered and fed so they grow at a more uniform pace. It also helps to select varieties that are resistant to cracking.

Probably the worst insect pest is the tomato hornworm, a large green caterpillar with a horn at the tail end. Because it is the exact color of the plants, it is not easily seen, except when the plants are defoliated. The worms have voracious appetites and can chew off the leaves of a single plant in a few days if they are not spotted and removed.

For other insects and diseases that may appear, spray or dust plants every 10 days with a general-purpose chemical.

Harvesting

If possible, allow tomatoes to ripen to a uniform bright red before picking. In very hot weather, however, the coloring process is slower and the fruits are likely to be soft when you judge them to be fully ripe. They should, therefore, be picked in the pink stage and complete ripening indoors at 16°–21°C/60°–70°F.

In the fall, just before the first frost, pick all the paler green fruits, which are beginning to soften, and store them in a frost-free place under cover until they turn red. They can be wrapped in newspaper or not, as you wish. Note that hard, dark-green fruits rarely ripen when handled in this way. Fruits that are touched by frost are unusable.

Dwarf tomatoes

Dwarf varieties of tomato can be grown outdoors in the usual way or in large pots outdoors and indoors. In the latter case, watering is required almost every day to keep the soil moist. Indoors, the plants can be brought to harvest stage on a warm windowsill, under fluorescent light or in a greenhouse. Thus tomatoes can be grown all year.

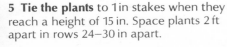

5 Tie the plants to 1 in stakes when they reach a height of 15 in. Space plants 2 ft apart in rows 24–30 in apart.

6 About six weeks after planting, rake in a small handful of balanced fertilizer around each plant. Repeat a month later, watering well each time.

7 Pinch out side-shoots as they develop, except on bush varieties. Do not thin the foliage.

8 In cool areas, spray the first fruit clusters with a fruit-setting hormone spray. Direct the spray at the back of the flowers. Barely dampen the flowers.

Squashes 1

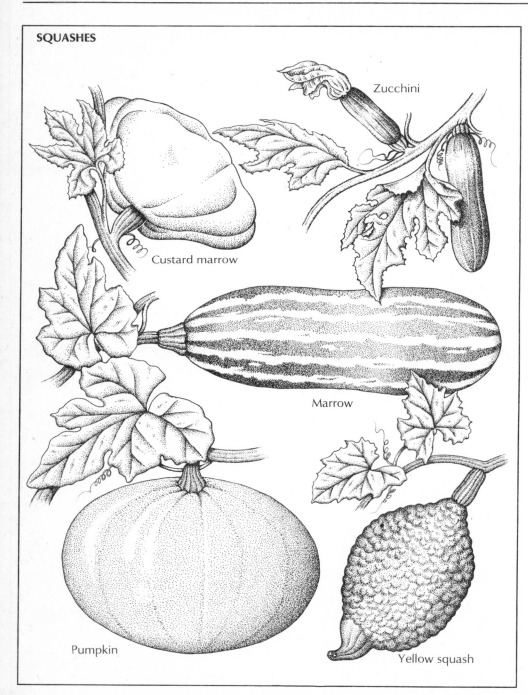

SQUASHES

Zucchini

Custard marrow

Marrow

Pumpkin

Yellow squash

Summer squash are extremely fast-growing, large, bushy plants that produce fruit in profusion, so do not overplant. Six to eight plants will usually give as much fruit as the average family can eat. Of course, the over-supply can be frozen for winter use but it does not freeze very well. Picked when very young, however, summer squash is delicious.

There are numerous varieties falling into three broad classifications: yellow squashes, which are either straight or crooked-necked and have smooth or warty rinds; zucchinis, which form long cylindrical fruits that are dark green, green-and-yellow striped, or yellow; and the patty pans, shaped like a creamy-white, flat, scalloped-edged bowl.

Cultivation

Summer squashes are very satisfying to raise because they are easy, handsome and yield abundantly about 50 days after planting. But they may suddenly die if attacked by borers, cucumber beetles, squash bugs or disease. For this reason, instead of trying to stretch out the life of one crop, it is wise to plant a succession of small crops at monthly intervals until 60 days before the first autumn freeze.

Squashes do not require exceptionally good soil but do best if you dig in an ample supply of humus and a little balanced fertilizer, such as 10-10-10. Drainage should be good; the location warm and sunny.

Planting After all danger of frost has passed, sow seeds in drills ½ in deep and about 4–6 in apart. Thin the plants to stand 2–3 ft apart. Rows should be about 4 ft wide for the yellow squashes and zucchinis; 5–6 ft wide for patty pans. Water plants well in dry weather. The large leaves and heavy foliage tend to discourage weeds close around the plants; but when an occasional weed does appear, pull it out by hand. Cultivating without breaking the leaves is difficult.

Pests and diseases

Spraying about once a week during warm weather with methoxychlor or malathion discourages most insect pests and also helps to control bacterial wilt, which is spread by insects. Dust young plants and the surrounding soil with rotenone or carbaryl to discourage vine borers. Mildew is controllable by spraying with zineb in periods of cool, damp nights and warm, humid days. A general-purpose vegetable and fruit spray can be used instead of these separate chemicals if wished. Be sure to spray under the leaves, where the bugs hide.

Harvesting

Cut off fruits with a sharp knife while they are still small. The best zucchinis are 6–8 in long; yellow squashes, 8–10 in; and patty pans no more than 3 in across. Much larger fruits are edible as long as it is possible to penetrate the skin easily with a fingernail, but they have less flavor than the smaller ones.

Chayote or mirliton

Chayote or mirliton is also known by several other names. Botanically it is called *Sechium edule*. It is a large perennial vine producing fairly small, green or white, pear-shaped fruits that are boiled and eaten like summer squashes. Unlike squashes, to which they are related, the fruits have only a single seed.

In the warmest zones, the plants can be grown as perennials but they are more commonly treated as annuals. However, they require such a long growing season that they cannot be relied on to produce fruit north of the warmest parts of zone 7.

Cultivation

Two or more plants must be grown to assure production of fruit. The soil should be fertile and rich in humus. Apply a balanced fertilizer, such as 10-10-10, before planting and make one or more side-dressings during development. Keep the plants well watered at all times.

From zone 8 southward, plant entire fruits directly in the garden after all danger of frost has passed. Let the stem end protrude slightly above the soil. The alternative—required in zone 7—is to plant the fruits in large pots indoors and move them outside after the last frost.

Space the plants 10 ft apart. If they are allowed to sprawl on the ground, they will also need at least 10 ft on each side. To conserve space, therefore, it is better to let them grow up a sturdy wire-mesh trellis fixed between posts.

Squashes 2

1 In spring dig in ample supplies of humus and a balanced fertilizer such as 10-10-10.

2 Sow the seeds after the last frost in drills ½ in deep and 4–6 in apart in the row. Space the rows 4–6 ft apart.

3 Thin the plants to 2–3 ft apart when they have 3–4 true leaves.

4 Water the plants well in dry weather and remove any weeds that appear.

5 Spray once a week with an insecticide to combat insect pests and bacterial wilt.

Harvesting

6 Cut off fruits with a sharp knife when they are still small and tender.

Chayote

From Zone 8 southward. Plant entire fruits direct in the garden after the last frost. Let the stalks protrude.

Zone 7. Plant indoors in large pots and move the young plants outside after the last frost.

Squashes 3

Winter squash

Winter squashes take three months or more to mature so only one planting per year is possible in most parts of the country. Most varieties trail across the ground and require a great deal of space. This can be reduced somewhat, however, if you plant squashes close to corn and let them run in among the stalks. The spacing can also be reduced to a 2 ft row if the plants are trained up a sturdy fence; however, the fruits are sometimes so large and heavy that they may tear loose or drag the fence down. To solve this space problem, seedsmen are now offering more dwarf, bushy varieties; but these have smaller and fewer fruits.

The most popular winter squashes are the dark-green, fairly small acorns; the orange-brown, dumbell-shaped butternuts; and the giant dark-green or blue-gray Hubbards. An increasingly popular newer variety is the spaghetti squash, which turns yellow when ripe and may grow to great size but is picked when 10 in long. This variety has spaghetti-like strands of flesh that are boiled and served with spaghetti sauce.

Cultivation

Like summer squash, winter squash does best when the soil is enriched with humus or manure and a balanced fertilizer before planting. Apply additional balanced fertilizer when the plants are about two months old. Keep the plants well watered and pull weeds faithfully. Mulching with grass clippings, hay or black polyethylene film when the plants are young solves both the watering and weeding problems.

Planting For an early crop seeds can be sown in individual peat blocks indoors about a month before they are to be planted out. Or the seeds can be sown in the garden about two weeks later and the seedlings protected from late frosts with cloches. However, because winter squashes are usually harvested late and stored for winter use, the normal practice is to sow the seeds directly in the garden after all danger of frost has passed and the soil is warm.

Sow about $\frac{1}{2}$ in deep in drills or hills (groups). Standard varieties should be thinned to 24–30 in apart in rows 7–8 ft wide. Bushier varieties are spaced 2 ft apart in rows 4–5 ft wide. By manually placing the developing stems where they are wanted, they can be prevented from smothering small plants nearby or invading lawn areas (where they do no harm but inhibit mowing).

Pests and diseases

Treat winter squash in the same way as summer squash.

Harvesting

Let winter squashes ripen fully before they are cut from the vines, but do not expose them to hard frost. If they are not ready to be picked when an early frost threatens, cover them with newspapers, plastic or anything light enough not to mash the plants. The fruits are ripe when the color is right and when the stems are pressed with a thumbnail. If the nail cannot penetrate the rind, the proper ripeness has been attained. Ripe fruits can be left in the garden for a long time (provided that they are not subjected to frost).

Pick squashes with about 1 in of stem and do not damage the rind. They can be stored for several months—perhaps until spring—in a dark, airy, slightly humid place at a temperature of 50°F/10°C. Somewhat higher temperatures will do no great harm but lower temperatures will ruin the fruits.

Pumpkin

This enormous winter vegetable, a cucurbit closely related to squashes, melons and cucumbers, is a favorite of children and gardeners who enjoy competing in pumpkin contests. But it takes so much space and has such limited culinary value that the average home gardener avoids it.

Cultivation

Pumpkins are raised like winter squashes, but require a little less sun and are therefore frequently planted—about 7 ft apart in all directions or in the middle of corn patches. They require a deep, fertile soil enriched with balanced fertilizer at planting time and again about two months later; lots of moisture; and good weed control. Mulching the soil is advisable. In addition to holding in moisture and keeping down weeds, an organic mulch helps to enrich the soil as it decomposes. Black polyethylene film has no nutritive value, but by keeping the pumpkins off the ground, it helps to prevent rot in damp weather.

If pumpkins are being grown for competition or exhibition, the need for moisture and plant food is especially important. Many competitors fertilize their plants weekly throughout the 3–4 month growing season. Use of a liquid fertilizer is recommended because a granular food is difficult to work into the soil between the many trailing stems. Water is sometimes supplied continuously by threading a cotton string through the stem of a fruit and immersing the other end in a bucket of water; but this is frowned upon by serious competitors.

Planting Sow seeds where the plants are to grow after all danger of frost has passed. Thin the plants to stand 24–30 in apart in rows 7–9 ft wide.

Pests and diseases

The same problems that beset squashes affect pumpkins and are controlled in a similar manner. To prevent ripening pumpkins from turning white or rotting where they touch the ground, slip sheets of plastic film or boards underneath. Clean straw can also be used to protect the plants.

Harvesting

Pumpkins can withstand a light frost but must be harvested before the first killing frost. Cut the stems about an inch above the fruits; take care not to bruise the rind; and store the fruits in a dark, dry, airy place at about 50°F/10°C.

For an early crop of winter squash sow seeds in individual peat blocks indoors about a month before the young plants are due to be planted out.

Thin pumpkin seedlings to 24–30 in apart and mulch the plants well to keep down weeds and to enrich the soil. Pumpkins require plenty of moisture. Black polyethylene film mulch keeps the fruits off the ground.

Sweet potatoes/Southern peas

SWEET POTATOES

Sweet potatoes, or yams, are very distantly related to ordinary potatoes, but, like them, have edible tubers. It is a perennial, but is grown as an annual in the USA.

Sweet potatoes

Sweet potatoes, or yams, are relatives of the morning glory. They are fairly small vines that sprawl on the ground. The below-ground tubers are long and pointed at the ends and have a sweet yellow or orange flesh. The flesh of the best varieties, grown mainly in the South, is moist and succulent; that of more northern varieties tends to be dry and mealy.

Sweet potatoes are most successful in zones 7–10 but can be grown in zone 6. The plants generally take more than four months to produce mature fruit.

Cultivation

Do not plant sweet potatoes in the same location more than once every three years. The soil should be a well drained, sandy or clay loam with a pH of 5.2–6.7. Sweet potatoes do poorly in very heavy or very light soils. Two weeks before planting, prepare the soil well and mix in 8 oz of a low-nitrogen fertilizer, such as 5-10-10, per 50 square feet. Then form the soil into ridges 8 in high and 24–30 in wide.

Buy seedling plants from a grower of certified seed potatoes. Plants can be raised from seed but it is rather demanding.

Plant the seedlings after all danger of frost has passed. Center them in the ridges and space them 1 ft apart. Water well. Plants require about 1 in of water every week. Cultivate regularly, taking care not to disturb the roots. Side-dress with a little low-nitrogen fertilizer about half way through the growing season.

Harvesting

Dig up the potatoes when the soil is dry and can be brushed off the tubers. If the soil is damp, don't attempt to brush or wash it off. Place the tubers in a shady place—never in the sun—until the soil is dry enough to brush off. The tubers must not be cut or bruised if they are to be kept for any length of time. Before digging up the tubers, cut off the tops to allow access to the roots. It is then easy to unearth them without damaging the tubers.

Harvesting should be done before frost strikes. If this is impossible, cut the frost-blackened tops from the plants immediately. If they are allowed to remain, the tubers will be spoiled. After the tops are off, the tubers can be dug anytime within the next few days.

Sweet potatoes can be cooked and eaten immediately after digging but they can be stored for only a short time. Ideally, they should be cured. This prolongs the storage period and also improves the sweetness of the flesh. However, it is difficult for the home gardener to cure tubers well because they should be held for seven to 10 days at high temperature and high humidity (best conditions call for a 29°C/85°F temperature and 90 percent humidity). After curing, the tubers are stored at a temperature of 13°–16°C/55°–60°F in a relatively humid storeroom.

Pests and diseases

Use of plants grown from certified tubers is the best way to protect against diseases.

Southern peas

Southern peas are also known as cowpeas, field peas and table peas. Closely related to beans, they produce long, slender pods crammed with seeds that are shelled and eaten fresh like peas. They are also canned, frozen and dried. The plants are about 2 ft tall and inclined to trail. Some varieties are more compact than others.

Southern peas are, as the name indicates, most widely grown in the South but they can be grown as far north as zone 6. On average, they require about 3 months to mature. Like beans, they require warm weather.

Cultivation

Since southern peas are leguminous plants widely grown simply as a green manure crop, they do not require rich soil. But it should be well drained and contain some humus. Mix in a low-nitrogen fertilizer, such as 5-10-10 before planting. This should carry them through the growing season.

Sow the seeds in the garden after all danger of frost has passed. Sow the seeds ½ in deep, 1–3 in apart in rows 2–3 ft wide. Do not thin the plants.

Water in dry spells. Except for keeping weeds hoed out, the plants require little attention. In fact, southern peas produce more food for less work than most other vegetables.

Harvesting

For eating fresh or for canning and freezing, the peas should be picked while the seeds are still green and have reached the desired size. For drying, leave the pods on the plants until they turn yellow or brown, then store in a cool dry place indoors.

Pests and diseases

The worst pest is the cowpea curculio. To control this, spray with toxaphene when blossoming starts and make twice-weekly applications for the next two weeks. Spray with carbaryl or malathion to control minor insects. If nematodes are present in the soil, fumigate the soil before seed sowing. Use of resistant or tolerant varieties of pea is the best way to avoid trouble from fusarium wilt and mosaic.

Watermelon

A favorite fruit on hot summer days, the watermelon is not a good vegetable for small gardens because it trails across the ground for 6–8 ft in all directions and the fruits are too large and heavy to permit growing on a trellis. If it is to be grown, put it in a sunny corner by itself.

Most favorite varieties—those producing dark green or striped white-and-green fruits up to almost 2 ft long—take too long to develop to be grown north of zone 6. But smaller varieties, such as New Hampshire Midget and Sugar Baby, require a shorter growing season and should succeed even in zone 3.

Cultivation

The soil for watermelons must be fertile and well drained. Mix in large quantities of humus and 10-10-10 fertilizer before planting. Generally, seeds are sown directly in the garden after all danger of frost has passed. For an earlier start and in colder climates, either sow seeds indoors about 4 weeks before they are planted out or sow them in the garden and keep them covered with cloches or polyethylene film. Sow the seeds or set seedlings in hills 8 ft apart and 8 ft from other vegetables. Thin to about two plants per hill.

Feeding and watering Keep the plants well watered and apply a side-dressing of balanced fertilizer or nitrate of soda when the plants start to run. Mulching the soil is advisable to keep out weeds, because these are hard to remove without damaging the vines. If a few large melons are prefered to a greater number of small ones, pick off the excess fruits when they are about 4 in across. Leave three to four fruits only per vine.

Watermelons are ripe enough to harvest when they give off a dull, muffled sound when rapped with the knuckles. When unripe, the sound is more like a metallic ring. Another sign of ripeness is the color of the rind touching the ground. If it is yellow, the fruit is ready; if white, it's not.

Pests and diseases

Watermelons are subject to the same problems that bother muskmelons and squashes, and are protected in the same way.

Peppers

Sweet peppers are in the same family as tomatoes and potatoes. They are grown for their large squarish fruits, which are usually harvested green although they can be left on the plant until they turn red.

Hot peppers (closely related to sweet peppers) produce much smaller fruits of varying shapes. All are green but turn red or yellow.

Cultivation

Peppers need similar growing conditions to tomatoes, although higher temperature and humidity is necessary. They grow in all but the very coldest areas.

Soil and situation Peppers must have well-drained, fertile soil. They need a sunny and sheltered site. They also require large amounts of moisture and the soil should be improved by the incorporation of well-rotted manure or garden compost during spring digging.

In greenhouses, peppers may be grown on the benches or in pots. Small, hot peppers can also be grown in the house on sunny windowsills or under fluorescent light.

Open ground crops should receive a base dressing of 1–2 oz per square yard of a balanced fertilizer at planting and should be fed again about six weeks later. Pot-grown plants require liquid feeding from an earlier stage and need very careful watering.

Plant raising High temperatures are needed to grow pepper plants satisfactorily and, even then, it takes 10–12 weeks from seed sowing until planting. A temperature of 21°C/70°F is needed for seed germination, reducing to 18°C/65°F for the remainder of the plant-raising period. Sow the seed thinly in a starting mixture in a seed tray and cover with a thin layer of the mixture. Water and cover with a sheet of glass and a piece of newspaper. Turn the glass daily to prevent condensation dripping on to the soil.

As soon as the seedlings appear, remove the covering; and when they are large enough to handle, prick them out into individual peat pots or plastic pots containing a good growing soil. Liquid feed to maintain growth. Alternatively, buy plants from a garden center.

Planting Plant peppers 18 in apart each way

after the last spring frost. Under glass, plant in 9 in pots and space the pots 18 in apart.

Training Peppers have a bushy habit and are encouraged to branch if the growing point is removed when the plants are about 6 in tall. Support is usually unnecessary except in windy areas.

Harvesting

From August onwards peppers can be harvested. Cut the fruits as required. Green fruits turn red if left on the plant for a further two or three weeks.

Pests and diseases

Spray aphids or red spider mite on sight with a low-persistence insecticide such as derris or malathion.

Diseases are not common on peppers but gray-brown sunken areas may appear on the fruits when the plants have been grown without sufficient water. The sunken areas go soft and may become colonized by gray mold (*Botrytis cinerea*). Always keep peppers well supplied with water, especially in isolated growing systems.

1 Late February. Sow the seed thinly on moistened soil. Cover with $\frac{1}{8}$ in of soil then glass and newspaper. Turn glass daily. Keep at 21°C/70°F until growing well.

2 As soon as the seedlings are large enough to handle prick them singly into peat pots. Feed to maintain growth.

3 When the plants are 6 in tall remove the growing point on each, leaving 3–4 branches. Support the plants with canes if necessary.

4 Throughout the growing season spray aphids or red spider mite on sight with a low-persistence insecticide, such as malathion.

5 August onward. Cut the green fruits as required. Leave the fruits on the plants for a further 2–3 weeks if red fruits are desired.

Eggplants

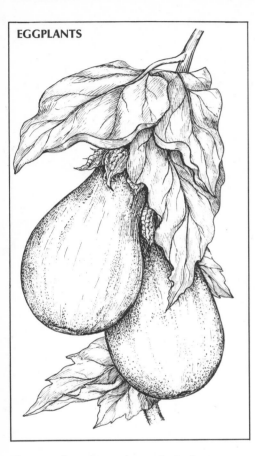

EGGPLANTS

The eggplant is a sub-tropical plant grown for its large egg-shaped fruits which give rise to its common name. The fruits are usually purple, but white-fruited types are also available.

Cultivation

Eggplants have requirements similar to tomatoes and peppers. They grow in zones 4–10. In the South, you can have two crops by sowing seed in early winter for a spring crop and in mid-season for a fall crop.

Soil and situation Eggplants must be grown in well-drained fertile soils and in a sunny, sheltered part of the garden. They should be given 1–2 oz per square yard of a balanced fertilizer before planting and should be fed again about six weeks later. Regular feeding

with a liquid fertilizer after the fruits begin to swell is helpful.

Plant raising The plant raising procedure is similar to that for peppers (see page 84) and, again, high temperatures are necessary. In early March sow the seed thinly in seed trays and keep them at a temperature of 21°C/70°F. Germination is slow and seedling growth also requires high temperatures. Prick out the seedlings into individual peat pots as soon as they can be handled. Maintain the temperature at 18°–21°C/65°–70°F and begin liquid feeding if plant growth slows down. Allow at least 8–10 weeks from seed sowing to planting.

Alternatively, purchase the plants from a grower or garden center.

Planting outside Do not plant eggplants outside until all danger of frost has passed and the soil has begun to warm up. Cover the soil with cloches for 2–3 weeks before planting and then put them back over the small eggplants to encourage establishment. Keep the cloches in place until the plants reach the glass.

Training Remove the growing point of each plant when 9–12 in high to encourage a branched habit. Eggplants are less bushy than peppers and only 3–4 branches should be allowed per plant. Space out and support the branches with string attached to overhead wires or bamboo canes.

Regular feeding and watering is necessary but "little-and-often" is the best policy to avoid the danger of waterlogging or drying out. Fruits develop readily in warm, sunny weather but good-sized eggplants are formed only if the number per plant is restricted to five or six. Remove any other flowers which then appear.

Harvesting

From August onward, cut eggplants with a sharp knife when they reach 6–8 in in length and have turned to a rich purple. Fruits that are only $\frac{1}{3}$ full size are also usable but have less flavor.

Pests and diseases

Aphids can be particularly troublesome on eggplants and the plants must be sprayed with a low-persistence insecticide.

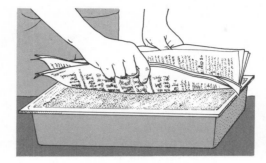

1 Early March. Sow the seed on moistened starting mixture. Cover with $\frac{1}{8}$ in of the mixture, then with glass and newspaper. Keep at 27°C/70°F and turn the glass daily.

3 When all danger of frost has passed, plant eggplants in soil previously warmed with cloches. Water in and replace the cloches until the plants reach the glass.

5 Remove all but 5–6 developing fruits on each plant, keeping them evenly spaced, and pinch out any extra flowers that form to encourage good-sized fruits.

2 As soon as they are large enough to handle, prick out the seedlings singly into peat pots. Keep at 18°–21°C/65°–70°F. If growth slows down, water and feed.

4 Pinch out the growing points when the plants are 9–12 in high, to encourage the growth of 3–4 strong branches. Support the plants with canes.

6 August onward. When the fruits are 6–8 in long and rich purple color, cut them with a sharp knife. Smaller fruits are usable but have less flavor.

Herbs 1

Most herbs are easy to grow and a selection of culinary types provides a variety of flavors to complement home-grown vegetables and enhance the flavor of everyday food. Many of them are perennial plants with invasive habits. Clean up the herb garden each spring to prevent the stronger plants from taking over, and weed it regularly by hand. Once every three or four years replant herbs using fresh stock. It is a good idea to site the herb patch as near to the kitchen as possible. Some of the herbs described on these pages also grow well in containers, provided they have good drainage.

PROPAGATING HERBS

Heel cuttings

1 Strip away a young side-shoot from its parent stem so that a heel, which is a thin sliver of bark and wood, also comes away at its base.

2 Trim the tail on the heel and any leaves near it. Dip the heel cutting in rooting hormone and plant immediately, preferably in a cold frame.

Root division

1 Lift the parent plant to be divided towards the end of the dormant season. Shake off the soil and wash the crown.

2 Cut off a piece with at least 1 developed bud. Dust the cut surfaces with fungicidal powder and replant.

Angelica (*Angelica archangelica*)

Angelica is a decorative biennial or monocarpic herb, which can sometimes be maintained as a perennial by the prevention of seeding. It is a tall plant and can reach a height of 6 ft. It has large, indented leaves and yellow-green flowerheads which appear in late summer.

Cultivation Angelica grows best in a rich, moist but well-drained soil. It grows in semi-shade or in an open position and it is quite hardy. Angelica is best grown from seed; it can be propagated by division but this often encourages flowering. In late summer (August to September) sow the seed outside, with a cloche over the drill in cold areas. In the following March transplant the seedlings, keeping them 12 in apart. Spring sowings are also possible. Angelica needs to be kept weed-free. Remove flowerheads to maintain growth because if angelica is allowed to seed the plants die. It can be grown in a container although its height is a drawback.

Harvesting Angelica is grown for its stems which should be cut before flowering. They are candied and used for cake decoration.

Basil (*Ocimum basilicum*)

Basil is a tender plant easily killed by frost when it is grown outdoors.

Cultivation Basil should be grown in well-drained soil which has been enriched with a liberal dressing of well-rotted organic manure. The site should be warm, sheltered and sunny. The best way of plant raising is to sow the seed in a heated greenhouse during March. Keep them at a temperature of at least 16°C/60°F; the seeds germinate quite slowly. Prick off the seedlings into small, individual peat pots and maintain the temperature at 13°–16°C/55°–60°F. Harden off the plants prior to planting in early June. Space the plants 9–12 in apart each way. Do not plant out earlier because the slightest hint of frost kills basil.

Alternatively, the seed can be sown directly outside in late May. The developing seedlings should be thinned to 9–12 in apart in each direction.

Water regularly during the season and remove flower stalks as soon as they appear, to prolong vegetative growth.

Basil is killed by the first frost but plants can be lifted in September and potted into 5 in pots with a rich potting compost. Cut the plants back hard to within 2–3 in of the base, and take them indoors. Re-growth then occurs to provide young leaves for use in autumn and winter.

Harvesting Pick the leaves as required throughout the summer.

Herbs 2

Borage (*Borago officinalis*)

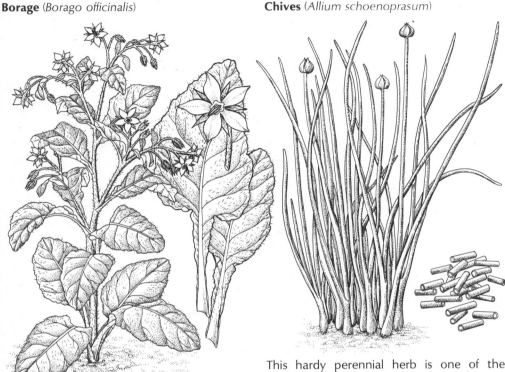

This hardy annual plant grows very readily in cool, temperate climates and has a number of culinary uses. The young leaves taste of cucumber and can be added to salads or used to flavor cool summer punches. The plants have bright blue flowers, which appear from May onwards, and hairy stems and leaves. Borage grows to a height of 3 ft very quickly.

Cultivation Borage tolerates almost any site and soil although the most rapid growth occurs in fertile soils and warm, sheltered sites. Sow the seed outside in February and, as soon as they are large enough, thin the seedlings to 12 in apart in each direction.

Seeds are shed on to the ground by the plants and these germinate in the summer or the following spring.

Harvesting Pick fresh, young leaves as required. The flowers can be used to garnish salads.

Chives (*Allium schoenoprasum*)

This hardy perennial herb is one of the smallest and most delicately flavored members of the onion family. Chives do not have bulbs like onions but are grown for their narrow grasslike leaves which are chopped and used in savoury dishes, soups and salads.

Cultivation Chives grow well in a rich, slightly alkaline soil. They flourish in full sun but tolerate semi-shade. In March or June take out a $\frac{1}{2}$ in deep drill and sow the seeds. When the seedlings are large enough to handle, thin them out until they are about 6 in apart. Do not cut any of the leaves during the early stages of growth. Later, cut off any flowers and, to ensure a continual supply of leaves throughout the summer, cut back the leaves to 2–3 in several times during the growing season. Water chives regularly and give them a little fertilizer in October and March. The clumps should be divided every two or three years and replanted 6 in apart. They can also be grown indoors in pots.

Harvesting Cut off the leaves with sharp scissors above soil level as required.

Dill (*Anethum graveolens*)

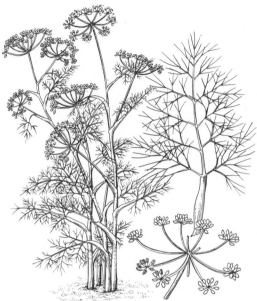

Dill is in the same family as fennel. It is grown for its aromatic leaves, which are used to flavor salads and fish dishes, and for its seeds. Dill vinegar is made by soaking the seeds in vinegar for a few days; the seeds are also used in pickling. The plant has feathery green-blue foliage and tiny yellow flowers arranged in flat umbels.

Cultivation Sunny, well-drained sites are ideal but the plants must never be short of water or the growth becomes weak and straggly. Sow dill directly into the permanent bed because the plants do not tolerate disturbance. Sow successively from April to June for a continual supply of young leaves to harvest.

Thin the seedlings to 12 in apart as soon as possible. Seeds which fall on to the soil germinate in the next season and produce large numbers of self-sown seedlings.

Harvesting Pick fresh leaves as required when the plants are 8 in tall. Harvest the seeds at the end of the season when they are dark brown in color and the plants have turned purplish-brown. The young leaves can be cut and dried for winter use.

Fennel (*Foeniculum vulgare*)

Fennel is an attractive perennial herb which can grow to 6 ft or more in height. It has feathery, blue-tinged foliage and yellow flowers and it is grown for its young shoots and seeds which can be used in sweet and savoury dishes. Fennel can be grown in pots or as a border plant.

Cultivation Fennel tolerates a variety of conditions but it grows best in a moist, well-drained and slightly acid soil. It needs full sun but it is quite hardy in winter. In February sow the seed in a $\frac{1}{2}$ in deep drill. Thin the seedlings to 12–15 in apart or remove all but the strongest if only one plant is required. Keep the plants weed-free.

Established fennel can be propagated by division. Divide or raise fennel from seed every three or four years to keep vigorous young stock.

Harvesting Pick fresh leaves regularly throughout the summer to maintain a constant supply. Allow the seeds to ripen fully and dry on the stem. In autumn, shake them off the stem and store in a warm, dry place.

Herbs 3

Tarragon (*Artemisia dracunculus*)

Marjoram (*Origanum majorana*)

Mint (*Mentha spicata*)

Parsley (*Petroselinum crispum*)

Tarragon is a perennial shrub which can grow to a height of 3 ft and it spreads, as does mint, by underground runners. Tarragon has widely-spaced leaves and clusters of white flowers.

Cultivation Tarragon grows well in poor soil but it must be well-drained. It should be grown in full sun. It is very seldom grown from seed and plants are usually acquired by root division, or less often from cuttings. Plant in spring when there is no longer any danger of frost. Leave a distance of 24 in between plants if more than one is being grown. Keep tarragon weed-free.

Renew tarragon every three or four years by lifting and replanting a few of the vigorous runners. Discard the older portions of the plant. Tarragon can be grown in suitably large containers.

Harvesting Cut the young leaves as needed in July. They may still be suitable in October. Cut the leaves for drying in June to July.

Sweet marjoram is a half-hardy annual. It is grown from seed each year although some forms are perennial. Pot marjoram (*Origanum onites*) is a hardy dwarf shrub which, as the name suggests, can be grown indoors in pots when it will continue to produce leaves for use during the winter.

Cultivation Sweet marjoram can be sown out of doors in mid-May in a warm, sunny site. Thin the plants to 12 in apart each way as soon as they can be handled. Alternatively, sow the seed in seed trays or pans under glass at a temperature of 16°C/60°F in early April. Prick out the seedlings into small individual peat pots and gradually harden off the plants before planting them outside in late May, when the danger of frost is over. Water the plants generously and keep down the weeds, especially in the early stages.

Pot marjoram (*Origanum onites*) is best propagated from heel cuttings taken in May or June. Otherwise, divide established plants in March and pot the plants. Keep them on the patio in summer and take them indoors in winter. Pot marjoram is deciduous and likely to lose its leaves if left outside in the cold months. Cut the plants back hard in March; new growth then appears from the base.

Harvesting Sweet marjoram can be used fresh, or the leaves can be removed and dried for winter use. Cut the shoots when they are about 8 in tall.

Common mint or spearmint (*M. spicata*) is the most popular kind of this hardy perennial herb. Apple or Bowles' mint (*M. × villosa alopecuroides*) is also common and it is considered by some people to have a more subtle and therefore preferable flavor.

Cultivation Mint grows anywhere if the soil is well dug and moist. It does equally well in a sunny or semi-shaded position. Since it is such an invasive plant underground it is advisable to restrict the roots by planting in a bottomless container sunk into the ground. Keep mint free of weeds and pinch out the flower buds when they appear to encourage maximum leaf-growth. Divide the roots each March and replant if possible in a fresh position. Otherwise, incorporate well-rotted compost or manure and a handful of bonemeal into the soil.

Mint is readily grown in pots or containers but should be kept clipped to maintain vigorous young growth.

Harvesting Pick fresh young leaves as required from May until the autumn. If dried leaves are required gather these before the plants begin to flower.

Pests and diseases If mint is attacked by the rust (*Puccinia menthae*), dig up all the roots and burn them. It is best to acquire new stock from a healthy source.

Parsley is a biennial plant which is best grown as an annual, although it will over-winter successfully and provide leaves for winter use if cloched. There are several varieties available, some with flat leaves, but the curly-leaved variety is most often grown.

Cultivation A rich, slightly alkaline, soil is ideal for parsley but poorer soils can be used if they are enriched with some well-rotted compost. Moisture is very important for successful parsley growing, and the plant grows best in a semi-shaded position. If parsley is grown in a sunny place it needs to be watered regularly.

The seed is sown in March. Germination, which is sometimes erratic, may take 6–8 weeks outdoors. This process can be speeded up by sowing the seed indoors in pots. When the seedlings are large enough to handle thin them out until they are 4 in apart. Weed regularly by hand when the seedlings are small and apply a liquid feed occasionally to increase leaf production. In the second year cut off the flower stalks to delay the plants' production of seed.

Throughout the winter parsley can be grown indoors, or in the greenhouse, in suitable containers for continual harvesting.

Harvesting Pick parsley fresh as required.

Pests and diseases Seedlings can be attacked by carrot fly. Before sowing sprinkle bromophos in the seed drill as a deterrent.

Herbs 4

Rosemary (*Rosmarinus officinalis*)   **Sage** (*Salvia officinalis*)   **Sweet bay** (*Laurus nobilis*)   **Thyme** (*Thymus vulgaris*)

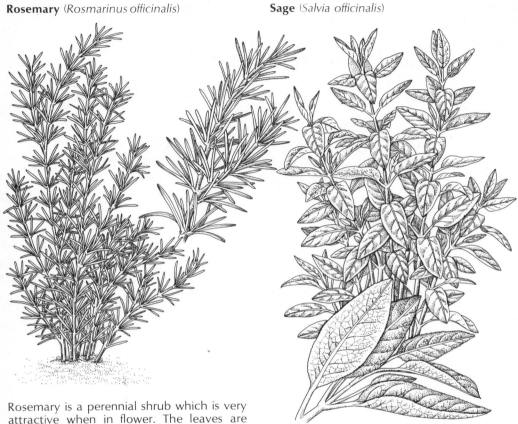

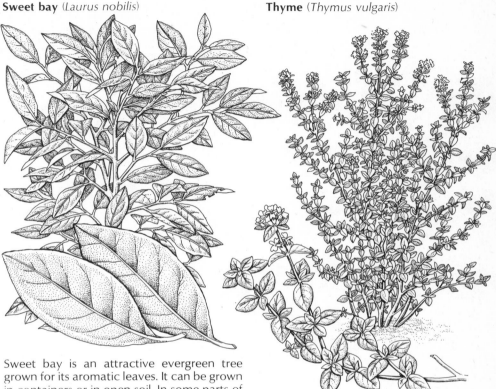

Rosemary is a perennial shrub which is very attractive when in flower. The leaves are needle-shaped and gray-green in color and the flowers, which appear from March to September, are pale to deep blue.
Cultivation Rosemary grows in any well-drained soil. It does best in a sunny sheltered spot although it may be grown in partial shade. Rosemary can be grown from seed sown in May and June but because seed is difficult to obtain and germination can be very slow, it is best to grow it from heel cuttings taken in early summer. Prune rosemary regularly to prevent straggly growth and to encourage a bushy habit.

Rosemary does well as a pot plant but it should be kept indoors during the coldest part of the winter.
Harvesting Pick fresh leaves and flowers as required but cut shoots for drying in the summer months only.

Sage is a small evergreen shrub 1½–2 ft high. The species most commonly grown, *Salvia officinalis*, may be grown from seed or propagated from heel cuttings.
Cultivation Sage tolerates any well-drained soil but grows best on a chalky loam. It requires a sheltered site in full sun. Sage shrubs grow well in any kind of container. Sow the seed under glass in March. Plant out the seedlings 12–15 in apart when there is no longer any danger of frost. Keep them weed-free and trim regularly when they are fully grown. Cut sage back lightly after flowering is over in July. Renew the shrubs every three or four years.
Harvesting Pick the leaves as required; they are best just before flowering. Cut leaves for drying in the active growing season.

Sweet bay is an attractive evergreen tree grown for its aromatic leaves. It can be grown in containers or in open soil. In some parts of the world it reaches a height of up to 50 ft.
Cultivation Sweet bay grows best in a dryish, well-drained soil which may be acid or alkaline. It grows well in full sun but a sheltered site is preferable because in severe winters the foliage, and occasionally the shoots, may be damaged. Buy a young, well-established tree from a nursery or propagate in late summer or early autumn (August to September) from cuttings of ripe shoots. Protect young trees in harsh weather to prevent the leaves turning brown. Sweet bay grows well in containers and makes a good ornamental tree because it can be clipped into shape and growth is restricted by the pot.

Place pot-grown trees indoors or in a frost-free shed during the winter months.
Harvesting Pick the young leaves as required and dry them slowly in the dark to make sure the color is retained.

Common culinary thyme is a small perennial bush about 10 in high. It has a beautiful scent and is a useful bee-plant.
Cultivation Thyme prefers a light, well-drained, neutral soil. Common thyme grows best in full sun although it is hardy. However, various other thymes grown mainly for ornament may require some winter protection.

Seed sown outdoors in March germinates fairly readily and the resulting seedlings should be thinned until they are about 12 in apart. Keep the thyme patch weed-free and trim the plants after flowering to encourage compact growth.

The plants should be renewed every three or four years. Propagate thyme by root division or heel cuttings. Common thyme grows well in containers.
Harvesting Pick the leaves for drying or immediate use before the plants flower.

Planning 1

The planting of tree, bush and cane fruits represents a long-term investment. Once planted there should be no need to move them until their cropping life is over. This could range from 20 to 50 years and more for tree fruits, and about 10–15 years for soft fruits. It is worthwhile, therefore, before planting to draw up a scale plan so that the plants are correctly sited.

The planner needs to take into account the approximate yield from each fruit to meet the family's requirements in relation to the amount of land available, the correct spacing and the right aspect.

Yield

The yield depends upon many factors, such as the fertility of the soil, the climate, and the variety and the size of the plant. As a guide, the table below lists approximate yields from reasonably mature plants of the fruits commonly grown outside.

Spacing

The eventual size and yield of a mature fruit plant are influenced by the environment, the variety and, with many tree fruits, the rootstock on which it is grafted. Trees grafted on vigorous rootstocks in time grow larger than trees grafted on dwarfing stocks, even though they may be the same variety. Nowadays, most trees are cultivated for small gardens and are usually grafted on non-vigorous stocks, except for the semi-dwarf or standard forms. Soft fruits are grown on their own roots.

The spacings given in the table below are intended only as a guide for the planner. For more detail, refer to the relevant fruit pages. Allow a wider spacing on very fertile soils.

Fruit against walls and fences

While in many gardens the bulk of the fruit crop comes from a plot of land specially set aside for this purpose, the use of walls, fences and trellises should not be neglected, particularly where space is limited. Their structure provides support for the plants and also for netting as protection against birds or frosts. Walls and solid fences have the added advantages of giving shelter and, where the aspect is sunny, extra warmth and light are reflected from the masonry or wood. The added warmth improves the quality of the fruits, promotes fruit bud development and makes it possible to grow the more exotic fruits where otherwise it might not be worthwhile.

Because wall and fence space is usually limited, use the restricted plant forms that are kept in shape and contained by summer pruning.

Apples and pears can be grown as cordons, espaliers or fans but stone fruits, such as apricots, peaches and cherries, do not respond to the cordon and espalier methods of training and are therefore grown only in fan-trained form. The climbing fruits, such as blackberries, hybrid berries and grapes, grow well against walls and fences. The grape vine in particular is perhaps the most versatile of all the trained fruits, being amenable to many forms of training against walls, fences or on pergolas but, of course, the aspect must be sunny.

The height of the supporting structure decides the shape or form in which the fruit is best trained.

Walls and fences up to 6 ft high are suitable for the low-trained tree forms such as the espalier, and for cordon and fan-trained gooseberries, red and white currants as well as blackberry and raspberry canes.

With walls and fences 6–8 ft high, it is possible to grow apples and pears (on dwarfing or semi-dwarfing stock) as cordons, fans or multiple-tiered espaliers, the number of tiers depending upon the height of the structure.

TREE FORMS

Oblique cordon

Espalier

Fan

Standard   Half-standard   Bush

There is no really dwarfing stock as yet developed for stone fruits, although it is anticipated there will be in the next five years, so the minimum height required for fan-trained apricots, peaches, nectarines, plums, and Morello cherries is 7 ft. There are successful peaches on semi-vigorous stocks grown on lower structures than this but they need regular pruning and tying down. The sweet cherry is a vigorous plant and needs a wall or fence of at least 8 ft. Trellis-work fencing gives structures extra height.

Aspect

The aspect of the wall, fence or trellis decides the kind of fruit that can be grown. In the northern hemisphere the warmest and sunniest aspect is the south-facing and the coldest and shadiest is the north, with the west and east somewhere between the two.

YIELDS AND SPACING

APPLES AND PEARS

Tree form	Yield Apples	Yield Pears	Spacing In rows	Spacing Rows apart
Bush	60–120 lb	40–100 lb	12–18 ft	12–18 ft
Dwarf bush	30–50 lb	20–40 lb	8–15 ft	8–15 ft
Dwarf pyramid	10–15 lb	8–12 lb	5–6 ft	6 ft
Espalier (2-tier)	20–25 lb	15–20 lb	10–18 ft	6 ft
Fan	12–30 lb	12–30 lb	12–18 ft	—
Single cordon	5–8 lb	4–6 lb	2½–3 ft	6 ft
Standard	100–400 lb	80–240 lb	18–30 ft	18–30 ft

OTHER TREE FRUITS

Tree form	Yield	In rows	Rows apart
Bush (Morello cherry)	30–40 lb	12–18 ft	12–18 ft
Bush (plum and peach)	30–60 lb	12–18 ft	12–20 ft
Bush, semi-dwarf and standard (sweet cherry)	30–120 lb	15–40 ft	15–40 ft
Bush or small tree (fig)	15–20 lb	18–20 ft	18–20 ft
Fan (all stone fruits)	12–30 lb	12–18 ft	—
Fan (fig)	15–20 lb	12–15 ft	—
Fan (sweet cherry)	12–30 lb	18–25 ft	—
Pyramid (plum)	30–50 lb	10–12 ft	10–12 ft
Standard (plum, peach and apricot)	30–120 lb	18–25 ft	18–25 ft

SOFT FRUIT

	Yield	In rows	Rows apart
Bush (black currant)	10–12 lb	5–6 ft	6 ft
Bush (gooseberry)	6–8 lb	4–5 ft	5 ft
Bush (red and white currant)	8–10 lb	5 ft	5 ft
Cordon (gooseberry, red and white currant)	1–3 lb	12–15 in	5 ft
Blackberry or hybrid berry	10–30 lb	8–15 ft	6–7 ft
Raspberry	1½ lb per ft of row	15–18 in	6 ft
Strawberry	8–10 oz per plant	12–15 in	2½–3 ft

Planning 2

South The southern, south-eastern and south-western aspects are best reserved for the sun-loving fruits, although most fruits would thrive in this situation. The soil at the base of a south-facing wall can become very dry, so ensure there is adequate moisture during the growing season by mulching and watering. This aspect is suitable for figs, peaches, nectarines, apricots, grapes, pears, plums, cherries and apples.

West The western aspect receives the hot afternoon sun. It is suitable for peaches, nectarines, apricots, sweet and sour cherries, grapes, pears, plums, apples, raspberries, blackberries, gooseberries, red and white currants.

East The eastern aspect is a dry situation receiving the fairly cool morning sun but shaded in the afternoon. Suitable fruits include the early pears, apples, plums, sweet and sour cherries, currants, gooseberries, blackberries and raspberries.

North The northern aspect is restricted to those fruits that are able to grow and ripen in cold situations with little sun. Suitable fruits are fan-trained sour cherries, early apples, cordon currants and gooseberries and blackberries. They will ripen later than those in full sun.

Wiring walls and fences

Horizontal wires firmly attached to the wall or fence are necessary to support the framework branches and for tying in the new growth. Use 14 gauge galvanized fencing wire for espaliers and cordons, and 16 gauge for fan-trained trees.

For espaliers, fix the wires so that they coincide with the height of the arms (tiers). Generally the tiers are 15–18 in apart but plant the espaliers first to see where the wires should be placed. The wires for oblique cordons are usually fixed every 2 ft, the highest wire being 6 in below the top of the wall or fence.

Fan-trained trees require horizontal wires every 6 in or two brick courses apart, starting at 15 in from the ground and continuing to the top of the wall or fence. Bolts to take the strain of the wires are not necessary on wires for fan-trained trees because the wires are placed closer together, so galvanized staples will suffice on wooden fences and lead anchors on walls.

Buying fruit plants

To ensure healthy new plants, it is best to buy fruit stock from a specialist fruit grower. Apart from having a better selection, the specialist is likely to stock varieties of a guaranteed high standard of purity, health and vigor.

Most state authorities inspect plants which are shipped in or out of the state to ensure that they are free of disease. Plants shipped within a state are, as a practical matter, usually inspected along with material going out of state, although they generally need not be inspected. Certified stock is usually healthy stock.

Also, before choosing any fruit plant check its pollination requirements. Some fruits such as sweet cherries, apples, pears and certain plums must be grown in compatible pairs or they will not produce fruit. Select the best varieties from the lists of recommended varieties and descriptions which head each fruit page. The varieties lists are given in abbreviated form for quick reference, and more detailed reading may be necessary.

WIRING WALLS AND FENCES

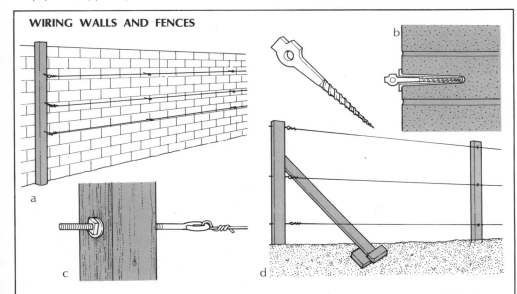

Wires must be held 1½–4 in away from walls by fixing 2 in square wooden battens (or 1½ in × 1½ in angle irons) to the masonry to hold the straining bolts and the ends of the wires (a). Screw or drive in 4 in galvanized or lead wall nails with anchors (b) every 5 ft to hold the wires between the battens. With the screw type, drill and plug the wall first. Wires should be kept taut by attaching straining bolts (c) to one end post. Use galvanized staples (d) to hold the wires on the intermediate and other end posts. Tighten the wires with the straining bolts before driving the staples home. A diagonal post is needed to brace the main post.

Planning a small fruit garden

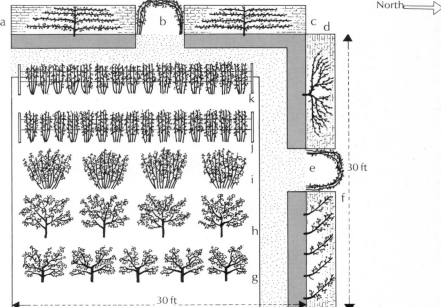

The above plot is a guide for planning a small intensively cultivated fruit garden. It can be modified to suit individual requirements. It contains: espalier pear (a); loganberry arch (b); espalier pear (c); fan peach (d); grape arch (e); cordon apples (f); gooseberries (g); red currants (h); black currants (i); June-fruiting raspberries (j); fall-fruiting raspberries (k).

Soft fruits

Introduction

Soft fruit is an umbrella term for several low-growing shrubs and perennials that bear soft, juicy fruit. They are not all closely related and they have a variety of growth habits. Botanically the best-known fruits can be placed into two groups: those belonging to the rose family (Rosaceae), including the raspberry, blackberry, loganberry and allied hybrids, and the strawberry; and those classified in the gooseberry family (Grossulariaceae) including the black, red and white currant, and the gooseberry. Three fruits not included in these two families are grapes (Vitidaceae), the melon (Cucurbitaceae) and the blueberry (Ericaceae). However, all the fruits in the soft fruit category have the common advantage of bearing fruit soon after planting—in some cases (such as the melon) within the same year. Also, soft fruits are particularly suitable for the small garden because they need far less room than do tree fruits such as apples, pears and plums.

Site

With good basic culture, all the soft fruits are easily grown and, once established, provide annual crops without fail. Although best grown in an open, sunny position, they do reasonably well in partial shade or in a site that gets afternoon sun only. Low-lying areas that are susceptible to late spring frosts should be avoided if possible.

If space in the garden is restricted, use walls and fences for grapes and climbing cane fruits, as well as for gooseberries and red and white currants as cordons or fans (see pages 90–91). Soft fruits such as strawberries, grapes and currants can also be grown in containers, in window boxes or in tubs on a patio, and climbing fruits can be trained over pergolas and arches.

In a small garden the fruits to be grown must be chosen carefully. If there is room, for example, for only six bushes it is tempting to grow one of each of all the main soft fruits. But it is more sensible and profitable to grow a minimum of three bushes of two favorite sorts only. In this way enough fruit can be picked for the family's needs, with some left over for jam-making perhaps, or for freezing.

Personal preference will, of course, dictate the choice of fruits. If only a few sorts can be grown, black or red currants, raspberries and strawberries are a good choice because, apart from their excellent taste, all are good croppers relative to their size and those in stores are seldom as fresh as those picked straight from the garden.

With the use of cloches, cold frames or polyethylene tunnels the season of some soft fruits (strawberries in particular) can be extended both in the early summer and in the fall.

Protection against birds

Another advantage of growing soft fruits is the comparative ease of providing protection against pests. Very few gardens escape bird damage to ripe fruit in summer and fall, or to fruit buds in winter and spring. This means some sort of year-round protection is needed. A permanent fruit cage is highly recommended because it provides both efficient bird protection and allows easy access to the plants for picking, spraying, pruning and top-dressing.

Clearing the site

Although most soft fruits grow well enough in any moderately fertile soil, it is always worth while doing some initial preparation. See pages 8–11 for details of soil preparation and drainage. A first essential is to make sure that all perennial weeds are removed. Nowadays there are selective herbicides for this purpose (see page 171), although some gardeners may prefer to double dig before planting which buries the weeds. Clean, cultivated ground needs single digging before planting (see pages 16–17), and hand picking occasional weeds during this operation is all that is needed.

Planting

Strawberry plants are set out with a trowel in much the same way as any bedding plant or young perennial. Raspberry canes and blackberry layers (plants) can usually be dealt with in the same way, depending upon how much root they have. At the most a small spade is all that is necessary.

Bush fruits generally have a more extensive root system and, because they are a fairly long-term crop, their planting ritual should be more elaborate. Plant bushes from November to March, depending on the region and weather and horticultural conditions.

Dig a hole which is deeper and wider than the roots when they are spread out. The bottom of the hole should be loosened with a fork and if little or no organic matter was dug into the area initially, a spadeful or two can now be worked in. Use well-rotted manure or garden compost, or peat and bonemeal.

Set the plant in the hole and spread out the roots. Fill in the hole with the soil, occasionally giving the bush a gentle shake up and down so that the soil filters among the roots and makes close contact with them. Firm the soil gently throughout with the feet. When all the plants are in position, rake the site over so that it is level and apply a light dressing of a balanced fertilizer.

Strawberries 1

JUNE-BEARING STRAWBERRIES

EARLY
'Dixieland' Large, firm berries. Especially good in South, but adapted to other areas.
'Earlibelle' Very early. Does best in deep South. Bright red berries turning dark red. Medium-large.

'Earlidawn' Very early. Big, tart berries and lots of them. Susceptible to verticillium wilt and should be avoided if this is a problem in the area.
'Holiday' Very early. Very productive. Solid red.
'Premier' Standard commercial variety, but good in home garden. Widely grown. Medium-size berries.

'Puget Beauty' Fine variety for the Northwest. Long, medium-large berries. Aromatic and sweet.
'Redglow' Especially flavorful, medium-big berries, but not in large quantities.
'Spring Beauty' High-yielding and puts out a great many runners. Berries orange-red, large and sweet.

MID-SEASON
'Catskill' Unusually large berries are bright crimson and extra sweet. Productive. High resistance to verticillium wilt.
'Dunlap' Also called 'Senator Dunlap'. Highly weather-resistant and adaptable. Fairly small, red berries with outstanding flavor.

The strawberry cultivated today has resulted from the interbreeding of a number of *Fragaria* species, principally the North American *F. virginiana* as well as the South American *F. chiloensis*. This intermingling of genetic characteristics has resulted in a fruit of great variety in taste and color, with a cropping ability and season of such versatility that it can be grown from the Tropics to the cool temperate regions of the world. It is no wonder the strawberry is the most popular soft fruit.

For the purposes of cultivation the strawberry is divided into three categories: the ordinary June-fruiting strawberry; the so-called ever-bearing strawberry that produces one crop in the spring and a second crop in the fall; and the alpine strawberry (*Fragaria vesca*, subspecies *alpina*), a mountain form of wild strawberry (see page 95).

Standard strawberries

The ordinary, or June-bearing strawberry, crops once only in the early summer. A few do crop again in fall and these are called "two crop" varieties, but they are cultivated in the same way as the others. The expected yield per strawberry plant is about 8–10 oz.

Cultivation

Some gardeners prefer to grow strawberries as an annual crop, planting new runners each year. This method produces high quality fruits but a lower yield than that of larger two- or three-year-old plants.

Soil and situation Most soils are suitable for strawberries, but they should be well drained. On waterlogged land, if a drainage system is not practicable, grow strawberries on ridges 2–3 in high. They prefer a slightly acid (pH 6.0–6.5) light loam in a frost-free, sunny situation. They will, however, tolerate some shade and because many varieties flower over a long period, the later flowers should escape spring frosts. Strawberries are readily attacked by soil-borne pests and diseases and a system of soil rotation should be practiced. Do not grow them for more than three or four years in any one site. For this reason, strawberries are best grown with the vegetables rather than with the more permanent fruit plants.

Soil preparation A strawberry bed will be down for three or four years, and the initial preparations should be thorough so that the land is made fertile and free from perennial weeds. In July dig in well-rotted manure or compost at about the rate of 14 lb to the square yard. Rake off any surplus because bulky organics on the surface encourage slugs, snails and millipedes. Once applied, no more organics should be needed for the life of the bed. Just before planting, lightly fork in a balanced fertilizer such as 10-10-10 at 3 oz per square yard.

Planting and spacing The earlier the planting, the better the maiden crop in the following year. Plant in early spring after the ground has started to warm up. It is not necessary to wait until frost danger has passed. In the warmest American climates, however, it is better to plant in October. Plant the runners in moist soil with the crown of the strawberry just level with the soil surface; planting too deep may result in the rotting of the buds and planting too shallow may cause drying out. Plant with a trowel or hand fork, spreading out the roots well. Replace the soil and firm it. Space the plants 18 in apart in rows 3 ft apart. On a light soil they can be 15 in apart with 2½ ft between the rows. Plants to be grown for two years need only 12 in spacing.

Pollination The flowers are pollinated by bees and such crawling insects as pollen beetles. Imperfect pollination results in malformed fruits. All modern varieties are self-fertile.

Watering and feeding Water regularly for the first few weeks after planting and whenever dry conditions occur during the growing season, but try to keep water away from the ripening berries because this encourages gray mold (*Botrytis cinerea*). The risk is less with trickle or drip irrigation because only the soil is wetted. Damp conditions overnight also encourage botrytis; water in the morning so that the plants are dry by nightfall. In mid-August each year, apply a balanced fertilizer at ½ oz per square yard along each side of the row. No other feeding is necessary unless growth has been poor. In this case apply sulfate of ammonia at ½ oz per square yard in April, taking care to prevent fertilizer touching the foliage because it will scorch it.

Weed control Weeds compete for nutrients and water. Keep the rows clean by shallow hoeing and tuck any runners into the row to fill gaps. Pay particular attention to cleaning up between the rows before mulching. Weedkillers may be used (see page 171).

In general, shallow cultivation of strawberries keeps weed growth in check. But care should be taken to weed strawberry beds each fall, and particular attention should be paid to the removal of all weeds.

1 In late winter or the preceding fall, dig in well-rotted manure or compost at a rate of 14 lb per square yard. Rake off any surplus manure.

2 About April, plant the strawberries 18 in apart in rows 3 ft apart. Spread out the roots, keeping the crowns level with the soil surface. Firm the soil.

3 For the first few weeks after planting and during all succeeding dry spells in the growing season, water regularly. Keep water away from ripening berries.

4 Up to July 15 in the first year, pick off all blossoms to force strength into the plants for a big crop next year.

5 When the fruits begin to swell, scatter slug pellets along the rows. Cover the ground beneath the berries and between rows with barley or wheat straw.

6 Protect the fruit from birds. Support nets with posts at least 18 in tall. Cover posts with jars or pots first.

Strawberries 2

MID-SEASON
'Cambridge Favourite' The most widely grown. Flavour fair. Fruits large, salmon scarlet. Cropping heavy and reliable.
'Redgauntlet' Widely grown. Flavour fair. Fruits large, scarlet. A heavy cropper. Will give a second crop in the autumn if protected in the spring. Some resistance to red core disease.

'Cambridge Aristocrat' Rich flavour. Highly fragrant. Long conical, crimson fruits. Light cropper.

LATE
'Cambridge Late Pine' Excellent aromatic, sweet flavour. A dull-red fruit. Medium/large fruit. Heavy cropper.

'Domanil' Good flavour. Fruits large, round; orange-red with orange flesh. Heavy cropper. Tall, vigorous plants.

Strawing down When the fruits begin to swell and weigh down the trusses, scatter slug pellets along the rows. Then put straw down around the plants. This is to keep the fruits clean, so tuck the straw right under the berries and also cover the ground between the rows to help to keep down weeds. Do not straw down earlier than this because the straw prevents the heat from the earth reaching the flowers, which may then be damaged by frost at night. Preferably use barley straw (which is soft) or, as a second choice, wheat straw.

Protection from birds One method of protection is to use barn cloches with netting over the framework. Alternatively, make cages using ¾ in or 1 in plastic netting, supported by posts and wire or string. The height should be at least 18 in; about 4 ft is the ideal height for picking in comfort. Put glass jars or plastic plant pots over the posts to prevent them tearing the netting.

Harvesting

The best time to pick strawberries is in the morning when the berries are still cool. Pick them complete with stalks; try not to handle the flesh because it bruises easily.

Alternatives to strawing down

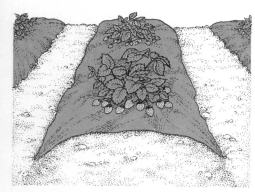

If straw is not available, strawberries can also be grown through black polythene. First, prepare the bed by raising a 3 in high ridge of soil. Water it well. Lay 150-gauge plastic over the ridge, tucking in the edges under the soil. Plant the

At the end of the season

Immediately after cropping cut off the old leaves (about 3 in above the crown) and unwanted runners using shears or a sickle. Tuck in runners needed to fill in any gaps in the row. In the second year a matted row can be grown by allowing runners to root in the row and reducing the space available, so that the quantity of fruit is greater but the quality suffers. The space between the rows is kept clear. Defoliation and the burning of the old straw or other debris is good horticultural practice because it is a source of pests and diseases, but it must be done as soon as cropping is over to avoid damaging fresh growth and reducing the crop the next year.

Propagation

Strawberries are easily propagated from runners which the parent plant begins to produce as the crop is coming to an end. The aim is to obtain well-rooted runners for early planting and it is achieved by pegging down the strongest runners so that they make good contact with the soil. In June or July choose healthy parent plants which have cropped well. From each select four or five strong runners. Peg them down either into moist

strawberries through slits in the plastic at 15–18 in intervals. Leave a 6 in run of soil between the plastic to enable rain to permeate to the roots. Alternatively, protection can be provided by placing mats around individual plants like a collar.

open ground or into 3 in pots buried level with the soil. Pot-grown runners are best because they are easier to transplant. Fill the pots with a potting compost such as John Innes No. 3, or a peat-based compost. Peg close to the embryo plant but do not sever it from the parent at this stage. For the pegs, use 4 in pieces of thin galvanized wire bent to a U-shape. Straightened out paper clips are ideal.

In four to six weeks there should be a good root system. Sever from the parent, lift and plant out into the new bed. Keep them well watered.

Planting under mist or in a closed propagating case are other useful ways of obtaining very early runners. With these, sever the embryo plants from the parents at the first sign of roots—root initials—and peg them into 1½–2 in peat pots.

Varieties

Strawberries soon become infected with virus diseases, so it is important to plant only virus-free stock. It is best to obtain plants from a specialist propagator who guarantees healthy stock rather than accept them from a dubious source.

Clearing up the bed

In August, after cropping, cut off the old leaves and unwanted runners with shears 3 in above crowns. Rake off the leaves, old straw and other debris and burn it. Fork up the compacted earth between the rows, leaving the ground weed-free.

PROPAGATION

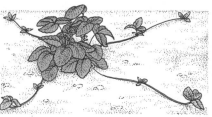

1 In June to August, select four or five runners from healthy, cropping plants.

2 With U-shaped wires, peg runners into open ground or into 3 in pots buried level and filled with a potting compost.

3 In four to six weeks they should have rooted. Sever from parents close to plants.

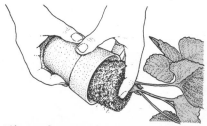

4 Lift out the potted runners and knock out from the pot. Plant out into the new bed and water well.

Strawberries 3

EVER-BEARING STRAWBERRIES
'Geneva' Excellent large, sweet berries, but have a tendency to rot in damp weather. Produces fairly late in the spring.
'Luscious Red' From Minnesota, therefore quite hardy. Long, pointed, medium-size berries.
'Ogallala' Drought-resistant plants doing best in cool climates. Berries are large, dark red and have a faint wild strawberry flavor.
'Ozark Beauty' Unusually productive. Big, sweet, wedge-shaped berries. Extremely popular.
'Superfection' Tart, rounded, light red berries. Among the most widely planted ever-bearing varieties.
'Chief Bemidji' Very hardy. Big, solid red berries.   Good for southern gardens as well as those elsewhere. Excellent producer over a long period. Huge, sweet, orange-red berries.
ALPINES June to October.
'Baron Solemacher' Superb flavor. Masses of tiny dark red fruits. Widely grown. Prefers slight shade.
'Alexandria' Sweet and juicy. Very bright red. Fruits long (over ½ in) and large for an alpine. Good cropper.
'Fraise des Bois' Good flavor. Fruits very small. Bright red. Prolific continuous cropper.
'Alpine Yellow' Strongly flavored, very small golden-yellow fruits. Not as heavy a cropper as the red varieties.

Ever-bearing strawberries

Ever-bearing strawberries have the characteristic of producing fruit in the spring and again in the fall. It is useful to cover the fall crop with cloches to extend the season, possibly in late October. It is best to grow ever-bearers for one year only because the size and weight of the crop deteriorate in the second year. Replant with new runners each year.

Cultivation

The basic requirements of soil, spacing, mulching and feeding are the same as for June-bearing strawberries. The soil should be highly fertile and moisture-retentive. Be sure to water well in late summer and fall.

Plant in the early spring and remove the first flush of flowers to ensure a good crop later in the season.

In the fall, when cropping is finished, clean up the rows, remove the old straw, surplus runners and one or two of the older leaves, and burn the debris. Cover with straw or hay in the late fall to protect against winter damage.

Do not fertilize the plants in the spring of the following year, but apply a balanced fertilizer immediately after all the spring berries have been picked to encourage a second, smaller, crop in the fall. Then remove plants entirely.

Alpine strawberries

Several varieties have been selected for garden and commercial cultivation. They make an attractive edging plant, having masses of small white flowers. They bear dark red fruits continuously or in flushes from June until November.

Cultivation

Alpine strawberries are usually grown from seed and kept for no more than two years before re-sowing. There are a few varieties that produce runners, but most do not. Maintaining virus-free stock is difficult.

Sowing Sow the seeds in March under glass. Sow into seed boxes containing a moist seed-starting mixture. Maintain them at a temperature of 18°–20°C/64°–68°F. Cover the boxes with glass and shade until the seeds germinate. When two true leaves appear, prick out the seedlings 1in apart into flats or peat pots.

Soil preparation, planting and feeding The soil should be rich, well drained and slightly acid (pH 6.0–6.5). Just before planting apply sulfate of potash at ½ oz per square yard. Once the danger of frosts is over, but by the end of May, plant out the seedlings in the prepared, moist soil. Plant in the open or in light shade. Space the seedlings 1ft apart with 2½ ft between the rows. Water them in dry weather (about 3–4 gal per square yard every 7–10 days). For better cropping, when the flowers appear, feed every two weeks with a liquid fertilizer.

Harvesting

Pick carefully. Slight crushing, sugaring, and overnight soaking brings out the flavor.

PROPAGATION

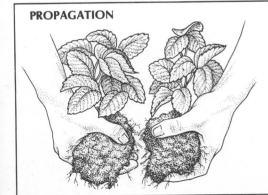

Some ever-bearing strawberries produce runners and are propagated in the same way as are June-bearing strawberries, but a few varieties do not and these are propagated by division.

From late August to early September, dig up a mature plant and break off the new crowns or buds with as many roots as possible. Transfer them to the new strawberry bed and plant them immediately in the usual way. Do not plant the crowns too deep or they will rot.

1 In March, sow into seed boxes of moist seed compost.

2 Cover with glass and shade until germination. Maintain a temperature of 18°–20°C/64°–68°F.

3 When the seedlings have two true leaves, prick out 1in apart into flats or individual peat pots.

4 Just before planting, apply sulfate of potash at ½ oz per square yard to moist well-dug soil, forking it in lightly.

5 Once the danger of frosts is over, plant out the seedlings in the prepared bed, 1ft apart in rows 2½ ft apart.

6 In dry periods, water the plants thoroughly every 7–10 days. For better crops, feed every two weeks with liquid manure.

Raspberries 1

STANDARD RASPBERRY VARIETIES
'Amber' Amber-yellow berries superior in quality to other yellows and comparable to most reds (which are generally better than the yellows). Fruits rather late. Not hardy in zone 3.
'Boyne' Red berries of good quality. Vigorous, very hardy plants grown in North Dakota and Manitoba.

'Canby' Canes nearly thornless. Large, sweet red berries ripening before
'Chief' Profuse small red berries, but of only fair quality.
'Early Red' Red berries of better-than-average flavor. Hardy and very early.
'Latham' Probably the most popular standard red raspberry. Very large, mildly sweet, firm fruits of moderate quality.

Hardy and tolerant of virus diseases.
'Sumner' Dependable variety well adapted to heavier soils. Big, red berries ripening over a long period.
'Taylor' Excellent large, conical, light red berries in profusion. Delicious flavor. Vigorous, hardy, erect plants.
'Willamette' Enormous, conical, dark red berries in abundance.

Like the strawberry, the raspberry is one of the quickest fruits to crop, bearing a reasonable amount in the second year and full cropping thereafter. A good average yield is 1½–2 lb per foot run of row.

Cultivation

Most red raspberries (there are also a few with yellow fruit) flower in late spring and the fruits ripen in early to midsummer, depending upon the variety and the weather: such varieties are called standard or summer-bearing raspberries.

The stems, or canes, are biennial in that they grow vegetatively in their first year, flower and fruit in their second year and then die back to ground level. The root system is perennial and of suckering habit, producing each growing season new replacement canes from adventitious buds on the roots and new buds from old stem bases.

Some raspberry varieties have the characteristic of flowering on the first year's growth on the topmost part. These are called ever-bearing raspberries as they produce a small

crop of fruit in early summer and a larger crop in early fall. All grow in zones 3–7. Because their cultural requirements differ in some respects, they are described separately (see page 98).

Soil and situation Red raspberries grow best on a slightly acid soil of pH 6.0–6.7 that is moisture-retentive but well drained. They can be grown in dry, sandy and limy soils of low fertility, provided plenty of water is given during dry weather and bulky organic manures are liberally applied. Raspberries will not tolerate poor drainage, and even temporary waterlogging can lead to the death of the root system and subsequent death of the canes. In alkaline soils above pH 7.0, iron and manganese deficiencies may occur. See pages 10–11 for reduction of soil alkalinity and correction of iron and/or manganese deficiencies.

The site must be sheltered because strong winds damage the canes and inhibit the movement of pollinating insects. Preferably, they should be planted in full sun, although they grow quite well in partial shade with a

minimum of half a day's sun, provided they are not directly under trees and the soil is not too dry.

Soil preparation Prepare the ground in late fall or late winter by forking out all weeds, particularly perennials. Then dig a trench along the intended row three spades wide by one spade deep. Cover the bottom of the trench with well-rotted manure or compost to a depth of 3–4 in and fork it into the base so that it is thoroughly mixed with the soil. With double-dug grassland there is no need for this operation because the buried turf takes the place of the organic manure. Finally fill in the trench and fork in a balanced fertilizer such as 10-10-10 at the rate of 3 oz per square yard.

Planting and spacing If possible the rows should run north-south so that one row does not shade another too much.

In early spring, plant the canes 18 in apart in the rows. If more than one row is planted, space the rows 6 ft apart, or 5 ft apart if using the single fence system. Spread the roots out well and plant them about 3 in deep; deep planting inhibits new canes (suckers).

After planting, cut down the canes to a bud about 9–12 in above the ground. Later, when the new canes appear, cut down the old stump to ground level before it fruits. This means foregoing a crop in the first summer but it ensures good establishment and the production of strong new canes in subsequent years.

Supporting the canes

To prevent the canes from bowing over when heavy with fruit and to keep the fruits clean it is generally advisable to support the canes. The usual method is a post and wire fence for which there are various alternative systems. It is easier to erect the fence before planting, although it may be left until the end of the first summer.

Single fence: vertically trained canes This is the most popular method and consists of single wires stretched horizontally at heights of 2½, 3½ and 5½ ft. It requires the least space of the various fencing systems and is ideal for the small garden. The fruiting canes are tied individually to the wires and thus are secure

1 In early fall, take out a trench in prepared ground three spades wide by one spade deep. Cover the bottom of the trench with a 3–4 in layer of well-rotted manure or compost and fork in thoroughly.

2 Then, fill in the trench and fork in 3 oz per square yard of a balanced fertilizer such as 10-10-10.

3 From March to April, plant the canes at 18 in intervals. Spread the roots out well and plant about 3 in deep. Cut down the canes to a bud about 9–12 in above the ground.

4 In late March, apply sulfate of ammonia at ½ oz per square yard. Mulch with a 2 in layer of garden compost, keeping it well clear of the canes.

Raspberries 2

EVER-BEARING RASPBERRY VARIETIES
'Fall Red' From New Hampshire and very hardy. Large, bright red berries of fine flavor and aroma. Ripens very early.
'Heritage' Flavor fair. Berries firm, small to medium, round, conical, light red. Cropping heavy. Requires a warm situation.
'Indian Summer' Soft, crumbly red berries of good flavor. Brilliant red. Abundant producer.
'September' Flavor fair. Berries crumbly, small to medium, conical, dark red. Cropping and vigor moderate.
Yellow autumn-fruiting raspberry
'Fallgold' Sweet, mild flavor. Berries medium to large, golden-yellow, conical. Canes vigorous, prolific.

against winter winds. They are exposed to the sun, which enhances the quality of the fruits and reduces the incidence of fungal disease. The system has the disadvantages that the new canes are at risk of being trampled on during picking and of being damaged by strong winds in July unless temporarily supported by string tied to the lower wires.

Drive in preserved $7\frac{1}{2}$ ft posts 18 in into the ground 12–15 ft apart. Use 14 gauge galvanized fence wire.

Erect the end posts first and strut them and then drive in the intermediate posts. Finally fix the wires to the posts using straining bolts at one end and staples on the intermediates and at the opposite end.

Double fence: parallel wires The double fence is erected in a similar way to the single fence but because the top wires are not as high, the posts are only $6\frac{1}{2}$ ft tall. Cross bars $2\frac{1}{2}$ ft long by 2 in across to carry the parallel wires are fixed to the end posts and to the intermediate posts. In exposed situations, double posts should be used instead of cross bars. Parallel wires are spaced 2 ft apart at 3 ft and 5 ft from the ground. Stretch wire as cross ties every 2 ft along the wires to prevent the canes falling down in the row.

This method has the advantage of enabling a larger number of canes to be trained in and a greater yield to be obtained from much the same area. Picking the fruits from the center is difficult, however, and there is a higher risk of fungal diseases because of the more crowded conditions.

In an exposed garden the untied canes may be damaged on the wires, so the canes should be tied to the wires.

Scandinavian system (training in a low "V")

This is a double fence system with only one set of parallel wires spaced 3 ft apart at 3 ft from the ground.

Drive two sets of posts $4\frac{1}{2}$ ft long 18 in into the ground, 3 ft apart every 12–15 ft in the row.

The fruiting canes are not tied but woven around the wires to form a "V" when viewed from the end of the row. The replacement canes are allowed to grow up the center unsupported.

With this method the fruit is presented at a low picking height and the replacement

canes are safe within the row. However, there is the risk of fungal troubles because of the crowded conditions of the canes on the wires and in the row. If more than one row is planted, space the rows 6 ft apart.

Single post system This is a method particularly suited to a very small garden. It consists of a single post to which each plant is tied. The posts are $7\frac{1}{2}$ ft long by $2\frac{1}{2}$ in top diameter, driven 18 in into the ground.

Initial pruning

In the first two seasons after planting, the number of canes may be few, but thereafter there should be more than enough.

In the second year thin out the weakest canes in the early spring so that the remainder grow more strongly, and pull out unwanted canes growing well away from the row. Allow about 8–10 canes to a plant.

Pruning and training established plants

As soon as fruiting is over, cut down to ground level the old canes which have fruited. Select the healthiest and strongest of the young canes, retaining about four to eight per stool.

If using the single fence system, tie the canes to the wires, 3–4 in apart. Either tie each one separately with a 6 in twist tie or secure them to the wires by continuous lacing using jute or strong string. Tie an occasional knot as a precaution against the string breaking later on.

With the Scandinavian system the canes are laced around a single wire, equally on each side. Gently bend them over at the point they reach the wire and then twist the canes around the wire. No tying is necessary. Do this in late August or early September when the canes are still supple. Depending upon the length of the canes, this could mean four or six canes being twisted around each other and the supporting wires like a rope. The average number of canes from each plant should be about four to six.

For the single post system the fruiting canes are tied to the posts and the replacement canes looped in as and when necessary.

Tipping the canes (This is not applicable to the Scandinavian system). In early spring, about March, cut the canes to a bud 6 in

above the top wire. This removes winter damage to the tips and encourages the lowest buds to break.

For very vigorous varieties grown on the single fence system, where tipping would remove a lot of the cane, loop and tie the canes back on to the top wire and then prune about 6 in off the tips. This method gives extra length of canes, hence more crop, but the top wire must be strong.

Feeding and watering

In early spring each year apply 1 oz of sulfate of potash per square yard. Every third year add 2 oz of superphosphate per square yard. In late March apply sulfate of ammonia at $\frac{1}{2}$ oz per square yard. The fertilizers should be applied as a top dressing covering about 18 in each side of the row.

Also, in late March, mulch with a 2 in layer of garden compost, damp peat or manure, keeping the material just clear of the canes. The mulch helps to conserve moisture in the summer and inhibits weed seeds from germinating.

Throughout the growing season keep down weeds and unwanted suckers by shallow hoeing. Be careful not to damage or disturb the roots of the raspberries. If preferred, herbicides can be used (see page 171).

In dry weather water the raspberries regularly but, to minimize the risk of fungal troubles, keep the water off the canes.

Protect the fruit from birds with netting.

Propagation

Raspberries are easily propagated by forking up surplus canes with as many roots as possible in early spring. The canes must be healthy and strong. Virus-infected plants should be dug up and burned.

Harvesting

Pick the fruits without the stalk and core, unless the raspberries are required for showing, when they are harvested with the stalk attached, using scissors. Picking of standard varieties continues for about a month. In general, pick raspberries when they are fresh, if possible, for better flavor. Use shallow containers to prevent the fruits from crushing each other.

SUPPORT SYSTEMS

Single post system

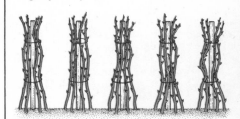

Drive $7\frac{1}{2}$ ft long $2\frac{1}{2}$ in dia. posts 18 in into the ground at each planting station.

Single fence system

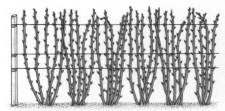

Drive $7\frac{1}{2}$ ft posts 18 in into the ground at 12–15 ft intervals. Stretch 14 gauge galvanized wires between the posts at $2\frac{1}{2}$, $3\frac{1}{2}$ and $5\frac{1}{2}$ ft.

Double fence system

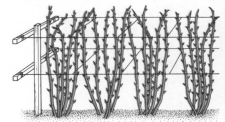

Drive $6\frac{1}{2}$ ft posts 18 in into the ground 12–15 ft apart. Fix 2 in dia. cross bars $2\frac{1}{2}$ ft long to the end posts and to each intermediate post. Then, stretch parallel wires 2 ft apart between the posts at 3 ft and 5 ft from the ground. Stretch wires as cross ties every 2 ft along the wires.

Raspberries 3

Pests and diseases

If aphids are present, spray with dimethoate, formothion or malathion in spring. An oil spray in winter gets rid of the over-wintering eggs. To prevent raspberry beetle grubs feeding on the fruits in summer, spray at dusk with malathion or derris when the first pink berry is seen.

The most serious diseases of raspberries are viruses, which cause the leaves to become mottled or blotched and the canes to be stunted. Seek expert advice before destroying canes because the symptoms are similar to those caused by raspberry leaf mite and bud mite. New canes should be planted elsewhere.

Canes affected by cane blight in summer will wilt, snap off easily and die. If fruiting spurs become blighted, cut out and burn affected canes. Spray new canes with bordeaux mixture.

Cut out and burn canes badly affected by cane spot and prevent it by spraying with liquid copper or thiram at bud burst and pre-blossom time, or with benomyl every two weeks from bud burst to petal fall.

Spur blight causes dark purple blotches around the buds and shoots wither in early spring. Cut out and burn affected canes. Spray new canes when they are a few inches high with benomyl, thiram or captan repeating two, four and six weeks later.

Prevent gray mold (*Botrytis*) on ripening fruit by spraying three times with benomyl at flowering and at two week intervals. Remove and destroy infected fruits.

Selecting healthy plants

It is important to buy only certified stock, wherever possible, to ensure the plants are virus-free and healthy. Healthy plants should last at least ten years before starting to degenerate from virus infection. When this occurs, remove the plants and start a new row in soil that has not grown raspberries or other *Rubus* species before. Alternatively, re-soil over an area 2 ft wide by 1 ft deep.

EVER-BEARING RASPBERRIES

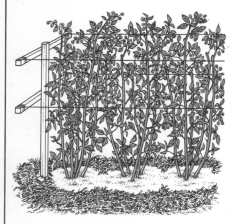

Ever-bearing raspberries bear their fruit on the top part of the current season's canes, extending back from the top over 12 in or more, depending upon the variety. The fruits ripen in early summer a little ahead of standard varieties and again from the beginning of September until stopped by the fall frosts. Ever-bearing raspberries should be picked as soon as ripe and, if necessary, every day. The fall crops can be quite heavy.

The cultural requirements (soil preparation, planting, spacing, initial pruning and feeding) are the same as for the summer-bearing kind. Use the parallel wire method of support described on page 97. The fruits are produced when the weather is becoming cooler, so they are best planted in the sunniest position possible, otherwise too few raspberries may ripen before the first frosts arrive.

Pruning established plants Such ever-bearers do not produce a large spring crop. It is better to grow them for fall use only and to put in standard varieties for summer use. Each February cut down all canes in the row to ground level. In the following spring, new canes are produced which crop in the fall. As the canes are not in the row for more than a year, it is not necessary to thin them unless they are particularly crowded. Pull out any which are growing away from the row.

The first year

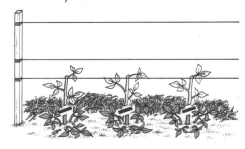

1 In spring, when the new canes appear, cut down the old stumps to ground level.

2 In June to September, as new canes develop, tie them 4 in apart on to the wires.

Second and subsequent years

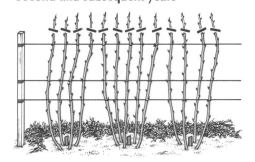

3 In March, cut the canes to a bud 6 in above the top wire. Mulch the plants.

4 In midsummer, fruit is carried on laterals from last year's canes. Thin out the weakest new growth to leave strong canes 4 in apart. Pull out new shoots growing away from the row.

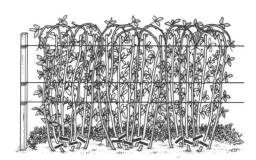

5 When fruiting is over, cut the fruited canes down to ground level. Tie in new canes 4 in apart. If growth is vigorous loop the new canes over to form a series of arches.

6 Each year in early spring, apply 1 oz of sulfate of potash per square yard as a top dressing 18 in each side of the row. Every third year apply 2 oz superphosphate per square yard.

Blackberries 1

The blackberry is a rambling cane fruit found growing wild in many milder parts of the United States. The canes are of arching habit, thick, strong and often aggressively thorned, although there are good thornless cultivated varieties. The plants are usually deciduous, but not always so in mild winters. They grow in zones 5–8.

A good average yield from a well-established blackberry plant is 10–30 lb of fruit, depending upon the size of the plant and the variety.

Cultivation

Cultivated blackberries are much larger and more luscious than wild varieties. They need little preventive spraying and can be planted in a spare corner of the garden to which their wide-spreading roots should be confined.

Soil and situation Blackberries grow in a wide range of soils and will tolerate slightly impeded drainage. If thin dry soils cannot be avoided, improve their moisture retentiveness and fertility with bulky organics.

Blackberries flower relatively late, from May onwards, and bloom over a long period, and so frost is seldom a problem. They are among the few fruits that can be successfully grown in a frost pocket, although this should be avoided if possible. They will also tolerate partial shade but fare better in full sun. Because of their rambling habit, they need some support.

Planting Prepare the ground in the fall. Fork out perennial weeds. Then, if the ground is poor, apply a 2–3 in deep layer of well-rotted manure, compost or peat over an area 2–2½ ft square at each planting site and dig it in thoroughly. Rake in 3 oz of a balanced fertilizer such as 10-10-10 over the same area.

Plant while dormant in early spring. Young plants, in the form of rooted tips or one-year-old bedded tips, can be obtained from a nursery. Using a hand trowel or fork, dig a hole wide and deep enough to take the roots spread out well. Plant the canes to the nursery depth. After planting, firm the soil and then cut down each cane to a bud at about 10 in above the ground.

Spacing Plant the canes 4 ft apart in rows 6 ft apart. One plant is often sufficient.

Support Support is generally necessary to keep the canes off the ground for easy picking and to keep the plants tidy. Individual plants can either be tied to sturdy stakes, or a wire fence trellis can be erected with wires every 12 in between 3 and 6 ft. Erect the wires before planting the canes.

Training The fruiting canes should be trained to keep them separate from the young replacement canes to facilitate picking and to reduce the risk of the spread of fungal diseases from the old to the new.

The three methods commonly used are the fan, weaving, and rope system trained one way. The fan is best reserved for less vigorous berries. The weaving system takes full advantage of the long canes of vigorous kinds but there is much handling at pruning time. The one-way system keeps handling to a minimum, but wastes space because young rods are trained along the wires only to one side of the plant. These fruit the following year. When new rods appear they are trained in the opposite direction.

Initial pruning In the first summer after planting, a number of young canes should spring up from the root system. Tie these securely to the lower wires in a weaving fashion. In the second summer these canes should flower and fruit. At the same time new growth springs from the base of the plant. This young growth should be secured and trained in the adopted method.

When fruiting is over, untie the old canes and cut them down to ground level. With the fan and weaving systems the young canes are then trained in to take their place. With the one-way system, the young canes are already tied in. The young growth will fruit in the next year, and so the cycle is repeated.

Subsequent pruning Pruning in the third and subsequent years consists of cutting out the canes that have fruited and replacing them with the new canes. If the replacement canes are few, the best of the old canes can be used again, but the older growth does not yield the best quality berries. Each April cut back any winter-damaged tips to a healthy bud.

Feeding and watering In early spring apply 2 oz of a balanced fertilizer such as 10-10-10 as a top dressing over one square yard around the base of each plant.

A little later, mulch with a 2 in layer of garden compost, peat or manure, keeping the material just clear of the canes. In dry weather water the plants but, to minimize the risk of fungal troubles, avoid the canes.

Pollination

All varieties are self-compatible and only one plant is needed.

Harvesting

Blackberries are ready for picking when they are black, plump and sweet. Some varieties turn black before they are fully ripe. Pick all fruit when it is ripe even if not required, because this helps the later fruit to achieve a good size.

Pests and diseases

Blackberries are prone to the same pests and diseases as raspberries (see page 98).

OTHER BERRIES

Boysenberries, dewberries, loganberries and youngberries are all closely related to the blackberry and red raspberry, but generally grow much larger and are of trailing habit. They grow only in warm climates, usually to zone 8, but sometimes to zone 7. All are available in thorny and thornless varieties.

Boysenberries have very large reddish-black fruits with a dusty bloom. They are soft, tartly sweet and have a delicious aroma.

Loganberries have light reddish fruits covered with fine hairs. They are tarter than boysenberries.

Youngberries are very similar to boysenberries, but the fruits are shiny and a little sweeter.

Dewberries are somewhat hardier and have sweet black berries sometimes measuring 1½ in long. They ripen a week or so earlier than blackberries. 'Lucretia' is generally considered the best variety.

Culture

All of these plants have the same requirements as blackberries. Because the canes run to great length, they should be trained on a trellis. Cut out those that have fruited after harvest in August. Cut back new canes, growing on the trellis, to 6–8 ft and remove all but 12–16 of the canes. Early the following spring, cut the laterals to 1 ft.

In areas where the plants are marginally hardy, remove the canes from the trellis in the fall and cover with straw. This should be some protection from frost.

PROPAGATION

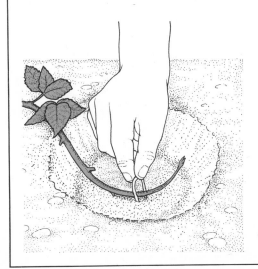

Blackberries (like black raspberries) are propagated by tip-rooting. The new canes are tip-rooted in August and September. A 6 in hole is dug with a trowel near the plant, and the tip of a young cane is bent down into it. The soil is then replaced and firmed. As new canes are produced, more tips can be buried. In the following spring, the rooted tips are severed from the parent plant with about 10 in of stem, and then dug up and planted out in a new position. A few varieties produce suckers, which should be lifted with as much root as possible and planted out in the new bed.

Another method is by leaf bud cuttings taken in July and August and rooted in a cold frame. This method is useful for rapid propagation when stock is limited, and when there are other growing restrictions.

Blackberries 2

Cultivation

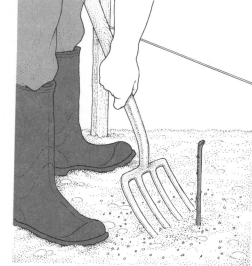

1 In fall, clear the ground of perennial weeds. If the ground is poor, dig in a 2–3 in layer of well-rotted manure over an area 2–2½ ft square. Fork in 2 oz of balanced fertilizer over the same area.

2 In early spring, dig a hole to take the plant with the roots spread out well. Plant to the same depth as it was at the nursery. Firm the soil and cut the cane to a bud 10 in above the ground.

3 Fork in 3 oz of a balanced fertilizer such as 10-10-10 per square yard around the base of each plant.

4 Later, apply a 2 in layer of garden compost keeping it just clear of the canes. During dry weather, water the plants but keep the water off the canes.

Weaving system

The second year

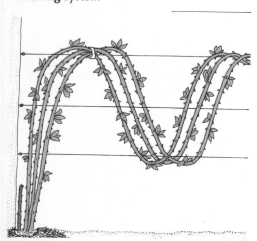

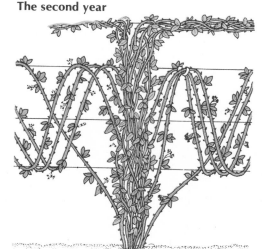

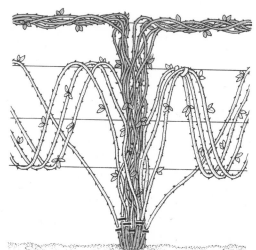

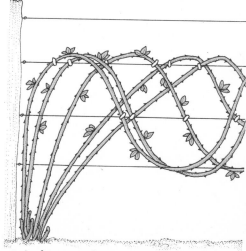

1 In summer, as the young canes appear, tie them to a strong wire support. Weave them in and out of the bottom three wires.

2 In summer, train the new canes up through the center of the bush and along the top wire. Fruit is carried on laterals of last year's canes.

3 After fruiting, cut out all fruited canes to base. If there are few new canes, retain the best of the old.

4 At the same time, untie the current season's canes and weave them round the lower three wires. In fall, remove the weak tips from the young canes.

Black currants 1

BLACK CURRANTS

EARLY
'Boskoop Giant' Juicy, moderately sweet, good flavor. A thin, rather tender skin. Berries very large. Cropping heavy. Bush very vigorous and slightly spreading. Susceptible to leaf spot.

'Blackdown' Sweet flavor. Berries firm, medium to large. Cropping good. Bush medium to large, rather spreading. Very resistant to American gooseberry mildew.

MID-SEASON
'Wellington XXX' Sweet, good flavor. Berries medium to large. A tough skin. A heavy cropper. Growth vigorous and spreading and needs careful pruning to keep upright. Sensitive to lime sulfur.
'Blacksmith' Good flavor. Skin rather thin and tender. Berries large. Cropping heavy. Bush vigorous, large and

spreading. Not suitable for the small garden.
'Ben Lomond' Flavor good, acid. Berries large, cropping very heavy. Bush upright and compact, spreads a little under the weight of the crop. Flowers late and has some resistance to frost. Carries a good resistance to American gooseberry mildew.

The black currant (*Ribes nigrum*) is a native of central and eastern Europe from Scandinavia to Bulgaria, also northern and central Asia to the Himalayas. It can be found growing wild, generally in damp woody places.

Selection in cultivation has given rise to stronger-growing and highly productive varieties. Black currants are grown on a stool system—that is, many shoots spring from below the ground rather than from a single stem. A well-grown black currant bush may reach 5–6 ft in height and spread and should last 15 years or more before it needs to be replaced. A good average yield from an established black currant is about 10–12 lb.

Cultivation

The black currant is an alternate host for white pine blister rust, a serious pest that kills those trees. Many of the states in which white pine grows forbid the planting of black currants because of the adverse effect on white pine.

Therefore, any gardener considering planting such fruit should first check with the state agricultural extension service or forestry department before ordering. Some nurseries will be able to advise if restrictions exist.

The black currant is the worst of the several alternate host plants of white pine blister rust. Consequently, black currants are difficult to find in American nurseries and only one variety, 'Boskoop Giant', is commonly offered by those nurseries that sell black currants.

Soil and situation Black currants can be grown in a wide range of soils. Ideally it should be slightly acid (about pH 6.5), highly fertile, moisture-retentive and well-drained, although black currants will tolerate slightly impeded drainage. Light soils need plenty of bulky organics. Excessively acid soils should be limed to bring the pH up to 6.5.

The site should be frost-free and sheltered from strong winds so that pollinating insects such as bees are not inhibited. Most varieties bloom early in the spring and the flowers are extremely vulnerable to frost. In frost-prone areas, plant late-flowering or more frost-tolerant varieties and cover the plants on frosty nights. Black currants will tolerate partial shade but prefer a sunny position.

Preparing the soil Prepare the ground in early fall, clearing away all weeds. Apply a 3 in layer of manure or compost over the whole area. If manure and compost are not available, apply a 2 in layer of peat with bonemeal at 3 oz per square yard. If the ground is fairly clean single dig the materials in, but if rough and weedy double dig the area. Rake in a balanced fertilizer such as 10-10-10 at the rate of 3 oz per square yard.

Planting and spacing Buy two-year-old certified bushes. Select plants with not less than three strong shoots.

Plant during dormancy in early spring. Space bushes 5 ft apart in the row (6 ft apart for more vigorous varieties), with 6 ft between rows.

Dig out a hole wide enough to take the roots spread out well. To encourage a strong stool system plant bushes about 2 in deeper than they were in the nursery—the soil mark on the stems gives an indication. Fill in the hole and firm.

Initial pruning After planting, cut all shoots to within 2 in of soil level. This encourages the production of strong young shoots from the base, and creates a good stool system for heavy cropping in the future, although it means foregoing a crop in the first summer. If the plants are certified free of disease, the pruned shoots may be used as cuttings. They root easily, so buy only half the number of bushes required and fill the vacant positions with two to three cuttings to each station.

After the hard initial pruning the young bush should produce three or four strong shoots from the base, each shoot being 18 in or more in length. If growth is poor, they should be cut down again in the winter. Assuming a strong bush has been formed, no pruning is required at the end of the first year; the young shoots are left to fruit in the following summer.

Pruning an established bush Black currants bear the best fruit on the wood produced in the previous summer, although they also crop on the older wood. Prune in early fall or at any time in the dormant season until early April.

The objective with an established bush is to stimulate a constant succession of strong young shoots to carry fruit in the next season

by fairly hard-pruning, cutting at or as near the base as possible, and by heavy feeding.

It is important to be able to distinguish the young wood from the old. This is fairly easy because the bark of the young shoots is much lighter in color than that of three years old or more.

There is no need to limit the number of main branches nor to have the center open. However, about a quarter to a third of the oldest wood should be removed annually. Cut back to a strong young shoot at or near the base or, if there is none, cut out the branch altogether.

Remove any thin mildewed shoots including those suffering from die-back in the center. Leave a working space between one bush and the next.

Feeding and watering Black currants thrive on heavy manuring and high summer moisture. Each March apply a balanced fertilizer such as 10-10-10 over the whole plantation at 3 oz per square yard. Additionally, in April apply sulfate of ammonia at 1 oz per square yard; on acid soils apply an artificial fertilizer containing calcium carbonate and ammonium nitrate. Follow this with a 3 in thick mulch of manure or compost around each bush.

In dry weather apply $4\frac{1}{2}$ gal of water per square yard every ten days, but keep the water off the stems as much as possible to lessen the risk of fungal trouble.

Weed control The bushes are shallow-rooted. Do not dig around the plant but keep the weeds down by shallow hoeing or by hand weeding or by using herbicides.

Pollination

Black currants are self-compatible and are pollinated mainly by bees.

Frost and bird protection

The flowers are extremely vulnerable to spring frosts which cause the fruitlets to drop. On nights when frosts are likely, drape the bushes with burlap or a few layers of bird netting (see page 92); remove the cover in the mornings. Net the fruits against birds when the first fruits begin to color.

Harvesting

Pick selectively when the currants ripen but

before they begin to fall or shrivel.

Pests and diseases

The most serious pests of black currants are aphids, the black currant gall mite, and red spider mite. Use a systemic insecticide against aphids, benomyl for gall mite, and malathion, dimethoate or derris to control red spider mite.

Of the diseases, the most troublesome are reversion disease, gooseberry mildew, leaf spot and botrytis. Bushes affected by reversion should be dug up and burned. Mildew can be controlled by regular spraying with benomyl; this will also control leaf spot. Alternative fungicides are zineb or thiram. For botrytis use benomyl at flowering time.

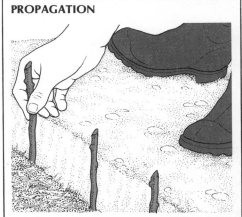

PROPAGATION

Black currants are propagated from cuttings 8–10 in long and about a pencil's width thick, from well-budded healthy wood of the current year's growth. Take the cuttings in October or November. Make a sloping cut just above a bud at the top and a straight cut just below a bud at the base. Insert the cuttings deeply with only two buds showing above the surface in well-drained light soil. Space the cuttings 6 in apart and firm them in the row.

At the end of the first growing season dig up and plant the rooted cuttings 12 in apart. Cut them down to within 1 in of the ground. This hard pruning should create a stooled bush.

Black currants 2

LATE
'Baldwin' (Hilltop strain). The most widely grown variety. Acid flavor, rich in vitamin C. Tough skin. Berries medium and hang well without splitting over a long period. Cropping moderate to good. Bush of medium vigor, fairly compact. Suitable for the small garden.
'Jet' Flavor good, acid. Berries firm, small to medium. Trusses extremely long, hang well, easy to pick. Cropping very heavy. Bush large and vigorous. Flowers very late. Carries some resistance to gooseberry mildew.

1 In early spring, clear the ground of weeds. Dig in a 3 in layer of manure or compost. Rake in a balanced fertilizer such as 10-10-10 at 3 oz per square yard.

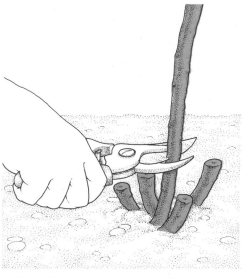

2 Dig a hole wide and deep enough to take the roots spread out well. Plant the bush 2 in deeper than it was at the nursery. Fill in the hole and firm the soil.

3 After planting, cut down all shoots to within 2 in of soil level.

The second year

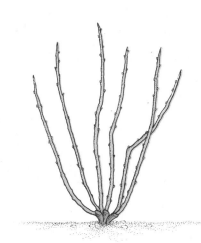

4 In the fall, the severe pruning has resulted in strong new shoots appearing from the base. These will fruit the following year. No pruning is required.

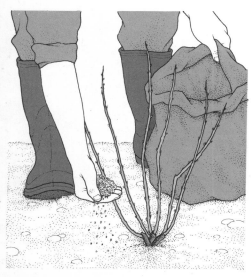

5 In March, apply a balanced fertilizer such as 10-10-10 at 3 oz per square yard. A month later, apply 1 oz sulfate of ammonia per square yard.

6 In July, the bush fruits best on last year's wood. New basal growths develop.

The third year

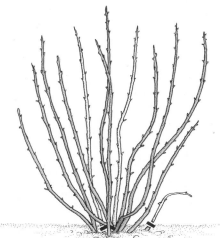

7 In winter, thin out weak shoots and any branches that are too low, broken or mildewed.

In subsequent years

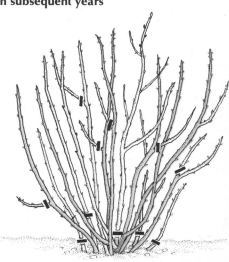

8 Every winter, remove about one-third of the bush. Cut out badly-placed, damaged wood. Cut back fruited branches to a strong shoot.

Red and white currants 1

RED AND WHITE CURRANT VARIETIES
'Cascade' Popular old variety with red, rather mild-flavored fruits in compact clusters. Early.
'Perfection' Reasonably productive, somewhat spreading plants with large bright crimson berries in mid-season.
'Red Lake' Vigorous, upright plant with big, light red berries in large clusters.

Fruits remain on the plant long after ripening.
'White Imperial' Choice white-fruited variety. Medium-size berries. Clusters are not always well filled.
'Wilder' Dependable, mid-season currant with big, dark red berries of good quality in mid-season. Vigorous, productive, upright plant.

'Viking' Late red fruits in sizeable quantities. May be immune to rust.

Red and white currants are basically derived from two European species, *Ribes rubrum* and *R. spicatum*. Red currants sometimes occur as garden escapes from bird-sown seed and *R. rubrum* is also found naturalized in many areas.

Cultivation

The fruit buds are produced in clusters at the base of the one-year-old shoots and on short spurs on the older wood. Because of this fruiting habit there is a permanent framework of branches, unlike the black currant for which a succession of young wood is needed.

The red currant is usually grown as an open-centered bush on a 4–6 in stem or leg, rather like a miniature apple tree, with a height and spread of about 5–6 ft. This method of growth makes cultivation around the plant easier and keeps the fruit clear of the ground. The red currant is also grown as a single or multiple cordon, and, more rarely, as a standard or fan. A well-grown bush should yield at least 8–10 lb of fruit and a single cordon about 2–3 lb. Plants should bear well for at least ten years.

The smooth-skinned, glistening red berries are attractive and ideal for jelly, pies, juice and for wine making.

Red and white currants are, like black currants, alternate hosts to white pine blister rust, and so have planting restrictions in many states. The state agricultural extension service or forestry department should be consulted before ordering.

The white currant is a mutation or sport of the red currant and for cultural purposes is treated in exactly the same way. The berries, of somewhat milder flavor than the red, are also useful for jelly and for wine making.

Soil and situation Ideally, the soil should be neutral to slightly acid (about pH 6.7). Red and white currants are less tolerant of poor drainage than the black currant but, provided the soil is reasonably well drained and not deficient in potash, they are tolerant of a wide range of conditions.

The flowers of the red and white currants are hardier than those of the black currant, so it is a useful plant for north-facing walls and fences and for shaded areas, provided the soil is not dry and over-hanging trees do not drip on the plants. They grow in zones 3–8. A sunny position is best if the berries are to acquire their full flavor. The site should be sheltered but not a frost pocket.

Soil preparation Prepare the soil in the fall or late winter by clearing away all weeds. Apply a light dressing of well-rotted manure or compost about 1½ in thick over the whole area. If farmyard manure or compost are not available, apply a 1 in layer of damp peat. If the ground is fairly clean, single dig the dressing in; but if weedy, double dig the area. Rake in a balanced fertilizer, such as 10-10-10, at the rate of 2 oz per square yard and sulfate of potash at ½ oz per yard.

Selection of plants Buy plants from a reliable source because certified stock is not available. One- or two-year-old bushes are usually supplied by the grower. Select a plant with a clear stem, or leg, of about 4–6 in with a head of about 3–6 evenly balanced shoots. The single (or multiple) cordon may be two or three years old and should consist of one (or more) straight stems with sideshoots.

Planting and spacing Plant during the dormant season in March or April, unless the plants are container-grown, when they can be planted at any time.

Space bushes 5 ft × 5 ft (5 ft × 6 ft on fertile land) and single cordons 15 in apart, or 12 in apart on light soils. Allow 12 in between each stem of a multiple cordon; for example, double cordons should be planted 24 in apart from the main stem at ground level. Cordons should be trained up a vertical cane for straight growth and support. If planting cordons in the open, before planting erect a wire fence with horizontal wires at 2 ft and 4 ft and tie canes to the wires at each planting station.

Next, take out a hole large enough to contain the roots well spread out, and plant the bush or cordon to the same depth as it was in the nursery. Fill in and firm the soil.

Feeding and watering Each March apply a balanced fertilizer, such as 10-10-10, over the whole planting at 2 oz per square yard and sulfate of potash at ½ oz per square yard. On light soils also apply a mulch of rotted manure, compost or peat 2 in thick around each bush. If manure, compost or peat are not available, apply sulfate of ammonia at 1 oz per square yard. Water copiously in dry weather.

1 In late winter, dig in a 1½ in layer of well-rotted manure. Then, rake in a balanced fertilizer, such as 10-10-10, at 2 oz per square yard and sulfate of potash at ½ oz per square yard.

2 In early spring, dig a hole large enough to take the roots well spread out and plant the bush to the same depth as it was at the nursery. Delay planting if the ground is very wet or frozen.

3 Each March, apply 10-10-10 at 2 oz per square yard and sulfate of potash at ½ oz per square yard. On light soils also apply a 2 in mulch of rotted manure, compost or peat around each bush.

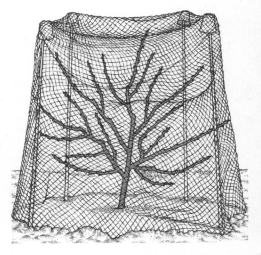

4 During the winter, protect the fruit buds with netting against attack by birds and frost at blossom time. Remove it during the day at flowering time.

Red and white currants 2

Pruning bush currants

The objective is to create a goblet-shaped bush with about 8–10 main branches growing upwards and outwards on a 4–6 in clear stem with an open center. Prune in the same way as the gooseberry bush (see pages 105–106) except that the leaders are pruned to outward-facing buds, unless the branches are drooping, when they are pruned to upward-facing buds.

Pruning the single cordon: initial pruning

On planting a one-year-old rooted cutting, shorten the central leader by about one-half to an outward-facing bud. Cut back all other laterals to about 1 in at a bud, and remove any buds lower than 4 in to create a short clear stem. If planting an older pre-shaped cordon, shorten the leader by one-third and prune maiden laterals to one bud.

In late June to early July cut back the current season's side-shoots to 4–5 leaves. Tie the leader to the cane as and when necessary throughout the growing season, but do not prune it.

Second and subsequent years A cordon is pruned in much the same way as a bush. Each summer at the end of June or early in July prune the current season's side-shoots to 4–5 leaves. Do not carry out summer pruning earlier than this or secondary growth may be stimulated. The leader is trained and tied to the cane, but not pruned in the summer until it has reached the required height, usually about 5–6 ft. From then on it is summer-pruned to 4–5 leaves.

Each winter, cut all the previously summer-pruned laterals to about 1 in at a bud. Prune the leader to a bud leaving 6 in of new growth. Once the leader has reached the required height, it is also pruned to leave one bud of the previous summer's growth. This helps to maintain the cordon at approximately the same height for some years.

Multiple cordons, such as the double- and triple-stemmed cordon, are pruned in exactly the same way as the single, except that in the early formative years suitably low placed laterals are used to form the main stems of each goblet-shaped bush.

Weed control

Red and white currants are shallow rooted. Do not dig around the plants but keep the weeds down by shallow hoeing or by using herbicides.

Pollination

Red currants are self-fertile and insect pollinated, so pollination is not a problem.

Frost and bird protection

Red and white currant flowers are fairly hardy, although they will not tolerate hard frosts. Cover them with burlap or two or three layers of bird netting on frosty nights.

The berries are extremely attractive to birds in the summer, as are the fruit buds in the winter. Net the bushes in the winter and at fruit ripening time. Remove the netting at flowering time, because it inhibits insect pollination.

Harvesting

Red and white currants are ripe in July or August and should be picked as soon as they are clear in color. Pick whole clusters to avoid injury to the delicate fruit.

Propagation

Propagate new red and white currant plants in the fall from hardwood cuttings, which should be 12 in long or more. Before planting the cuttings, remove all the buds except the top three or four. Insert into the soil with the third bud within 2 in of the soil surface and label the cuttings. After they have rooted (in about a year's time) plant out the cuttings. This method produces rooted cuttings with four good branches and a short leg.

Pests and diseases

The most serious pests are aphids and, to a lesser extent, sawflies and currant fruit flies. Control aphids with a systemic insecticide rotenone.

Occasionally anthracnose and cane blight can be troublesome. Early season sprays of ferbam give satisfactory control of anthracnose. If the canes are blighted, cut back to healthy wood and burn the prunings.

The first year: Cordon

1 In winter, when planting a one-year-old shorten the central leader by about one-half to an outward-facing bud. Cut back all laterals to 1 in at a bud and remove any lower than 4 in.

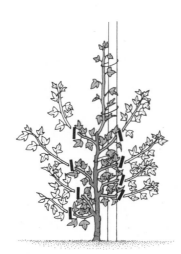

2 From late June to early July, cut back the current season's side-shoots to 4–5 leaves. Tie the leader to the cane as it extends but do not prune it.

Second and subsequent years

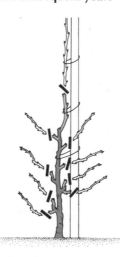

3 In winter, prune the leader to a bud leaving 6 in of new growth. Cut all previously summer-pruned laterals to 1 in at a bud. In later years, cut the leader back to one bud.

4 From late June to early July, prune the current season's side-shoots to 4–5 leaves. Tie the leader to the cane as it extends.

Gooseberries 1

GOOSEBERRIES
'**Chautauqua**' Large, greenish-yellow fruits. Rather early. Planted small, it is inclined to spread.
'**Downing**' Excellent medium-size green berries. Very productive and widely planted.
'**Fredonia**' Large, dark red berries. Late.
'**Glendale**' Dull red, medium fruits.

Large, vigorous plant. One of the best varieties for warmer regions since it withstands heat better than the average variety.
'**Pixwell**' Medium-large red berries. Produces heavily. Plant is less thorny than most gooseberries.

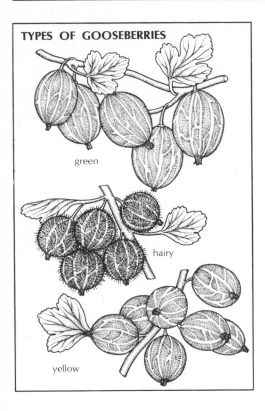

TYPES OF GOOSEBERRIES

green

hairy

yellow

The gooseberry (*Ribes uva-crispa*) is a deciduous thorny shrub growing in zones 3–8.

Like the red currant, the gooseberry bears its fruit on spurs on the older wood and at the base of the previous summer's lateral growth. For this reason it is grown with a permanent framework of branches, usually in the form of an open-centered bush on a short stem, or led, of about 4–6 in. It is also widely grown as a cordon in single or multiple form and occasionally as a standard on a 3½ ft stem or as a fan.

The fruits may be smooth or hairy, yellow, white, green or red according to variety.

A well-grown bush should reach a height and spread of 5 ft and crop well for 12 years or more. A good average yield from a bush is 5–6 lb, and from a cordon 1–2 lb.

Like currants, gooseberries are alternate hosts of white pine blister rust and can be planted only in areas where this disease is not a problem. The local state agricultural extension service or forestry department should be contacted before ordering plants.

Cultivation

One-, two-, or three-year-old bushes can be bought from a grower. A one-year-old bush should have about 3–5 shoots evenly placed around the stem, a two-year-old about 5–7 and a three-year-old 6–8 primary and secondary branches. Gooseberries are self-fertile, so they can be planted singly.

Soil and situation The soil requirements of the gooseberry are similar to those of the red currant. The soil should not be allowed to become potash-deficient. The plant tolerates a little impeded drainage, provided it occurs below 18 in. The ideal soil, however, is a slightly acid (pH 6.7), well-drained medium loam.

The gooseberry is tolerant of cool, partial shade, but grows best in an open sunny site, which should be sheltered against strong winds, especially at flowering time in early April. Do not plant it in a frost pocket.

Soil preparation Prepare the soil in the fall or late winter. It is essential to eliminate perennial weeds because the gooseberry is thorny and not easy to weed around. On light soils, dig in a 1½–2 in layer of well-rotted manure or compost over the whole area. On rich soils there is less need for bulky organics because too much of them encourages soft growth, which is prone to snapping and to mildew. Rake in a balanced fertilizer such as 10-10-10 at 2 oz per square yard and sulfate of potash at ½ oz per square yard.

Planting and spacing Plant during the dormant season in March or April, preferably when the soil is warm.

Dig a hole wide and deep enough to contain the root system with the roots well spread out. Before planting, clean off any suckers at the base of the plants and any shoots too near the ground, then plant it to leave a clear stem of 4–6 in. Fill in the hole and firm the soil.

Space the bushes 5 ft apart, or on highly fertile ground 5 ft by 6 ft apart, and single cordons 1 ft apart. Allow 1 ft space for each stem of a multiple cordon. For straight growth and support, train a cordon up a cane. If growing cordons in the open, erect a wire fence with horizontal wires at 2 ft and 4 ft and tie the canes to it.

Feeding and watering Each March apply a balanced fertilizer such as 10-10-10 over the whole plot at 2 oz per square yard and sulfate of potash at ½ oz per square yard. Mulch around the base of the plant with a 2 in layer of well-rotted manure, compost or peat on light soils, but less on medium or fertile soils. In the absence of bulky organics apply sulfate of ammonia at 1 oz per square yard.

Water copiously in dry weather but do not water irregularly or heavily at the ripening stage because this causes the fruit to split.

The second year

1 Clear the soil of perennial weeds. Rake in a balanced fertilizer such as 10-10-10 at 2 oz per square yard and sulfate of potash at ½ oz per square yard.

2 In early spring, dig a hole wide and deep enough to take the roots spread out well. Plant the bush so that there is a clear stem of 4–6 in above ground.

3 At the same time, cut back each framework branch by one-half to an inward- and upward-pointing bud. Clean off the suckers at the base and any shoots too near the ground.

4 In winter, shorten the leaders by one-half to inward- and upward-facing buds. Select well-placed shoots to form further permanent branches and cut back by one-half. Remove suckers and low stems.

Gooseberries 2

Formative pruning: Bush

Most varieties have a tendency to form drooping growth and, in order to maintain an erect bush, counteract this habit by pruning the leaders to inward- or upward-facing buds or back to upright laterals. The center of the plant is kept open to make picking and spraying easier, to ripen the wood and fruits, and to improve air circulation (which lessens the risk of mildew).

When planting a one-year-old bush, cut back each framework branch by one-half to an outward-facing bud if the shoot is upright. Cut back to an inward-facing bud if the shoot is weeping.

The second year (or a two-year-old bush)

In late winter, shorten the leaders by one-half. Select well-placed shoots to form further permanent branches and cut back by one-half. Remove any suckers or low-growing shoots growing from the stem.

The third year (or a three-year-old bush)

The bush should have developed a main framework of about 6–8 branches with well-spaced leading shoots; it is at the start of its cropping life. In winter, shorten the leaders by one-half to a bud facing in the required growth direction. Cut out shoots crowding the center and shorten those not required

for the framework to about 2 in. Thereafter, prune the bush both in the summer and in the winter.

Pruning an established bush

Each summer, in late June to early July, prune all laterals (that is, the current season's growth) back to five leaves. This opens up the bush and removes any mildew and aphids at the tips of the shoots. Do not prune gooseberries earlier because this might induce secondary growth. Do not prune the leaders unless they are affected by aphids or mildew.

Each winter, cut back the leaders by one-half to a bud facing in the required direction. If the branch is weeping badly and there is a suitably placed upright lateral on it, then cut back to this.

Next deal with the laterals that were pruned the previous summer. Where smaller quantities of large high-quality dessert fruits are required, cut all of these laterals back to about two buds. Where a large amount of fruit is required, pruning should be moderated accordingly. Vigorous varieties should be pruned less severely because this could encourage excessive growth. Cut out dead and diseased wood, and any growth crowding the center of the bush.

As the bushes become older and branches less productive or too spreading, leave in some suitably placed strong, young shoots to replace the old which are then cut out.

The third year

Pruning a single cordon Prune in the same way as the red currant cordon (see page 104).

Weed control

As with most bush fruits, the gooseberry is shallow rooted. Keep the weeds down by light hoeing or with herbicides.

Protection against frost and birds

The gooseberry flowers early, during April, and spring frosts can substantially reduce the crop. On frosty nights protect the plants when they are in flower. Cover with burlap or two or three layers of bird netting, but remove it during the day to allow in light and give access for pollinating insects.

The fruit buds are attractive to bullfinches and sparrows in the winter and the ripening fruits to blackbirds and thrushes in the summer. Net the bushes in the winter and when the fruits begin to ripen. For further information on netting against birds, see under separate headings (page 92).

Thinning and harvesting the fruits

For large dessert fruits start thinning the fruits in June, removing every other one, and use the thinnings for cooking.

For small or medium dessert fruits, do not thin the fruits but leave them to ripen and develop their full flavor. Pick gooseberries for cooking when they are a good size, but still green, from late June.

Propagation

Propagate gooseberries using 12 in hardwood cuttings taken from healthy shoots in late September. First remove the weak tip and all but four buds from the upper part of the cutting. This produces a miniature, open-centered bush on a short leg. Dip the base of the cuttings in a hormone rooting powder. Insert the cuttings in the open ground with their lowest buds 2 in above the soil surface. Leave the cuttings in the nursery bed for the growing season. Lift and replant, exposing more of the stem.

Pests and diseases

The pests and diseases that plague the gooseberry are similar to those that attack the currants. For example, aphids and anthracnose (see page 104).

The third year

5 In winter, shorten the leaders by one-half to a bud facing in the required growth direction. Cut out shoots crowding the center. Shorten laterals not required for the framework to about 2 in.

6 When the fruits are large enough for cooking, thin the fruits by removing every other one. Cover the bush with burlap or bird netting to protect the fruits from birds.

The established bush

1 In late June to early July, prune all the laterals produced that season to five leaves. This opens up the bush and removes aphids at the tips of the shoots. Do not prune the leaders.

2 In winter, cut back the leaders by one-half. Cut back laterals pruned in the previous summer to about two buds. Cut out diseased and dead wood and growth that crowds the center.

Heathland fruits 1

BLUEBERRIES
The following varieties are derived from *Vaccinium corymbosum*. They will set fruit with their own pollen but for maximum crops at least two varieties should be planted together.
'Berkeley' Very large, light blue berries of good flavor. Medium vigor.
'Bluecrop' Fast-growing variety with big clusters of large, light blue berries. A consistently heavy cropper of good quality. Bush upright, then spreading. Vigorous.
'Earliblue' Similar to 'Bluecrop' but the berries ripen earlier.

There are numerous closely related blueberry-like shrubs growing wild in the United States. They are known as bilberries, blueberries, deerberries, farkleberries, and huckleberries. Almost all belong to the genus *Vaccinium*, but huckleberries have the botanical name of *gaylussacia*. The most important of such berries are the low-bush blueberries, but even those are seldom cultivated in the accepted sense.

However, where they are the dominant plant (blueberry barrens), they are often managed commercially by burning over every two to three years in winter. This eliminates weed growth from the base. They are not cultivated because they provide less fruit and much smaller (but generally tastier) fruit than the taller high bush varieties.

They are, however, easy to cultivate, requiring almost the same conditions as the high bush blueberries. They tolerate drier soils and need full sun for good crops. Low-bush blueberries grow in zones 3–5.

They are best planted 12–15 in apart each way in beds 3 ft wide with access paths in between. Feeding is the same as for high bush blueberries.

Pruning as such is not necessary, but in the second or third year cut back hard half the plants to promote young, vigorous stems. One or two years later the other half is cut back. Thereafter the plants are treated regularly in this way. Harvesting and storing is as for high bush blueberries. Pests and diseases are not a problem.

High bush blueberries

The principal species of high bush blueberry is *Vaccinium corymbosum*. It forms bushes to about 12 ft in height with narrow oval leaves about 2 in long and white, sometimes pink-tinted flowers in dense clusters. The fruits are $\frac{1}{2}$ in wide. The blueberry is a decorative shrub, especially in the fall when the leaves turn red, and it can be grown as an ornamental with rhododendrons and other acid soil shrubs.

In the deep South, where *V. corymbosum* does not grow, cultivated blueberries have been developed from the native species, *V. virgatum*. These are known as rabbiteye blueberries and grow to 15 ft, but are otherwise similar to *V. corymbosum*.

Soil and situation Blueberries require moist but well-drained acid soil with a pH of 4.0–5.5 If the pH is much above the upper limit, chlorosis occurs and the plants may die. Suitably acid sandy or clay soils should be liberally enriched with peat moss or oak or pine leaf-mold at not less than one large bucketful per square yard.

As with most members of the heather and rhododendron family (Ericaceae), blueberries rely upon an association with a fungus for their existence. The fungus thrives where organic matter is abundant, so it is important to apply plenty of peat or acid leaf-mold to the soil. If the soil is thin and sandy, apply the organic material to the whole site. For most soils, it is usually sufficient to dig out 1 ft square holes at each planting station and till these with an equal mixture of peat and soil, or leaf-mold and soil.

Include some coarse sand if the surrounding soil is heavy. Dried blood at 2 oz per hole may also be added if the soil is poor. Alternatively, apply sulfate of ammonia to the soil surface at $\frac{1}{2}$ oz per hole after planting. It is also possible to grow bushes in large pots or tubs.

The site may be in sun or slight shade and should be sheltered from strong winds. Blueberries derived from *V. corymbosum* are hardy and grow in zones 5–7, but do not thrive if the temperature falls regularly below −28°C/−18°F. A frost-free growing season of at least five months is needed and ideally a warm summer with plenty of rain. Rabbiteye varieties grow in zones 7–9.

Planting Two- to three-year-old plants are usually available in containers. In fall or spring set out the plants 5 ft apart in rows 6 ft apart. If the plants are pot-grown, gently knock them out of their containers and carefully spread out the perimeter roots without breaking up the root ball, fill the planting holes with an equal mixture of peat and compost and firm fairly lightly. Then, using a trowel, make a small hole large enough to take the root ball, set the plant in the middle and firm the soil. Larger plants are planted as described in the Introduction to Soft Fruits (page 92).

Pruning Regular pruning is not essential. If young plants fail to branch naturally, in spring cut back the longest stems by about one-third. After the third year, bushes that are becoming dense should be thinned, removing the oldest, barest stems to ground level or to a low strong side-shoot.

Feeding and watering In spring, apply a dressing of dried blood at 2 oz per square

High bush blueberries

1 Before planting, dig out a 1 ft square hole at each planting station. Fill it with an equal mixture of peat, or leaf-mold, and soil.

2 In spring, plant the bushes 5 ft apart in rows 6 ft apart. With a trowel make a hole large enough to take the root ball. Set the plant in it. Firm the soil.

3 In spring each year, apply a dressing of sulfate of ammonia at 1 oz per square yard. At the same time, mulch with peat, oak leaf-mold, sawdust, or chopped bark.

The established bush

4 In late winter, cut back some of the fruited branches that have become twiggy to a vigorous shoot. Cut close to base any damaged or dead branches.

Heathland fruits 2

'Jersey' A vigorous variety of erect habit bearing large handsome foliage. The large, light blue berries are sweet and of good flavor. Excellent as a dual purpose bush for the shrub border.
'Rancocas' This variety produces a good crop of quality, small fruits over a long harvesting period. Good shapely habit. The following varieties are derived from

Vaccinium virgatum. Two different varieties must be planted.
'Tifblue' Large, bright blue berries of excellent quality. Ripens in mid-season (late May–June).
'Woodward' Very large, medium blue, tasty berries. Mid-season.

yard or sulfate of ammonia at 1 oz per square yard. On poorer soils, every other year in winter apply a general fertilizer, such as 10-10-10, at 2–3 oz per square yard. To maintain the humus content, mulch annually in spring with peat, oak-leaf mold or pine needles to a depth of 1–2 in. Other important sources of humus are composted sawdust and chopped bark.

Blueberries need plenty of moisture in the summer. In dry weather, water them copiously, preferably (although not necessarily) with collected rainwater.

Harvesting and storing
The berries should be picked when they are blue-black with a white waxy bloom and start to soften. They should be eaten fresh within a few days, but if spread thinly on trays and kept in a cool cellar or refrigerator they will last for at least a couple of weeks.

Pests and diseases
Blueberries have few problems that cannot be taken care of with a general-purpose fruit spray. The spray should be used if and when problems arise. Birds, however, are a prime nuisance and once the berries have formed, protection is essential (see page 92).

Cranberries
The common or small cranberry (*Vaccinium oxycoccus* or *Oxycoccus palustris*) has long wiry stems with tiny, narrow, pointed leaves. The small, pink flowers are carried in clusters. The fruits are about $\frac{1}{3}$ in wide, red or pink, sometimes with brown-red spots. Cranberries are sold in the market and are the fruits of *Vaccinium macrocarpum* (*Oxycoccus macrocarpus*). This is a slightly more robust species than the common cranberry with blunt-tipped leaves and much larger fruits. It grows from zone 6 northward.

Cultivation
In the United States, the cranberry crop is of rather minor importance and has developed into a highly specialized form of agriculture including the construction of artificial bogs which can be flooded and drained. It requires moister conditions than the blueberry to thrive and, ideally, a soil of greater acidity.

Despite this, cranberries are easy to grow if the right rooting medium can be provided.
Soil and situation Cranberries need a constantly moist soil of high organic content with a pH of 3.2–4.5. A naturally moist, acid soil is ideal, but if not naturally peaty, fork generous amounts of moss peat into the top 6–9 in. Or, prepare trenches as described in the box opposite. Cranberries should be cultivated in a sunny site.
Planting Plant one- or two-year-old divisions, rooted cuttings or seedlings 12 in apart each way in spring. Any long trailing stems should be partly buried, or held down by sand or small pegs to prevent them from being blown about. Rooting usually occurs along the pegged-down stems.
Pruning and feeding No pruning is required, but any semi-erect wispy stems can be sheared off annually in early spring. Feeding is not usually necessary, but if growth is poor, apply sulfate of ammonia at $\frac{1}{2}$ oz per square yard. Plants in peat-filled trenches benefit from a light dressing of general fertilizer every other year. An old matted bed can be rejuvenated by almost covering it with a layer of fine peat and sand.

Harvesting and storing
See high bush blueberries (see page 107).

Pests and diseases
A malathion spray when the flower buds are swelling and again as the flowers fade provides control of grubs that attack the fruit.

Varieties
Among the vigorous and free-fruiting varieties of *Vaccinium macrocarpum* are 'Early Black', 'Hawes', 'McFarlin', 'Searless Jumbo'. 'Stevens' is a particularly good new variety.
Highbush Cranberry The only similarity this shrub has to the cranberry is its small, acid, red fruit appearing in midsummer. The plant is actually *Viburnum trilobum*—a 10 ft ornamental deciduous shrub with large flower clusters in spring. It is not quite as hardy as the true cranberry.

Plant it in the spring in sun or partial shade and grow like any strictly ornamental viburnum. Fruit production starts when the plant is about three years old. Pick while firm.

PREPARING THE CRANBERRY BED

Where the soil is acid but not naturally moist, dig shallow trenches about 3 ft wide by 9 in deep and line them with heavy-duty polyethylene. Return the soil with peat to the waterproofed trench and lightly firm. Spread and rake in sulfate of ammonia at $\frac{1}{2}$ oz per square yard.

This trench method can be used on alkaline soils, filling in this case with pure peat moss or a mixture with up to half by bulk of coarse washed sand. The same fertilizers should be used.

Before planting, unless the ground is already wet, soak the bed thoroughly. It is best to use rainwater as this is the most natural nourishment.

Cranberries

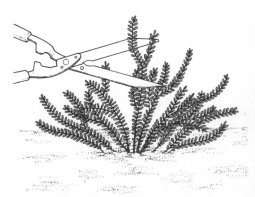

1 In spring, plant the divisions, cuttings or seedlings 12 in apart in the prepared ground. Bury any trailing stems.

2 In early spring, shear off any semi-erect wispy stems. If growth is poor, apply $\frac{1}{2}$ oz sulfate of ammonia per square yard.

Grapes 1

AMERICAN GRAPE VARIETIES
'Beta' Small, black berries. Early. Not good for eating but fine for juice and jelly. Very hardy.
'Brighton' Medium-sized red fruits in medium-size clusters. Mid-season. Self-unfruitful. Hardy.
'Catawba' Medium-size, purple-red fruits of fine flavor. Often made into wine. Late. Hardy.
'Concord' Best known of all large, black-fruited varieties. Delicious flavor. Mid-season. Hardy.
'Delaware' Superb small, red grape. Early. Vines are fairly weak but hardy.
'Extra' Large blue fruits with a flavor typical of the wild post oak grape. Grown in the Southeast.
'Fredonia' Large, black fruits of the 'Concord' type and among the best. Ripens ahead of 'Concord'. Hardy.
'Golden Muscat' Popular yellow-fruited variety ripening late. Large, full clusters. Distinctive muscat flavor.
'Nimrod' Greenish-white, seedless variety similar to the following. Hardy. Not a slipskin.
'Interlaken Seedless' Descended from famous 'Thompson Seedless' grape. Small, greenish-white fruits without slipskins. Mid-season. Hardy.
'Niagara' Delicious white variety with large fruit in large clusters. Strong foxy flavor. Mid-season. Hardy.
'Norton' Recommended for juice. Small blue fruits. Hardy.

The art of growing grapes, or viticulture, has a long and illustrious history. The vine grows wild in the temperate regions of North America, western Asia, southern Europe and parts of North Africa and it is thought to have originated in Asia Minor.

The vine is a perennial deciduous climber that clings to supports by tendrils. The leaves are hand- or heart-shaped and 4–8 in in size.

The grapes most commonly grown by home gardeners in the northern part of the United States are the so-called American, or bunch, grapes, descendants of wild grapes. The blue, black, green, red and yellow berries usually have slip-skins (separable from the pulp) and ripen from mid-summer on. They are largely self-fruitful. Although American bunch grapes can be grown from zones 3–10, they do best in zones 5–7.

Muscadine grapes are generally grown in the South (zones 7–9). These form much larger vines up to 90 ft long and produce fruits singly or in loose clusters. Several self-fruitful varieties are available but most varieties are self-unfruitful. Since the fruit of self-fruitful varieties is inferior to that of self-unfruitful varieties, self-fruitful varieties are best used to pollinate the self-unfruitful varieties.

Vinifera, or wine, grapes are descended from European grapes and are best employed in wine-making. A number of varieties, all with skins inseparable from the pulp, are eaten at table and are considered among the best grapes for this purpose. Some varieties are also used for raisins. All vinifera grapes are self-fruitful, producing berries in extremely large clusters. They grow best in California, but there are numerous hardy varieties that can be grown as far north as zone 6. There are also many new hybrid varieties resulting from crosses of American and vinifera grapes. These combine characteristics of the parents and are therefore difficult to classify.

Cultivation

Grapes are sun-loving plants and must be grown where they will be exposed to the sun all day or at least for the greater part of the day. But the base of the plant need not be in full sun although it is essential that the upper part of the plant catches as much strong sunlight as possible. (Grapes growing wild in forests often take root at the foot of trees and soon clamber above the trees).

The location selected for the vines should have good air drainage. In colder areas, protection from winter winds is necessary.

Soil

The vines are fairly tolerant of a wide range of soils, although the soils must be deep and well drained, and not too sandy. The plants require a soil pH of 5.5–7.0. If there is any possibility that the soil may become badly waterlogged, a good drainage system should be installed.

Two or three weeks before actual planting, prepare the soil by double-digging to break up any hard layers and to clear away perennial weeds. Dig in leafmold or well-rotted manure at the rate of about one wheelbarrow load per 20 square feet. Also rake in a balanced fertilizer such as 10-10-10 at the rate of 3 oz per square yard.

Planting

Plant one-year-old vines in early spring before they start to leaf out. Dig large, deep holes; spread out the roots; firm them well; and water thoroughly. Then cut off all but one strong cane and trim this back to eight buds.

Maintenance

Except for pruning and training, grapes do not demand a great deal of attention.

In dry spells, they should be watered deeply, but, as the fruit begins to mature, the water supply should be reduced somewhat. This helps the maturation process and also inhibits succulent growth. In the fall, however, after the fruit has been picked, one heavy watering is necessary to help protect the vines from winter injury.

Unless the plants are doing poorly, they need little fertilizer. Give each plant 2–4 oz of ammonium nitrate or a somewhat more balanced fertilizer in early spring. This should carry them through the growing season.

Keep encroaching weeds pulled. An application of an organic mulch around the plants discourages weed growth in addition to supplying the necessary nutrients for healthy growth.

Training and pruning

The training and pruning of grapes are matters of critical importance. The main purposes of training are to keep the large, fast-growing vines under control, to facilitate care and harvesting, and to expose all parts of the plants to the sun. The purposes of pruning are to maintain vigorous growth, to provide new canes for the next year, and to limit the number of fruit-producing buds so that the vines do not produce too much small fruit of inferior quality.

Various training systems are used for all three types of grapes.

American bunch grapes

Four-Arm Kniffin system This is the most popular method of training American bunch grapes since it gives good production and requires little summer tying of the vines.

The trellis required consists of 4–6 in posts and galvanized steel wires. Space the posts 16 ft apart. Sink the end posts 3 ft into the ground and brace them with diagonal struts or guy wires. Sink the intermediate posts 2 ft. The posts normally extend 5 ft above ground,

Staking and planting

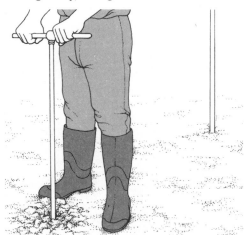

1 Bore or dig holes and drive 8 ft posts 3 ft into the ground, spaced according to the pruning system to be followed. Stretch wires between the posts, spaced according to the pruning system.

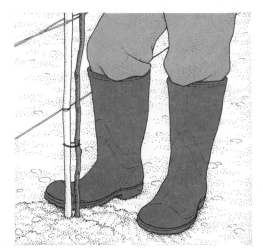

2 In early spring, plant the vine to the nursery depth between posts in prepared ground. Firm the soil and water well. Cut back the vine to one cane and eight good buds.

The first year

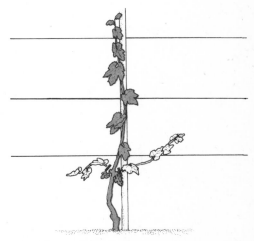

3 For both pruning systems, allow one rod to develop. Pinch back to one leaf any other shoots. Leave two good buds (Kniffen) or three (Guyot).

Grapes 2

'Ontario' Very early white fruit of excellent quality for eating and jelly. Hardy.
'Portland' Large white fruit in big clusters. Best very early variety. Hardy.
'Seneca' Small white fruit in large clusters. Delicious flavor. Early. Not a vigorous variety but hardy.
'Van Buren' Very early 'Concord' type

with medium-size blue fruits. Hardy and worth trying in zone 3.
'Worden' Large purplish-black fruit. Descended from 'Concord' but ripens about 10 days earlier. Hardy.

MUSCADINE VARIETIES
'Burgaw' Reddish-black fruits of only fair quality. But the vines are self-

fruitful and good pollinators.
'Dearing' One of the best self-fruitful varieties. Very sweet white fruits. Good pollinator.
'Dulcet' Small, sweet reddish-purple fruits. Early. Self-unfruitful.
'Hunt' Large, black grapes of excellent quality. Makes a fine jelly. Early. Self-unfruitful.

'Magoon' Small, early, black fruits of good quality. Self-fruitful.
'Scuppernong' Most famous muscadine variety. Bronze-colored fruits of distinctive flavor. Early. Self-unfruitful.
'Thomas' Very sweet, smallish, red-black fruits of excellent quality. Mid-season. Self-unfruitful.

but increasing the height to 6 ft exposes the vines to more sunlight and is especially recommended for short-season areas.

Use 9-gauge wire at the tops of the posts and 11-gauge at 30 in above ground. The wires can be stapled to the posts or run through holes drilled in the posts. Drilled holes give greater security. If staples are used, do not drive them down tight because it may be necessary to tighten the wires when they sag under the weight of the vines.

Plant the grape vines between posts. If planted at the base of posts, they may be injured by any wood preservative in the treated posts, and would undoubtedly be damaged when the posts had to be replaced.

The first year When the two top shoots on the young plant are about 1 in long, rub off all other shoots.

The second year Select the strongest cane for the trunk and tie it to the top wire. Cut the cane just above the wire and remove all other canes. If no cane reaches the top wire, tie the strongest one to the bottom wire and extend it to the top wire the next year. If no cane reaches either wire, reduce the vine to

a single stem with two or three buds and start all over again.

The third year Pick four good canes for the arms; cut them back to approximately 10 buds in length; stretch them out along the top and bottom wires in both directions from the trunk; and tie them. Cut four other canes back to two or three buds for renewal spurs and remove all other canes.

Subsequent years Each year cut off the 10-bud fruit-bearing canes of the previous year and replace them with the renewal spurs (which are shortened to approximately 10 buds). The renewal spurs are replaced with new renewal spurs cut back to two or three buds. All other canes are removed.

The actual number of buds that should be left on fruit-bearing canes each year depends on the variety of grape and the growing conditions. Until the home gardener has raised grapes for some time, the best way to determine how hard to prune is as follows. First rough-prune the vine, leaving a few more buds than needed. Weigh the wood removed. For the first pound of wood, leave 30–40 buds, more or less equally divided

between the four fruit-bearing canes, on the plant. For each additional pound of wood removed, leave eight more buds on the vine. (This weighing plan is used not only for the Four-Arm Kniffin training system, but also for all other training systems.)

All pruning is done in early spring while the vines are dormant and after danger of severe freezes has passed. If pruning is done too early, heavy frost can compound the winter injury already suffered by the plant, and the gardener cannot be certain which canes are alive and which are dead. Pruning late does no serious damage, but there is a good chance that some of the buds meant to be saved will be destroyed. If the cut canes "bleed", there is no need for worry as this does no great harm.

Munson system This is an excellent system for humid climates because the grapes are carried well above ground where they are exposed to more air currents.

The trellis consists of sturdy and large posts (4 × 6s are recommended) with stout 24 in crossarms 5 ft above ground. Brace the cross-arm. Staple two No 9 wires to the ends of the

crossarms on the top edge. Run a third wire through the posts 6–8 in lower.

Train the new vine, as above, to a single trunk extending to the bottom wire. In the third year, prune it to two fruit-bearing canes and two renewal spurs. Tie the canes along the lower wire, and as the young shoots develop, drape them over the upper wires, allowing them to hang down.

Each year thereafter replace the arms with the canes from the renewal spurs and replace the spurs.

Modified Chautauqua system This system is used where tender grape varieties need winter protection. The trellis is made with 4-in posts and three No 9 wires spaced 12, 28 and 44 in above ground.

In the first year, simply let the vine grow upward and tie it to the wires. In the fall of the same year, select the best cane for the trunk, reduce it to 30 in long, and remove all other canes. Lay the trunk on the ground and cover it with about 8 in of soil for a measure of protection.

In the spring, pull the cane out along the bottom wire at an angle and tie it. As new growth develops, tie to the other wires.

Prune the new growth to short two-bud spurs in the fall. Keep the cane closest to the end of the trunk to form an extension of the trunk. Remove the vine from the trellis and bury it as before.

In following years, repeat this procedure. Let the trunk grow to a maximum length of about 7 ft.

Muscadine grapes

Muscadines can be trained by any of the systems described, but the vine is such a strong, rampant grower that it is often cultivated on arbors. In this case, train the young vine to a trunk 6–7 ft long before allowing it to branch out to the sides along wires, spaced about 2 ft apart, forming the arbor roof.

In the Four-Arm Kniffin system, train and prune the vine to form a trunk and four strong arms. Do not cut the arms back until they meet those of the neighbouring vines. Thereafter, annually prune out deadwood, weak canes, and side growth on the trunk and the tendrils. Cut the remaining canes back to two or three buds.

Kniffen system—The second year

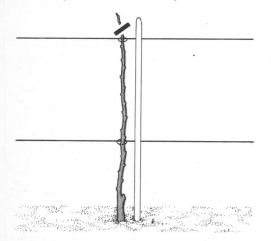

1 In spring, select the strongest cane, tie it in and cut off just above the top wire. Remove all other canes.

The third year

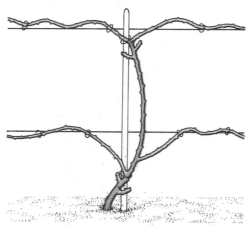

2 In spring, select four vigorous canes and tie them in to form arms. Prune them to ten buds each. Prune four other canes to form four renewal spurs for the next year.

Fourth and subsequent years

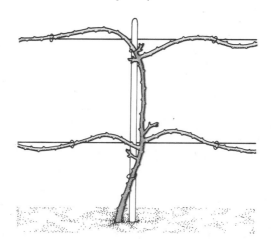

3 In spring, cut off the old fruiting arms. Tie in four new canes chosen from the renewal spurs. Cut each new cane back to six buds. Cut four new canes back to two buds to form renewal spurs.

Grapes 3

'**Topsail**' Sweetest of all muscadines. Medium-large, greenish-bronze fruits. Mid-season. Self-unfruitful.

VINIFERA VARIETIES
'**Baco No 1**' Also called 'Baco Noir'. Black grape for making red wine. Early. Hardy.
'**Cardinal**' Large, dark red fruits with a slight muscat flavor. Early.
'**Csaba**' Medium-size, yellowish-white fruits with a slight muscat flavor. Very early. Hardier than most.
'**Flame Tokay**' Very large, red fruits for eating. Mid-season. Tender.
'**Johannisberg Riesling**' Medium-size, greenish-yellow fruits with russet spots. Early. For making white wine.
'**Perlette**' Large, yellow to pale green berries in big, compact clusters. Very early.
'**Seibel 5279**' Pink-white fruits for wine-making and eating. Early. Hardy to zone 6.
'**Seyve-Villard 5247**' Very large, lavender fruits for making rosé wine. Early. Hardy vines have a bushy habit.
'**Thompson Seedless**' Famous green to yellow grape. Early. Favorite seedless table grape.
'**Zinfandel**' Medium-size red to black fruits for making red wine. Medium-early.

In the warmest regions, pruning should be done after the first killing frost in the fall or early winter. Further north, prune in early spring. Muscadines pruned at this time bleed great deal, but there is no damage to the plants.

Vinifera grapes
The Four-Arm Kniffin system is the method generally chosen in warm climates, but a modification called the Spur system is used for varieties such as 'Csaba' and 'Cardinal'. The Spur system allows the fruit-bearing arms to be permanent, that is they are not renewed annually. Each arm has 6–8 vertical fruiting spurs and each spur has 2–3 buds that produce fruit shoots.

In cold climates, where tender varieties need winter protection, the Modified Chautauqua system can be used.
Guyot system This is actually two systems. In the single Guyot system there is one fruit-carrying arm while in the double Guyot system there are two fruit-carrying arms. The double Guyot system is the more popular and is described below.

Double Guyot system—The second year

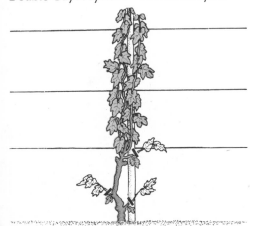

1 In spring, cut the vine down to within 15 in of the ground, leaving three buds. Train the resulting shoots vertically. Pinch back any laterals to one leaf as they develop.

Each year, allow three new main stems to develop. Retain two for fruiting and cut back the others to produce replacement stems for the next year. The fruiting canes are trained close to the ground to take advantage of its radiated warmth.

The trellis consists of 4-in posts spaced 8–10 ft apart. Brace the end posts. Attach a No 12 wire to the posts 15 in above the ground and two No 14 wires so they cross at each post.
The first year At planting, cut the vine down to about 6 in from ground level if the vine is on its own roots or, if it is a grafted plant, 6 in above the graft union, leaving at least two good buds. During the summer following planting, train one shoot up the post and pinch out all others to one leaf.
The second year In the spring, cut the vine down to within 15 in of ground level, leaving three good buds. During the summer, train in three shoots vertically. Pinch back any laterals to one leaf as they develop. In the next spring, the vine should be pruned as for an established vine (below).

Pruning an established vine Each spring

Third and subsequent years

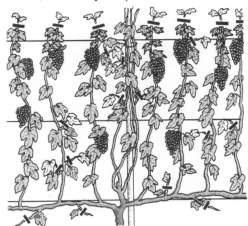

2 From April to August, train three shoots vertically from the center. Pinch back any laterals produced on them to 1 in as they develop. Tuck in the vertical fruit-carrying laterals through the double wires. Cut them back to three leaves.

(except the first) cut back the arms that bore fruit the previous summer to the replacement spurs. Do not allow fruit on the plants in the second year after planting, but allow them in the third. Tie down on to the lowest wire one replacement shoot to the left and one to the right. Cut down the remaining spur to three or four buds to provide replacement spurs for the following year. Cut back the immature wood on the replacement spur, leaving about 2–2½ ft of strong growth either side.
Third and subsequent years From April to August, tuck in the vertical fruit-carrying laterals between the double wires. Cut them back to two or three leaves above the top wires, as necessary, and remove any sub-laterals. Train the three replacement spurs from the center for the following year up the post. Pinch back any sub-laterals on the replacement spurs to one leaf and remove any blossom. Remove any surplus spurs coming off the main stem.

Thinning
Thinning of the fruit is recommended for vinifera grapes, but not for American and

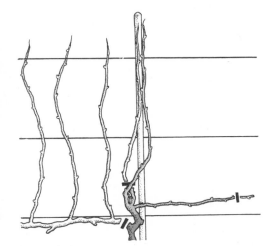

3 In November, cut out the two arms that bore fruit in summer to the replacements. Tie down one replacement shoot to the left and one to the right. Cut back each to leave 2–2½ ft of strong shoot. Cut down the remaining shoot to three buds.

Muscadine grapes. Viniferas are very heavy producers, and thinning is needed to improve fruit size. Thinning of varieties with very large or compact fruit clusters is done by removing individual berries immediately after fruit set. On varieties with loose or straggly clusters, remove some of the immature flower clusters appearing with the new growth in the spring.

In addition, with all vinifera varieties, it helps to remove entire fruit clusters soon after fruit set. The number of clusters left depends on the size and vigor of the vine. Keep about 20–30.

Harvesting
Even when grapes are fully colored, they are not ripe because they need a finishing period for sugars to form. This period can vary from 4–8 weeks. Once picked, grapes do not continue to ripen.

Pests and diseases
Grapes are not greatly bothered by pest and disease problems. But it is advisable to spray the plants in late winter with dormant oil. A general-purpose fruit spray should be applied when the new growth is about 8 in long, just before bloom and two weeks thereafter.

Mildew should be sprayed with a fungicide whenever it appears. Spraying with carbaryl takes care of Japanese beetles, which have a particular liking for grape vines. Repeat treatment as necessary.

It is almost impossible to cover grape vines securely with nets to protect them from birds. But the individual fruit clusters can be enclosed in mesh or with paper bags.

In some years, wasps are even worse than birds, attacking the fruit just as it is ready to harvest and quickly destroying entire bunches. Only paper bags can keep wasps in check.

Disease or pest infestation should not prove a hindrance in viticulture if the grape vines are tended so that they remain in a healthy condition. Soil balance is the greatest determinant influencing grapevine health while weather is the most unpredictable factor. Wet, humid weather usually means mildewed grape vines.

Melons

MELON VARIETIES

'Burpee Hybrid' An outstanding Muskmelon. Heavily netted, ribbed fruits to 6 in across. Delicious, sweet, deep orange flesh. Resistant to mildew.
'Crenshaw' An extremely large winter melon with superior, thick, salmon-pink flesh of finest flavor.
'Delicious 51' Large, oval Muskmelon of

excellent flavor, but flesh is rather soft.
'Early Hybrid Crenshaw' Almost exactly like the winter melon but matures in only 90 days so can be grown in areas with fairly short summers.
'Gold Star' Medium-size fruits with juicy, deep-orange flesh. Vigorous vines.
'Hale's Best 36' A famous old melon of fine flavor and good size.

'Harper Hybrid' Very thick-fleshed fruits with an unusual tang. Medium-size.
'Harvest Queen' Large melons of top-quality.
'Heart of Gold' Fruits medium size, long and oval. Orange flesh.
'Honeydew' Winter melon with smooth creamy-white skin and green flesh. Fruits range from medium to huge.

Delicious to eat.
'Honey Drip Hybrid' Like a small Honeydew. Matures in only 85 days—almost a month less than 'Honeydew'.
'Persian' Enormous winter melon with superb, bright orange flesh.
'Supermarket' Prominently ribbed fruits with thick orange flesh of musky flavor. Resistant to mildew.

Gray-green or ochre-colored melons with rough, netted skins are known to most Americans as cantaloupes, but the true cantaloupe is a hard-shelled European fruit that is rarely grown in the United States. Gardeners wishing to attempt to grow it usually have to order seeds from a foreign supplier.

Melons Americans grow fall into two categories: Muskmelons and Winter or late melons. Muskmelons mature in roughly 90 days and can be grown in zones 5–10 and even into zones 3 and 4, if the quick-maturing varieties are chosen. Winter melons, including the 'Casaba', 'Crenshaw', 'Honeydew', and 'Persian' varieties, are larger fruits with variously colored skins and most of them take about four months to mature, so they are grown primarily in warmer climates.

Cultivation

A popular misconception about melons is that they cannot be planted with cucumbers, squashes or other members of the cucurbit family because they are cross-pollinated and this changes the flavor and aroma of the melons. This does happen if seeds from melons grown the year before are used. But the use of fresh seed every year eliminates the problem.

Melons are tender and vulnerable and cannot be sown outdoors until the soil is warm and all danger of frost is past. In short-season areas, this makes melon-growing by this common method impossible.

Soil The soil for melons should be reasonably fertile but not too rich, with a pH of 6.7–7.0. Good drainage is essential. Dig the soil well before planting and mix in considerable humus to improve fertility and moisture retention. Also mix in about 24 oz of 5–10–10 fertilizer per 50 square feet.

Sowing the seed In the North, therefore, seeds are sown in flats or peat pots indoors about 3–4 weeks before the mean date of the spring freeze. When the plants have two or three true leaves, they are moved into the garden and grown under cloches or polyethylene tunnels, usually about two weeks after the last frost.

Planting Further south, however, direct sowing in the garden is a simpler and better method. Sow the seeds in $\frac{1}{2}$ in deep drills

about 6 in apart and thin them to stand 2 ft apart. In setting out transplants, space them 2 ft apart. The rows should be 5–6 ft wide. The alternative is to sow seeds or plant seedlings in gently rounded mounds (hills) 6 ft wide and a few inches high at the center spaced 4 ft apart. Allow two or three plants per hill.

Furrows about 10 in wide can be dug on the south side of the hills to a depth of about 6 in to allow watering without wetting the foliage. Water well, especially during dry spells, but do not keep the soil soaked.

If nematodes are a problem in the garden, the soil should be fumigated before planting.

Watering and feeding Melons need plenty of moisture throughout the growing season and this should be provided by deep weekly watering in dry spells. Pull out weeds as they appear. Mulching the plants with organic matter or black polyethylene film is a good idea to hold in moisture and keep down weeds. When the vines begin to run, side-dress them lightly with balanced fertilizer or nitrate of soda.

For example, apply 4-8-4 balanced fertilizer carefully at $\frac{1}{2}$ oz to each mound in a circle around each mound after thinning the plants. Keep the fertilizer well clear of the plants and cover the dressing with nearby soil. The dressing should ideally be applied 4–6 in away from each plant.

Harvesting

When melons start to turn their characteristic mature color, they are ripening and will soon be ready for picking. In the home garden, however, actual harvest should not start until the fruits pull away from the stem easily. At this time they are in prime eating condition. Do not leave them on the vine any longer, because they begin to deteriorate within a couple of days. Ripe melons have a strong, fruity scent.

Pests and diseases

Melons are attacked by a few insects, but these are not generally very troublesome and can usually be controlled by spraying with malathion or carbaryl when they appear. But diseases can be difficult, especially in warm, humid weather. The best protection against disease is to plant resistant varieties.

Melons under cloches

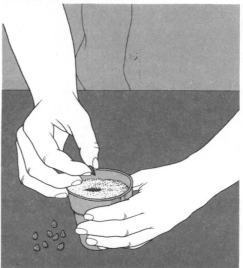

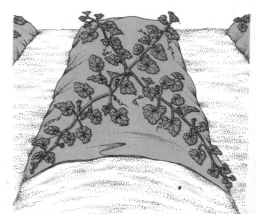

1 About four weeks before the expected date of the last spring frost, sow melon seeds in peat pots indoors. Harden off gradually before removal to the garden.

2 Plant out under cloches when the danger of frost is past. Make a hole wide and deep enough for the root ball to fit into comfortably.

Melons in the open

1 Dig soil well before planting and incorporate humus and 5-10-10 balanced fertilizer at 24 oz per 50 square foot. Mound up the soil.

2 Mulch the plants with black polyethylene and water well. Train as usual. Check for dryness at regular intervals thereafter. Mulching will help to warm cold soil.

Tree fruits

Introduction

Tree fruits (also sometimes referred to as top fruits) form a group comprising all the larger growing fruits which, in the natural state at least, attain tree form. The exceptions to this are the fig, elderberry, mulberry and quince, which may have several main stems and be more shrub-like in appearance; they are, however, still generally classified as tree fruits.

Botanically, the most familiar tree fruits are members of the rose family (*Rosaceae*), including the apple, pear, plum, cherry, peach, apricot and quince; the mulberry and fig are outsiders belonging to the mainly tropical family Moraceae. Also included in the tree fruit section are some of the most popular nuts, such as almonds, chestnuts, filberts, hazelnuts and walnuts.

Tree fruits are not difficult to grow provided the soil is well drained but moisture-retentive and of a moderate to good depth (see pages 8–9). The site must be sunny and not prone to severe late spring frosts.

Unlike growing soft fruits, cultivating tree fruits in the garden is a long-term project. Full fruiting capacity is reached by the tree only after several years, but with care it will then continue for a lifetime. However, the fruit grower is compensated by the fact that the fruiting season for tree fruits is much longer than that of soft fruits. Furthermore, if fruits such as peaches or figs are grown in a greenhouse the season can be prolonged.

Rootstocks

Apples, pears, cherries and plums can all eventually make sizeable trees if grown on their own roots; some even become too large for most gardens. For this reason they are grafted on to rootstocks which control their eventual size. Usually apples are grafted on to a range of apple rootstocks to produce dwarf or less vigorous trees which are ideal for the small garden (see page 116). Pears are traditionally grafted on to quince rootstocks and this lessens their vigor and ultimate size. A dwarfing rootstock for cherries has proved harder to find but a less vigorous one has now been produced, although it is not as dwarfing as some of the apple stocks that are now widely available.

Pruning and training

For all tree fruits, initial training and subsequent pruning is necessary to keep them in good shape and productive throughout their lives. Methods of training, particularly pruning, can seem daunting to an amateur but this need not be so if the instructions with each fruit entry in this book are followed closely. There is also a companion volume on pruning in this series.

Pruning terms The terms used frequently in fruit tree pruning are defined as follows. Maiden describes a one-year-old, for example, a maiden tree. A scion is a variety grafted on to a rootstock of another tree; the union is where the two join. A branch is a limb that arises from the trunk. Primary branches are the first formed, and secondary branches arise from the primary ones. A leader is a main central stem of a tree or a shoot selected to extend a main branch; a lateral is a side-shoot. Spurs are short laterals that bear flower buds and which can occur naturally or be induced by selective pruning of the laterals. Flower buds, or blossom buds, are unopened flowers, often referred to as fruit buds. Wood buds open to give rise to a shoot, as opposed to a flower. Suckers are shoots that grow from below the ground or below the union.

Choice of site

The site should be chosen with care and the soil cleared of perennial weeds either with a selective herbicide (see page 171) or by hand weeding during digging. If some weeds still persist, herbicide treatment can be given again after the tree is planted, but take care to choose one which will not damage the tree.

Protection against birds

In areas where bird damage is expected (and few rural or suburban districts are exempt), protection is necessary. For small tree forms, such as dwarf bush trees, cordons or espaliers, this can be provided by a fruit cage, ideally one with tubular steel or metal alloy poles and netting, although 7 ft headroom is a minumum. It is generally impracticable to protect larger tree fruits against bird damage.

Wall- and fence-trained trees

If there is no room in the open garden for free-standing tree fruits, good use can be made of walls and fences if restricted tree forms such as fans, cordons or espaliers are grown. North-facing walls can be used in this way for Morello cherries. Some plums are even more successful on walls than in the open, ripening well in the sheltered and warmer environment. Figs are often best grown on a warm wall (see pages 90–91).

Pollination

Unlike most soft fruits which will produce an adequate crop even if only one plant is grown, many tree fruits are totally or partially self-incompatible, or self-unfruitful. This means that some varieties cannot produce a good crop of fruit if their flowers are fertilized with their own pollen. In such instances at least two different compatible varieties must be grown close enough for bees to be able to carry pollen from one to the other. Sweet cherries provide the best example of self-sterility, but practically all the tree fruits set heavier crops if two or three varieties are planted together. They must, of course, flower at the same time and produce plenty of good pollen.

Storage

If it is decided to plant enough apples and pears to provide fruit for the late fall to winter period, storage facilities are necessary. This can be provided by a cool but frost-free cellar or shed. Late apples and pears finish ripening many weeks after they have been picked, and so they should not be stored with mid-season varieties until this ripening has taken place because the gases given off by the earlier varieties shorten the storage life of the later ones. Deep freezing is suitable for these two fruits only if they are to be used in cooking when thawed.

Fruit under glass

Figs, peaches and nectarines produce luscious fruits under glass in cool areas. Artificial heat is not required although ripening can be hastened by its use early in the season. Wall or roof space not less than 10 ft long is needed for a well developed peach or a fig rooted in the floor of the greenhouse. Alternatively, much smaller trees can be grown in large pots and housed in all but the smallest greenhouse. Space outside should be set aside where hardy potted trees can be kept with the roots protected during the winter after the fruit has been picked. For fruit in the greenhouse, see pages 254–255.

Pollination

Pollination is the transfer of pollen from the anthers or male parts of the flower to the stigmas or female parts of the flower. This results in fertilization and the eventual production of fruit. It is usually carried out by bees or other insects or by the wind. Occasionally, it is necessary to pollinate by hand.

The flowers of most garden fruits contain both anthers and stigmas. Some fruits, such as melons and hazelnuts, bear separate male and female flowers on the same plant.

Some fruit trees, such as peaches, nectarines, apricots and certain plums, are self-compatible—that is they can be fertilized by their own pollen. Others, such as nearly all sweet cherries, elderberries and many varieties of apples and pears are self-incompatible (self-unfruitful); they must be grown with another variety of the same fruit that flowers at the same time so that the two varieties can fertilize each other.

Pollination groups

Different varieties of plums, apples, pears and cherries are divided into pollination groups according to when their flowers are open and ripe for pollination. Those varieties in the same pollination group will cross-pollinate because their flowers are open at the same time. Those in adjacent groups are also acceptable because in most years their seasons of flowering overlap. However, a plant that blossoms very early cannot be counted on to cross-pollinate another plant that blossoms very late.

Incompatibility groups

Not all varieties of the same fruit can cross-pollinate, even when they are in the same pollination group. This is called cross-incompatibility. These varieties are divided into incompatibility groups and will not set fruit with their own pollen or that of any variety in the same incompatibility group. They will cross-pollinate with varieties in another group or in adjacent groups (provided they flower at the same time).

Ineffective pollinators

Some varieties of apples and pears, although not strictly cross-incompatible, are ineffective pollinators. This can occur for a number of reasons.

Most varieties are diploid, that is, they have the normal number of chromosomes. A few are triploid, that is they have $1\frac{1}{2}$ times the normal number. Triploids are poor pollinators and should be grown with two diploid varieties to pollinate each other and the triploid.

Some varieties of pears are known to be ineffective pollinators. Also some varieties of both apples and pears flower only every two years (biennially) or, irregularly. These cannot, therefore, be relied upon to pollinate other varieties.

Many triploids, ineffective pollinators and irregular flowering varieties are good varieties in their own right and popular with gardeners. If planting these varieties, remember to plant other varieties near them to provide the necessary pollen.

The following list gives the specific pollination nature of a selection of popular garden tree fruits from apples to sweet cherries.

Specifics

Apples No variety is completely self-compatible, so more than one variety should be grown.

Apricots Usually self-compatible with a few exceptions (for example, 'Moongold' and 'Sungold' should generally be planted together).

Crabapples Self-compatible.

Nectarines Self-compatible.

Peaches The great majority of varieties are self-compatible.

Pears No variety is fully self-compatible. Plant two or more varieties. Most bloom at about the same time.

Plums Most varieties are self-incompatible, and even those that are self-compatible bear more reliably if planted with another variety. European plums cannot pollinate Japanese plums or vice versa. Native plums are pollinated by other native varieties, sandcherry-plum hybrids or Japanese varieties, if a native variety has been crossed with a Japanese.

Quinces Self-compatible.

Sour cherries Self-compatible. Sweet cherries are not suitable pollinators for sour cherries, but sour cherries can pollinate sweet cherries, although most flower too late.

Sweet cherries Self-incompatible. Two or more varieties are needed. However, some varieties, such as 'Bing', 'Emperor Francis', 'Lambert' and 'Napoleon' do not pollinate one another.

STRUCTURE OF BLOSSOM (APPLE)

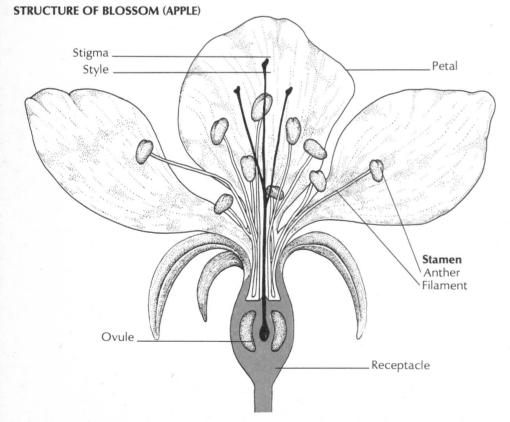

Stigma
Style
Petal
Stamen
Anther
Filament
Ovule
Receptacle

HAND POLLINATION

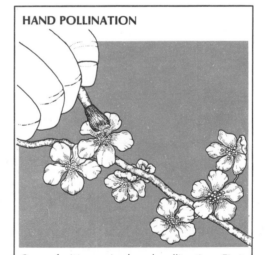

Some fruits require hand pollination. First draw the finger-tip over the anthers. A deposit of yellow grains on the finger indicates pollen is being shed. Pollinate at midday and when the weather has been warm and dry for two or three days.

Very gently transfer the pollen from the anthers to the stigmas by using a soft camel-hair brush or a piece of cotton wool on a matchstick.

Carry out hand pollination every day until flowering is over.

Planting fruit trees

Good establishment, healthy growth and eventual successful cropping of a fruit tree depend a great deal on how well it is planted.

Preparation
Before planting prepare the ground in early fall as described on pages 16–17. Then, for each tree, prepare an area 3 ft square by single digging clean ground and double digging weedy land. Prepare the ground over-all for closely planted trees such as those on dwarfing rootstocks. Apply lime if the pH is less than 5.8.

Just before planting, fork in a balanced fertilizer, such as 10-10-10, at a rate of 3 oz per square yard with bonemeal at 2 oz per square yard.

Time to plant
Plant in the dormant season from late October to April; but spring planting is generally recommended. Container-grown trees can be planted at any time. Do not plant when the soil is frozen hard or very wet.

If the tree arrives from the nursery when the soil conditions are not right, heel it in in a sheltered part of the garden. If the ground is too cold and hard to heel in, keep the tree in an unheated, frost-free place such as a cool basement. Unpack the upper parts of the tree but keep the roots in damp straw wrapped in burlap until planting.

Staking
Mark out the planting position and drive in a stake to a depth of 18 in on heavy soils and 24 in on light. Standard trees require 7½–8 ft posts, semi-dwarfs 6–6½ ft and dwarfs 3½–4 ft. Central-leader trees need a stake as long as the height of the tree plus the depth into the soil. A large-headed standard, such as a sweet cherry, is best supported by two stakes 18 in apart with a crossbar (to which the tree is tied) nailed just below the stake tops. The top of the stake should be 2–3 in clear of the tree's head to avoid chafing the lowest branches. Stakes come in a variety of materials.

Trees on very dwarfing rootstocks, for example apples on Malling 9, are best staked permanently. But for trees on more vigorous stocks, the stake can usually be removed after four or five years, depending on the vigor. Before removing the stake, check if the anchorage is sound by rocking the tree.

Planting
If the roots are a little dry, soak them for an hour before planting. Keep them covered.

On the day of planting, dig out a hole deep and wide enough to take the roots fully spread out. Mound the soil in the center. Keep the fertile top-soil separate from the lower layers. Fork the bottom and prick the sides of the hole to allow the roots to develop outwards. Dig in into the base rotted-down sods or a bucketful of well-rotted manure, compost or peat. Trim off with shears any broken or long tap roots. If planting a container-grown tree, gently tease out the soil and roots around the edge of the rootball.

Place the tree on the mound with the stem 2–3 in away from the stake. Ensure that the lowest branches clear the top of the stake. Plant the tree to the same depth as it was in the nursery, indicated by the soil mark. Keep the union between scion and rootstock at least 4 in above the soil surface to prevent the scion from rooting.

Fill in the holes; this is easier if one person holds the tree while another fills it in. Sprinkle a little of the fertile top-soil over the roots first then return the remaining soil a spadeful at a time. Occasionally shake the tree gently so that the soil falls among the roots. Finally, firm the soil and level off the surface.

Next, mulch the tree with well-rotted manure compost or peat over an area 18 in in radius to a depth of 2–3 in, keeping the material 1–2 in clear of the trunk to prevent fungal diseases from infecting the base.

Tie the tree to the stake. A one-year-old can be secured with plastic chainlock strapping using a figure of eight tie, but older trees need a more substantial tie with a cushion between stake and tree to prevent chafing. There are a number of proprietary makes, or one can be made.

Dwarfs require one tie placed 1 in from the top of the stake. Semi-dwarfs and standards require two ties, one at the top and one half-way down. Nail the ties to the post to prevent them slipping down.

Where animals are particularly trouble-some, protect the trees with wire netting.

Each year in April, July and October check the tree ties and if necessary loosen to avoid constriction. Re-tie home-made ties.

Planting against a wall
The soil at the foot of a wall can become very dry and poor, especially if it is protected from rain-bearing winds or is sheltered by overhanging eaves.

Where the soil is poor and the drainage is bad, construct a drywell or a single line of tiles 3 ft deep to take the water away (see pages 10–11). Re-soil over an area at least 6 ft × 3 ft wide × 2 ft deep with a fibrous, medium chalky loam, if possible made from sods stacked for six months before use. Add rubble to the loam in the ratio ten soil to one rubble. Two weeks before planting thoroughly mix in base fertilizer at the rate of 8 oz per 2 gal bucketful of soil.

The tree should be planted about 9 in from the wall base. During the growing season, water it whenever the soil is dry, applying 4 gal at a time around the base of the tree.

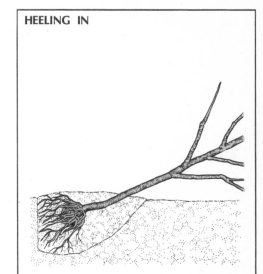

HEELING IN

Take out a shallow trench. Unpack the tree and lay it in the trench at an angle. Cover the roots with moist, friable soil.

1 If the roots are dry, soak them for an hour before planting. Trim off broken or long tap roots with shears.

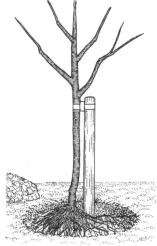

2 Drive in stake. Dig a hole deep and wide enough to take the roots fully spread out. Mound the soil slightly in the center.

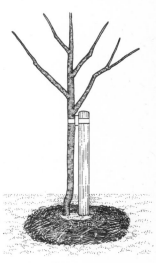

3 Set the plant on the mound 2–3 in away from the stake with the union at least 4 in above the soil surface. Replace the soil, firming gently. Mulch well.

Apples and pears 1

APPLE VARIETIES
Apples are self-unfruitful. Plant two or more varieties that blossom at the same time.
'Baldwin' Only fair eating quality; better for cooking. Dull, red, medium-large fruits. Late. Slow to start bearing. Usually a biennial producer and a poor pollinator.

'Cortland' Big, red, dark-stripped fruits of fine flavor. Mid-season. Reliable.
'Cox's Orange Pippin' Famous English apple generally considered the finest dessert apple grown. Flesh tender, yellow, juicy, aromatic. Fruits medium, round, conical; golden-yellow with brown-red flush and russet. Late. Does not succeed in many areas.

'Dudley' Large, greenish-yellow fruits with red blush. Coarse yellow flesh, but tasty. Mid-season. Hardy.
'Golden Delicious' Medium-sized, conical, yellow fruits. Late. Excellent quality for eating. Biennial bearer.
'Golden Russet' Very old variety. Medium-large fruits highly flavored and of top quality. Russet-yellow. Late.

'Granny Smith' Pure grass-green fruits with shiny skin. Hard, crisp, white flesh. Very late. Excellent for cooking.
'Gravenstein' For cooking and eating. Big, red fruits. Mid-season. Poor pollinator; plant with two other varieties.
'Grimes Golden' Medium-size, yellow-green fruits in mid-season. Good pie apple and also good to eat.

Introduction and rootstocks

The domestic apple (*Malus domestica*) is of complex hybrid origin but it has evolved, under human influence, from various species, all of them belonging to the series Pumilae. It has been estimated that up to 1980 there were at least 6,000 named varieties of apples in the world.

Like the apple, the pear (*Pyrus communis*) has long been cultivated. It is a native of Northern Europe. In the United States, apples are grown in zones 3–8 and pears in zones 5–8. In both cases, however, a very few varieties will grow further north or further south of these zones.

Site

Ideally, the site should be frost-free, in full sun, and sheltered from strong winds. Pears flower in late April to early May and apples in the first half of May, when they are at risk from spring frosts. The gardener in a frost-prone site should consider growing trees on dwarfing stocks or using the restricted forms whose small size makes it practicable to protect them by covering the trees on frosty nights. With apples, the alternative is to plant varieties that flower late, but this is not applicable to pears because even the later varieties flower in the danger period.

Ample sunshine is important, particularly for pears, if the fruits are to develop their full color and flavor. Apples will tolerate some shade, provided they receive at last half a day's sun in the growing season. Where there is a choice, allocate the sunniest position for pears and dessert apples, and the less sunny positions for cooking apples, for which color and flavor are not so critical.

Shelter is essential because both kinds of fruit are insect pollinated and strong winds inhibit the insects' flight, which results in poor pollination. Wind-breaks, either living or artificial, should be provided on exposed sites or, again, choose apples and pears on dwarfing stocks or in restricted form because they are easier to shelter than are taller trees (see pages 90–91).

Soil

The ideal soil for both apples and pears is a medium well-drained loam, not less than 24 in deep and slightly acid (pH 6.7). They are, however, tolerant of a wide range of soils. Pears and dessert apples require good drainage, whereas cooking varieties can be grown in heavy soil and marginally poorer drainage, but the soil must never be waterlogged.

Light sandy soils are acceptable provided bulky organics are incorporated and heavy mulching and watering is practiced. Thin soils over limestone are unsuitable because lime-induced chlorosis and lack of water and nutrients generally occur. Deep soils over limestone can support apples and pears quite satisfactorily.

Soil preparation

In late winter, prepare the soil by clearing away perennial weeds over an area 3 ft square. Fork in a compound fertilizer such as 10-10-10 at 3 oz per square yard.

Planting and staking

In early spring, plant the tree to the same depth as it was at the nursery, spreading the roots out well (see page 115).

Standard trees and semi-dwarfs require stakes and tree ties. The restricted forms are supported by wall or fence wiring.

Selecting the rootstock

Apples and pears are not grown on their own roots for a number of reasons. Some will not root easily, some are prone to root troubles, and some make large unproductive trees. To overcome these problems, apple and pear varieties are grafted by the nursery on to various rootstocks.

The rootstock is the most important influence on the eventual size of the tree. An apple grafted on to a dwarfing stock, for example, will stay small, whereas on a vigorous stock it will eventually become large. It can also affect how long it is before the tree will fruit and its cropping capacity, so it is important to know the rootstock on which the tree is grafted or, when ordering a new tree, to indicate to the nursery what size of tree is required so that the appropriate rootstock is selected.

The stocks most widely used are listed right. The size of the tree quoted under the rootstock is an estimate.

ROOTSTOCKS

Apples

M7: Semi-dwarfing tree that can be controlled by training and pruning and grown to a height of about 15 ft.

M9: Very dwarfing One of the most dwarfing stocks, M9 is widely used, making a tree about 6–10 ft in height and spread. It soon bears fruit, usually from the third year onwards, sometimes even in the second year. It requires good soil conditions and will not tolerate neglect, or competition from grass and weeds. The root system is brittle and such a tree requires staking throughout its life. An excellent stock for the small garden. Used for dwarf, dwarf pyramid and cordon.

M26: Dwarfing M26 makes a dwarf tree 8–12 ft in height and spread. It tolerates average soil conditions. It soon bears fruit, usually within three or four years of planting. It requires staking for the first four or five years, longer on exposed sites. Used for dwarf pyramid, and cordon and occasionally espalier and fan. It is a suitable stock for the small garden.

M27: Extremely dwarfing It is too soon to comment about its suitability for garden use but first reports are that it will make an ideal tree for growing in pots and in small gardens. It needs careful feeding and watering.

MM106: Semi-dwarfing MM106 makes a tree 12–18 ft in height and spread. It is tolerant of a wide range of soils. Trees on this stock soon bear fruit—usually within three or four years—and can produce heavily in later years. Such a tree requires staking for the first four or five years. Used for cordon, espalier and fan.

MM111 and M2: Vigorous The trees on these stocks make trees 18–22 ft in height and spread, but their growth varies according to soil and variety. They make large trees on good loamy soils, but only medium-sized trees on poorer sandy soils. Used by nurseries for half-standard and standard trees, espaliers and occasionally cordons and fans. They are slow to fruit in comparison with the more dwarfing stocks, sometimes taking seven to eight years. They are too vigorous for most gardens except where the soil is poor.

Pears

Pears are usually grafted on to quince rootstocks, which make them small to medium-sized trees. Some pears have a weak and spreading habit, and others are vigorous and upright, therefore the sizes given below are only an approximation.

There are three rootstocks: Quince C, Quince A and Pear. Both Quince C and A are suitable for the garden.

Quince C: Moderately vigorous Quince C makes a pear tree about 8–18 ft tall. It bears fruit in four to seven years. It is suitable for highly fertile soils and vigorous varieties, but not where conditions are poor. Used for cordon, dwarf pyramid and espalier.

Old stocks of Quince C may be infected with a virus, so where possible obtain stock certified as virus-free. If in doubt, use Quince A because there is not much difference in vigor between the two.

Quince A: Medium vigor Slightly more vigorous than Quince C, it is the stock upon which most pears are grafted. It bears fruit in four to eight years. Pears on Quince A make trees between 10–20 ft in height and spread. It is used for all forms of pear tree except standards.

Certain pear varieties are not compatible with quince and these have to be double worked by nurseries. This means a piece of pear graftwood compatible with both the quince rootstock and the pear variety, such as 'Beurré Hardy', is used as an intermediate between the two. Varieties requiring double working include 'Bristol Cross', 'Dr Jules Guyot', 'Doyenné d'Eté' and 'William's Bon Chrétien'. If this is not done, the pear could eventually separate at the graft union.

Pear stock: Very vigorous Pears grafted on to pear rootstock make very large standard trees, and, consequently, are too big for most gardens.

Apples and pears 2

'Haralson' Tart, juicy, medium-size red fruits. Mid-season. Especially popular in Midwest.
'Idared' White, somewhat juicy flesh of fair flavor. Big, ribbed fruits are yellow with red flush on sunny side. Moderately vigorous, spreading tree. Late.
'Jonathan' Mid-season cooking and eating apple. Red fruits are small to

medium-size with tart flesh. Susceptible to fire blight.
'Lodi' Big, yellow fruits for cooking and eating. Early. Much planted in Oregon.
'Macoun' Dark red, medium-size, flavorful fruits in mid-season. Excellent flavor. Heavy thinning of fruit required.
'McIntosh' Large, red, beautiful fruits of excellent flavor. Mid-season. Heavy

producer. A favorite in the Northeast.
'Melba' Excellent early-season dessert apple; small and red striped. Heavy bearer in alternate years.
'Milton' Tasty, large, often poorly-shaped fruits. Pinkish-red. Mid-season.
'Northern Spy' Fruits large and red-striped. Delicious flavor. Late. May not start bearing until 10 years old. Often a

biennial bearer. Very particular about needing well-drained soil. Poor pollinator.
'Red Delicious' (or simply Delicious). Probably most widely grown American apple. Red, conical fruits of excellent eating quality but poor for cooking. Late. The many sports have a richer red color but offer few positive advantages, and often revert permanently to the original.

Selecting the tree form

Just as important as the correct choice of rootstock is the choice of tree form.

There are two basic types of trees, those that are planted in open ground and pruned in the winter, and those that are grown in restricted form, usually against a wall or fence, and pruned mainly in summer. The restricted form of tree is not widely available in the general market and it may be necessary to seek out a nursery specializing in this form.

Where a gardener has plenty of land and a heavy yield is the main criterion, the unrestricted winter-pruned trees planted in the open are the best choice. Where the gardener has little room, or prefers the neat look of well-trained summer-pruned trees, or wants to fill a blank space on a wall or fence, then the restricted forms should be chosen.

Trees in the open

The tree forms commonly grown in the open are the dwarf, semi-dwarf and standard. These are all open-centered trees and they differ only in the length of stem or trunk before the first permanent branch and in the size of the head, or framework.

Dwarf tree The dwarf tree has an open center and is goblet-shaped with a short stem of about 18–24 in. It is used only for apples because there is as yet no truly dwarfing stock for pears. Dwarf apples are grafted on to a Malling 9 rootstock or the equivalent and, because of their small size, are suitable for any garden. The soil must be very fertile, however, and the trees have to be fed and watered regularly or they will be stunted. Gardeners with less fertile soils should choose trees on more vigorous rootstocks.

Dwarf trees are easy to prune, spray and pick, and they soon bear fruit, but obviously their cropping capacity is not as great as that of larger trees. It is best not to plant dwarf bush apples in a lawn because they cannot compete with grass but if this is unavoidable, maintain a grass-free area for at least 2 ft around the base by mulching and water the tree regularly.

Semi-dwarfs The semi-dwarf tree has a clear stem or trunk of about 20–30 in before the first primary branch is reached, and its total

full-grown height is roughly midway between the height of a dwarf and a standard tree.

Semi-dwarf apples develop into moderately-sized trees which bear fruit in about three to six years, depending on the rootstock used, the variety of the apple, and the growing conditions.

Semi-dwarf apples and pears are suitable for the medium to large garden and can be planted in a lawn provided the grass does not inhibit the young tree's growth. They are not suitable as shade trees because the head is too low.

Standard The standard has a clean stem of 6–7 ft, and, in the case of a few varieties, may reach an ultimate height of 40 ft. But they should be kept much smaller by pruning, about 20 ft at most. The gardener needs a long ladder for picking fruit and a powerful sprayer for pest and disease control. Vigorous trees are slow to bear fruit but, because of their large size, they eventually yield heavy crops.

Restricted tree forms

The restricted tree forms are used where trees have to be contained in some way, for example, against a wall or fence. They are ideal for the small garden or where space is limited. However, because they are restricted, the yield in comparison with trees in the open is relatively small.

The main restricted tree forms for apples and pears are the cordon, the espalier and the dwarf pyramid. The fan is occasionally used.

The cordon is intended for a low fence. If closely planted, many varieties can be grown in a relatively small space and the gardener can more easily meet the cross pollination requirements (see pages 121–122).

The espalier may be planted against a low or high fence, depending upon the number of arms it is intended to have. Its long horizontal arms require more room than the cordon. It is a handsome form (see pages 123–124).

The fan requires a high wall, the height depending on the kind of fruit grown (see pages 90–91). Unlike the cordon or espalier it cannot be planted against a low fence unless the gardner is prepared to increase the height with trellis work. The fan is used mainly

for stone fruits such as peaches, cherries and plums, and for this reason it is described only on those pages.

The dwarf pyramid The dwarf pyramid is a small tree, pyramidal or Christmas tree-like in shape and kept this way by summer pruning. If, like the cordon, it is closely spaced, many

---

TREES IN THE OPEN: SPACING AND YIELDS

Dwarf tree
Spacing Plant the trees 8–10 ft apart.
Yield A good average yield from an established tree is about 40–60 lb.

Semi-dwarf tree
Spacing Plant 18–20 ft apart.
Yield 70–90 lb.

Standard tree
Spacing Plant 30–35 ft apart.
Yield A good average yield from a well grown standard apple is 60–120 lb and from a pear 40–100 lb.

---

trees can be planted in a relatively small area. Close attention to summer pruning is necessary, however, to maintain space between the framework branches and adjoining trees, otherwise a row of dwarf pyramids can soon degenerate into an unproductive hedge.

Although a restricted form, the dwarf pyramid is intended for planting in the open, not against a wall or fence (see pages 125–126).

Varieties

The choice of varieties depends upon the personal preferences of the gardener. Nevertheless, when making the final selection, ensure that the varieties will pollinate each other (see page 114).

Many triploid varieties are very vigorous and are not suitable for growing in restricted form unless grafted on to the dwarfing rootstocks Malling 26 for apples and Quince C for pears.

The description of the apple and pear varieties gives the season when the fruit is mature and fit to eat or cook. The picking date and maturity are not necessarily the same and this varies from locality to locality.

TREE FORMS

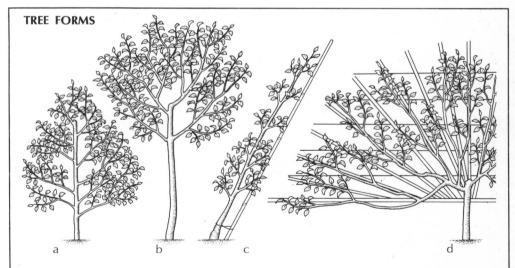

The dwarf tree (a) is made up of the top, an inter-stem of 18–24 in, and the rootstock. The standard tree (b) has a clear stem of 6–7 ft grafted onto a vigorous rootstock. The cordon (c) is planted and trained obliquely. The fan (d) is shaped.

Apples and pears 3

'Rhode Island Greening' Excellent cooking apple. Very large, green and very tart. Late. Extremely productive but often on a biennial basis. Poor pollinator.
'Roxbury Russet' Ancient variety that stores exceptionally well. Pale green with russeting. Excellent cider apple and also suitable for various kinds of cooking. Late.

'Rome Beauty' Splendid cooking apple. Big, red fruits. Very late. Heavy producer. Susceptible to fire blight.
'Sheepnose' Large, oblong, ribbed fruits are deep black-red when fully ripe. Prized for cooking. Late.
'Spitzenburg' Brilliant orange fruits with gray spots. Fine eating apple also used for cooking. Late.

'Stayman Winesap' Big, juicy, red-striped dessert apple. Late. Poor pollinator.
'Summer Pippin' Medium-large, green, very early cooking apple. Productive but likely to bear biennially.
'Summer Rambo' Early cooking apple. Large fruits may be almost entirely green or have red stripes. Poor pollinator.
'Tydeman's Red' ('Tydeman's Early').

Medium-sized red fruits of better quality than most early apples. Popular in Northwest.
'Wealthy' Favorite in northern Midwest. Medium-size, red-striped. Early. For eating and cooking.
'Winesap' Small, red, crisp apple for eating and cooking. Late. Does best in Virginia's Piedmont area. Poor pollinator.

Trees in the open
The dwarf, semi-dwarf and standard tree forms are commonly grown in the open.

Selecting the tree
A nursery can supply one-year-old, two-year-old or three-year-old trees. Trees older than this are not recommended because they may not establish well.

A one-year-old, or maiden, tree consists of a straight stem with or without laterals. A maiden with laterals, sometimes called a feathered maiden, is a better choice because if the laterals are suitably placed they can be used as primary branches, and a year is saved in the formative pruning stage. The maiden is the least expensive type, but it requires initial shaping and takes longer to bear fruit.

Trees of two and three years old will have already been partly shaped by the nursery and, being older, bear fruit sooner.

Soil preparation and planting
Prepare the soil in the late winter (see page 115). Plant the tree while dormant, in March or April, driving in a stake first.

Pruning
Prune in late winter, but not when the air temperature is below freezing.

The first winter The work of forming the head begins with the maiden tree.

Unfeathered At planting, shorten the maiden tree to 24 in for a dwarf bush or to 30 in if a standard is to be formed. Cut back to just above a bud, making a sloping cut away from the bud and ensuring there are three or four good buds beneath it. This cut stimulates the formation of primary branches the next year.

Feathered Cut back the main stem to a lateral at about 24 in for a dwarf or 30 in for a standard, ensuring there are two or three suitably placed laterals just beneath it. Remove all others flush with the main stem. Shorten the selected laterals by about two-thirds to an outward-facing bud.

The second winter (or the two-year-old tree) In the dormant season, select three or four strong leaders to form the primary branches, taking care to select those that are evenly spaced and have formed wide angles with the main stem. The wide angles ensure a stronger joint; a narrow-angled branch may break

off under the weight of the crop later on. Notice the effect of apical dominance, that is, the topmost shoot is the most upright and it is often unsuitable because it is too central and forming a narrow angle with the stem. If this is so, cut it out, heading back to the next branch. Next, shorten the selected primary branches by one-half and shorten the less vigorous ones by two-thirds. Cut each to an outward-facing bud. The remaining shoots are removed altogether. Protect the cuts.

During the summer, the branch growth following the hard pruning should be strong, with secondary branches forming.

In the third winter (or the three-year-old tree) Select about four more widely-spaced branches. The framework now consists of about eight branches. Shorten these by one-half or, if weak, by two-thirds, cutting back to outward-facing buds. Prune back to about four buds those laterals not required for secondary branches and those competing with the leaders. If the tree is growing vigorously, some laterals on the outer part of the tree can be left unpruned to form flower

buds. Shoots crowding the crotch of the tree should be removed. The center should be open, but not completely barren of growth. Growth from the main stem lower than the primary branches should be cut off to maintain the clean leg. Protect the cuts with a tree paint.

The fourth winter The tree is entering the cropping phase of its life, but a little more formative pruning is still necessary, as described for the third winter. Weak varieties may need further formative pruning for the next two or three winters.

Winter pruning the cropping tree By the fourth or fifth year the tree should start bearing fruit. From then the pruning guidelines are flexible, exactly how much is pruned depends on the condition of the tree.

Before pruning an older tree, remember that the harder the tree is pruned, the more growth is obtained, but in consequence the less fruit is produced. Thus, a heavily pruned tree will be vigorous but unfruitful, whereas a lightly pruned tree may crop heavily, but the fruit will be small and the framework weak and badly shaped.

Pruning a feathered maiden

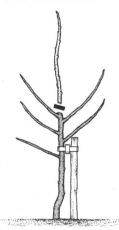

1 In late winter, prepare the soil and drive in a stake. Plant a maiden tree to the same depth as it was at the nursery. Tie to the stake. Cut the main stem back to a bud or lateral at about 24 in for a dwarf, 30 in for a standard.

The second year

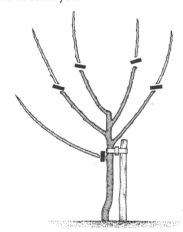

2 In late winter, select four of the primary branches that have formed wide angles to the stem. Cut back vigorous ones by one-half and less vigorous ones by two-thirds. Prune to outward-facing buds. Remove unwanted branches.

The third year

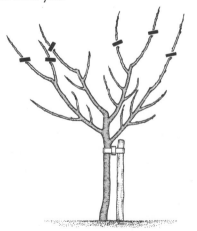

3 In late winter, select a further four well-placed new growths to form permanent branches. Cut back vigorous ones by two-thirds. Prune to outward-facing buds.

Fourth and subsequent years

4 In late winter, the branch framework has now been formed and leader pruning can cease, unless growth is weak. Leave laterals on the outer parts of the tree unpruned. Cut back laterals on the inside to about 4 in.

Apples and pears 4

'Yellow Transparent' Among early apples, probably the best. Used for cooking. Greenish-yellow fruits ripen unusually early; consequently, apple can be grown with reasonably consistent success in Alaska.
'York Imperial' Lopsided red fruits of fair to good eating quality but fine for processing. Late. Bears biennially.

Pruning the cropping tree

Before pruning apple or pear trees that are past the formative stage, it is important to distinguish between the spur-bearing and the tip-bearing varieties. A spur-bearing variety produces fruit buds on the two-year-old as well as on the older wood, where they are carried on short stubby shoots called spurs. Where these shoots become very branched, typically on old wood, they are called spur systems. The spur-bearer is the most common type of apple and pear tree.

A tip-bearing variety produces fruit buds at the tips of slender shoots made in the previous summer. A few spurs are also produced on the older wood, but considerably fewer than on a spur-bearer. The tip-bearer has a more gaunt appearance in comparison. There are also partial tip-bearers, which produce spurs on the older wood as well as fruit buds at their tips. For pruning purposes they are treated as spur-bearers.

There are three basic pruning techniques: spur pruning, renewal pruning, and regulatory pruning.

Spur pruning As mentioned above, spur-bearing varieties form spurs naturally, but they can also be induced to form spurs. Each winter cut back a proportion of maiden laterals to four or five buds. Choose those that have insufficient room to extend as secondary branches.

In the following summer, a lateral so pruned produces one or two shoots from the uppermost buds, but usually the lower buds develop into flower buds by the end of the growing season.

In the second winter, cut back the laterals to the topmost flower bud, thus removing the previous summer's growth. However, where there is room and no risk of the spur overlapping an adjoining branch, extend the spur system by cutting back to three or four wood buds on the previous summer's growth.

After some years, a spur system may become crowded and complicated and, as a result, the fruits are too numerous and therefore small. Then spur thinning is undertaken by reducing the length of the spur systems, cutting away the weakest buds and those buds growing on the undersides of the branches.

Renewal pruning of spur-bearers This also depends upon the tendency of many apple and pear varieties to produce flower buds on unpruned two-year-old laterals. It is best reserved for the strong laterals on the outer part of the tree, where there is room for such growth.

The renewal system of pruning is a method that encourages regular cropping by the removal of fruiting laterals that have passed their peak in growth. Young laterals are trained to take the place of the old laterals. This system is only effective when done by experienced gardeners and so should be practiced with great care.

In the winter, select a proportion of strong, well-placed laterals on the outer part of the tree and leave them unpruned. Prune the others as described in spur pruning. During the following growing season, the terminal bud on each unpruned lateral extends to produce a further maiden shoot, while most of the remaining buds develop into flower buds.

In the second winter, cut back the laterals to the topmost flower bud. In the following summer the cut-back laterals produce fruit.

In the third winter, half the laterals that have fruited can be retained as an elongated spur system. The others are cut back to leave a 1 in stub. This severe shortening stimulates the production of a new lateral from the stub, and so the cycle is repeated.

To sum up, at any one time the tree carries a number of one-year-old laterals unpruned, two-year-old laterals pruned back to a flower bud, and three-year-old laterals which are stubbed back to 1 in after fruiting—or left if there is room.

Regulatory pruning This applies to the tree as a whole rather than to specific parts of it as in spur or renewal pruning. Basically it entails keeping the center open by removing crowding and crossing branches and cutting out dead, diseased and broken wood. There is no need to prune the leaders after the early formative years except with poorly growing varieties, which require the stimulus of hard pruning.

The framework branches, laterals and spurs also should not be crowded. As a rough guide, in an old tree no main branch should directly over-shade another by less than 18 in, nor should branches be closer than 18 in when side by side. Laterals should be spaced about 18 in apart and spurs not less than 9 in along the framework of branches.

If in later years, as a result of light pruning, the tree over-crops (with consequent small fruit) and growth is weak, adopt a policy of harder pruning to reduce the number of flower buds and to stimulate new growth. Simplify some of the over-long spur systems, and where they are crowded cut out some of them altogether. Increase the amount of renewal pruning.

Pruning of tip-bearers In the winter, prune lightly on the regulatory system (see above). Leave any maiden shoots less than 9 in long unpruned because they have fruit buds at their tips. Prune longer laterals back to four buds. This induces short shoots in the following summer with fruit buds at their tips—spur pruning in effect.

Always prune the leaders of tip-bearing varieties because this induces more laterals to bear fruit in the following year.

SPUR PRUNING

The first year

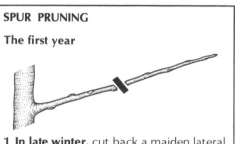

1 In late winter, cut back a maiden lateral to four buds.

The second year

2 In late winter, cut back the lateral to a flower bud.

Third and fourth years

3 In late winter, a spur system begins to be formed.

RENEWAL PRUNING

The first year

1 In late winter, select a strong well-placed lateral and leave it unpruned.

The second year

2 In late winter, extension growth has occurred. Flower buds have formed on last year's wood. Cut back to the junction between old and new wood.

The third year

3 In late winter, cut back the fruited lateral to leave a 1 in stub.

4 In October, at the end of the growing season, a strong new lateral has been produced from the 1 in stub. This is left unpruned to repeat the cycle.

Apples and pears 5

PEAR VARIETIES
Plant two or more varieties together to assure fruiting.
'Anjou' Excellent dessert pears even after long storage. Medium-large, oval. Yellowish-green with slight russeting. Does best in West. Late.
'Baldwin' Tender with good flavor. Early. Can be grown in zone 9.

'Bartlett' Favorite pear for eating and processing. Juicy, sweet fruits. Medium-large. Yellow. Vigorous, productive. Mid-season. Trees susceptible to fire blight. Do not plant with 'Seckel' as that variety does not pollinate it.
'Beurre Bosc' Long-necked, medium-large fruits are yellow overlaid with bronze. Smooth, juicy, rich flavor.

Productive, but very susceptible to fire blight. Late.
'Clapp's Favorite' Symmetrical, medium-large fruits. Excellent quality and flavor. Pick while quite firm, because fruits soften rapidly. Early. Very susceptible to fire blight.
'Comice' Outstanding dessert fruit; juicy, delicious, melting flavor. Medium-

large. Yellow. Late. Grows in zones 5–8, but is by far best at higher elevations.
'Duchess' Very large fruits. Greenish-yellow. Fine flavor. Often self-fruitful, but is more reliable when planted with another variety.
'Flemish Beauty' Grows in zone 4. Spicy-flavored, medium-large, rounded fruits. Mid-season.

The central-leader tree

The success of this form, which is not common in the United States, depends upon producing wide-angled branches off the central leader. Depending on the training method, it is referred to as a vase shape or modified-leader form. Therefore buy a feathered maiden, because the laterals on such a tree are naturally formed at the correct angle. Such a form may be used if the gardener does not desire maximum fruit production, but only wants a specimen of beauty.

Soil preparation and planting

Prepare the soil in the early fall (see page 115). This form requires a long stake to support the central leader. The stake should be 8–8½ ft long by 1½–2 in top diameter.

Drive the stake in first, 18 in deep on a heavy soil and 2 ft deep on a light soil. Plant the tree and tie it to the stake.

Pruning and tying down in the first year (or the one-year-old tree)

During the dormant season from November to February, select three or four laterals to form the first tier of branches starting at not less than 24 in from the ground. Choose strong, well placed laterals coming off the main stem at a wide angle. Prune these back by one-half to an outward-facing bud. Remove the rest of the laterals entirely. Cut back the central leader to the third bud above the topmost selected lateral.

By August the original laterals will have extended and possibly new laterals will have been produced. A new central leader will have grown on. Tie the leader to the stake using a figure of eight tie with soft thick string. Choose three or four good laterals that form a wide angle with the main stem and gently tie the extension growth of each down to 30 degrees above the horizontal with soft

thick string secured to 9 in long wire pegs pushed into the ground. Remove any upright laterals and those directly beneath the central leader.

Pruning in the second winter

Cut back the central leader by about one-third of the previous summer's growth to a bud on the opposite side to that of the previous year. The technique of cutting to an opposite bud is called "zig-zagging" and helps to maintain the more or less straight growth essential in the central leader. Remove any upright laterals and those competing with the leader. Prune each remaining lateral by one-quarter to a downward-facing bud. Check the string ties to ensure there is no constriction and remove any where the branch has set at about 30 degrees.

In August, again tie down suitable new laterals to form branches.

Pruning the cropping tree

In the third and subsequent years a similar procedure is followed. The central leader is pruned by one-quarter (if weak by one-third) to induce the lower buds to produce new laterals. The more vigorous the leader is, the lighter it is pruned. Branches are allowed to grow from the central stem at regular intervals, choosing those with a wide angle. Narrow-angled laterals are removed. The higher placed branches must be kept shorter than those beneath to allow sunlight to reach the lower parts. After the laterals at the very top have fruited, they must be pruned on the renewal system (see page 119). Tying down is discontinued once the branches have set at the required angle.

Each winter cut back the extension growth of the central stem to a weaker side branch once it has reached a height of 7–8 ft. Tie up the side branch to the stake as the new leader.

The second year

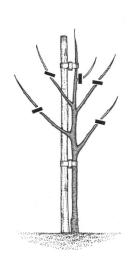

1 In November to March, prepare the ground and drive in a stake. Plant the feathered maiden tree to the same depth as it was at the nursery. Tie it to the stake.

2 At the same time, select three or four laterals to form the first tier of branches at about 24 in from the ground. Prune them back by one-half to an outward-facing bud. Remove remaining laterals entirely.

3 Then, cut back the central leader to the third bud above the topmost selected lateral. Protect the pruning cuts with a wound paint.

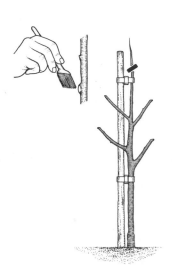

4 By August, the original laterals will have extended and a new central leader will have grown on. Tie the leader to the stake. Tie down the extension growth to 30 degrees above the horizontal using soft string.

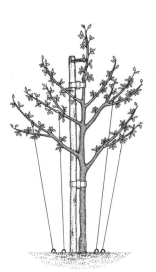

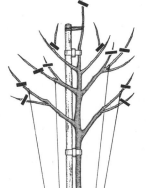

5 In winter, cut back the central leader by one-third of the previous year's growth to an opposite-facing bud. Remove any upright laterals. Prune remaining laterals by one-quarter to a bud.

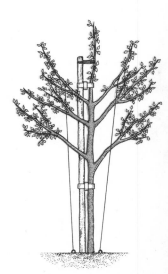

6 Every year, check the string ties. Remove the ties where the branch has set at 30 degrees. In August, tie down new laterals. Cut back the leader to a weaker lateral. Tie it up as the new leader.

'Gorham' Fruits large and yellow with light brown russet. Melting, sweet musky flavor. Late. Vigorous, but susceptible to fire blight.
'Kieffer' Grows from zones 4–9. Only fair quality when fresh, but processes very well. Big, yellow fruits. Late.
'Lincoln' Recommended for region around Oklahoma. Large, good-quality

fruits. Mid-season to late.
'Magness' New hybrid descended from 'Comice' and 'Seckel'. Medium-size, sweet, aromatic fruits. Greenish with russeting. Mid-season. Tree resistant to fire blight, but thorny. An unreliable pollinator; plant with two other varieties.
'Maxine' Fruits of only fair quality, but the tree is highly resistant to fire blight,

and is therefore recommended for areas where this disease is a particular problem. Large, yellow fruits. Late.
'Moonglow' Large, smooth, sweet, mild-flavored fruits. Big fruits are yellow with rosy blush. Early. Highly resistant to fire blight. Heavily spurred tree produces at an unusually early age.
'Orient' Very large, rounded fruits in

mid-season. Spreading, vigorous tree resistant to fire blight. Grows in zone 9.
'Seckel' Small, brownish, yellow, red-blushed fruits of delicious flavor. Late. Productive, but slow to produce. Not pollinated by 'Bartlett'.
'Tait Dropmore' Very hardy, growing into zone 3. But medium-size fruits are of only fair quality. Mid-season.

Apples and pears 6

Restricted tree forms: The cordon

A cordon consists of a single straight stem furnished with side-shoots or fruit spurs which are kept short by summer pruning and sometimes by winter pruning. It may be planted and trained vertically or obliquely, usually the latter because it requires less height and its growth is more easily controlled. There are also multiple cordons, with two or more stems.

The single stem apple cordon is not difficult to care for and is an ideal way for the amateur gardener to experiment.

The cordon is a form that, perhaps more than any other, is suited to the small garden. It is closely planted, so many varieties can be grown in a relatively small space and the gardener can more easily meet the cross-pollination requirements of apples and pears. Cordons can be grown against walls and fences or out in the open on a wire fence.

Choice of rootstock

For apple cordons, the dwarfing rootstock Malling 9 is the most suitable where space is very limited and the cordons are to be kept down to a height of 5–6 ft. The soil must be fertile, however. If in doubt about the soil, obtain trees on a slightly more vigorous stock.

For pears, the cordons must be grafted on to Quince A or C rootstocks.

An apple cordon crops high quality fruit early and heavily because it is raised on dwarfing rootstock. Other fruits that can be grown on the cordon system include gooseberries, red currants, sweet cherries, and white currants.

Selecting the tree

Cordons of one, two or three years old can be planted. If selecting a maiden tree, preferably choose one with plenty of laterals because these are the foundation of the fruit spurs to come. Two- or three-year-old cordons will be quicker to bear fruit, but they must be well furnished with spurs and laterals.

Spacing

Space the cordons 2½ ft apart on medium to good soils or 3 ft apart on poor, shallow or sandy soils with the rows 6 ft apart.

Support system

Cordons may be planted against a wall or fence or out in the open on a wire fence. On walls and wooden fences erect horizontal wires every 2 ft as described on pages 90–91. Out in the open drive in wooden posts every 12 ft to hold the wires. The posts may be 2½ in × 2½ in oak or 3½ in top diameter in other woods. Set the posts 2 ft deep or 3 ft in sandy soils. The end posts should be strutted. Alternative materials include iron, steel or concrete posts. Erect the wires at 2 ft, 4 ft and 6 ft and use 10 gauge wire for the upper wire and 12 gauge for the other two. Securely tie 8 ft bamboo canes to the wires at an angle of 45 degrees, with the tops pointing towards the north if the rows run north-south, or to the east if they run east-west. Space the canes at 2½–3 ft intervals to correspond with the planting stations.

Planting and training oblique cordons

Prepare the soil in the early fall (see page 115). Plant in the dormant season, unless using container-grown plants, which can be planted at any time. Against walls and solid fences, the cordon should be planted 6–9 in away from the structure to allow room for the growth of the trunk. Set the cordon at an angle of 45 degrees with the union between stock and scion uppermost, and then securely tie the cordons to the cane using thick soft string or plastic chainlock strapping in a figure of eight. If the one-year-old tree has laterals, shorten those over 6 in long to four buds. Thereafter, prune each summer. Do not prune the leader.

It is not wise to allow a cordon to crop in the first year after planting, so in the spring remove any flowers, taking care not to cut the growing shoot just behind the blossom.

Summer pruning: Modified Lorette System

Summer pruning is necessary to confine the growth to the limited space available. It also induces the production of fruit spurs close to the main stem. The Modified Lorette System is the simplest method.

Summer prune in about mid-July for pears and in the third week of July for apples in

warm climates. Prune seven to ten days laterals arising from existing side-shoots or all mature shoots of the current season's growth that are growing directly from the main stem. Cut back those mature sublaterals arising from existing side shoots or spurs to one leaf beyond the basal cluster or rosette of leaves. Mature shoots have a stiff woody base, dark leaves and are 9 in or more long. Leave immature shoots until mid-September. Do not prune shoots that are shorter than 9 in because they usually have fruit buds at their tips.

Pruning the cropping tree

Each May, once the cordon has passed the top wire and reached the required height (usually 7 ft), cut back the extension growth to its origin. Each July subsequently, cut the leader to 1 in. From mid-July onwards the remaining shoots on the cordon are pruned on the Modified Lorette System (see above).

If, later on, there are secondary growths from shoots pruned in July, cut them back to mature wood just before leaf-fall. In areas

The first year

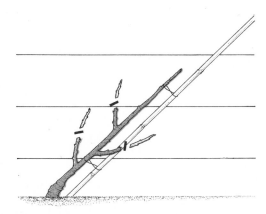

1 In late winter, plant the maiden tree with the union uppermost, against a cane secured to wire supports at about 45 degrees. Do not prune the leader. Cut back any feathers to four buds.

Second and subsequent years

2 In spring, after a further year's growth spurs will have formed on the cut-back feathers. Remove any flowers as they appear, leaving intact the growing shoot behind the blossom.

3 In late July, cut back laterals longer than 9 in arising directly from the main stem to three good leaves from the base, ignoring the basal cluster. Cut back sub-laterals from existing spur systems to one leaf beyond the basal cluster.

Apples and pears 7

where secondary growth is prolific after pruning, for example in high rainfall regions, delay pruning until later in the summer. If much secondary growth still occurs, then stop summer pruning altogether and prune in the winter instead, pruning to one bud from existing spurs and three buds on laterals arising directly from the main stem.

Winter pruning

Normally neither the leader nor the side-shoots are pruned in the winter except when a tree makes too much secondary growth, or makes poor growth, or to renovate it.

When a young cordon does not produce sufficient side-shoots, resulting in bare areas of stem, laterals may be induced by pruning the leader (previous summer's growth) by up to one-third of its length. Treat newly planted tip-bearers in the same way.

Neglected cordons can be brought back into shape by winter pruning. Thereafter prune them in the summer. Overlong or complicated spur systems should be reduced to two or three fruit buds.

LOWERING THE CORDON

When the cordons reach the top wire they may be lowered to obtain a longer stem. Lowering also helps to check the vigor of an overvigorous cordon. Lower carefully five degrees at a time and not lower than 35 degrees, so that there is no risk of breaking the stem. Lowering the angle slows down the movement of sap and limits extension growth while encouraging fruit bud protection.

MULTIPLE CORDONS

Cordons may also be formed with two, three or more arms, trained either vertically or at an angle. The training of a multiple cordon is initially similar to the formation of the first horizontal arms of an espalier. Thereafter each stem of the multiple cordon is treated as a single cordon. Vertically trained cordons are generally more vigorous and often less fruitful than those trained at an angle of about 45 degrees. The angle can be reduced further (see Lowering the cordon).

Secondary growths

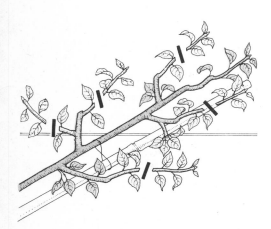

Just before leaf-fall, if further growth has developed from pruned shoots, cut it back to mature wood. In high rainfall areas, where much secondary growth occurs, stop summer pruning and prune from November to March instead.

The fruiting cordon

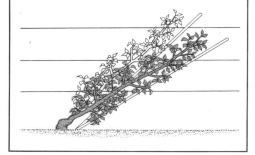

1 In May, when the leader has passed the top wire and reached the required height of about 7 ft, cut back the extension growth to its origin.

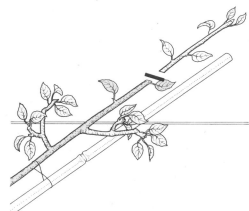

2 Each July, cut back the leader to 1 in. Cut back to three leaves all mature laterals longer than 9 in growing directly away from the main stem and those from existing side-shoots and spurs to one leaf beyond the basal cluster.

OVERCROWDED SPUR SYSTEMS

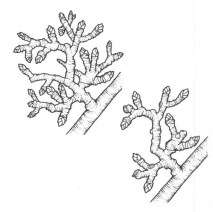

As the tree matures thin out in the winter by reducing overlong overlapping or complicated spur systems to two or three fruit buds. Remove buds that are weak on the underside and shaded parts of the branches.

Apples and pears 8

Restricted tree forms: The espalier

An espalier consists of a central stem from which horizontal fruiting arms (tiers) grow at about 15–18 in intervals. The tree is trained in one plane and makes a handsome boundary marker or can be used to cover walls or fences.

Choice of rootstock and spacing

If a small espalier apple is required, for example, against a low fence, the tree should be on the Malling 9 rootstock. This means obtaining a maiden tree and shaping it, because pre-formed espaliers on this stock are not usually available. For more than one espalier, plant 10 ft apart.

Where more vigorous trees are required, to clothe a large wall for example, they should be on vigorous rootstock and spaced 15–18 ft apart. Pears should be on Quince A or C rootstock.

Selecting the tree

The number of horizontal arms or tiers required depends upon the height of the wall or fence. Most nurseries that sell trees for espaliering supply two-tier and three-tier espaliers and further arms can be trained in if required. A formed espalier is much more expensive but crops sooner.

Support system

On walls and fences erect the horizontal wires to coincide with the espalier arms (as described on pages 90–91); usually each tier is 15–18 in apart. Out in the open, drive in posts to hold the wires every 12–18 ft, depending upon the spacing of the espaliers. The end posts should be strutted. Plant the espaliers centrally between the posts. Use 10 gauge galvanized wires and strain tight with straining bolts on the end posts.

Soil preparation and planting

In late winter, prepare the soil (see page 116). Plant in March or April. To allow room for the trunk to grow when sited against a wall or fence, the espalier should be planted 6 in away.

Formative pruning

Formed espaliers may be obtained or the gardener may prefer to start off with a maiden tree. The formative pruning steps in the first, second, and subsequent years are described below in as much detail as possible.

The first year Plant an unfeathered maiden tree in late winter or early spring. Cut back the stem to within 15 in of ground level, making sure that room for a short leg is left, together with three good topmost buds. The two lower ones should point in opposite directions.

In spring carefully direct the shoot from the top bud vertically up a cane and the others to the right and the left. It is difficult to obtain horizontal shoots in the first year without a check to growth and it is best to train the two shoots initially at angles of about 45 degrees to the main stem. This can be achieved by tying them to canes secured to the wire framework.

During summer the angle can be varied so that a weaker shoot is encouraged to catch up by raising it a little towards the vertical.

In November, at the end of the first growing season, lower the two side branches to the horizontal and tie them to the wire supports. Prune back the central leader to within 18 in of the junction, with the lower arms to coincide with the next wire. The intention is to promote a further three growths—one to continue the central axis and the other two to form a second tier of side branches. Shorten surplus laterals from the main stem to three buds. Prune the two horizontal leaders to downward-pointing buds, removing about one-third of each shoot. If growth has been particularly satisfactory, perhaps because of a good growing season, the leaders can be left unpruned.

Second and subsequent years The next years are a repetition of the first, with subsequent tiers of branches being trained in. In late winter lower the side branches to the horizontal and secure them to the wire supports. Cut back the central leader to within 18 in of the last tier of arms at the next wire. Cut back unwanted laterals from the main stem to three buds. The horizontal leaders should be cut back by one-third, cutting to downward-pointing buds, if growth has been quite poor.

Cut back competing growths from the main stem to three leaves during the summer from July to September.

The first year

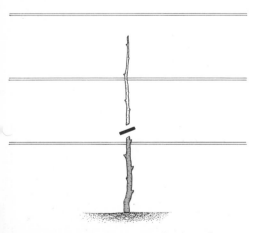

1 In late winter, plant an unfeathered maiden tree. Cut back the stem to within 15 in of ground level. Leave room for a short leg and select three good upper buds for training.

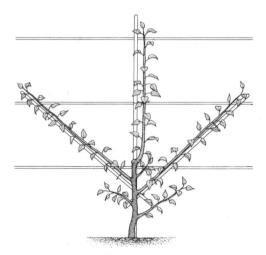

2 From June to September, train the shoot from the top bud vertically up a cane. Train the shoots from the two lower buds at an angle of 45 degrees to the main stem. Tie them to canes fixed on the wire support.

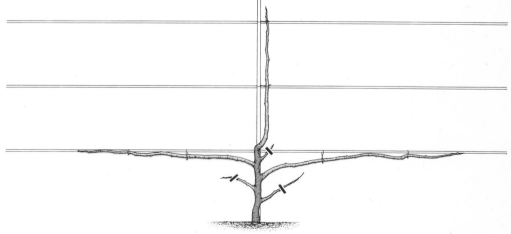

3 At the end of the growing season, lower the two side branches to the horizontal and tie them carefully to the wire supports with soft string. Cut back surplus laterals on the main stem to three buds.

Apples and pears 9

There is a tendency for vertical shoots to grow from the horizontal arms. These laterals are pruned in summer, cutting each back to three leaves above the basal cluster. Do not tie the extension growth of the horizontal arms until the end of the summer because early tying checks growth. In winter train and prune both the horizontal and vertical leaders

in the same way as before. This regime of winter and summer pruning should continue until the desired number of tiers has been built in.

The number of tiers finally achieved depends on soil, site and inherent vigor, but four or five is usual. Eventually both the central axis and the horizontal arms fill their

allotted space. From then onwards cut back the new terminal shoots to their origin each May and summer prune subsequent growth.

The fruiting stage
Each summer The fruits are carried on spur systems on the horizontal arms. The spurs are formed by the summer pruning of laterals

on the Modified Lorette System in the same way as for cordons. Regard each arm as a horizontal cordon (see pages 121–122).

Winter After a few years of fruiting, the spur systems may become complicated and should be simplified by removing clusters of weak buds and by cutting back some of the spurs to two or three fruit buds.

Second and subsequent years

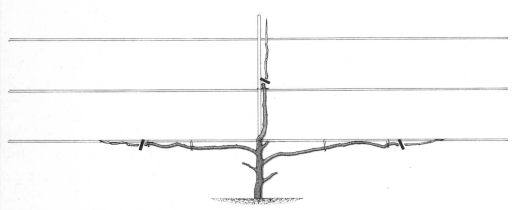

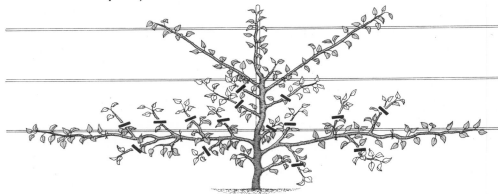

4 At the same time, cut back the central leader to within 18 in of the lower arm at the next wire, leaving three good buds to form the central leader and two new horizontal arms. If growth is weak, prune back the horizontal leaders by one-third, cutting to downward-pointing buds.

5 From July to September, train the second tier of branches in the same way as in the previous years (see caption 2). Cut back competing growths from the main stem to three leaves. Cut back laterals from the horizontal arms to three leaves above the basal cluster.

Mature tree

6 In winter, cut back the central leader to within 18 in of the lower arm, leaving three good buds to form the new central leader and two new horizontal arms. Cut back surplus laterals on the main stem to 3 buds. Tie down the extension growth of each arm to the horizontal. If growth is poor, prune back the leaders by one-third.

7 In May, when the final number of tiers is produced and the tree has filled its allotted space, cut back the new terminal growths of the vertical and horizontal arms to their origins. From now on prune them each summer as if they were cordons.

Apples and pears 10

The dwarf pyramid
The dwarf pyramid was evolved by commercial fruit growers as an easier method of producing apples and pears intensively. The pear, in particular, when grown on Quince rootstock, responds well to this method of training and in recent years the technique has been extended to plums. With apples and pears the aim is to produce a central-leader tree some 7 ft high with a total branch spread of about 4 ft through the tree, tapering to the top to form a pyramid.

It is essential to keep such a closely planted and compact tree under control. This control is exerted by a combination of summer pruning, early cropping, the complete removal of any vigorous upright shoots, and the choice of a rootstock capable of sustaining the required balance between steady cropping and the renewal of bearing wood.

Choice of rootstock
Malling 9 and Malling 26 rootstock are suitable for apples in most gardens and either Quince A or the re-cloned Quince C (when generally available) can be used for pears.

Planting and staking
In early fall, prepare the soil (see page 116). Plant in the dormant season from November to March. Individual stakes are not necessary unless planting only one or two trees. With a row of trees, support them by erecting two posts at the ends of the row, and stretch two horizontal wires between them, one at 18 in and the other at 36 in. Tie the trees to these, using string or strapping.

Spacing
Space apples on M9 rootstocks at 4–5 ft apart, and apples on M26 rootstocks and pears 5–6 ft apart. Allow the wider spacing on fertile soils. The rows should be 7 ft apart.

Pruning and training
The first year A start is made with a maiden tree, which is cut back to about 20 in on planting during the dormant season in early spring. Prune to a bud on the opposite side to the graft. The result of this initial pruning is the production of four or five strong shoots. The uppermost shoot, which will become the leader, grows vertically.

The first year

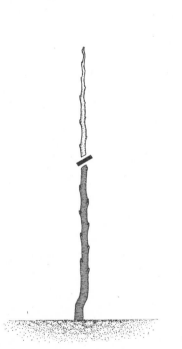

The second year

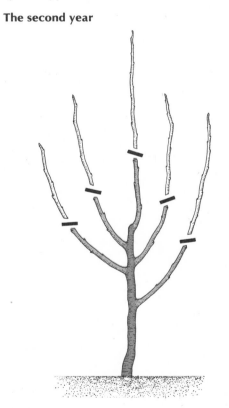

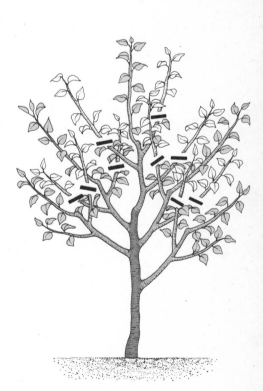

1 In early spring, at planting cut back the maiden to a bud within 20 in of ground level.

2 From July to August, four or five strong shoots will have been produced. No pruning is necessary.

3 In late winter, cut back the central leader to leave 9 in of new growth. Cut to a bud that points in the opposite direction to the last pruning. Cut back side branches to downward-pointing buds to leave 8 in of the maiden extension.

4 In late winter, cut back laterals not required for the framework to three leaves or 3–4 in and sub-laterals to one leaf beyond the basal cluster. Leave leaders unpruned.

Apples and pears 11

The second year In the following winter prune the central leader to leave about 9 in new growth, taking care to cut to a bud that points in the opposite direction to the last pruning. This is aimed at keeping the successive stages of the central stem as straight as possible, in a series of zig-zags. It would be easier not to prune the leader at all because the stem would be straighter if left untouched, but such pruning is necessary to stimulate the annual production of side branches during the formative stages. These side branches, perhaps four in number and evenly spaced around the tree, are pruned back to within 8 in of the maiden extension, cutting each to a downward-pointing bud to maintain the horizontal direction.

During the following summer begin summer pruning, starting in mid-July for pears and about the end of July for apples. Cut back laterals (the current season's growth) longer than 9 in arising directly from the side branches to three leaves, and laterals from existing spurs to one leaf beyond the basal cluster. Leave immature shoots until September and then prune them in the same way.

Do not prune the leaders in summer.

Third and subsequent years Prune the central leader in winter. Aim to leave about 9 in of new growth, cutting to a bud that is pointing in the opposite direction from the bud to which the stem was pruned in the previous winter. This stimulates the production of new side branches. Cut back any secondary growth that may have occurred as a result of summer pruning to a mature bud.

Every summer, prune the current season's growth on the side branches using the Modified Lorette System (see page 121), treating each side branch as if it were a cordon. Prune the branch leaders to six leaves.

When the tree reaches 7 ft, further extension growth should be stopped by cutting back the leader to its origin each May. Prune any other shoots that need restriction, such as vigorous upright shoots at the top or branch leaders growing into adjacent trees.

In winter it is occasionally necessary to shorten branches to a downward-pointing shoot in an attempt to maintain the essential horizontal position of the fruiting arms. Trim overcrowded spurs at the same time.

Third and subsequent years

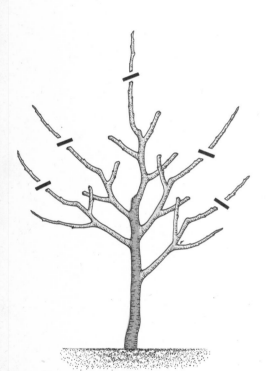

5 From November to February, prune the central leader to leave about 9 in of new growth, cutting to a bud on the opposite side to the previous pruning.

6 From July to August, throughout summer cut back laterals to three leaves or 3–4 in and sub-laterals to one leaf beyond the basal cluster. Prune the leaders of the side branches to six leaves.

7 In late winter, prune the central leader to leave 9 in of new growth. Remove entirely any over-vigorous shoots. Shorten branches to downward-pointing buds as necessary to maintain the horizontal position of the fruiting arms.

THE MATURE TREE

When the tree has reached the required height of about 7 ft, cut back the leader to its origin each May. Thin fruiting spurs as necessary. Maintain the central stem and retain the pyramid shape by close pruning and removal of vigorous shoots.

Apples and pears 12

Cultivation

Feeding and mulching Apply fertilizers as a top dressing over the rooting area, which is roughly equivalent to the spread of the tree and slightly beyond. Inorganic fertilizers can scorch grass, therefore brush well in and water the grass if the weather is dry. If the soil tends to be acid, with a pH lower than 6.7, sulfate of ammonia should not be applied because it makes the soil more acid. Instead use an artificial fertilizer containing calcium carbonate and ammonium nitrate. It does not affect the pH.

In early March, mulch newly planted and young trees with well-rotted manure, compost or peat to a depth of 2 in over a radius of about 18 in, but keep the mulch just clear of the stem.

Dessert apples In mid-winter apply sulfate of potash at $\frac{3}{4}$ oz per square yard. Every three years, in mid-winter apply superphosphate at 2 oz per square yard. In late winter apply sulfate of ammonia or the fertilizer mentioned above, at 1 oz per square yard.

Dessert apples in grass See cooking apples.

Cooking apples The same rates and timings given for dessert apples apply except that extra nitrogen is necessary, so double the application of sulfate of ammonia or the fertilizer mentioned above. This also applies to dessert apples grown in grass.

During heavy rainfall in spring and summer, and in high rainfall areas, some apple varieties suffer from magnesium deficiency (see pages 260–262). At the first signs, apply three foliar sprays at 14-day intervals, using 8 oz magnesium sulfate in $2\frac{1}{2}$ gal water, plus a spreader ($\frac{1}{4}$ fl oz washing-up liquid). To avoid a recurrence, apply the magnesium sulfate as a top dressing in April, at 2 oz per square yard over the rooting area.

Pears, dessert and cooking Pears benefit from additional nitrogen, but if too much is given, vigorous growth is encouraged which, in turn, encourages fire blight. In the first year, therefore, apply only a few handfuls of balanced fertilizer such as 10-10-10. From the second year until the tree starts to bear, apply 8 oz of ammonium nitrate. Then increase the application to 16 oz and then, when the tree is about 10 years old, apply 24 oz. Thereafter, apply 32 oz per year.

Watering To ensure good establishment and strong growth, young trees (especially newly planted ones) need to be watered in the growing season whenever the soil is dry. As a guide, apply 4 gal per square yard every ten days throughout dry periods.

Cropping trees also respond to irrigation by producing heavier crops of larger and better quality fruit. Lack of water may induce a biennial bearing pattern (see page 129). The total amount of water needed is about 4 in (18 gal per square yard) in July, 3 in ($13\frac{1}{2}$ gal per square yard) in August and 2 in (9 gal per square yard) in September.

Obviously, in cool wet regions these totals will be met by natural rainfall, but in dry areas some water must be applied, the actual amount depending upon the rainfall. Apply 2 in (9 gal per square yard) at a time under the trees, starting in early July. Use a slow-running hose as a soaker and keep the water on the ground rather than on the foliage, irrigating over the rooting area.

Fruit thinning The main purpose of fruit thinning is to obtain larger and better quality fruits. In heavy cropping years if the fruits are not thinned, the resultant crop will consist of small, medium to poor quality apples or pears and, as with lack of water, the strain imposed upon the tree might put it into a biennial habit. Much depends upon the condition of the trees: trees with healthy foliage and a strong framework can carry more fruit than can weaker trees. Young trees should not be allowed to crop so heavily that the branches are bowed down and the tree cannot make the essential strong growth needed for its framework.

Some varieties naturally shed some of their fruitlets in late June or early July which is called the June drop, but this may not be sufficient. Start lightly thinning before this in mid-June by removing the malformed fruits, and then complete the task after the June drop in about mid-July.

Cooking varieties should be thinned harder than the dessert fruits.

Use sharp scissors or press the fruitlet with the thumb and finger, leaving the stalk behind. In the final thinning, dessert apples should be spaced on average 4–6 in apart with about one fruit per cluster and occasionally two where there is a good show of supporting leaves. Cooking apples should be spaced on average 6–9 in apart.

With apples, sometimes the "king" or "crown" fruit produced in the center of a cluster is virtually stalkless and malformed. If this is the case, remove it, but if the apple is well shaped, leave it because the king fruit can be the best in the cluster.

Pears need less thinning than do apples. Start thinning after the natural drop in late June, but not until the fruitlets turn downwards. Thin to two fruits per cluster and occasionally to one where the foliage is poor or sparse.

Supporting heavily laden branches Prop up heavily laden branches well before there is a risk of the branches breaking. Use forked poles or stakes but place a cushion of soft material such as a piece of rubber tire between the prop and the branch.

Weak branches can be tied to stronger ones with rope or webbing. Small trees can

Manuring

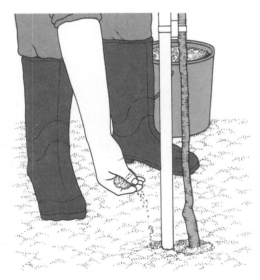

1 In mid-winter, apply sulfate of potash at the recommended rates. In late winter apply sulfate of ammonia.

Mulching

2 In early March, mulch newly planted and young trees with a 2 in layer of well-rotted manure or compost over a radius of 18 in.

Watering

3 In summer, apply 4 gal per square yard every ten days in dry periods.

Apples and pears 13

be supported by "maypoling". This involves driving a tall stake into the ground near the stem of the tree and tying rope or thick string from its top to each branch that will benefit from support.

Protection from wasps and birds

Apples and pears (especially the early varieties) sometimes need protection against wasps and birds. The trees can be netted or collars placed around the fruit stalks against birds but wasps are more difficult to combat. One remedy is to find and destroy the wasps' nest. They can also be trapped in jam jars partly filled with beer and sugar. However, these two methods guarantee only partial control and the most positive (if tedious) protection against wasps is to enclose each fruit, or cluster of fruits, in a muslin bag or piece of nylon stocking.

Harvesting and storing

The time for picking apples and pears varies according to the season and the locality so it is not possible to give exact picking dates. As a guide, the earliest varieties of apples are ready for picking in late July to early August.

Apples A good test for ripeness is to lift the fruit in the palm of the hand and if it leaves the spur easily with its stalk intact, it is ready. Another sign is the first windfalls (discounting drops from strong winds and codling moth attack). With the later ripening varieties, the color of the pips is an indication. They should be beginning to change color from white to straw-coloured and eventually to brown. With dessert apples in particular the skin of the fruits becomes more brightly colored.

Early varieties are best picked when slightly immature because they soon go mealy. Pick those apples that have colored rather than clearing all the apples in one go. Usually those apples in full sun are ready first and those in the middle of the tree last. Handle the fruits very gently because bruised fruits do not keep. Put the fruits carefully into a picking container lined with soft material and transfer them just as gently into their final container.

Late apples reach maturity in storage sometime after picking, depending upon the variety. Most should be off the tree by about the third week of October, but there are a few varieties which keep better and acquire more flavor if left on as long as possible, birds and winter gales permitting. These include 'Granny Smith' and 'Idared'.

Store only sound fruits (see page 113 for details of storage).

Pears The correct time for picking pears is harder to assess than it is for apples. The best test of readiness is to lift the pear in the palm of the hand and with a slight twist and tug, it should leave the spur with its stalk intact. There is also an almost imperceptible change in the ground color of the skin from dark green to lighter green.

Early and early mid-season pears (August to September) must not be left on the tree until they are fully ripe otherwise they may go "sleepy", that is very soft, mealy and brown at the center. Pick them when they are almost ready but still firm, and then let them mellow in storage. Their storage life can be extended considerably by keeping them under cool conditions (3°–7°C/37°–45°F).

Late pears should be left on the tree until they leave the spur easily; the first sign of windfalls is an indication. The fruits are hard at this stage but will mellow in storage. Keep them under cold conditions and bring the pears into room temperature to finish ripening whenever required. (See page 113 for details of storage).

Pests and diseases

Apples The most troublesome diseases are scab, mildew and canker and the most troublesome pests are aphids, leaf-eating caterpillars, sawfly and codling moth larvae.

Scab and mildew can be controlled by regular spraying with benomyl or captan starting at bud burst and finishing in July. If canker occurs, cut out the rotting wood and paint the clean wounds with a canker paint. In bad attacks also apply liquid copper sprays after harvest and at 50 per cent leaf-fall, and the following year at bud burst. Check that the soil is not badly drained (see pages 8–11).

Use a systemic aphicide against aphids.

Thinning

4 In mid-June, thin the fruits using sharp scissors or press the fruitlets off with the thumb and finger, leaving the stalk behind.

In mid-July, thin again to leave one or two dessert apples per cluster 4–6 in apart, cooking apples 6–9 in apart. Pears need less thinning; leave two fruits per cluster.

Maypoling

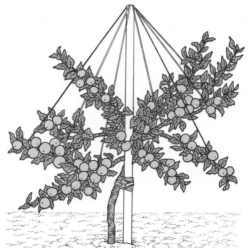

5 On small trees, to support branches with a heavy crop, drive a tall stake into the ground near the stem of the tree. Tie a rope from its top to each branch.

Grassing down the orchard

6 After four or five years, sow grass in the orchard. Sow a fine lawn mixture at 2 oz per square yard, leaving a grass-free area of 2 ft radius around the base of each tree.

Apples and pears 14

Spraying with dimethoate one week after petal fall controls sawfly larvae. Use a general-purpose fruit spray against codling moth caterpillars in mid-June and again at the end of June.

Pears The most troublesome disease of pears is scab and the most troublesome pests are aphids and leaf-eating caterpillars.

For scab spray with captan or benomyl at bud burst, repeating every two weeks as necessary until late July.

The whole business of pest control can be greatly simplified if a general-purpose fruit spray containing an insecticide and fungicide is used on a systematic schedule throughout the growing season.

In winter, during dormancy, spray with a dormant oil. Then use the general-purpose spray (1) just before blossoms open, (2) when three-fourths of the flower petals have fallen, (3) two weeks after petal fall, and (4) every 10–14 days thereafter until about three weeks before harvest.

Adding a "sticker" (a gluey liquid) to the spray keeps it from being rapidly diluted by the rain. If the "sticker" is not used, it may be necessary to increase the frequency of spray in wet or very humid weather to every seven days.

Propagation
Apples and pears do not come true from seed nor are they satisfactory from cuttings, so they are propagated by budding or grafting on to suitable rootstocks, a task normally performed by the fruit tree nursery.

Biennial bearing
Biennial bearing or the carrying of a heavy crop one year and little or none in the next, is a common problem with apples and pears. Certain varieties are prone to it, although almost any variety can fall into this habit. It is more likely to happen to trees which are starved or receiving insufficient moisture, which makes them unable to carry a heavy crop and at the same time develop fruit buds for the following year. Frost destroying the blossom one spring can sometimes be the start of biennial bearing. Once the tree is into this cropping pattern it is difficult to correct, although there are certain techniques the

---

BIENNIAL BEARING

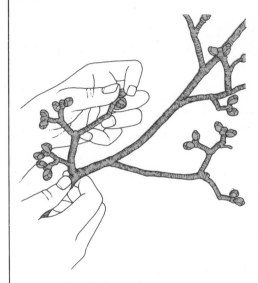

1 In spring, before a heavy crop year, rub one-half to three-quarters of the fruit buds from the spurs, leaving one or two per spur.

2 Each March, apply 4 oz per square yard of a balanced fertilizer, such as 10-10-10, and sulfate of ammonia at 2 oz per square yard. Mulch small trees with a 2 in layer of well-rotted manure over a radius of 2 ft.

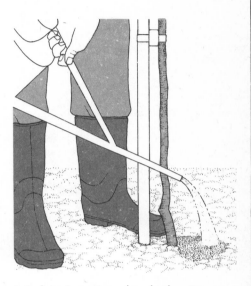

3 In late August, apply a further 2 oz per square yard of sulfate of ammonia. In dry weather water copiously, giving at least 1 in of water ($4\frac{1}{2}$ gal per square yard) over the rooting area every ten days until rain restores the balance.

---

gardener can try which sometimes improve the situation.

In early spring before an expected heavy crop year, half to three-quarters of the fruit buds are rubbed off the spurs, leaving about one or two per spur. This lessens the burden of too heavy a crop in that year and may enable the tree to develop fruit buds for the next year.

In conjunction with bud rubbing, a policy of more generous feeding and watering should be adopted in "on" and "off" years. But remember the danger of over-feeding pears.

First, clear away grass or weeds from the base of the tree over a radius of at least 2 ft.

Each March apply a balanced fertilizer such as 10-10-10 at 4 oz per square yard and sulfate of ammonia at 2 oz per square yard. Small trees should also be mulched with well-rotted manure or compost to a depth of 2 in over a radius of 2 ft but keep the material clear of the stem.

In late August apply a further 2 oz per square yard of sulfate of ammonia. Throughout the growing season, whenever the conditions are dry, the tree should be irrigated copiously by applying at least 1 in of water ($4\frac{1}{2}$ gal per square yard) over the rooting area every ten days until rain restores the balance.

If bud rubbing does not work, an alternative technique is to induce the tree to crop biennially over half the tree by removing half the blossom. Alternate branches are selected and marked in some way. Half the branches are designated to crop in the even years (1980, 1982, and so on) and half the branches are designated to crop in the odd years (1981, 1983, and so on). Each spring, those branches not selected to crop in that par-

ticular year must be rigorously deblossomed. At first this deblossoming represents quite a task, especially with a large tree, but after the third or fourth year it should be found that the branches have accepted this alternate pattern and very little blossom removal is necessary. However, a careful watch should be kept to see that the tree does not slip back into the full biennial cropping. As with the first technique, generous feeding is recommended.

Grassing the orchard
After four or five years, sow grass seed throughout the orchard. Grass checks the vigor of the trees and promotes color in the fruits, so grass down dessert fruits, but not cooking apples or cooking pears for which size is more important than color. Delay grassing if the trees are growing poorly.

Plums 1

EUROPEAN PLUM VARIETIES

'Fellemberg' Large, oval, purple fruits with sweet firm flesh. Mid-season. Hardy, productive tree. Self-fruitful.
'French damson' Large, dark blue fruits of excellent quality. Remain on trees for a long time without too much deterioration. Mid-season to late. Self-fruitful.
'Green gage' Excellent flavor. Small, yellow-green fruits with russet dots and pink flesh. Juicy. Freestone. Mid-season. Self-fruitful.
'Imperial Epineuse' Very large prune-plum with reddish-purple skin. Semi-clingstone. Mid-season. Self-fruitful. Brown rot is troublesome.
'Oneida' Reddish-black prune-plum of good size and quality. Freestone. Self-fruitful.
'Shropshire' Small, blue, very tart fruits in mid-season. Self-fruitful.
'Stanley' Large, bluish-purple fruits. Juicy, rich flavor. Mid-season. Reliably self-fruitful.
'Yellow Egg' Large, oval yellow fruits of quality. Juicy and sweet. Late. Self-fruitful.

A classification of plums

Plums grow in varieties of color, shape, and size and are known by different names in various parts of the world. Understandably, therefore, confusion often occurs among gardeners and botanists over names in the plum family.

The plum is a deciduous tree ranging in height from 15–30 ft when mature. It bears small fruit and is popular with gardeners. For reasons of simplification, the plum can be classified into three broad categories or groups: European, Japanese and native. But there are several other fruits which are also called plums, and these will be described briefly at the end of this section.

The European plum, primarily a blue fruit growing in zones 5–7, is further sub-classified simply as plum, or as, for example, gage, damson, or bullace. These fruits are recognized in the United States as plums, but a varietal name, such as green gage plum, damson plum, or Stanley prune plum, is appended for more precise identification.

The Japanese plum is a red fruit somewhat larger than the European plum, and grows in zones 5–9. Native plums, the best of which are for the most part hybrids, are the results of crosses with Japanese plums. The fruits are red or yellow and fairly small. These trees grow in zones 3–7.

All plums can be canned or made into jams or jellies, but not all are ideal for immediate consumption. The Japanese plum is generally the best of the many plums available for eating when ripe and fresh, but many of the European plums are also excellent eating.

Since the plum does not form a very large tree, it is generally grown as a free-standing tree in the open. Standard, semi-dwarf and dwarf specimens are available. Some of the European varieties can be fan-trained against a warm wall or a fence, or as a pyramid, a very good form for the small garden. It is not suited to such restricted forms as the cordon or espalier.

Pollination

As a rule of thumb, plums are self-unfruitful. The numerous exceptions to this rule are noted in the lists of varieties (above). A general safeguard, however, is to plant any variety of plum in the proximity of another variety to ensure a good set of fruit. But it should be realized that European and Japanese plums cannot pollinate each other. Native plums are pollinated either by other native varieties, by sandcherry-plum hybrids or, in the case of crosses between native and Japanese plums, by Japanese varieties.

Cultivation

The cultivation of all the various types of plums is broadly the same. The major variations are in pruning.

Yield A good average yield from a fully-grown plum tree in the open ranges from 30 to 120 lb.

Soil and situation Plums require a deep, moisture-retentive, well-drained soil with a pH from 6.5 to 7.2. Shallow soils over light, sandy subsoils are unsuitable. The plums grow best in clean soil. Control grass and weeds around the tree by shallow hoeing. Avoid too deep cultivation because this encourages suckering. Plum varieties on vigorous rootstocks can be surrounded with grass, but a clean area 2 ft square should be maintained right around the base of the tree.

Plums flower early, and so a sheltered, frost-free site must be chosen because this is essential to avoid irregular cropping. Japanese plums, which bloom very early, should be planted on a north-facing slope or the north side of a building or wall in order to retard blooming and thus protect the plums from late frosts.

Soil preparation In the fall or early spring, prepare the ground by thoroughly clearing away perennial weeds over an area 3 ft square. Fork in a balanced fertilizer such as 10-10-10 at 3 oz per square yard and bonemeal at 2 oz per square yard just before planting. If the soil is light, also fork in well-rotted manure or compost at one 2-gal bucketful per 2 square feet.

Planting and spacing Plant bare-root trees in March or April while the tree is dormant. Container-grown trees can be planted at any

1 In autumn, prepare the ground, clearing away perennial weeds. Lightly fork in 3 oz of a balanced fertilizer and 2 oz of bonemeal per square yard.

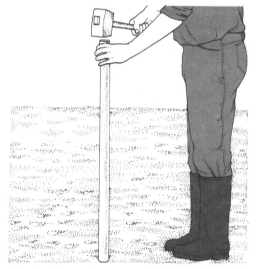

2 For trees in the open, drive in a stake. For fan-trained trees construct a system of wires on the wall. Plant the tree and tie it to the stake or to the wall wires.

3 In February, apply a balanced fertilizer at 4 oz per square yard. One month later, apply sulphate of ammonia at 1 oz per square yard. Mulch the tree with a 1–2 in layer of compost or manure.

4 Thin the fruits when they are the size of hazelnuts and once the stones have formed within the fruits. Repeat when the fruits are twice this size to leave them 2–3 in apart on the branches.

Plums 2

JAPANESE PLUM VARIETIES
'Abundance' Big, red fruits. Sweet and juicy. Extremely susceptible to brown rot.
'Elephant Ear' Big, red fruits with red flesh of outstanding flavor. Mid-season. Does best in dry western areas.
'Methley' Purple-red fruits with delicious red flesh. Very productive, but inclined to bear bienially. A good variety for warm climates.
'Queen Ann' Large, heart-shaped fruits of a dark mahogany color. Tree is weak.
'Santa Rosa' Large, red fruits changing to reddish purple when fully ripe. Excellent flavor. Mid-season. Widely grown and prolific.
'Shiro' Golden-yellow fruits ripening in early August.

time. Dig a hole wide and deep enough to take the roots fully extended. For trees in the open, before planting drive in a stake to reach just below the lowest branch. For fan-trained trees, construct a system of supporting, horizontal wires spaced 6 in apart (see pages 90–91). Plant the tree to the same depth as it was in the nursery. Return the soil and firm it well. Tie to the stake with a tree tie and cushion or tie in the branches of a fan to the wall wires. Water well. Trees in the open require staking for the first two or three years.

Space trees grown in the open 20 ft apart. Fan-trained trees are spaced 15–20 ft apart.

Pruning
Since Japanese and native plums grow more vigorously than European varieties, they require more pruning. This includes cutting back the head to some extent almost every year.

The first year In late winter, cut back the central stem of the maiden tree to a bud at about 2–3 ft for a dwarf, or 4–5 ft for a standard. It may be necessary to grow the tree on for another year to acquire the needed height for a standard before cutting it back. Shorten all laterals to about 3 in to help thicken the stem.

In July or August, select four to five evenly spaced primary branches around the stem at the top. Pinch out the growing points of all others at four or five leaves, including those lower down the main stem.

The second year In late winter, select four branches that have formed wide angles with the stem. Cut back each leader of those selected by one-half to outward-facing buds. Remove the remainder, including the lower laterals of the last year to thicken the stem.

In the summer, remove any suckers that appear from the ground as well as shoots on the main stem below the head.

The third year Repeat the procedures adopted in the previous spring and summer, but allow more secondary branches to develop to fill the increased space, providing up to eight strong, well-placed outward-growing branches. In late winter, cut these back by one-half to two-thirds of the maiden growth to outward-facing buds. Leave shoots on the outer parts of the head not required for leaders. Prune back unpruned laterals on the inside of the tree to 3–4 in.

Little pruning of European plums is necessary in subsequent years. Generally, all that is needed is to cut out dead, broken, rubbing and crossing branches and to thin out the head when it becomes crowded. Japanese and native plums require the same general treatment, but, as noted above, may need some heading back.

Pruning the fan-trained tree Starting with a maiden tree, the framework of a fan-trained plum is built up in the same way as a fan-trained peach (see pages 136–139). Thereafter, the pruning is different because, unlike the peach, the plum fruits on short spurs on three- and four-year-old wood as well as on growth made in the previous summer. However, the older wood tends to become bare with age and from damage by frost or birds. The aim in pruning is to encourage spur formation and, when necessary, to replace worn-out branches.

In the early years, extend the framework, as with the peach, to fill in the wall space; then follow the steps below.

In the spring of later years, cut out a proportion of the old, worn-out wood back to young replacement branches. Paint the wounds.

Feeding and watering
In early spring, apply a balanced fertilizer, such as 10-10-10, at 4 oz per square yard. Mulch young trees with a 1–2 in layer of well-rotted manure or compost over a radius of 18 in, keeping the mulch clear of the stem.

Water well and regularly in dry weather during the growing season, applying 1 in of water ($4\frac{1}{2}$ gal per square yard) every ten days until rain corrects the balance. Avoid irregular heavy watering because this can cause splitting of the fruits, especially near the ripening stage.

Thinning the fruits
Thin the fruits (if the tree carries a heavy crop) after the stones have formed within the fruits

The pyramid plum: the first year

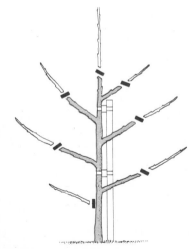

1 In March, cut back the leader to 5 ft. Cut back to the stem all laterals up to 18 in from the ground. Cut back the remaining laterals by one-half.

2 In late July, shorten the new growth of the branch leaders to 8 in to downward-facing buds. Shorten the current season's laterals on the branches to 6 in. Do not prune the central leader.

Second and subsequent years

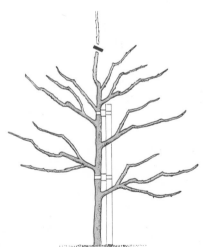

3 In March, shorten the central leader by two-thirds of the previous summer's growth until the tree has reached about 9 ft, then shorten the central leader to 1 in each May to keep the tree at this height.

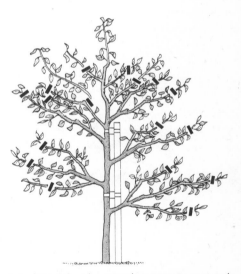

4 In late July, shorten the current season's growth of each branch leader to eight leaves. Shorten the laterals to six leaves. Cut out any vigorous shoots at the top of the tree.

Plums 3

NATIVE PLUMS
'Red-coat' Medium-size dark red fruits not very good for eating, but fine for cooking. Freestone. Mid-season.
'South Dakota' Medium-size, red fruits. Very sweet. Mid-season.
'Superior' A Japanese-native hybrid. Large, red fruits of superior quality. Mid-season. Not so hardy as true natives,

but hardier than Japanese varieties. Very productive.
'Tecumseh' Medium-sized, juicy, red fruits. Early.
'Underwood' Excellent quality. Big, dark red fruits. Early.

to avoid loss of flavor and the possibility of a biennial pattern of bearing. Thin once when the fruits are about the size of hazelnuts, and again when they are twice this size. On most European and native plums, fruits left on the tree to ripen should be 2–3 in apart; however, allow 4 in in the case of very large varieties. Japanese plums should be thinned to 3–4 in apart. Do not tug the fruits off because this may tear away the following year's fruit buds; cut the fruit stalk with scissors or shears.

Supporting the branches

It is essential to support very heavily laden branches because they may break and spoil the shape of the tree. Such wounds also increase the risk of bacterial infection. Support individual branches with a clothes prop or forked stake driven into the ground at an angle. Wrap the branch with burlap where it meets the crotch of the support. Alternatively, the branches of dwarf trees can be supported with ropes tied to a central stake in maypole fashion (see illustration 5 on page 128).

Protection against birds

The fruit buds of the plum are susceptible to bird damage in winter and the ripe fruit is also at risk in the summer. Where necessary and practicable, protect the tree with lightweight nylon or plastic netting.

Harvesting and storing

Plums ripen from midsummer on. They do not ripen simultaneously and it is necessary to go over the tree several times. Pick fruits intended for canning, jam and cooking while still slightly under-ripe. Pick all fruits with the stalks intact.

Plums cannot be stored for prolonged periods, but they will keep for two to three weeks if picked when a little under-ripe and kept in a cool place, at about 6°–7°C/42°–45°F.

Propagation

Plums are propagated by budding or grafting, a task normally carried out by the nursery. For more details see the **Propagation** section in this book (pages 172–203).

Pests and diseases

Spray trees with dormant oil in late winter. Then apply a general-purpose fruit tree spray when the petals fall and at 10–14 day intervals until approximately a month before harvest. Brown rot is a problem if the weather is warm and humid at time of bloom or in the three-week period before harvest. To control it, spray with captan at 3–4 day intervals.

Sandcherry-plum hybrids

These small ($\frac{1}{2}$ in to $1\frac{1}{4}$ in diameter) plums are also known as cherry plums. They are the result of crossing native sandcherries with plums, usually native but sometimes Japanese. Accordingly, the deciduous plants range from shrubs no more than 4 ft high to trees about 25 ft high. The fruits have purple, red or green skins and yellow to purple flesh. Sandcherry-plum hybrids are most commonly grown in zones 2–6, where true plums do not thrive.

The many varieties all fruit from mid-August to September.

Cultivation

The sandcherry-plums are grown like plums and in dry regions require about as much space. In wetter areas, however, spacing can be reduced considerably. The best fruit is borne on young growth, so the plants must be pruned rather hard every year. A good procedure is to remove entire branches after they have fruited for about three years. The plants are self-unfruitful; plant two or more varieties.

Beach plums

The beach plum is generally associated with Cape Cod, where it grows wild in profusion, but it can be grown throughout zones 6–8 near the ocean.

Cultivation

The beach plum grows in indifferent soil so long as it is well-drained, but needs full sun. A little balanced plant food can be applied in early spring, the plants can be mulched with leaves, and then pretty well forgotten. Watering is required only in long dry spells.

The plum fan

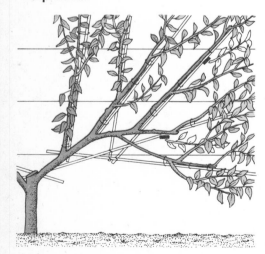

1 For the first three years, follow the formative pruning steps for the peach fan (see pages 138–139) extending the framework to fill in the wall space. Prune only in spring or summer.

Fourth and subsequent years

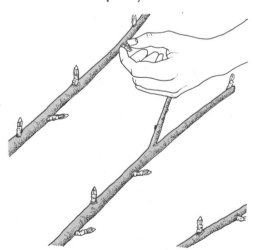

2 Each spring, as growth begins, rub out shoots growing directly towards the wall and breastwood.

3 From late June to late July, as new shoots are made, pinch out the growing points of shoots not wanted for the framework when they have made six or seven leaves. This begins to form the fruit-bearing spur system.

4 After cropping, between mid-August and mid-September, cut back the pinched-out shoots to three leaves to encourage fruit buds to form at the bases of the pinched-out shoots the following year.

Sweet and Duke cherries 1

SWEET CHERRY VARIETIES

'Bing' Undoubtedly the best known. Large fruits in mid-season are very deep red, almost black, with firm, sweet flesh. But subject to cracking. Mid-season.
'Black Tartarian' Excellent purple-black fruits of medium size. Semi-early.
'Early Rivers' Very large crimson-black fruits of excellent flavor. Vigorous,

somewhat spreading tree. Early.
'Emperor Francis' Big red and yellow fruits. Mid-season. Juicy and of excellent flavor. Productive.
'Giant' Very similar to 'Bing' and considered to be better by some gardeners.
'Lambert' Large, purple-red fruits. Very sweet. Late. Unusually hardy: the variety

The cultivated sweet, or dessert, cherry is a hybrid between *Prunus avium* and *P. cerasus*. It is a hardy deciduous tree which is cultivated in many areas of Europe and western Asia. It bears clusters of attractive, white flowers in spring and bears fruits, ranging in color from yellow and pink to almost jet black, from June onwards in cool temperate areas. It grows in zones 6 and 7, and in protected locations in zone 5.

The Duke cherry is thought to be a cross between the sweet and sour cherry and it is intermediate in character between the two. 'May Duke', 'Olivet', 'Reine Hortense' and 'Royal Duke' are good varieties, but are difficult to find.

Cultivation

Although this delicious fruit merits a place in any garden, it has one serious drawback—its extreme vigor. Despite the introduction of increasingly dwarfing rootstocks, the cherry remains quite vigorous and is therefore not suitable for a small garden. It is often grown as a fan on a wall, but the wall must be fairly high. In the open it is grown as a standard. By using the less vigorous rootstock Colt, it could be grown as a pyramid. Treat Duke cherries in the same way as sweet cherries.

Yield The yield from the different kinds of cherry can vary enormously depending, of course, on the size, age and form of the tree and the climate. A good average from a fan is about 30 lb and from a well-grown standard 100 lb.

Soil and situation Cherries grow in any good, well-drained soil but it must be deep, ideally more than 2½ ft. The pH should be between 6.7 and 7.5. Light, sandy and shallow soils are not suitable.

Cherry blossom is susceptible to frost and young trees to wind damage so the site should be sheltered from winds, in full sun and not in a frost pocket.

Soil preparation In the spring clear away weeds over an area 3 ft square, single digging clear ground and double digging weedy ground. Just before planting, fork in a balanced fertilizer such as 10-10-10 at the rate of 3 oz per square yard with bonemeal at 2 oz per square yard.

Planting and spacing Plant when dormant in March or April. Container-grown trees can be planted at any time. Dig a hole wide and deep enough to take the roots fully extended. For trees in the open, before planting drive in a stake to reach just below the lowest branches. Standard cherries require two stakes and a crossbar. For fan-trained trees, erect a system of horizontal wires on the wall using 14 gauge wire and spaced 6 in or two brick courses apart (see pages 90–91).

Plant the tree to the same depth as it was at the nursery. Return the soil and firm it well. Tie to the stake with a tree tie and cushion, or tie in the branches of a fan to the wall wires. Space fan-trees 18–25 ft apart; half-standards and standards at 30–40 ft apart and dwarfs 25–35 ft apart.

Pruning the fan-trained tree

The sweet cherry fan is pruned as shown in the step-by-step instructions below. Prune in spring as the buds burst and not in winter because of the risk of bacterial canker. If the maiden tree is well feathered use two strong laterals, one to the left and one to the right at the first wire to form the initial ribs. Tie these to canes fixed to the wires at 35 degrees.

Pruning dwarf, semi-dwarf or standards

The first year: the maiden tree Prune in the early spring just as the buds begin to open. The head is formed by cutting back to three or four suitably placed buds in the same way as for the apple (see page 118). The objective is to obtain three or four well-placed primary branches by the end of the summer. Pinch out any flowers that are produced. Shoots lower down on the main stem should be pinched back to four leaves. These help to stiffen the stem and should not be removed until the cherry is four years old. Protect the pruning cuts.

The second year In spring, prune each leader by one half to an outward-facing bud. Summer prune the pinched-back shoots on the main stem by pinching out the growing points. Weak or diseased branches should be entirely removed.

Pruning the fan-trained tree: the first year

1 In spring, prepare the soil. Dig a hole wide and deep enough to take the roots fully extended. Plant the tree against a wired wall for fan-training (or with two stakes and a crossbar for standards).

2 Each April, apply a top dressing of balanced fertilizer at a rate of 3 oz per square yard over the rooting area. Mulch with a 2–3 in layer of well-rotted manure over a radius of 18 in.

1 In spring, tie two strong laterals to canes fixed to wires at 35 degrees. Head the center stem back to the uppermost of the selected laterals. Remove all other laterals and protect the cuts.

The second year

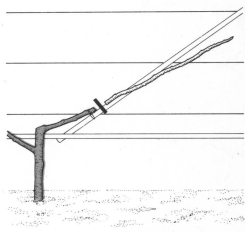

2 In spring, select suitable buds and shorten each leader to about 12 in. This encourages shoots to develop in the summer which are used as the ribs of the fan.

Sweet and Duke cherries 2

is grown commercially in Montana. **'Napoleon'** Also called 'Royal Ann'. A favorite among fruit packers, but likely to be difficult for the home gardener because fruits crack in wet weather and are often afflicted with brown rot. The tree is also only semi-hardy and demands perfect soil. Mid-season fruits are red and yellow

'Seneca' Probably the best of the early cherries. Soft, juicy, purple-black fruits. **'Windsor'** Large purple-red fruits with yellow flesh. Very late.

The third year By the third spring six to nine well-spaced leaders should have been formed. Prune them lightly, leaving about 24 in of the previous summer's growth. Prune laterals competing with the leaders back to three buds. Upright laterals in the center should be cut out because these may grow too vigorously and spoil the shape of the tree. Where there is room, leave other laterals unpruned.

Fourth and fifth years No more leader pruning should be necessary. In the fourth spring clean up the trunk by removing the pinched-back shoots. Protect the wounds by sealing them with bituminous paint.

Pruning an established tree
Very little pruning is necessary while the tree is well furnished with cropping wood and of manageable height. Each year cut out dead, broken, crowded or crossing branches, cutting them flush to avoid any snags. Prune in the spring and protect the wounds by sealing them with bituminous paint.

Grassing down For the first four or five years the soil around trained trees must be kept clear by maintaining a 3 ft wide border along the length of the wall over the spread of the tree. The border may then be planted to grass if the tree is developing in a satisfactory manner.

Dwarf and standard trees should also be grassed down after five years. For the grass mixture (see page 128). Keep the grass clear of the trunk of the tree, as not to do so will encourage pests or diseases.

Feeding and watering In March or April apply a balanced general fertilizer, such as 10-10-10, at 3 oz per square yard as a top dressing over the rooting area. Young trees, both fan-trained and in the open, should also be mulched to a depth of 2–3 in over an overall radius of 18 in.

Cherries against walls require watering in dry spells during the growing season. Once a good set of cherries has been achieved, water the border soil copiously in times of drought. Apply 1 in (4½ gal per square yard) over the rooting area every seven days (ten for the sour cherry) until rain falls. Keep the

tree accustomed to moist soil conditions. Do not suddenly give heavy applications of water after the soil has become dry because this may cause the fruits to split and so spoil the subsequent crop.

Pollination
With one exception (the variety 'Stella') sweet cherries are not self-compatible, in fact, cross-incompatibility occurs. Most Duke cherries are self-compatible and can be planted singly but a few are not.

Protection against frost and birds
It is feasible to protect the blossom of a fan-trained tree against frost, but hardly practicable with a tall standard. Drape the fan with burlap or netting. Other birds destroy the buds in the winter while starlings and blackbirds eat the ripe fruits. Protect the tree by covering it with adequate netting.

Harvesting
Leave the cherries on the tree until ripe unless they start cracking. Pick with the stalk on

using scissors or shears: if fruits are pulled off and the stalk is left hanging it encourages brown rot. Cherries should be eaten as soon as possible after picking as they can deteriorate quite quickly.

Propagation
Cherries are propagated by budding, or by grafting on to rootstocks, tasks normally carried out by the nursery but which can be done by keen amateurs if great care is taken in the exercise.

Pests and diseases
Tent caterpillars, cherry slugs, and brown rot are the most troublesome problems. Cherry slug and tent caterpillar as well as most other problems can be controlled by a regular spray program. The program should include the application of a dormant oil in late winter or early spring followed by consistent use of a general-purpose fruit spray after petal fall. To prevent brown rot, spray the plants with captan during periods of warm and humid weather conditions.

The third year

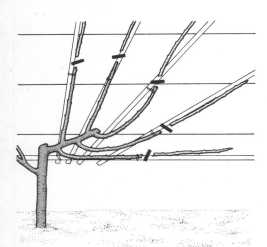

3 In spring, cut back all leaders to suitable buds, leaving 18–21 in of new growth.

Fourth and subsequent years

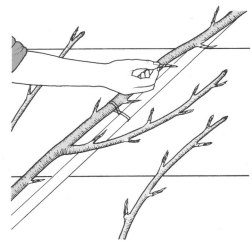

4 In spring, when most of the wall space has been filled, rub or cut out any breastwood or laterals growing directly towards the wall.

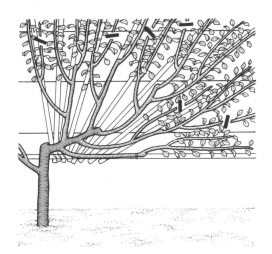

5 In late July, cut back to six leaves any laterals not wanted for the framework. When growth reaches the top of the wall, cut back to a weak lateral just below. Or, bend and tie down the shoots.

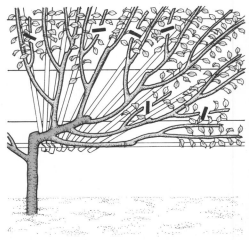

6 At the end of September, cut back to three leaves the laterals that were pinched out in July to encourage fruit buds to form at the base of the shoots in the following year.

Sour cherries

'Early Richmond' Very early soft fruits of medium quality.
'Meteor' Big, light red fruits. The tree is very hardy and does not grow much over 12 ft.
'Montmorency' Most widely grown sour cherry. Unusually large, attractive, crack-resistant fruits that may be eaten fresh when fully ripe but tart enough to make

excellent pies and jams.
'Morello' (or 'English Morello'). Most widely planted sour cherry in England, but much less common in the United States. Large, dark red, almost black fruits with a bittersweet flavor when fully ripe. Tree is hardy and small, but not overly productive.
'North Star' Only 8 ft tall, this Minnesota

variety is hardy yet grows even into the cooler areas of zone 8. Fruits are big and juicy.

The sour cherry is a culinary fruit derived from *Prunus cerasus*. It is a hardy deciduous tree that is much less vigorous than the sweet cherry and can be grown in a small garden. There are two types of sour cherry: the Morello with dark red, almost black fruits and red juice; and the Amarelle, with red fruits and colorless juice. Both are self-compatible and can be planted singly in zones 4–7.

Cultivation

Usually grown as a small tree in the open, or as a fan on a wall, the sour cherry can also be grown as a central leader tree in pyramid form.

The sour cherry begins to bear fruit in its third or fourth year. A maiden tree can be planted but a few years are gained if a two- or three-year-old tree already partly shaped by the nursery is obtained.

Soil and situation Provided the soil is well drained, the sour cherry is tolerant of a wide range of soils but it prefers one that is neutral to slightly alkaline (pH 7.0).

The sour cherry flowers early in spring and so should not be planted in a frost pocket. It will tolerate partial shade and can be grown as a fan on a north-facing wall.

Planting and spacing Plant the tree when dormant in early spring. Prepare the soil and plant, stake and tie as for the sweet cherry (see page 133). Bush and central-leader trees should be staked for the first four or five years. For fan-trained trees, erect a support system of horizontal wires on the wall before planting. Use 14 gauge wire and stretch the wires at every 6 in or two brick courses (see page 91).

Space trees grown in the open 20–25 ft apart. Fans are spaced 12–15 ft.

Control weeds and grass by shallow hoeing or use weedkillers (see page 171). Leave a border of uncultivated soil around the tree.

Pruning the fan-trained tree

The formative pruning and training is the same as for a peach fan (see page 136), taking care to cut the leaders back hard in the first three years of training so that a head with plenty of ribs arising close to one another is formed.

Pruning the cropping tree is based on the fact that the sour cherry fruits almost solely on the growth made in the previous summer. As with the peach, the aim is to obtain a constant supply of strong new shoots to carry the next season's cherries.

In spring and early summer, thin out the new shoots to about 4–6 in apart along the framework branches. Leave one replacement shoot at the base of each fruit-carrying lateral. Tie the young shoots to the wires while they are still flexible. Do not pinch out the growing points of the young shoots, but let them extend where there is room.

After harvesting in mid-summer, cut out the laterals that have fruited back to the young replacement shoots.

Some sour cherries are relatively weak growing and the fruiting laterals do not readily produce replacement shoots near the base. If these fruiting laterals are left unpruned and no replacements form, they become extremely long with the base and center of the fan bare and the crop carried only on the perimeter. When this happens, in March, cut out a proportion of the three- and four-year-old branches back to younger laterals to stimulate the development of new growth.

Pruning the bush and pyramid

The initial training for these forms is the same as for the open-centered bush and pyramid plum. The leaders are cut back in early spring as growth begins to establish the framework.

Mature trees bear fruit along young wood formed in the previous season. In March cut back a proportion of the older shoots to one-year-old laterals or young shoots so that the old growth is continually replaced.

As the trees become older, the center may become bare and unproductive. Each year after harvesting, cut back one-third of the main branches to within about 3 ft of the head to produce vigorous young replacement branches. Protect the cuts with a wound paint.

Routine cultivation

For feeding, watering, protection, thinning, harvesting, propagation, pests and diseases see Sweet and Duke cherries (pages 133–134).

Fan-trained tree

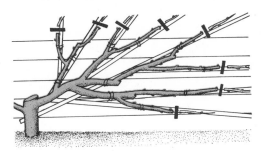

1 For the first three years, follow the eight steps for formative pruning of a peach fan (see pages 136–139), cutting the leaders back hard.

3 After harvesting, cut out the laterals that have fruited back to the young replacement shoots.

The mature tree

2 In March, cut back some of the older shoots to one-year-old laterals or young shoots to replace the older growth.

Fourth and subsequent years

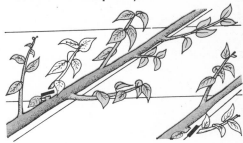

2 In spring and early summer, thin out new shoots to 4–6 in apart along the framework branches. Tie in young shoots to the wires.

Pyramid plum tree

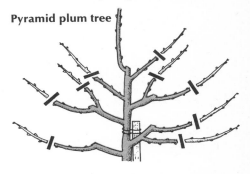

1 For the first three years, follow the steps for the initial pruning of a pyramid plum. Cut back the leaders in early spring.

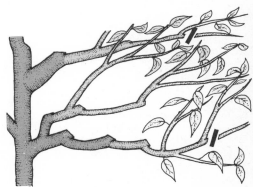

3 After harvesting, if the tree is bare and unproductive, cut back one-third of the main branches to within 3 ft of the head.

Peaches and almonds 1

highest quality. Mid-season. Brown rot is a problem.
'Golden Jubilee' Large freestone fruits susceptible to bruising. Early.
'Halehaven' Large, delicious fruits. Freestone. Ready for picking about three weeks before Elberta. Tree is hardier than most.
'JH Hale' Famous variety but now used mostly for commercial canning. Large, freestone fruits in mid-season. Must be planted with another variety to ensure fruiting.
'Keystone' Grown in deep South. Freestone. Early.
'Redhaven' Excellent peach for eating out of hand. Semi-freestone. Fruits of medium size are all-over pink and have very little fuzz. Hang on trees even when fully ripe. Early. Very productive.
'Rio Oso Gem' Large, firm freestone fruits. Mid-season.
'Southland' Medium-size freestone fruits especially good for canning and freezing. Flesh does not turn brown when exposed to air. Early.
'Sun Haven' Medium to large fruits are

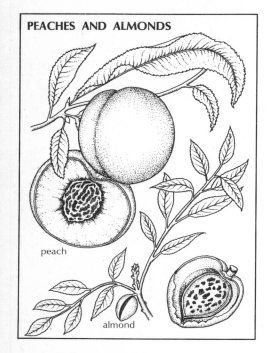

PEACHES AND ALMONDS

peach

almond

Peaches, nectarines and almonds (outdoors)
The peach (*Prunus persica*) is a small deciduous tree with long, tapering light green leaves and attractive pink flowers borne singly in the early spring. Despite its name, the peach did not originate in Persia, but almost certainly in China where it was cultivated for many centuries before being introduced to Europe. The peach is grown throughout the warm temperate regions of the world (zones 6–8).

The nectarine is a smooth-skinned sport, or mutation, of the peach. Generally the fruits are smaller than peaches and often considered to have a better flavor. For most cultural purposes, however, it is treated in exactly the same way as the peach.

The almond tree is similar in size, habit, leaf form and flower to the peach, but it blossoms even earlier and therefore in cooler areas the blooms are frequently destroyed by frost or affected by cold. For this reason in northern latitudes (zone 7) it is grown largely for its beautiful blossoms. The almond tree is a reliable producer of nuts in zone 8 and especially in zone 9. It does best in the hot Sacramento and San Joaquin valleys of California.

Cultivation
The peach and the nectarine are self-compatible and single trees can be planted. The almond is only partly self-compatible and two or more varieties should be planted.

Yield The yield from a peach or a nectarine can vary enormously depending upon the size of the tree and the environment. A good average. yield from a fan is about 30 lb and form a bush 30–100 lb.

Soil and situation The peach is tolerant of a wide range of soils but it is essential that they are well drained. To improve the drainage of a heavy soil place brick and stone rubble and chopped sods in the bottom of the planting hole. The ideal soil is a medium to heavy, moderately limey loam, not less than 18 in in depth with a pH of 6.7–7.0.

The peach is quite hardy, preferring a cold winter and a sunny dry spring rather than a warm, wet winter which causes the buds to open only to be damaged by subsequent frosts. The site must be in full sun and sheltered from cold winds and ideally not in a frost pocket. The peach flowers very early so it is ideally grown as a fan on a wall or fence with a southerly aspect where it can be protected against frost at flowering time and benefit from the warmth of the structure. When planted in the open, as it generally is, the peach can be placed on a northern slope or the north side of a building so that it will bloom late after frost danger is past.

Soil preparation Where there are poor soils at the base of a wall, it is worth while preparing the border specially (see page 115).

On good soils, however, it is sufficient to fork in a balanced fertilizer such as 10-10-10 at the rate of 3 oz per square yard with bonemeal at 3 oz per square yard over an area of two square yards.

Selecting the tree For a tree to grow in the open buy a well-feathered maiden tree. For a fan obtain a fan that is already partly formed. Choose one with 5–12 shoots (depending upon the age of the tree) that are evenly spaced to form the first ribs of the fan.

Planting Plant during the dormant season, usually in March or April. If planting a container-grown tree, it can be planted generally at any time. In the prepared soil, dig a hole wide and deep enough to take the roots fully spread out. Plant the tree to the same depth as it was at the nursery. Give each tree grown in the open a space of about 20 ft in diameter.

A fan must be planted 6–9 in away from the wall or fence to allow for growth, with the stem inclined slightly towards its support structure (see page 115).

After planting, apply a 2–3 in mulch of well-rotted manure, compost, peat or mushroom compost for 18 in around the tree.

A system of horizontal wires is necessary to support the fan. Fix the wires to the wall or fence every 6 in or two brick courses apart, starting at 12 in above the ground (see pages 90–91). Tie canes to the wires where needed with thin wire.

Pruning and training
Stone fruits such as the peach are pruned in late winter or early spring.

The fan-trained tree
The first year In March, starting with the feathered maiden tree, cut back to a lateral at about 24 in above the ground, ensuring that there are two good buds, or laterals, beneath it, one to the left and one to the right. Cut all remaining laterals to one bud. If there is not suitable lateral, cut back to a wood bud which is slender and pointed. If in doubt, cut to a triple bud which consists of two round flower buds and one wood bud.

In the early summer select three strong shoots. Train the topmost shoot vertically and of the other two, train one to the left and one to the right, choosing those that come from just below the bottom wire. Remove all other buds or shoots entirely.

As the two side-shoots lengthen, tie them to canes at an angle of 45 degress. When both these shoots are about 18 in long, in June or July, cut out the central shoot entirely. Protect the wound with a wound paint to prevent disease or pest infection.

The second year In March, cut back the two side-shoots to a wood or triple bud at 12–18 in from the main stem. This will induce new shoots in the coming summer. Protect the cuts with wound paint.

In summer, select four strong shoots from each arm. One to extend the existing rib, two equally spaced on the upper side and one on the lower side of the branch to give the tree a total of eight ribs by the end of the season. Pinch back all other shoots as they develop to one leaf.

Carefully train each new shoot to a cane to extend the wings of the fan. Keep the center open at this stage.

The third year In March, shorten each leader by about one-third, cutting to a downward-pointing wood bud. Paint the wounds.

In the summer, allow the leading shoot on each of the eight ribs to extend. Also select three more shoots on each branch and train these outwards, tying them to canes on the wires, to fill in the remaining space on the wall or fence. Rub out buds growing directly towards the structure and breastwood. Of the remaining buds, allow young shoots to grow every 4 in on the upper and lower sides of the ribs. Pinch back to one leaf any surplus shoots. Repeat this process as and when necessary throughout the summer. When the selected laterals have made 18 in of growth, pinch out the growing points, unless they are required as part of the framework. In late summer tie them to canes on the wires. Fruit will be borne on these laterals in the following summer.

Fourth and subsequent years From this point onwards the tree must be regarded as a cropping tree. The wall or fence should now be more or less completely covered with framework branches on which every 4 in are fruit-bearing laterals.

The peach carries its fruits on shoots made during the previous summer so pruning is aimed at a constant and annual renewal of young shoots. It follows also that the shoots which have borne fruits are cut out to make room for the new young ones.

Each late spring, about May, remove shoots growing directly towards and away from the wall or fence but leave one or two leaves or shoots which have flower buds at the base. Next deal with the previous summer's laterals which should be carrying both blossom and

Peaches and almonds 2

PEACHES
'Elberta' Standard variety by which others are usually judged.
'Freestone' Large, yellow fruits with a bright blush. Sweet yellow flesh, but a little coarse. Mid-season. Large, productive tree, but fairly tender.
'Blake' Large, yellow fruits of fine flavor and texture. Freestone. Mid-season.

'Bonanza' This dwarf starts bearing when only 3 ft tall and never grows over 7 ft. Good for container growing. Large, yellow fruits of fair quality.
'Champion' Old, white-fleshed variety of good flavor. Large fruits in mid-season. Freestone.
'Crawford' Most famous of the peaches grown in the United States almost 200

years ago. Fruits almost entirely red and of fine flavor. Clingstone. Late.
'Dixired' Best very early variety. Moderate-size fruits of nice flavor. Semi-freestone.
'George IV' Excellent freestone peach with white flesh of rare flavor. Mid-season.
'Georgia Belle' Freestone. White flesh of

side-shoots. Select one side-shoot at the base as the replacement, one in the middle as a reserve and one at the top to extend the fruit-carrying lateral. Pinch back the remaining side-shoots to two leaves. When the basal side-shoot and the reserve lateral are 18 in long and the fruit-carrying lateral has a further six leaves, pinch out the growing points of each.

Pruning the standard tree The formative pruning is the same as for an apple (see page 118).

In the cropping years the objective is to encourage plenty of strong new growth each year to carry fruit in the next summer. This new growth is then cut back 50 per cent or more in the early spring of the year if it is to bear fruit. Long branches at the top of the tree should be removed at the same time. It is occasionally necessary to cut back some of the older wood which has become bare to young healthy replacements. Avoid, however, making large wounds because peaches are susceptible to bacterial canker.

Feeding and watering In early spring each year apply a balanced fertilizer such 10-10-10 at the rate of 3 oz per square yard as a top dressing over the rooting area. Replenish the mulch if necessary.

Trees over the age of three years need nothing more than nitrate of soda or ammonium sulfate unless a soil test indicates the soil has a potassium or phosphorus deficiency.

Keep the soil moist at all times until just before the fruit begins to ripen. Ample water is essential to good production. But it is also important to keep the tree accustomed to moist soil conditions at all times. In other words, do not suddenly apply a lot of water near ripening time because there is the risk of splitting the fruits. Because the soil at the base of a wall tends to dry out rapidly, fan-trained peaches must be watered with special care. Direct water at the base of the tree so that moisture gets to the roots. Do not wet the foliage.

Frost protection
Protection of the blossom against frost is also essential from pink bud stage until the danger of frost has passed. Drape the fan-trained tree with burlap or bird netting. Remove during the day.

Planting

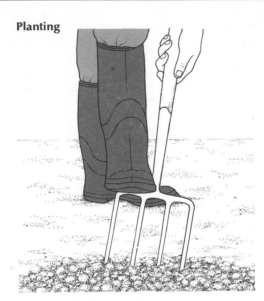

1 Before planting, fork in 3 oz per square yard of a balanced fertilizer, such as 10-10-10, with 3 oz bonemeal. Repeat every March.

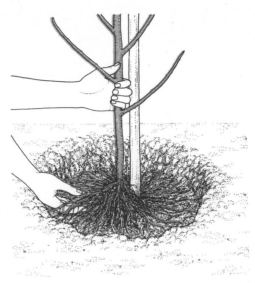

2 In March or April, plant during the dormant season. A fan should be 6–9 in away from the wall or fence with the stem inclined towards it.

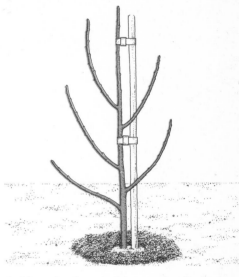

3 After planting, mulch to a depth of 2–3 in with manure or compost for 18 in around the tree. Replenish every year in late winter.

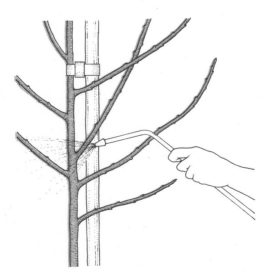

4 In March, spray with a copper fungicide or Bordeaux mixture against peach leaf curl. Also spray with dormant oil.

Thinning

5 From early May to July, thin the fruits, starting when they are the size of large peas.

Harvesting

6 From August onwards, pick the fruit when the flesh feels soft at the stalk end. Hold the fruit in the palm of the hand, lift and twist it slightly.

137

Peaches and almonds 3

bright red with yellow cheeks. Freestone. Ripen 40 days before Elberta. Very hardy.
'Springtime' White-fleshed, clingstone fruits grown in the South. Ripen two months before 'Elberta'.
'Vedette' A freestone originated in Canada and suitable for zone 5. Early.

NECTARINES
'Cavalier' Small fruits with firm, aromatic flesh. Freestone. Vigorous.
'Cherokee' Large, semi-clingstone of excellent quality. Very early.
'Lexington' Freestone. Tree is unusually hardy and vigorous.
'Pocahontas' Mild, good quality, semi-clingstone fruits. Less troubled by brown

Thinning

To obtain good-sized fruits it is essential to thin the fruits. Thin over a period, starting when the fruitlets are the size of large peas and stopping when they are the size of walnuts. Peaches should be 9 in apart and nectarines 6 in aprt after the final thinning.

Harvesting peaches and nectarines

The fruit is ripe when it has a reddish flush and the flesh feels soft near the stalk end. Hold the peach in the palm of the hand, lift and twist it slightly. It should part easily from the tree. Store the fruits in a cool place until they are to be eaten. They will keep for only up to a week and for long-term storage they must be canned or frozen without the stones.

Pruning the fan-trained tree after harvesting

Immediately after cropping, not later than the end of September, cut out the laterals which carried the fruits back to the replacement shoots. Tie in the young shoots and cut out any dead or broken branches.

Once the peach has reached the required height and spread, remove any unwanted extension growth by cutting to a lateral further back along the branch. Cut out bare wood back to strong young replacements. Protect the wounds with a wound paint.

Harvesting and storage of almonds

Harvest the nuts when the husks split and the nuts fall naturally. Remove the nuts from the husks and dry them thoroughly in well-ventilated conditions: in sunshine is ideal, or in an airing cupboard. Keep the nuts off the ground by laying them on wire netting to allow air circulation. Once dry they should be kept in cool and dry conditions.

If squirrels are troublesome, harvest the nuts slightly earlier and dry both husk and nut initially before splitting them open.

Propagation

Peaches, nectarines and almonds are propagated by budding or grafting, a task normally carried out by the nursery, but it can be performed by the keen amateur.

Pests and diseases

Peaches and nectarines are attacked by a number of diseases and insects but this need not cause worry if a consistent spray program is followed faithfully. A dormant oil can be sprayed on in late winter. Then, after about 75 per cent of the petals have fallen, apply a general fruit-tree spray and continue with this at about two-week intervals for the next wo months, or even up to within a month of harvest. Such treatment will take care of most problems.

To control brown rot, especially troublesome on nectarines and, in some years, just about as bad on peaches, spray with captan. Do this every three days if there is a spell of hot, humid weather at the time of bloom. Captan spraying can also be carried out in the three-week period prior to harvest as well as during a hot and humid spell.

Leaf curl causes first leaves to thicken and curl as well as tinting them red and yellow. To control this, apply a liquid copper fungicide before the buds open in the spring. Bordeaux misture can also be employed, and, if so, it is mixed and applied with dormant oil. Almonds require regular spraying with a general-purpose fruit spray.

The fan-trained tree: the first year

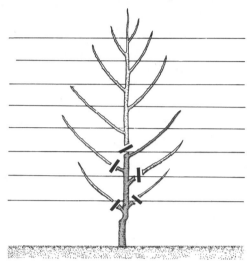

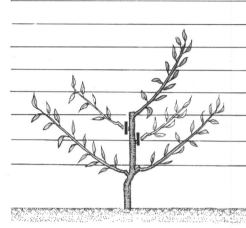

1 In March, cut back a feathered maiden peach to a lateral about 24 in above the ground, leaving one good bud on each side beneath it. Cut remaining laterals to one bud.

2 In early summer, select three shoots. Train the topmost vertically, and one to the left and one to the right. Remove all other buds or shoots.

The second year

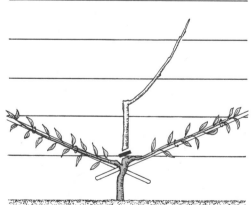

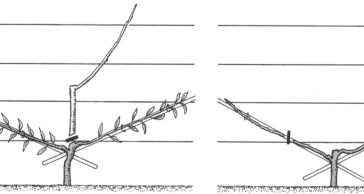

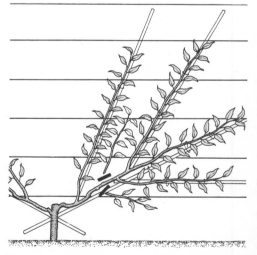

3 In June or July, tie the lengthening side-shoots to canes set at an angle of 45 degrees. Later that summer, cut out central shoot and protect cut with wound paint.

4 In March, cut back the two side-shoots to a wood or triple bud at 12–18 in from the main stem. Protect the cuts with wound paint.

5 In summer, select four shoots on each arm, one to extend the existing rib, two spaced equally on the upper side and one on the lower. Stop other shoots at one leaf.

Peaches and almonds 4

spot than the majority of nectarines.
'Redbud' Early freestone with white flesh.
'Redchief' Bright red fruits with strongly flavored white flesh. Medium-size. Freestone. Mid-season. Better-than-average resistance to brown rot.
'Rivers Orange' Small freestone fruits covered all over with a red blush.

ALMONDS
'Hal's Hardy' Self-fruitful variety with hard-shelled nuts of medium quality. Does best in zones 7 and 8.
'Nonpareil' Most common variety and most widely planted. Early nuts with paper-thin shells, uniform and excellent.
'Texas Prolific' (or simply 'Texas'). Late hard-shelled variety of good quality.

The third year

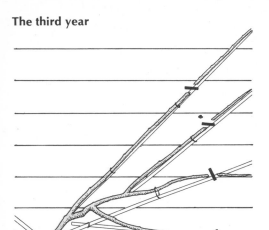

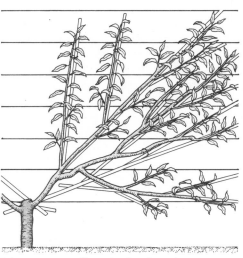

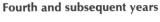

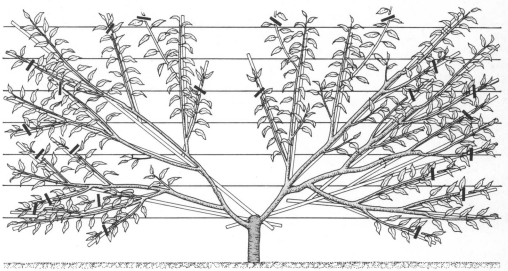

6 In March, shorten each leader by one-third by cutting to a downward-pointing wood bud. Protect the cuts.

7 In summer, allow the leading shoots on each rib to extend. Train three shoots on each branch outwards, tying them to canes. Allow shoots to grow every 4 in.

8 In late summer, when the selected laterals have made 18 in of new growth, pinch out the growing points of each and tie them to canes on the wires. These laterals will bear fruit the following summer.

Fourth and subsequent years

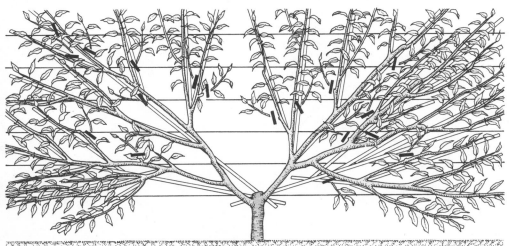

9 Each year in about May, remove shoots growing directly towards and away from the wall or fence. Leave shoots with flower buds at their base one or two leaves.

10 Select two replacement laterals on each leader: one at the base and a reserve in the middle. Allow a lateral to extend the fruit-carrying lateral. When the basal and reserve laterals are 18 in long and the extension has six leaves, pinch out the growing points. After harvesting, cut the fruited laterals back to their replacements.

Apricots

'Alfred' Good flavor. Fruit medium to large, round and flattened, orange with pink flush; flesh orange and juicy. Ripens late July to early August. Tends to biennial cropping. Flowers early.

'Early Moorpark' Rich flavor. Fruit round to oval, yellow with crimson flush and darker mottling; flesh deep orange and juicy. Ripens late July. Heavy cropping.

'Farmingdale' Very good flavor. Fruit medium, roundish, orange-yellow with red flush; flesh orange and moderately juicy. Ripens late July. Heavy cropper. Vigorous, fairly disease-resistant tree.

'Moorpark' Very popular variety. Rich sweet flavor. Fruit large, uneven round, pale yellow with reddish-brown flush. Ripens late August. Regular.

'Moongold' Sweet, firm, slightly flattened, yellow freestone fruits in mid-July. Hardy to zone 4, sturdy and vigorous. Plant with 'Sungold'.

'Riland' Grown mainly in West. Medium-size fruits with excellent flavor. Red-blushed skin. Early.

'Royal' Popular old variety widely grown in California. Medium-big, fine textured

fruits with orange skin. Mid-season.

'Sungold' Mild, sweet flavor. Freestone. Medium-size round fruits colored gold with orange blush. Ripens a week later than 'Moongold' with which it should be planted to ensure pollination.

The apricot (*Prunus armeniaca*) is a hardy deciduous tree. It is a native of China and is widely grown in California and Washington, but can be raised successfully elsewhere in zones 5–8.

Cultivation

A dwarf tree is best for the garden where space is limited. Even this can reach a height of 8 ft and a span of 15 ft. Buy a two- or three-year-old tree.

Soil and situation The apricot needs a well-drained but moisture-retentive and slightly alkaline soil with a pH range of 6.5–8.0. Light, sandy soils are not suitable.

Warmth in summer is essential and, although the apricot can be grown in the open in warm temperate areas, it thrives best fan-trained against a south- or west-facing wall in the cooler regions. It can also be grown successfully in containers.

Shelter the tree from frost and wind to encourage pollinating insects and to protect the ripening fruit. Keep the soil around the tree clear of weeds and grass so that ample moisture can reach the roots.

Planting In all but the mildest climates, where fall planting is safe, apricots should be planted only in the spring. To prepare the ground, clear away perennial weeds over an area 3 ft square. Dig in well-rotted manure or compost at a rate of one 2-gal bucketful per square yard. Plant the tree, water well, and mulch lightly.

Plant fan-trained trees 15 ft apart and 6 in from the wall or fence. Plant bush trees 15–20 ft apart.

Formative pruning and training The formative pruning of the fan-trained apricot is the same as that of the fan-trained peach. The formative pruning of the bush apricot is the same as that of the bush plum, but prune it in early spring before growth begins.

Pruning the cropping tree Mature fan-trained apricots are pruned in the same way as are fan-trained plums. Mature bush apricots are pruned in the same way as sour cherries (see page 135).

The apricot carries the best quality and most abundant crops on short spurs on two- and three-year-old wood. Extensive pruning is not necessary because it results in a poor crop. Every four to six years, cut out the older shoots that have fruited to make room for new young ones. This means cutting out some of the lateral and sub-lateral branches of a fan-trained tree. Retain and tie in the same number of new shoots to replace them. Do not prune or pinch back these shoots until the second season, but only if required.

Thinning Thin the fruits at intervals from the time they are the size of cherries until they are almost full size. First remove misshapen fruits and those growing towards the wall. Later, thin pairs and clusters so that those left to ripen have 3–4 in between them.

Feeding Root dryness is a common problem with wall-trained trees. Water generously until the root area is soaked, especially if the weather is dry when the fruit is setting or when it starts to swell.

In late winter, sprinkle an artificial fertilizer containing calcium carbonate and ammonium nitrate around the tree at a rate of 1 oz per square yard and apply a general fertilizer, such as 10-10-10, at a rate of 2 oz per square yard. Every four years, if necessary, apply ground limestone to maintain the pH at a little above 7.0. In late spring, mulch the root area to 1 in.

Pollination Most apricots are self-compatible but, because the flowers open early in spring when few insects are about, hand pollination is sometimes necessary (see page 114). The new and very hardy 'Moongold' and 'Sungold' are not self-fruitful and must be planted together.

Protecting the blossom The apricot is highly susceptible to frost damage. Protect it with polyethylene or netting.

Harvesting

Depending on the variety, apricots ripen from midsummer to early fall. Pick the ripe fruit carefully and try not to break the skin.

Pests and diseases

Spray trees on the same schedule and with the same materials as peach trees. The trees are very susceptible to brown rot if the weather is humid and warm at the time of bloom and in the three weeks before harvest starts. To control this, spray frequently with captan during these periods.

1 In early spring, in prepared ground dig a hole large enough for the roots. Plant at the same depth as at the nursery. Mulch well.

The first year

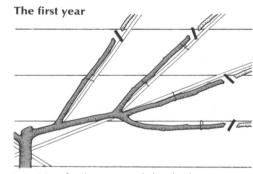

3 In March, shorten each leader by one-third, leaving about 30 in of growth.

The second and subsequent years

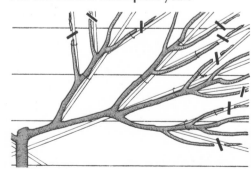

5 In spring, rub out buds pointing towards or away from the wall or fence. Prune the leaders by one-quarter.

A three-year-old fan-trained tree

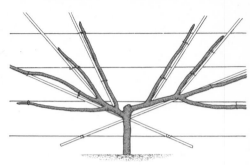

2 Erect supporting horizontal wires 9 in apart on the wall or fence. Tie in the young branches to the canes on the wall wires.

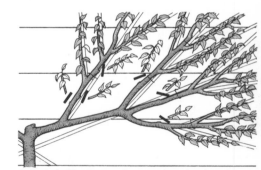

4 In July/August, select and tie in three additional shoots from each pruned leader. Pinch out all remaining shoots.

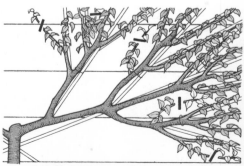

6 Early in July, pinch off the tips of side-shoots at six leaves. After cropping, cut back these laterals by one-half.

Passion fruit

Passion fruit (outdoors)
The passion fruit (*Passiflora edulis*), a native of southern Brazil, is most commonly grown in Hawaii, but will do well anywhere in zone 10 if protected from cold during the first winter. It is well distributed throughout the Tropics. A vigorous, evergreen climber, the passion fruit plant has deep glossy green leaves and white fragrant flowers. The flowers blossom intermittently throughout the winter.

The fruits (technically berries) are $1\frac{1}{2}$–$2\frac{1}{2}$ in long and oval in shape. Although basically a sweetish fruit, when eaten fresh it has a pleasant, somewhat aromatic tartness. Two forms are recognized: *P. edulis edulis* with deep purple fruits; and ·*P. edulis flavicarpa* with deep yellow fruits.

Soil The passion fruit plant will grow in almost any soil provided the soil is quite well drained, contains a large amount of humus, and is not extremely acid. Soil infested with nematodes should be fumigated before the plants are set out.

Planting and training Select a location that is protected from strong winds. Support is essential so provide a system of wires as described for grapes (see pages 109–111) or follow the instructions as given in the paragraph below.

The support system should preferably be erected against a wall but may be freestanding.

The illustrations and captions on this page indicate ways to prepare the soil and to plant the passion fruit vine, to hand pollinate the flower, and to train the vine to facilitate natural development.

Grow the plants on a trellis made with three 9-gauge wires. The top wire should be no less than 6 ft above ground and probably at least 7 ft; the middle wire is 18 in lower; and the bottom wire another 18 in below that. Since the vines are extremely heavy, the wires should be run through the posts, not just stapled to them. Space the posts 10 ft apart.

Plant one vine at the base of each post and help it to grow upwards (which usually happens very quickly) by hanging a secured string down the post to which the vine can attach itself and climb.

Feeding and watering Before planting, apply a balanced fertilizer at 3 oz per square yard, and make a similar application about eight weeks after planting. One-year-old and older plants are fed at a slightly higher rate four times a year, that is: before the beginning of active growth; prior to the summer and winter crop; and midway between each growth period.

In Hawaii, a 10-5-20 fertilizer is recommended. Elsewhere use a fertilizer with a lower nitrogen content. Keep the plants watered during dry spells when they are in active growth.

Pruning Pruning should be done sparingly after the winter crop is gathered. Just remove trailing stems and cut out excess growth as necessary to keep the plants from becoming too large and heavy.

Pollination
Passion fruit that is raised from seed may be self-incompatible. If possible obtain clones of the purple-fruited form that are known to be self-compatible. If only seed-raised plants are available, plant two seedlings about 2 ft apart, and allow the shoots to intermingle after initial training. Hand pollinated flowers usually do produce larger fruits than naturally pollinated ones so, where practical, hand pollination is worth while (see page 114). The flowers are short-lived and should be pollinated soon after they open.

Harvesting and storing
For really juicy and good flavored fruits, do not pick passion fruit until it is fully ripe. When mature the fruit attains a strong color, and the skin hardens and begins to shrivel. Once gathered, the fruit should be used as soon as possible but it can be stored a few weeks if kept cool.

Pests and diseases
To control fruit flies, spray with malathion as the flies appear. This treatment may also eliminate mites, the other most serious pest; if not, use a sulfur spray. Always spray when the flowers are closed so that too many insect pollinators are not killed. Flowers of the purple passion fruit open in the early morning and close before noon while flowers of the yellow passion fruit open after noon and close at night.

Second and subsequent years

1 Before planting, apply a balanced fertilizer at 3 oz per square yard. Make a similar application about eight weeks after planting.

2 In spring or early summer, plant two or more seedlings 2 ft apart in the prepared soil. Pinch out the growing tips.

3 During flowering, pollinate with a small brush. Liquid feed every 14 days until the fruits ripen. For further details, see hand pollination, page 114.

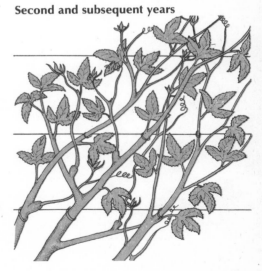

4 In spring, train in the new growths onto the 3-wire trellis support system by initially guiding them into position and then allowing them to develop naturally.

Citrus fruits 1

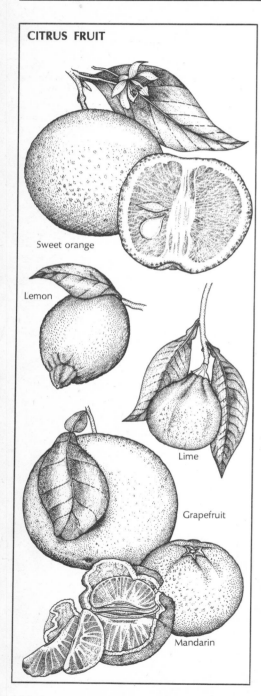

CITRUS FRUIT

Sweet orange

Lemon

Lime

Grapefruit

Mandarin

Citrus fruits can only be grown in the warmest of American climates. Fruits such as the orange, grapefruit, lemon, lime, kumquat, mandarin (including tangerine and satsuma), shaddock, tangelo, and calamondin thrive only in certain zones. For example, the lemon and the lime are restricted to zone 10, while some varieties of other citrus fruits can be cultivated in the southern sections of zone 9. The kumquat, the hardiest species of citrus fruit along with the calamondin and mandarin, can even be grown in zone 8 if the location is well sheltered and sunny.

All citrus trees make attractive evergreen garden specimens as well as being producers of large quantities of enjoyable fruit. With a few exceptions, citrus trees are self-fruitful, making it unnecessary to plant more than one tree of any kind.

Tree selection

The chosen citrus plant should preferably be selected from trees developed by the nursery and grafted on reliable rootstock. Those grown from fresh seeds are inclined to be overly large and may be unsuited to the area in which they are to be grown.

Selection of the right rootstock is difficult for the amateur gardener who has to choose from a wide range of rootstocks, each with characteristics peculiar to the given stock. The nurseryman, preferably a grower who knows local requirements, should be consulted before a choice is made. As a general guide, the gardener should buy either a one-year-old plant having a trunk of $\frac{1}{2}-\frac{3}{4}$ in in diameter, or a two-year-old plant measuring $\frac{3}{4}-1\frac{1}{4}$ in. The trunk of the plant should be measured one inch above the graft. If possible, the plant should be state-registered as free of serious viral disease.

Cultivation

Citrus trees are not very particular about soil, but do best in loam or sandy loam. Drainage must be excellent and the pH between 6.0–6.5. If the water table is very high or the topsoil is underlain by clay, construct a mound of earth at least 18 in high, 8 ft across at the top, and 12 ft across at the bottom.

Before planting, turn over the soil thoroughly and remove weeds. Mix in a good supply of humus and about 6 oz of balanced fertilizer per square yard.

Locate the trees where they will receive sunlight all day long. Avoid low areas where frost may collect. In regions with occasional freezes, place the trees on the south side of a building, wall or hedge, or near a pond. Oranges and grapefruits require a space of 25–30 ft diameter, calamondins, kumquats, lemons and limes need 15 ft, while other species of citrus fruit benefit from 20 ft of space.

Planting Plant the trees in late winter or early spring after the frost danger is past. Spread the roots out well in the holes. The top roots should be at about ground level and the trunk just a little higher than it was in its nursery container.

After the hole is filled in and the soil firmed, ridge up the soil in a 2 ft diameter circle around the trunk to form a watering basin, and fill this with water. Then, to protect the tree from sunburn, wrap the trunk from the ground up to the lowest branches with loose-fitting newspapers or wrapping paper. Tie the papers in place and leave them on for the next year.

Watering and feeding Citrus trees need considerable moisture, a minimum of 36 in per

1 In late winter or early spring, plant the young, grafted nursery tree in thoroughly turned soil mixed with humus and balanced fertilizer. Spread the roots out well.

2 After the hole is filled in and the soil is firmed, ridge up the soil in a 2 ft diameter circle around the trunk to form a basin. Fill with water.

3 To protect the tree from sunburn, wrap the trunk with paper from the ground to the lowest branches. Use loose-fitting newspapers or wrapping paper.

Citrus fruits 2

year at all times, but especially in the first three years. In dry climates, such as California, build a shallow watering basin that extends about a foot beyond the branch tips of each tree. Also build a ridge of earth close around the tree trunk to keep it dry. Fill the basin with water as necessary. In California first-year trees should be watered every 7–10 days during dry weather, second-year trees every 2 weeks, and older trees every 2–6 weeks.

After they have been planted and have put out leaves, citrus trees should be fertilized on a regular basis to produce good crops. Always just scatter the fertilizer on the ground and water it in. Do not dig fertilizer in, or apply it in holes, because it may burn the roots.

The type of fertilizer and the amount used as well as the schedule by which it is applied varies considerably between citrus regions. In Florida, for instance, a 6-6-6 balanced fertilizer containing magnesium, manganese and copper is recommended, while in Louisiana a 6-12-6 or 8-8-8 fertilizer is used. But, in Arizona, California and Texas, ammonium sulfate is usually satisfactory alone. Established trees should be fed four times a year.

The best way to determine how to care for citrus trees is to send a soil sample to the state agricultural extension service for analysis. On the basis of the analysis, the service can suggest a precise feeding regimen.

Mulching Citrus trees are frequently grown in bare ground, but an organic mulch should be maintained under the tree canopy. This is of benefit to both the tree and the gardener. The mulch should be kept 6 in away from the trunk of the tree to protect it from moisture, fungi and other pests. Mulch not only helps to hold in moisture and keeps down weeds, it also contributes to soil fertility.

Frost protection
Until a citrus tree has developed a low-hanging canopy, the trunk should be banked with soil in late November if the area is subject to occasional freezes. After November, the gardener can take several precautions if frost is predicted. For example, the trees can be covered with large sheets of fabric, fans can be set up to keep air circulating around the trees, or tree heaters can be placed near and under the trees. Tree heaters are not permitted in some areas.

Trees damaged by frost should not be pruned until growth starts again and the damage has been assessed. If the damage is severe, delay pruning for six months. This gives the trees a chance to recover from the shock of freezing.

Harvesting
The first fruits of young trees up to about four years old are of poor quality and should be either pulled from the tree when immature or thrown away at harvest time.

When harvesting fruits in later years, cut the stems close. Do not pull the fruits. Take care not to bruise or cut the rinds if the fruits are destined for storing.

Allow the fruits to ripen on the tree before picking. Citrus fruits, unlike other fruits, do not have to be picked as soon as ripe because they do not deteriorate immediately, indeed they may be safely left for a long time. Fruits picked soon after they ripen can be stored for a considerable period in open boxes at 16°C/60°F. The longer the ripe fruits are left on the tree, the shorter the storage period. Juice from citrus fruits can be canned, and peel from oranges and grapefruit candied.

Pests and diseases
Citrus fruit trees are susceptible to many diseases, as well as attacks from insect and animal enemies. The best method of warding off most disease is to begin with healthy, virus-free plants on recommended rootstocks, and to prevent wet soil from remaining in contact with the trunks for long periods. Eternal vigilance seems the only remedy against deer, armadillos, gophers, land turtles and other animals that damage trees.

To control insects, follow a regular spray schedule as recommended by the state agricultural extension service.

Serious burning of tree trunks, caused by long exposure to the sun, can be prevented by whitewashing until the branch canopy is large and dense enough to shade the trunks.

There is no reliable preventative measure to stop the splitting of fruit because the precise cause is not known, although this may be the result of an extremely uneven water supply or lack of minor nutrients in the soil. Or it may be a combination of these detrimental factors. Take advice from state agricultural extension services about local pest and disease problems.

4 After the trees have been planted and have put out leaves, scatter fertilizer on a regular basis. Always water the fertilizer in.

5 Maintain an organic mulch under the tree canopy. The mulch should be kept 6 in away from the trunk of the tree to hold in moisture and keep down weeds.

6 In late November, bank the tree with soil as a frost protection precaution. The tree will eventually develop a low-hanging canopy that will help ward off frost.

7 After November, two frost protection methods are to cover the trees with large sheets of fabric and/or to set up fans to keep the air circulating.

Pecans

The pecan tree is a hickory species (*Carya illinoiensis*) that can attain a height of 150 ft in the wild, but is usually trained to grow to a much lower height in the orchard or garden. It is a handsome, if craggy, specimen in the large garden. To ensure a harvest of pecan nuts, it is necessary to plant two trees of different varieties, that is, a variety that sheds pollen early and a variety that pollinates later. Even if this precaution has been taken, a crop is not a certainty unless the fruit has had five to seven months of warm weather to mature without unfavorable conditions such as drouth. Good management is essential.

Pecans are probably the most popular nuts in the United States and among the most widely grown next to peanuts, which are not true nuts. They do best in zone 8, but are also productive in zones 7 and 9. Small crops of pecans may even be harvested in zone 6 and the southern part of zone 5 with careful cultivation.

Cultivation

Although the pecan tree will tower above other trees within a number of years and so obtain the necessary sunlight to thrive, it should not be planted in semi-shaded areas. Nursery pecan trees that are one year old and 4–6 ft in height should be given plenty of space to develop rapidly and more than average care if they are to survive the first summer. Choose nursery trees that have been freshly dug from the field.

Soil of enough depth to accomodate the long tap root ($2\frac{1}{2}$–4 ft) and large lateral root system of the pecan tree should be chosen. A well-drained, humus loam is preferable. If the soil contains much sand, mix in large amounts of organic matter; if there is too much clay, mix in gravel as well as organic matter. Soils infested with nematodes should be fumigated before planting.

Planting Make the planting holes at least 6 in deeper than the roots of the young tree and at least 30 in across. This can be done, for example, by using a 12 or 14 in power auger or post hole digger. Trim the roots only if they are damaged. Set the tree and fill the hole with loose soil. Thoroughly water the basin formed around the tree until it is full to settle the soil, then add more soil to raise a mound.

Watering and feeding Irrigate deeply throughout the first growing season. Mulching with organic matter to a depth of 6 in is advisable. After the trees have developed leaves, work in 4 oz of 10-10-10 fertilizer, and make a second similar feeding about six weeks later, but not after the beginning of August.

Maintenance of a good moisture supply at all times during the growing season is essential. During dry weather, soak the ground thoroughly so the water penetrates to the root ends.

Fertilize the trees in early spring with ammonium sulfate or another nitrogen product, applying about 10 oz per year of tree age. If the ground under the trees is cultivated or mulched, scatter the fertilizer over the entire root area, scratch it in lightly and water well. In a lawn, where the nitrogen would probably kill the grass, drop the fertilizer into holes made with a crowbar at 2 ft intervals throughout the root area.

Such care will help to counteract the tendency of some trees to bear in alternate years. It also helps to assure that the kernels fill out properly.

Pruning and training When the young trees are planted, cut the top back, leaving a 36 in trunk. Wrap the trunk with burlap or paper to within 6 in of the top to prevent sunscald, retard drying, and to discourage pests. Maintain the wrapping for two years, replacing and renewing it as necessary.

Train one of the upper branches as an extension of the trunk by tying it to a stake when the tree starts putting out growth. From this will arise the main (scaffold) branches. There should be four or five of these, spaced about 18 in apart, up and down the trunk and growing out in different directions. Do not remove the branches below the scaffolds, which start at 5 or 6 ft above ground, for three or four years.

Once the basic structure of the tree is well developed, little pruning is necessary. Just cut out dead and damaged branches as well as upper branches that prevent sunlight from penetrating the base shape formed by the scaffolds. Remove also branches which cross over others and which cut off light from the main branches.

Harvesting

Pecan trees do not start to bear heavily until they are about ten years old, but nuts can be gathered in small quantities after the fifth year. The nuts are ready for picking when the husks open at the tips and the color begins to fade. They can be allowed to fall naturally or can be knocked out of the trees with lightweight bamboo poles. Dry pecan nuts thoroughly before bagging. Halved pecans can be added to crocked fruit mixtures.

Pests and diseases

Keeping fallen nuts, leaves and twigs raked up is the best way to protect trees. For safety's sake, however, young trees should be sprayed with dodine or zineb when the first leaves show and the buds burst; repeat when the leaves are half developed. Then use a combination of dodine and malathion or zineb and malathion when the tips of the new nuts begin to turn brown, repeating the treatment at 3–4 week intervals. Dodine is used for varieties susceptible to scab and

Planting and training

1 Make the planting hole 6 in deeper than the roots of the tree and 30 in across, using a power auger if necessary. Set the tree and fill the hole with loose soil. Water the basin to settle the soil and then mound in additional soil.

zineb for those tolerant or resistant to scab.

To prevent rosette, a physiological disorder resulting in the yellowing of the leaves, thickening of leaf veins and a bunching up of small leaves at the ends of short twigs, apply zinc sulfate to the soil at a rate of 16 oz per in of trunk diameter. Spread this over the entire root area and work it in thoroughly using a rake or a garden fork.

Varieties

There are three groups of pecan varieties: Eastern, Western, and Northern. Eastern varieties are fairly resistant to scab and other diseases, and grow best in the southeast. Western varieties, on the other hand, are extremely susceptible to scab and other diseases. They grow in moderately dry climates from central Texas to areas westward of that state. Although Northern varieties are tolerant of disease and mature more rapidly than the other varieties, crops are small or non-existent. They are grown more for ornament than utility.

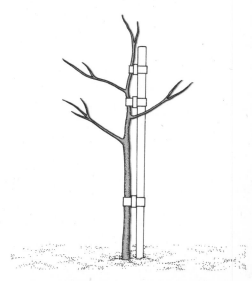

2 Train one of the upper branches as an extension of the trunk by tying it to a stake when the tree starts giving out growth. From this will arise the four or five main scaffold branches protruding from the trunk about 18 in apart.

Physalis

The physalis is variously known in different countries and within the United States as Cape gooseberry, golden berry, ground-cherry, husk tomato and, in Hawaii, as poka. Botanically, it is *Physalis pruinosa* syn. *P. Peruviana* or *P. edulis*. It comes from Peru, although it is now cultivated in many areas of the world, and is related to the ornamental Chinese lantern plant (*P. alkekengi*), which also has edible but indifferent-tasting fruit.

The distinctive feature of this fruit is its lantern-like calyx or husk which conceals the golden, cherry-sized fruit. The husk protects the berry from birds and insects, aids the storage of the fruit, and is attractive, as are the small yellow-white blossoms with their purple-black markings. The leaves are large and slightly heart-shaped. The fruit is sweet with a distinctive taste. It can be eaten raw, cooked or preserved. It has a high vitamin C content. Each plant will produce about 1–2 lb of fruit.

Cultivation

The Physalis is a half-hardy perennial usually grown in zones 3–10 as an annual. It can be grown in the open in sheltered areas, or under glass or in pots. It responds to much the same treatment as its relative the tomato.

Soil and situation Do not grow the Physalis in ground just used for tomatoes or potatoes, because it is subject to the same pests and diseases, which may still be present in the soil. A sandy, well-drained soil of pH 6.5 is ideal but it will tolerate a wide range of soils, including limey soil if well laced with humus. It should be planted in a sunny sheltered position.

Propagation The Physalis is grown from seed indoors. The seeds should be sown in gentle heat in early spring. Sow the seeds individually, ¼ in deep, in seed trays filled with any proprietary starting mixture. The pots should be covered with glass. A temperature of 18°C/65°F is necessary for good germination. When the seeds germinate in 10–14 days remove the glass. When the seedlings are large enough to grip, prick them into 3 in pots filled with potting mixture.

Planting and staking Prepare the site, which should be cultivated to a fine tilth. No extra fertilizer is needed unless the soil is poor, when a 2-gal bucketful of well-rotted manure should be applied per square yard. An alternative to manure is a dressing of fertilizer such as 10-10-10 at 2–3 oz per square yard.

Plant out after all danger of frost has passed, setting the plants 2½ ft apart. For a slightly earlier start, grow under cloches or tunnels until the danger of frosts and cold winds is past. Plants can be stunted by a cold wind as late as early summer so provide shelter in the form of screens when necessary.

The plants should be supported with individual stakes 3 ft high or with a network of posts and wire. If the plants have not produced flowers by the time they are 12 in high, pinch out the growing points to induce branching and thereafter regular pinching is not needed. Watering should be carefully regulated, for if the plants are given too much moisture they produce growth at the expense of fruit. Give a liquid fertilizer sparingly only after the first flowers appear. Tomato fertilizers are suitable.

Growing under glass In areas where the frost-free season is less than about 80 days, or summers are cool, protection is essential. Grow the plants in pots which can spend the early and fruiting stages inside and the summer in the open.

Seed should be sown in the same way as for outdoor plants. Instead of planting out, the plants should be potted on into 10 in pots filled with about equal amounts of loam and humus. Plants should be staked individually. Or if stood outside, the stakes should be secured to a wire stretched between stronger stakes driven into the soil.

Although plants can be retained for the following year and potted on into larger containers, it is recommended that new seeds are sown each year and the plants discarded after fruiting because thereafter they do not crop so heavily.

Harvesting

In cold regions, fruits grown outdoors may not be ripe by the time of the first frosts. Pot-grown plants can be put back under glass to ripen. The fruits are ready to pick when they turn golden-yellow and the husks have a papery texture. Ripe fruits can be left on the plants for several weeks, the peak of flavor being reached 2–3 weeks after ripening. If frost threatens outdoor plants, gather all those berries that have a hint of yellow color.

Pests and diseases

Outdoor plants should be regularly inspected for aphids, which may gather on the tips of shoots. When seen, spray with malathion.

1 In early spring, sow seeds ¼ in deep in seed trays filled with a proprietary starting mixture. Cover the seed trays with glass. Maintain a temperature of 18°C/65°F.

2 In 10–14 days, when the seeds germinate remove the glass. When the seedlings are large enough to grip, prick out into 3 in pots.

3 After last frost, plant out the seedlings 2½ ft apart. For an earlier start, protect with cloches. Remove the cloches when the danger of frosts is past.

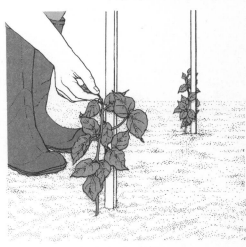

4 During the growing season, provide support for the plants. When 12 in high, if they have no flowers, pinch out the growing points. When flowers appear, feed sparingly.

Preparing the site 1

When preparing a site for a lawn begin at least two to three months before the planned sowing or sodding dates. This gives sufficient time for the soil to settle and for weeds to be brought under control. For fall sowing or winter sodding begin preparations in early summer if leveling or draining the site is going to be necessary, or if there are many weeds present. For spring sowing the draining can be done in fall but leveling is best carried out during summer since the soil needs to be dry.

Clearing the site
The first step is to clear away builders' rubble, bricks, discarded gravel and rubbish, if present. Remove any heaps of sub-soil left by the builders—do not spread them over the site. Next, carefully dig out any tree stumps or broken-off roots. If they are left in the soil they may become colonized by fungi, even if the pieces of wood are quite small, and in time produce unsightly and recurring crops of toadstools. If the new site is heavily infested with weeds use the appropriate weed-killers or fallow the land during the spring and summer months (see page 161).

Recently vacated building sites may have been subjected to considerable soil disturbance, and in some cases much of the fertile top-soil will have been lost. First establish the nature and depth of the top-soil by making trial excavations on the nearest accessible undisturbed site. Ideally, there should be at least 6 in of top-soil, but a minimum depth of 4 in is acceptable. If there is less, purchase sufficient top-soil from a local supplier or dig in materials such as lime, fertilizers and manure to improve the existing soil.

Grading
The term grading means the elimination of surface irregularities. This is done by relating site levels to nearby fixed levels such as house foundations, walls or paths. It is not essential to have a perfectly level site; a fall of 1:80 is quite acceptable and has the advantage of assisting surface drainage.

Grading can be expensive and on larger sites need not be necessary since a gentle slope or undulations can be visually pleasing.

When grading major irregularities first remove all top-soil and heap it clear of the site. Then even out the level of the sub-soil and replace the top-soil to an even depth.

Minor irregularities can be corrected by adding a little top-soil. Do not, however, take it from higher points on the site since this may leave the top-soil very thin in places which will cause the grass to grow irregularly. Instead, bring in top-soil from elsewhere in the garden.

Where there are steep slopes it is preferable to draw the soil forward to make a single level area since sodded banks can be very difficult to maintain. Alternatively construct two or more terraced lawns with retaining walls and connecting steps (see page 149).

Leveling
Few people may take the trouble to establish the level of the site properly by using a spirit level, straight edge and pegs. Usually they rely instead on a "good eye", or pegs and garden line. However, for finer ornamental lawns and areas where games are to be played it is always advisable to do this task properly. For this, the following equipment is required: a straight-edged board about 7 ft long, a large spirit level, a tape measure or marked cane, a handful of marked pegs and a mallet. Hammer in the master peg at a selected point, leaving about 4 in of the peg above the surface. Then drive in the other pegs at 6 ft intervals to form a grid system. Establish the master peg at the required level then, working from it, adjust the other pegs with the straight edge and spirit level until they align with the master peg. Next, add or remove soil (sub-soil or top-soil) until the soil surface is level either with the top of each peg or to a predetermined peg marking. Where a slope is required, establish across-slope levels in the same manner. Down-slope levels can then be established with pegs and line or, more accurately, with a spirit level, using pairs of marked pegs at each station.

Digging
Digging serves two purposes: it allows improvement of soil texture (and hence aeration and drainage) and it relieves compaction. It is advisable to dig all lawn sites unless, of course, they have recently been plowed. Lawn sites that have been vacated by builders should be deeply dug because such sites almost invariably are compacted to a considerable depth.

When digging, take out a trench a spit deep, then fork over the bottom of the trench to the full depth of the fork. On heavy soils incorporate gritty material or lime-free, medium-grade sand ($\frac{1}{5}-\frac{1}{2}$ mm) to improve soil texture and porosity. Also add well rotted stable manure, garden compost, leaf-mold or moist granulated peat at up to 14 lb per square yard. On sandy soils improve moisture retention and encourage deeper rooting by incorporating similar dressings of organic materials. Dried sewage can also be used at up to 2 lb per square yard.

Break up organic materials when digging them in; if they are left in large lumps, surface irregularities may occur as they gradually decompose. Finely broken organic matter can also be worked into the sub-soil, but do this in moderation, otherwise settling may occur at a later date.

Soil pH
If soils are very acid (low pH) or very alkaline (high pH) some of the nutrients in the soil can become "locked up" and be unavailable to plants. The ideal pH level for most lawn grasses is between 6 and 6.5, that is, slightly acid—simple test kits are available for measuring the pH of the soil. Grasses can grow at higher or lower pH levels and it is not essential for the soil pH to be at this level, but with increasing acidity or alkalinity growth problems occur. Few lawn sites will require the pH to be altered. Possibly some heathland development sites will be too acidic for a lawn, but those developed from agricultural land almost always have a satisfactory pH value.

Where tests show that the soil is too acid (below pH 6) apply lime in the form of carbonate of lime (either ground chalk or ground limestone). If there is uncertainty as to how much lime is needed, apply only a moderate dressing of 2 oz per square yard on sandy soils and 4 oz per square yard on clay soils. Lime needs may vary considerably according to the texture of the soil, and very acid soils may need further treatment. Test the soil again after one or two years. Ensure

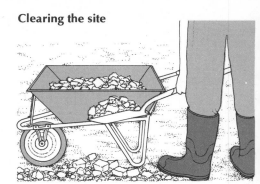

1 Remove any debris left by builders, such as rubble and bricks. If they have left heaps of sub-soil, remove these as well.

2 Carefully dig up and remove any tree stumps together with all their roots, including those that have broken off.

3 Test the depth of the top-soil and, if necessary, purchase sufficient to bring it up to a minimum depth of 4 in.

Preparing the site 2

that sufficient lime is added to raise the pH to the required level, otherwise there may be problems with diseases, and coarse grass and weed could become established.

On alkaline soils reduce the soil pH by adding sulfur or acid peat materials. Note that on strongly alkaline soils the incorporation of acid peat materials will benefit early growth of seedling grasses, but it will not appreciably reduce alkalinity.

Final preparations

The final stage of preparation is the creation of a firm, even, fine-particled soil surface. If the soil is heavy then digging may have left the surface very rough. However, if it has been subjected to a long period of weathering after digging, or if the soil is light, then the surface should be in a reasonable condition. On larger sites that have been worked with a cultivator or tiller there will be few clods to break down, but the soil will have been less

thoroughly prepared than if it were well dug.

For fall sowing, begin the final preparation of the seedbed during the summer. This will allow several weeks fallowing during which germinating weed seedlings can be killed periodically by light hoeing or spraying with cacodylic acid, glyphosate or preferably a mixture of the two. For seed sown in spring, germination will be slower and, although it is still advantageous to prepare the seedbed a few weeks in advance of sowing, the weather conditions may prevent this. In this case it is better to take advantage of favorable conditions and sow immediately after preparation. For laying sod, fallowing is less important, but take advantage of favorable weather conditions for early preparation, particularly on heavier soils.

The first step is to break down clods and lumps into fine particles. On smaller sites use a heavy metal rake or a garden fork reversed. On larger sites use a cultivator or tiller set to a

shallow level of penetration. Breaking down clods should be done when the soil is fairly dry since this reduces the risk of compacting the soil.

The second step is to firm, or consolidate, the soil. On smaller sites this can be done by light treading. Very short or overlapping steps are taken with body weight mainly on the heels, the ball of the foot providing balance. Alternatively, use the head of a rake. Ensure that uniform pressure is applied over the entire surface so that all soft spots are located and firmed. As with breaking down, do not firm when the soil is wet.

After firming, rake the soil level, remove stones and debris and firm again. If hollows are still present, repeat the process until the surface is uniformly consolidated and heel pressure makes only a slight indentation. Do not allow the soil to become so compressed that surface drainage is impaired. Keep a close check on the level as firming progresses.

With larger areas, manual firming by treading or using a rake is not practicable and this job is then best done by using a water-weighted roller.

Pre-sowing fertilizer

If a site is known to have been heavily manured and fertilized in recent years, a dressing of fertilizer is not essential. However, where there is any doubt regarding soil fertility apply an inorganic fertilizer with proportions roughly 6–12–4 (see page 165), at the rate of 2 oz per square yard. Rake this in thoroughly seven to ten days before sowing, if possible. However, sowing can, if necessary, be done immediately after applying fertilizer. Use the fertilizer at once—if stored it will soon set hard.

If sowing is not done immediately after applying fertilizer, give the site a final raking to remove all small stones and debris so that it is ready for sowing when planned.

Grading major irregularities

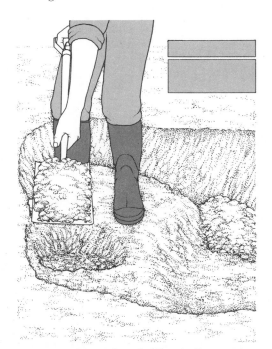

1 Dig up all the top-soil from the site and pile it up to one side, leaving just the sub-soil beneath.

2 Even out the sub-soil, filling hollows with sub-soil taken from bumps, and then replace the top-soil.

Grading steep slopes

1 After removing the top-soil from the slope, transfer the sub-soil from the higher half of the slope to the lower half.

2 Level out the sub-soil and firm it. Finally return the top-soil evenly over the surface.

Preparing the site 3

Leveling the site

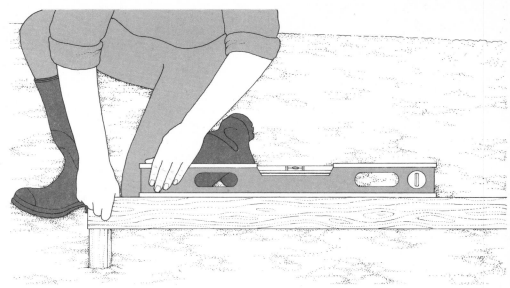

1 Hammer the master peg into the soil at a suitable point, leaving about 4 in of the peg showing above the surface. Then drive in the remaining pegs at 6 ft intervals to form a square grid system.

2 Adjust the height of the secondary pegs with a spirit level and straight-edged plank or board, working away from the master peg. Continue until the tops of all the pegs lie in the same horizontal plane.

Creating a sloping site

3 Add or remove soil until it is either level with the top of each peg or comes up to a predetermined marking on each peg. Ensure that all the soil has been evenly firmed before removing the pegs.

Establish the across-slope levels as above. The down-slope levels are determined by using a pair of pegs, with the soil being added or removed up to a fixed distance below the top of the down-slope peg, and to the top of the up-slope peg.

Preparing the site 4

Firming the soil

Lightly tread over the site, taking short or overlapping steps and with the weight of the body on the heels. Alternatively, firm the

soil with the head of a rake. Then rake the soil level, remove any debris present and firm again.

TERRACING A STEEP SLOPE

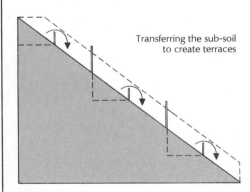

Transferring the sub-soil to create terraces

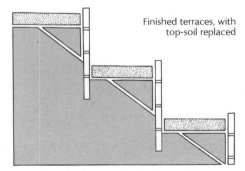

Finished terraces, with top-soil replaced

The first step is to decide how many terraces are required and to mark out their dimensions. Starting at the lowest terrace, remove the top-soil and place to one side or on the next highest level. Next, stretch a line across the terrace to divide it into an upper half and a lower half. Then move

sufficient sub-soil from the upper half to bring the two halves level. Finally, replace the top-soil. If necessary, construct a retaining wall before replacing the top-soil and beginning work on the next terrace. Do not forget to include a ramp for mowers if needed.

DRAINING

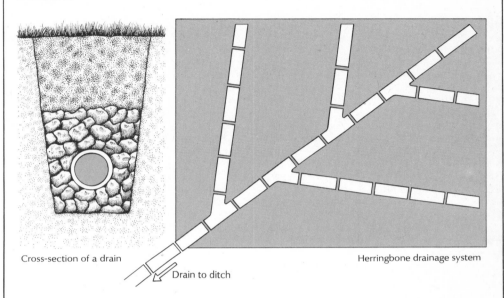

Cross-section of a drain

Drain to ditch

Herringbone drainage system

When constructing a new lawn, a thorough working of the top-soil and breaking up of the sub-soil, with textural improvement where necessary, should ensure that surplus moisture is not held at the surface. If, however, the site is known to be wet in places then some form of drainage should be installed.

For a small lawn or wet corner, a drywell provides sufficient drainage. To build one, first dig a hole 2–3 ft square by at least 3 ft deep at the lowest part of the lawn. Fill it with clinker, broken bricks or stone to 8 in from the surface and add a 2 in layer of coarse sand, grit, or upturned sods to prevent the soil from washing through to the coarse material below. Finally, fill in the hole by adding a 6 in layer of top-soil.

A more satisfactory method of draining, though not often necessary, is tile draining. On a very wet site a herringbone or grid system may be needed, but usually a single line of drainpipes laid diagonally across the site, or through a wet section and feeding

into a drywell, is sufficient. For this use agricultural clay or 3 in diameter plastic lateral or collector pipes. If several lines are being laid, space them about 10 ft apart on heavy soils, and up to 30 ft apart on light soils. Their depth should be about 2 ft and they should have a fall of between 1:80 and 1:100. A herringbone or grid of lateral 3 in pipes should feed into a 4 in main drain laid at a depth of $2\frac{1}{2}$ ft. This in turn should be connected to a main drain or ditch—check beforehand with the appropriate authorities that this is permissible.

Pipe drainage should be installed only after the site has been leveled. Excavate the soil carefully so that, firstly, the pipes will just fit into the bottom of the hole and, secondly, the top-soil and sub-soil are kept separate. Place a small piece of sod with the grass down over the joints between the pipes, then cover with clinker or gravel to within 8 in of the surface. Finally, add a 2 in layer of coarse sand, grit or fine gravel, then replace the top-soil, discarding the sub-soil.

Lawn grasses 1

Of the many kinds of grasses that exist in nature only a few are suitable for creating lawns. The most important qualities needed in lawn grasses are that they should tolerate close mowing, drought and cold. They should also be resistant to diseases, be hard-wearing and have a naturally low-growing habit. Since no single species of grass possesses all these qualities, lawns almost invariably contain a mixture of different grasses to provide the optimum blend.

Many seedsmen supply good basic proprietary mixtures of grasses, and these are perfectly satisfactory in a wide range of conditions. If, however, problems are experienced in establishing lawn from seed on the more difficult kinds of soil it could be worth while studying the qualities and preferences of the main types of lawn grasses and then over-seeding or modifying a proprietary mixture with the appropriate species or strains. New varieties having improved characteristics are introduced from time to time, and the best varieties available should be sought. They are usually the most expensive but are a worthwhile investment. Note that particular named varieties are only available commercially in large quantities.

Types of grasses

Which grasses are appropriate for a particular lawn depends in the first instance on the climate. On this basis, the types of grasses available can be divided into three groups: cool-season grasses, warm-season grasses and extreme-season grasses. Cool-season grasses are most suitable for climates found in the northern half of the country. South of a line through Tennessee these grasses become dormant during hot dry spells and are then susceptible to crabgrass. Cool-season grasses are usually grown from seed.

Warm-season grasses are suited to areas south of around Virginia. They are usually started from plugs or sprigs rather than seed. The last category, extreme-season grasses, are used for areas that have an extreme climate, whether this be hot or cold, wet or dry.

Within these categories, the most appropriate mixtures depend on the soil conditions, the degree of shade, the local climate and how hard-wearing the lawn needs to be.

Cool-season grasses

Kentucky bluegrass (*Poa pratensis*) is the most popular of all cool-season grasses. It has a tufted growth with slender creeping rhizomes, and is tough and hard-wearing. However, it is rather slow to establish and dislikes wet, heavy or acid soils. If buying a seed mixture that contains Kentucky bluegrass ensure that there is at least 45 per cent of this grass present. The most popular of the many different varieties of Kentucky bluegrass available are Merion, Newport, Park, Prato and Windsor.

Rough-stalked bluegrass (*Poa trivialis*) has a loosely tufted habit with short creeping rhizomes. It has a lighter color than Kentucky bluegrass and is more suited to wet heavy soils, but is less tolerant of wear.

Chewings' fescue (*Festuca rubra* spp *commutata*) has a dwarf, densely tufted habit and tolerates poor soils.

Creeping red fescue (*Festuca rubra* ssp *rubra*) is a hard-wearing grass with slender creeping rhizomes that is tolerant of wet, dry or cold conditions. It is, however, less tolerant of close mowing than Chewings' fescue. The strain slender creeping red fescue (*Festuca rubra* ssp *littoralis*) is suited to close-mown lawns.

Creeping bentgrass (*Agrostis palustris*) is a tufted stoloniferous grass that thrives in wet areas, though it has some resistance to drought. On its own it needs frequent attention and is susceptible to diseases; it is thus best used in mixtures.

Italian rye grass (*Lolium multiflorum*) is an annual grass that germinates rapidly and is useful for protecting a lawn site while slower-germinating perennial grasses develop. However, it is a coarse grass and seed mixtures should not contain more than 20 per cent.

Perennial rye grass (*Lolium perenne*) is less coarse than Italian rye grass and grows well on almost any type of soil, being particularly suitable for heavy soils in cool moist regions that have mild winters. It is not so tolerant of close-mowing as Italian rye grass.

Warm-season grasses

Bermuda grass (*Cynodon* spp) is the most important of the warm-season grasses. It is a deeply rooting grass that spreads by means of both surface runners and rhizomes; in a

Bermuda grass

Chewings' fescue

sunny site it is a vigorously growing grass, though it will also tolerate shade. It needs frequent mowing and edging, and can become invasive.

St Augustine grass (*Stenotaphrum secundatum*) is a coarse dark-colored grass that needs little mowing and will tolerate shade and bad weather. In dry conditions it needs frequent watering. It grows best on a well drained fertile soil. Do not spray this grass with weed-killers based on 2,4-D.

Japanese lawngrass (*Zoysia japonica*) is a hard-wearing dense grass that needs a fully sunny site. It will grow on almost any type of soil, even poor ones, and does especially well on heavy soils. It is particularly effective at preventing crabgrass from establishing. A disadvantage of this grass is that it is very slow to establish and may take more than two years to form a dense sod.

Manila grass (*Zoysia matrella*) is a finer denser grass than Japanese lawngrass, to which it is

Lawn grasses 2

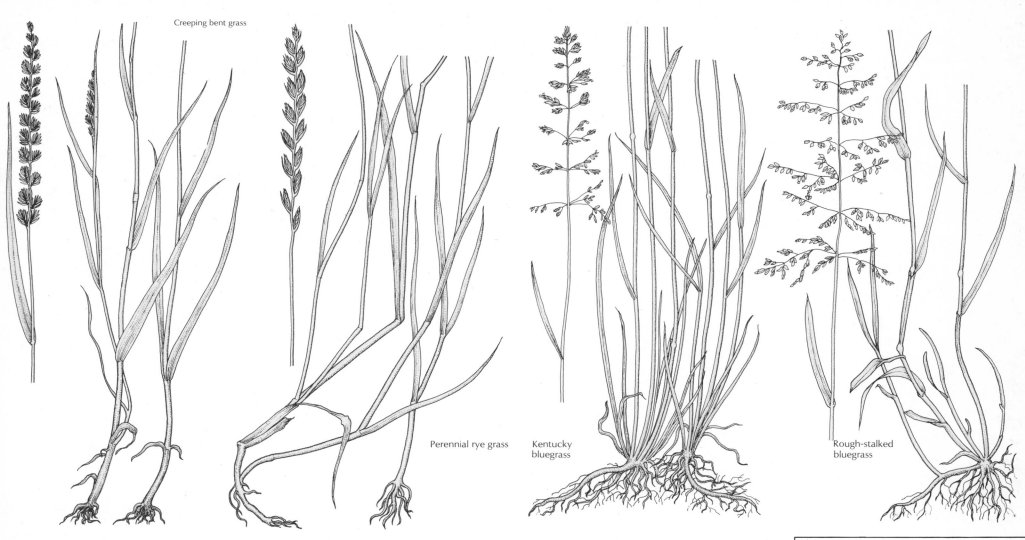

Creeping bent grass

Perennial rye grass

Kentucky bluegrass

Rough-stalked bluegrass

related, but is less hardy. It will grow in either full sun or partial shade. Like Japanese lawn-grass, it can take a very long time to establish.
Bahia grass (*Paspalum notatum flugge*) is a rapidly spreading stoloniferous grass that is ideal for poor sandy soils and areas that are not fertilized.
Centipede grass (*Eremochloa ophiuroides*) is a tufted grass that grows well on poor soils and needs little maintenance. It is thus ideal for utility lawns.

Extreme-season grasses
Apart from the grasses discussed below, a number of cool- or warm-season grasses may be satisfactorily grown in regions having extreme climates, so long as suitable grass is chosen. If using cool-season grass, plant sod rather than seed because the seed may not establish successfully.
Buffalo grass (*Büchloe dactyloides*) is a native warm-season tufted grass that spreads by stolons. It is resistant to drought and very

bad weather generally, and requires little mowing or other attention.
Blue grama (*Bouteloua gracilis*) is a creeping warm-season grass that is hardy and drought-resistant. It prefers a heavy soil, and is frequently used to prevent erosion in dry places.
Crested wheatgrass (*Agropyron desertorum*) is a long-lived drought-resistant grass. It becomes dormant in extremely hot weather and will not withstand much flooding.

CHOICE OF GRASSES

Grasses most tolerant of close mowing:
Italian rye grass
Chewings' fescue
Bermuda grass

Hardest-wearing grasses
Kentucky bluegrass
Bahia grass

Seed or sod?

The most common methods of establishing lawns in the United States are to sow seeds or lay sods. At one time sodded lawns were much more common than seed lawns. However, in recent years there have been considerable improvements in the quality, variety and availability of seed mixtures, and sowing is now an increasingly popular alternative.

A point that is often overlooked when comparing seeding and sodding is that, whichever process is decided upon, the site needs to be prepared thoroughly. In particular, it is not sufficient simply to rake over the site before laying sods.

There are various factors to consider when making a choice between seeds and sod. To help the gardener decide which method to use, the various advantages and disadvantages of each are listed below.

Advantages of seed
The most important advantages that seed has over sod are that it is much cheaper to buy and there is less work involved in sowing than in laying sod. The gardener can choose a mixture of seeds to suit his or her own particular requirements or conditions, whereas with sods, the gardener has much less variety to choose from. A further advantage of seeds is that it can be stored easily and will not deteriorate. Unlike sodding, sowing can, therefore, be delayed until the weather conditions are exactly right.

Disadvantages of seed
Seed takes much longer to establish than sod, and it is some months before the lawn can be used: a lawn sown in late summer will not be usable until the following June, and a spring-sown lawn will not be able to tolerate normal wear and tear until late fall. The soil surface requires a more careful final preparation and, if the site is weedy, it must be left fallow for a time to ensure a reasonable freedom from weed seeds. These may also be carried on to the site by birds and wind, where they quickly become established and compete with the grass seedlings for water and nutrients. A lawn created from seed is more dependent on good weather for successful establishment than is a sodded lawn and, in

hot damp conditions especially, is much more susceptible to disease. There is also the risk of disturbance to the seedbed from birds, cats, dogs or moles to be borne in mind. Lastly, grass seed is sown in either the spring or early fall, which are often busy periods in the garden.

Advantages of sod
The most obvious advantage of sod is that the lawn can be created and used almost immediately, although it is advisable to allow a period for rooting into the bed before general use. Since laying sod has an instant visual effect, it is a much more attractive proposition than seeding for people moving into a newly built house with a featureless garden. Other points in favor of sodding are that is is easier to achieve a neat, well defined edge to paths and borders with sods than with seed, and they can be laid in late fall or winter, at which time it is too late for sowing grass seed. Another advantage of being able to lay sods in the fall or winter is that there are few other pressing tasks in the garden at this time of year. Lastly, and importantly, sodding gives immediate stabilization of the soil against wind and water erosion.

Disadvantages of sod
The inexperienced buyer may fail to notice weeds, weed grasses or other defects that may be present in low-quality sod, for example, variations in thickness and shape, which will both require attention before sodding can proceed. Laying to a good standard is much more difficult than sowing, and takes both skill and time. Sod will deteriorate if a long period of bad weather prevents laying, so the operation needs to be planned well in advance. The lawn site should be completely prepared before the sods are ordered and they should be laid as soon as possible after delivery, since they will deteriorate rapidly, even if they are stored carefully. To store sods, stack them grass upwards three or four deep. Rolled or folded sods should be similarly stacked. During the summer the sods must be laid within twelve hours of delivery otherwise they will perish. At other times store only for a day or two.

SPRIGS AND PLUGS

Another method of establishing lawns, and one commonly used in the warmer parts of the United States, is to plant sprigs or plugs. Sprigs are short lengths of surface runners with grass blades and roots attached; plugs are small round pieces of sod about 2–4 in in diameter. Both are planted at suitable intervals on the site so that they will spread out to provide a dense tightly knit lawn.

Plant in spring or fall and prepare the site as thoroughly as for sowing or sodding.

Sprigs

To plant sprigs, first chop them into 2–3 in lengths and scatter them evenly over the site, ensuring that each sprig is no more than 1 in from its neighbor. Cover them lightly with sifted top-soil, then

lightly roll. Keep the site well irrigated with a lawn sprinkler, but do not use a hose or a watering can because their heavier spray may dislodge the sprigs. Mow as for new lawns raised from seed.

Plugs

The first step when plugging is to create the holes into which they are to be planted. This is best done with a special plugging tool, spacing the holes at 8–12 in intervals to form a grid. Then water each hole and after it has drained away insert

the plug and firm it down, either by hand or by pressing down with the heel. Then rake over the surface between the plugs and water the site thoroughly. Keep the site well irrigated and hoe regularly to control weeds until the grass has spread.

Growing lawns from sod 1

Buying sod

Since sods are a relatively expensive means of creating a lawn, they should always be examined carefully before being purchased, and again when they are delivered. Do not hesitate to reject sub-standard sods on delivery. Failure to do so will very likely create problems both with laying the sods and with subsequent care of the lawn.

The most important points to look for are the quality of the grass, the soil and the roots, and whether there are weeds present. Check also the grass components in the sods and how much of each is present. The grass should be uniform in appearance, with no broad-bladed coarser grasses present, and it should be suitably mown since long shaggy grass may hide defects. The soil should be either loamy or light and sandy, not heavy and clayed since a clay soil could adversely affect the lawn later on. The sods should have a good root system and a reasonable level of organic matter, a high level may give poor rooting, which will subsequently create problems. The sods should be weed-free, or virtually so. If there are many weeds present, it indicates that the sods have been poorly managed. Such sods usually break apart when handled, and if laid, there would be immediate problems with weeds.

The last point to check is that the size and thickness of the sods should be uniform. The size of the sods may be 12–18 in wide and 4–9 ft long. For the inexperienced the smallest size is the simplest to lay. The sods should have a soil thickness of $\frac{1}{2}$–$\frac{3}{4}$ in. Thinner sod will establish satisfactorily if its quality is good and the roots are well developed, but more care is needed both when laying and with the subsequent lawn. If the sod is thicker or irregular, it will have to be trimmed to an even and satisfactory thickness. To do this lay each sod grass-side down in an open-ended box of suitable depth. Then, using a long-bladed knife, preferably one with two handles, shave off the unwanted soil.

When to sod

The best period for sodding is between October and February, though not when frost or rain is present. The advantage of sodding during this period is that newly laid sod is then rarely subjected to the stress of drying winds or hot sunshine, and it usually inter-roots before such conditions occur.

Lawns may be established satisfactorily at other periods, but in warmer, drier conditions there is increasing need for artificial irrigation. This has the disadvantage that, unless this is very carefully applied, it can affect the level of the lawn and its firmness.

Before laying

Always apply fertilizer before laying, unless the soil is already rich and well manured due to, for example, vegetables having been grown there regularly. The fertilizer encourages the sods to knit together and the roots to establish. Apply either superphosphate at 2 oz per square yard or the following mixture, which also supplies nitrogen and potash: 1 oz superphosphate, $\frac{3}{4}$ oz bone meal, $\frac{3}{4}$ oz hoof and horn meal and $\frac{1}{4}$ oz sulfate of potash per square yard. Apply the fertilizer a few days before sodding begins, and rake it well into the soil.

Lay the sods as soon as possible after they have been delivered. This should be done within twelve hours during hot summer weather. In cool conditions they can be stored for a day or two by rolling or folding them and stacking them three or four deep.

If storing sods for more than a day, place them flat in a shaded site and keep them well watered otherwise exposed roots will dry up and shrivel. Before laying the sods, check each one and remove any coarse grasses or rosetted weeds.

The final step is to mark out the precise dimensions of the lawn and allow 1–2 in overlap if there is sufficient sod. This can be trimmed back when the sod is well established to leave a neat, sharp edge.

Laying sod

Begin by laying a row of sods along the most accessible side of the soil bed, using a tautly stretched garden line as a guide. Always ensure that each sod is laid as close as possible to the previous one. Lay in straight lines and do not at any time stand on the prepared bed. Work forwards, facing the unsodded area, standing or kneeling on broad planks. Avoid walking on the newly laid sod by using planks as pathways. This spreads the weight and prevents depressions being formed by heavy boots or heels.

Stagger successive lines of sod by using half sods in alternate rows. The sods will then hold together more firmly when mown during the early stages of inter-rooting. If a short piece is needed to finish a row, greater stability is obtained by laying the last whole sod to the edge with the short piece fitted in behind. Keep a constant watch on the soil level and have a bucket of ordinary soil and a rake handy for adjusting minor irregularities or for packing extra soil under thin sods. Never attempt to level a piece of sod by beating it with a spade since this will cause local compaction. Instead, lift the sod, remove a little soil and then re-lay it.

After laying

When the laying has been completed, firm the sod by rolling with a light garden roller to eliminate air pockets and help settle the sods. Alternatively, construct a simple sodding board by attaching a pole, such as a broom handle, to the center of a 9 in by 15 in wooden board. Firm the sod, gently pressing down on the turfing board. If the level of the surface needs improving, top-dress with a sandy mixture at 3–4 lb per square yard. This will also protect the lawn from drying out. Apply as an overall dressing, working it well into the crevices between the sods with a broom or the back of a rake. If good top dressing materials are in short supply, fill a bucket with a mixture of sand and sifted soil, and top-dress along the crevices between sods, afterwards brushing it in.

Irrigate the new lawn thoroughly and regularly during dry periods—sod laid in the spring or summer is particularly susceptible to drying out and, if neglected, will often deteriorate rapidly.

When the grass begins to grow in spring top with the mower and from then on adopt the programme of maintenance for established lawns given on page 158.

Do not be in too much of a hurry to use new lawns. Give them time.

Trimming sod

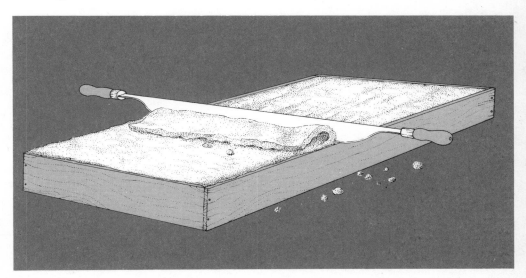

Place the sod grass-side down in a box of the correct height. Then take a knife whose blade is at least as long as the sod is wide, and pull this along the top of the box to shave off unwanted soil. If possible, the knife should have two handles.

Growing lawns from sod 2

Laying sods

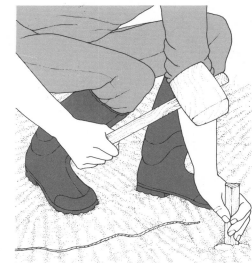

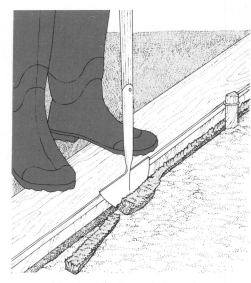

1 Apply a dressing of fertilizer a few days before laying. Do not feed if the soil is already rich and well manured.

2 Rake in the fertilizer, incorporating it well into the soil.

3 Mark out the exact shape of the lawn and allow for the sods to extend an inch or two beyond its edges. This can then be

trimmed back after the sods have been laid and have settled down to leave a neat, sharply defined edge.

4 Lay the sods in straight lines, ensuring that each sod is as close as possible to the preceding one. If a segment of sod is needed

to complete a row, lay a whole sod at the end and place the segment behind it. Allow 1–2 in overlap at the edge.

5 Stagger successive rows of sod by laying half sods. Do not walk on newly laid sod instead lay down planks as pathways. They

will spread out the weight and so avoid risk of compaction.

Growing lawns from sod 3

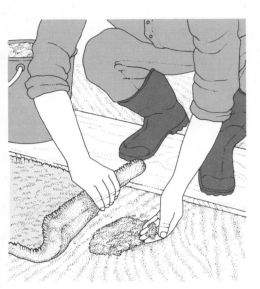

6 Correct irregularities in the soil level as sodding progresses. Have some soil at hand for packing under thin sods.

7 After the laying has been completed roll the lawn with a light garden roller, if one is available.

8 Apply a sandy top dressing mixture at 3–4 lb per square yard if the surface of the lawn is uneven.

9 Work the dressing well into the crevices between sods, using either a broom or the back of a rake.

SEEDLING SOD

An alternative to laying sods of established grass is to lay seedling sods. These come in large lightweight rolls, about a yard thick, and are well rooted and of uniform thickness. Seedling sod is raised in special sod nurseries by one of two methods. One method uses long, polyethylene-lined troughs filled with water. Buoyant soil-less compost is then spread on the water, and on this is laid a thin strip of polyurethane foam upon which the grass seeds are sown. The second method is to grow the sod on a thin layer of soil-based rooting medium over a hard, impenetrable base. In the first method, the sod is held together by the foam, and in the second method by the densely intermingled roots. When laid the foam base gradually disintegrates.

Seedling sod is best laid during cool, moist conditions in spring or early fall because it is more susceptible to cold and drought than ordinary sod. Also, it needs a period of good growing conditions in which it can quickly establish itself. Do not attempt to lay seedling sod in the summer unless it can be adequately irrigated. Give the sod an initial cut after two or three weeks, and do not cut it closer than 1in during the first six weeks after laying. Then cut it to the appropriate height for the grass and the time of year.

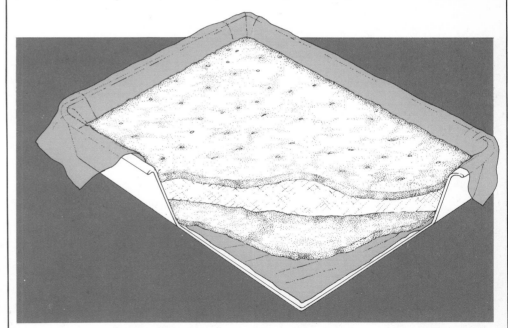

This technique can be adopted by gardeners who wish to raise small squares of sod for repair work. Line a seed box or a deep tray with polyethylene, then introduce a $\frac{1}{2}$ in layer of well firmed seed compost and cover with a piece of cheesecloth. Add a second layer of compost and sow grass seeds on the surface at the standard rate (see page 150). Then place the box in a sunny position and keep it constantly moist. Once the seeds have germinated, feed it weekly with a liquid fertilizer. The sod will be ready for laying about three weeks after germination.

Growing lawns from seed

Sowing

Seeds may be sown either by hand or by seed drill. For hand-sowing divide the grass seeds into two equal portions, adding dry soil, if wished, to facilitate distribution. Sow half the seeds by traversing the plot lengthways, then sow the remaining half crossways. This method gives a more even coverage than a single application. Divide large areas into smaller sections or small plots marked out in square yards to facilitate accurate sowing.

If hiring a drill first ensure that it can be calibrated to apply grass seeds at the required rate. To check that a drill is applying the correct rate of seeds, mark out two separate square yard areas on concrete or a strip of burlap. Scatter $\frac{1}{2}$ oz of seed by hand on one square, then run the drill over the other square. The density of seeds should be equal in the two squares.

Apply the seeds to the seedbed in parallel strips using the previous run's wheeltrack as a guide. Again, sow half the seed lengthways and half crossways. If space allows lay a strip of burlap along the edge of the lawn and over-run since the drill may distribute the seed unevenly when it is being turned.

Sow during a period of calm, dry weather when the surface of the seedbed is dry and soil does not adhere to boots or to the wheels of a seed drill. There should, however, be moisture just below the surface.

After sowing, lightly rake over the seedbed. Do this carefully since the seeds may not germinate if buried too deeply, and it may also make the distribution uneven. Then roll the surface to firm it and improve germination. If after a few days there has been no rainfall then irrigate gently but thoroughly with a garden sprinkler. Do not use a hose or a coarse-rose watering can since they may redistribute the seeds. If sparrows or other seed-eating birds are troublesome locally, use seed that has been treated with a bird deterrent. Usually a more serious problem created by birds is dust-bathing. Help to prevent this by stretching black thread 3–4 in above the seedbed. Alternatively, lay some leafless twiggy brushwood lightly over the bed after sowing.

When to sow

The two most suitable periods for sowing grass seeds are early fall and spring. The best time for fall sowing is mid-August to mid-or late September, depending on the temperature. During this period the soil temperature is still high and moisture is usually plentiful, both conditions that encourage a quick germination period of seven to ten days. This enables seedling grasses to become well established before the first frosts in October or early November. Do not sow much later than these recommended times since germination may be poor and seedlings will not establish well. They may not then survive prolonged cold or wet weather.

If seed is to be sown in spring do this during April since the soil is beginning to warm up at this time and there is a full growing season ahead. Note that germination is slower at this time of year and there is a greater risk of the weather being dry than in fall.

After germination

The soil surface is often slightly lifted at germination. Therefore, when the young grasses are about 2 in high (3 in for utility turf) lightly roll when the surface is dry using a light garden roller or a rear-roller cylinder mower with the front roller and blades lifted clear of the grass.

Two or three days later, when the grass has recovered from rolling and is growing vertically again, cut it with a sharp-bladed mower. Remove no more than about a third of the grass growth. It is preferable to use a side-wheel cylinder mower, or rotary mower since they have no front roller to flatten the grass before cutting. If using a front-roller machine, lift or remove the front roller before mowing. After this first mow, fall-sown grass may need further cuttings before the spring, depending upon the rate of grass growth. With spring-sown grass progressively reduce the height of cut to the normal mowing height for an established lawn (see page 159 for details).

First season of growth

Use the lawn as little as possible during the first season of growth. If there are any surface irregularities, gradually eliminate them by top-dressing lightly with compost at intervals beginning after the first cut. Feed the lawn regularly according to seasonal requirements, and irrigate as necessary. This will quickly establish a vigorous grass coverage of sufficient density to prevent mosses and weeds from establishing.

Damping-off diseases

Fungal diseases may kill both grass seeds and young grasses. Damping off may cause young seedlings to become yellow or bronze and collapse at or near ground level, or brown shriveled patches may occur, depending on the species of fungus responsible. At the first sign of attack water with a copper fungicide at $\frac{1}{2}$ oz in 1 gal water per square yard.

Seed dressings based on 75 per cent captan used at the rate of $\frac{1}{2}$ oz per 14 lb of seed will provide a useful degree of protection where sowing under difficult conditions.

Sowing grass seeds

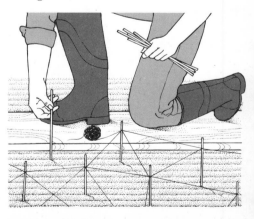

1 Divide the seeds into two halves and, if sowing by hand, broadcast one batch walking lengthways across the site and the other batch walking crossways.

2 If a seed drill is being used, lay a strip of burlap along the edge of the site and over-run. Again, sow half the seeds lengthways and the other half crossways.

3 After sowing, lightly rake over the entire seedbed, taking care not to bury the seeds too deeply, otherwise they may not germinate.

4 Prevent birds from dust-bathing by inserting small twigs or sticks at intervals in the seedbed. Then twine black thread among them 3–4 in above the soil surface.

Weed control in new lawns

In established lawns most weeds can be easily controlled by applying selective lawn weedkillers, combined with appropriate cultural measures. These weedkillers may, if used on new lawns, damage young seedling grasses before they are well established. For this reason do not use selective lawn weedkillers on newly seeded lawns earlier than three months after germination, and preferably not until at least six months have passed. However, it is important to control weeds in these early stages to prevent them competing with the young grass.

Annual broad-leaved weeds
Seeds of annual broad-leaved weeds are likely to be present on any site selected for a lawn and it is always advisable to deal with them well in advance of sowing to allow for a period of fallowing. Even so, weed seeds may still be introduced to the site unknowingly if fresh soil is used in the final stages of preparation. Seeds may also be carried in on the wind from surrounding areas. A few scattered weeds are no real cause for concern. They can be removed by hand (see below) with little effort, or left to be controlled by the mower—annuals such as groundsel, fat hen and mayweed soon die out once the grass has become strong enough for it to be mown regularly. Where strong-growing annual weeds are numerous they may smother grass growth, particularly where it is slow because of bad weather, or poor and weak because of inadequate preparation of the site. Common chickweed can be particularly troublesome since it grows strongly from very early in the year.

Weedkiller treatment can be used where annual broad-leaved weeds are numerous. Control them by spraying with bromoxynil. This weedkiller will kill broad-leaved annual weeds without harming young established grasses. Do not, however, apply before the grass has developed beyond the second-leaf stage, that is, not until the seedling grasses have at least two leaves. Use only formulations that are specifically recommended for weed control in new lawns. Note that mixtures of bromoxynil and mecoprop should only be used on established lawns and are not suitable for new lawns.

Grass weeds
The most troublesome weeds in new lawns are seedling perennial grasses such as cocksfoot (*Dactylis glomerata*) and quack grass (*Agropyron repens*). In high-quality turf, redtop (*Agrostis alba*) can be troublesome. None of these weeds can be controlled by bromoxynil in new lawns; they are checked to some extent by frequent close mowing but tend to persist indefinitely.

Seeds of coarse grasses may be present in grass seed mixtures as an impurity and it is advisable always to purchase seed of reliable quality from a reputable supplier. It is much more likely, however, that seeds were already present in the soil at the time of sowing.

Crabgrass (*Digitaria sanguinalis*) is perhaps the most troublesome lawn weed for American gardeners. It is an annual weed that seeds throughout the summer, forming thin seedheads that radiate from the tips of the stems. With the first frosts, the plant turns reddish-brown and dies, though the seeds remain dormant in the soil over winter and germinate the following spring. The only way to control this and other grass weeds is by hand-weeding.

Hand-weed in fine weather when the soil surface is firm, and not soft and wet from recent rain. If hand-weeding causes any serious disturbance to the lawn grasses, irrigate after weeding with a lawn sprinkler to resettle the grass roots. Thorough fallowing prior to sowing will minimize problems with all grass weeds.

Perennial weeds
Even after thorough preparation and removal of perennial weed growth, the deeply penetrating roots or rhizomes of some broad-leaved perennials may remain. Suitably deep cultivations during preparation should, however, ensure that little growth appears prior to mowing. Once the lawn has established, the use of selective lawn weedkillers will soon eradicate such recalcitrant weeds.

Newly laid turf
Do not use selective weedkillers on newly laid turf until it is well established and growing strongly. Purchase only good quality, weed-free turf.

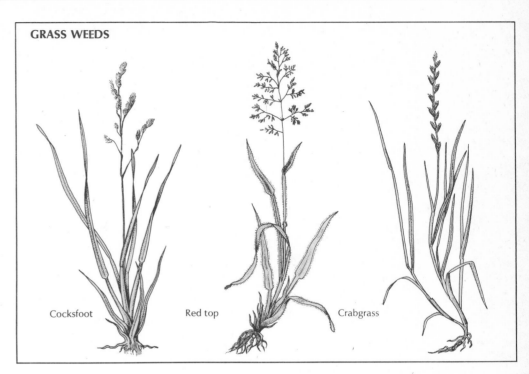

GRASS WEEDS

Cocksfoot   Red top   Crabgrass

Controlling broad-leaved weeds

Spray broad-leaved weeds with bromoxynil, using only those formulations that are recommended for use on new lawns. Do not spray until the grass has developed at least two leaves.

Controlling grass weeds

Remove grass weeds by hand-pulling, using one hand to grasp the weed and the other to press down the soil around the weed and keep it firm. This will prevent the surrounding grasses from being disturbed.

Month-by-month guide

This program provides a useful indication of the approximate times when particular operations or treatments can be undertaken effectively. It is important for the gardener to decide firstly the precise requirements of his own lawn and secondly when the soil and weather conditions are most suitable for carrying out each operation. This program does not give the details of these operations. For these, consult the relevant pages elsewhere in the book.

JANUARY
Remove any accumulations of dead leaves.
Check drains if water is standing on the surface for any length of time after rain, and drain persistently wet sites.
Overhaul the mower and other lawn tools before the start of the new season.

FEBRUARY
From February check regularly for signs of worm activity or unhealthy grass following mild spells. Disperse worm casts regularly.
Complete all major sodding work by the end of the month.
Apply a mosskiller in late February if weather is settled; if still cold leave until March.
Top-dress lightly if necessary.
Towards the end of the month, begin preparations for spring sowing if soil conditions and weather are suitable.

MARCH
Scatter worm casts and lightly rake to remove debris; then mow with the blade set high.
Roll before mowing if the lawn has been lifted by frost.
Treat against worms if they become very troublesome.
Re-align ragged lawn edges.

APRIL
Increase the frequency of mowing according to the weather and grass growth.
Continue checking at intervals for signs of unhealthy grass.
Apply a light dressing of a spring feed in early to mid-April; a few days after feeding apply a weedkiller if necessary.
Remove patches of coarse grass and re-seed.
Seed-in sparsely grassed areas and new lawns.
Check newly sodded areas and top-dress lightly if necessary to improve levels or fill joins.

MAY
In early May adjust the mower to the summer cutting height.
Continue weedkilling; if very mossy apply a mosskiller.
From May onwards irrigation may be needed in drier periods.

JUNE
Mow frequently; if patches of creeping weeds are troublesome lightly scarify before mowing.
Continue weedkilling and irrigation as necessary.
Spike, lightly top-dress and irrigate areas that are subjected to heavy wear.

JULY
Mow regularly; scarify patches of creeping weeds and surface-running grasses before mowing.
Feed warm-season grasses with a light dressing of a general lawn fertilizer.
Apply weedkillers and irrigate as necessary.

AUGUST
Mow regularly.
In cooler areas sow grass seed during late August.
Examine the condition of the lawn and carry out fall renovation: scarify to remove matted growth or thatch, spike and top-dress, and seed-in sparse patches.

SEPTEMBER
Apply a lawn weedkiller during dry weather, but not if there is drought.
Apply a lawn sand to control moss.
Feed both cool-season and warm-season grasses with a general lawn fertilizer.
With the onset of cooler, moister conditions check regularly for signs of unhealthy grass and worm activity.
In warmer areas seed-in new lawn sites.

OCTOBER
Modify the cutting height of the mower towards the end of the month, since the rate of growth is now slowing.
Switch or brush to remove early morning dew and encourage rapid drying if the weather is fine.
Spike and top-dress if unable to do so in September.
Apply a second dose of lawn weedkiller if some weeds survived the September treatment.
Prevent accumulation of fallen leaves because this can create conditions in which diseases may establish.
Lay sodded lawns from this month onwards.
Apply a second fall feed to both cool-season and warm-season grasses.

NOVEMBER
A final mow may be necessary, but do not attempt mowing in frosty conditions, nor when the soil is heavy after a recent fall of rain.
Continue clearing up leaves.
Continue sodding when conditions are suitable.

DECEMBER
Apply lime this month if it is needed.
Continue with sodding and leaf clearance where necessary.

Table of operations
This table provides a simplified version, for quick and easy reference, of the month-by-month guide to lawn maintenance given on this page. As stated previously, the exact timings of the various operations depend very much on the weather conditions, the state of the soil and the nature of the lawn.

In this table, heavy shading indicates that the particular operation or treatment will be necessary, or almost always so, during the period concerned. Where the shading is lighter, it indicates that the operation is optional or, in the case of treatment, that it may sometimes be necessary. For example, the best time for sodding is the fall but, if conditions allow, it can also be done in winter.

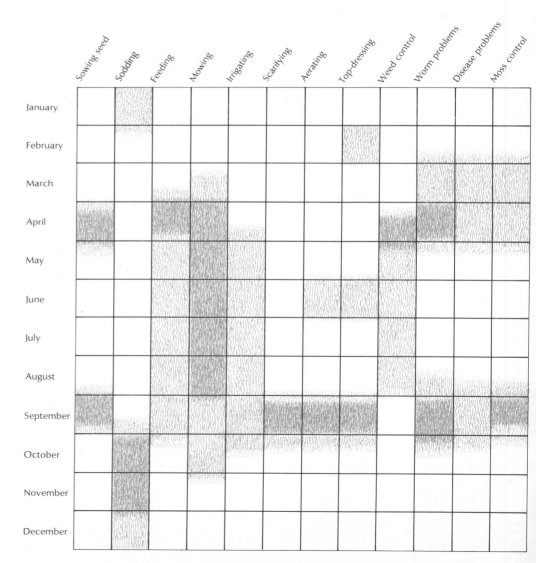

Mowing 1

The purpose of mowing a lawn is to keep the grass short enough to be neat and attractive, but without hindering its ability to grow strongly. Mowing a lawn too close weakens the grass and allows moss and lawn weeds to become established. On the other hand, where lawns are allowed to grow too long, coarser grasses become increasingly dominant and finer grasses deteriorate. The best approach is to mow regularly but not too closely. Apart from keeping the grass to a reasonable length, it encourages tillering, which increases the density of the turf, and deters moss and weed development. Further advantages of this approach are that the yield of mowings is lower and the lawn quicker and easier to mow if the grass is mown regularly rather than sporadically.

Height of cut

The most suitable height of cut is determined by the kind of grasses present and the time of year. Cool-season grasses should be cut to a height of $1\frac{1}{2}$–2 in, since at this height lawn weeds will not easily flourish. Warm-season grasses need closer mowing and should be cut to a height of 1 in. Bermuda grass, however, requires an even lower mowing height of $\frac{5}{8}$ in. Leave the grass slightly longer during hot dry weather unless the lawn can be adequately irrigated.

Between the fall and early spring, when growth is slow, increase the height of cut by $\frac{1}{4}$ in. This leaves the lawn less open to moss and weed infestation. Where the soil is moist and soft adjust the height of cutting to compensate for any sinking of the mower's wheels or rollers.

Do not cut any lawn to below $\frac{5}{8}$ in because all grasses are weakened when cut below this level. On the other hand, lawns should not be allowed to grow longer than 2 in since above this height coarser grasses begin to dominate over the finer grasses.

Frequency of mowing

Once the most suitable height of cut has been established, mow with sufficient frequency to keep the grass as close to the desired height as is practicable. Increase or decrease the frequency of mowing according to the rate of growth. This varies from season to season, and may be influenced by factors such as weather conditions, feeding, irrigation, the varieties of grass being grown and the general health of the lawn itself.

Fine lawns should be mown at intervals of two to three days Mow average lawns at least every seven days and preferably at intervals of three to five days. For other lawns mow at least once every seven days. Never allow the grass to grow long then cut it very short on the pretext that it saves time.

Removing the mowings

Most gardeners remove the mowings from a lawn, usually by means of a grass-box. There are a number of reasons for doing this. In wetter weather mowings cling to the surface, impeding aeration and becoming increasingly unsightly as they slowly decompose. Seeds of weeds and annual meadow grass are scattered and will infest other areas, as will severed stems of white clover and speedwell. Leaving the mowings on the lawn also encourages worm activity and the mowings make the grasses softer and lusher. In milder, moister falls, this causes the lawn to be more susceptible to diseases, many of which thrive in such conditions.

There are, however, some advantages in leaving the mowings on the lawn. Firstly, mowing is less arduous without a grass-box. Secondly, the mowings act as a mulch, increasing drought resistance and deterring moss. As they decompose, they return nutrients to the soil to give a greener, lusher lawn. Nevertheless under normal conditions always remove the mowings from the lawn. Return them only in hot dry conditions when irrigation is not available.

After gathering the mowings do not simply lump them on to the compost heap. Grass mowings contain a high percentage of moisture, and if heaped when they are still fresh they decompose into a green-black glutinous mass. Small quantities can be added to the compost heap when fresh as long as they are layered thinly with other garden waste. Larger quantities should be dried before composting. Do this either by spreading them out thinly, or by making a loose heap of the cuttings and turning it frequently.

HEIGHT AND FREQUENCY OF CUT

This chart indicates the height and frequency to which different quality lawns should be cut for the period late spring to early fall. The figures given are only a rough guide, and should be varied according to the weather and the state of the lawn. Outside this period the height of cut should be increased by $\frac{1}{4}$ in.

Type of grass

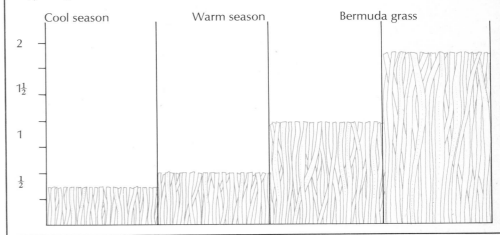

Composting mowings

Small quantities of mowings can be added to the compost heap in thin layers, which should be alternated with other refuse.

Dry large quantities before composting by spreading them out thinly, or by making a loose heap and forking it over.

Mowing 2

Mowing problems

Ribbing is a series of narrow, parallel strips of alternating longer and shorter grass. This effect occurs with cylinder-bladed mowers that have a low cylinder speed and a low number of blades, which cause them to give few cuts in relation to distance traveled. Ribbing may also occur when the grass is too long for the mower setting; if this is so, increase the height of cut.

The washboard effect is the occurrence of irregular waves or corrugations; the grass alternates from long on the crest of each wave to short between crests. It is caused by the grass always being mown in the same direction and usually occurs where powered mowers are used. Change the mowing pattern and vary the direction of mowing with successive cuts.

Lacerated grass or uneven cutting are caused by having blunt or incorrectly set blades, or by the mower having a damaged bottom plate. Check the mower and adjust or repair it as necessary.

Scalping occurs where there are surface irregularities. Increase the height of cut and improve the level of the lawn: correct minor irregularities by top-dressing and major ones by lifting a sod and adding or removing soil as necessary.

Retarding growth

On areas of coarser grass the chemical growth retardant maleic hydrazide can be used to check growth. It acts by inhibiting cell division within the grass, and retards growth for as much as 12 to 14 weeks. It also has an inhibiting effect on the development of seed-heads. This is a very useful method of controlling grass growth on verges, churchyards, steep banks and other places where mowing is difficult. If the grass is weedy apply a weed-killer as well since maleic hydrazide is mainly effective against grasses, and weeds may continue to grow strongly.

Maleic hydrazide is not suitable for finer lawns because treated grass would soon lose its freshness of appearance in comparison with regularly mown grass. There is also the risk of deterioration through wear and tear, which in untreated lawns is normally compensated by continuous growth.

HOW TO MOW

1 Always plan the direction of mowing to minimize overlapping, reversing and abrupt changes of direction, since these will all increase compaction and wear.

2 Mow when dry. Wet mowings clog the machine and grass-box, and lengthen the mowing time. During the fall and spring mow on sunny days in the early afternoon when the grass has dried. If dew is heavy disperse it two or three hours before mowing using a supple bamboo cane, rake or besom.

3 Scatter worm casts before mowing.

4 During the colder months, do not top when cold winds are blowing. The leaf-tips may be wind-scorched and seared, and remain unsightly until the next cut.

5 If the grass contains weeds or unwanted surface runners, rake it occasionally before mowing to lift unwanted growth.

6 Move steadily forward if using a hand-propelled mower. Repeated backward and forward movements result in an uneven cut.

7 Always mow at right-angles to the line of the previous mow since this helps to control weed grasses and bents and to smooth out irregularities in the mowing.

SEASONAL GUIDE TO MOWING

March: top with the blade set $\frac{1}{4}$ in higher than the summer height of cut.

April: increase frequency according to the weather and growth of the grass.

May–August: adjust to summer heights and frequencies.

August–October: reduce frequency as growth rate slows.

Late October: adjust to the seasonal height of cutting.

November–February: occasional topping may be necessary during mild winters.

Producing a banded finish

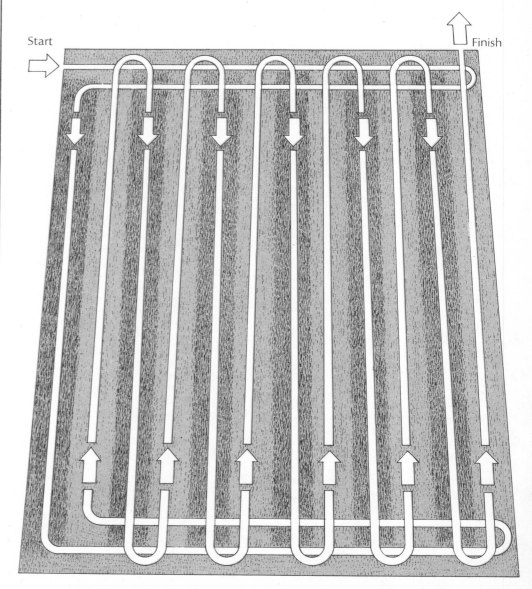

Start / Finish

A neat, banded finish of contrasting light and dark strips can be obtained by using a mower with a rear-mounted roller. Work across the lawn and mow each succeeding parallel strip in the opposite direction to the previous one.

Weed control in lawns

The weeds most troublesome in established lawns are crabgrass and the low-growing perennials of creeping or rosette-type growth, such as clovers, speedwell, daisy and plantain, which can adapt to or are unaffected by regular close mowing.

Sowing or laying clean sods on a thoroughly cleaned and fallowed site will ensure a weed-free start (see pages 146–149). Regular mowing with a grass-box, careful feeding and attention to irrigation will keep the lawn densely leaved and healthy, making it difficult for weeds to establish themselves.

Weeds may reach the lawn in various ways: as seeds blown by the wind; carried by birds; brought in on muddy footwear, machinery or tools; or concealed in unsterilized soil or badly made compost used for top dressing. Runners may be introduced on borrowed mowers or fertilizer spreaders, or they may encroach from weedy paths or flower beds.

Always use a grass-box when mowing since this minimizes the spread of lawn weeds. Sections of runners of certain weeds can regrow if not removed from the lawn, while the seeds of lesser yellow trefoil, which seeds freely, are easily scattered.

Hand-weeding with a hand fork or grubbing tool is a useful approach when dealing with scattered weeds, but it is essential to firm the surrounding grass carefully after extracting each weed. Hand-weed only during good growing conditions in spring when the grass will grow quickly to fill in the bare patches. Later in the year, when there are drier conditions, slower grass growth and more weed seeds, there is a much greater risk of bare patches being recolonized by weeds—or moss if a wet period follows a long spell of warm, dry weather. If large numbers of weeds are present in the lawn then hand-weeding is no longer practicable and weedkillers must be used.

Weedkillers

Lawn sands containing sulfate of ammonia and sulfate of iron are occasionally advocated for spot treatment of lawn weeds. However, there is often strong weed regrowth, and lawn sand has now been superseded by selective lawn weedkillers.

These do not harm narrow-bladed erect grasses but kill or check broad-leaved weeds. Some weeds can be killed by a single treatment, others may need several.

Most proprietary brands of lawn weedkiller contain two or occasionally three active ingredients, such as mecoprop, MCPA or 2,4-D. A product with two different active ingredients will give control of a wider range of weeds than a product containing a single ingredient. To decide which is best, list the different kinds of weeds in the infested lawn. Then check the proprietary mixtures and choose one that carries the manufacturer's recommendations for use in controlling the listed species.

If some weeds are not killed by the first application, repeat the treatment after four or five weeks. Some weeds may survive a second treatment. If so, confirm their identities then try another means of control. This may, in some cases, involve a change to a different weedkiller or some cultural measure that will help to weaken or check its spread.

Form and methods of application

Most lawn weedkillers are sold in concentrated liquid form, to be applied after dilution with water. Coarse-jet low-pressure sprayers can be used for larger areas. These include haversack sprayers with a lance and boom attachment or wheeled models with a forward-mounted boom. For smaller lawns, where the danger of spray drift into surrounding plants is greater, it is better to use a watering can with a fine rose or dribble bar attachment since the droplets are larger than those produced by a sprayer and there will be less risk of them being carried by the wind. Some lawn fertilizers incorporate weedkillers in dry form, which allows the two operations of feeding and weedkilling to be combined into one.

Lawn weedkillers are also available in aerosol or solid stick form for spot-treating isolated weeds. Some aerosols have the advantage that they leave a foam marker which persists for some time after weed treatment. Although spot treatment is a more economical approach than overall spraying where few weeds are involved, there may often be some localized temporary scorching

of the grass since it is difficult to gauge the amount being applied.

Apply lawn weedkillers in spring and early fall, ideally during fine warm conditions when the soil is thoroughly moist and grass growth is vigorous. The weedkiller is then rapidly translocated throughout the weed and the vigorously growing grass will fill in the space as the weed dies. Apply a nitrogenous

fertilizer one or two weeks before the weedkiller is used to encourage recovery of the turf. Then apply the weedkiller evenly with the aid of canes and twine.

If it is at all possible to avoid, do not apply lawn weedkillers during the summer since in hot weather there is a considerable chance that lawn grasses will be injured. Similarly do not apply during dry weather.

Spot-treating weeds

Spot treatment with a lawn weedkiller in aerosol or solid stick form is a simple and economical method of control if there are only a few isolated weeds present.

HOW TO USE LAWN WEEDKILLERS

Do not apply when the temperature is very hot or cold, nor when the soil is very wet or dry.

Do not apply immediately before rain, otherwise much of the weedkiller may be washed into the soil.

Do not apply when windy, otherwise the spray may be carried to affect nearby garden plants. If this does happen, spray the plants immediately with large amounts of clean water.

Do not apply immediately before mowing or much of the treated leaf surface may be removed before the weedkiller can reach the roots. Allow three or four days where possible before resuming mowing.

Do not apply at a rate stronger than that recommended by the manufacturer. Too high a concentration may kill weed foliage before the weedkiller can reach the roots, and this would allow the weed to revive. It may also cause the grasses to be badly damaged.

Do not mow immediately before weedkiller application or there will be a much-reduced leaf-surface area to receive and absorb the weedkiller.

Do not use fresh mowings as mulches for at least two weeks following treatment of lawns. Freshly treated mowings can be composted but the compost should not be used for at least six months.

Moss control in lawns

Of the hundreds of mosses that occur in the United States relatively few are troublesome as lawn weeds. Of these the most common are the following. *Hypnum cupressiforme* (and its forms) has yellow to golden-green trailing stems, and often colonizes large areas. *Brachythecium rutabulum*, with bright green, creeping, irregularly branched stems, is common in poorly drained lawns. *Ceratodon purpureus*, with short erect stems and densely tufted growth, is often found on poor, acid, heathland soil. *Bryum argenteum* is a cushion-type moss which has an attractive silvery sheen to its foliage.

Contrary to widespread opinion, the presence of moss in a lawn does not necessarily show the need for lime, for example, mosses such as *Hypnum cupressiforme* var *lacunosum* naturally inhabit chalk grassland. Other species are natural to all forms of grassland. Moss colonizes lawns for various reasons. Poor fertility or weakness due to attacks by pests or diseases, lack of aeration, bad drainage, excessive shade or mowing too closely will all result in weak, sparse grass that allows moss to establish.

Moss can be temporarily controlled by using mosskillers but, unless the reason for infestation is established and then corrected, moss will return. Examine the lawn and identify factors causing weak growth. Feed regularly if previous feeding has been sporadic. Top-dress regularly to improve moisture retention if the soil is light and sandy; irrigate regularly and thoroughly if the lawn is prone to drought. Aerate if surface drainage is impeded and carry out deep spiking if there is compaction through heavy usage. Watch for signs of waterlogging during the winter months and, if necessary, check and clear existing pipe drainage systems or install a new system. Do not set the mower blades too low; close and frequent mowing can weaken grass, letting weeds and moss establish themselves. On very acid soils a light winter application of lime in the form of ground chalk or ground limestone will slightly reduce acidity and usually discourage the mosses present. First determine by soil testing that liming is likely to be beneficial since excessive use of lime, or use when not required, can improve conditions for coarser grasses, clovers and other weeds while suppressing growth of the finer-leaved, more desirable grasses. If lime is necessary, apply at 2 oz per square yard (see page 146).

Where moss is troublesome in grass under trees there is often little that can be done. Lifting the tree canopy by removal of the lower branches will let in more light but grass growth may remain poor and sparse if the soil is light, dry and full of roots. A permanent solution to this problem is to replace the grass with ground cover (see page 166).

Moss spores, which are released during the summer, may allow moss to spread on lawns where the grass is weak and sparse. The spore-producing bodies develop well above the level of the moss foliage and on a well mown lawn are unlikely to survive to maturity; mosses can, however, reproduce from vegetative cells and the simple act of mowing or raking can spread moss about the lawn. When mowing always use a grass-box to collect mowings, and rake inwards toward the center of moss patches.

Mosskillers

Moss grows most strongly during cool moist conditions in the fall and spring; therefore these are best periods for applying chemical mosskillers. Lawn sands consisting of sulfate of ammonia, sulfate of iron and lime-free sand have been used to kill moss for many years and are still a useful means of control. Proportions vary in proprietary mixtures. A suitable formula is three parts sulfate of ammonia, one part calcined sulfate of iron and ten parts medium grade lime-free sand (not builders' sand). Apply at 4 oz per square yard during fine weather, ideally on a moist, dewy morning with a fine day ahead. Water the lawn 48 hours later if there has been no rain. One to two weeks later carefully rake out the blackened dead moss. Lawn sand is not a long-term control but it does stimulate grass growth, especially when applied in spring.

Dichlorophen is an effective chemical mosskiller and the active ingredient in some proprietary lawn moss eradicants. It is marketed as a concentrated liquid formulation. Apply it with a sprayer or watering can to wet the moss thoroughly.

Moss control program: fall

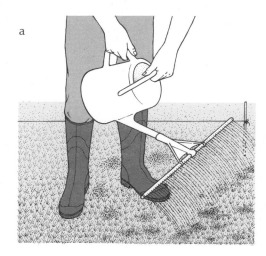

a

b

In early September apply a mosskiller, using either a sprayer or a watering can (a). A week or two later rake out blackened and dead moss. Then apply a lawn fertilizer suitable for the fall (b), followed by a top dressing of six parts sand, three parts sandy loam soil and one part granulated peat; apply it at the rate of 4 lb per square yard. If necessary, seed-in bare patches at 1 oz per square yard, then rake in.

Moss control program: spring

c

d

In mid- to late March, apply a mosskiller during fine weather. One or two weeks later, rake out the dead moss, taking care not to disturb any young, developing stoloniferous grasses (c). Feed the lawn with a general lawn fertilizer. Then apply a light top dressing at the rate of 2–3 lb per square yard (d). As with the fall program seed-in any bare patches at 1 oz per square yard and rake in.

Preparing the site

Planning

The first step in preparing to plant ground cover is to draw a plan of the site. If the site is large, mark in any variations in soil conditions, exposure to wind and the degree of sun or shade. These can then be more easily taken into account when ground cover plants are being selected.

The choice of plants depends, in the first instance, on whether ground cover is needed to occupy a difficult site where little except weeds will grow, or whether it is needed because the site, though satisfactory, cannot be maintained to an acceptable level of appearance. In the former case the ornamental value of the ground cover is of less importance than its ability to grow satisfactorily under the conditions, and the choice may be confined to a single species, such as English ivy or St John's wort.

With the latter, the less stringent conditions usually allow a considerably wider choice of cover plants, and more emphasis can be placed on their ornamental qualities. Thus groups of plants with contrasting or complementing colors can be grown, for example, heathers that differ in both the color of their foliage and of their flowers. Variations in height between adjoining groups can also be utilized, as can the contrast between leafy clump-forming plants and those that form a dense carpeting cover.

Weeding the site

The first step in preparing the site is to clear it of weeds. Established annual weeds are mostly shallow rooting and are easily removed when the site is forked over before planting. If the site has been neglected for a year or two, seedling growth after planting may be a problem, in which case a period of fallowing would be helpful.

Perennial weeds are a more serious problem, and it is essential to clear the site of all traces of such weeds before planting. If this is not done, strong-growing perennials such as bindweed, gout weed and quack grass will compete with the ground cover and weaken it. They will also be extremely difficult to eradicate once the ground cover is established. Do not plant until the site is completely free of perennial weeds, even if

this means that planting ground cover has to be delayed for a season or more.

To eliminate perennial weeds it is necessary to kill or remove the underground parts, such as rhizomes. If the weeds are to be dug out, this can be done at any time of the year, but weedkillers are only effective when the weeds are in active growth. The roots of some weeds, particularly bindweed and horsetail, penetrate too deeply for them to be dug out completely. If they are present, it is better to leave infested plots unplanted and spray in late spring or early summer with ammate when the weeds are growing strongly. Even then there may be some regrowth later in the year, in which case, spray again. Horsetail is very persistent, but control is improved if the weed is crushed before spraying.

Improving the soil

Irrespective of the nature of the site and the choice of plants, thorough and careful soil preparation is essential. The fact that some types of ground cover plant will grow in poor soils and difficult habitats does not mean that they will provide effective cover if they are planted into unprepared soil. The site should

be prepared as thoroughly as for any other kind of plant, since to obtain good cover the plants need to establish rapidly and remain healthy and effective for some years after being planted.

The texture of all types of soil will be improved by digging in a heavy dressing of organic matter or humus. Any type of decomposing vegetation can be used: garden compost, stable manure, leaf-mold or leaf litter, peat, pulverized bark or spent mushroom compost. However, the last of these is usually strongly alkaline and should not be used where acid-loving plants are to be grown. Use well decomposed materials on lighter soils. On heavier clay soils dig in coarser materials since they help to improve the aeration and drainage. A suitable quantity of dressing is roughly one heaped barrowload of manure for every 25 sq ft, dug in to a spade's depth.

Organic manures are rich in trace elements but contain relatively small amounts of major plant foods, and these foods are hardly present at all in peat and pulverized bark. Therefore, to ensure that a sufficient supply of nutrients is available to encourage early

growth, apply a general balanced fertilizer at 1–2 oz per square yard before planting, working it well into the top few inches of soil with a hoe or fork.

Another factor to take into account is the soil pH, although many ground cover plants are tolerant of all but extreme conditions. There are several soil testing kits on the market which will provide a good indication of the soil's acidity. Excessively acid conditions can be modified by dressings of lime, but the improvement is not immediate. Do not apply lime without establishing that it is needed. With alkaline or limy soils, on the other hand, the pH cannot be reduced appreciably. Digging in acid peat or pulverized bark in quantity will improve the texture, but it will have little effect on the alkalinity. On some neutral or slightly alkaline soils the pH can be reduced by means of chemicals, but the process is slow and complicated. Whether the soil is acid or alkaline, it is simpler to choose plants that are tolerant of a particular type of soil than to attempt to change substantially the basic character of the soil.

Planning

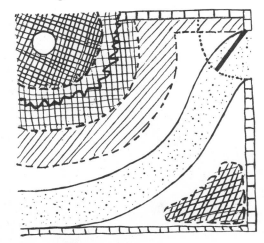

Draw a plan of the site, marking in any areas that are shaded or exposed to wind, and features such as walls, gates, paths, trees and shrubs.

Weeding the site

Remove all traces of weed growth. Dig out shallow-rooted perennial weeds and use ammate against deep-rooted ones. Fork over to control annual weeds.

Improving the soil

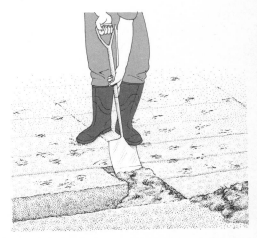

Dig in organic matter to a spade's depth, at one heaped barrowload per 25 sq ft. Before planting, fork in a general balanced fertilizer at 1–2 oz per square yard.

Planting and spacing

Ground cover plants must be planted carefully and correctly, at the appropriate spacings and at the right time of year, to ensure that they grow away quickly and vigorously.

When to plant
The best period for planting ground cover is in early spring. At this time the soil is beginning to warm up and there is ample moisture available, both of which are conditions that encourage plants to produce new root growth quickly. They will also have a full growing season ahead in which to become well established and are, therefore, less likely to be damaged by severe winter conditions later on. Do not plant during hot, dry summer weather because such conditions may check their growth. Also avoid planting late in the year because the roots may not establish properly and the plants will deteriorate or even die during the winter.

Container-grown plants can be planted out at any time of the year as long as the soil conditions are suitable. The ground should not be heavy with recent rain, bone dry, frozen or covered with snow.

If planting has to be delayed because the soil or weather conditions are not right, the plants must be protected from hot sun and drying winds. Store plants with bare roots by heeling them in. To do this, dig out an angled trench in a cool position in friable soil. Insert the plants close together and cover the roots with earth to the level of the planting mark. This is the point on the stem where there is a slight color change that indicates the depth at which they were planted. Store container-grown plants by plunging them to the rim in gravel, sand, grit or similar porous material. Alternatively, stand them in a cool, sheltered site and protect the containers with straw or bracken. Check their water requirements regularly.

Even if there is no delay to planting, always cover bare-rooted plants with damp burlap to protect them during site preparation.

How to plant
First, dig out a planting hole that is wide enough to take the roots when they are fully spread out. Where necessary, tease out the roots of container-grown plants that have become compacted. Ensure that the hole is deep enough to allow the plant to be inserted at the correct level. The soil level should be up to the planting mark on bare-rooted plants, or at the point where the roots and shoots meet if they are herbaceous. With container-grown plants the soil level should be the same as it was in the container, or marginally deeper.

Insert the plant carefully. Return the soil around and between the roots and firm it well. Water in evergreen plants. Finally, lightly fork over the soil to give a smooth surface.

Planting distances
It is important to decide the correct planting distance for each kind of ground cover plant in order to achieve 75–100 per cent cover in one or two years. The planting distance is determined by a number of factors. The most important are the natural growth habit of the plant and the soil and climate conditions, all of which influence how quickly it will cover a given area and what its ultimate spread is likely to be.

The size of the plants should also be taken into account. Young, well rooted plants establish faster and grow more rapidly than larger, older plants, and will usually provide good cover by the end of the first season. However, more plants are required and this can be expensive.

The recommended planting distances for individual plants are in the section on specific ground cover plants, pages 152–153.

Planting ground cover

1 Cover bare-rooted plants with damp burlap as soon as they have been lifted. This will protect the roots until they can be planted out.

2 If planting is delayed, store bare-rooted plants by heeling them in up to the level of the planting mark.

3 To plant ground cover, first dig out a planting hole sufficiently deep and wide to accommodate the roots.

4 Tease out the roots of plants if they were raised in a container, since they may have become compacted.

5 After inserting the plant, replace the soil and firm it down well. Then lightly fork over the surface.

Maintenance

One of the main factors to be considered when selecting ground cover plants is that they should not require a high degree of maintenance. However, a certain amount of work is necessary in the early stages to ensure that the plants establish successfully.

Weed control

During the first year after planting it is essential to keep weeds under control, otherwise they will compete with the plants for water, nutrients and light. Clear weed seedlings by hand-weeding or hoeing. Continue hand-weeding to kill weed seedlings as they appear and to remove any perennial weeds that have escaped treatment when the site was being prepared. Alternatively, spot-treat perennial weeds very carefully with ammate

The weedkiller trifluralin can be used to control germinating weed seeds among many established ground cover plants; simazine can also be used, though its range of application is more limited. However, since some plants are intolerant of simazine, it should not be used without first checking the manufacturer's recommendations.

A safer and more effective approach is to apply a 2–3 in mulch of peat or pulverized bark. Well rotted garden compost or leafmold can also be used, but they may contain viable weed seeds. Apply the mulch between the plants, taking care not to cover the growing shoots if they are herbaceous. Carpeting plants only require a light sprinkling of mulch between the spreading shoots. The mulch suppresses most weed development and, as it breaks down, will provide nutrients for the plants. Mulching encourages carpeting plants to take root and give more rapid cover. It also helps to keep the soil cool and to conserve moisture. Renew mulches each spring until good cover has formed.

Fertilizers

Once the plants are established they should not be neglected completely. Feeding, though not essential, greatly improves their appearance and vigor. Feed every two years in early spring as new growth appears, applying either a balanced inorganic fertilizer or an organic one such as bone meal.

Alternatively, use a slow release fertilizer; these are particularly suitable for ground cover plants since they release nutrients over a period of several months. Apply inorganic fertilizers carefully around the plants to avoid scorching the leaves.

Where plants have suffered a check, or where newly planted ground cover is slow to grow away, apply a foliar feed in late spring or early summer.

Pruning

As with feeding, pruning is not essential, but it does benefit the appearance and vigor of ground cover plants. Remove old flowering stems, dead twigs or damaged shoots when necessary, and examine all plants annually in late winter or early spring.

More severe pruning may be needed to prevent vigorously spreading plants from becoming invasive, and plants such as heathers and vincas from becoming straggly. Do this in February or March for deciduous woody plants, or in April for evergreens. Some young woody plants may need to be pruned back to encourage lower branching.

Tidy up deciduous herbaceous plants in late autumn when the foliage has died down. Cut back old flowering stems and remove dead leaves, but do not harm the crowns of plants that retain some foliage over winter.

PROPAGATION

Many ground cover plants can be easily propagated, either by division, layering, taking cuttings or sowing seeds. Some general points concerning propagation are discussed below. For the methods of propagating a particular plant, see the propagation section on pages 172–203.

One of the simplest methods of propagating a plant is to divide and replant it, or to replant runners that have taken root. However, this inevitably disturbs the existing plants and can check their growth. A better method, though not always possible, is to peg down runners into pots of compost. Once they have taken root they can be severed from the parent and planted out. With clump-forming or suckering plants the only alternative to division is to grow several stock plants in a nursery bed and gradually build up the stock over several seasons.

Another method of propagation is to take cuttings. In most cases these will require two to three years to become sufficiently sturdy to be planted out. Most woody plants can be propagated from softwood cuttings taken in June or July; they will root satisfactorily if placed in a mist unit or a propagator with bottom heat. Others can be rooted from hardwood cuttings taken in the fall and planted in a cold frame or plastic tunnel. Certain herbaceous perennials can be propagated from leafy cuttings taken in late summer and planted under glass.

Many ground cover plants can also be raised from seed, but considerable attention is needed to produce well rooted plants within a few years of germination.

Weeding

Hand-weed regularly to remove weed seedlings as they appear, and any perennial weeds that develop.

Feeding

Feed the plants every two or three years in early spring. Apply inorganic fertilizers carefully to avoid scorching the leaves.

Pruning

Examine plants annually in late winter or early spring, removing any dead foliage, damaged shoots or straggly growth.

Problem sites 1

Shaded sites
A indicates a moist soil
B indicates an average soil
C indicates a dry soil
If a plant prefers one of these conditions, then a letter in bold type is used; a letter in normal type indicates that the plant will tolerate these conditions.

☆ indicates that the plant requires an acid, lime-free soil.

One of the most common reasons for growing ground cover is to utilize those awkward sites in a garden where little other than weeds will grow. This section discusses these sites in turn, the difficulties that they present and points concerning site preparation and planting. For each site, a list of suitable ground cover plants is given, usually in tabular form. If only a few plants can be recommended, they are given within the text.

Shaded sites

One of the most important factors that limits the choice of plants for a particular site is the degree of shade present. Many plants grow poorly in shade and may become distorted by developing only towards the light. The soil conditions at the site may also be extreme, for example, under the canopy of larger trees the soil is often poor and dry, and there may be many tree roots near the surface. On the other hand, in low-lying poorly drained sites or open woodland, the soil may be perpetually moist.

To prepare the site, the first step is to mark out the extent of the shaded area; do this on a sunny day in spring or fall. Decide on the degree of shade possessed by the site and the nature of the growing conditions there, then choose the appropriate plants accordingly. Plant the cover in fall if possible because, if the plants are evergreen, they benefit from the moister winter conditions and may receive some winter sunshine. Also, many deciduous plants will begin growing in

spring well before the trees come into full leaf.

Prepare the site thoroughly and, after planting, water in evergreens to help their roots settle in the soil; if the weather is dry, water in deciduous plants as well. Mulch the plants in spring and, for at least the first season after planting, keep a close check on them to ensure that they have sufficient water.

If the plants are growing under large mature trees, there will be little change in the soil conditions from year to year. However, under young, rapidly growing trees both the extent and the degree of shade will increase annually. If, in the latter case, existing plants show signs of deterioration, replace them with plants that are more tolerant of the increasing shade and dryness. Where planting under young trees anticipate the change in the shade as the trees mature by choosing plants that possess a greater tolerance to shade than is needed at the time.

Moist sites

With the exception of aquatics, few plants can survive prolonged wet or waterlogged conditions. Therefore, where possible, drain the site if the soil remains very wet or waterlogged for long periods, particularly if this occurs in winter.

Some plants, including a few with good ground cover qualities, can survive in moist to wet soils. Their roots have low oxygen requirements and they can establish and grow in conditions where those of many plants would rapidly decay.

DEGREES OF SHADE

In the list on the right and in the text that follows, the degree of shade that a plant needs, or tolerates, is indicated by the terms light shade, partial shade, moderate shade and deep shade.

Light shade usually refers to a site that is open to the sky, but is screened from direct sunlight by some obstacle such as a high wall or a group of trees.

Partial shade describes a site where the sun is excluded for all but two or three hours in a day, either early morning or late evening. Note that several hours of

sunlight in the middle of the day qualifies a site as sunny.

Moderate shade has little or no direct sun, but there is some reflected or transfused light. It often occurs in woodlands or larger shrubberies.

Deep shade is usually encountered under the canopy of larger deciduous trees that have low branches and dense foliage, for example, maple, beech and horse chestnut. This type of shade is also found under clumps of conifers or among overgrown shrubberies.

PLANTS FOR SHADED SITES

Medium or deep shade

GROUP 1

	A	B	C
Galeobdolon argentatum	A	B	C
Hedera canariensis		B	
Hedera colchica		B	
Hedera helix and var hibernica		B	
Vinca spp	A	B	C
Waldsteinia ternata	A	B	C

GROUP 2

	A	B	C
Asarum spp	A		
Euonymus fortunei var radicans			C
× Gaulnettya wisleyensis ☆	A	B	
Gaultheria shallon ☆		B	C
Leucothoe fontanesiana	A	B	
Mahonia aquifolium		B	C
Pachistima canbyi ☆	A	B	
Pachysandra terminalis		B	C
Prunus laurocerasus		B	C

GROUP 3

	A	B	C
Acanthus mollis latifolius		B	
Brunnera macrophylla	A	B	
Hosta spp	A	B	
Iris foetidissima		B	C
Pulmonaria spp	A		

GROUP 4

	A	B	C
Asperula odorata		B	
Blechnum spicant	A		
Convallaria majalis	A	B	
Duchesnea indica		B	C
Euphorbia robbiae			C
Gaultheria procumbens		B	
Geranium nodosum	A	B	
Geranium phaeum	A	B	
Geranium punctatum	A	B	
Lamium maculatum	A	B	C
Luzula maxima		B	C
Mitchella repens ☆		B	
Omphalodes spp	A	B	
Rubus spp		B	C
Sarcococca humilis		B	C
Symphytum grandiflorum	A	B	
Tellima grandiflora	A	B	C
Tiarella spp	A	B	
Viola labradorica	A	B	C

	A	B	C
Viola obliqua	A	B	C
Zebrina pendula	A	B	C

Light or open shade

GROUP 2

	A	B	C
Arctostaphylos uva-ursi ☆	A	B	
Bergenia spp and hybrids	A	B	
Cotoneaster spp	A	B	C
Cotoneaster 'Gnome'		B	C
Erica herbacea		B	
Euonymus fortunei f carrierei		B	
Hypericum × moserianum		B	C
Juniperus conferta		B	C
Juniperus × media 'Pfitzeriana'			C
Juniperus sabina var tamariscifolia		B	C

GROUP 3

	A	B	C
Alchemilla mollis		B	
Coronilla varia		B	
Geranium endressii 'Wargrave Pink'	A	B	
Geranium psilostemon	A	B	
Geranium sylvaticum	A	B	
Polygonum campanulatum	A		

GROUP 4

	A	B	C
Ajuga reptans	A		
Campanula spp		B	
Ceratostigma plumbaginoides		B	C
Cornus canadensis ☆	A		
Cotula squalida		B	C
Dichondra carolinensis	A	B	
Epimedium spp		B	
Geranium ibericum	A	B	
Geranium macrorrhizum	A	B	
Geranium × magnificum	A	B	
Geranium platypetalum	A	B	
Geranium procurrens	A	B	
Glechoma hederacea	A	B	C
Lotus corniculatus	A	B	C
Lysimachia nummularia	A		
Ophiopogon japonicus	A	B	C
Potentilla alba	A	B	
Prunella grandiflora	A	B	
Vaccinium vitis-idaea ☆	A	B	
Viola cornuta			
Viola garden hybrids		B	

Problem sites 2

Moist sites
A indicates moist shade
B indicates cool, damp shade
C indicates a moist sunny site
If a plant prefers one of these conditions, then a letter in bold type is used; a letter in normal type indicates that the plant will tolerate these conditions.

☆ indicates that the plant requires an acid, lime-free soil.

Hot, dry sites
☆ indicates that the plant requires an acid, lime-free soil.

The roots of moisture-tolerant plants are usually rather fleshy, with the plants spreading by means of stolons or rhizomes to form a dense leafy cover. Some are plants of wet pasture or meadowland. Others are native to cool moist woodland or its fringes. They have large soft-textured leaves and pale delicate flowers; they come into growth and flower early in the year before the development of dense overhead leafy cover.

Plants with these qualities and characteristics can be used along the damp margins of streams and ditches where, for most of the year, conditions are too wet for other plants. They can also be used to provide good summer cover in poorly drained, low-lying areas and in damp woodland where deep leaf-mold provides a moist root run throughout the summer months.

Plant in the spring where possible. Planting in the fall is acceptable, but even moisture-tolerant plants may deteriorate over winter in very wet conditions when their roots are not well established.

In suitably moist conditions there will be little need for summer watering except in very dry seasons, but, if the site is drier than anticipated, herbaceous plants may die down prematurely during the summer, giving a shorter season of good cover and the possibility of weeds establishing during the late summer or fall. There may also be some leaf-fall from evergreen, reducing the density of cover and giving rise to similar problems of weed seedling development. In either case, water the plants to prevent this.

For the purposes of the table on this page, a moist soil is defined as one that is uniformly moist, or relatively so, throughout the year. It may, however, become wet occasionally during periods of heavy and extended rainfall. Sites that are very wet in the spring and very dry during the summer do not come into this category. Few if any ground cover plants will provide satisfactory cover in such situations.

Cool, damp shade relates to sites both under trees and in open shade where the soil remains cool and moist throughout the year. Under trees, this is usually due to the presence of a good depth of moisture-retentive leaf-mold or humus.

PLANTS FOR MOIST SITES

GROUP 1
Galeobdolon argentatum		**B**	C
Vinca spp		**B**	
Waldsteinia ternata	A	**B**	C

GROUP 2
Arctostaphylos uva-ursi ☆		B	**C**
Asarum spp	**A**	B	
Bergenia spp and hybrids	A	**B**	C
Calluna vulgaris			**C**
Cotoneaster spp		B	**C**
Daboecia cantabrica			**C**
× Gaulnettya wisleyensis ☆		**B**	C
Leucothoe fontanesiana ☆		**B**	
Pachistima canbyi ☆	A	**B**	C
Pachysandra terminalis		**B**	

GROUP 3
Brunnera macrophylla	**A**		
Geranium spp	A	**B**	C
Hosta spp	A	**B**	C
Polygonum campanulatum	A	B	**C**
Pulmonaria spp	A	**B**	C

GROUP 4
Ajuga reptans	**A**	B	C
Asperula odorata	A	**B**	
Campanula spp		B	**C**
Ceratostigma plumbaginoides	A	**B**	C
Convallaria majalis	A	**B**	
Cornus canadensis ☆	A	**B**	C
Cotoneaster dammeri		**B**	C
Epimedium spp		**B**	
Gaultheria procumbens		**B**	
Geranium spp	A	**B**	C
Lamium maculatum	A	**B**	
Lotus corniculatus			**C**
Lysimachia nummularia	**A**	B	C
Mitchella repens	**A**	B	
Omphalodes cappadocica	**A**	B	C
Potentilla alba		**B**	
Prunella grandiflora		**B**	C
Symphytum grandiflorum	**A**	B	
Tellima grandiflora		**B**	C
Tiarella spp	A	**B**	
Vaccinium vitis-idaea ☆	A	**B**	
Viola spp and hybrids	A	**B**	C
Zebrina pendula	**A**	B	C

PLANTS FOR HOT, DRY SITES

GROUP 1
Hedera spp (not variegated varieties)
Hypericum calycinum
Vinca spp and varieties

GROUP 2
Anthemis cupaniana
Arabis albida
Aubrieta deltoidea
Aurinia saxatilis
Ballota pseudodictamnus
Cerastium tomentosum
Cistus parviflorus
Cotoneaster spp
Cytisus spp
Daboecia cantabrica (not on very dry sites)
Dianthus spp
Dryas octopetala
Erica herbacea (not on very dry sites)
Euonymus fortunei var radicans
Euonymus fortunei f carrierei and varieties
Genista spp
× Halimiocistus sahucii
Hebe spp
Helianthemum hybrids
Hypericum × moserianum
Iberis sempervirens
Juniperus communis and varieties
Juniperus conferta
Juniperus horizontalis and varieties
Lithodora diffusa ☆

Mesembryanthemum
Phlomis fruticosa
Salvia officinalis
Senecio 'Sunshine'

GROUP 3
Liriope muscari
Nepeta × faassenii
Origanum vulgare

GROUP 4
Acaena novae-zelandiae
Antennaria dioica
Anthemis nobilis
Artemisia stelleriana
Ceratostigma plumbaginoides
Cotoneaster dammeri
Geranium 'Russell Prichard'
Muehlenbeckia axillaris
Phlox douglasii
Phlox subulata and hybrids
Potentilla alba
Potentilla calabra
Saxifraga "mossy" hybrids
Sedum spathulifolium
Sedum spurium
Stachys byzantina 'Silver Carpet'
Thymus serpyllum
Veronica prostrata
Viola labradorica
Viola obliqua

Hot dry sites
There is a wide choice of plants for covering dry, sunny sites since there are many that grow naturally in such conditions. The main problem facing these plants is that they tend to lose more moisture through their leaves than they can absorb through their roots. Plants that are native to this type of habitat have had to adapt themselves to overcome this, for example, by having very small or narrow leaves and a dense system of branches, which help to shade the roots from the drying effects of the sun. Other plants have thick-skinned fleshy evergreen leaves, or leaf surfaces that are densely covered with fine hairs, making the plant appear silvery.

In many cases the root systems of such plants have also adapted, becoming extensive and deeply penetrating. This enables them to obtain sufficient moisture from the soil and allows their roots to escape the desiccating effects of summer heat on the upper soil layers. However, this places an important limitation on the type of site on which these plants will grow: it must be well drained throughout the year and, in particular, not become wet and heavy during the winter since much of the root system would die in such conditions. Plants with woolly or hairy leaves are particularly susceptible to this effect because, although they are perfectly hardy to frost, in their natural habitats the

Problem sites 3

Slopes and banks
A indicates a sunny site
B indicates a lightly shaded site
C indicates a deeply shaded site

☆ indicates that the plant requires an acid, lime-free soil.

climate is dry throughout the year. Thus, unless the soil is very well drained they may suffer or even die during a winter in which cold frosty weather alternates with milder wetter intervals.

Before planting it is important to dig in a dressing of well rotted farm manure, garden compost, leaf-mold or peat, particularly if the soil is light. This is because the plants will have been raised in rich compost and kept well irrigated. They may, therefore, suffer a considerable check to growth and be slow to establish if they are planted into unimproved soil. By digging in a dressing, the ability of the soil to retain moisture will be increased temporarily, and so the risk of early losses will be reduced.

Planting should be done either in the spring or the fall when the soil is cool and moist. If possible, it is better to plant in the fall, since this allows the roots to become well established before the following summer, when the site will become hot and dry. Mulch the plants in spring to help them conserve moisture during the summer.

Slopes and banks

Most slopes or banks are, by their nature, well drained, and those in full sun on lighter soils usually become quite dry in the summer. Therefore, when choosing plants, it is usually important to select those that are tolerant of drier, well drained soils.

Gentle slopes (those with an angle of less than 20 degrees) provide few problems and allow a wide choice of plants as there is usually little risk of surface erosion. However, if water drains on to the site from higher ground, choose stem-rooting or suckering plants rather than clump-forming plants.

On steeper slopes, grow either suckering shrubs or plants whose branches or stems take root as they spread, since they will consolidate loose surfaces and prevent erosion. Evergreen plants are also useful since they protect the surface from the impact of heavy winter rains, which can rapidly erode unprotected slopes. English ivy is a valuable ground cover plant in deep shade where few other plants can survive.

Begin planting at the top of the site and

PLANTING ON SLOPES AND BANKS

On gentle slopes (a) plant in shallow hollows since this facilitates mulching and watering. On steeper slopes (b) create terraces, holding them in place with boards and pegs. On banks of porous rock, plant in pockets chipped from the rock face (c). If the rock is non-porous, either train plants up or trail them down the bank (d) or plant them through matting pegged to the rock (e).

PLANTS FOR SLOPES AND BANKS

GROUP 1	Planting distance	
Hedera colchica	36–48 in	A B C
Hedera colchica varieties	36–48 in	A B
Hedera helix	36 in	A B C
Hedera helix variegated varieties	24–36 in	A B
Hedera helix var hibernica	36–48 in	A B C
Hypericum calycinum	15–18 in	A B C
Vinca major	18 in	A B C
Vinca major var oxyloba	24 in	A B C
Vinca minor	9–12 in	A B C
Also for milder climates:		
Hedera canariensis 'Azorica'	36–48 in	A B C
Hedera canariensis 'Gloire de Marengo'	36–48 in	A

GROUP 2		
Arctostaphylos uva-ursi ☆	15 in	A B
Calluna vulgaris and varieties ☆	9–18 in	A B
Cotoneaster conspicuus 'Decorus'	72 in	A B
Cotoneaster 'Gnome'	18–24 in	A B
Cotoneaster microphyllus	18–24 in	A B
Cotoneaster 'Skogholm'	18–24 in	A B
Daboecia cantabrica and varieties ☆	15–18 in	A
Erica herbacea and varieties	12–15 in	A B
Erica vagans and varieties ☆	12–15 in	A
Euonymus fortunei var radicans	12–18 in	A B C
Euonymus fortunei f carrierei 'Variegatus'	12–18 in	A B C
Gaultheria shallon	36–48 in	A B C
Genista hispanica	24 in	A
Genista pilosa	15 in	A B
Helianthemum hybrids	18 in	A
Juniperus communis, ssp depressa and varieties	24 in	A
Juniperus horizontalis and varieties	18–24 in	A
Juniperus × media 'Pfitzeriana'	48–72 in	A B C
Mesembryanthemum	2–8 in	A
Also for milder climates:		
Ceanothus thyrsiflorus repens	36–48 in	A
Juniperus conferta	24 in	A B
Phlomis fruticosa	30 in	A

GROUP 4		
Cotoneaster dammeri	24 in	A B
Lotus corniculatus	18–24 in	A B
Luzula maxima	15 in	A B C
Polygonum vacciniifolium	9–12 in	A
Rubus tricolor	36 in	A B C
Stephanandra incisa 'Crispa'	36 in	A
Symphoricarpos × chenaultii 'Hancock'	36 in	A B

Problem sites 4

work downwards. On gentle slopes dig a shallow hole for each plant with a trowel, drawing the soil forwards. Alternatively, dig a shallow trench across the slope. These holes will help the site to retain mulches and water. If the digging exposes sub-soil, or if the soil is poor, dig out larger planting holes and fill them with richer soil or work in some good planting compost.

On steeper slopes, construct small terraces by drawing soil forwards to create a series of levels. Hold the back of each terrace in place with boards and wooden stakes or pegs; after a year or two, when the plants are well established, these can be removed. Do not use logs to hold the terrace back because they will decay and may become infested with honey fungus which will endanger woody plants in the garden.

On a newly cut bank where the soil is sandy there is considerable risk of erosion. Prevent this by firmly pegging down coconut matting or a similar, decomposable, material before planting so that the surface is held firm. Then make holes in the matting and plant through these with spreading, stem-rooting plants that will root down through the matting as it rots to provide good consolidation against erosion. Alternatively, if the underlying material is porous rock, chip pockets out of it and plant in these.

On very steep banks where erosion is likely to occur and it is virtually impossible to plant, the most satisfactory answer is to construct a retaining wall. Alternatively, plant sprawling climbers at the base of the slope and train them up the face, or plant them close to the crest of the slope to trail downwards. The strong-growing species of ivy are suitable for this, as are certain climbers which, though of little merit as ground cover in general, are very useful in this type of situation. They include *Clematis montana* 'Tetrarose', *Clematis orientalis*, *Lonicera henryi*, *Lonicera japonica* 'Halliana' and *Parthenocissus quinquefolia*.

Large areas

As the cost of maintaining a garden has escalated in recent years, the designs of many larger gardens have had to be modified. This has usually been done by increasing shrub plantings and putting down larger areas to grass. However, both methods have several disadvantages. Shrub plantings may take several years to develop into good cover and, in the interim period, will need regular weeding, mulching and pruning. Unless they are carefully selected and positioned, shrub plantings may grow to blot out attractive garden features. With grass there is the expense of fertilizers, weedkillers and mowing equipment. It also needs regular maintenance throughout the growing season.

A much more satisfactory solution to the problem of large areas is to plant ground cover, since it is visually pleasing and requires little maintenance.

As with any other kind of site, the choice of cover plants must be related to the nature of the site and its soil type, but where the planting is to replace a prominent garden feature, or will occupy a strategic position in a new garden, then strong emphasis should be placed on having attractive plants.

Apart from the ornamental aspects, the two most important factors when choosing plants are their height and planting distances. As stated above in connection with shrub plants, height may detract from other features in the garden. The planting distance will, of course, affect the cost of the ground cover. Before planting, measure the site carefully, then calculate the precise number of plants required by referring to the spacing recommendations. Where large numbers of plants are required, obtain quotations and, if the cost is too great, consider alternative selections. The planting distances may be slightly increased where the soil conditions are good, but this may delay the development of effective coverage for a season.

Exposed coastal gardens

Many plants do not grow well in coastal gardens because their shoots and leaves become badly scorched by the salt present in sea winds, even when they are growing some distance inland. There are, however, a number of plants that have become adapted to this type of habitat. For example, marram grass, sea holly and sea pink can be found close to the high-tide mark, where they are frequently drenched by sea spray during stormy weather. Similarly, gorse, Cornish

PLANTS FOR LARGE AREAS

GROUP 1	Height	Planting distance
Galeobdolon argentatum	6–9 in	24–36 in
Hedera canariensis 'Azorica'	6–9 in	36–48 in
Hedera canariensis 'Gloire de Marengo'	6–9 in	36–48 in
Hedera colchica and varieties	6–9 in	36–48 in
Hedera helix	6–9 in	24–36 in
Hedera helix var *hibernica*	9–12 in	36–48 in
Hypericum calycinum	9–12 in	15–18 in
Vinca major and var *oxyloba*	6–9 in	18–24 in
Waldsteinia ternata	3–4 in	12 in
GROUP 2		
Bergenia spp and hybrids	6–12 in	9–24 in
Calluna vulgaris varieties	6–18 in	9–18 in
Cotoneaster 'Gnome'	3–4 in	18–24 in
Daboecia cantabrica	15–18 in	15–18 in
Erica vagans and varieties	9–18 in	12–15 in
Euonymus fortunei f *carrierei* and varieties	24 in	30 in
Genista hispanica	24 in	24 in
Juniperus × *media* 'Pfitzeriana'	36 in	48–72 in
Juniperus sabina var *tamariscifolia*	15–18 in	24–30 in
Leucothoe fontanesiana	36 in	36 in
Pachysandra terminalis	3–4 in	12 in
Prunus laurocerasus varieties	36 in	36 in
Senecio 'Sunshine'	36 in	36 in
GROUP 3		
Brunnera macrophylla	12 in	15–18 in
Geranium endressii 'Wargrave Pink'	18–21 in	12–18 in
Geranium psilostemon	30 in	12–18 in
Hosta spp, particularly *H. sieboldiana*	12–18 in	15–24 in
Polygonum campanulatum	18–24 in	18–24 in
GROUP 4		
Asperula odorata	4–5 in	24 in
Ceratostigma plumbaginoides	8–12 in	24 in
Dichondra carolinensis	6 in	6 in
Geranium procurrens	18–24 in	18–24 in
Luzula maxima	12 in	15 in
Mitchella repens ☆	– 4 in	24 in
Rosa 'Max Graf'	36 in	48–60 in
Rosa × *paulii*	36–48 in	48–72 in
Rosa 'Temple Bells'	18–24 in	30–36 in
Rosa wichuraiana	12–18 in	60–72 in
Rubus tricolor	12 in	36 in
Stephanandra incisa 'Crispa'	24 in	36 in
Symphoricarpos × *chenaultii* 'Hancock'	24 in	36 in
Tellima grandiflora	6 in	12 in

Problem sites 5

Exposed coastal gardens
A indicates a light sandy soil
B indicates a medium to medium-heavy soil
If a plant prefers one of these conditions, then a letter in bold type is used; a letter in normal type indicates that the plant will tolerate these conditions.

☆ indicates that the plant requires an acid, lime-free soil.

Exposed inland gardens
☆ indicates that the plant requires an acid, lime-free soil.

PLANTS FOR COASTAL GARDENS

Fully exposed sites

GROUP 2		
Arctostaphylos uva-ursi ☆	A	**B**
Calluna vulgaris ☆	A	**B**
Cerastium tomentosum	**A**	B
Cistus spp	**A**	
Cotoneaster spp	A	**B**
Cotoneaster 'Gnome'		**B**
Cytisus spp	**A**	B
Daboecia cantabrica ☆	A	**B**
Dianthus spp	**A**	
Erica herbacea and varieties	A	**B**
Erica vagans and varieties ☆	A	**B**
Euonymus fortunei var *radicans*	A	**B**
Euonymus fortunei f *carrierei* and varieties	A	**B**
Genista spp	**A**	
× *Halimiocistus sahucii*	**A**	
Hebe spp	**A**	B
Juniperus communis and varieties	A	**B**
Juniperus conferta	A	**B**
Juniperus horizontalis and varieties	A	**B**
Potentilla fruticosa var *mandschurica*	A	**B**
Senecio 'Sunshine'	**A**	
GROUP 4		
Artemisia spp	**A**	
Cotoneaster dammeri	A	**B**
Potentilla spp	A	**B**
Rosa wichuraiana	**A**	
Sedum spp	**A**	B

Less exposed sites

GROUP 1		
Hedera spp	**A**	B
Hypericum spp (and Group 2)	**A**	B
Vinca spp and varieties	**A**	B
GROUP 2		
Arabis albida	A	B
Aubrieta deltoidea	A	B
Bergenia spp and hybrids		**B**
Dryas octopetala	**A**	
Helianthemum hybrids	A	B
Lonicera pileata	A	B
Mahonia aquifolium		**B**
GROUP 3		
Alchemilla mollis		**B**
Geranium spp (and Group 4)		**B**
Polygonum spp (and Group 4)		**B**
GROUP 4		
Campanula spp		**B**
Euphorbia robbiae		**B**
Ophiopogon japonicus	**A**	**B**
Phlox spp and varieties	A	B
Rubus spp		**B**
Saxifraga "mossy" hybrids	A	B
Stachys byzantina	**A**	
Symphoricarpos × *chenaultii*		**B**
Thymus serpyllum	**A**	
Vaccinium vitis-idaea ☆		**B**

EXPOSED INLAND GARDENS

The following plants provide good ground cover in gardens that, although inland, are still exposed to severe weather, for example, northerly gardens. The same considerations apply to these plants as to those growing in coastal gardens.

GROUP 1	
Hedera helix and var *hibernica*	*Iberis sempervirens*
Vinca major and var *oxyloba*	*Juniperus communis* and varieties
Vinca minor	*Juniperus horizontalis* and varieties
Waldsteinia ternata	*Leucothoe fontanesiana* ☆
	Pachysandra terminalis
GROUP 2	**GROUP 4**
Arctostaphylos uva-ursi ☆	*Cornus canadensis* ☆
Calluna vulgaris and varieties ☆	*Gaultheria procumbens* ☆
Cotoneaster spp and varieties	*Sarcococca* spp
Erica herbacea and varieties	*Symphoricarpos* × *chenaultii* 'Hancock'
Euonymus fortunei and varieties	*Vaccinium vitis-idaea* ☆

heath and thrift survive on sea cliffs, even though they are fully exposed to salt-laden gale-force winds.

Before selecting ground cover plants, study the site carefully and note whether any part of it is protected against the prevailing wind. Also take into account the soil type and growing conditions.

Prepare the site thoroughly before planting by digging in a dressing of well rotted farm manure, garden compost, leaf-mold or peat. This is particularly important on sand, silt or dry limy soil. On drier soils, dig in fresh moist seaweed at up to 20 lb per square yard. This will increase temporarily the capacity of the soil to hold moisture, and so reduce the risk of early losses and encourage quick establishment.

Plant in the spring to give the ground cover a full growing season ahead in which to become well established before there is any serious risk of exposure to severe weather conditions. After planting evergreens, water them in well to settle the roots. With all plants, whether deciduous or evergreen, apply a good surface mulch after planting.

Rose beds

Rose beds are very susceptible to weeds since the plants are spaced fairly far apart and are often rather gaunt and leafless towards the base. This problem can be overcome by using weedkillers (see page 171), but an alternative approach is to grow ground cover. The use of ground cover does, however, have one serious drawback: it can interfere with pruning and feeding. Roses need feeding regularly in order to maintain their health and vigor. This can be done by using foliar nutrient sprays, but the best method is to apply mulches of farm manure or garden compost. However, these cannot be laid down effectively where ground cover has been planted. A compromise is to use ground cover plants of moderate vigor and height to provide a broad edging to rose beds without letting them encroach within the boundary defined by the stems of the outermost rose bushes. This will allow the roses to be mulched and pruned, while at the same time providing an attractive border.

Suitable plants for such ground cover include *Geranium sanguineum* var *lancastriense*, *Hebe pinguifolia* 'Pagei', *Helianthemum* hybrids, *Viola*, *Nepeta* × *faassenii* and "mossy" hybrids of *Saxifraga*.

If ground cover is to be planted throughout a rose bed, then the choice is limited to low-growing plants with some shade tolerance. On drier soils, suitable plants include *Lamium maculatum*, *Saxifraga* × *urbium* and *Campanula portenschlagiana*. On moister soils plant *Viola*, *Lysimachia nummularia* 'Aurea' or *Prunella grandiflora*.

Bulbs

In most gardens, bulbs are grown on sites that, for most of the year, are bare earth, for example, at the front of shrubberies or flower beds. This has the disadvantage that the site is readily colonized by weeds after the bulb foliage dies down in early summer. Some bulbs have to be grown in open ground since they need a high dormancy temperature, or "baking", to induce flower bud development, but others, particularly spring-flowering kinds, can be grown successfully under ground cover. The cover must not be so dense that it smothers the bulbs, yet it should be vigorous enough to suppress weed growth. The best plant to use for dwarf bulbs is *Cotula squalida*, which has a very low-spreading habit and gives medium density cover. It tolerates dry or moist conditions and full sun or light shade.

With taller, stronger-growing bulbous plants such as daffodils, *Muscari armeniacum* or bluebells, the density of cover is not so critical. Suitable plants for ground cover include *Ajuga*, *Pulmonaria*, *Viola*, *Mitchella repens*, *Veronica prostrata* and *Lysimachia nummularia* 'Aurea'.

Weed control

ANNUAL WEEDS
Annual meadow grass
(*Poa annua*)
Fat hen (*Chenopodium album*)
Shepherd's purse
(*Capsella bursa-pastoris*)
Chickweed (*Stellaria media*)
Mayweeds (*Matricaria* spp)
Groundsel (*Senecio vulgaris*)

Annual nettle (*Utrica urens*)
Speedwells (*Veronica* spp)

PERENNIAL WEEDS
Docks (*Rumex* spp)
Couch grass (*Agropyron repens*)
Creeping thistle
(*Cirsium arvense*)
Bindweed (*Convolvulus* spp)

A weed is a plant growing where it is not wanted. Thus one of last year's potatoes which comes up in this year's carrots is a weed. Weeds compete with crops for light, water and nutrients and they also create a micro-environment around plants in which gray mold (*Botrytis cinerea*) and damping-off diseases flourish. Weeds also act as hosts for pests, such as aphids and whitefly, and diseases, such as club-root of brassicas.

Annual weeds and perennial weeds
Annuals are plants that complete their life-cycle within a growing season, and they are often able to undergo more than one life-cycle in a season. Annuals are also characterized by the production of very many seeds so that the weed seed population in the soil is constantly replenished. Perennial plants live from year to year and usually have underground organs—stems or roots—which enable them to survive through the winter. Thus docks (*Rumex* spp) have thick, fleshy tap roots and couch grass (*Agropyron repens*) has underground stems or rhizomes.

Controlling perennial weeds
Weed control begins with winter digging prior to growing the first crops. Cut down any woody perennials, such as brambles (*Rubus* spp), and dig out all the roots. Double dig the whole of the garden in the first instance and remove all perennial weed roots and rhizomes. Burn them all and never use them for compost making. Once the land has been cleared of perennial weeds, they should never be a problem again, unless, of course, they are imported with organic materials such as farmyard manure.

Controlling annual weeds
Annual weeds continually reappear, however, and all fertile garden soils have a large reservoir of weed seeds. Weed seeds are also blown in on the wind and carried by birds and by man.

When winter digging, the gardener should skim off annual weeds and dig them into the bottom of each trench along with organic manure or garden compost. Digging brings up annual weed seeds which were buried in previous seasons. Many will germinate, but subsequent cultivations should kill the young weed seedlings that emerge. They will have appeared by the time cultivations take place to prepare the land for sowing or planting. Remove these and the next flush of weed seedlings will appear with the sown or planted vegetables.

Hoeing against weeds
Hoeing is the main method of weed control in the growing crop. It is largely a matter of personal preference which type of hoe to use, but in every case the blade must be kept constantly sharpened so that the weeds are severed from their roots rather than pulled up with them.

Choose a warm, drying day so that the weeds wilt and die quickly after hoeing. Care is needed when hoeing closely around crop plants because any damage caused is quickly colonized by disease organisms. Keep the hoe in the upper, surface layers of the soil so as not to bring up more weed seeds to germinate and grow. The dry soil produced by surface hoeing acts as a mulch which in itself inhibits weed growth.

Mulching against weeds
Weeds can also be controlled by using mulches. The use of dry soil as a mulch has already been mentioned but materials such as black polyethylene, well-prepared compost, or peat can also be used. Black polyethylene forms a complete physical barrier to weed growth; it also warms up the soil and conserves moisture. It is usually necessary to bury the edges of the polyethylene to prevent it blowing away and holes must be cut in it through which vegetables can be planted or sown. As well as eliminating weeds, a black polyethylene mulch can bring crops forward and hasten their maturity by as much as three weeks but, unfortunately, pests can thrive in the moist conditions produced. Organic mulches, such as peat, perform similar functions but have the advantage that they can be dug into the soil at the end of the season, thus improving its structure and fertility. Straw is not recommended as a mulch material because the bacterial action required to break it down can lead to a nitrogen deficiency in certain soils.

Using chemicals against weeds
The amateur's vegetable garden is extremely productive and a large number of crops are grown in a very small area. The danger of spray drift and persistence from chemical weedkillers is therefore considerable. Against annual weeds non-persistent contact weedkillers such as paraquat or diquat, do have a place, however, but they must be applied at low level with a dribble bar when there is no wind and, therefore, no danger of drift. These materials are inactivated rapidly on contact with the soil but they kill any green tissues with which they come into contact.

More toxic and persistent weedkillers should not be used in the home vegetable garden because the risks involved are too great. Whenever using chemicals always follow the manufacturer's instructions.

Hoeing

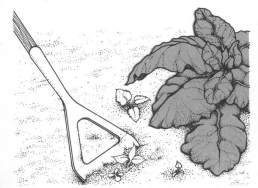

Carefully hoe annual weeds, keeping the blade level with the surface layers of the soil. Choose a warm, drying day for hoeing and keep the blade sharp.

Digging perennial weeds

During winter digging remove all perennial roots and rhizomes and burn them.

Mulching

Use black polyethylene (or organic mulches) to act as a barrier against weed growth, to conserve moisture and to warm up the soil.

Chemical weed control

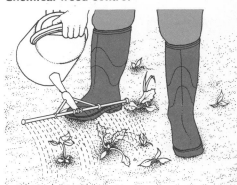

Use a dribble bar to deliver herbicides at ground level just on top of each weed. Never apply herbicides on a windy day and follow the manufacturer's instructions.

Tools and equipment

To propagate plants successfully, it is necessary to have a clean and tidy working area, efficient and effective tools and equipment and to follow a standardized procedure. Failure in any part of the system leads to frustration and, more importantly, delays that will reduce the probability of success.

Most important of the gardener's special tools and equipment for plant propagation are a sharp knife, a pair of shears, a dibble, suitable compost and a selection of pots and seed trays. Not all tools or fancy bits of equipment will necessarily enhance the success of propagation, but the important ones will because they make the gardener's job easier, and if the job is easier it often succeeds more readily.

The use of suitable tools gives the plant material the very best start. To avoid tearing and crushing, for example, always use a sharp knife or razor blade and a clean sheet of glass when preparing a softwood cutting for planting. If the plant material is damaged, it will die and become a site for possible rots to infect the cutting. By the same token it is important

not to push a cutting into the compost; always first make a hole with a dibble of suitable size, and then plant the cutting in that hole. A dibble should be approximately the same diameter as the cutting to be planted.

Although many people will use a kitchen table, drain-board or greenhouse bench, the most suitable place to make cuttings, graft or sow seeds is a bench in the garden shed with a convenient shelf for all the bits and pieces of equipment, tools, rooting powders, etc. The height of the bench will be a critical factor to the comfort of the gardener if considerable time is to be spent propagating or potting plants. Incorrectly sited benches will encourage or enhance backaches and cricks in the neck. It is also important to have good lighting placed directly over the workbench itself.

Plant propagation in many ways is akin to surgery, and nowhere is there more routine and standardized procedure than in an operating theater—where all concentration is centered on the patient.

Therefore the secret of success for a gardener lies in having all the required tools and equipment readily to hand and clean and in good working order, so that any technique of propagation can proceed smoothly and all concentration can be centered on the plant material.

After use it is important to clean, service and restore all equipment to its correct place so that it is readily accessible.

Basic tools and equipment

Knives (1), safety razor blades (2) and shears (3)
Sharpening stone (4)
Oil for lubrication (5)
Cleaning rags (6), solvent (7) and emery paper (8)
Pressers (various) for firming compost (9)
Dibbles (10)
Sieve ($\frac{1}{8}$ in mesh) (11)
Labels and soft lead pencil (12)
Notebook for records (13)
Polyethylene bags and tape (14)
Raffia, twine, etc. (15)
Split canes 12 in or 15 in (16)
Hand sprayer (17)
Watering can (18)
Fungicides (19)
Pesticides (20)
Rooting powders (21)
Panes of glass for covering seed trays (22)
Panes of glass for cutting (23)
Pots (24) and seed trays (25)
Composts (26) and fertilizer (27)

WORKBENCHES

To find the correct height for your workbench, stand up straight, drop your arms to the side; then raise your forearms at right angles to your body and drop your wrists— the bench should be at the height indicated by your fingertips.

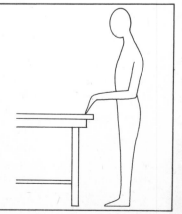

Environmental control

The main problem in propagation is to ensure survival of the propagated material (be it seed, cutting or graft) until it establishes as a new young plant. If the correct material has been used at the start, and as long as any treatments or cuts have been made correctly, then success is directly related to the control of the environment. The quicker the regenerative processes can be induced the less chance there is for things to go wrong.

In plant propagation there are two environments: the aerial environment, which can be broken down into humidity, temperature, gaseous balance and light transmission; and the environment of the medium (soil and compost), which covers temperature, moisture status, aeration and its reaction (acidity/alkalinity). Any equipment therefore should be measured in relation to the effect it has on these factors.

An ideal environment is one that allows minimum water loss from the plant material, cool air temperatures, adequate light penetration for photosynthesis, a normal atmospheric balance between compost and air, good drainage and warm soil/compost temperatures with a neutral acidity/alkalinity reaction. The degree to which a particular system of environmental control operates will limit the propagation techniques that can be used successfully within it. In general, the "softer" or less hardy the plant material the greater will be the degree of environmental control needed to achieve success. The vagaries of the normal climate are too great for all but the easiest and hardiest plants to be propagated successfully outdoors.

Cold frames

To provide initial control over the environment, place a box with a lid of glass on ordinary soil. This cold frame environment helps to increase soil temperatures, reduce temperature fluctuation, maintain humidity and allow light penetration, and it can be used for the propagation of a wide range of hardy plants. Its main disadvantage, which is shared with all enclosed environments, is that air temperatures build up when conditions are sunny. This necessitates either airing the frame to reduce the temperature, and thereby losing humidity, or shading the glass to cut down the light input, and so reducing photosynthesis.

There are many plastics substitutes used in place of glass, but because of their heat/light transmission characteristics they are less satisfactory in the late autumn to spring period as they do not conserve heat so effectively as glass.

The most manageable cold frame to construct is made with "Dutch lights," which are single panes of glass held in separate wooden frames 4 ft 11 in long by 2 ft 6¾ in wide. These can be laid side by side across a base frame with a distance between backboard and frontboard of 4 ft 9 in. For propagation the backboard is best made at a height of about 12 in and the frontboard at 9 in. The slope of the roof should be pitched in a southerly direction. The cold frame can be made more reliable by improved sealing of any cracks in the structure and by double glazing with two layers of "lights"—the lid of a cold frame being called a "light."

Greenhouses

The next step in the sequence of environmental control is the greenhouse, where slightly more sophisticated pieces of equipment for environmental control can be used. Greenhouses can, of course, be of a wide variety of shapes and sizes. Wooden-framed greenhouses are expensive to purchase, maintain and keep clean. Metal greenhouses are less expensive, cheaper to maintain and easier to keep clean, but unless they have an adequate internal structure they are subject to considerable distortion and damage if exposed to high-velocity winds.

A closed case, which is a frame with a lid of glass in a greenhouse, provides a high-temperature system for propagation of house plants and less hardy subjects. Accurate control of temperature can be attained by installing a thermostatically controlled soil-heating cable, which will provide bottom heat, into some sand at the base of the closed case.

Mist propagation units

The ultimate environmental control is provided by a mist unit. This is an open system that automatically maintains the moisture level while allowing the full penetration of light and the use of bottom heat without an increase in air temperature. However, such a system requires both electricity and water in the greenhouse.

Propagators

The alternative compromise is the so-called "propagator." This is a portable unit and can be used either in the greenhouse or indoors provided that adequate light is available. It consists of a fiberglass base fitted with a thermostat and heating cables and a Plexiglas-type dome, which provides the closed environment. All sorts of variations are available so make sure that the propagator you buy is sufficiently large for your needs.

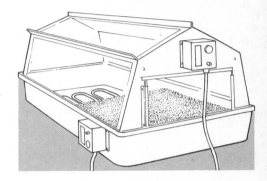

Polyethylene tents and tunnels

At the other extreme is a cheap and simple arrangement that provides a sufficiently effective closed environment for easily propagated plants. Place a polyethylene bag over the top of a pot or tray, and support it either by one or two bamboo rods or by a loop of wire with an end stuck in the compost; seal with a rubber band. Make a tunnel over plants outdoors by supporting polyethylene sheeting with wire and then sealing the ends.

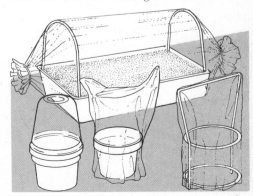

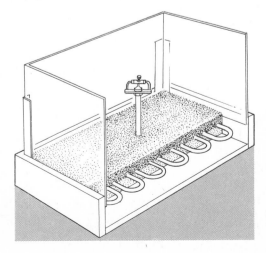

Composts

Basically a compost is a soil substitute for propagating and establishing plants. To carry out this function a compost requires certain properties—to be well aerated, to retain water, to hold nutrients and to conduct warmth. Thus in constituting a compost the components used should be chosen to establish these particular conditions as well as maintaining them throughout the life of the compost. In order to prevent the occurrence of pests, diseases and weeds the component materials should also be sterile.

The only component of a compost that is not initially sterile is the loam. To sterilize it place the loam in a broad, flat container such as a meat tin and put in the oven at 82°C/180°F for 30 minutes. Best results are obtained if the loam is dryish and if the tin is covered with foil so that the steam generated encourages the sterilizing effect. Cool and riddle the loam before use.

Cuttings compost

The formulation of a compost for rooting cuttings really only requires two considerations: the retention of sufficient moisture to help prevent desiccation of the cutting, and the provision of an aerating agent so that air can always circulate within the medium.

Conventionally, peat has been used as the water-retentive component and, although various peats are available, sphagnum moss peat is best as it retains a good structure for a long period. For most reliable use and to achieve uniformity it should be riddled through a $\frac{1}{4}$ in sieve.

Sand is used as the aerating agent, and it also allows adequate drainage—peat by itself tending to become waterlogged. In horticultural parlance sand usually means grit, and for these purposes a washed and crushed lime-free grit providing a particle size of between $\frac{1}{8}$ in and $\frac{1}{16}$ in across is the most desirable. The particles should also be "sharp," that is they should not be rounded but have points and corners and thus be irregular in shape.

Although these two components provide the basic compost they can be substituted with such items as sedge peat, well-weathered sawdust, perlite, vermiculite and graded coal dust—in fact by any material that has suitable physical properties, and that is chemically inactive and biologically more or less sterile.

Cuttings composts are usually formulated by evenly mixing equal parts by volume of peat and grit, although it is often difficult to assess how much sieved peat there is in a particular mix. In the end there is no substitute to determining the "feel" of the compost and whether it has the right properties.

Compost for germinating seedlings

The composition of a compost for seedling germination does not differ greatly from that produced for cuttings, except that a little more attention needs to be paid to the nutrient and chemical aspects.

The basic components are peat and sand and for germination pure and simple this is sufficient. However if the seedlings are to remain in the compost for some time, add loam to act as a buffer in holding nutrients and controlling drying out. The amount of sterilized loam required need not be great: a formula of 2 parts by volume peat, 2 parts sand and 1 part loam is satisfactory.

As seeds are much more sensitive to the acidity in such a compost, lime in the form of ground limestone should be mixed in with the sand at the rate of $1\frac{1}{2}$ oz per bushel of compost.

Although it is not usual to include complicated nutrient mixes in seed composts, it is important to ensure that sufficient phosphate is available. Therefore also mix $\frac{3}{4}$ oz superphosphate per bushel of compost in with the sand.

Potting composts for growing on young plants

The formulation of composts for the establishment and growing on of young plants follows on from seed composts in much the same pattern. It is necessary to prepare a compost that allows the development of a root system; contains adequate water to support the plants and sufficient nutrients not to check growth; has a suitable acidity/alkalinity status; and does not dry out too easily.

Nowadays such composts are based on the use of peat, although traditionally the John Innes concepts were based on the use of sterilized loam. The recommendation of loam as a base for composts has had to be discontinued because it is no longer feasible to obtain a standard material on which a recipe can be formulated. Peat is capable of being relatively standardized and so currently forms the basis. It is important, however, to realize that loam has a steadying and controlling influence on both water and nutrient availability that peat does not provide, and so peat-based (that is, loamless) composts require a higher degree of management and maintenance. Therefore it is prudent to use loam as a minor component merely to provide the buffering action and so ease management. In practice the aim is to produce a loamless compost with added loam!

Young plants also need nutrient in the compost and this should be added at the rate of 4 oz fertilizer base per bushel of compost unless the manufacturer recommends otherwise.

There are, of course, many available proprietary brands of peat-based composts, all of which have been tried and tested successfully. Their main disadvantage is their capacity for drying out and the difficulty of rewetting a dried compost, although this latter factor is less of a problem if a wetting agent has been incorporated. Their chief advantage is that they are ready mixed and come packed in handy-sized plastic bags.

If a peat-based compost proves difficult to rewet, then add a small quantity of wetting agent or spreader such as soft soap. Do not use wash-up liquids.

How to mix composts

The important aspect of mixing compost is to obtain an even and uniform end product. Thorough mixing of the ingredients is essential. It is also easier if you have a bushel or half-bushel box on which to base the formula as lime and fertilizers are normally added at a bushel rate. (A bushel is the amount that will fit into a box 22 in × 10 in × 10 in without compacting.)

Evenly layer the ingredients into a pile on a clean concrete floor. The lime and fertilizers should be sprinkled into each sand layer. The whole should then be well mixed with a clean shovel.

SIEVING PEAT

Riddle peat through a $\frac{1}{4}$ in sieve before mixing thoroughly with other ingredients to make the required compost.

Rooting hormones/Wounding

Certain chemicals will promote or regulate growth responses in plants when used in minute dosages, and they are used by gardeners not only for plant propagation but also to achieve a variety of other responses, such as encouraging fruit trusses to set.

These plant-growth-regulating substances work at very low concentrations and within very critical limits; a substance that sets fruits at one concentration and produces roots on stem cuttings at another may be used as a weedkiller at yet another. Thus it is exceedingly important to follow dosage instructions exactly in order to obtain the desired results.

It is also important to realize that these chemicals do not constitute a panacea for success: they will not induce rooting responses if the inherent ability of the stem to produce roots is not present. Their action is merely to enhance the innate capacity of the stem to produce its roots both in greater quantities and quicker than might otherwise have been the case. If the stem cutting is propagated from a healthy plant and at the correct season, then the use of such hormones is usually of no advantage whatsoever. They should be used with knowledge, and only as and when they are likely to achieve an effect.

The majority of rooting hormones available on the market are constituted as powders, the base simply being finely ground talc. Talcum powder is used because it is extremely soft and it lacks an abrasive quality, so causing no damage to the cutting. Mixed in with the talcum powder is the rooting hormone. Normally this is a chemical, β-indolyl-butyric acid, known as IBA. Occasionally either IAA (β-indolyl-acetic acid) or NAA (naphthoxy-acetic acid) is substituted. The concentration for hardwood cutting propagation is normally 0.8 percent IBA in talc; softwood concentrations are usually much less—about a quarter of this figure. All-purpose hormone powders are usually based on NAA.

In many cases fungicidal chemicals are also incorporated into the powders, so helping against any rots that may develop in the cuttings.

Rooting hormones are also made up in liquid formulations, where the chemicals are dissolved either in water or in an organic solvent such as alcohol.

It is important to emphasize that these hormones should not be used on either leaf or root cuttings. For these cuttings chemicals are not yet commercially available to aid regeneration.

How to apply rooting hormones

In order to know how to apply rooting hormones, it is important to understand one or two basic premises. First, that the concentration of hormone applied to induce root formation is not the best concentration to cause root development. Second, although the hormone may be absorbed through the bark, most of the hormone will be taken up through the cut base of the stem cutting.

In actually applying the hormone therefore take care to touch only the basal cut surface onto the powder so that no powder adheres to the outside of the stem; do not dip the cutting even as deep as 1 in.

By applying the hormone the roots are induced to form, but if they emerge and come into contact with the hormone still on the bark this may cause the roots to die off. In many cases this does not happen totally, but it may cause losses in some plants or under certain conditions; it is prudent to adopt a system that is suitable for all plants.

If there is difficulty in getting sufficient hormone powder to adhere to the cut surface at the base of the cutting then the cutting should first be dipped in water. This is an especially valuable hint with softwood cuttings, which will benefit from the water anyway.

Make up water-based formulations by dissolving a pill in a specified amount of water. Then stand the base of the cutting in the solution for 12–24 hours. As the concentration of water-based rooting hormones is much lower than powder-based ones, the bark is not adversely affected and so the cutting can be left standing in any depth of the solution.

If an alcohol-based solution is used, dip the base of the cutting in solution and allow to drain so that the alcohol can evaporate, leaving the hormone on the cuttings.

Correct way to apply rooting hormones

1 Dip the base of a stem cutting into water.

2 Push the base of the cutting on to the hormone powder.

Incorrect method

Ensure no hormone powder adheres to the outside of the stem cutting.

WOUNDING STEM CUTTINGS

Since certain chemicals are capable of enhancing root production on a stem cutting, it is possible that other techniques may also cause a surge in natural hormone production that could improve rooting.

In some plants there exists in the stem between the bark tissues and the wood tissues a sheath of material that is capable of inhibiting root development. However, when part of this sheath is damaged, then roots will be produced normally. This damage is achieved by a technique known as wounding.

The commonest method of wounding is to remove a slice of bark from the bottom inch or so of the cutting, using a sharp knife so that the wood tissues are just exposed. Alternatively make three or four 1 in long incisions in the bark at the base of the cutting as deep as the wood tissues.

The technique of wounding can be very effective with rhododendron, daphne and juniper, but it is unwise to use it as a matter of course as it provides another possible site for infection and rotting. It may only be necessary on older, hardwood cuttings; softwood cuttings do not normally require wounding. The need to wound a cutting will only be discovered in the light of experience—a continued failure to root a cutting, which cannot be attributed to any other cause, may then suggest that the cutting may respond to wounding.

Fertilizers

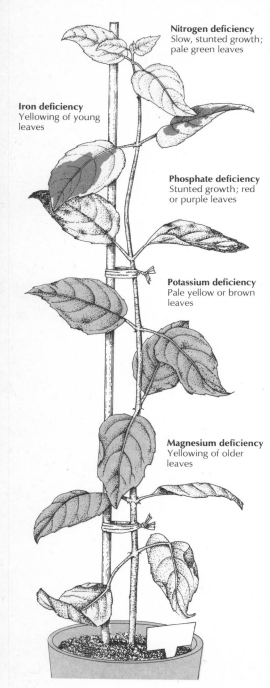

Nitrogen deficiency
Slow, stunted growth; pale green leaves

Iron deficiency
Yellowing of young leaves

Phosphate deficiency
Stunted growth; red or purple leaves

Potassium deficiency
Pale yellow or brown leaves

Magnesium deficiency
Yellowing of older leaves

There is much misunderstanding of the role that plant nutrients play in the growth of the plant and hence they are often misused in the propagation and establishment phases of plant production.

The three so-called major elements that are required for successful plant growth are nitrogen, potassium and phosphorus. These materials are needed in addition to carbon, hydrogen and oxygen as the basic building blocks of plant material. At a secondary level elements such as calcium, sulfur and magnesium are needed in fair quantities, while trace elements, which include iron, manganese, boron, molybdenum and cobalt, are used by the plant in small to minute quantities.

Nitrogen is required wherever and whenever plant growth is anticipated. A shortage of available nitrogen is typified by the slow, stunted development of the plant and pale green leaves. It is usually taken up by the plant in the form of either nitrate or ammonium salts. Nitrogen's role in the plant is predominantly as a basic ingredient of protein and it is thus a necessary feature of developing new plant tissue. Often it is referred to as being "important for leafy growth," which is essentially true because leaves constitute a major part of plant tissue; however it is equally a necessary component of stem, root, flower and seed production. As a protein component it is also a vital feature of chromosome development.

The role of potassium in the plant is rather less easily explained. Potash, as it is commonly called, is needed as a catalyst wherever chemical reactions occur. It is especially associated with the food-making process of photosynthesis and with supplying nourishment around the plant. This again explains its general association with "leafy growth." However potash is equally important in virtually all parts of the plant where chemical reactions are occurring. Potassium deficiency in plants is usually manifest when the edges of the leaves turn pale yellow, and as this discoloration moves inward the outer edges turn brown and appear scorched.

Phosphorus, which is normally used in the form of phosphate, has two major roles to fulfil in plant growth. First it is an essential component of those very specialized proteins that constitute the chromosomes. Second it is the basis on which the energy needed for plant growth and development is collected, transported and released within the various chemical reactions of the plant. A phosphate shortage is much more difficult and uncertain to describe especially when it is only a marginal amount, but generally stunted growth associated with a purple or red leaf discoloration is a typical symptom; however a similar situation often arises with root damage caused by pests or rots.

Most other plant nutrients occur in sufficient quantities as minor components or impurities in the main fertilizers, and they do not specifically need to be applied as individual fertilizers.

The only two nutrients that may cause problems are magnesium and iron. The prime role of magnesium is in the formation of chlorophyll, the green coloring in the plant. A lack of it is typified by a yellowing of the older leaves as the plant transfers magnesium from its older parts to its newly created parts so causing the "chlorosis" in the old leaves.

Iron has a similar function to magnesium but it is not reusable in the plant. Its deficiency causes the young leaves to turn yellow although the veins remain green, and by this characteristic it is possible to distinguish a shortage of this element from a magnesium deficiency.

The correct use of fertilizer

It is important to ensure that sufficient nutrients are available to young plants. If composts are correctly formulated they should contain an adequate amount. However, seedlings, for example, are germinated in a compost containing only phosphate; as soon as they begin to show green leaves they will benefit from feeding with nitrogen and potash to encourage growth.

Although it is possible for the gardener to make up his own soluble feed it is far simpler and much more reliable to use one of the several proprietary brands of liquid feeds that are readily available. If a plant shows signs of, for example, potash deficiency, buy a proprietary brand of liquid fertilizer with a high balance of that particular nutrient, and not one with only that nutrient in it, and use it as recommended.

Organic fertilizers such as bonemeal and dried blood are too slow acting to have any real beneficial effect on a plant with a nutrient deficiency.

In the closed environment of pot or seed tray, inorganic fertilizers such as nitrate of soda, sulfate of ammonia, sulfate of iron, sulfate of potash and superphosphate should also be avoided as they may have too drastic a chemical effect on the plant and also upset the balance of the other nutrients.

If the gardener is plagued with regular magnesium deficiency substitute magnesian limestone (Dolomite limestone) for ordinary limestone in the compost.

Acid-loving plants and ericaceous ones such as heathers and rhododendrons are liable to have an iron shortage and this can be treated with a chelated iron compound either in the compost or as a foliar feed.

When applying a foliar fertilizer, always follow the manufacturer's instructions exactly. Water the nutrients over the plant's leaves using a fine rose.

APPLYING A FERTILIZER

Make up a nonfoliar fertilizer according to the manufacturer's instructions. Then water on to the compost, protecting the plant's leaves with the hand. Alternatively, place the plant pot in a bowl. Pour in a dilute solution of fertilizer. Leave overnight to absorb.

Sowing in containers

To assist with germination and the establishment of a new plant, it is often helpful to soak seeds in water for 12–24 hours before being sown in a compost that will provide adequate aeration, sufficient water-holding capacity, a neutral acidity/alkalinity reaction and sufficient phosphate. Thus a "sowing" or "seed" compost should be used.

Before choosing a pot, pan or tray decide how much seed is to be sown; the container should be large enough to allow the seedlings space to develop to the size at which they are to be pricked out.

Heap the container with compost and then, to ensure it is evenly distributed and there are no air locks, very lightly firm it to the corners and base using the fingers. Do not compact the compost.

Using a sawing action, strike off the compost with a presser board or other piece of wood so that it is level with the top of the container. Then with a presser board that fits into the container, lightly and evenly firm the compost to $\frac{1}{4}$–$\frac{3}{8}$ in below the rim, ensuring that the surface is level.

The container is now prepared for sowing. The seeds should be sown evenly over the surface either by sowing large seeds one by one or gently shaking small seeds direct from the packet. When shaking, keep the packet low over the compost to prevent the seeds being unevenly distributed. If the seeds are very fine it is easier to distribute them evenly, and see where they are sown, if they are mixed thoroughly with some dry fine sand. Sow the seeds by shaking across the container, using about half the seeds; then turn the container through 90 degrees and sow the rest of the seeds in the same way.

Gently shake some compost over the container through a $\frac{1}{8}$ in sieve so that an even and uniform layer covers the seeds. As a general rule seeds do not need to be covered by compost deeper than their own thickness.

Finally label the seeds and water them in by standing the container in a shallow bath of water so that the water moves up by capillary action. Do not stand the container in so much water that it overflows the rim onto the seeds and compost. After watering stand out to drain.

Alternatively water the compost from above, using a watering can with a fine rose. Start pouring the water away from the container and once an even flow is attained direct it over the seeds; similarly, to stop, move the water away from the container and then stop the flow, so that no drops fall on to the compost.

Cover the container with a piece of glass and place in a warm dark place, for example an airing cabinet. Otherwise, cover with glass and a sheet of paper and leave in any warm (21°C/70°F) environment.

1 Soak large seeds in water for 12–24 hours before sowing in compost.

2 Fill a container with compost until it is heaped above the rim.

3 Firm the compost into the corners and base using the tips of the fingers.

4 Strike off the compost using a sawing action until it is level with the rim.

5 Firm the compost lightly to $\frac{1}{4}$–$\frac{3}{8}$ in below the rim using a presser board.

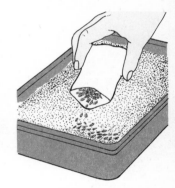

6 Sow half the seeds across the container, keeping hand low to prevent bouncing.

7 Turn container through 90 degrees. Sow the remaining seeds.

8 Cover the seeds by sifting on compost, keeping the sieve low over the seeds.

9 Label the seeds with their full name and date of sowing.

10 Water in the seeds from above the compost, using a can with a fine rose.

11 Cover the container with a pane of glass to keep the seeds moist and warm.

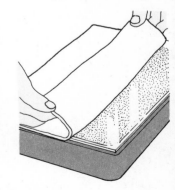

12 Place a sheet of paper over the glass to minimize temperature fluctuations.

The developing seed 1

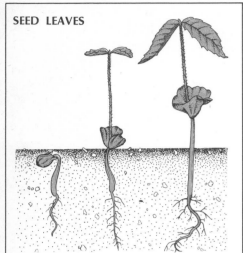

SEED LEAVES

When the seed begins to germinate, the embryo produces a root and seed leaves. These seed leaves are usually different from the true leaves that will follow.

Germination

The germination of seeds covers the entire process, from subjecting a resting seed to suitable conditions to cause it to develop to the stage at which the seedling produces true leaves and establishes as a young plant. If a seed is subjected to the conditions required for germination, and it fails to germinate, despite the fact that it is alive, then the seed is described as being dormant.

Water is vital to allow plant growth to get under way. So, if the seed has not been soaked before sowing, it is important that the compost should be watered immediately after sowing.

Once the seed has sufficiently imbibed, the embryo inside the seed begins to produce root and stem systems, which eventually break out of the seed.

To grow, the embryo uses its food reserves. When oxygen is combined with carbohydrates in these food reserves, the energy necessary for growth is produced. Thus the germinating seed will have a massive oxygen requirement, which can only be satisfied by a well-aerated environment within the compost.

All growth processes within the seed are chemical reactions activated by the addition of water. To develop successfully, the seed needs an increasing quantity of water, and the compost must be capable of holding these amounts.

As all the processes involved are basically chemical reactions they will obey normal physical rules, the simplest of which implies that the higher the temperature is raised, the faster will be the rate of the reaction. In practice, this means that the warmer seeds are kept, the quicker they will germinate. As all these reactions are taking place in a biological context, there are biological limitations as to how high the temperature can be raised. In practice there are also economic considerations, because high temperatures are costly to maintain. Experience suggests that a germination temperature of 21°C/70°F is a reasonable compromise for most flower and vegetable seeds, and this is why an airing cabinet is an excellent place for seeds to germinate.

Protection

To Keep seeds moist and warm cover the container with a sheet of glass so that water condenses on the glass and falls back into the compost. To minimize temperature fluctuations cover the glass with a sheet of paper.

As soon as the seedlings emerge, both paper and glass should be removed. Spray the seedlings regularly with water and place them in a well-lit area, out of strong direct sunlight to avoid scorching.

Spray germinating seeds with Captan or copper fungicides regularly or they may succumb to damping-off diseases.

If the seedlings are to be kept in their container for some time they should be given a liquid fertilizer diluted according to manufacturer's instructions, because many seed composts contain only a phosphate fertilizer.

Pricking out

As soon as seedlings can be handled, transplant them into a more suitable compost, leaving enough space for unrestricted

The developing seed

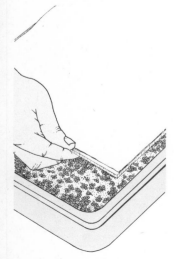

1 Remove the glass and sheet of paper as soon as the seedlings appear. Place in a well-lit area.

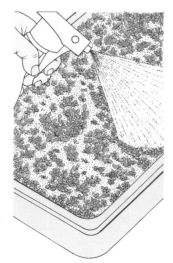

2 Spray seedlings regularly with water, but do not allow compost to become waterlogged.

3 Water in a fungicide to prevent or contain any outbreak of damping-off diseases.

Pricking out

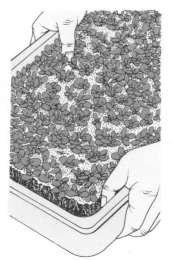

4 Knock the sides of the container on the workbench to loosen the compost and seedlings.

5 Loosen the compost further with the dibble, lifting a clump of seedlings.

6 Lift one seedling free of compost by holding its seed leaves and gently pulling.

The developing seed 2

development of the young plants. This is known as pricking out or potting on.

Fill a container with John Innes No. 1 compost or a compost of similar structure (see page 174), and firm to the base with the tips of the fingers. Strike off compost level with the rim. Lightly firm with presser board so that the compost is $\frac{1}{4}-\frac{3}{8}$ in below the rim of the container, which is now prepared.

Water the seedlings; then loosen them by knocking the old container so that the compost comes away from the sides. Hold a seedling by its seed leaf and gently lift with the aid of a dibble, keeping its root system intact. Never hold the seedling by its stem.

With the dibble, make a hole in the fresh compost big enough to take the roots. Drop in the seedling and gently firm the compost back round the roots with the dibble. Repeat this operation for each seedling, spacing at 24–40 seedlings per tray.

After the tray has been filled, water in the seedlings and return them to the warm environment (21°C/70°F) so that they can re-establish as quickly as possible.

Hardening off

After the seedlings have been pricked out, they have to be gradually weaned to a stage at which they can be planted out and survive cool temperatures, fluctuating water conditions and the effects of wind without their growth rate being affected. In the plant world this process is generally referred to as hardening off.

Most seedlings will have been germinated in a protected environment during the early part of the year to produce a plant of sufficient size to be planted out as soon as the danger of frost is passed. Because so many seedlings are produced in the early part of the year, and they are not hardy, and in most gardens there is a premium on any space that provides sufficient protection, plants tend to be grown at a high density.

The problem with crowding plants together is that an increase in fungal diseases both on the stems and leaves and in the compost is likely to result; the plants tend to become spindly as they compete for light; and the varying plants have different watering needs

so more day-to-day care and attention are needed, which is of course time consuming.

Once the pricked-out seedlings have re-established, move them to a cooler environment. For this purpose there is no real substitute for a cold frame, which should be kept firmly closed. Over the course of a few weeks increasingly air the frame during the day by raising the lid, until the frame is continually aired during the day and night: indeed the lid may be completely removed during the day if it is warm. Eventually the lid can be discarded altogether.

Frosts as severe as −4°C/25°F are sufficient to penetrate into the cold frame, so, if this level of cold is expected, provide some insulation to protect half-hardy plants. The best and most easily manageable insulation should be light yet thick; fibrous matting and similar materials are useful and effective.

Regularly check the seedlings in the frame to ensure that they are not drying out excessively. They should not however receive too much water. If anything it is better to err on the side of dryness rather than risk water-

logging. Under these cooler conditions wet composts are increasingly susceptible to fungal root rots. Similarly, the close density of plants creates conditions under which leaf diseases are capable of taking hold. It is, therefore, important that all plants in the frame are sprayed regularly with a fungicide, either Captan, which will prevent the diseases spreading, or a systemic fungicide such as Benlate, which should prevent an outbreak of the diseases.

Another aspect of seedling management is the necessity for feeding. Many pricked-out seedlings will spend several weeks in the potting compost before being finally transplanted, and there is no point in starving them and preventing them developing to an adequate size. Thus the seedlings should be regularly fed using a proprietary liquid fertilizer at the intervals stated on the manufacturer's instructions. Avoid excessive feeding as it will produce overvigorous plants that will check their growth on transplanting; it will also increase the risk of disease in the cold frame.

Hardening off

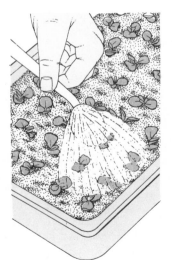

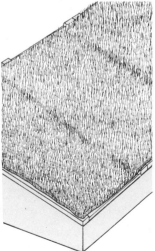

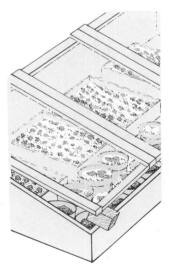

7 Hold the seedling in one hand. Make a hole with the dibber in the fresh compost in a new container.

8 Place the seedling in the hole and firm the compost back with the dibble.

9 Water in the seedlings once the seed tray is completed. Place in a warm (21°C/70°F) area.

10 Cover cold frame with fibrous matting to insulate seedlings against damage caused by frost radiation.

11 Raise the cold frame lid to allow the seedlings to harden off.

12 Water, using a fine rose, to ensure seedlings do not dry out. Add a fungicide and liquid feed regularly.

Root cuttings 1

Some plants propagated successfully from root cuttings

ALPINE PLANTS	Morisia	Eryngium	Romneya	Rhus (sumac)	Robinia
Anchusa	Primula denticulata	Limonium		Rubus	
Anemone	Pulsatilla	Papaver	SHRUBS		CLIMBERS
Arnebia	Verbascum	Phlox	Aesculus parviflora	TREES	Bignonia
Carduncellus		Statice	Aralia	Acacia (mimosa)—some species	Campsis
Erodium	HERBACEOUS PLANTS	Verbascum	Chaenomeles	Ailanthus (tree of heaven)	Eccremocarpus
Geranium	Acanthus		Clerodendrum	Catalpa (Indian bean tree)	Passiflora
Lactuca	Anchusa	SUBSHRUBS	Daphne genkwa	Koelreuteria	
		Dendromecon	Prunus (plum and blackthorn)	Paulownia	

When to take root cuttings

When propagating plants from root cuttings it is vital to understand how seasonality affects the capacity of root cuttings to produce stem buds.

The subject of "on" and "off" seasons appears to have been virtually unconsidered until the mid-twentieth century. However, recent research has established that fluctuations in the ability of roots to produce stem buds do exist and that it is pointless to propagate while the plant's response is inhibited by adverse seasonal influences.

It is this fluctuation in the capacity to propagate that has probably produced the uncertainty which has led to the propagation of plants from root cuttings being virtually ignored by nearly all gardeners.

It is therefore necessary to determine whether the plant from which root cuttings are required does have different seasonal responses, and, if so, what is the best time to take cuttings.

Without prior guidance, the natural inclination for the gardener would be to take such cuttings in the growing season, but experience has shown that this has met with little success; although results sometimes improved if cuttings were taken very early or very late in the season.

A few plants can produce new plants equally well at any time of the year, but these are relatively uncommon. Perhaps the best example is the horseradish, which can make itself into a pernicious weed by virtue of this characteristic: when the roots are broken, it is capable of establishing itself as a new plant from each root piece.

Virtually all other plants demonstrate a seasonal response. Early observations suggested that plants propagated most successfully during the winter, but experience has shown that, although this is typically true for woody plants, the real feature is not the winter but the dormant season. Many herbaceous plants and more especially alpine plants are not necessarily dormant during the winter. Some alpines, for example the Pasque flower (*Pulsatilla vulgaris*), start growing in the new year and if root cuttings are made after this period they do not respond; success is only achieved during their dormant season, which is in the late summer and early autumn.

Although propagation from root cuttings is likely to succeed throughout a plant's dormant season, it is best to keep to the mid-part of that season, as a maximum response may not exist while the dormancy is still developing or once it is phasing out.

Preparing the plant

Before propagating from root cuttings, it is preferable to prepare the parent plant itself so that it will develop roots that will have a high capacity to regenerate stem buds and so produce new plants.

This ability to produce adventitious stem buds on a severed root is already present in most plants, but it can be enhanced. Lift a healthy plant prior to the growing season and shorten any top growth. Reduce its root system by cutting off the roots close to the crown of the plant, using a knife. Then return the plant to the ground. The pruning upsets the natural root/shoot balance of the plant, and it will grow quickly during the following season to bring the plant back to its normal equilibrium between root and shoot. As a result of this treatment the vigorous, quickly grown roots will exhibit a very high level of ability to develop stem buds.

The roots will have developed fastest at the beginning of the season, and the rate will gradually have declined as the season progressed until, as the dormant season approached, growth will have ceased altogether. At the point where any root started its growth in the spring, and where it grew fastest, will also be where it has the greatest capacity to produce buds; in other words, there is a direct correlation between the rate at which a root grows and its ability to produce stem buds. If, therefore, plenty of root material is available, it is best to take a root cutting only from the top of the root where it began its development in the early spring.

In order to obtain cutting material, lift the parent plant and shorten any top growth. Wash it free of soil either in a bucket of water, or by hosing it down. It is then possible to distinguish the young roots which are suitable for propagation. Cut these close to the crown

Preparing the plant

1 Lift a healthy plant from the ground during the dormant season.

2 Cut back any top growth. Shake any excess earth off the roots.

3 Wash the roots in a bucket of water or hose them clean.

4 Cut off the roots close to the crown, using a sharp knife.

5 Return the plant to its position in the garden.

6 Leave the plant to re-establish during the growing season.

Root cuttings 2

of the plant, at right angles to the root. Return the parent plant to the garden.

Discard the thin root end by slicing with a sloping cut. Slice off any fibrous lateral roots on the cutting to ease handling and planting later on.

The removal of roots from the parent plant for propagation will have had the additional effect of root pruning and so will cause the development of further roots for propagation in the ensuing propagating season.

Size of a root cutting

The size of a root cutting may not be critical if only one cutting is made from each root, but, with roots that regenerate readily and from which it is possible to make more than one cutting, the optimum size of a root cutting becomes very important. It is therefore necessary to determine the minimum size for a root cutting so that maximum use can be made of the available root.

The size of the root cutting depends on two factors. First, the cutting requires sufficient food to initiate and develop a stem bud to the stage at which it produces green leaves and can begin to support itself. Second, the cutting requires sufficient food reserves to support itself while this regenerative process is going on.

The size of the cutting, therefore, is made up of the regenerative portion and the survival portion. The size of the survival portion depends on how long the cutting will take to regenerate, and this is reliant on the temperature in which the cutting is propagated: the warmer the environment the quicker the stem will develop. A root cutting taken and planted in the open ground during the winter may not produce a shoot until May, but if it had been placed in a propagator in a temperature of 18°–24°C/65°–75°F, it might well have regenerated in about four weeks. The amount of food reserve required for survival between these two temperature environments is dramatically different.

The size of the regenerative portion needed, however, will remain constant whatever the temperature of the propagating environment, so a rule of thumb measurement for the size of a root cutting is based on the variable factor—temperature.

As a plant's roots will have been pruned a year before the cuttings are taken, all roots will show one year's growth and therefore be approximately the same thickness. Thus the cutting length is unaffected.

An open-ground cutting should be at least 4 in long as it will need to survive for some 16 weeks. A cold frame/cold greenhouse provides a warmer environment, and regeneration will occur in about eight weeks and so a smaller survival portion is required and the cuttings need only be just over 2 in long. In a warm (18°–24°C/65°–75°F) greenhouse or propagator, regeneration time is reduced to four weeks, halving the survival time and the required food reserve once again so that in this environment root cuttings need only be about 1 in long.

Recognizing the top of a root cutting

When propagating plants from root cuttings it is very important to notice the "polarity" of the cutting—that it has a top and a bottom and therefore a "right way up." Most people suggest that root cuttings should be planted horizontally because the cuttings have been made in such a way that the top and bottom cannot be recognized, and there is no other way in which polarity can be recognized because roots have no leaves and axillary buds. However, stem cuttings are not planted on their side, so it is unreasonable to expect root cuttings to be, no matter in what direction their roots subsequently grow. Cuttings planted vertically and the correct way up will usually develop to a maximum level provided that the cuttings were taken from a healthy plant and they were given suitable conditions (see page 40). Cuttings planted on their side rarely achieve more than a 40 percent success rate.

In order to recognize the top of a root (that is, the end nearest the crown of the plant) so it can be planted the right way up, make a flat cut at right angles to the root where it was severed from its parent; at the bottom end cut away the thin portion using a sloping cut. Always cut roots in this way so, whatever subsequently happens to the root cutting, it will be possible to recognize its correct polarity and so ensure that it is planted the right way up.

Obtaining cutting material

7 Lift the plant in the middle of the dormant season. Cut any top growth.

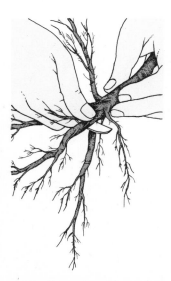

8 Wash its roots. Then cut off the young roots close to the crown and set aside.

9 Return the plant to its usual position in the garden.

Taking a root cutting

10 Cut off any fibrous lateral roots on undamaged young roots.

11 Make a right-angled cut on a root where it was severed from its parent.

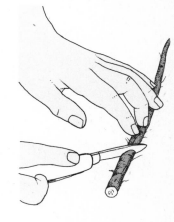

12 Cut away the thin root end at the appropriate length, using a sloping cut.

Root cuttings 3

Treatment

After all the initial aspects have been considered and the root cutting has been made, the next step is to consider the question of what treatment the cutting may need in order to enhance its chances of producing a stem bud and then surviving until the bud develops and establishes as a new plant. At present there are no growth-promoting substances available for root cuttings, so that it is not possible to enhance bud production in this way. The special powders produced for inducing roots on stems should not be used on root cuttings as they will actually depress bud production.

The best way to protect a root cutting is to treat it with a thin powder film of fungicide such as Captan. The root cutting, when planted, will be more or less completely surrounded by soil or compost and as such could easily become waterlogged and so subject to all sorts of fungal rots. The survival of the cutting will very much depend on protecting it against this possibility.

Place the cuttings in a polyethylene bag, add some fungicidal powder, using about one teaspoonful of Captan for every 100 1in cuttings. "Balloon" the bag by twisting the top and then shake it vigorously. Once the cuttings are coated with a powder film, they are ready for planting.

It will be apparent why it is important to be able to recognize the top and bottom of the cuttings after such processing.

Planting

Root cuttings need to be planted in a medium that will support them, prevent them drying out, allow adequate aeration and, when regeneration starts, provide basic nutrients. All these features can be found in the ground outdoors and the root cuttings will do well there provided that the soil is reasonably light or they are placed under a cold frame in soil to which peat and grit have been added. However, except perhaps for a few very vigorous herbaceous perennials, it is more convenient to plant root cuttings in a container and then plant them out just as soon as they are established.

Select a container of suitable size for the number of root cuttings to be propagated, allowing 1–1½ in for each cutting. For example, plant seven cuttings in a 3½ in pot. Fill the container with a peat-based compost containing loam, which will act as a buffer to prevent excessive drying and will maintain an even level of nutrients. Strike off the compost with a presser board so that it is level with the rim. Then press the soil down to at least $\frac{3}{8}$ in below the rim of the container.

Make a hole in the compost with a dibble and then plant the root cutting. Place the top of the cutting just level with the top of the compost. Firm back the compost around the cutting. Space the remaining root cuttings evenly round the container.

Cover the cuttings with grit. Strike off with a presser board until the grit is level with the rim of the container. This weight of grit tends to compress the compost slightly so causing the tops of the cuttings to be pushed farther up into the grit. This will provide almost perfect aeration for the bud that will develop at the top of the root cutting. Do not water. Label the container and stand it in an environment (propagator, cold frame, etc.) that is appropriate to the size of the root cutting (see **page 181**).

Some plants, for example *Romneya coulteri*, do not like being dug up and having their roots disturbed. Therefore, place only one or two of their root cuttings in a small pot and treat as one plant, disturbing their roots as little as possible when transplanting them once they are established.

Aftercare

Keep watering to a minimum to maintain a well-aerated compost, which encourages bud development and reduces the likelihood of rotting. In fact there is probably no need to water at all if the root cuttings were initially planted in a reasonably moist compost and a humid environment is maintained.

Very often when the bud first develops, it produces a stem and green leaves but no root system. This will grow later from the base of the new stem. Even if the new roots do develop from the cutting, they too will not appear until after the stem and green leaves have grown. Do not water until the roots appear as the cutting is still liable to rot.

Place in a well-lit area once the stem appears. Harden off any young plants propagated in a warm (21°C/70°F) environment before planting out or potting up. Apply a liquid fertilizer, according to the manufacturer's instructions.

Treating root cuttings

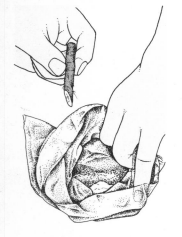

1 Place the root cuttings in a bag filled with some fungicidal powder.

2 Close the bag and shake until all the cuttings are covered with fungicide.

3 Fill a pot with compost. Make a hole with a dibble. Plant cutting vertically.

Planting root cuttings

4 Plant remaining root cuttings 1–1½ in apart. Cover the pot with grit.

5 Strike off the grit until level with rim. Label, and leave cuttings to develop.

6 Do not water until the roots have appeared. Then apply a liquid fertilizer.

Tuberous roots

Some herbaceous perennial plants die back to a crown of buds each dormant season, and their roots are modified to store food. These specialized swollen roots are described as tuberous roots. They can be distinguished from modified stems by their structure and from root cuttings by their inability to produce adventitious buds on isolated roots and so grow a new plant.

There are two basic kinds of tuberous roots: those that develop annually, such as on dahlias, and those that are perennial and simply increase in size, such as on begonias.

Annual tuberous roots develop from lateral roots at the crown of the plant. During the growing season, certain of these develop as food stores, swelling up and producing a cluster of such roots. Each year the new shoot system develops at the expense of the food store in the tuberous roots, which eventually die and disintegrate.

Perennial tuberous roots are much simpler in their development. Usually the emerging radicle of the seedling begins to modify as a food storage organ, and this increases in size as and when food is available.

The division of tuberous roots is not a widely used technique as many plants with tuberous roots can be propagated more satisfactorily by stem, leaf and leaf bud cuttings. Success depends on how well the roots are stored. Lift the plant at the end of the growing season. Clean the crowns and dust with a fungicide. Wrap each plant in thick newspaper and place in a frost-free environment, below 5°C/42°F.

Just before the growing season, divide the tuberous roots into portions, each with at least one crown bud, from which the new stem will develop. Protect all cut surfaces from rotting by dusting with a powder fungicide such as Thiram or Captan. Then place the divisions in a warm (21°C/70°F), dry, airy area for a couple of days so that the cut surfaces seal themselves quickly by developing a corky layer of tissue, to give added protection. Pot up the divisions in John Innes No. 1 compost if they are to be transplanted within a month or so; otherwise plant them in John Innes No. 2 compost. Label them; do not water. Place in a frost-free area. Set in the light once a shoot appears.

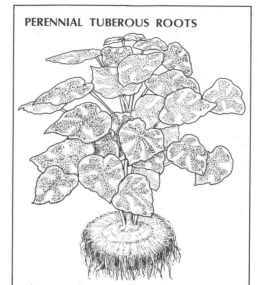

PERENNIAL TUBEROUS ROOTS

Plants such as begonias have only one tuberous root, which is perennial and extends sideways each year.

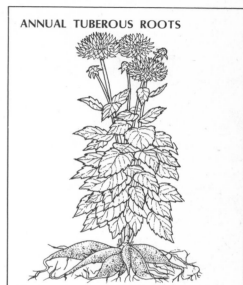

ANNUAL TUBEROUS ROOTS

Some tuberous rooted plants such as dahlias produce annual storage roots that die and disintegrate after one season.

1 Lift a plant at the end of the growing season. Clean the crowns thoroughly.

2 Dust the entire crowns with a fungicidal powder. Lift on to some newspaper.

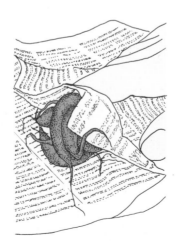

3 Wrap up the plant. Store in a frost-free place until the buds begin to swell.

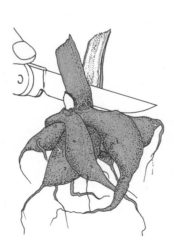

4 Divide the swollen roots into portions, each with at least one crown bud.

5 Dust all cut surfaces with fungicide. Leave in a warm, dry, airy place.

6 Pot up the cuttings once the cut surfaces have formed a corky layer.

Tubers

Some plants that produce tubers
Artichoke, Chinese
Artichoke, Jerusalem
Caladium
Nymphaea sp: (Water lilies)
Potato
Tropaeolum sp.—especially
   T. tuberosum

Tuberous pea

Some plants that develop tubercles
Achimenes
Begonia evansiana
Dioscorea batatas

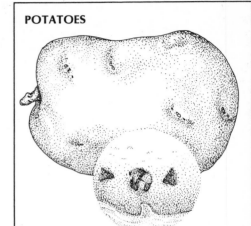

The name "tuber" in horticultural terms has been much misused and has on occasions covered almost any swollen food storage organ that is chiefly underground.

A tuber is, in fact, a swollen underground stem, modified as a food storage organ. It often is of roundish (usually terminating) growth and is normally annual. The leaves are scaly and membranous, and the axillary buds provide the following year's shoots.

Within these limitations the number of plants producing true tubers is not very great. The commonest is the potato. Those plants, such as Jerusalem artichokes, that produce opposite rather than spirally arranged buds, such as potatoes, often have a knobby shape. Some water lilies (*Nymphaea* sp.) produce small tuberlike structures that develop from the main rootstock toward the end of the growing season.

Although potatoes are prolific producers of tubers, this is unusual. Normally, plants that develop tubers do so only in very small numbers.

Any increase in numbers must be achieved artificially. As the tuber is normally an organ that allows a plant to survive its dormant period, the season to propagate tubers by artificial division should be just before growth would commence in the spring.

Cut the tuber with a sharp knife so that each piece has at least one good dominant bud or "eye." Then dust all the cut surfaces with a fungicide such as Captan to reduce the possibility of fungal infection. Stand the pieces on a wire tray and keep in a warm (21°C/70°F), dry environment, for example an airing cabinet, for a couple of days. A protective corky layer, which enhances their survival, will then develop. These tuber "seeds" should not be kept in the dry for any longer than necessary, otherwise the tuber itself will desiccate.

Therefore plant them out immediately in a hole twice their depth. They will then quickly produce roots and shoots and establish as a new plant. Label them clearly at all stages of propagation.

POTATOES

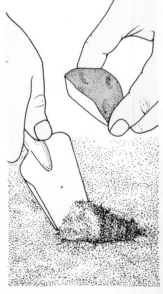

A potato tuber is marked by a scar at one end, where it was attached to the parent plant, and by "eyes," or nodes, placed spirally over its surface.

TUBERCLES

Just a few plants produce very small tubers from the axillary buds. These buds modify into tubers and eventually fall off the parent stem.

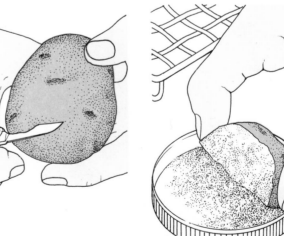

1 Cut a tuber into pieces with a sharp knife. Ensure each piece has at least one good "eye."

2 Dust all the cut surfaces with a fungicidal powder. Stand on a wire tray in a warm (21°C/70°F), dry place.

3 Plant the tuber pieces in the open ground as soon as a protective corky layer has formed. Label them clearly.

Rhizomes

Some plants that develop rhizomes
Arum lily (*Zantedeschia* sp.)
Asparagus
Begonia rex
Bird of paradise
  (*Strelitzia reginae*)
Canna

Couch grass
Crabgrass
Ferns—some species
Iris, bearded
Lily of the valley
  (*Convallaria majalis*)
Mint
Mother-in-law's tongue

(*Sansevieria* sp.)
Peony
Rhubarb
Smilax
Solomon's seal (*Polygonatum*)
Thistle, creeping

A rhizome is a stem that grows laterally at or above the soil surface, although in some plants it is underground. Normally, a rhizome stores food, but the degree to which it does this varies from species to species.

A rhizome is a perennial, and it is propagated artificially by division at an opportune season of the year: in most cases this is after flowering, when the rhizome is about to extend and produce new roots.

It has two ways of growing. In one, typified by the German or bearded iris, a terminal bud develops and flowers; the plant sends out extension growth through a lateral bud. The following season, this extension growth develops its own terminal bud, which flowers, and the plant continues to extend through its lateral buds. In the other way of growing, typified by mint and couch grass, its extension growth develops continuously from the terminal bud and occasionally from a lateral bud, which usually produces flower spikes.

In habit, rhizomes may also vary: "crown" rhizomes, such as asparagus, have virtually no extension growth annually and develop as a spreading crown, whereas other kinds of rhizomes, such as mint, couch grass and crabgrass, make rapid and continuous growth and spread over large areas of ground in a relatively short time.

Perhaps the most prolific of garden plants to be propagated using rhizomes are bearded irises. The best time to divide their rhizomes and establish new plants is immediately after flowering, when the old root system dies down and a new root system begins to develop. Lift the clump of rhizomes with a fork and knock off as much soil as possible. Cut away and discard any old rhizomes, just leaving the current season's flushes of growth. Cut back their roots to 2–3 in, and shorten the leaf blades to reduce water loss before the new root systems develop. The prepared rhizomes are now ready for planting.

As a general rule, a rhizome should be replanted at the same depth as it was growing; for irises this is more or less in the surface soil. Usually, a rhizome has two rows of roots longitudinally on each side underneath. Therefore, when replanting, dig out two linear shallow trenches and place the roots in these. Firm back the soil over these roots and label the rhizome clearly. If necessary, settle in by watering.

CROWN RHIZOMES

Less easy to propagate are the "crown" rhizomes, such as peony and asparagus, which have what is traditionally referred to as herbaceous perennial rootstock. Fairly massive cuts are needed to divide such rootstock into suitable pieces for propagation: each piece requiring at least one well-developed bud.

Divide crown rhizomes in late winter before the buds enlarge and before the new season's root system begins to develop. Make a few relatively large divisions, unless quick bulking-up is essential, when it is better to plant small divisions in pots filled with John Innes No. 1 compost or similar (see page 12) in order to give them good conditions in which to become established. Dust the cut surfaces thoroughly with a fungicide to prevent bacterial and fungal rots. Leave them in a warm (21°C/70°F), dry atmosphere for the surface to dry out and develop the beginnings of a protective corky layer. Then plant out the divisions. Label them clearly.

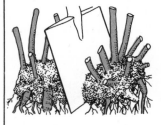
1 Divide crown rhizomes in late winter.

2 Dust the cut surfaces with a fungicidal powder.

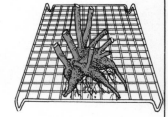
3 Plant out after two days in a warm, dry area.

1 Divide rhizomes after flowering, when the old root system dies down.

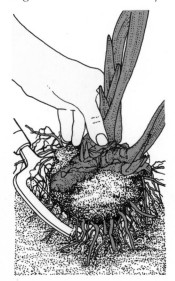
2 Lift a clump with a fork. Knock off as much soil as possible from the roots.

3 Cut away and discard any old rhizomes from the current season's growths.

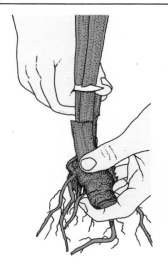
4 Shorten the leaf blades and cut back the roots to 2–3 in.

5 Replant each rhizome on a ridge with its roots in trenches either side.

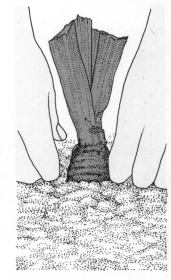
6 Firm back the soil over the roots. Label and settle by watering.

Corms

Some plants that develop corms
Acidanthera
Crocosmia
Crocus
Gladiolus
Ixia
Ixiolirion
Montbretia
Tritonia

Corms look very similar to bulbs and are often confused with them. However, structurally they are very different. A corm consists of a stem that is swollen as a food store and that is shorter and broader than a bulb. The leaves of the stem are modified as thin, dry membranes that enclose the corm and protect it against injury and drying. Each leaf has a bud in its axil, the top of the stem usually develops as a flowering stem, and the roots are produced from the corm's base, which is often concave. In some kinds of corm, several buds at the top of the stem may grow out and flower.

Each year a new corm develops around the base of each stem. Increase, therefore, is

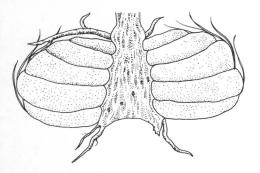

directly related to the number of stems produced by a corm. Normally, most plants developing corms will propagate naturally to give a sufficient increase, but should it be necessary to bulk up supplies more quickly then an artificial technique should be used.

Always buy corms from a reputable specialized grower, because it is vital to propagate from disease-free corms.

Cut a large, healthy corm into several pieces just prior to the season for planting and ensure each piece has at least one bud. Dust the cut surfaces with a fungicidal powder such as Captan or Thiram, in order to reduce the risk of rotting. Set the pieces on a wire cake-tray and place in a warm, dry environment, such as an airing cabinet, for 48 hours. This will cause the cut surfaces to seal. Then plant singly in a pot or in the ground, and label clearly.

If the corm is too small to cut up satisfactorily, then the lateral buds can be induced to develop more readily by removing the main stem either by snapping it off or digging it out with a knife. Then dust the cut surface with fungicidal powder and plant out the corm in the ground. During the growing season it will produce several shoots, which will eventually become new plants.

Propagation by division

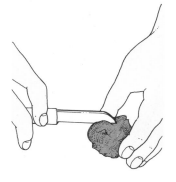

1 Cut a corm into several pieces, each with at least one bud, just before planting in autumn.

2 Dust the cut surfaces with a fungicidal powder. Set pieces on a wire tray. Leave in a warm, dry place.

3 Plant each piece in a pot or in the open ground once it has developed a corky layer. Then label.

Propagation by inducing lateral buds

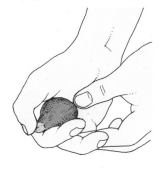

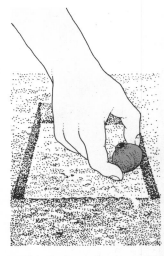

1 Lift the corm in autumn. Snap off the main stem or dig it out using a pointed knife.

2 Dust all the cut surfaces with a fungicidal powder.

3 Dig a hole twice the depth of the corm in the open ground. Plant it out immediately and label.

CORMELS

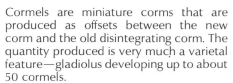

Cormels are miniature corms that are produced as offsets between the new corm and the old disintegrating corm. The quantity produced is very much a varietal feature—gladiolus developing up to about 50 cormels.

The level of cormel production will be influenced by the depth at which the main corm is planted; the deeper the corm is in the ground, the more cormels produced.

Collect the cormels when the corm is lifted from the ground before winter and store them below 5°C/41°F in a dry, frost-free environment with air circulating round them. Soak any cormels that become dry in tepid water for 24 hours before planting the following season. Plant them outdoors close together and label. They will normally take two years to reach flowering size.

Bulblets and bulbils

Some lilies that produce bulblets
Lilium auratum
L. bulbiferum
L. canadense
L. longiflorum
L. pardalinum

L. speciosum
L. tigrinum

Some lilies that produce bulbils as a result of disbudding
Lilium candidum
L. chalcedonicum

L. dauricum
L. × hollandicum
L. leichtlinii
L. × maculatium
L. × testaceum
Ornamental onions
—some species

Bulblets

Bulblets are tiny bulbs that develop below ground on some bulbs.

Plants that produce bulblets can be artificially induced to increase their bulblet production. This is done by removing the flower stem, and burying it until bulblets develop in the leaf axils.

Dig a trench 6 in deep; slope one side up to ground level. Pinch out any buds or flowers on the stem and then twist it out of the bulb, which should remain in the ground. Lay the stem in the trench along the slope, leaving part of it sticking out of the ground. Spray the stem with a liquid fungicide to prevent disease. Then fill the trench with sand or a light compost and label.

By autumn, bulblets will have developed in the leaf axils at the lower end of the stem. These can be detached and planted straight into the ground at twice their own depth or be left *in situ* for a year.

This is a surprisingly easy method of producing bulblets, and the only difficulty that is likely to arise is the potential rotting of the stem before the bulblets are produced.

Bulbils

Bulbils are tiny bulbs that grow on a stem above ground. This natural process is an extremely prolific way of increasing stock.

A number of lily species such as *Lilium candidum* can be artificially induced to produce bulbils by disbudding the plant just before flowering. Bulbils will develop in the leaf axils during the remainder of the growing season. Collect them as they mature.

Fill a pot to the rim with John Innes No. 1 compost or similar (see page 174). With a presser board, strike off the excess compost and then firm gently to within $\frac{3}{8}$ in of the pot rim. Set the bulbils 1 in apart on the compost surface and gently press them so they make contact with the compost. Cover generously with grit. Strike off the grit level with the rim of the pot. Label and place in a cold frame. Leave for at least twelve months, until autumn of the following year. Then transplant into the open ground.

Certain other plants can also be artificially induced to produce bulbils; some of the ornamental onions will develop them in the flower heads.

Bulbil propagation

1 Disbud a suitable plant stem just before it begins to flower.

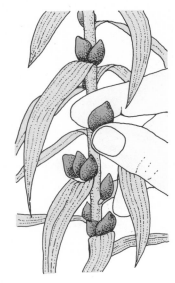

2 Pick off any bulbils as they mature in the leaf axils on the stem.

3 Set them 1 in apart in a compost-filled pot. Cover with grit and label.

Bulblet propagation

1 Pinch out any buds or flowers on a suitable plant.

2 Twist the stem out of the bulb, leaving the bulb in the ground.

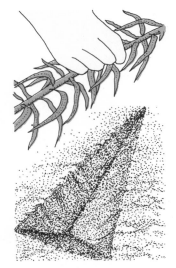

3 Lay two-thirds of the stem along the sloping side of a trench 6 in deep.

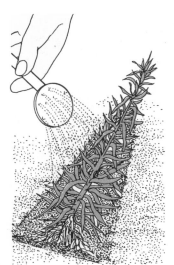

4 Spray the stem with a liquid fungicide such as Captan or Benomyl.

5 Fill the trench with sand or a light compost. Label clearly.

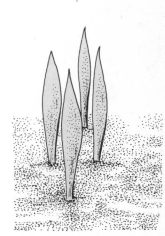

6 Leave during the summer. Detach the bulblets in autumn and replant.

Division 1

Some herbaceous plants with fibrous crowns
Achillea
Alchemilla
Alyssum
Aster
Aubrieta
Caltha

Campanula
Chrysanthemum
Doronicum
Erigeron
Gentiana
Geranium
Helenium
Hemerocallis

Lupine
Lythrum
Mimulus
Monarda
Polemonium
Prunella
Pyrethrum
Raoulia

Rudbeckia
Sagina
Scabiosa
Solidago
Tiarella
Trollius
Veronica

Herbaceous plants with fibrous crowns

Dividing a plant is a common way to propagate many herbaceous perennials, and it is also used to rejuvenate favorite plants and keep them in a vigorous condition. Propagation by division is also successful with shrubs, such as sumac, that produce suckers; with semi-woody perennials, such as New Zealand flax, that produce a crown of offset shoots; and with most plants with modified stems, such as bearded iris (see pages 184–187).

Herbaceous plants with fibrous crowns

The commonest method of propagating plants by division is that used for herbaceous perennials, such as chrysanthemums, with fibrous roots and a relatively loose crown. Normally, the central part of the crown becomes woody over the course of two or three years. As this woody area does not produce many shoots and generally loses vigor, it is discarded and the remainder of the clump is divided into suitable-sized portions for planting out and reestablishing a new crown.

The only variable feature of this form of propagation is the time at which division is carried out. As a general rule, the most opportune time to divide such plants is directly after flowering, as this is when the new vegetative shoots are being produced and the new root system is developing. In very late-flowering subjects, this would be the following spring.

Lift the parent plant and shake off as much soil as possible. Then wash the crown in a bucket, or hose it clean of any residual soil. The plant can be divided without this preliminary preparation, but it is much easier to deal with clean plants, especially if the soil is wet and muddy. Shorten any tall stems above the ground to prevent unnecessary water loss, especially if the division takes place in summer. Break off a piece with at least one good "eye" from the periphery of the crown, where the young shoots are generally produced; avoid the central woody crown, which is of no value and should be discarded. If the piece proves rather intractable to remove, cut it off, using an old carving knife or similar blade. Plant out the new clump as quickly as possible to the same depth as it was growing previously. When replanted it should be labelled and watered in—indeed "puddled" in would be more appropriate.

1 Lift the plant that is to be divided directly after it has flowered.

2 Shake off as much soil as possible.

3 Wash the crown and its roots in a bucket, or hose it clean.

4 Shorten all tall stems above the ground to minimize water loss.

5 Break off a piece with at least one good "eye" from the edge of the crown.

6 Divide any intractable pieces with an old carving knife or similar blade.

7 Make a hole and replant the new clump at once. Firm the soil and label.

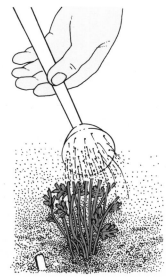

8 Water very thoroughly, using a watering can with a spray attachment.

9 Keep the new clump free of weeds.

Division 2

Some herbaceous plants with
fleshy crowns
Astilbe
Hosta

Some alpine plants dividing
naturally
Aubrieta
Autumn gentian

Campanula
Primula—European species
Thalictrum

Some semiwoody
herbaceous plants
Cortaderia
Phormium
Yucca

Some woody shrubs
Aronia
Blackthorn
Lilac

Herbaceous plants with fleshy crowns

Many herbaceous plants, such as hostas, develop a compact, fleshy crown that is not easy to pull apart.

The best way to propagate these plants is by division toward the end of their dormant season, when buds will begin to shoot, indicating the most vigorous areas.

Lift the parent plant and shake off as much soil as possible. Wash the crown thoroughly. With a convenient-sized knife, cut the crown into pieces. The size of divisions will depend on preference, but must include at least one developed shoot. Avoid latent buds, which do not always develop satisfactorily. Dust the cut surfaces with fungicidal powder to reduce the chances of fungal rots. Do not allow the divisions, especially from really fleshy rooted plants such as hostas, to dry excessively. Therefore replant the divisions either in the ground or in a pot as quickly as is feasible. Label them clearly.

Naturally dividing alpines

There are a number of alpine plants, such as campanulas, which lend themselves to propagation by division because their crowns separate naturally into individual new plantlets each season.

After flowering, or in the spring if the plant flowers in the autumn, as does *Gentiana sino-ornata*, lift the plant and tease apart the divisions. Replant as soon as possible. Label and water in well.

This is a very simple but effective system of increasing plants. If the crowns are lifted and divided fairly frequently the rate of increase can be quite dramatic. However, plants left *in situ* for a long period tend to produce only a few large divisions.

Semiwoody herbaceous plants

Some perennials with upright, swordlike leaves, for example *Phormium*, increase in size by producing a sort of offset that develops into a large crown of individual shoots, each with its own root system.

To propagate these plants, it is best to divide them in the spring, although it can be done at any time of the year. Lift them and shake out the soil, if necessary hosing or washing the crown clean. Pull the various pieces apart. Cut the clump with a spade or hatchet if it is hard and woody in the middle, and replant the divisions fairly quickly to avoid the roots drying.

Woody shrubs

There are a few woody shrubs, such as blackthorn, that produce suckers, which then develop into individual clumps of stems. Lift these plants in the dormant season and wash thoroughly. Divide the clump of stems into convenient-sized portions. Normally the main core of the clump will be woody and will carry few roots. This will be of little value for propagation purposes, so take the new pieces from the younger, more vigorous growth on the outside of the clump.

Cut back the branches fairly drastically to reduce water loss, as the buds will break in the spring before sufficient roots have been produced. Replant the divisions back in the ground as soon as possible and label.

Lift relatively isolated suckers individually in the dormant season and use to establish new plants.

If the plant has been grafted—as may happen with Japanese quinces—then it is the rootstock, not the cultivated variety, that is divided.

IRISHMAN'S CUTTINGS

Plants, such as Michaelmas daisies, that produce particularly loose crowns can be propagated by separating off single stems on the periphery of the crown so that each has an adventitious root system. These single stem portions are described as "Irishman's cuttings," and they should be planted at once.

Herbaceous plants with fleshy crowns

1 Lift the plant to be divided toward the end of its dormant season.

2 Wash the crown well. Cut off a piece with at least one developed bud.

3 Dust the cut surfaces with a fungicidal powder. Then replant immediately.

Woody shrubs with suckers

1 Remove isolated suckers from woody shrubs during the dormant season.

2 Cut back part of the roots and top growth.

3 Replant immediately; label and water in well.

Offsets/Runners

Some plants developing offsets	Some plants developing runners
Agave	*Ajuga reptans*
Crassula	*Geum reptans*
Echeveria	Grass—some species
New Zealand flax (*Phormium*)	Potentilla, herbaceous
Pineapple	*Saxifraga sarmentosa*
Sempervivum	Strawberry
Yucca	

Offsets

An offset is a plantlet that has developed laterally on a stem either above or below ground: the stem arises from a crown bud and usually carries no other buds.

Most plants, such as sempervivums, that produce offsets first grow a miniature plant with only minimal roots. A root system will not fully develop until late in the growing season.

To speed up this process of propagation, pull away the offset from its parent, usually in spring. Either plant out in the garden or pot it up, using a cuttings compost with added grit, which will drain freely and so ensure good root development.

Where offset development is poor, it is possible to stimulate offsets by removing the plant's growing tip. This has the same effect as removing a terminal bud.

Although the term offset is normally used for a plantlet that is separated from its parent during the growing season, it is also used to describe slower-developing shoots that are produced by mainly monocotyledonous plants such as yuccas. Eventually these shoots should be sufficiently mature to be separated from the parent and planted on.

A pineapple plant produces offsets that can be used for propagation once its fruit is nearly mature. These offsets are variously described as slips, ratoons or suckers. Cut them off the plant close to the crown and plant out.

Many corm and bulb plants, such as fritillarias, each year produce miniature reproductions of themselves from the bases of the newly developing corms or bulbs. These are known as cormels (see page 186) and bulbils and bulblets (see page 187).

1 Pull an offset away from the parent plant, preferably in spring.

2 Plant the offset in a pot filled with a cuttings compost with added grit.

Cut off pineapple slips close to the crown and plant out individually.

Runners

A runner is a more or less horizontal stem that arises from a crown bud and creeps overground. The leaves are normally scale-like, and rooting may occur at the nodes. The lateral buds develop as new plants, and eventually the stem of the runner deteriorates, leaving a new isolated plant. The classic example of this kind of natural vegetative reproduction occurs in the strawberry plant.

New plantlets usually root down and produce new plants quite successfully. However, unless controlled, a mat of new plants tends to develop, and these are not easily lifted and separated without damage, so thin out the runners regularly.

To produce large, well-established individual plants, dig in plenty of good compost for rooting; in early summer, thin out some of the runners, and pin down the rest into the compost, evenly radiating them around the plant. This method will induce early rooting, but the rate of development will not be quite as fast as for pot-grown runners.

These are obtained by placing a pot under each runner.

Dig a hole in the ground beneath a developing plantlet. Set a pot containing good compost into it and then push back the soil to keep the pot in position. Pin down the runner, using wire bent in the shape of a staple, so that the plantlet will root in the pot.

1 Thin out some runners in early summer to encourage strong growth.

2 Fill a pot with John Innes No. 1 compost. Firm to within $\frac{3}{8}$ in of the rim.

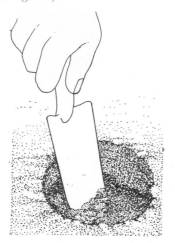

3 Dig a large hole in the ground beneath a plantlet. Set the pot in the hole.

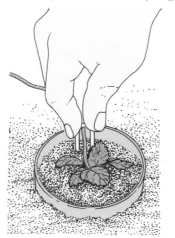

4 Pin down the plantlet in the middle of the pot, using a wire staple.

5 Pin down any other plantlets in a star-shaped pattern round the parent plant. Sever their connecting stems once they are fully established.

Layering/Simple layering 1

Layering is one of the oldest techniques used by gardeners to propagate woody plants. A stem is encouraged to develop roots before it is removed from the parent plant. This method is easy as it avoids any complicated environmental control to ensure the stem survives while the root system is developing. The early gardeners had probably observed this process when it occurred naturally under certain conditions. To do it artificially they just repeated the conditions and modified the technique.

As with any method of propagation, it is necessary to consider both the stem from which the layer is to be made and what soil is suitable to encourage rooting.

The condition of the stem will have a significant effect on the eventual success of propagating by layering. For greatest success, the gardener should develop vigorous, rapidly grown stems with their high capacity to produce roots. Certain methods of layering, such as stooling, encourage this capacity in stems as part of the normal system of management, but in others, such as simple layering, it is necessary to prepare the stems by pruning the parent plant well before propagation can take place. When pruning bear in mind that, with most methods of layering, the branches to be layered will have to be brought down to ground level.

The soil around the parent plant will also require preparation so that it will induce the stem to form roots. Rooting will be encouraged primarily by the exclusion of light, but also by the availability of oxygen and the presence of sufficient moisture and warmth.

The exclusion of light from the stem, that is blanching it, is extremely important when encouraging roots to start growing. The sooner light is excluded from the stem, the more effective is the response. So, the earlier a stem is buried or earthed up the more likely it is to root. This effect cannot be overemphasized, as lateness in earthing up is probably the commonest reason why a stem fails to produce roots, provided that it is basically vigorous and capable of producing roots.

The soil for layering must have a good water-holding capacity, good aeration and adequate drainage. Thus, especially if plants are to be layered in an ordinary garden border as opposed to a purpose-developed layer bed, the soil must be dug deeply to provide good drainage and so reduce the chances of waterlogging. It can be further lightened and improved by the addition of peat and/or grit, depending on the heaviness of the soil.

Warmth will improve rooting, so ensure the layered stem and soil are placed where they will receive adequate sunlight. However, warmth will only be effective if the soil is moist, so water the layered stems during dry periods.

In most methods of layering, the soil should be carefully forked away from the layer once it has rooted, so it can be lifted. Do not allow the roots to dry out, otherwise they will die.

Layers that may have difficulty rooting successfully should be well established before they are lifted. To encourage this, sever the newly rooted layers from the parent plant about three to four weeks prior to lifting and replanting.

This weaning can be further enhanced by pruning the stems so that there is a greater balance of root to stem.

Simple layering

Simple layering is perhaps the easiest and most effective method of layering a wide variety of woody plants, and it is a technique that can be carried out with minimum disturbance to the parent plant.

A stem is buried in the soil behind its tip so that roots are induced in this area. Once the root system is established, the stem can be severed from the parent. The roots are encouraged to develop because the plant foods and hormones are restricted where the stem is buried. To be successful, the gardener must use stems that have a high capacity to produce roots, and they should also be near ground level.

Twelve or more months before layering, rigorously prune a low branch or branches on the parent plant so that young, rapidly grown shoots are produced. These will be more amenable to the bending and manipulation involved in the actual layering operation, and because of their rapid growth will have the required capacity to produce roots.

Layering is normally done in late winter/early spring, as soon as the soil can be worked down to a tilth.

As the technique is likely to be carried out in the garden and not in a purpose-prepared nursery bed, it is important to prepare the soil both thoroughly and effectively. Dig as deeply as possible. Then add peat and grit in sufficient quantities to convert the existing soil into a rooting medium with good water-holding capacity, good aeration and adequate drainage.

Trim a rapidly grown stem of side-shoots and leaves for about 4–24 in behind the tip. Pull the stem to ground level and mark its position on the soil 9 in behind its tip. Dig a trench from that point, with one straight side about 4–6 in deep and the other sloping up to ground level near the parent plant.

The secret of inducing root formation is to restrict movement of food and hormones in the tissues of the stem: this is usually achieved by bending the stem at least at a right angle. However, in plants that are particularly difficult to root, the stem should first be girdled by cutting into the stem with a knife or by binding the stem tightly with a piece of copper wire at the bend.

Bend the stem at right angles 9 in behind its tip and set it in the trench against the straight side with its tip exposed above the trench. If the stem is whippy, peg it down with heavy wire staples. Bury the stem with soil, firm in and water well.

Keep the soil reasonably moist, especially in dry periods. Rooting will normally occur during the growing season.

In autumn, sever the layered stem from the parent plant so that the new plant can accustom itself to an independent existence.

About three to four weeks later, cut off the growing tip to encourage the roots to establish. Pot up or plant out the layer and label it. If rooting is not well advanced by autumn, leave the layer to establish for a further year before lifting and transplanting it.

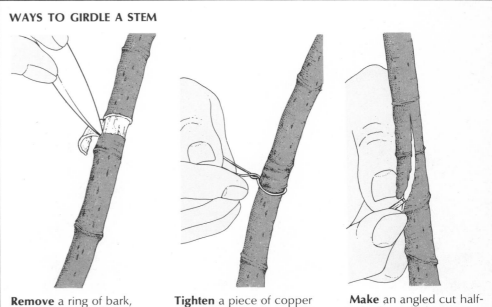

WAYS TO GIRDLE A STEM

Remove a ring of bark, about $\frac{1}{3}$ in wide, from round the stem, using a sharp knife.

Tighten a piece of copper wire round the stem. Twist it finger tight.

Make an angled cut halfway through the stem. Keep the cut surfaces apart with a match.

Simple layering 2

1 Prune some low branches off the parent plant during the dormant season to induce vigorous growth.

2 Cultivate the soil well round the plant during the following late winter/early spring. Add peat and grit.

3 Trim the leaves and side-shoots off a young, vigorous stem for about 4–24 in behind the growing tip.

4 Bring the stem down to ground level and mark its position on the soil 9 in behind its tip.

5 Dig a trench from that point. Make one straight side 4–6 in deep. Slope the other toward the plant.

6 Bend the stem at right angles 9 in behind its tip. Peg it down in the trench against the straight side.

7 Return the soil to the trench to bury the stem. Firm it in well.

8 Water well, using a watering can with a coarse rose. Keep the soil moist, especially in dry periods.

9 Sever the layered stem from its parent plant in autumn.

10 Cut off the growing tip from the rooted layer about three to four weeks later.

11 Lift the layered stem if its roots are well advanced. Otherwise, leave for a further year.

12 Replant either in the open ground or in a pot and label. Leave to establish.

Tip layering

Some plants responding to tip layering
Blackberry
Boysenberry
Loganberry

Rubus phoenicolasius
(Japanese wineberry)
R. thyrsoideus 'Plenus'
R. ulmifolius bellidiflorus
Veitch berry

Tip layering is a specialized technique used for the various members of the genus *Rubus*, such as blackberries and loganberries. If the growing tip of such a plant is buried in the soil, it will naturally swell, develop roots and establish itself. This phenomenon is modified to suit the gardener.

Tip layering is an invaluable technique for propagating a few plants, as it can be carried out in the garden on one part of a plant without disturbing the flowering or fruiting ability of the rest of it.

The members of the genus *Rubus*, especially the fruiting varieties, are prone to virus infections, and they should be propagated only from known virus-free stocks.

Select a new strong stem as it develops from the crown of the plant during the spring. As soon as it reaches 15–18 in long, pinch out the tip to encourage branching. The growth of these stems is rapid and vigorous, and soon the stems can be pinched out again. Continue to do this until midsummer, when about six to eight tips should be well developed.

It is at this stage that the stems can be layered. However, as the roots of these particular plants are fine, fibrous and easily damaged, the soil for layering should be well prepared so that once the layers have rooted they can be lifted with minimum damage to their root system.

Dig and cultivate the soil thoroughly, if possible dig in a deep layer of organic matter to conserve moisture and prevent the roots drying. Improve the top 6 in by adding some peat and grit.

Pull down a stem and make a mark where its tip touches the ground. Start digging a trench at this spot, making it 4 in deep. Give it smoothed vertical sides except for one which should be sloped toward the parent plant. Smoothed vertical sides will help any shoots to grow vertically and so produce a manageable plant.

Place the tip in the deepest part of the trench and pin it down with a heavy wire staple. Replace the soil, firm and water.

In about three weeks, shoots should appear above ground level.

In September cut back the original stem at the crown of the parent plant, so that the layer can establish as an independent plant.

Cut off the rest of the original stem and shorten the growing tip before lifting the rooted layer in autumn after leaf fall. Replant the layer immediately and label it.

Protect any layers that cannot be replanted straight away by wrapping their roots in damp newspaper, which is then placed in a plastic bag. Close the bag and tie the neck tightly so the roots will not dry out.

Propagation by tip layering in this way can be repeated each year.

1 Pinch out the tip of a 15–18 in basal shoot of the current year's growth.

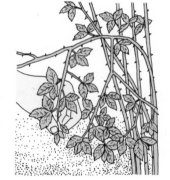

2 Continue to pinch out the tips until six to eight tips have developed.

3 Cultivate the soil well. Add peat and grit to the top 6 in of the soil.

4 Pull down a stem. Dig a trench 4 in deep where its tip touches the ground.

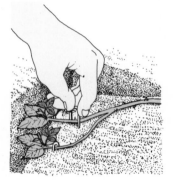

5 Place the tip in the deepest part of the trench. Pin it down with a staple.

6 Replace the soil, firm and water, using a can with a coarse rose.

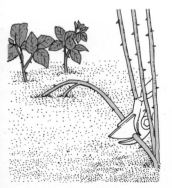

7 Cut back the original stem at the crown of the parent plant in September.

8 Cut off the rest of the stem once the rooted layer has dropped its leaves.

9 Shorten some of the top growth that the layer may have made.

10 Lift the layer very carefully to avoid damaging its fine, fibrous roots.

11 Plant the rooted layer at once in well-cultivated soil. Label it clearly.

12 Place layers that cannot be planted at once in damp newspaper in a plastic bag.

Making a stem cutting 1

Some plants suitable for propagation by leaf bud cuttings
Aphelandra
Camellia
Clematis

Ficus elastica (rubber tree)
Haberlea
Ivy
Mahonia
Ramonda
Vine

Leaf bud cuttings

Leaf bud cuttings can be taken from any type of stem—soft wood, green wood, semiripe wood, hard wood or evergreen. Each cutting consists of a leaf, a bud in its leaf axil and a very short piece of stem. The leaf supplies food to support the cutting and the regenerative processes; the bud provides the basis for the new stem system; and the piece of stem is where the first roots are produced.

To be successful, the gardener must use stems that have a high capacity to produce roots. Therefore, prune the parent plant rigorously should it be a woody plant. This will encourage new stems, which will grow rapidly and so have a high rooting potential.

For leaf bud cuttings, select one of these new stems with an undamaged leaf that is fully expanded and mature. If the leaf is immature, the cutting will complete leaf growth before it starts producing roots, and this increases the chances of peripheral problems, such as rotting. Also, ensure that there is a viable bud in the leaf axil. (For example, some virginia creepers do not have a bud in every leaf axil.)

Make the cuttings with a razor blade, knife or shears, depending on the hardness of the stem. Cut close above the bud so that as small a snag as possible is left. This minimizes the likelihood of rotting and die-back, which might endanger the bud.

Make the basal cut about 1–1½ in below the top cut so that sufficient stem is available to anchor the cutting firmly in the cuttings compost. This is especially important with plants that have big leaves and are liable to rot.

Plants with big leaves are also difficult to plant at a realistic spacing, so reduce their leaf area either by removing some of the leaf or by rolling the leaf and placing a rubber band round it so that it takes up less room. Dip the cutting in a rooting hormone.

In a pot filled with cuttings compost make a hole with a dibble. Plant the cutting with its bud about level with the compost surface. Firm sufficiently to prevent rocking. Label and water in with a fungicide. Place hardy cuttings in a cold frame and less hardy cuttings in a well-lit, more protected environment, such as a mist unit or closed case.

DOUBLE LEAF BUDS

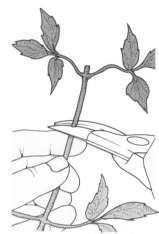  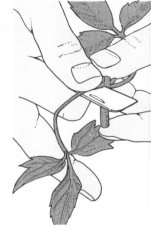

1 Cut a stem with leaves that grow opposite each other just above a bud and again 1–1½ in below it.

2 Split the stem down the middle, using a sharp knife, to make two cuttings.

OR Remove one leaf. Dip the cutting in a rooting hormone. Then plant and label clearly.

Leaf bud cuttings

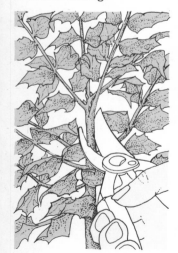   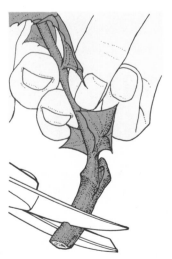  

1 Prune the parent plant, if suitable, to encourage new stems with a high rooting potential.

2 Select a new stem with an undamaged mature leaf and a viable bud in its axil, later in the season.

3 Make an angled cut just above the bud.

4 Make a straight cut 1–1½ in below the top cut.

5 Roll up or cut a large leaf. Dip the leaf bud cutting in a rooting hormone.

6 Plant in a pot with its bud about level with the compost surface. Firm well. Then water in a fungicide.

Making a stem cutting 2

Heel cuttings

The taking of heel cuttings is a traditional way to propagate plants from stem cuttings. It is a widely used method of removing a stem cutting from a plant, and it is quite possible to make heel cuttings of softwood, greenwood, semiripe, hardwood or evergreen stems.

A young side-shoot is stripped away from its parent stem so that a heel, that is a thin sliver of bark and wood from the old stem, also comes away at the base of the cutting.

The reason for taking a stem cutting with a heel is to give the cutting a firm base so that it is well protected against possible rots. It also exposes the swollen base of the current season's growth, which has a very high capacity to produce roots.

Heel cuttings are often used for stem cuttings that take some time to develop roots, for example those that are planted in autumn and have to survive through the winter before rooting, or those hardwood cuttings that are planted in a cold frame. Heel cuttings are also made from softwood and greenwood stems that are left to develop in partially controlled environments, such as a propagator. Heel cuttings can be taken at any time of year.

Hold the bottom of the side-shoot between the thumb and forefinger and pull down sharply so it comes away with a long tail.

If the side-shoot does not pull off readily, place a knife blade in the angle close against the parent stem and cut away the side-shoot with a heel.

Trim the tail on the heel and any leaves near it. Remove some of the tip on semiripe and hardwood cuttings. Dip the cutting in a rooting hormone.

Plant hardwood cuttings straight into the ground; semiripe and subshrub cuttings in a cold frame; and less hardy cuttings in the protected environment of a propagator. Label and water them in with a fungicide.

Mallet cuttings

Mallet cuttings have a hardwood plug at the base of each cutting to guard against rotting organisms. Their use is restricted to semiripe and hardwood cuttings, and they are especially successful for many *Berberis* when propagated in the autumn and planted in cold frames.

Mallet cuttings are most successfully made from stems with a feathered habit, that is from a stem with small side-shoots.

Prune back the parent plant in winter to encourage vigorous stem growth, which has a high capacity to produce roots.

Take mallet cuttings from these new stems in the later part of the growing season. Cut horizontally with scissor-type shears across the parent stem immediately above a suitable side-shoot. It is important to make this top cut as close to the side-shoot as possible because the longer the snag the greater the likelihood of die-back and hence potential rotting.

Make a further horizontal cut about $\frac{3}{4}$ in below the top cut so that the side-shoot is isolated with a small "mallet" of parent stem. Split this piece of mallet with a knife if it is thick. Trim any leaves at the bottom.

Dip the base of the mallet stem in a rooting hormone. Make a hole large enough to take all the mallet and part of the side-shoot with a dibble. Plant semiripe cuttings in a cold frame and hardwood cuttings in the open ground. Label and water with a fungicide.

Heel cuttings

1 Hold the bottom of a side-shoot between the thumb and forefinger. Pull down sharply.

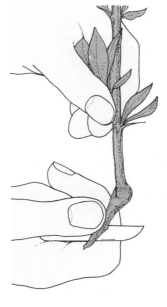

2 Neaten the long tail on the heel and any leaves near it. Dip the basal cut in a rooting hormone.

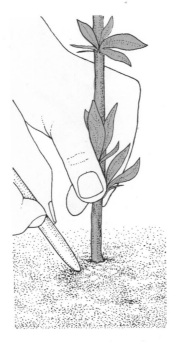

3 Make a hole in the soil or compost. Plant the cutting. Label it and water with a fungicide.

Mallet cuttings

1 Cut horizontally with shears across the parent stem just above a side-shoot.

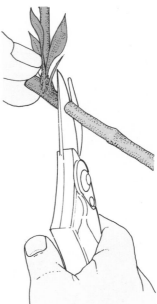

2 Make a basal cut about $\frac{3}{4}$ in below the first cut. Remove any leaves at the bottom.

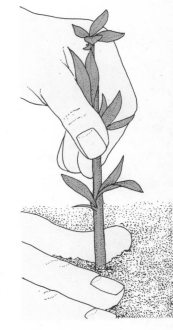

3 Dip the basal cut in a rooting hormone. Plant the cutting and label it. Water with a fungicide.

Soft woods 1

Soft wood is the most immature part of a stem, and, when propagating, it is the most difficult kind of cutting to keep alive. However, soft wood does have the highest capacity of all kinds of stems to produce roots: the younger and the more immature the cutting, the greater will be its ability to develop roots, and so propagate successfully.

Soft stem growth is produced continuously at the tip of any stem during the growing season. As it matures, the stem gradually hardens and becomes woody. The faster the growth at the tip, the more stem without wood will be present.

Softwood cuttings, then, are taken in spring from the fast-growing tips of plants. Growth when the buds first break is remarkably rapid, and, if cuttings are made as soon as there is sufficient growth, the highest rooting potential will be available. Tips of plants taken slightly ·later in the season, around the beginning of June, will be slower growing, more mature and have a lower capacity to root, and they are referred to as greenwood cuttings.

It is possible to obtain softwood cuttings later in the season by forcing the plant, that is by increasing temperatures well above the norm, which will accelerate growth. This can be done, for example, by placing deciduous outdoor plants in the warmth of a greenhouse, or by placing houseplants in a temperature of about 29°C/85°F. The very highest capacity to produce roots can be achieved by pruning the parent plant vigorously in winter, which will encourage rapid growth; by increasing the temperature around the plant in spring; and by then taking the cutting as soon as sufficient tip growth is available.

Softwood cuttings are extremely susceptible to water loss. Their immature leaves have not fully expanded and so have not completely developed their own mechanisms for reducing water loss. Even a relatively minor water loss will hinder the roots developing. By the time a cutting is wilting all root development will have ceased.

The secret of success is to collect the cuttings in small batches and to maintain them in a fully turgid condition before planting them.

Fill a container with cuttings compost and firm to within $\frac{3}{8}$ in of the rim.

Take a cutting in early morning when the stem is fully turgid. By midafternoon normal water loss from the plant will exceed uptake, and the plant will be under water stress.

If the stem has grown less than 4 in since bud-break, remove it with a heel, that is with the swollen portion at the base of the stem that had the very fastest growth when the new stem started to develop at bud-break.

Place the cutting in a polyethylene bag or a bucket of water immediately. Keep the polyethylene bag shaded to avoid "cooking" the cutting—a major cause of failure.

Plant the cutting as soon as possible. If it cannot be dealt with quickly, keep it cool in the vegetable compartment of a domestic refrigerator, where the low temperature will prevent excessive water loss.

1 Prune woody plants hard in winter to promote stems with a high capacity to produce roots.

2 Fill a container with cuttings compost. Firm to within $\frac{3}{8}$ in of the rim.

3 Cut the fast-growing tip off a stem in the early morning in spring.

4 Place the cutting at once in the shade in a polyethylene bag or a bucket of water.

5 Cut the base of the stem $\frac{1}{8}$ in below a leaf joint if the cutting is more than 4 in long.

OR Trim the tail if the cutting was taken with a heel.

Soft woods 2

If there is more than 4 in between the tip and the base of the cutting, place the cutting on a sheet of glass and make a nodal cut—that is a cut at the base of the stem just ($\frac{1}{8}$ in) below a bud or leaf joint. This provides as hard and solid a surface as possible and will help prevent rotting.

If the cutting was taken with a heel, neaten the tail that will also have come away with the stem.

Remove the leaves on the bottom third of the cutting, which will be reliant on the remaining leaves to produce sufficient food to keep it alive until its roots are fully established.

Dip the base of the cutting in a powder fungicide such as Captan to protect it against rotting. Softwood cuttings do not need to be treated with a rooting hormone, but the "softwood" strength (0.2 percent IBA) can be mixed in with the powder fungicide if desired.

Make a hole with a dibble and plant the cutting up to its leaves in the compost, taking care not to damage the base of the cutting. Plant cuttings so their leaves do not touch. Label and firm them in by watering from above the compost, using a watering can with a fine rose; pressing by hand may damage the cuttings.

Place the cuttings as quickly as possible in a well-lit propagating environment such as a mist unit, a closed case or a polyethylene tent that will conserve moisture within the cuttings.

The advantage of a mist unit is that it keeps the top of the cuttings cool, whereas air temperatures are high in a closed case or polyethylene tent. A high aerial temperature will force the cuttings to grow upward, and food will be diverted from the important function of root initiation. If the cuttings are shaded to reduce the aerial temperature, then the light intensity penetrating to the leaves of the cuttings is decreased, and this reduces food production and hence the rate of regeneration.

The problem then becomes a vicious circle that is not easy to resolve without a mist unit, which maintains both a cool, aerial environment and high water status within the cuttings.

Softwood cuttings, because they are the immature part of a plant, are susceptible to all the vagaries of their environment: so the longer they take to root, the greater are the chances of them succumbing to some outside influence. Thus the speed with which they regenerate is vital. The rate of root production will be dependent on the temperature surrounding the base of the cuttings; in general, the higher the temperature, the faster the roots are produced. Best rooting will occur with a temperature around the base of the cuttings of 21–24°C/70–75°F.

Spray softwood cuttings with a liquid fungicide at least once a week to protect them against rotting and disease.

Harden off the cuttings once they have rooted successfully, gradually weaning them from their controlled environment; finally pot them up in John Innes No. 1 compost or similar (see page 174) and label.

6 Remove the leaves off the bottom third of the cutting. Dip the basal cut in a powder fungicide.

7 Make a hole with a dibble in the compost. Insert the cutting up to its leaves. Plant any more cuttings.

8 Label the cuttings clearly. Water from above the compost. Place in a well-lit protected area.

9 Spray the cuttings with a dilute solution of liquid fungicide at least once a week.

10 Harden off the cuttings gradually when they have rooted.

11 Pot them in John Innes No. 1 compost once they are weaned and label.

Green woods

Some plants suitable for propagation by greenwood cuttings
Berry fruits
Ceanothus

Chrysanthemum
Delphinium
Forsythia
Geranium
Gooseberry

Philadelphus
Vines—fruiting and ornamental

The essential but subtle distinction between softwood cuttings and greenwood cuttings is their speed of growth. Externally they may appear to be very similar, but greenwood cuttings are taken from the soft tip of the stem after the spring flush of growth has slowed down. The stem is, then, slightly harder and woodier than for softwood cuttings because the tip is not growing away from the hardening stem so fast as it was in the spring. In fact, as the season progresses greenwood cuttings become harder and harder. However, it should be emphasized that greenwood cuttings require just as much environmental control as softwood cuttings.

Use greenwood cuttings to propagate a wide range of trees and shrubs, such as gooseberries, that will root easily, and the majority of herbaceous plants, such as chrysanthemums. However, plants that are difficult to root should be propagated from softwood cuttings and not from greenwood cuttings, which have a slightly reduced ability to develop roots.

Prune back woody plants rigorously in winter to encourage rapidly grown stems with a high capacity to root, which can be used for propagation in the growing season.

Take cuttings from these stems once their growth rate has begun to decline, which will usually be about the beginning of June for most outdoor plants.

Fill a container with cuttings compost and firm to within $\frac{3}{8}$ in of the rim.

Take a cutting from a fully turgid stem with all its current season's growth, early in the morning. Place the cutting immediately in a bucket of water or a polyethylene bag in a shaded position, because it is vitally important to maintain the turgidity of a greenwood cutting. If it suffers water loss, its rooting will be hindered.

Place the cutting on a pane of glass and with a knife reduce the cutting to about 3–4 in. The cutting's length will very much depend on the amount of soft growth available. Discard the leaves from the bottom half of the cutting. Dip the base of the cutting in a rooting hormone powder of "softwood" strength (0.2 percent IBA).

Make a hole in the compost and plant the cutting up to the leaves. Label it and water with a fungicide. Place in a closed case, mist unit or polyethylene tent, to prevent excessive water loss and wilting. Ensure the cutting receives adequate light to make the food

needed for root production, as the cutting has little or no food reserves.

Rooting should take between three and eight weeks. Take the rooted cutting out of the propagating environment but keep it well protected, gradually hardening it off. Then repot in John Innes No. 1 compost or similar (see page 174), and label clearly.

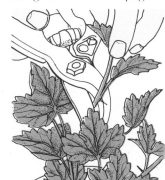

1 Prune woody plants in winter to encourage strong, vigorous stems with a high capacity to root.

2 Fill a container with cuttings compost. Cut off all of a vigorous stem early in the morning.

3 Place the cutting at once in a bucket of water in the shade.

4 Place the cutting on a pane of glass. Reduce to about 3–4 in, using a sharp knife.

5 Trim the leaves from the bottom half of the cutting, slicing them flush with the stem with a sharp knife.

6 Dip the base of the cutting in rooting hormone.

7 Make a hole with a dibble in the compost. Insert the cutting up to its leaves. Label the container.

8 Water with fungicide. Place in an environment that will control water loss and give shaded light.

9 Harden off the rooted cutting. Repot and label as soon as it has established.

Semiripe woods

Some plants that can be propagated from semiripe cuttings

Currant, flowering
Deutzia
Diervilla
Dogwood, colored-bark
Forsythia
Philadelphus
Plum, colored-leaf
Weigela

During the late summer, annual stem growth slows down and plant stems become harder. Cuttings taken at this time are called semiripe cuttings. As they are thicker and harder than softwood cuttings, they are more capable of survival. However they are still susceptible to the same problems of water loss because the cuttings carry leaves.

Semiripe cuttings have relatively high levels of stored food and can therefore survive and produce roots in poor light.

Many deciduous plants, such as deutzias, that root fairly easily are propagated from semiripe cuttings, and some evergreen plants can also be increased in this way.

Prune the parent plant at the start of the dormant season, so that strong, fast-grown stems are available for propagation the following season. These will have a greater ability to produce roots than unpruned stems.

Prepare the soil in the cold frame by digging deeply. Add peat and grit to improve drainage and its water-holding capacity. Cover the surface with a 1 in layer of fine (builder's) sand to make a better rooting medium. If only a few cuttings are to be taken, fill a container with cuttings compost and cover with a 1 in layer of fine sand.

Take semiripe cuttings from a main stem with all the current season's growth or from side-shoots if the main stem has feathered growth, that is a series of small side-shoots growing on the main stem.

Remove the tip of the stem if it is soft, but leave it if the apical bud has set and growth has ceased for the year. Shorten the cutting with shears to 4–6 in long, depending on the vigor of the particular plant.

Cut off the lower leaves flush with the stem so that about 2 in of stem is clear at the base.

Treat the basal cut surface with a rooting hormone powder. The strength for semiripe cuttings is 0.4 percent IBA.

Make a hole with a dibble in the soil in a cold frame. Plant the cutting about $1\frac{1}{2}$ in deep, so its base just enters the soil below the sand layer. Space the cuttings as close as is feasible, but this is not likely to be much less than 3–4 in apart. Label them clearly.

Water in the cuttings using a dilute fungicidal solution; this also firms the sand around the cutting. Close the frame tightly and shade it to prevent the leaves from scorching. Air the cold frame from the lower end if the temperature rises above 27°C/80°F. Water sufficiently to rewet and develop high humidity should conditions become dry.

As semiripe cuttings are usually deciduous, they will drop their leaves in autumn. At this stage remove all the fallen leaves from the frame so that they do not rot and cause disease.

Insulate the frame with matting once the leaves have fallen to protect the cuttings against frost in winter. Once the cuttings have no leaves, light is not necessary for the plants to manufacture food and so the matting can be left in place all the time.

Rooting may start fairly quickly if the weather is mild; otherwise it will occur during the late winter or spring.

Leave the rooted cuttings *in situ* during the following growing season. Feed them regularly with a liquid fertilizer and water when dry. Remove insulation and air the cold frame by raising its lid during the day as soon as the danger of frost is over. Eventually remove it altogether. Lift the new plants and transplant them after leaf fall in the autumn. Label the new plants clearly.

1 Prune the parent plant at the start of the dormant season to encourage strong stems to grow.

2 Prepare the soil in the cold frame by digging deeply. Add peat and grit. Cover with 1 in fine sand.

3 Cut off a shoot with all its current season's growth in late summer. Remove the tip only if it is soft.

4 Shorten the cutting to 4–6 in. Cut the leaves off the bottom 2 in of the stem.

5 Treat the basal cut surface with some rooting hormone. Dibble in a cutting $1\frac{1}{2}$ in deep.

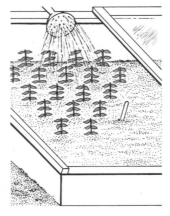

6 Plant the remaining cuttings 3–4 in apart. Label and water with a fungicide. Seal and shade the frame.

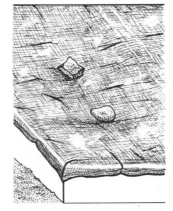

7 Rewet the soil if it dries. Remove any fallen leaves. Insulate the cold frame with matting.

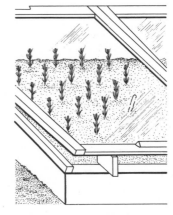

8 Remove the insulation and air the frame once the danger of frost is over. Apply a routine liquid feed.

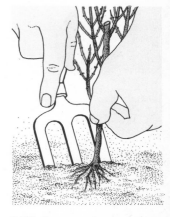

9 Lift the new plants and transplant them once their leaves have dropped in autumn. Label them clearly.

Leaf petiole cuttings

Some plants responding to propagation by leaf petiole cuttings
Begonias—other than
  Begonia rex
Peperomia caperata
P. metallica
Saintpaulia

The simplest and most reliable way to produce new plants from leaf cuttings is to use a complete leaf with its stalk. The disadvantage of this method is that it develops only a few new plants from each leaf.

Rotting and disease are the main causes of failure so always use clean tools, containers and composts.

Leaf petiole cuttings can be taken at any time of year provided a new, fully expanded leaf is available.

Make up a cuttings compost of equal parts sifted peat and grit. Fill a container that is large enough to take the leaf petiole cuttings. Firm the compost to within ⅜ in of the rim of the container.

Slice a suitable leaf cleanly through the leaf stalk, using a sharp knife or a single-edged razor blade to ensure the least possible damage. Leave about 2 in of the leaf stalk attached to the leaf blade.

Make a small hole with a dibble in the compost to a depth just sufficient to hold the cutting. Plant at a shallow angle so that the leaf blade is almost flat on the compost. The shallower the base of the stalk is planted into

the compost the more the air can circulate around it, which will encourage a quick response. Then firm the compost around the stalk. When the cuttings are all planted, label them and water in a dilute fungicide such as Captan or Benlate, using a fine rose.

Place the cuttings in an environment that maintains a steady high humidity, so that the cuttings do not dry out. The temperature, especially for houseplants, needs to be relatively high, and this is best provided by using a propagator that is heated at the bottom—ideally at about 20°C/68°F.

Expose the cuttings to sufficient light for them to manufacture food and develop the new plantlets. Too much sunlight may scorch the cuttings. In general, light shade is the best compromise.

The new plantlets will develop on the cut surface of the leaf stalk within five to six weeks, and several may appear at this point. Leave them until they can be handled and separated into individual plants, potted on and hardened off. If it is likely to be some time before they are large enough to be potted on, then liquid feed the plantlets.

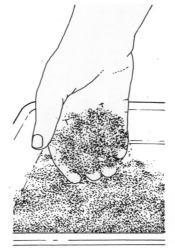

1 Fill a container with equal parts sifted peat and grit.

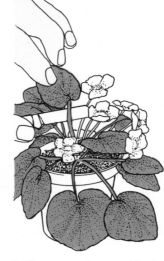

2 Slice an undamaged leaf that has recently expanded fully away from the plant.

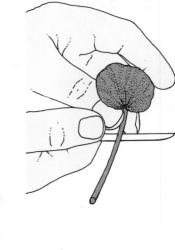

3 Cut through the leaf stalk about 2 in from blade, using a sharp knife.

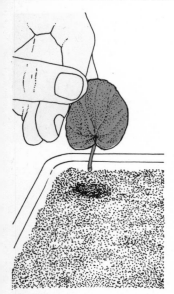

4 Make a shallow hole and insert the cutting at the angle shown.

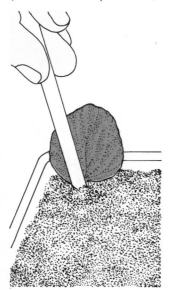

5 Firm the compost gently round the cutting. Plant the remaining cuttings.

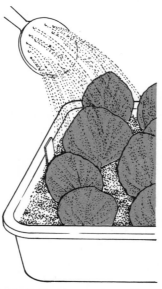

6 Label and water in a dilute fungicide such as Captan, using a fine rose.

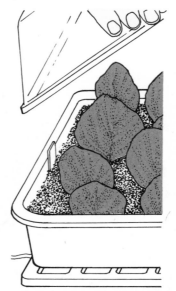

7 Place the cuttings in light shade in a propagator that is heated from below.

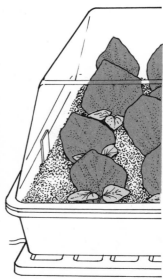

8 Apply a liquid feed once the new plantlets have started developing.

9 Pot on the plantlets once they can be handled. Label and harden them off.

Foliar embryos

Some plants that develop
foliar embryos naturally
Asplenium
Cystopteris
Mitella
Tolmiea menziesii
  (piggyback plant)

Some plants that require
leaf separation for
stimulation of plantlet
development
Cardamine
Kalanchoe
Sedum
Tiarella

A few plants are capable of developing isolated groups of simple cells in certain areas of their leaves. As a result these cells, or foliar embryos, are capable of developing into new plantlets. Given certain growing conditions some of these plants, such as *Mitella*, have foliar embryos that develop naturally into plantlets. Other plants such as *Cardamine* will only respond in this way if the leaves are separated from the parent plant.

The position on the leaf of these embryos is fixed according to each plant's characteristic and it is not influenced by the way the actual plantlets develop. The plantlets in *Kalanchoe* leaves, for example, arise between the jagged edges of the leaves; in *Mitella* and *Cardamine*, the plantlets appear at the junction of the leaf stalk and leaf blade. *Sedum*, however, produces only one plantlet and this is at the base of each sessile leaf.

Collect the plantlets from those plants that produce them naturally. With some of these plants, such as *Kalanchoe*, the plantlets fall off once the roots begin to develop. Plant them in cuttings compost in a labeled seed tray. Repot them separately once they have established properly.

Although other plants such as *Asplenium* and *Cystoperis* develop foliar embryos naturally, it is best to remove the leaf together with the plantlets to allow them slightly longer to become established before separating them from the parent leaf. Place the leaf flat on some cuttings compost in a seed tray. Pin it in position with a light wire staple if it does not sit flat on the compost. Label and leave on a shaded greenhouse bench. Ensure that the parent leaf does not become desiccated. Separate the plantlets and pot on once they have rooted and established. This should take seven to eight weeks.

Some plants, such as *Tiarella*, will only be stimulated into developing plantlets from foliar embryos if their leaves are severed. Cut off a leaf as soon as it has expanded fully. Set it on some cuttings compost in a seed tray. Label; then place in a warm (21°C/70°F), humid, shady environment such as a polyethylene tent until the plantlets develop and establish (five to seven weeks); then separate and pot on. Succulents, such as *Sedum* and *Kalanchoe*, can be left on an open bench in a greenhouse to develop their plantlets. Certain *Kalanchoe* respond best if the leaves are stimulated in spring to produce plantlets.

Establishing naturally produced plantlets

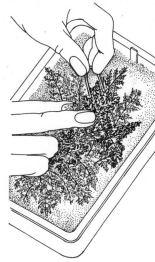  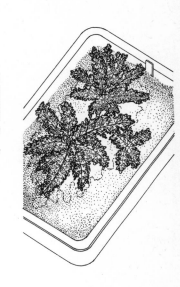

1 Cut off a leaf together with its plantlets. Fill a container with some cuttings compost and firm.

2 Pin the leaf flat on the compost with a wire staple. Label and place on a shaded greenhouse bench.

3 Ensure the leaf does not dry out. Separate the new plantlets and pot on once they are rooted.

Stimulating plantlet development

1 Cut off a leaf as soon as it has expanded fully. Fill a container with some cuttings compost.

2 Set the leaf on the compost. Label. Place in a warm (21°C/70°F), humid, shaded environment.

3 Leave until the plantlets develop and establish. Then separate, pot on and label.

WHERE FOLIAR EMBRYOS CAN DEVELOP

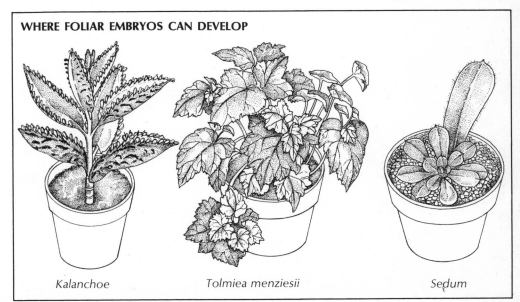

Kalanchoe   *Tolmiea menziesii*   *Sedum*

Grafting/Whip-and-tongue 1

Grafting is a technique of joining two parts of different plants together in such a way that they will unite and continue their growth as one plant.

One part, called the scion, is usually a stem from the plant to be propagated. This is grafted onto a root system from another plant, which is called the rootstock (also, the stock or understock). All the various techniques of joining plants are called grafting, although, when buds only are joined to the rootstock, it is sometimes called budding.

There are two basic grafting positions: apical grafting, in which the top of the rootstock is removed and is replaced with the scion; and side grafting, in which the scion is grafted on to the side of the rootstock and the rootstock above the graft is not removed until after a union is achieved.

Because time-consuming preparation work is necessary before two plants can be joined, grafting is superficially a less attractive technique than other relatively easy methods of vegetative propagation, such as taking stem cuttings or layering. However, some plants such as witch hazel are not easily propagated by any other vegetative method if selected forms are required, and so they are grafted onto rootstocks.

Perhaps the most useful reason for grafting is to transfer the benefits of a particular rootstock on to another plant. Various fruit-tree rootstocks, for example, have been developed to control both the size and fruiting vigor of other varieties of fruit tree. Other advantages that a rootstock might possess are resistance to pests and diseases; toleration of high soil-moisture levels and salt concentrations; and toleration of high alkalinity levels in the soil. The more rootstock incorporated into a new plant, the more influence the rootstock will have.

Another advantage of grafting is that more than one scion can be joined onto a plant. This is particularly useful with fruit trees as a suitable pollinator variety can be grafted into a tree or bush already grafted with another variety, or it may allow a decorative stem to be grafted on and then be top worked with another variety.

There are a number of problems associated with grafting. The main one is ensuring two plants are compatible. This limitation determines which variety and species of plants can be grafted onto which rootstocks; in general, it is normal to graft varieties onto their own species or very closely related ones.

To graft successfully, it is vitally important to position the various tissues of the stem correctly so that the stem can make a quick and continuous union. The cambium is the actively growing part of the stem that lies just under the bark. This cambium layer on both the scion and the rootstock must be positioned so they are absolutely adjacent to each other, or at least in as much contact as possible.

The successful formation of a graft also depends on making and matching cuts quickly and cleanly: the cut surfaces must be placed in contact with the minimum of delay. Should the surfaces dry out, the tissues will die and so make an effective barrier to the development of a successful union.

The making of a graft union is only partly due to successful carpentry. Much also

THE ADVANTAGES POSSESSED BY VARIOUS ROOTSTOCKS

Rootstock	Advantage	Plant
East Malling series (EM)	Controls vigor	Apple
Malling Merton series (MM)	Resists woolly aphids and controls vigor	Apple
Colt, F12/1	Controls vigor	Cherry
East Malling quince	Controls vigor	Pear
Brompton, Pixie, St Julien A	Controls vigor	Plum
Rhododendron 'Cunningham's White'	Tolerates up to pH7	Rhododendron
Rosa chinensis 'Manetti'	Tolerates soil moisture and salt concentration	Roses (pot grown)
Rosa laxa	Does not produce suckers, has few thorns and has long hypocotyl	Roses

Whip-and-tongue grafting

 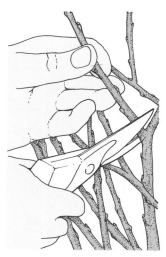  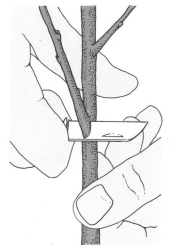 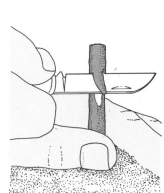 

1 Select a plant that will be suitable as rootstock. Plant it outdoors. Label and leave for a growing season.

2 Select a plant that is suitable as scion material. Cut off some vigorous hardwood stems for scions.

3 Bundle these scions together. Heel them into the ground in a well-drained, cool place. Label.

4 Trim the bottom 12–15 in on the rootstock of all branches just before the leaf buds break.

5 Cut back the rootstock to where the scion is to be grafted. Make a 1½ in sloping cut at the top.

6 Lift the scions from the ground. Make a top cut just above a bud about four buds from the base.

Grafting/Whip-and-tongue 2

depends on providing suitable conditions for the tissues to develop and grow to form a successful union. In effect, this means that water loss must be prevented and warmth must be provided round the grafted parts by carefully covering them until they have joined together.

Traditionally, the grafted parts have been covered and tied together with raffia, but most grafts are now enclosed by ½ in wide clear polyethylene strip. This has the advantage of completely surrounding and sealing the cut areas, so reducing water loss to a minimum. The graft union on indoor grafted plants is taped with rubberized strip before being placed in a humid atmosphere to develop.

Once the grafted parts have successfully united, the development of the new plant depends on preventing any further competition from the rootstock. Therefore, always remove all subsequent growths from anywhere on the rootstock.

Although it is theoretically possible to graft at almost any time of the year, the best season for most grafting is in the spring.

Shield-budding, however, must normally wait until midsummer when the bark lifts easily from the wood on the rootstock.

Whip-and-tongue grafting
Whip-and-tongue grafting is commonly used to propagate fruit trees, although the technique can be employed successfully for trees and shrubs with tissues that will also readily unite at relatively low temperatures.

Select a plant that will be suitable as rootstock and plant it outdoors. Label it and leave it to establish for one growing season.

In midwinter, select a plant that is suitable as scion material. From it take some hardwood stems with all their previous season's growth. Bundle these scions together and heel them into 6 in of soil in a well-drained cool position. Firm back the soil and label them. When the scions are eventually grafted in spring, they will be less developed than the growth on the rootstock.

Prepare the rootstock once its sap has started to rise; this is usually just before the leaf buds break. Trim to make a single stem with no branches.

Fruit trees (especially apples) are grafted at 9–10 in above soil level to avoid problems such as collar rot. Ornamental plants, on the other hand, are grafted as close to the ground as feasible, to avoid unsightly bulges that may occur with certain rootstock/scion combinations.

Cut back the rootstock to the appropriate height with a pair of sharp shears. Then make a 1½ in sloping cut across the top, using a sharp knife.

Lift the scions from the ground. Select one that has a similar diameter at its base to that of the rootstock top. Take a sharp knife and make a top cut close above a bud about four to five buds from the scion base. Then make a sloping 1½ in cut across the base of the scion, ending it just below a bud; ensure the cut is at the same angle as the rootstock cut.

This is a splice or whip graft. To provide rigidity, add a tongue to the cuts.

The tongue is made from single cuts on both the scion and rootstock. From one-third of the way down the sloping cut on top of the rootstock, make a shallow, single ½ in slice down into the rootstock.

Make the scion tongue by cutting for ½ in from one-third of the way up the scion sloping cut, keeping the knife blade at the same angle as the tongue on the rootstock.

Slip the scion into the rootstock so they interlock. If the rootstock is thicker than the scion, move it to one side until there is good contact between the two cambial layers. Bind with clear polyethylene grafting tape to hold the join firmly. Seal the top of the scion with tree paint and label.

For a wide range of trees and shrubs, including apple and pear trees, the grafted parts can then be left to unite. Cherry trees, however, should have their scion and grafted area covered with a polyethylene bag—the increased temperature hastening development.

Remove the grafting tape and polyethylene bag as soon as the cut surfaces start callusing, which means the two grafted parts are beginning to join.

Cut off any growth that the rootstock may produce and, if required, reduce the scion shoots to just one to promote a single-stemmed tree or shrub.

7 Make a 1½ in basal cut at the same angle as the rootstock cut. End it just below the bottom bud.

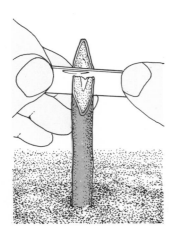

8 Make a shallow, single ½ in slice into the rootstock from one-third down the sloping cut.

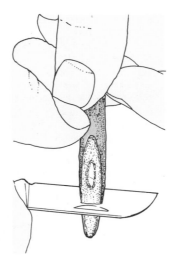

9 Make a shallow, single ½ in slice into the scion from one-third up the scion sloping cut.

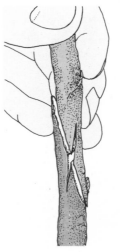

10 Slip the scion into the rootstock so they interlock.

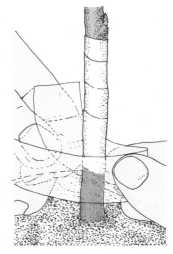

11 Bind the join firmly with clear polyethylene tape. Dab the top of the scion with tree paint. Label.

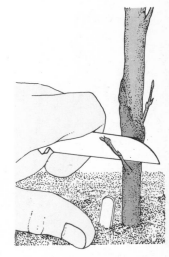

12 Remove the polyethylene tape once the cut surfaces start callusing. Cut off any rootstock growth.

Roses: introduction

Most people grow at least a few roses in their garden or against the walls of their house, but to many gardeners the correct way to prune roses remains a complicated and mysterious process.

In the wild, roses produce strong new shoots from near the base of the plant each season. In the following years the secondary, or lateral, growth from these shoots becomes progressively weaker. When strong new shoots appear, the food taken in by the roots is directed to this new growth and the original shoots are gradually starved out. Eventually the old shoots die and remain as dead wood before falling to the ground—a natural but long-winded method of pruning. The purpose of pruning is to short-circuit nature by cutting away the old worn-out shoots and so encourage the production of vigorous, disease-free new growth and the largest number of flowers for the rose gardener.

Pruning is a simple operation, but because roses range in size from miniatures, which are less than 1ft tall, to vigorous climbers, which may reach 30–40ft, they require a variety of pruning techniques to keep them healthy, flowering, and within control.

Rose "eyes" or growth buds are located in the axils of the leaves. If the leaf has fallen they can be seen just above a leaf scar. Always cut close to a bud.

There are certain general principles that apply to pruning all kinds of roses.

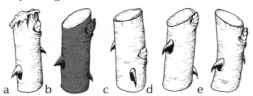

1 Always use sharp shears and a knife; a ragged cut caused by blunt tools may cause the shoot to die back (a). The cut must not be more than $\frac{1}{4}$ in above the eye and must slope gently away from it (b). If you cut too high the snag will die back (c); a cut that is too low may damage the eye or allow disease spores to enter the wound (d). A cut in the wrong direction allows moisture to gather by the eye (e).
2 Cut back into healthy wood. If the pith is brown or discolored cut the shoot back until healthy white pith is reached.

3 Cut to an outward pointing eye to encourage an open-center habit. With roses of spreading habit it is sometimes useful to prune some branches to inward-pointing eyes to obtain more upright growth.

4 Vigorous modern roses often produce two or three shoots from one eye after pruning. As soon as possible reduce these to one shoot by pinching out the young growth. Never allow more than one shoot to grow from a pruning cut.

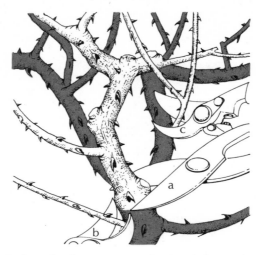

5 Completely cut out any dead and diseased stems (a) and weak, spindly growth (b). This may mean cutting it out to ground level or, with a lateral growth, to the junction with a healthy stem. Where two branches cross, cut one back below the point where they cross (c). With shrub and climbing roses this is not always easy, but wherever possible at least prevent branches rubbing against each other or on their supports.
6 Keep all branches well spaced to allow free air-flow through the plant and to allow light to reach the leaves. This lessens the likelihood of such diseases as black spot, rose mildew and rose-rust, which all thrive under stagnant air conditions.
7 Burn prunings to reduce the possibility of spreading disease.

You may not know to which group the roses in your garden belong, particularly if you moved into your house in late autumn or winter and there are no labels on the plants. If you are not sure how to deal with them, confine your winter pruning to the points made in the section on general principles. Next summer you can see from the way they flower to which group they belong and prune accordingly. Pruning techniques may vary slightly in different conditions, and with experience you will quickly learn how to deal with them to suit your soil and climate.

SUCKERS

Most roses are budded on to the selected rootstock of a wild rose species. During the growing season shoots may arise from below the budding point. These are sucker growths from the rootstock, which can quickly weaken, and eventually replace, the rose variety concerned. They must be removed as soon as they are seen.

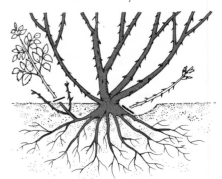

Trace the sucker back to the root from which it springs and pull it off at the point of origin. Never cut it off at ground level; this only encourages basal buds to produce several more suckers.

With standard roses, which are budded at the tops of stems of wild rose rootstocks, shoots may arise from below the budding point on the stem. These are treated as suckers and carefully pulled off, or pared away with a sharp knife.

Time of Pruning

Time of pruning differs to some extent with the group of roses concerned and further details are given in each section.

Winter pruning

Winter pruning is best carried out between mid-February and mid-March, depending on locality, season, and prevailing weather conditions. Earlier pruning from December to January can lead to precocious growth and this is often damaged in severe weather. Later pruning in April often involves wasting the plant's energy by cutting off young growth already produced. The best guide is to prune —weather permitting—when the growth buds about halfway up the most vigorous stems are beginning to swell.

After winter pruning put a good mulch of well-rotted compost or manure around the bases of your roses. Pruning encourages a constant supply of young, vigorous shoots and these will only be produced if sufficient food is available for the new growth.

Frost damage may occur in some seasons, particularly with fluctuating spring weather of warm spells followed by frosty periods. If new shoots are damaged by frost the main shoots must be cut back to dormant eyes.

EXHIBITION PRUNING

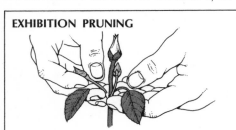

Rose-growers who exhibit at national and local shows aim to provide high-quality blooms for a given date. This involves considerable experience and an intimate knowledge of individual rose varieties. It is not the purpose of this book to attempt to provide a guide for would-be exhibitors. Suffice it to say that it usually involves harder initial winter pruning to limit the number of shoots produced and, for Hybrid Tea roses, disbudding to only one flower per stem.

Summer pruning

Summer pruning is confined to the removal of flowers or flower clusters and is carried out through the flowering season.

Some roses, such as 'Scarlet Fire' and *Rosa*

Hybrid Tea

Correctly cut Hybrid Tea inflorescence
Cut back to a strong outward-facing shoot or eye below the inflorescence.

Floribunda

Correctly cut Floribunda inflorescence
Remove the whole truss by cutting back to the first strong outward-pointing eye or shoot.

moyesii are grown for their autumn display of brightly colored hips as well as their flowers. With these roses the flowers should be left on the bush, but with most roses it is best to remove all flower clusters as soon as they

Incorrectly cut Hybrid Tea inflorescence
The stems are cut too long and will weaken the plant.

Incorrectly cut Floribunda inflorescence
The individual flowers in the truss have been cut off leaving weak stems.

fade. This prevents the plant wasting food on unnecessary seed production, and it removes a possible source of disease—the decaying petals (particularly in wet weather). Removing the roses also encourages fresh growth and bloom in repeat-flowering roses.

Cut back to the first convenient strong eye or young shoot below the flower stem or flower truss. Normally this should be an outward-pointing eye, but occasionally it may be inward-pointing to maintain a well-shaped plant. If only the flower and its stalk are removed weak stem buds just below the inflorescence will grow and produce thin, straggly shoots.

Never cut a flower stem longer than is really required and never take more than one or two long stems from a single bush. Leaves manufacture much of the plant's food so cutting off too many leaves when it is in active growth will weaken the plant.

In late summer the removal of faded flower clusters should be discontinued or kept to a minimum to avoid stimulating further growth shoots, which may be damaged in winter.

BLIND SHOOTS

Some varieties of Hybrid Teas and Floribundas and climbers produce a few shoots that are "blind" and do not flower. These blind shoots should be cut hard back as soon as they are seen, to encourage vigorous growth from buds lower down on the shoot, otherwise the flowering potential of the plant is diminished.

Autumn pruning

In very windy areas it is worth shortening any very long growths by 6–12 in during November. This reduces the risk of damage by windrock to the roots.

Hybrid Teas and Hybrid Perpetuals

Hybrid Teas and Hybrid Perpetuals are pruned in the same way. The aim is to encourage the production of strong basal growths to form an open-centered, cup-shaped plant with an evenly spaced framework of shoots.

Hybrid Teas and Hybrid Perpetuals flower on the new (current) season's growth and most benefit from a moderate to fairly severe annual pruning. This keeps the plants bushy and ensures a constant supply of strong young shoots. Annual pruning is from mid-February to mid- to late March. Some variation will occur depending on local soil conditions and the prevailing weather.

Very vigorous roses, 'Peace' for example, should be pruned only lightly as hard pruning stimulates very robust but often flowerless shoots. Other vigorous cultivars, such as 'Chinatown' and 'Uncle Walter,' produce their flowers on tall, 5–6 ft stems. An alternative method of growing these cultivars is to peg down the stems horizontally. A different pruning technique is required.

The first year

First-year, or newly planted, Hybrid Teas or Hybrid Perpetuals are usually bought in autumn from the nursery with 3–4 strong shoots. Cut back main shoots slightly if not already done, and then prune long, coarse or damaged roots before planting. In late February to mid-March cut back each shoot to 2–4 eyes or 6 in from ground level. This encourages strong basal growths to be produced. If the soil is very sandy and lacking nutrients, more moderate first-year pruning to 4–6 eyes or 9 in is advisable. This first pruning is followed by more severe pruning in the second year.

Second and following years

In the second and following years Hybrid Teas and Hybrid Perpetuals should be moderately pruned. Cut back the strongest (thickest) shoots to 4–6 eyes or 9 in and the less vigorous shoots to 2–4 eyes or 6 in. This method of pruning gives the best all-round results. As the plant becomes older, one or two old stems should be cut out to the base.

The first year

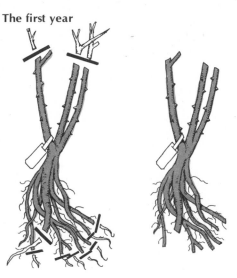

1 Autumn. Open ground bush as received. Cut back the main shoots slightly, if it is not already done. Prune long, coarse or damaged roots before planting.

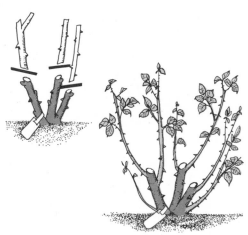

2 Mid-February to mid- to late March. Cut back each shoot to 2–4 eyes or 6 in from ground level. By June or July new shoots will have grown.

3 September to October. At the end of first season's growth, tip back flowered stems and cut out any soft, unripe shoots.

Second and following years

4 Mid-February to mid- to late March. Cut out dead or diseased wood. Cut out weak stems. Cut out crossing stems. Cut out inward-growing stems.

5 At the same time, cut back strong stems to 4–6 eyes or 9 in and less vigorous stems and remaining laterals to 2–4 eyes or 6 in.

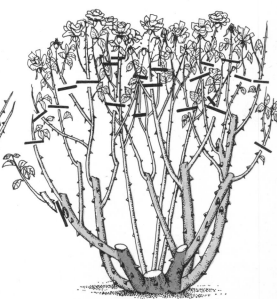

6 September to October. At the end of the season's growth, tip back flowered stems and cut out any soft, unripe shoots.

Floribundas

Floribunda roses are more vigorous than most Hybrid Teas and Hybrid Perpetuals and produce a succession of large clusters of moderate-sized flowers. It is sometimes difficult to prune Floribundas to obtain the optimum number of blooms. Severe annual pruning, as used for Hybrid Teas and Hybrid Perpetuals, can weaken Floribundas within a few years, but light pruning creates large bushes filled with weak, spindly growth.

Moderate pruning of each shoot to 6–8 eyes or 12–18 in is often recommended and proves reasonably successful, particularly in windy areas. It does not, however, always produce the almost continuous summer display which can sometimes be achieved, and some of the older wood tends to die away without replacement basal shoots forming.

A combination of light pruning of some shoots to produce early flowers and harder pruning of other shoots can encourage renewal of basal growths and provide later flowers. This has proved the most satisfactory method. Annual pruning is from mid-February to mid-March, depending on local soil and weather conditions.

The first year
First-year Floribundas are usually received with 3–5 strong shoots and often weak, spindly laterals. Between mid-February and mid-March cut back each strong shoot to 3–5 eyes or 6–9 in and remove all weak shoots.

The second year
In mid-February to mid-March of the second year all the main one-year-old basal, or near-basal, shoots must be shortened by approximately one-third of their length and any remaining laterals should be cut back to 2–3 eyes or 4–6 in. Strong shoots from older wood (pruned back at planting to 3–5 eyes) must be cut back to 3–5 eyes or removed completely to keep the center of the bush open.

Third and subsequent years
In the third and subsequent years this renewal program is continued between mid-February and mid-March. Prune back strong one-year-old shoots lightly by one-third and cut back two-year-old wood to 3–5 eyes or 6–9 in from ground level. If the bush is crowded cut out some old growths to base.

The first year

1 Autumn. Open-ground bush as received. Cut back main shoots slightly if not already done. Prune long, coarse or damaged roots before planting.

2 Mid-February to mid-March. Cut back all growths to 3–5 eyes or 6–9 in from the base. Remove all weak shoots. By April or May new shoots will begin to form.

3 October. Growth at end of first season. Tip back main growths and cut out any soft, unripe shoots.

The second year

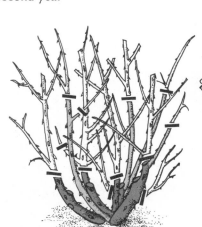 

4 Mid-February to mid-March. Cut out dead or diseased wood, weak stems, crossing and inward-growing stems. Prune back one-year-old basal shoots by one-third. Cut back older wood to 3–5 eyes or 6–9 in and remaining laterals to 2–3 eyes or 4–6 in.

5 October. Growth at end of second season. Tip back main growths and cut out any soft unripe shoots.

Third and following years

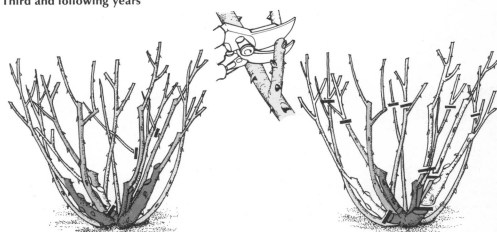

6 Mid-February to mid-March. Cut out dead or diseased wood. Cut out weak stems. Cut out crossing stems. Cut out inward-growing stems.

7 At the same time, prune back all main one-year-old basal shoots by one-third and their laterals to 2–3 eyes or 4–6 in. Prune older wood hard to 3–5 eyes or 6–9 in from ground level and, if the center of the bush is crowded, cut out some old growths to base.

Climbers and Ramblers 1

Climbing and rambling roses either bloom freely in glorious unruly tangles or produce only a few poor-quality flowers. However, with pruning and training they will provide a regular supply of good-quality blooms each year.

For convenience, the ramblers and climbers have been divided into five groups, but these are not rigid divisions and some overlap of pruning techniques occurs.

Wherever sufficient space is available it is always a good idea to train new extension shoots of climbing roses as near to the horizontal as possible. But be sure to provide allowance to create a balanced plant. Vertically placed shoots frequently form on only a few flowering laterals, at the tips. Horizontally placed shoots will produce flowering laterals along most of their length and create a far better display.

The provision for new shoots depends on adequate feeding, particularly in Group 1, where virtually all the old wood is removed annually. To avoid wind breakage and make training into a balanced framework easier, make sure that all new long growths are tied in as they develop.

Group 1 includes the true ramblers, varieties such as 'Dorothy Perkins' and 'Excelsa,' derived from *Rosa wichuraiana*. They flower in June and July on laterals of long, flexible, basal shoots (canes) produced the previous season.

The first year
Prune all vigorous shoots back to 9–15 in from the base at planting and remove completely any weak growth. This hard initial pruning encourages vigorous, balanced growth during the first season, but no flowers are produced until the following year.

Second and following years
Pruning of established plants consists of cutting to the base all the shoots that have bloomed. This should be done soon after flowering, usually between August and September. The developing young basal growths are tied in to replace the old shoots, and the young shoots will produce flowering laterals the following summer. Where the site allows, train most of the new shoots as near to the horizontal as possible to encourage maximum development of flowering laterals.

Sometimes only a few basal growths are produced. if this happens, retain some of the strongest old shoots and cut back their laterals to 2–3 eyes or 4–6 in from the main stem after flowering.

The first year

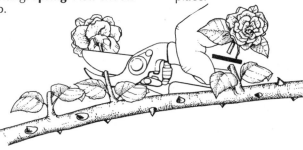

1 Autumn. Plant as received with 3–4 shoots about 4–5 ft long. Prune back shoots to 9–15 in and trim uneven and coarse roots before planting. **Spring.** New shoots begin to develop.

2 June to September. Strong shoots have developed from the pruned growth and from the base of the plant. Train them into place.

Second and following years

3 June to July. Plant flowers on lateral shoots produced on previous year's growth. Young basal shoots develop; train these more or less horizontally and tie in.

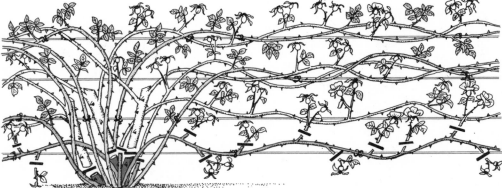

4 August to September. Cut out flowered shoots to base leaving one or two to fill in framework if required. Cut back laterals to 2–3 eyes or 4–6 in. Tie in all new growth.

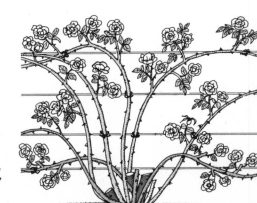

5 October. Shoots fully trained in at end of the second season's growth.

Climbers and Ramblers 2

Group 2 includes many well-known vigorous rose varieties such as 'Albertine' and 'Chaplin's Pink.' They flower once in summer on the laterals of long shoots produced the previous year. They differ from true ramblers in producing very few basal shoots each season, most of the new growth coming from higher up on the old stems. The aim of pruning is to remove old wood in proportion to the new.

The first year
Newly planted varieties in this group are treated in the same way as those in Group 1.

Second, third and following years
Pruning of established plants takes place soon after flowering. Completely cut away one or two old growths and train any basal shoots that have started to develop in their place. If no basal shoots are forming cut back one or two old stems to 12–18 in from base.

Cut back old wood higher up on the plant to a point where a vigorous new leading shoot has started to grow. Keep leading shoots at full length and train them as near to the horizontal as possible. Any shorter laterals should be cut back to 2–3 eyes or 6 in.

The second year

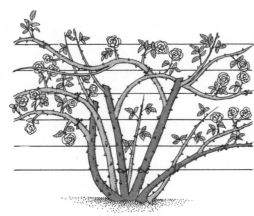

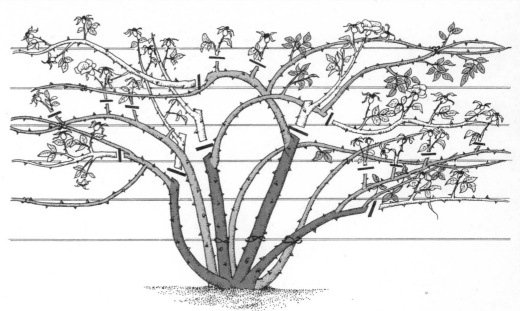

1 June to July. Plant flowers on lateral shoots produced on previous year's growth. Allow one or two basal growths to develop and some leader shoots develop higher up.

2 August to September. Cut back old growth to main replacement leaders. Cut back flowering laterals to 2–3 eyes or 6 in.

Train replacement leaders as near to the horizontal as possible. Cut back weak leaders to 2–3 eyes or 6 in.

Third and following years

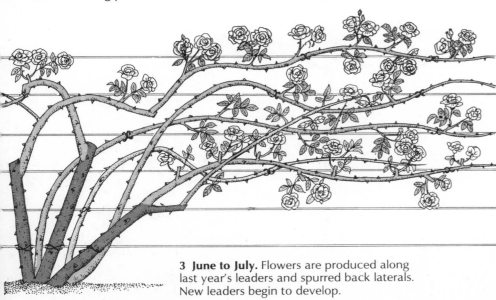

3 June to July. Flowers are produced along last year's leaders and spurred back laterals. New leaders begin to develop.

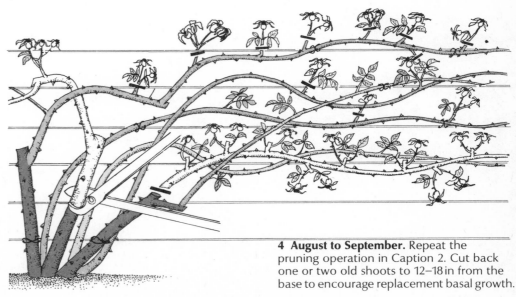

4 August to September. Repeat the pruning operation in Caption 2. Cut back one or two old shoots to 12–18 in from the base to encourage replacement basal growth.

Climbers and Ramblers 3

Group 3 contains the ramblers and climbers that produce their blooms on the current season's growth, and includes climbers of Hybrid Tea style and climbing sports of Hybrid Teas and Floribundas. Most, although by no means all, of the roses in this group are repeat-flowering. Their long, flexible shoots make them ideal for training against walls and fences and on pergolas.

The first year

Newly planted roses in this group should not be pruned back at planting, although the roots should be trimmed and any damaged tips and very weak growth removed. This is because many are climbing sports from bush varieties and hard pruning at planting may cause them to revert to bush form.

It is essential to build up a strong, evenly spaced framework of branches, as roses in this group do not readily produce vigorous basal growths once established, but they develop most of their young shoots higher up on existing main stems. Horizontal or angled training of new leader shoots at an early stage will help to prevent the base of the plant becoming too bare.

Second and following years

Apart from maintaining the plant within its allotted space, pruning and training of mature roses in this group is restricted to summer pruning flowering laterals during the growing season as the flowers fade. Diseased, dead and weak wood should be cut out in late autumn or winter before any growth begins. At the same time train new growths into gaps in the framework and trim all flowered laterals back to 3–4 eyes or 6 in.

With old plants it will occasionally be necessary to cut back weak and exhausted shoots to a few inches from the base. This should encourage one or two vigorous basal shoots to be produced.

The first year

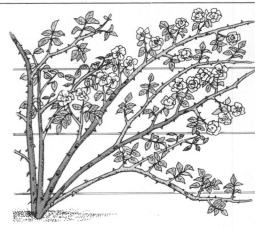

1 Autumn or early spring. Plant as received with 3–4 shoots 4–5 ft long. Trim any uneven and coarse roots. Slightly tip back any unripe or damaged growths. Do not prune except to cut out any weak side shoots. Begin to train shoots.

2 July to August. Tie in framework of new shoots as they develop. Some flowers are produced at the tips of new growths and on laterals. New shoots develop and should be tied in. Summer prune.

Second and following years

3 October to March. Prune back flowered laterals to 3–4 eyes or 6 in. Cut out weak wood and tie in leading shoots.

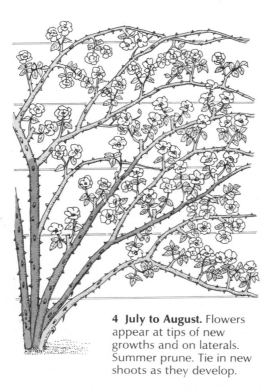

4 July to August. Flowers appear at tips of new growths and on laterals. Summer prune. Tie in new shoots as they develop.

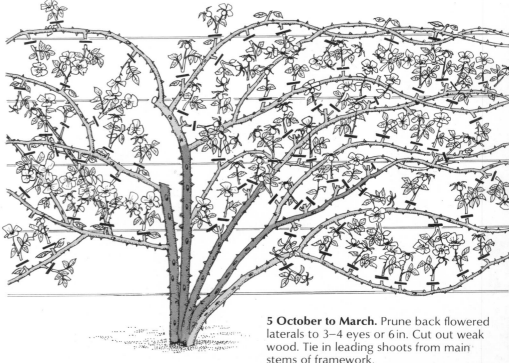

5 October to March. Prune back flowered laterals to 3–4 eyes or 6 in. Cut out weak wood. Tie in leading shoots from main stems of framework.

Climbers and Ramblers 4

Group 4 includes pillar roses, which are repeat-flowering and produce their blooms on the current season's wood. They differ from roses in Group 3 because they are more moderate, usually upright in growth and seldom exceed 8–10 ft in height. Their shoots are generally less flexible than in Group 3 and, as their name indicates, they are suitable for growing against pillars or for training in positions where horizontal space is limited.

The first year

Newly planted varieties in this group are treated in the same way as Group 3. Before planting, trim the roots and remove any damaged tips and weak growth. In view of their naturally upright habit do not train the leader shoots at an angle as in Group 3.

Second and subsequent years

Pruning of mature pillar roses involves routine removal of all flower trusses as they fade in summer. In late autumn or early winter, cut away weak, diseased and dead wood and shorten some leaders and laterals on main growths just enough to maintain a symmetrical shape. To stimulate growth at the base of the plant, cut back the lower leaders by two-thirds of their length. In old plants where growth is crowded, cut out one or two of the oldest stems to ground level.

The degree of trimming differs with the rose variety and the space available. Some of the more vigorous varieties of pillar rose, which have flexible growth, particularly of the lateral shoots, may require more severe restrictions.

VIGOROUS CLIMBERS

Group 5 includes climbing species, or near-species, and hybrids of tremendous vigor. These often produce flexible 20 ft growths each season. These roses are typified by the exuberant *Rosa filipes* 'Kiftsgate' and the Banksian roses. If grown unrestricted in trees it is impractical and quite unnecessary to prune or train them at all, except for the removal of dead, diseased and weak wood where this is possible.

When they become too overwhelming the renovation procedure as illustrated on page 20 should be employed.

Initial planting and training is as for Group 3, but laterals need only very light pruning.

HORIZONTAL TRAINING

Many climbing roses can be trained to grow horizontally along the ground, instead of on a wall or other support.

A similar method is used with vigorous Hybrid Tea, Hyrid Perpetual and shrub roses. The flexible trailing shoots of several varieties derived from *Rosa wichuraiana* are admirably suited for this kind of training. They can be used to cover banks and other areas where fairly dense ground cover is required.

The shoots are pegged down close to ground level and the same pruning methods are used as when these rose varieties are grown more conventionally as climbers.

The first year

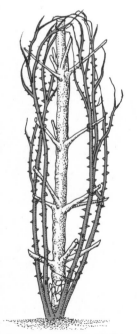

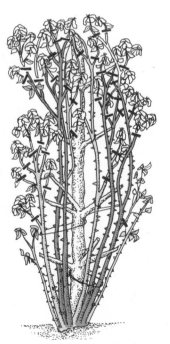
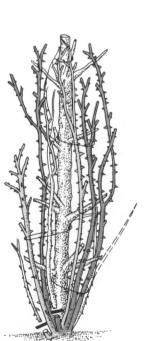

The second year

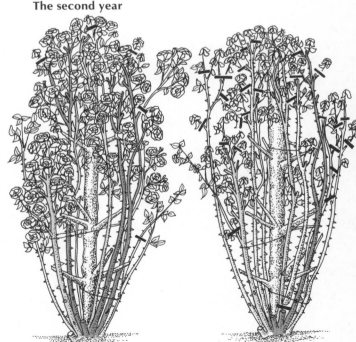

1 Autumn to early spring. Plant with shoots tied into a post or pillar.

2 June to August. Plants flower on laterals of the old growth. New growth has developed from previous year's stems and from the base. Summer prune.

3 November. Cut back flowered laterals and some new leaders sufficiently to maintain the symmetry of the plant.

4 At the same time, cut out weak, diseased and dead wood. Tie in new shoots.

5 June to August. Plants flower on laterals of the old growth. New growth has developed from previous year's stems and from the base. Summer prune.

6 November. Cut back flowered laterals and some new leaders sufficiently to maintain the symmetry of the plant.

Species and Shrub Roses 1

Shrub and species roses are grown less often than Hybrid Teas and Floribundas, but are increasing in popularity. Grouped together or planted singly in shrub or mixed borders, shrub roses are extremely rewarding during summer and autumn, particularly in informal settings, where modern bedding roses may look out of place.

It is often recommended to leave shrub roses entirely unpruned, "to grow naturally," or suggested that only very minor trimming is necessary. Generally shrub and species roses left to their own devices will grow and flower well for a few years, but this *laissez-faire* approach, although appealing, will not always provide the best display of roses.

To obtain the best results it is necessary to carry out a certain amount of pruning annually, even though it may be no more than a gentle manicure.

In order to simplify the process, as much as possible, three groups have been identified. The divisions are arbitrary and not rigid, and inevitably overlap occurs and slight modifications of pruning techniques may be needed for a few individual roses that do not fit neatly into the groups defined here.

Pruning shrub and species roses involves exactly the same general principles that apply to other roses (see page 204): that is, to encourage strong basal, or near-basal growths and to replace older stems that have lost their vigor and flower sparsely.

It is important also to take into account that the flowers of some varieties may be produced on the current season's growth late in the year as well as on laterals and sublaterals from older growth. Flowers of some varieties are produced mainly during June and July in one flush, but other varieties may be repeat-flowering and produce bloom until the autumn. Attractive fruits (hips) are a feature of some varieties and therefore do not need their spent flowers removed.

The following general points always apply:
1 No initial pruning is required when planting, beside the removal of coarse and damaged roots and the shortening of unripe or damaged shoots.
2 A sturdy framework of well-spaced shoots should be built up and thin weak growth should be removed after flowering. Dead and diseased wood should be cut out.
3 Regular pruning to remove spent flowers is desirable unless dealing with varieties grown for their fruits. Repeat-flowering shrub roses, such as the hybrid musks, benefit considerably from this manicuring because their growth energy is put into producing new flowering laterals rather than into fruits.
4 Slight tipping back by a few inches of all vigorous shoots in winter will encourage flowering laterals and sublaterals the following summer. It also helps to remove a possible source of disease.

Group 1 brings together the following kinds of roses, which require only minimal pruning for many years:
Species roses (other than climbers) and their close hybrids
Rosa spinosissima, the Burnet rose, and hybrids derived from it
Rosa rugosa, the Japanese rose, and hybrids derived from it
Gallica roses
Hybrid musk roses.

Almost all of these roses are of a fairly dense, bushy habit and flower mainly on short lateral and sublateral shoots produced from second-year or older wood. They do not regularly produce vigorous basal growths once established.

The first and second year
In the first year and second year after planting, pruning is more or less confined to points 1 to 4 mentioned in the introduction to this section. Occasionally a badly placed shoot may need to be cut out to the base.

Third and following years
In the third and following years one or two older main growths, which only flower sparsely, may be cut out in winter. This will encourage basal replacement shoots and maintain a sturdy vigorous framework. More drastic treatment may occasionally be necessary with very old bushes. In winter cut out several old and poorly placed main branches to leave a well-spaced framework.

The second year

1 February to March. Tip back all vigorous shoots. Cut out to the base any badly placed shoots. Basal shoots have developed.

2 June to August. Plant flowers on laterals of old wood, new basal shoots develop.

3 September. Summer prune. After flowering cut out thin, weak growth. Cut out dead and diseased wood.

Third and following years

4 February to March. Tip back all vigorous shoots and laterals if required. Cut out one or two older main shoots that have flowered sparsely.

5 July to August. Plant flowers on laterals of old wood, new basal shoots develop.

6 September. Summer prune. After flowering cut out thin, weak growth to maintain a well-spaced framework. Cut out dead and diseased wood.

Species and Shrub Roses 2

Group 2 consists of roses that flower mainly on short lateral and sublateral shoots produced from second-year or older wood. This group includes "old roses" such as the Albas, Centifolias, Moss roses and most Damasks. A large number of modern shrub roses, which do not repeat-flower but have one main flush of bloom in midsummer, are also included.

The first year

First-year roses are treated in the same way as those in Group 1. Tip back unripe or damaged shoots and remove coarse or damaged roots.

Second and following years

Mature roses in Group 2 differ from those in Group 1 by their regular production of vigorous basal, or near-basal, shoots, which may grow to 5–8 ft in one season. In the second year these long shoots produce an abundance of flowering laterals, which often weigh them down so that the shoots are almost resting on the ground and in danger of breaking.

This growth habit necessitates a different pruning technique from Group 1 so that the natural habit is maintained while preventing the top-heavy flowering shoots from snapping or dragging their blooms in the mud.

In addition to the general points 1–4 of the introduction to this section all the vigorous, long shoots of the current year are pruned back by up to one-third of their length and the laterals on older main growths are cut back to 2–3 eyes or 6 in from the stems during the winter. Care must be taken not to shorten these long shoots too much or the elegant arched habit can be lost and the potential of producing an abundance of flowering laterals is diminished.

This annual pruning with the removal each year of one or two old spent growths, should keep all roses in this group flowering profusely and growing strongly and healthily for many years ahead.

The second year

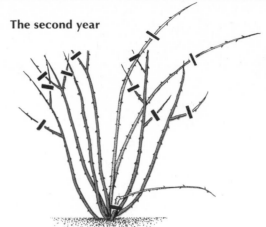

1 February to March. Cut back long new basal growths by up to one-third. Cut back laterals on flowered shoots to 2–3 eyes or 4–6 in. Cut out any badly placed shoots.

2 June to August. Plant flowers on cut-back laterals of old wood. New basal shoots develop. Summer prune.

Third and following years

3 September to November. Tip back extra-long growths to minimize wind-rock. No other pruning is required.

4 February to March. Cut back long new basal growths by up to one-third. Cut back laterals on flowered shoots to 2–3 eyes or 4–6 in. Cut out to base any badly placed and old shoots that flower sparsely.

5 June to August. Plant flowers on cut-back laterals of old wood. New basal shoots develop. Summer prune.

6 September to November. Tip back extra-long growths to minimize wind-rock. No other pruning is required.

Species and Shrub Roses 3

Group 3 can be regarded as a variant of Group 2. It includes most of the China roses and a number of modern shrub roses such as 'Fountain.' Of the "old roses" many Bourbons, such as the well-known 'Zephirine Drouhin' and 'Mme Isaac Pereire' are also part of this group. Certain very robust Hybrid Teas and Hybrid Perpetuals can be included in this group and treated as border shrubs.

The first year
First-year plants in this group are treated in the same way as those in Group 1.

Second and following years
Mature roses in Group 3 differ from those in Group 2, because they flower more or less recurrently throughout summer and autumn on both the current season's shoots and on laterals and sublaterals from second-year or older wood. Many also produce long, flexuous or robust growths. These come from either the base or higher up the plant on strong, established stems. These new shoots often develop sprays of flowers at their tips during the current season, unlike roses in Group 2.

Severe, or moderately severe, winter pruning of all these roses produces vigorous but sometimes sparsely flowering—or even non flowering—shoots. The blooms are often delayed and intermittent rather than continuous. Light pruning is needed to achieve the best results.

Group 3 roses tend to produce fresh flowering laterals and sublaterals all summer and they quickly build up into dense twiggy tangles. Dead-head and slightly thin during the flowering period. This treatment helps to encourage continuity of flower. Otherwise winter pruning is similar to that of Group 2 with more emphasis on removing twiggy growths that have lost their vigor.

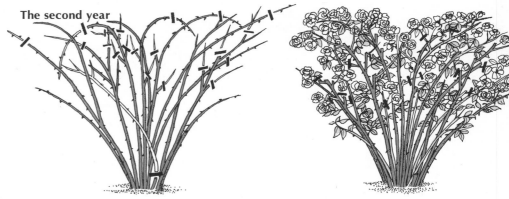

The second year

1 February to March. Cut back very long, new basal or near-basal one-year shoots by up to one-third. Take care to maintain the arching habit. Cut back laterals on shoots which flowered last season to 2–3 eyes (3–6 in). Cut out weak or badly placed shoots.

2 June to July. Plant flowers on laterals from previous season's wood. Basal and near-basal shoots are developing. Summer prune.

Third and following years

3 August to September. Flowers are produced on laterals from current season's growth. Twiggy sublaterals have developed from summer-pruned growth.

4 October. Tip back extra-long growths to minimize wind rock.

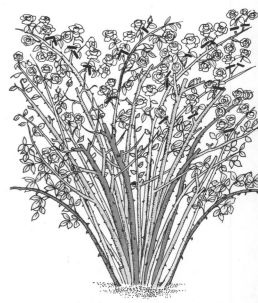

5 February to March. Cut back very long, new basal or near-basal one-year-old shoots by up to one-third. Take care to maintain the arching habit. Cut back laterals on shoots that flowered last season to 2–3 eyes (3–6 in). Cut out to base any old, badly placed or weak shoots. Mulch well.

6 June to July. Plant in flower on laterals from previous season's wood. Basal and near-basal shoots are developing. Summer prune.

Standard Roses

Hybrid Tea and Floribunda roses are frequently grown as standards, or half-standards among bedding roses. They give height in the garden, where they can be extremely effective, particularly if used in a formal context. They are usually budded on stems of *Rosa rugosa* or common briar, but have become less popular in recent years as the head is often frequently top-heavy and the slender stem requires careful staking to maintain the formal habit. Initial pruning, and subsequent treatment, is similar to that given to the same varieties when grown as bushes.

Light pruning leaves a fairly large head on a standard which is vulnerable to wind damage, particularly in exposed gardens. Moderately severe pruning appropriate to the variety should be practiced.

With Hybrid Teas cut back strong shoots to 3–5 eyes or 6 in. With Floribundas cut back one-year-old growth to 6–8 eyes or 10 in and two-year-old shoots to 3–6 eyes or 6 in.

BUDDING STANDARD ROSES

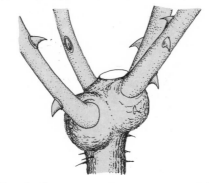

Standard roses are best propagated by inserting growth buds each side of the stem in order to obtain an even head; if only one bud is used one-sided growth normally occurs, so before you buy a standard make sure it is double-budded.

Weeping standards

Climbing roses are budded on tall stems of *Rosa rugosa* or common briar so that the long trailing growths hang down.

Weeping standards of rose varieties in Group 1 of ramblers and climbers (page 208) can be most attractive when correctly grown. Pruning is quite simple. In August to September cut out all of the two-year-old shoots that have flowered and leave the vigorous young shoots to flower the following season. If insufficient young growths are produced leave a few of the two-year-old shoots in appropriate positions and cut back their laterals to 2–3 eyes or 6 in.

Varieties in Group 2 of ramblers and climbers (page 209) are less satisfactory when grown in this way, and are seldom seen. Pruning should be confined to cutting out surplus older wood and cutting back laterals to 2–3 eyes or 6 in after flowering. Tie down any vigorous young growths as they appear.

The first year

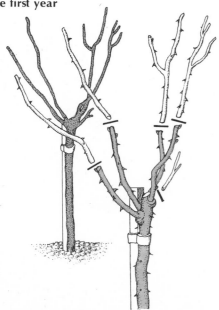

1 February to March. Cut back strong stems to 3–5 eyes or 6 in.

2 October to November. At the end of the season's growth, tip back main stems and cut out any soft, unripe shoots.

Second and following years

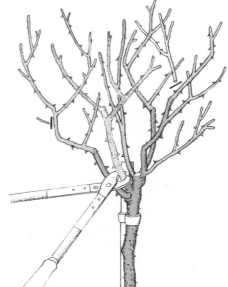

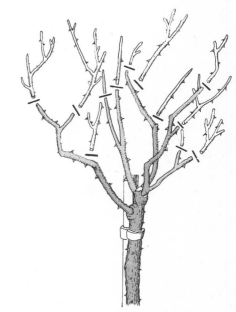

3 February to March. Cut out dead, diseased, weak and crossing stems.

4 At the same time, cut back new shoots to 3–5 eyes or 6 in and remaining laterals to 2–4 eyes or 4–6 in.

Shrubs: introduction 1

There is a commonly held, but quite incorrect, belief that all shrubs should be pruned, and pruned hard, each year. This often takes the form of a "haircut" or involves slaughtering the branches to keep the plant within bounds. Both treatments result in a misshapen ugly specimen with few or no flowers.

The other extreme of leaving the shrub entirely unpruned is preferable. Many deciduous and most evergreen shrubs will grow well enough by themselves and give adequate flowers without being pruned at all, if there is enough room for the plants to develop and the soil is reasonably fertile.

There are several groups of shrubs where correct pruning is beneficial to producing regular and abundant flowers together with healthy, vigorous growth and foliage. These same species, left unpruned, may still flower fairly well, but the quality and quantity of bloom and growth is poor compared with correctly pruned specimens.

An understanding of the basic principles behind pruning and knowledge of the growth habit and the method of flowering of the plant concerned is important, particularly the age of the wood on which flowers are borne.

Placing of the shrub in the garden also has an effect on pruning. Never try to fit a shrub which naturally grows to a large size into an area where limited room is available and constant pruning will be necessary. This may seem obvious, but frequently one sees large shrubs cut back several times a year, just to fit a particular space. The result is an ugly plant with a mass of growth and virtually no flowers. So, if you want to grow a *Philadelphus* in a site where only a 4ft spread is possible choose 'Manteau d'Hermine' (3ft × 3ft) or 'Erectus' (5ft × 3ft) which will fit, not 'Burfordensis' (12ft × 6ft) which is far too large.

Feeding and watering are also important if the shrub is to be pruned so that it produces healthy vigorous growth over a number of years.

When pruning any shrub try to obtain the best decorative effect whether it is grown for the flowers, fruit, foliage or the beauty of its winter stems. The pruning techniques will vary from shrub to shrub, depending on the plant and the effect required.

In some circumstances shrubs may be pruned by different methods to obtain different effects. The purple-leaved varieties of the smoke bush, *Continus coggygria*, are an example. If left virtually unpruned, this plant will form a large 10–12ft shrub, valued for the colored foliage and smokelike plumes of flowers. But the young plants may also be cut back hard each spring to form smaller shrubs with masses of long unbranched stems with large bright purple leaves.

Also try to create and maintain a well-balanced and attractive overall shape and

appearance for the plant. Many shrubs are naturally neat and symmetrical in outline and require no more than the removal of the occasional awkwardly placed shoot that destroys this symmetry.

Others are unruly and may grow unevenly, presenting a lop-sided shape with weak, twiggy growth on one side and strong healthy branches on the other. These plants require pruning to restore them to a reasonable shape. Strong shoots should be lightly pruned (a), which will result in moderate growth, while the weak wood (b) should be cut back hard to stimulate vigorous shoots, which will help to balance the shape (c). Do not cut back the strong shoots hard (d) and leave the weak unpruned (e) so that the overall height is the same. This will result in further strong growths being produced from the hard-pruned side but not from the unpruned growth, which will accentuate rather than correct the lack of balance (f).

In many, but not all, shrubs pruning will encourage the production of vigorous, basal or near-basal shoots. These will maintain the vitality of the plant and provide replacement growth for the older, worn-out branches. Pruning will also ensure an even distribution of flowers. The exceptions are such shrubs as the Japanese maple, witch hazel, and most evergreens.

Shrubs: introduction 2

To keep shrubs in a healthy condition involves the three "D's" of pruning—the removal and burning of all dead, diseased and damaged growth as soon as possible. It is obligatory in the case of all plants.

Pruning cuts. All pruning cuts should be made correctly as shown. Incorrect cuts can result in die-back and disease problems. Cuts should be made just above an outward-pointing bud or shoot or above a strong pair of opposite buds so that the resulting shoots will be well placed in relation to the other new growths on the plants.

Reversion. Occasionally branches of shrubs with variegated foliage may revert to the original green-leaved form of the species. If this occurs it is most important to completely remove the nonvariegated branches as soon as they are seen. They are frequently more robust than the variegated shoots, and if allowed to remain they will—like suckers—gradually become dominant, and eventually the shrub almost reverts to its green-leaved form. Examples include *Elaeagnus pungens* 'Maculata' and *Kerria japonica* 'Picta.'

Newly planted shrubs. When plants are taken from the nursery or garden center any shrub should be well shaped and bushy with a strong root system (a), and not one-sided (b). Most evergreens should need no pruning at planting, besides removing damaged shoots or tipping back a wayward branch.

With such deciduous shrubs as *Deutzia* there may be some weak growth present and to encourage strong basal growth this should be cut out completely. Terminal growth should also be shortened slightly to a strong bud, or strong pair of buds. Sometimes more drastic initial pruning is required. Details are given in the appropriate group.

Suckers. Although most modern shrubs are propagated vegetatively from cuttings and are on their own roots, a few are still budded or grafted on to stocks. These may occasionally produce sucker growths from the root-stocks and it is important to remove these as soon as they are seen. The sucker shoots should be traced back to their point of origin and carefully cut or pulled off. The dormant buds at the base of each sucker should be removed at the same time. Cutting them off at ground level merely results in a further cluster of suckers from these dormant buds. If the suckers are left they will gradually take over and replace the grafted plant.

Early training. Most shrubs produce a number of vigorous basal shoots during the first year or two after planting. These shoots will form the basic framework of the shrub and it is important to make sure that they are evenly spaced. Often they are too close, or cross, and if left unpruned they will spoil the balance and overall symmetry of the shrub (c). If shoots are ill-placed cut them out (d).

It is particularly important to do this with shrubs that do not naturally renew their growth from basal replacement shoots when they are older. When these shoots form a permanent, woody framework on which both extension growth and flowers are borne. Examples of shrubs in this category are

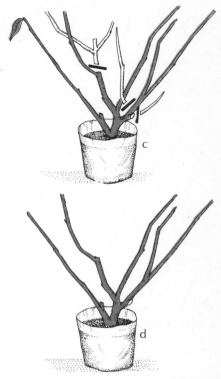

magnolias, *Hamamelis*, and many evergreens, including rhododendrons and camellias.

In many cases it is desirable to keep deciduous shrubs open in the center to allow free air circulation. This avoids stagnant conditions, which invite the spread of disease.

A number of deciduous shrubs such as the Japanese maple, *Acer palmatum*, naturally form an intricate network of crossing branchlets. Pruning, after the initial year or two, is unnecessary and undesirable except the removal of dead or diseased wood. Over-pruning may ruin the natural habit of the plant. Pruning of crossing branches should be confined to early training with shrubs of this habit.

Root pruning. This is seldom practiced with ornamental shrubs, but is occasionally useful to check excessive top growth. It is sometimes used in preparing large shrubs for transplanting.

Deciduous Shrubs 1

Group 1 includes

Acer palmatum (Japanese maple)
Acer japonicum (Japanese maple)
Amelanchier
Buddleia globosa
Clethra
Colutea
Cornus florida
Cornus kousa
Corylopsis

Cotinus (unless treated as in group 4)
Cotoneaster (deciduous species)
Daphne (deciduous species)
Euonymus (deciduous species)
Fothergilla
Hamamelis
Hibiscus syriacus
Magnolia (deciduous species and
    hybrids)

Potentilla fruticosa
Rhus
Stachyurus
Styrax
Syringa (Lilac)
Viburnum (deciduous species and
    hybrids)

Group 1 consists of a number of deciduous shrubs that do not regularly produce vigorous replacement growths from the base or lower branches of the plant. The extension growth of these plants is produced on the perimeter of a permanent framework of older branches. The growth habit can be thought of as the crown of an oak tree without its trunk.

These plants require the minimum of pruning once they are established, but for the first few years after planting it is important to build up a framework of sturdy branches, removing the weak, crossing and misplaced shoots in the dormant season so that a symmetrical and balanced plant results. Open-center plants in this group, such as *Hamamelis* and *Magnolia* x *soulangiana*, may need removal of only the occasional misplaced shoot or shoots or branches that cross.

Pruning of the mature shrub is restricted to removing any dead, damaged or diseased growth as seen and to maintaining the overall symmetry of the shrub by pruning back weak and wayward growths.

Occasionally vigorous shoots will be produced from near the base or on the framework of mature plants. These may be used as replacement growths for old branches in the framework if they are suitably placed. But more usually, these growths are produced in an awkward position and should be cut out completely.

When old branches are removed always use a wound paint on the cut surfaces to protect the plant from such diseases as coral spot, which can be troublesome.

JAPANESE MAPLE

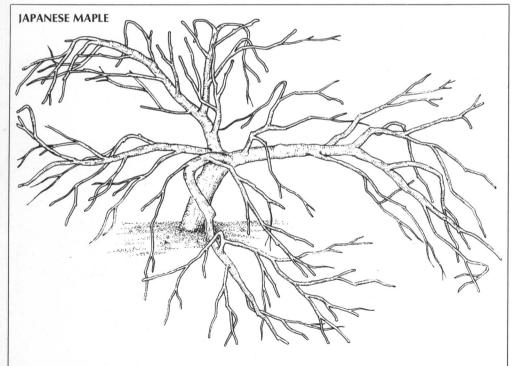

An intricately branched form of *Acer palmatum* (Japanese maple). Note the basic framework branches. After the initial framework is formed no further pruning is needed except for the removal of dead, diseased and damaged shoots as seen. The normal habit should be maintained and the crossing branches left unpruned.

The first year

1 November to April. *Magnolia stellata* at planting. Remove weak shoots and crossing branches. Create a balanced framework by removing any unruly growths.

Third and following years

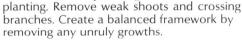

3 March to April. Minimum pruning is now required. Allow the plant to develop its natural habit, but always remove the dead, diseased and damaged wood.

The second year

2 March to April. Cut out any badly spaced extension growth and laterals produced during the first growing season. If growths are well-spaced leave them alone.

4 April. The mature plant in flower.

Deciduous Shrubs 2

Group 2 includes
Buddleia alternifolia
Cytisus scoparius and its hybrids
Deutzia
Dipelta
Forsythia
Hydrangea × macrophylla
Kerria
Kolkwitzia

Neillia
Philadelphus
Ribes sanguineum
Spiraea × arguta
Spiraea thunbergii
Stephanandra
Tamarix (spring-flowering)
Weigela

Group 2 includes deciduous shrubs that flower on shoots that are produced during the previous growing season. The flowers are formed either on short laterals produced from this one-year-old wood as in *Deutzia, Philadelphus, Ribes sanguineum* or directly from the one-year-old branches as in *Forsythia*. Many spring and early summer-flowering shrubs belong to this group. They require renewal pruning to maintain them at a reasonable height and to ensure that there will be each season a regular supply of strong young shoots from low down on the plant. Unpruned shrubs in this group quickly form many twiggy branchlets, often becoming ungainly with fewer flowers of poor quality.

The first year
The plant will usually be two to three years old when you buy it at the nursery. Pruning when planting is limited to cutting out weak and damaged growth and cutting back main shoots a few inches to a strong bud or pair of buds. This ensures that during the first growing season the plant's energy is concentrated on producing a strong basic framework of branches. Little flower is produced the first year. Immediately after flowering cut back any flowering laterals to a strong developing shoot and remove thin weak branch growth.

The second year
Flowers will be borne either on short lateral branchlets or direct from the stem. One or more strong growths will develop below the flowering branchlets. Once the flowers have faded remove all the one-year-old wood that has produced flowers. Cut back the branches to the lowest (usually also the strongest) of the developing new shoots, provided this does not spoil the balance and shape of the plant. If the flowered wood is not pruned away immediately after flowering, many weaker shoots develop from lateral buds.

Third and following years
During the second year branchlets that have borne flowers should be cut out immediately after flowering, in the same way. In addition completely cut out one-quarter to one-fifth of the old stems to the base, taking care to balance the shape of the plant.

Deutzia provides a typical example of a shrub in Group 2. The time of pruning will differ slightly, depending on the flowering period of the shrub. Prune immediately after flowering.

The first year

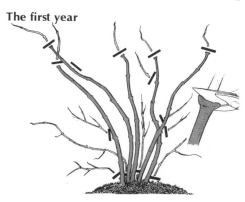

1 Autumn or early spring. Young *Deutzia* at planting. Cut out all weak growth and tip back the main shoots to a strong pair of buds (or an outward-pointing bud for shrubs with alternate buds). Add a good mulch of manure.

4 July. Immediately after flowering cut back the stems that have flowered to vigorous young growths developing lower down on the main stems. Remove any weak growth. Make sure the overall balance and symmetry of the shrub is maintained.

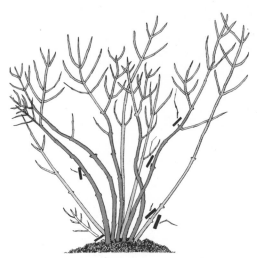

2 October to November. A few strong basal growths and many laterals from the main branches have developed during the first season. Cut out any weak or misplaced shoots to maintain a symmetrical framework. Mulch well in early spring.

5 October to November. The vigorous young shoots have grown several feet and produced laterals on which the following season's blooms will be borne. Mulch well in early spring.

The second year

3 June to July. Flowers are produced from short laterals along many of the upper shoots which grew last season. As the flowers fade strong shoots will grow from the base of the plant and from low down on the main stems.

Third and following years

6 July. Immediately after flowering cut back the stems that have flowered to vigorous young growths developing lower down on the main stems. Remove any weak growth. If the main stems are becoming crowded cut out one-quarter or one-fifth of the oldest stems to the base. Mulch well.

Deciduous Shrubs 3

Kerria

Group 2 also includes a few shrubs such as *Kerria*, which produce almost all of their new growth from ground level. They flower on one-year-old wood, but require a slightly different pruning technique. Immediately after flowering the shoots that have flowered should be cut out to the base or occasionally to a point low down on the shoot where vigorous young growth is appearing. If flowering wood is left most of it will die back naturally by the following winter, but it is unsightly.

The first year

1 Autumn or early spring. Young *Kerria* at planting. Cut out any thin weak growth. Leave the vigorous stems and their laterals as these should flower this season.

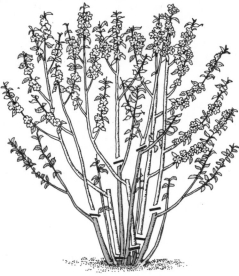

2 May. Cut out the flowered shoots to the base or, with very strong stems, to points low down where vigorous young shoots are forming. Basal growths develop. Mulch well.

Second and following years

3 May. Cut out the flowered shoots to the base or, with very strong stems, to points low down where vigorous young shoots are forming. Basal growths develop. Mulch well.

Hydrangeas

Hydrangeas are included in Group 2. Pruning the Hortensia hydrangea (*H. × macrophylla*), which includes the familiar Mop-head and Lace-cap kinds, frequently causes difficulties. They flower late in the season and there is a tendency to prune them hard each spring in the belief that the resultant strong growths will flower in late summer or autumn. Unfortunately this does not occur.

Only cosmetic pruning is needed for young plants. And plants left unpruned will usually flower quite freely. They tend to produce a good deal of twiggy growth if left entirely unpruned, and, with plants three or more years old, a proportion of the older wood should be cut out to the base in early spring to encourage a constant supply of vigorous young replacement shoots each season. Do not remove the previous year's flower heads in winter as these provide some protection to the growth and flower buds, which may be damaged in severe weather. Remove them in early spring.

1 Late March to April. Cut out one-third to one-quarter of the older exhausted shoots to the base. Cut out any weak thin shoots still remaining. Cut back the old flower heads to leave only a strong pair of buds.

2 September. The upper growth buds on the pruned shoots have grown and the strongest have produced flower heads. New vigorous basal shoots have developed but will not flower until next season.

BROOMS

Many brooms (*Cytisus scoparius* and its hybrids) are included in Group 2. They are deciduous shrubs, although the bright green young stems make them appear evergreen. They flower in May and June along the entire length of the previous season's wood.

No pruning is required at planting. Once the blooms have faded cut back the flowered wood by two-thirds of its length to where young growths are developing. The pruning principle is the same as for *Deutzia* and similar shrubs, but brooms should not be cut back hard because shoots do not grow very well from old wood. It is essential to prune even one-year-old plants after flowering to prevent them becoming leggy and top heavy.

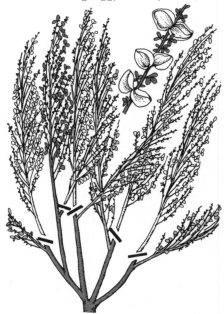

1 June to July. In second and subsequent years, immediately after flowering, cut back the flowered wood by two-thirds to vigorous young growths developing near the base of the previous season's wood.

Deciduous Shrubs 4

Group 3 includes
Buddleia davidii
Caryopteris
Ceanothus (deciduous)
Ceratostigma
Fuchsia (hardy)
Hydrangea paniculata
Perovskia

Prunus glandulosa
Prunus triloba
Romneya
Spiraea × bumalda
Spiraea douglasii
Spiraea japonica

Group 3 includes those deciduous shrubs that bear their flowers on the current year's growth. When pruned back hard in early spring they produce vigorous shoots that flower in summer or early autumn. If left without pruning they soon develop into unkempt, twiggy bushes that gradually deteriorate in the quality and quantity of flowers that they produce.

It is convenient also to include in Group 3 a small number of deciduous shrubs, typified by *Prunus triloba*, which flower early each year on the previous season's wood. They also respond to hard pruning in March or April, by which time they will have flowered already, producing long, wandlike shoots which bloom the following spring. The pruning technique is exactly the same.

The basic requirement is to prune early in the year so that there is a maximum amount of time for the flowering wood to develop. This may simply mean cutting out all growth to ground level between March and April of each year for small subshrubby plants, such as hardy fuchsias, *Leycesteria* and *Perovskia* or allowing a framework of woody branches to develop to the required height and then cutting back the growths close to the framework each spring, as with *Buddleia davidii*. Variation in the height of the growth and flowers on a single plant can be achieved quite simply by pruning a few of the basic framework shoots higher or lower than the remainder. This is useful in a place where the plant is only being seen from one side and allows a greater surface area of flower to be presented to the viewer. This hard pruning is carried out in March to early April each year just as the growth buds begin to swell and the position of the new shoots can be seen.

In windy areas it may be necessary to trim back the flowered growths in late autumn to minimize wind-rock, but normally only the spring cut-back is required.

It is most important to feed shrubs pruned by this method to ensure that adequate healthy growth is produced each season.

The first year

Initial pruning is aimed at building up a strong well-spaced framework of branches. In the first season pruning is usually less severe than in subsequent years so that the root system is able to become well established. Remove all weak and damaged growth at planting. Cut back the remaining growths by one-quarter to three-quarters of their length in March to April, the more vigorous shrubs such as *Buddleia davidii* being pruned more severely than less robust species, such as *Perovskia* and the deciduous *Ceanothus*.

The second year

In March to April cut back hard the previous year's growth to developing buds just above the older wood. With fuchsias, *Leycesteria* and similar subshrubs which may not develop a woody basal framework cut back almost to ground level. In mild areas these subshrubs may become woody and are than treated using the framework principle. Apply a good mulch of compost or manure around the plant to encourage vigorous new growth.

Third and following years

The pruning sequence is exactly the same as in the second season. After a number of years the basic woody framework may become congested and slight thinning of the old woody stumps may be needed. Always apply an annual basal mulch to ensure continued vigorous growth.

Because of the slight variations in the degree of pruning needed to form the initial framework three examples which require marginally different techniques are provided of shrubs in this group. Failure to feed regularly may result in weak spindly growth.

This method is suitable for deciduous shrubs such as *Ceanothus, Caryopteris, Spartium junceum* and other shrubs in Group 3 which are less vigorous than *Buddleia davidii* (see page 223) it is important to let them grow unchecked during the first season, and only remove the weak growth and badly placed shoots that will spoil the symmetry of the plant, so that a sturdy natural branching system is developed. If they are cut back hard at planting they may produce only weak growths or die back completely.

The first year

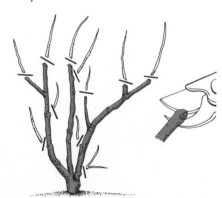

1 March to early April. Cut out any damaged or very weak growths. Tip back main shoots by 1–2 in to strong outward-pointing buds. Cut out entirely any badly placed shoot.

2 August to September. Strong shoots have grown from upper buds on last season's growths and these will flower during late summer.

The second year

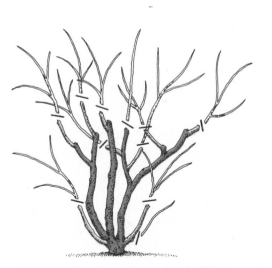

3 March to early April. Cut back all last season's growths by one-half to strong outward-pointing buds. Remove entirely any weak straggly shoots.

Third and following years

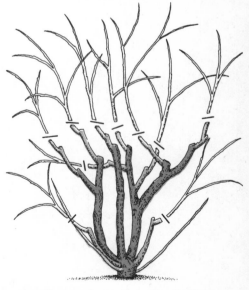

4 March to early April. Cut back all last season's shoots to within one or two buds of the previous season's growth. The basic framework of woody stems is formed.

Deciduous Shrubs 5

Group 3 includes such shrubs as *Perovskia* (Russian sage), *Leycesteria formosa*, hardy fuchsias and *Ceratostigma*, which may not develop a woody framework and are cut back almost to ground level.

The second year

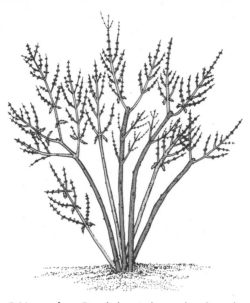

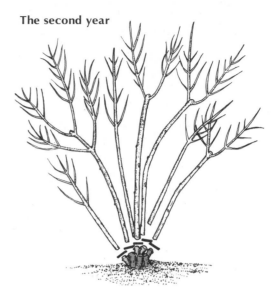

CREATING A FRAMEWORK

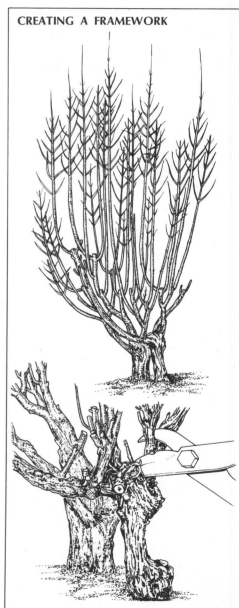

The first year

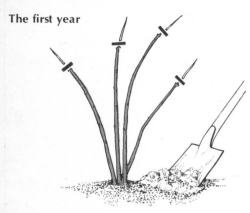

1 March to April. *Perovskia* as planted. Cut back any weak, thin tips by a few inches to a pair of strong buds. Add a good mulch to the base of the plant.

2 November. Basal shoots have developed during the summer and last year's shoots have produced lateral growths. The grey stems remain attractive in winter.

3 March to April. Cut back all stems almost to ground level, above strong pairs of buds.

Third and following years

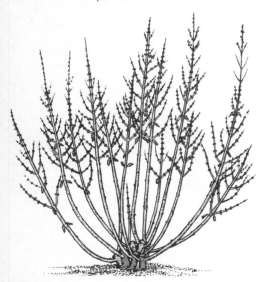

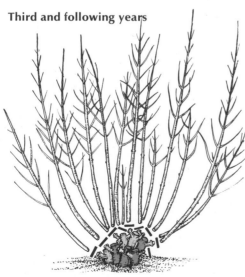

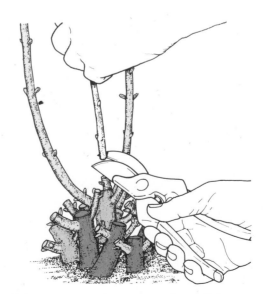

4 September. Strong growths have developed to a height of 2–3 ft. Laterals are produced towards the top of each shoot. Flowers are borne on laterals and shoot tips.

5 March to April. Cut back all stems almost to ground level, above strong pairs of buds.

Take care not to leave snags that will die back during the year.

If required *Perovskia* can be grown on a framework of woody basal shoots. Early training and subsequent pruning is exactly as shown under deciduous *Ceanothus*.

Deciduous Shrubs 6

Group 3 includes vigorous shrubs such as *Buddleia davidii* that should grow on a framework of woody branches, which is allowed to develop to the required height.

The first year

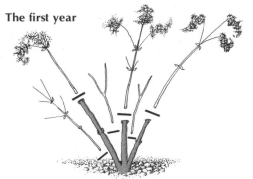

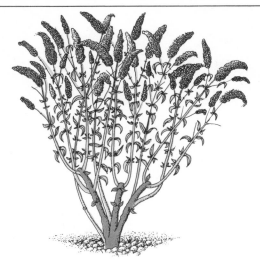

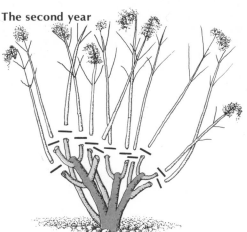

The second year

1 March to early April. *Buddleia davidii* as planted. Cut back all main shoots by one-half to three-quarters of their length to points where vigorous shoots are developing or the buds are swelling. Cut out remaining weak growth entirely. Mulch well.

2 July to August. Long wandlike growths have been produced from the pruned branches and also from the base. These will flower near the tips in late summer.

3 March to early April. Cut back new shoots hard to within one or two pairs of buds of the previous year's growth. Cut back any basal or near-basal growths that have developed the previous season to the required height. Mulch well.

4 October. The plant has flowered on terminal shoots and upper laterals of the current season's shoots. In windy gardens cut back all main shoots by one-third to minimize wind rock.

The third year

Fourth and following years

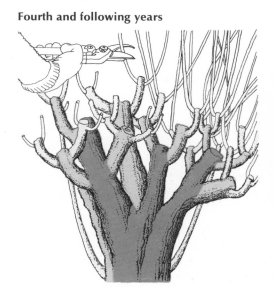

5 March to early April. Cut back as in caption 3. The main framework is now formed. Any basal or near-basal shoots that

develop in future years may be used to fill gaps in the framework or cut out if not required. Mulch well.

6 March to early April. Carry out normal pruning. When the framework becomes very woody and congested remove any badly placed "stumps," leaving the

remainder as well spaced as possible. Train in any new shoots as required to replace the old framework wood that has been cut out.

Deciduous Shrubs 7

Group 4 includes
Cornus alba
Cornus stolonifera
many *Salix* species
Rubus cockburnianus
Cotinus coggygria
Corylus maxima 'Purpurea'
Sambucus (Golden-leaved and
purple-leaved forms)

Group 4 includes shrubs that are pruned hard in early spring each year so that the most attractive decorative effect is obtained from their foliage or the bark of their stems during the winter. The technique is very similar to the one described in Group 3. Most of the shrubs included here would flower on wood produced the previous year, but pruned by this method, they do not bloom at all. With the right feeding the foliage of variegated or purple-leaved variants of such shrubs as *Cotinus coggygria* and *Cornus alba*, or of those such as *Rhus typhina*, grown for autumn color, will be two or three times larger.

Many shrubs with beautifully colored bark, such as the red- and green-stemmed dogwoods, some willows and the white-stemmed brambles, also react well to this drastic pruning, producing vigorous, unbranched new growth. They also show more pronounced color than unpruned specimens.

As with Group 3 the basic framework can usually be varied in height to suit the position of the shrub. The exceptions are species such as the white-stemmed brambles, which do not build up a woody framework but sucker to produce canelike growths from the base of the plant.

Cotinus coggygria

This method is used to increase the decorative value of the shrubs in Group 3 that have colored or variegated foliage, such as the purple-leaved smoke bush, *Cotinus coggygria* 'Foliis Purpureis'. It is also very effective with the golden elder and purple hazel, and useful in small gardens, where the same plants if left unpruned would be too large.

The technique is very similar to the method of pruning *Cornus alba* (see page 225), but the plant is allowed to develop a woody stem or group of stems to the required height before being pollarded.

The first year

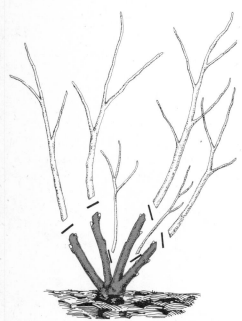

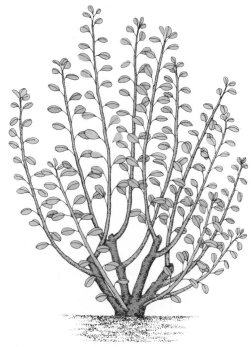

The second year

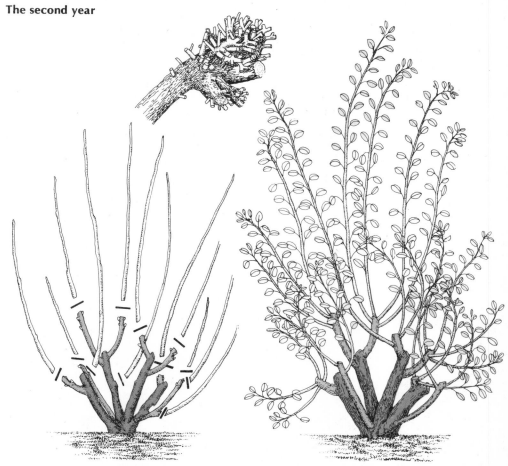

1 March to early April. *Cotinus coggygria* 'Foliis Purpureis' at planting. Cut back all main growths to 12–18 in to create the base framework. Cut out any weak basal growths. Mulch the plant well.

2 July to August. Vigorous unbranched shoots have developed with larger and more handsome foliage than that of an unpruned bush.

3 March. Cut back hard the previous season's growths to above a bud within 1–2 in of the framework. If a higher framework is needed cut back these growths to the appropriate height. Remove any surplus or weak growths to ensure that the framework branches are well spaced.

4 July to August. The established plant with a strong, basic, woody framework and numerous vigorous growths.

Deciduous Shrubs 8

Rubus cockburnianus

This method is suitable for such shrubs as *Rubus cockburnianus* and its relatives, the white-stemmed brambles. These are grown for the effect of their white, branched stems in winter. They do not form a woody framework but sucker from the base to produce annual replacement shoots, similar to their relative the raspberry.

Pruning simply consists of cutting all growths down to ground level between March and April each year. If the previous season's growths remain they will flower in summer, but they will not be particularly decorative. It is better to remove these before active growth starts. Pruning will encourage the plant's energy to go into producing vigorous new growths rather than being shared between flower and shoot production.

Where growth is poor one or two of the previous year's shoots may be left at pruning time, this provides food for the plant early in the season and helps to stimulate basal growth during the summer.

The first year

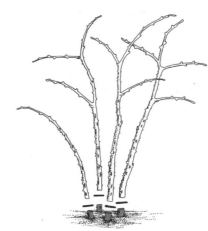

1 March to April. White-stemmed bramble at planting. Cut out all growth close to ground level. Mulch well.

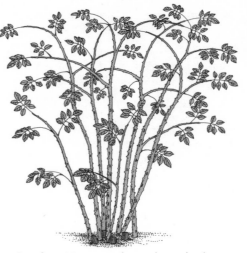

2 October. Vigorous shoots branched towards the top have grown during spring and summer. In autumn the foliage falls and the stems remain attractive during winter.

Second and following years

3 March to April. Cut out all growth close to ground level.'

Cornus alba

This method is applicable to *Cornus alba* and many willows grown for the colored bark of the young shoots. They usually withstand hard pruning immediately after planting.

The first year

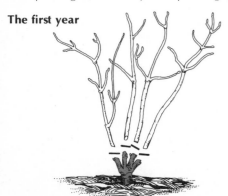

1 March to early April. *Cornus alba* at planting. Cut back hard all main shoots to within a few inches of the base. Cut out any weak basal growths. Mulch the plant well.

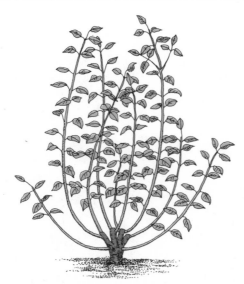

2 October. Vigorous whippy, usually unbranched shoots have grown during spring and summer. Once the leaves have fallen the colored stems form an attractive feature throughout the winter.

The second year

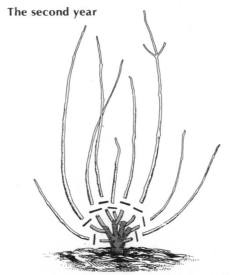

3 March to early April. Cut back hard all main shoots to within a few inches of the base. Cut out any weak basal growths. Mulch the plant well.

POLLARDING

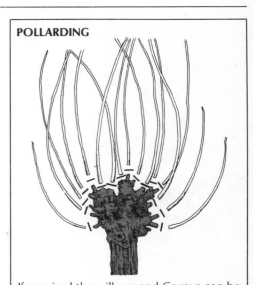

If required the willows and *Cornus* can be allowed to develop a single woody stem or stems to the required height and then pruned back in the same way. This method of pruning is usually known as pollarding.

Evergreen Shrubs 1

Group 5 includes the evergreen shrubs. Most evergreens are naturally bushy and reasonably compact in habit. Provided sufficient room is available they should be allowed to develop naturally with only minor pruning. This usually amounts to no more than the removal of spent flowers or wayward shoots and branches that would detract from the overall symmetry of the shrub.

Dead, diseased and mishapen shoots can be removed at any time of year. But any winter-damaged growth is best cut back between April and May, just as the growth buds are beginning to swell. This gives the maximum period for new shoots to ripen before winter. Pruning earlier in the year makes the plant vulnerable to wind and frost damage, while summer and autumn pruning will produce soft growth. This will almost certainly be damaged or killed during the following winter.

A small number of evergreen shrubs or subshrubs benefit from harder pruning, it helps them to maintain a compact habit or increase their flowering potential. This may involve cutting such plants as cotton lavender (*Santolina*) almost to ground level each spring or shearing over old growths of the rose of Sharon (*Hypericum calycinum*) and *Mahonia aquifolium*.

Early training

Early training is confined to slightly shortening any lateral growths which spoil the overall symmetry. Occasionally the leader shoots of young evergreen shrubs such as camellias may be spindly, rather weak, and lack any lateral branchlets. In these circumstances the leader should be cut back a few inches at planting. This will encourage laterals to grow from lower down. The uppermost new lateral should be trained to replace the leader. Do not cut the leader back more than a few inches, hard pruning may stimulate too much lateral growth and no adequate replacement leader shoot will develop. If the weak leader shoot is left, a plant which is bushy at the base and thin at the top will develop.

The pruning and management of *Eucalyptus* differs from that of other evergreens because of its unusual growth characteristics; it is described separately.

Training

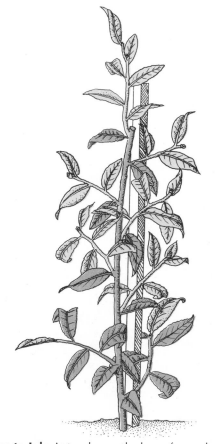

April to May. A young camellia with a well-developed leader. Cut back the uppermost vigorous lateral slightly; if left, unbalanced growth may result.

April to May. A young camellia with a weak leader and few laterals. Prune back the weak leader to a strong bud to stimulate vigorous lateral growth.

June to July. Lateral growths have formed. The uppermost lateral is trained in as the replacement leader.

DEAD-HEADING

Some evergreens, rhododendrons for example, flower and seed abundantly. Unless seed is required to increase stock the spent flower trusses should be removed as soon as possible. This will prevent the plant forming seed pods and directing its energy into producing strong new shoots and flower buds for next season's display. Dead-heading should be carried out immediately after the flowers fade and before seed pods begin to form. Carefully snap off the spent flower truss between finger and thumb. Take care not to damage the growth buds, which are present in the leaf axils directly below the flower truss.

Evergreen Shrubs 2

Lavender

Unpruned lavenders develop into woody, gnarled shrubs with bare lower stems sparsely topped by grey foliage. It is not worth while trying to rejuvenate mishapen or unkempt plants; they seldom produce satisfactory young growth if cut back into the old wood. It is better to replace them with young plants, which should be pruned hard in April to establish a low bushy habit.

Pruning consists of clipping over the bushes every April. Remove an inch or so of the previous season's growth to stimulate fresh young shoots that produce flowering spikes later in the season. Tidy gardeners will remove the old flower stems in early autumn to keep a neat appearance in the plant. Other gardeners may prefer to remove the stems the following April when undertaking annual pruning. In cold climates it is worth leaving these old flower stems until the April pruning because they help to protect the foliage from severe weather conditions.

Do not prune lavenders immediately after flowering as is sometimes recommended. This only stimulates late young growth that is liable to winter damage.

Heathers

Tree heathers (*Erica arborea* and its allies) do not require regular pruning. However, the removal of awkwardly placed or wayward branches is occasionally necessary. This should be carried out in April. Renewal pruning in April to May can be successful with tree heathers and some larger species and hybrids.

Most summer- and autumn-flowering heathers (*Calluna vulgaris, Erica ciliaris, E. vagans, Daboecia cantabrica* and their variants) benefit from regular trimming. If left unpruned they usually become leggy with shorter, less attractive flower heads.

Trimming should be carried out between March and early April because the russet or bronze coloring of the old flowers is attractive during the winter months. The old flower spikes of those heathers, which are grown for their brightly colored winter foliage, should be trimmed after flowering in October. They may require a further trim in March to early April.

Winter-flowering heathers are naturally either compact or spreading in habit, and when they have finished flowering in April can be gently trimmed to remove the old flower heads. No further pruning is required.

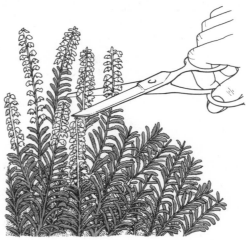

1 March to early April. Trim back the previous season's flower head to a point just below the lowest flowers on the spike. Use shears (or scissors on young plants), taking care to follow the natural growth habit of the individual plants. Avoid the flat "table-top" cut by varying the angle at which the blades of the shears are held.

2 August to September. *Calluna vulgaris* in flower; a compact plant with long flower spikes. Do not trim the old flower heads, they are attractive throughout winter.

The first year

1 April. Young lavender as received 9 in tall. At planting prune hard to remove straggly shoots and encourage new growth.

2 September. Vigorous bushy growth is produced during spring and summer. A few flower spikes develop during the first season.

Second and following years

3 April. Clip over the bush removing all old flower spikes and 1 in of the previous season's growth. Follow the natural outline of the plant with the shears so that a flat "table-top" appearance is avoided.

4 September. Old plant after flowering showing the form that should be created by regular pruning.

Climbing and Wall Plants: introduction

House walls and fences add an extra dimension to gardening by providing suitable locations to grow a wide range of climbing plants and trained shrubs. Many people grow a climbing rose or a clematis against the house, but wall or fence space that is readily available is seldom used effectively.

All houses walls, fences, the sides of sheds and garages—whatever their aspect—could and should be ornamented with plants. Apart from the obvious advantage of masking some of the less attractive areas of the house, planting is a method of merging house and garden, creating the single living unit that in Mediterranean countries is achieved by the vine-covered patio that links them together. Walls and fences also provide shelter for slightly tender plants that are not hardy in the open garden.

It is also possible to create additional vertical growing space by means of pergolas, arbors, pillars and other devices or to plant climbers to scramble through trees or, occasionally, hedges.

When considering the pruning of the many plants that can be used in these vertical plantings it is important to bear in mind the growth habits and the details of basic cultivation that can affect the training and subsequent pruning of climbers and wall shrubs.

The plants used can be divided into various groups based on their growth habit.
1. The natural clingers, such as ivy and Virginia creeper, which support themselves by aerial roots or sucker pads. No support system is needed.
2. The twiners, a large group, including honeysuckle, clematis and wisteria, which climb by means of curling or twining leaf tendrils, leaf stalks or stems. A support system to which they attach themselves is required.
3. The scramblers and floppers, which clamber through other plants in the wild using hooked thorns (roses) or by rapid elongation of their willowy shoots (Solanum crispum). A support system is needed to which the growth can be easily tied.
4. Shrubs which are slightly tender and benefit from the protection of a wall or fence. They may either be lightly pruned if space allows or trained and hard-pruned if space is limited. Examples include the evergreen

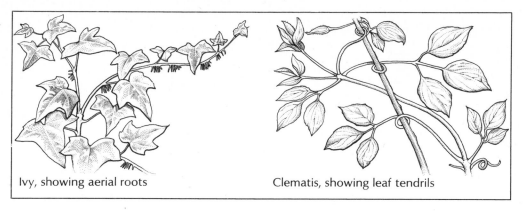

Ivy, showing aerial roots

Clematis, showing leaf tendrils

Ceanothus, Carpenteria californica and Fremontodendron. If the plant is trained to stay close to the wall it requires support systems to which the growths can be tied.

Many hardy shrubs can be trained against walls or fences in the same way and it is particularly useful to do this in small gardens, where space does not allow such large plants as Philadelphus and Forsythia to be grown in the open.

Select a plant to fill the area comfortably without the need for constant restriction to keep it within bounds. A rampant Virginia creeper on a bungalow, however attractive initially, will require constant and prompt attention to prevent its questing growths from dislodging tiles and damaging the gutters. A well-trained clematis, Ceanothus or pyracantha is much more satisfactory in the same position.

The dullest fence can be enlivened and the hard, straight edges lost by growing Clematis montana vertically to the top of the fence and then training and pruning the growth horizontally along the upper 6–12 in as far as is required. Even the difficult areas of low walls beneath windows can be clothed with trained shrubs such as Caryopteris, Daphne odora or variegated Euonymus if correct initial training and pruning is carried out.

Aspect is very important in deciding what plants to grow. It is no use planting sun-loving Ceanothus on a north-facing wall or fence. They may grow but they will seldom thrive, often becoming straggly and unkempt, whereas pyracanthas will grow, flower and fruit well.

Never plant directly against a wall or fence, always leave 9–12 in between the plant and its support system. The soil close to the wall is usually very dry. There may be difficulties with poor growth, die-back or sparse flowering.

Unless the plant climbs naturally by suckers or aerial roots some artificial system of supporting it against a wall or fence is required. Make certain the support system, which should be erected before planting, is adequate to support the plant in strong winds or heavy snowfalls. Careful training and pruning can be ruined in a very short time by failure to provide a strongly anchored support system of wire, chain-link or trellis.

Initial training and subsequent pruning

All the precepts of good pruning apply equally as much to climbers and wall plants. In particular the "3 D's," the removal of all dead, damaged and diseased wood, should be carried out regularly.

The gardener prunes to obtain the maximum coverage and the maximum effect of foliage, flower and fruit. This makes it necessary to restrict the natural habit of the plants concerned, and particularly where space is limited pruning must be aimed, in part at maintaining balanced and not excessive growth, which would require fairly drastic annual pruning of very vigorous species.

The importance of early training to establish a sound basic framework of branches cannot be overemphasized. Gardeners will often be reluctant to cut back vigorous growth on young plants, but in some situations this is essential to obtain maximum coverage of the wall or fence and to avoid the problem of excessive growth outward from the supports that is particularly prevalent with wall shrubs. The aim of the gardener must be to maintain growth as close to the wall or fence as possible.

Initially this involves considerable directing and tying in of shoots to cover the area of wall or fence concerned and cutting back outward-pointing growth (breastwood) to encourage lateral (sideways) growth.

The pruning of established plants will vary to some extent with the mode of growth. Some climbers such as ivies and Virginia creeper which cling with aerial roots or sucker pads will require no more than the removal of wayward shoots. With other shrubs regular annual pruning is needed to keep the plants neat, within bounds and free-flowering.

Generally follow the rules for pruning shrubs. Those plants which flower on the previous year's wood before midsummer, for example Ceanothus impressus, Forsythia suspensa and Clematis macropetala, are pruned immediately after flowering. Those which flower after midsummer on the current season's shoots are pruned either in late winter (Clematis × jackmanii) or in early spring (Ceanothus × burkwoodii and Ceanothus Autumnal Blue').

Some plants require a more complicated program if they are to flower profusely. Summer pruning—cutting back laterals and breastwood to form flowering spurs—is used. The leading shoots are trained in as required to fill space in the framework while the lateral and breastwood shoots produced during the growing season are cut back leaving only 2–5 leaves on the shoots, the severity of pruning depending on the plant concerned.

This technique is particularly applicable to the Japanese or flowering quinces (Chaenomeles) and Wisteria. They both need firm control to prevent unruly overvigorous growth, which, if left, results in a limited number of flowers. Summer pruning encourages flower bud formation on the spurred-back laterals, the food being channelled into forming flower buds on the spurs rather than into forming long growth shoots.

Clematis 1

The complicated instructions for pruning *Clematis* that are often found can be reduced to three categories based on the age of the growth on which the flowers are produced.

Some *Clematis* flower entirely on the current year's growth, while a number of spring-flowering species and hybrids produce all their bloom on short shoots from the previous year's wood. A third group, which includes many well-known hybrids such as 'Nelly Moser', produce flowers from last season's growth during early summer and a further display of rather smaller flowers in late summer and autumn from the current year's young shoots.

Vigorous species such as *Clematis montana* can be grown through trees and left unpruned unless they become completely out-of-hand. If this occurs it is simple to renovate them by cutting the old stems hard back to within 2–3 ft of ground level in late winter or early spring. In most instances dormant buds on the old, woody stems are stimulated into growth and within a few seasons they should be flowering freely. As with all renovation techniques it is important to feed and water the plants well.

Left unpruned most *Clematis* develop into tangled masses of growth, bearing their flowers high up above the bare woody stems. The following techniques aim to provide the maximum coverage and the most lavish flowers in the space available.

Pruning at planting is important but often overlooked. Many *Clematis*, particularly the larger-flowered hybrids, will tend to grow rapidly upwards on a single stem during the first season after planting unless checked at an early stage.

At planting the stem should be cut back to the lowest pair of strong buds to encourage the plant to produce further basal growth. The two stems produced from these buds can be stopped again to increase the number of basal shoots, but this is usually unnecessary.

This initial pruning applies to all *Clematis*, whether planted dormant in January or February or in leaf during spring or early summer. Most *Clematis* species will break naturally to form bushy, well-furnished plants, but it is a practice to prune them at planting to ensure that this occurs.

Group 1 contains all the *Clematis* species and hybrids that flower in summer and autumn entirely on the new growths produced during the current season. If left unpruned they begin growth in the spring from where they flowered the previous season and rapidly become bare at the base with flowers at the top only.

Pruning is very simple and consists of cutting back all of the previous year's growth virtually to ground level in late January or February. The pruning cuts should be made immediately above the lowest pair of strong buds on each stem.

Examples of *Clematis* in this group are *C. orientalis, C. tangutica, C. texensis* hybrids such as 'Gravetye Beauty' and 'Etoile Rose,' *C. viticella* and its derivatives; and among the large-flowered hybrids *C. × jackmanii*, 'Ernest Markham,' 'Hagley Hybrid' and 'Perle d'Azur.'

The first year

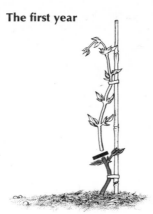

1 January to February. A newly planted *Clematis*. Cut back to the lowest pair of strong buds. Mulch well.

2 May to June. Train in the strong young growths and any basal growth. Flowers may appear in late summer.

The second year

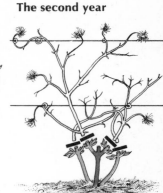

3 January to February. Cut back all growths to the lowest pair of strong buds on each stem. Mulch well.

Third and following years

4 May to June. Train in young growths and further basal growth as it develops.

5 July to September. Flowers are produced on the current season's growth.

6 January to February. Cut back all growths to the lowest pair of strong buds on each stem. Mulch well.

Clematis 2

Group 2 consists mainly of vigorous spring-flowering species, which flower between April and June on short shoots from growth produced the previous summer.

Examples of species in this group are *Clematis montana* and its forms, *C. chrysocoma*, *C. alpina* and *C. macropetala*.

The first two species are very hardy and attempting to restrict them to limited areas on a wall or fence usually results in a good deal of work. They thrive best given ample space on a house wall or in a tree and left unpruned or merely sheared over after flowering to keep them tidy. If left unpruned they may require rejuvenation after a few years. This involves cutting them to near ground level in winter.

The first and second years
Initial pruning at planting will encourage vigorous growth that can be gently guided to cover the area available and to form the basic framework over a two-year period.

Third and following years
Once this has been achieved the pruning of mature plants consists of cutting away all the flowered wood to within a few inches of the main framework immediately after flowering.

This stimulates vigorous long growths that can be trained or guided in as required, or allowed to cascade naturally. This growth will provide next season's flowering display and must not be winter-pruned.

The first year

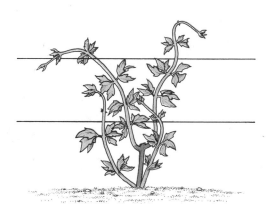

1 January to February. A newly planted *Clematis* with a single main stem. Cut back the stem above the lowest pair of strong buds. Mulch well.

2 May to June. Train in the strong young growths and any further basal growths that may have developed.

The second year

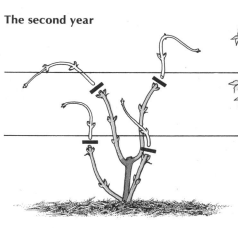

3 January to February. Cut back all the main growths trained in the previous summer by one-half their length to a pair of strong buds. Mulch well.

4 April to June. Train or guide the new shoots as required. Prune back any laterals that have flowered low down on the plant to one or two pairs of buds from the base.

5 July to September. Train or guide in new growth as required.

Third and following years

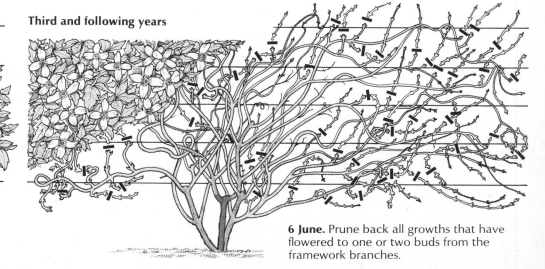

6 June. Prune back all growths that have flowered to one or two buds from the framework branches.

Clematis 3

Group 3 contains all the hybrids that provide large, sumptuous flowers from May to July on the previous year's wood. While the flowers are being produced on side-shoots from the old wood new growth is being formed. This produces further crops of medium-sized blooms during late summer and early autumn.

Popular varieties in this group include 'Lasurterr,' 'Nelly Moser,' 'The President,' 'Henry,' 'Mme le Coultre,' 'William Kennett' and the double-flowered 'Duchess of Edinburgh' and 'Vyvyan Pennel,' which may produce single blooms late in the season.

The growth habit of Group 3 Clematis makes them difficult to prune satisfactorily without a good deal of work, and they may be left entirely unpruned or only lightly pruned until they become straggly and out of control. Then the rejuvenation process described in the introduction can be applied. Alternatively they may be treated as Group 1 and pruned back hard to base each January to February, but then they will only flower in late summer.

Neither of these treatments allows the full flowering potential of these Clematis to be exploited, but a simple renewal system can be instituted with mature plants to provide the maximum flower during summer and autumn. It involves the same basic training as Group 1, but mature plants are renewal-pruned with one-quarter to one-third of the old shoots being cut to within a foot or so of the base. This is done between May and July, depending on the variety, immediately after the first flush of bloom has been produced on the previous season's growth. Alternatively the renewal pruning can be carried out annually in January or February, but this means a smaller display of flowers in early summer.

Strong shoots arise from the pruned-back stems and will grow vigorously during summer and possibly provide a few autumn blooms. Ample feeding to maintain vigor is required, but using this method the gawky "bird's-nest" effect so commonly seen is avoided.

This renewal system works more easily with wall- or fence-grown plants, where the shoots can be spaced out evenly. On pergolas or grown among shrubs Clematis in this group are best left unpruned or trimmed after the initial flowering as it is difficult to disentangle the cut-back stems.

The first year

1 January to February. A newly planted Clematis with a single main stem. Cut back the stem to above the lowest pair of strong buds. Mulch well.

2 May to June. Train in strong young growths and any basal growths which develop. A few flowers may be produced in late summer.

The second year

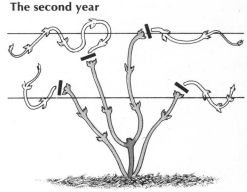

3 January to February. Cut back all the main growths trained in the previous summer by one-half to a strong pair of buds. Mulch well.

4 June to September. Train or guide in new growths as required. The basic framework has been established. Some flower will be produced in summer and autumn on the new growth.

Third and following years

5 June to July. Plant will flower on old wood. Immediately after flowering cut one-quarter to one-third of the mature shoots to within a foot or so of the base. Water and feed well.

6 August to September. Plant flowers on young shoots. Guide into place basal shoots that develop from the cut-back stems.

Wisteria 1

The pruning of *Wisteria* baffles most gardeners as the tremendous vigor of their whiplike summer shoots seems almost impossible to control. It is however, quite possible to keep them restrained and trained into a reasonably confined space—although they are capable of clambering a hundred feet or more up a tree or along a wall. Successful control demands a good deal of attention from the gardener as pruning needs to be carried out twice during a season to ensure adequate flowers and to confine the plant's naturally robust growth.

The first year

A young *Wisteria* planted in winter or early spring will normally produce one or two vigorous basal growths that increase rapidly in length. Few or no lateral shoots develop naturally at this stage. If the plant is to be grown in espalier form to cover a wall or fence the main shoot must be cut or tipped back to 2½–3ft from ground level at planting.

This stimulates two or three lateral buds to develop and these new shoots should be trained into the positions required. Tie in the upper shoot vertically and the other growths at an angle of approximately 45 degrees. If the laterals are trained in a horizontal position initially their growth may be checked. At this stage the branches are flexible and easily positioned on the support system.

The second and following years

The following winter cut back the leading shoot leaving 2½–3ft of wood above the uppermost lateral. Bring down the laterals to a more or less horizontal position. At the same time cut back the horizontal leaders of those laterals by about one-third of their length.

This stimulates further lateral growth and a similar training process is carried out during the following years to form a new vertical leader and further well-spaced horizontal laterals to form the arms of the espalier.

Train in a new horizontal leader for each pruned-back lateral and cut back surplus laterals or sublaterals in early August to within 6–9in (4–5 leaves) of the main framework branches to form flowering spurs.

This process is continued annually until the desired number of well-spaced lateral branches is obtained. The aim should be to produce an espaliered plant with horizontal branches not less than 15–18in apart. This allows the long pendulous inflorescences to hang down gracefully from the spurs without crowding those on the branches below.

Further basal growth that develops should be cut out completely as soon as it is seen.

The first year

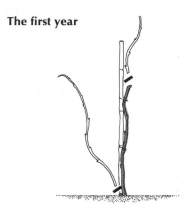

1 Winter to early spring. Young *Wisteria* at planting. Prune or tip back the strongest growth to 2½–3ft from ground level. Stake this main shoot. Remove to base any surplus shoots that are present.

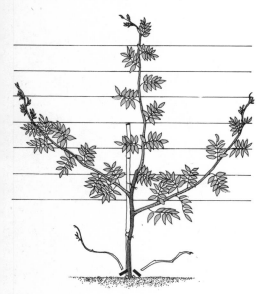

2 June to early August. Two or three vigorous shoots develop from lateral buds. Train in the uppermost vertically. Tie in other laterals on the support framework at approximately 45 degrees. Remove any new basal growths. Tie in further extension growth. If sublaterals are produced, cut them back in early August to 6–9in.

The second year

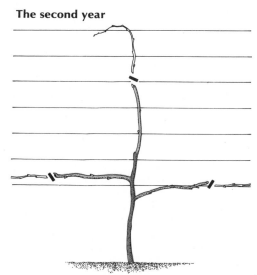

3 December to January. Cut back the vertical leader to within 2½–3ft of the uppermost lateral. Bring down the laterals trained at 45 degrees to a horizontal position and cut back their leaders by one-third.

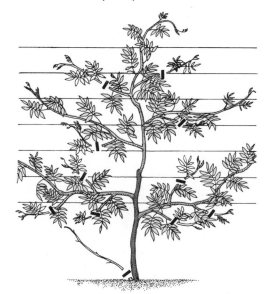

4 June to early August. Vigorous shoots develop from lateral buds on the vertical leader. Train in the uppermost vertically as the new leader. Tie in other laterals on the support framework at an angle of about 45 degrees. Remove any further basal growth. In early August cut back any surplus laterals and sublaterals to 6–9in.

The third year

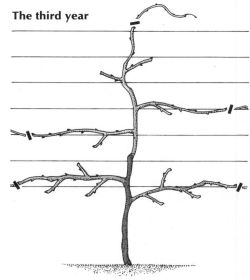

5 December to January. Cut back the vertical leader to within 2½–3ft of the uppermost lateral. Bring down the laterals trained at 45 degrees to a horizontal position and cut back their leaders by one-third. Cut back last season's growth of leaders on horizontally trained branches by one-third.

Wisteria 2

The mature plant
Once the basic framework of branches has been trained to fill the area available any further extension growths, which may reach 10–12 ft in a season, and lateral growths are pruned back in early August to within 6 in (4–6 leaves) of the main branches to form flowering spurs. This summer pruning is followed by a further shortening of these spurs in winter (December and January) to 3–4 in leaving only 2–3 buds on each spur shoot. The following season's flowers are borne on these spurs. In winter the plump flower buds are easily distinguished from the flattened growth buds so the flowering potential is easy to predict.

A difficult procedure that will provide more flower buds involves pruning back the extension growths to 6 in at two-week intervals during the summer. This stimulates further laterals to form and constant pinching back produces more congested spurs.

Wisteria can be grown in a number of ways and trained as espaliers, fans, and as low-standard shrubs or semi informally to be used against walls or fences. The same pruning technique is used for mature plants, but the initial training will differ slightly with the method used. Wherever possible it is best to train the main branches more or less horizontally as the maximum display is obtained from plants trained this way.

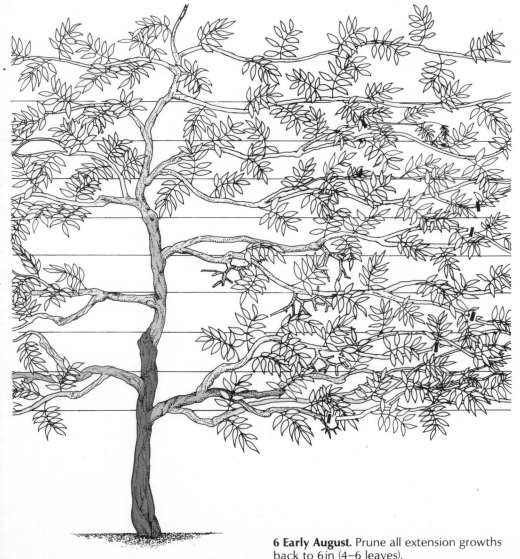

6 Early August. Prune all extension growths back to 6 in (4–6 leaves).

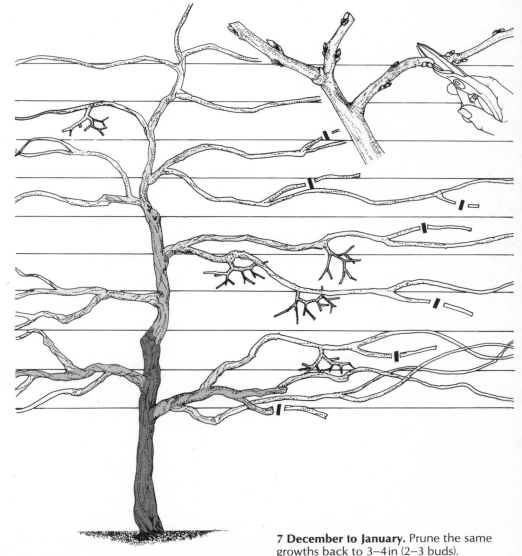

7 December to January. Prune the same growths back to 3–4 in (2–3 buds).

233

Ceanothus and Honeysuckle

The shrubby evergreen *Ceanothus* species and hybrids are suitable for training as wall plants, where their abundant blue, powder-puff flower heads show to the best advantage. Most *Ceanothus* flower in May on growth produced the previous summer, but a few, such as 'Autumnal Blue' and 'Burkwoodii,' flower on both last season's and the current year's growth and require slightly different pruning treatment.

The first year

Ceanothus should always be planted in spring as pot-grown plants. Training consists of tying in the main shoot vertically as it grows and fanning out the laterals to fill the available space as evenly as possible. Growth is rapid and it is important to tie in the young shoots regularly during spring and summer to ensure that they are guided in the direction required. If left they will tend to grow away from the support structure and become difficult to manage as the growth ripens. Breastwood is produced abundantly and, if not suitable for training into the framework, should be clipped over once in June to encourage dense, tight growth and to maintain the plant close to the wall or fence.

Second and following years

Continue training and tying in extension growth until the space provided has been filled. Immediately after flowering clip over the previous season's growths, which will normally have flowered during May, to within 3–4 in of the framework. The dense growth produced during the summer provides flowers the following spring.

It is important to prune a wall-trained evergreen *Ceanothus* regularly each season so that a compact mat of growth is maintained against the support structure. If it is left unpruned it will quickly grow away from the wall or fence and is liable to be damaged by strong winds or snow. *Ceanothus* resent hard pruning into old wood and it is difficult to maintain the neatly tailored look which is so attractive with well-grown specimens if regular training is not carried out.

Pruning of the few evergreen *Ceanothus*, which flower mainly on the current season's growth, is carried out in April. The initial training and method of pruning is the same. Pruning in early spring means the loss of any early bloom, but ensures that the plant maintains a tight habit and flowers generously in summer and autumn.

The first year

1 April to May. Tie in the leader vertically. Spread out and tie in lateral growths. Cut out badly placed shoots and trim back breastwood to 2–3 in.

2 June to July. Rapid extension growth has occurred. Tie in leader and lateral shoots. Trim breastwood to 3–4 in from the supports.

The second year

3 June. A few flowers have been produced on last year's side-shoots. Cut back breastwood to 3–4 in from the framework.

HONEYSUCKLE

The climbing honeysuckles can be divided into two groups for pruning purposes, based on their flowering habit.

The first group, typified by *Lonicera japonica*, the rampant Japanese honeysuckle, produces flowers in pairs in the axils of leaves on the current season's growth. The only pruning necessary is to restrict the exuberant growth. This involves clipping away any unwanted growth in March or April each season. This stimulates fresh young growth which quickly covers the sheared surface and will flower later in the season.

The second group includes the much more popular Dutch honeysuckle *L. peri-clymenum* 'Belgica' and a number of related species and hybrids such as *L. × americana, L. × brownii, L. sempervirens, L. × tellmanniana* and *L. tragophylla*. These bear flowers on laterals produced from the previous season's growth.

If space allows they may be permitted to climb through old trees or on walls and left completely unpruned so that the growth wanders and cascades in a natural manner. They tend to form "birds'-nests" on bare stems (like some *Clematis*) and if they are to be grown in positions where tangled growth and bare stems will be unsightly, mild pruning is required immediately after flowering each season. This simply involves cutting back some of the old weak growths and some of the shoots which have flowered to a point where vigorous young growth is developing. The young growth can be tied in to the framework as it develops, but is more effective if left to cascade down so that an informal curtain of flowers is produced.

Third and following years

4 July to September. Tie in leader and main lateral shoots as they develop.

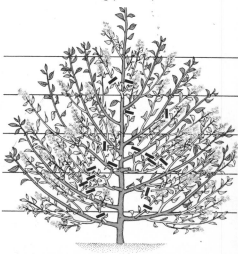

5 June. Cut back all breastwood that has flowered to within 4–6 in of the framework. Tie in extension shoots as they develop.

Chaenomeles and Pyracantha

Most varieties of the common "Japonica" or "Flowering Quince" are excellent plants for training against walls or fences. They flower well even on northern and eastern aspects, where they are particularly useful for early spring color.

The first year
Although *Chaenomeles* can be trained formally as espaliers or fans a less exact arrangement than that described for *Wisteria* better suits their growth habit.

The basic framework is built up by training in a leader and spacing out more or less horizontally any laterals against the wall or fence. If several basal shoots are present on the young plant these can be spaced out evenly against the support structure as it is not essential for a main leader to be established unless a formal espaliered plant is required.

Most *Chaenomeles* produce laterals and sublaterals freely without the need to stop the main shoots. These are trained in as required to complete the basic framework. Very little flower is produced during the first year or two after planting.

Cut back any outward-pointing shoots (breastwood) or sublaterals not required to form part of the framework to 4–6 leaves from the base after they have made their initial summer growth.

Further sublaterals usually develop on these cut-back shoots and these should be pruned to 2–3 leaves in late summer so that a stubby spur system is formed.

Second and following years
After flowering in spring vigorous extension growth is produced. Unless any shoots are required to train in to fill gaps in the framework summer-prune all new growths to 4–6 leaves from the base in June to July. Cut back any secondary shoots produced from this summer-pruned growth in early autumn, again to 2–3 leaves. This summer pruning builds up flowering spurs that are covered in bloom the following spring. In time these spurs may become congested and some will require to be thinned out each winter to maintain a balanced plant. This winter thinning may be done annually on established plants, pruning back all the summer growth originally cut to 4–6 leaves to two buds in winter if required. It produces a neater plant, but specimens which are only summer-pruned with an occasional winter-thinning of spurs flower equally well.

PYRACANTHA

Pyracantha is ideal for covering walls and can easily be trained to form almost any pattern of growth and grow around the windows and doors of houses. It also lends itself to formal training as an espalier, cordon or fan and is particularly valuable for northern and eastern aspects.

The first year
If a formally trained plant is required, the training is similar to that used for espalier apples. Usually it is more convenient to use the less formal system described for *Chaenomeles*, making sure that the basic framework branches are well spaced and that excess lateral growths and breastwood are cut back in July or early August to form spur shoots and to maintain growth close to the wall or fence.

Mature plant
The bunches of white flowers, which are followed by red or yellow berries, are formed in the leaf axils of short spur growths on the previous year's shoots. After flowering growth shoots appear during late June and July, hiding the young berries. On mature plants these need to be summer-pruned so that the fruit can be seen to full effect. Cut back the young growth as soon as the berries begin to ripen in mid- or late July or August to within 3–4 in of the main framework. Secondary growth often occurs and a second trimming in early September can be given if needed. This pruning not only exposes the fruits so that they ripen well and can be seen but also produces the next season's flowering spurs.

The first year

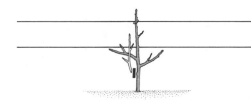

1 October to March. Train in the leader vertically. Space out laterals more or less horizontally. Cut out any awkwardly placed shoots that cannot be trained.

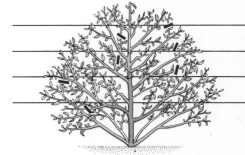

3 August to September. Train in late growth. Cut back any breastwood or surplus laterals to 2–3 leaves.

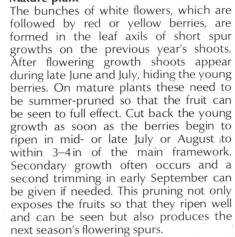

5 August to September. Cut back summer growth (sublaterals) to 2–3 leaves from base.

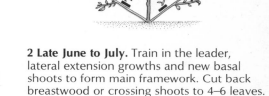

2 Late June to July. Train in the leader, lateral extension growths and new basal shoots to form main framework. Cut back breastwood or crossing shoots to 4–6 leaves.

Second and following years

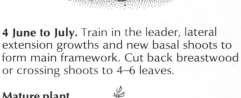

4 June to July. Train in the leader, lateral extension growths and new basal shoots to form main framework. Cut back breastwood or crossing shoots to 4–6 leaves.

Mature plant

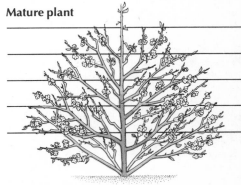

6 March to April. When the allotted space is filled stop the leader and main laterals.

Introduction/Hygiene 1

Of all the branches of horticulture, growing under glass is the most specialized. Not only is the constant maintenance of the plants necessary, but the environment must be controlled to give acceptable growing conditions.

The ideal environment The basic aim should always be to create an ideal environment for healthy growth, but perfection is seldom possible, and never possible if a mixed collection of plants is grown, for plants have differing needs. In theory at least, the fully automated greenhouse can be programmed to provide the correct levels of heat, light, humidity and ventilation whatever the conditions in the outside world. But in practice this is rarely the case. Freak weather conditions, a breakdown of equipment or a simple power failure can quickly upset the automated system. In the end, it is the skill of the gardener that counts. Automatic equipment can at best work to only fairly wide tolerances and has the disadvantage of providing the same levels of water, heat and so on for all the plants in the greenhouse. It is most important to get to know the limitations of the individual greenhouse and the degrees of tolerance of the plants being grown. This knowledge goes to build up the intuitive skill which all good growers have, to know when to water and ventilate, when to damp down, shade or feed for the very best results. All this takes patience and practice and the beginner must be keen enough to spend time with his plants, noting what happens to them under different conditions.

Record keeping There is much to be said for keeping a greenhouse diary or notebook. Record in it the daily maximum and minimum temperatures, when seeds are sown or cuttings taken, when plants are potted, fed, staked, and stopped. In addition, comments can be made from time to time on the vigor, appearance and health of the plants. Over the seasons, a valuable record of the prevailing conditions is built up.

The daily routine

It is important to establish a regular daily routine when gardening under glass. To fail to do so is likely to lead to the disappointments of poor-quality plants and frequent failure of seedlings and young plants.

Summer A routine for an imaginary summer day could be as follows. Once the morning sun is fully on the greenhouse, check the temperature. If it is about five degrees above the desired minimum temperature for the plants being grown, open the ventilators by half to two-thirds. If temperatures continue to climb, open up fully around mid-morning. Damp down, shade if required and check that there are no dry plants (but leave the main watering operation until later). In early afternoon, go over the watering thoroughly and damp down again if conditions are hot. If it is not particularly hot, damp down in late afternoon. As soon as direct sunlight is off the greenhouse the blinds can be rolled up and when the temperature drops back to about five degrees above minimum, shut down the ventilators. During a warm spell the temperature may not drop so low even after nightfall and the greenhouse can then be left open day and night. All depends on the minimum temperature being maintained.

Cleaning the greenhouse

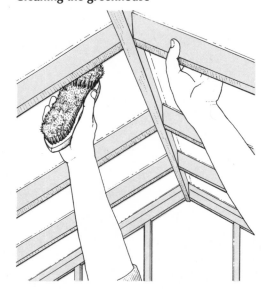

In late summer, scrub the framework of the greenhouse to remove pest and disease organisms. First empty the greenhouse. Use a dilute sterilizing agent.

Winter Much the same procedure is followed in winter, but if the weather is cold and temperatures do not rise, ventilation and damping will not need to be carried out and watering will be minimal.

While this sort of routine is ideal for the plants, it is not easily carried out by the gardener who may have to be away all day. Happily, it can be modified and compromises made. Full ventilation and essential watering can be carried out just before leaving in the morning and the main watering and damping down done on arriving home. Damping down during the day, while desirable for most plants, is not essential. Automatic watering and ventilation help to optimize conditions in greenhouses left unattended during the day.

In the winter a daily check over in the morning or evening is enough. If automatic ventilators and capillary watering are installed, then a weekly check over should suffice in winter.

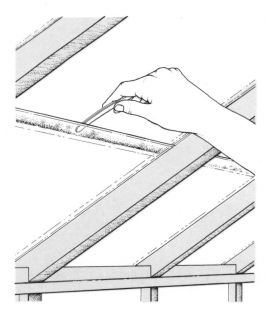

In autumn, wash the glass thoroughly using a non-toxic detergent. Remove dirt and algae from glass overlaps with an alloy plant label.

Hygiene

Along with the right environment and routine care, a good level of hygiene must be maintained to ensure healthy, vigorous plants. The need to keep the greenhouse and particularly the glass clean is often overlooked. It is surprising how much dirt can settle firmly onto a sheet of glass in the open, even in areas where air pollution is low. This considerably cuts down light intensity, the effects of which are particularly noticeable in winter. Plants which need good light, such as tomato, lettuce and freesia, look thin and pale and lack substance.

Glass should be washed thoroughly in autumn, using a suitable non-toxic detergent. Where the glass overlaps, dirt accumulates and algae flourish, forming a dark band. Remove this dirt with a metal plant label or a sliver of sheet metal. Glass washing should be carried out at intervals during the winter, especially in areas of air pollution. At other times of the year it is usually not

At the same time, scrub surfaces such as paths and walls to remove algae, using a dilute solution of a proprietary algicide.

Introduction/Hygiene 2

so important and in summer the layer of grime can even be beneficial, acting as partial shading.

At least once a year the framework of the greenhouse should be scrubbed to remove pest and disease organisms such as the eggs of red spider mite and spores of fungal diseases. To do the job properly the greenhouse should be empty so that a sterilizing agent, a chemical fluid, can be added to the washing water. Late summer is a good time to wash the greenhouse, when all but the tenderest plants can be stood outside.

In a humid greenhouse a film of green algae can form on all moist surfaces including walls and floors, and can become slippery. All such surfaces should be scrubbed, using one of the proprietary algicides in the water.

Hygiene should not stop at keeping the greenhouse clean. All used pots and seed flats should be thoroughly washed and scrubbed before re-use to minimize the spread of disease. Remove any "tide-marks"

of soil or chemicals around the insides of the pots. Soak clay pots in water to ensure cleanliness. Perhaps the chief cause of infection of soil-borne rots is the use of dirty containers for propagation. It is of great importance to ensure that containers are clean.

In order to avoid cross-infection, always remove containers and used soil from the greenhouse when not in use. Spent soil provides ideal conditions for the multiplication of both damping off fungi and sciarid flies. It is important to wipe tools clean after use to ensure they do not become a potential source of infection.

It is futile to go to great lengths to sterilize soil, or to go to the expense of buying sterile soil mixes, if they are left lying about open to the elements. All mixtures and their components should be kept bagged and covered to maintain their reliability. Do not attempt to re-use spent soil mixes, even if sterilized, as the chemical balances will be out of proportion.

PEST AND DISEASE CONTROL

Good greenhouse hygiene, as outlined in the previous section, is an essential starting point in the avoidance of pests and diseases. However, problems will inevitably occur because it is impossible to avoid introducing infected material into the greenhouse. The following pages detail pests and diseases met with in the greenhouse and prescribe remedies. On this page methods of control are discussed.

Control methods
Because the greenhouse is a closed environment it is often easier than in the open garden to control pests and diseases. Some pests, such as snails, can be removed by hand, but most greenhouse problems will have to be dealt with by chemical means. Some biological control is possible for a few greenhouse pests (see below). Good growing practice is the first line of defence, for healthy sturdy plants are less susceptible to disease than sickly ones.

Applying chemicals Choose a chemical which will not harm the plants being grown, but which is effective against the problem concerned. Remove any plants likely to be harmed by the chemical, or cover them with plastic sheeting secured with string or elastic bands. Carefully follow the instructions given on the next page for the use of chemicals in the greenhouse. When spraying, open all ventilators and the door. Many pesticides are also available as dusts which are applied from a puffer pack. Use dusts on flowers and on plants sensitive to moisture on foliage.

Fumigation Chemicals can also be applied in smoke form, a process called fumigation. First check carefully that none of the plants present will be damaged by the fumigant to be used. The manufacturer's instructions will contain a list. Remove any such plants from the greenhouse. Fumigants are available as simple pyrotechnic smokes which resemble slow-burning fireworks, or as solids which are vaporized on electric elements. Fumigants should be applied at a measured rate depending upon the cubic capacity of the greenhouse. Measure the capacity by the formula length × breadth × average height. Fumigation can be used against specific pests or as a general hygiene measure every six months.

Apply fumigants in the evening, then leave the greenhouse closed overnight. Seal any leaks and close all ventilators before application. To sterilize the greenhouse, empty it of plants and burn sulfur at the rate of 1 lb per 1000 cu ft. The burning sulfur produces sulfur dioxide gas, which is highly poisonous. Leave the greenhouse as soon as the sulfur is ignited.

Biological control
In the open, many harmful pests are kept under control by predators such as birds or other insects. In the closed greenhouse environment, such natural balances break down, leading to pest problems. In an effort to avoid over-use of chemicals, biologists have investigated the possibility of biological control. This means introducing a predator to attack concentrations of harmful pests. Some predators have been found to be regularly effective and are available commercially. A predatory mite, *Phytoseiulus persimilis*, controls greenhouse red spider mite. A ladybird, *Cryptolaemus montrouzeri*, can be used against mealybugs; a parasitic wasp, *Encarsia formosa*, for greenhouse whitefly; and a bacterium, *Bacillus thuringiensis*, attacks caterpillars.

If biological control is used chemical means must be ruled out until the predators have had a chance to work, which limits its application if more than one pest is found. Predators are a cure rather than a prevention: they cannot work until their prey, the pest, is present. The critical time to introduce predators is when the pest first appears. The predator can then breed and build up a large enough population to eradicate the pests. Predators will only breed faster than the pests when the daytime temperature exceeds 21°C/70°F and light intensity is good.

While biological control avoids chemical build-up on plants, a point especially to be borne in mind with food crops, it is a less certain and more complicated method of pest control than the use of chemicals. The use of predators has to be carefully timed. This may involve investigating sources of supply well before the trouble is likely to arise and taking swift action once the pests are noticed.

After use, wash and scrub seed boxes and pots to minimize the spread of disease. Store containers neatly and do not allow debris to build up. Potting soil should be kept in a bin with a tight-fitting lid to avoid staleness and possible contamination. Remove spent soil from the greenhouse after use.

The year in a cold greenhouse 1

The year in a cold greenhouse

This calender details sowing and harvesting times for basic cold greenhouse crops and lists planting, sowing and potting on times for ornamentals.

Regular tasks such as watering, feeding, damping down, shading and ventilating are not listed every month. The timing of these procedures is to a large extent dependent upon day to day conditions and on the crops being grown. Follow the instructions given under individual crops, and act according to the basic principles discussed in the first two sections of this book.

Pest and disease control is another regular task that must be attended to whenever problems arise. The worst period for pests is from April to October, but problems such as whitefly and red spider mite can appear in any of the 12 months. For the control of pests and diseases, see page 237; for the specific types, see pages 260–265.

Using a cold greenhouse

A cold greenhouse is one which possesses no form of artificial heat. It is, in effect, no more than a protective covering against extremes of cold, wet and wind. A cold greenhouse can form a vital and interesting adjunct to the garden provided its limitations are recognized and the plants to be grown carefully selected.

The most important limitation of the cold greenhouse is that of temperature. In winter, if the outside temperature drops to around 7°C/20°F it is likely that there will be several degrees of frost inside the greenhouse. It is wise to recognize this and to avoid trying to over-winter plants which are not frost-hardy. It is possible to give protection against frost by plunging pots and covering plants with polyethylene or burlap, but these provide limited defense against severe frosts.

Conditions and choice of plants

A cold greenhouse will suit those plants that are hardy outdoors, and will in most cases allow them to be grown better. It also suits annuals, including fruits and vegetables, which are half-hardy outdoors. A cold greenhouse can extend the growing season at either end, allowing crops to be taken earlier and later than outdoors. Ornamental annuals and biennials can be raised from seed in the predictable conditions a cold greenhouse offers, and various propagation techniques carried out.

Despite the lack of artificial heat, the gardener has various techniques available to allow him to alter the environment of a cold greenhouse. The basic principles explained in the section on Running the Greenhouse (pages 236–237), apply here, though with the narrow tolerance of many cold greenhouse plants extra care is needed.

Ventilation The most effective method of temperature control available is ventilation. In very cold conditions it can be colder in the greenhouse than outside if the doors and lower ventilators are not opened for a few hours in the middle of the day. Cold air is heavy and collects in a pool at ground level, but will flow out if given the chance.

Most ventilation is concerned with trapping solar heat. Once outside temperatures start to rise in spring, ventilators should be opened a little in the morning and closed some hours before sunset. This regime may well cause the thermometer to rise five degrees above normal; this heat surplus not only acts as a cushion against the rapid drop in temperature as night falls, but also improves the growing atmosphere. Some of the surplus heat is absorbed by the soil, paths and structure generally, moderating night temperatures as it is given off into the cooling air. This mechanism is exploited by several solar heating systems.

At all times the aim is to produce a buoyant atmosphere, one in which the air within the greenhouse is moving up and around rather than lying stagnant.

Air movement The circulation of air is a vital factor in cold greenhouse management. Even in a closed-up cold house in winter, imperfections in glazing can allow air to escape sufficiently fast to give two complete air changes per hour. In high summer well-ventilated greenhouses can have 120 air changes per hour, which helps to keep internal temperatures close to those outside. If through a deficiency in ventilation air changes drop to 30–40 per hour, summer greenhouse temperatures can rise as high as 43°C/110°F, to the detriment of plants.

January

Plan the year's crops and order seeds and seedlings. Ventilate the greenhouse on sunny days.
Sow onions for transplanting. Sow early radishes in soil borders or peat pots.
Bring in plunged bulbs to flower in the greenhouse (*Babiana, Chionodoxa, Crocus,* daffodils, *Fritillaria, Iris, Leucojum, Ornithogalum.*)
Bulbs which have finished flowering can be planted out into frames.
Sow lily seed. Begin sequence of chrysanthemum cuttings later in the month.

February

Ventilate as necessary. Water sparingly.
Sow lettuce, early bunching turnips, carrots, parsnips and early beets (until March), bulb onions (until April). Sow tomatoes in heat later in the month.
Bring potted strawberries in to crop in late spring.
Bring in remaining plunged bulbs to replace those which have finished flowering.
Pot on and divide ferns if necessary.
Pot on over-wintered coleus, fuchsias and pelargoniums.
Sow and place in a propagating case: *Abutilons,* tuberous and fibrous begonias, *Coleus, Celosias, Gloxinias, Streptocarpus.*
Pot on annuals sown in autumn.
Re-pot evergreen azaleas.

March

Sow lettuce, celery, carrots, mustard and cress.
Sow in heat: eggplants, sweet peppers, dwarf beans, tomatoes if not sown in February.
Prick out lettuce seedlings. Pot out late in month.
Sow for transplanting: broad beans, runner beans, brassicas, leeks, celery, peas, sweetcorn, chives, thyme.
Continue to bring in pot strawberries.
Sow half-hardy annuals and alpines.
Pot on over-wintered annuals. Take pelargonium and dahlia cuttings.
Plant out rooted cuttings taken in winter. Plant hippeastrum bulbs in pots.

April

Sow according to needs: lettuce, radish, mustard and cress, beets, endive. parsley. Sow sweetcorn, celeriac, dwarf French beans, cucumbers.
Harvest early radishes and lettuce, chicory, seakale and rhubarb.
Complete sowing half-hardy annuals. Sow biennials for spring flowering under glass. Prick out March-sown seedlings. Begin to harden off bedding plant seedlings. Take fuchsia cuttings, pot rooted dahlia and other cuttings. Pot up tuberoses for flowering. Start feeding camellias.

May

Plant eggplants, sweet peppers, okra and cucumber, melons.
Harvest early carrots, early bunching turnips, beets.
Plant out tomatoes after last frost.
Harden off bedding plants and plant out after frosts have ended.
Take cuttings from regal pelargoniums. Sow *Calceolaria, Freesia, Schizanthus* for winter flowering.

June

Harvest lettuce, radish, endive, mustard and cress, beans, parsley.
Continue to sow biennials. Pot on cyclamen seedlings.
Take cuttings of pinks. Plunge azaleas outside and feed every 14 days.

The year in a cold greenhouse 2

Excessive summer temperatures can be reduced by damping down floors and walls with city water, which rarely rises above a temperature of 10°C/50°F. Damping down also promotes a degree of humidity enjoyed by most plants. Excessive transpiration caused by very dry, hot conditions gives a severe check to plant growth. Shading, used in conjunction with ventilation, is also important in controlling summer conditions.

Thus the management of a cold greenhouse is an amalgam of attention to ventilation, atmospheric moisture, warmth and light. Holding the environmental balance is a complicated art in which experience is an important factor.

Plants for the cold greenhouse
Most annuals, biennials and shrubs, provided they are hardy, can be successfully overwintered in a cold house. The advantage of doing so is that they flower two to three weeks earlier than plants grown outdoors. Their condition, not having had to contend with winter weather, is better than that of outdoor plants. Blooms are more spectacular as wind and rain damage is not a problem.

Alpines and similar plants can also be grown in an unheated greenhouse, but they require conditions which preclude the growth of many other plants.

Many food crops can be grown in a cold house, providing cash saving over shop prices and, often produce of a higher quality. Tomatoes, the most popular crop, are covered in detail on pages 244–245. The following pages also detail the cultivation of fruits and other salad and vegetables. Another aspect of garden food production that a greenhouse can assist is the raising of seedlings for transplanting outdoors. This frees the gardener from dependence on commercially raised plants, and makes the growing of unusual vegetables, and the obscurer varieties of common ones, possible. As with flowers, the quality of crops grown under glass will be higher than those grown outdoors, due to the lack of weather damage. This is especially true of salad crops and strawberries.

Over-wintering Successful over-wintering is more likely if certain precautions are taken. During the coldest spells, plants must be kept on the dry side. It is best that the roots do not freeze for these are often more tender than the tops. Ground level beds should be deeply mulched with bracken or straw and the bases of shrubs and climbers wrapped. Large pots and tubs must be wrapped either with straw, glass fiber, or any other approved insulating material that can be secured in place with netting or burlap and wire twine. Smaller pots are best plunged in peat or sand.

Winter sets limitations on what can be grown permanently in the unheated greenhouse. From about mid-spring to late autumn the full range of cool greenhouse plants thrive happily. From late spring to early or mid-autumn even warm greenhouse plants succeed. With a heated propagating case, such plants can be over-wintered.

Flowering plants from seed
A wide range of hardy and tender annuals and biennials is readily available to provide color and interest in the cold greenhouse for a large part of the year. These plants can be used as the main display or to fill in gaps between non-flowering permanent plants or fruit and vegetable crops. Hardy annuals can be sown in late summer or early autumn. They will over-winter well in a cold greenhouse and flower late the following spring, well ahead of their normal season. This technique can be used for hardy biennials, but these need to be sown in early summer and may be grown outside or in an open cold frame until late autumn. Routine seed sowing and pricking off into flats or pans is all that annuals and biennials initially require (see pages 178–179). Thereafter place the young plants singly into 5 in pots, or space three out into 6 or 7 in containers. A fairly rich soil mix is recommended, a John Innes potting No. 2 being very satisfactory. Once the young plants are 3–4 in tall, pinch out their tips to encourage branching and a more bushy habit. As soon as they are growing more strongly, in late winter or early spring, commence liquid feeding and repeat at 10–14 day intervals. At about this time, insert twiggy sticks or canes for support.

July
Harvest sweet peppers, lettuce, radishes, mustard and cress, parsley, tomatoes left in the greenhouse.
Take hydrangea cuttings.
Take half-ripe cuttings.

August
Sow lettuce, radishes, mustard and cress, winter endive.
Sow cyclamen seeds. Take fuchsia cuttings, pot on half-ripe cuttings.

September
Sow lettuce, radishes, mustard and cress, alpine strawberries.
Plant late in month: apricots, peaches, grape vines.
Harvest lettuces, parsley, radishes, mustard and cress.
Lift seakale roots late in month, pot up and blanch.
Sow hardy annuals for spring flowering under glass.
Pot on hardy biennials for spring flowering.
Bring in evergreen azaleas, pot-grown chrysanthemums. Plant bulbous irises and hyacinths in pots.

October
Sow lettuce for crops in spring.
Plant fruit trees.
Continue to pot up and blanch seakale.
Bring in tender bedding perennials for over-wintering.
Repeat sowings of annuals. Prick out annuals sown in September.
Pot on biennials. Sow sweet peas.
Over-winter chrysanthemum stools and dahlia tubers.

November
Sow onions for transplanting.
Box up rhubarb crowns, chicory and remaining seakale. Insulate boxes if necessary.
Bring in pots of herbs for winter supply.
Plant grape vines.
Cut back chrysanthemums to 6 in after flowering to encourage growth for cuttings. Prick out October-sown sweet peas. Pot on annuals. Bring plunged bulbs into the greenhouse as shoots appear.

December
Harvest chicory.
Bring in remaining plunged bulbs for spring flowering.
Take advantage of quiet period to do cleaning and maintenance jobs on greenhouse and equipment.

Ornamentals 1

Growing annuals from seed

To gain good benefit from the protected environment that the cold greenhouse affords, sow seeds of annuals in autumn for flowering in spring and early summer. Choose from the many available according to personal preference. Annuals can also be grown in a cool greenhouse where they will be protected from frost. In a cold house, plunge the pots in sand or ashes to prevent roots from freezing.

Sowing In September and October prepare flats of seed mix watered with a dilute fungicide such as Captan. Broadcast the seed thinly, cover it with ⅛ in of sieved mix and water it in using a watering can fitted with a rose to prevent disturbance. Until the seedlings emerge, light is not necessary, but once germination has occurred, put the boxes on a bench or shelf where they will receive good light, but do not risk being scorched by any late summer sunshine. Keep the seedlings well watered, adding dilute fungicide to the water once a week, and ventilate the house as the weather allows, taking care to make sure that seedlings become hardened but are not damaged by unexpected frost.

Pricking out and potting on When the seedlings are sturdy and large enough to handle, prick them out into peat blocks or flats filled with John Innes No. 1 or a similar potting mix or soil. Continue to water and apply dilute fungicide, and to ventilate the greenhouse during the daytime. By late autumn the seedlings should be large enough to be potted on. Depending on the eventual size of the plants, place between one and three seedlings in each 3 in pot. After this first potting on, and throughout the winter, water the plants sparingly to prevent the soil from becoming over-damp and to minimize the risks of disease. Ventilate the house as much as air temperature allows, which will depend on the severity of the winter. In February or March, carry out the final potting on, planting specimens singly or in groups, depending on the ultimate size, in labeled 4–5 in pots filled with John Innes No. 2 or an equivalent mix. If necessary, provide plants with support in the form of canes, brush or wire netting. Increase ventilation and watering as air temperatures rise in spring to help provide a good display of blooms.

Bulbs

The word bulb is a generic term often used in gardening to include plants that also grow from other vegetative storage organs such as corms and tubers. Many such plants are ideal for the cold greenhouse and a planned succession will provide color nearly all the year round. Once in flower, bulbs can be left in the greenhouse or taken indoors. Select bulbs from the suggestions given, but consult the catalogs and reliable nurseries for a wider choice of named varieties.

Winter and spring flowering bulbs

When growing bulbs for winter and spring flowering, remember that only those that have been specially treated are suitable for forcing. Untreated bulbs will flower satisfactorily under glass, but later than prepared forcing bulbs. This special treatment is applied, for example, to hyacinths and some tulips, narcissi, and bulbous irises, but not to crocuses, which will not flower if forced too quickly. Hyacinths, tulips, narcissi, grape hyacinths, the attractive bulbous irises and crocuses all lend themselves well to cultiva-

Annuals for spring flowering

1 September–October. Make two or three repeat sowings in seed mix which has been watered with a fungicide.

2 When seedlings appear, place on the bench or a shelf. Water, shade and ventilate carefully.

3 When they are large enough to handle, prick out seedlings into peat blocks or flats of well-drained mix or soil.

4 Late autumn. Pot on into 3 in pots, placing 1–3 seedlings, depending upon the variety, in each pot.

5 Winter. Water carefully and sparingly and provide ventilation whenever air temperatures allow.

6 February. Pot on into final pots, using John Innes No. 2 or equivalent. Provide supports, using canes or wire netting.

Ornamentals 2

tion. in the cold house, although cultural details differ slightly. All these bulbs can be planted in autumn for winter and spring flowering. For hyacinths, set each bulb in potting soil or mix so that it is half exposed, then plunge the pot in a frame (see also page 257). When shoots appear six to eight weeks later, remove pots to a shady place in the greenhouse for a week before placing them in full light. Keep the house well ventilated but make sure that the ventilators are closed during very cold weather to maintain as high a temperature as possible. Return the plants to a shady spot after flowering, and allow the foliage to die away naturally. Bulbs should not be forced two years in succession. Plant forced bulbs in the open garden after one season under glass.

The requirements of narcissi and tulips are similar except that bulbs should be planted with only their "noses" above the soil level while bulbous irises and grape hyacinths are best completely covered. When planting crocus corms, give them a 2–3 in covering of soil. Crocus cannot be forced. If given heat, the flowers abort.

Summer and autumn flowering bulbs

The ambitious gardener can use the cold house to grow many unusual and spectacular summer and autumn flowering bulbs. For a lengthy show of color, plant *Agapanthus*, *Hippeastrum*, *Tigridia* and *Polianthes* in spring. *Nerine* in August and *Ixia* from October to November. All these bulbs differ slightly in their needs, but all will need good ventilation, even watering, and a mix such as John Innes No. 2. After flowering allow the leaves to die down then lift the vegetative underground organs and store them in a dry and, if necessary, frost-free place. *Agapanthus* and others with fleshy roots should be plunged in their pots in frames and watered sparingly.

Camellias in containers

Most camellia varieties provide a good display if grown within the protected environment of the cold house as they flower earlier in the year and outdoors their blooms are often spoiled by frost. In very large greenhouses camellias can be planted out in the soil, but for the amateur, containers, which restrict plant growth to manageable proportions, are

best. Containers can be moved outside in summer to free greenhouse space. Place them in a sheltered spot with light shade. If the pots are plunged, camellias can be left outside until late autumn.

Soil Camellias in and out of containers need an acid, lime-free, loam-based soil made up by volume of 7 parts medium loam, 3 parts moss peat and 2 parts coarse acid sand. This should be mixed with a well-balanced fertilizer at the rate of 4 oz to the bushel. A slow-release fertilizer is a useful addition.

Potting on When a camellia plant is bought from a nursery, check whether it needs potting on. If a tight mass of roots is visible when the plant is removed from its container it needs a pot 2 in larger in diameter. Prepare the new pot by crocking it well to supply good drainage. Place a layer of soil in the base of the pot, put in the plant and fill in with soil all round the roots. Shake the pot, top it up, then press the soil down round the sides. Give the pot a sharp tap on the greenhouse bench to help settle the soil. Water by immersion to ensure that the rootball is thoroughly soaked.

Watering and feeding Care must be taken not to overwater the plants. It is also essential to make sure that the rootball does not become too dry in the center. Water by immersion to maintain evenly moist soil mix. Because the plants dislike lime, try to collect rainwater for them, particularly in hard water areas. Give liquid fertilizer only between April and August, choosing a formula high in nitrogen in April to June and one high in potash for the remainder.

Ventilation and shading Good ventilation is essential for camellias. Even in winter the greenhouse ventilation should be left open during the day. In summer, if the air temperature in the house exceeds 27°C/80°F the glass on the south side of the house should be painted with shading paint to prevent scorching, and in hot weather the plants will also benefit if the house is damped down every day. Move pot-grown camellias outside in summer if possible. Place them in slight shade and water well.

Care after flowering Any re-potting and pruning should be carried out after plants have flowered.

Bulbs

1 Early autumn. Choose equal-sized hyacinth bulbs and pot in potting soil so that the bulb is half-exposed. Use half pots or ornamental containers.

2 After potting, plunge the bulbs in the greenhouse or in a frame by covering with peat, grit or weathered ashes. Keep the soil moist.

3 Six to eight weeks later, when shoots appear, remove from the plunge bed and stand the pots in a cool, shady frost-free place such as beneath the staging.

4 A week later, move into full light. Flowering will take place in early spring. After flowering, keep the bulbs cool and slightly shaded while the foliage dies away.

Ornamentals 3

Evergreen azaleas
Many evergreen azaleas can be grown in pots in the cold greenhouse to provide color in winter and early spring. Many early flowering varieties are now available and it is wise to consult a catalog or visit a well-stocked nursery before deciding which ones to choose.
Soil mix Like camellias, azaleas need lime-free soil. Proprietary peat mixes can be used for azaleas, but remember to check that they contain no lime. Alternatively, the gardener can make up his own mix using equal parts by volume of leaf mold, fibrous peat or moss peat, and coarse sand. Add a balanced slow-release fertilizer.
Care of plants Azaleas grown in pots can be plunged in the garden in a sheltered partially shaded place during the summer months after their flowering season is over. If the garden soil is not lime-free, plunge in sand. They should be watered regularly and given liquid fertilizer every two weeks. In September, bring the pots back into the greenhouse to protect plants from winter cold and damp. Keep the greenhouse well ventilated during the day except during the worst weather, and water the plants regularly, preferably with rain water which is almost guaranteed lime-free. Make sure that the pot soil never dries out completely as it is almost impossible to get peat-based mixes thoroughly wet again once they have become dehydrated.

After flowering, remove withered flowers and re-pot plants into slightly larger pots. Tease out some of the spent soil from the edges of the rootball and re-pot into fresh soil. Carefully work the fresh soil around the roots and gently firm it with the fingers. After potting, immerse the plants in water. Keep the plants in the greenhouse until the danger of frost has passed, then plunge them outdoors in a sheltered partially-shaded place for the summer months.

Fuchsias
The cold greenhouse is an excellent place to grow fuchsias as their blooms are easily spoiled by bad weather. Pendulous species such as *Fuchsia triphylla* and its varieties are also attractive planted in hanging baskets.

Cultivation Fuchsias can be grown from rooted cuttings taken in April and planted in 3 in pots containing John Innes No. 2 or a similar mix, then potted on, using John Innes No. 3, into 5 or 6 in pots in which they will flower. Throughout the spring and summer keep the greenhouse well ventilated but damp it down once a day in hot weather to increase the humidity. In summer, shade the glass with shading paint, or put plants in the shade of larger specimens of other genera. Water the plants well and take care that they do not dry out as this may cause the buds to drop. After flowering, reduce watering so that the soil is kept barely moist until growth restarts in spring. Ventilate the house during the day. Plunge the pots in sand or ashes to protect them from frost, and cover the plants with polyethylene if frost is forecast.

Pelargoniums
Hundreds of different varieties of pelargoniums—popularly known as geraniums—are available for the greenhouse gardener to choose from and all make excellent shows of color from spring to autumn. Regal pelargoniums, which flower in early spring, need heated greenhouse conditions. In March, take cuttings of plants over-wintered in greenhouse or frame. Insert individual cuttings in 2½ in pots filled with John Innes seed compost or a mixture of equal parts by volume of peat and sand. Place the pots in a propagating case or a closed frame on the greenhouse bench. When the cuttings have rooted, pot them on into 4 in pots filled with John Innes No. 2 or an equivalent mix.

During the growing season, keep plants well watered and shade the greenhouse glazing once the air temperature exceeds 13°C/55°F. Give plants good ventilation. After flowering, cut the pelargoniums back and leave them in their pots or plant them in boxes and store them in a frost-free frame to save space (see page 257), or on the greenhouse benching. In winter, cut down the amount of water given, but allow as much ventilation as the weather permits. In very cold weather it is essential to provide a little artificial heat to prevent plants from being damaged by frost. Take fresh cuttings in March and repeat the cycle.

Evergreen azaleas

1 After winter flowering is over remove the withered flowers and re-pot the plants. Use larger pots if the plants are in 3, 4 or 5 in pots.

2 Scrape away some of the spent soil and remove the old drainage crocks from the base of the plant. Work fresh soil around the roots, firming it well.

3 Water the plants by immersion in rain water so that the peaty mix in which the plants are grown never dries out.

4 Plunge plants outside in their pots from June to September in a partially shaded position. Water regularly. Plunge in sand if soil contains lime.

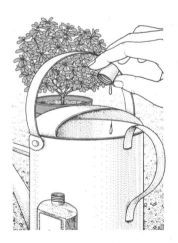

5 Feed plants once every 14 days in spring and early summer, reducing to every 3–4 weeks in mid-summer. Stop feeding in mid-August.

6 Return plants to the greenhouse in September to flower during the winter. Ventilate freely and water well, if possible with rain water.

Fruits

FRUIT VARIETIES

STRAWBERRIES
'Gorella'
'Redgauntlet' (early)
'Trellisa' (perpetual)
'Baron Solemacher' (alpine)
'Cambridge Favorite'
'Royal Sovereign'

MELONS
'Charantais'
'Ogen'
'Sweetheart'

GRAPES
'Black Hamburg'
'Muscat Hamburg' (muscat)
'Madresfield Court' (black)

'Buckland Sweetwater' (white)
'Foster's Seedling' (white)
'Muscat of Alexandria' (white)
'Alicante' (black)
(Mrs. Pearson' (white)

PEACHES
'Duke of York'
'Hale's Early'

APRICOTS
'Alfred'
'Moorpark'

NECTARINES
'Early Rivers'
'Lord Napier'

A cold greenhouse can be used to grow a variety of fruit crops, the best choice being melons, strawberries, grapes, peaches, apricots and nectarines. The more stable environment of the greenhouse, and the protection it affords, allows the production of earlier, more reliable fruit crops compared with outdoor culture, especially in districts with cooler than average summer temperatures. The greatest limitation of the cold greenhouse for growing fruit is that many of the crops, but particularly grapes, peaches, apricots and nectarines, take up a great deal of space. If possible, it may be best to devote a whole greenhouse to fruit culture but if this is not practical, select fruit that will not occupy the whole house or block light from other plants. Alternatively, cultivate plants in pots to restrict their growth to manageable proportions.

Choosing a greenhouse

For small-growing crops such as melons and strawberries a house of conventional dimensions will be suitable but a larger house is necessary to accommodate other fruit adequately unless they are grown in pots. When choosing a greenhouse for growing fruit remember that a vigorous grape vine will need a border at least 8 ft long and that a peach, apricot or nectarine will require a greenhouse with a wall or glass sides at least 12 ft high. When selecting a greenhouse for fruit growing ensure that it is well ventilated. Fruit trees should be grown against a south-facing wall.

Planting

Vines, peaches and their relations and melons can all be planted direct into the border soil of the greenhouse, which should be prepared according to the individual requirements of each crop. Strawberries, however, are best cultivated in pots or barrels. If space is limited it is also possible to cultivate grapes, peaches, apricots and nectarines—and even plums, apples, pears and cherries—in pots, although for the last four of these it is essential to select varieties grown on dwarfing rootstocks. Container culture has the added advantage that it is possible to provide exactly the right type of soil but it is important

to give plants the maximum possible light. It will be difficult for plants to thrive, and for fruit to ripen, if plants in pots are shaded by a thick vine or a vigorous peach.

Training and support Except for strawberries, all the types of fruit suggested for the cold greenhouse will need some system of wires on which they can be trained and this should be combined with a support system. Always remember to arrange the training system before planting because inserting wires behind growing plants is not only difficult but can lead to damage.

Ventilation

The exact needs of fruit crops vary in detail but good ventilation is essential. Peaches, for example, ideally need ventilation from the roof and sides of the house. When growing a crop that takes up a good deal of space in the greenhouse always make sure that the growth of the plant does not interfere with the ventilation system or make windows difficult to open.

For full details of cultural practices see pages 90–145.

CULTIVATION

Grapes Construct a training system of horizontal wires 9 in apart and 15 in from the glass. Plant in November in well-drained porous border soil containing loam, peat and grit with added base fertilizer and limestone. Water to give a thorough soaking in early spring. Mulch. Keep the soil thoroughly damp, watering every 7–10 days in hot weather, and reduce watering as fruit ripens. Ventilate from January to March then close the vents until May or when the air temperature exceeds 18°C/64°F.

Peaches, apricots and nectarines Construct a training system of wires placed 10 in apart and 10 in from the glass. Plant in October in border soil enriched with peat and add lime at 1 lb per sq yd. Mulch. Water well after planting and from the time growth starts. Ventilate during the day only after fruit has set. Close the house at night.

Melons

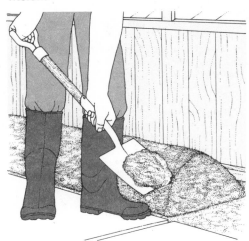

1 Prepare a soil mix of 2 oz steamed bonemeal and 2 oz compound fertilizer to one 2 gal bucketful of soil. Place this on top of the border soil in a ridge 1 ft high.

3 As the plants grows tie stems to canes and laterals to the horizontal wires. Pinch out the growing point when plant is 6 ft tall. Pinch back side shoots to two leaves beyond each flower. Increase ventilation.

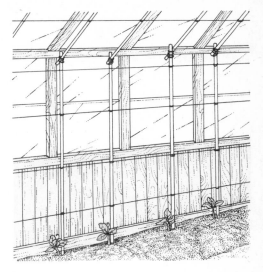

2 Stretch wires along the sides 1 ft apart and 15 in from the glass. Tie in two canes per plant, one from soil to eaves, the other from the eaves to the house ridge. In May plant the seedlings raised in heat.

4 Thin the fruit to four of the same size per plant when fruits are walnut-sized. Water the plants very well and liquid feed them every 7–10 days. As fruits enlarge support them with netting slings.

Tomatoes 1

Tomatoes are an excellent choice of crop for a cold greenhouse for they are tender plants that profit greatly from the protection glass affords. A heated propagating case can be used in a cold greenhouse to provide the added heat necessary for raising plants from seed. All greenhouse-grown tomatoes need careful attention to watering, feeding and care in controlling pests and diseases.

Raising tomato plants
Without the use of a heated propagating case it is usually best to purchase tomato plants rather than raise them from seed. Choose strong plants with no trace of disease.

Seed sowing Seed may be sown in a heated propagating case in early January for planting eight weeks later. Sow seed thinly in John Innes No. 1 compost placed directly in the case or in flats or pans which are placed in it. Seeds sown too thickly are likely to suffer from damping-off diseases. Set the propagator thermostat to 18°C/65°F. At this temperature germination and emergence should take place in 7–10 days. Keep the seedlings evenly moist but not waterlogged.

Pricking out When the seedlings have developed their first true leaves 10–12 days after sowing, carefully prick them out singly into individual 3 in peat or plastic pots filled with a proprietary potting soil or mix. Insert a small dibble beneath the roots of each seedling and hold the seedling by its leaves to prevent damage. Use the dibble to make a hole big enough to take each seedling without restricting its roots. Water the seedlings gently to firm the soil round their roots and replace them in the propagator.

Temperature control Keep the seedlings at 18°C/65°F until they begin to shade each other, then turn the thermostat down to 16°C/60°F. About a week before planting, reduce the temperature to 10°C/50°F. Apply a balanced liquid feed and support plants with a small cane if they become too tall to support themselves.

Planting
While seedlings are maturing, decide which growing system will be used. The main choices are between greenhouse soil, ring culture, 9 in pots placed direct on greenhouse soil, growing bags or straw bales (for full details see page 78). If plants are to be grown directly in greenhouse soil, double dig and enrich the lower spade depth with well-rotted compost or manure. For pot or ring culture fill pots with John Innes No. 2 or 3 or an equivalent mix. Plant tomatoes when the young plants are 6 to 9 in tall. This is usually when the flowers on the first truss are just opening. Immediately before planting, water plants thoroughly and destroy any plants that show signs of disease. Make a hole in the chosen growing medium big enough to accommodate the roots without crowding. Place the top of each rootball level with the soil surface. Plants raised in peat pots should be made thoroughly wet before planting (tear down one side of the pot wall if necessary to prevent drying out) and planted complete with the pot. Space plants about 18 in apart each way. Give planted tomatoes a thorough watering in and keep them moist to make sure the roots become well established.

Support In the greenhouse tomato plants are usually best supported on soft garden string tied to a horizontal wire near the greenhouse roof at one end and to the stem of the plant, under the lowest true leaf, at the other. Each plant is then twisted loosely round the string as it grows. Take care not to damage the plant stem by pulling the string too tight. Alternatively, plants in pots or grown direct in greenhouse soil may be loosely tied to bamboo canes for support.

Watering and feeding
The success of greenhouse-grown tomatoes depends on meticulous attention to watering and feeding throughout the life of the plant. Plants will be damaged by drying out which causes flower drop, or waterlogging which is a particular hazard for plants grown in isolated systems such as growing bags, for it quickly kills off plant roots. Plants in growing bags will only thrive if the growing medium is kept uniformly moist, which may mean watering three or four times a day in hot weather. Ring culture also demands much water because drainage is very rapid. The most stable water supply is achieved with plants grown directly in greenhouse soil. In all systems, irregular watering will cause fruit to split.

Raising from seed

1 Early January Sow 2–3 seeds per sq in in propagator filled with sieved soil. Sprinkle over ⅛ in layer of soil and cover with newspaper.

2 Prick out seedlings 10–12 days after sowing using a small dibble. Transfer to 3 in pots filled with John Innes No. 1 or an equivalent mix.

Planting

3 Place pots in propagator and set thermostat to 18°C/65°F. Water sparingly but often. Liquid feed before planting.

4 Mid–late April When flowers on first truss are just opening water plants well. Remove plants from pots and place 18 in apart in chosen growing medium.

Tomatoes 2

Greenhouse grown tomatoes should be liquid fed with a proprietary fertilizer mixed with the water according to the manufacturer's instructions. A balanced fertilizer will provide nitrogen to encourage vegetative growth and potassium to improve quality.

Trimming and de-leafing

As tomato plants grow they develop side shoots in the junctions (axils) between leaf and stem. These must be removed while they are small or they will use up water and nutrients needed by the productive parts of the plant. Snap off each side shoot cleanly between finger and thumb, preferably in early morning when the plants are turgid. Avoid pulling which leaves scars that are easily invaded by disease-causing fungi.

When plants are 4–5 ft tall, remove the lower leaves up to the first truss. Use a sharp knife and cut cleanly leaving no snags. De-leafing allows more light to reach the plant base, improves air circulation and helps to combat fungal diseases. As the trusses crop make sure any yellowing or diseased leaves are removed.

Pollination and fruit setting

If fruit setting is a problem it can be improved by assisting pollen dispersal. Spray the plant with a fine droplet spray, shake the plant gently or tap the flower trusses.

Stopping

In a cold greenhouse tomatoes will not usually produce more than six or seven fruit trusses per season so it is best to snap off the growing point two leaves beyond the sixth or seventh truss. Continue to remove further sideshoots, which will often be stimulated into growth by the stopping process.

Harvesting

Ripe fruit should be ready for picking in mid-May from seed sown in early January. Harvest time depends upon sowing time. If climate allows, crops can for instance be sown in June for September–December crops.

Pests and diseases

Greenhouse tomatoes are notoriously susceptible to pests and diseases which are described in detail on pages 260–265.

Support

1 Bamboo canes can be used for support. Tie the plant on loosely with soft garden string so that stems are not damaged.

2 Snap off side and basal shoots between thumb and forefinger. If possible de-shoot in early morning when the stems are turgid.

3 Spray the flowers with a fine droplet spray or shake the plant gently to disperse pollen and improve fruit setting.

4 Liquid feed growing plants following manufacturer's instructions. Water them as necessary.

Stopping

5 Snap off growing point 2 leaves above top truss when 6–7 trusses have set fruit. Remove any lower leaves that turn yellow.

6 Pick ripe fruit by snapping the stalk, leaving the calyx on the fruit. Ripe fruit left under hot sun will soon lose its firmness.

TRAINING SYSTEMS

Vertical training Plants are carefully twisted round soft string attached below lowest true leaf and to a horizontal wire 6–8 ft above ground level.

V-training Plants are twisted round strings set alternately at 60° to the ground. This system is good for straw bale culture with plants placed closer than 18 in.

Vegetables and salads 1

The greatest advantage of the cold greenhouse in salad and vegetable growing is that it can be used to extend the growing season at both ends of the year. In warmer parts of the country, an unheated greenhouse can also provide winter crops. Those summer crops normally grown outside, such as tomato and cucumber, can be grown under glass for faster maturing and protection against rain, hail and wind. With good planning a greenhouse can provide food for the kitchen almost all the year round. It is also very useful for raising young vegetable plants which are later planted out into the garden.

The most significant limitation of the cold house is implicit in its description—because it is unheated, the gardener must wait until the house temperature reaches a suitable point before certain seeds can be sown. Also, the winter temperature in the cold house precludes the growing of many out of season crops. When considering which crops to grow, make maximum use of space. Catch crops such as carrots and radishes can be grown between tall crops before they develop.

Leaf crops

Good choices for the cold house include salad greens, seakale and herbs.

Lettuce Sow lettuce seed in pots then prick them out into peat blocks or pots before planting them in greenhouse soil. If seed is sown in small quantities at fortnightly intervals from early spring until autumn, a constant supply can be assured. To prevent diseases, particularly botrytis, it is important to ventilate the house well in all but the worst weather. The crop needs adequate light and attention to watering. Give a few thorough waterings rather than many small ones. The crop will be improved by a thorough soaking about 10 days before harvesting.

Mustard and cress As long as the greenhouse temperature is 10°C/50°F or above, mustard and cress can be sown at weekly intervals. Sow seed on a moist tissue in a shallow dish and place it in the dark under a bench, lightly covered with a dark cloth or newspaper if necessary to exclude light. Once the seeds have germinated, move the dish up into a lighter place and keep the seeds well watered.

Winter endive Sow seed as for lettuce in late August to early September and put in a well-lit position. Ventilate the house and water the seedlings regularly. When plants are fully grown, tie them round loosely with raffia and place a large plastic pot over selected plants to blanch the leaves. Cover the drainage hole of the pot and support it on crocks to allow free air circulation.

Seakale From late September to late October, lift seakale crowns from the garden and trim off the side roots and any yellowing foliage. Trim the main roots to about 6 in. Allowing 3 crowns per pot, plant the crowns in 9 in plastic pots filled with rich soil mix such as John Innes No. 3. Cover each pot with another of the same size turned upside down and place under the greenhouse staging. Ideally the crowns need a temperature of about 10°C/50°F, so if the house gets too cold insulate the pots with newspaper or burlap.

Herbs Many herbs will continue growing through the winter if plants are potted up and brought into the cold house for protection during winter. Herbs that benefit most from such protection include parsley, chives, mint, French tarragon, pot marjoram, rosemary, thyme and sage. Water plants well and ventilate the house during the day in all but the worst weather. In spring, begin sowing seeds of annual and biennial herbs as soon as the greenhouse temperature is high enough.

Root crops and bulbs

Small quantities of root crops can be raised in the cold house for harvesting weeks before the main outdoor crops. Seed sowing can begin in February–March in peat pots or directly into slightly acid greenhouse border soil prepared according to crop requirements. If the vegetables are to be eaten really young and tender, make more sowings at three or four week intervals. Thoroughly water and well ventilate the house once the temperatures begin to rise in April.

Pods

Select dwarf varieties of bush beans for cold greenhouse cultivation and make two sowings, one in spring for early summer cropping,

Lettuces

1 Sow seed in 3½ in pots filled with potting soil. Cover the seeds lightly and water using a fine rose. Repeat sowings every 2 weeks.

2 Prick out as many seedlings as required into small individual peat blocks or pots. Water well and increase the ventilation according to the weather.

3 When plants have 4–5 true leaves plant the peat blocks or pots 8 in apart into the greenhouse border soil. Water well and ensure good ventilation.

4 Harvest lettuce by carefully pulling up whole plants and trimming off the roots, or cut plants below lower leaves. Remove discarded matter from greenhouse.

Vegetables and salads 2

the other in July for autumn harvesting. Pre-germinate the seeds and sow four or five seeds round the edges of a pot filled with John Innes No. 2 or equivalent mix. For the spring sowing wait until early April in cool areas, or germinate the seeds indoors. Water the plants well once flowers appear and ventilate the house in warm weather.

Vegetable fruits

Cucumbers, sweet peppers and eggplants, as well as tomatoes whose culture is described in detail on pages 244–245, can all be grown in the cold greenhouse.

Cucumbers Pre-germinate cucumber seeds then sow them singly in 3 in pots filled with John Innes No. 1 or a similar mix. Allow 4 to 5 weeks from sowing to planting and time the operation so that planting can take place in late May, if necessary germinating the seeds indoors. Preferably, plants should be planted in growing bags (2 plants per standard bag) or singly on straw bales. At planting time or before, erect a system of supporting strings tied to horizontal wires near the greenhouse roof, or insert bamboo canes on to which plants can be loosely tied. Developing plants should be well watered and given liquid feed and the atmosphere in the house should be kept as humid as possible. Pinch and trim the plants as shown in the illustrations and remove any male flower.

Sweet peppers These vegetable fruits are best grown in the cold greenhouse in pots. Because the seed needs a temperature of 21°C/70°F for germination, seeds must be germinated in a propagating case and the seedlings hardened off, or the gardener can buy plants from a nursery. Allow 10 to 12 weeks between sowing and planting in late May. Sow seed thinly on moistened soil covered with $\frac{1}{8}$ in of compost and then with glass and newspaper. When seedlings are large enough to handle, prick them out into 3 in pots filled with John Innes No. 3 compost or plant 3 plants in a standard sized growing bag. Place pots 18 in apart on the border soil or greenhouse staging. When plants are about 6 in tall, remove the growing point to encourage bushy growth, and support and tie them to bamboo canes if necessary. Keep plants well watered and liquid fed and venti-late the house in warm weather. Watch for aphids and red spider mites. Spray with malathion or derris if pests are seen.

Eggplants These need very similar cultural conditions to peppers, and plants can be raised from seed in the same way or purchased from a nursery. Aim for planting in early May and allow two plants to a standard size growing bag. Pinch out the growing points when plants are 9–12 in high and allow only 5 or 6 fruit to develop on each plant. Remove any extra fruits, leaving the remaining ones well spaced, and pinch off any extra flowers that form. Water and feed often but sparingly and ventilate the house in hot weather. Watch out for pests and spray against those that appear as for peppers.

Raising seed

Seeds of many vegetables can be raised in the cold house for planting out once the weather is suitable to provide earlier, more reliable crops. Sow seed in peat blocks or pots for easy planting later on and keep house well ventilated.

Cucumbers

WITLOOF CHICORY

In November, lift witloof chicory roots from the garden and cut off the leaves to within $\frac{1}{2}$ in of the crown. Trim the roots to 9 in and take off any side shoots. Store the roots horizontally in boxes of dry sand outside under a north wall until they are needed. From mid-November onwards plant 3 or 4 chicory roots at weekly intervals in a 9 in plastic pot filled with sand so that each crown is $\frac{1}{2}$ in above the top of the soil. Water sparingly and cover with pot to keep out light. Place under the bench and keep well ventilated. The chicons will be ready after 4 weeks.

1 Late May Plant seedlings raised in heat in 9 in pots filled with potting soil. Water and liquid feed regularly. Keep the greenhouse humid.

2 June–July Tie growing plants to canes for support. Pinch out growing points as main stems reach the roof. Ventilate frequently, but carefully, as humidity is important.

3 June onwards Keep single laterals in each leaf axil and stop them at 2 leaves. Remove male flowers if appropriate. Harvest by cutting the stems with a sharp knife.

The year in a cool greenhouse 1

A cool greenhouse, one provided with a heating system that ensures that temperatures do not fall below 4.5°C/40°F, provides an environment suitable for a vast range of plants. Nearly all the plants from the world's temperate zones can be cultivated, and the choice extends into those from the subtropical and tropical regions. A distinction is made between those plants that can be grown in winter in a cool house, such as salads and chrysanthemums, and those such as sub-tropical bedding plants which are dormant at cool greenhouse temperatures but survive the winter undamaged, when they would die in the open garden or an unheated house. In addition, all those plants which will tolerate cold greenhouse conditions can be grown in a cool house. In many cases their growing seasons will be longer. It is possible to raise a wider range of out-of-season food crops and ornamentals given the minimum temperature of a cool house.

To many gardeners, the cool greenhouse is the norm and a cold or warm house is a deviation from it. When gardening literature and catalogs are consulted, it will be noticed that "greenhouse plants" tends to mean those to be grown in a cool house.

While there are very many plants to choose from for growing in a cold house, it is often worth experimenting to try to widen the range still further. Plants rarely have an absolute minimum temperature which kills them, unless it be frost level which, by freezing the cells, can cause physical damage. Many plants thought to need higher temperatures than the cool house minimum can in fact be acclimated to the prevailing conditions. A lot depends upon avoiding extremes and sudden changes. If the balance of the environment—heat, humidity and ventilation—is carefully watched, plants thought tender may survive and go on to flourish. Among those worth experimenting with are the many house plants available, and sub-tropical flowering plants such as those fostered by Victorian conservatory gardeners for winter blooms.

Management

The principles of cool greenhouse care are those outlined earlier in this book for the running of any greenhouse. The one main difference in the running of a cool house is the need to manipulate the heating system.

An inefficient heating system is undesirable for three reasons. First, if the system is not running correctly it will not be able to maintain the necessary temperature and plants will suffer. The second reason is that inefficiency in the use of fuel will lead to rapidly escalating bills. Heating a greenhouse is expensive, and if the system used keeps the temperature unnecessarily high, or burns fuel inefficiently, the cost will be magnified. Third, certain kinds of heating system, those which burn gas or oil, can harm plants if they are not adjusted correctly. Badly set wicks and burners can cause the heater to give off poisonous fumes.

Thermostats The sensible management of a heating system centers around the use of thermostats. These devices sense temperature changes and act as switches, turning the heating system on and off as required. They are most often used with electrical systems, which are easily controllable and capable of producing heat quickly. Gas and oil systems can also be fitted with thermostats—as are domestic central heating boilers.

A thermostat is only useful if the system it controls has sufficient capacity. The heaters must be capable of maintaining the desired temperature without running constantly. The specialist suppliers use formulae designed to calculate the size of heating installation necessary. Once a large enough system has been installed, thermostatic control will

January
Check draft-proofing, insulation (if fitted) and heating system. Set thermostats to night minimum of 4.5°C/40°F. Water plants in flower, water others sparingly. Maintain a dry atmosphere to discourage mildew.
Sow canna, fuchsia, pelargonium.
Bring in bulbs for flowering as they show growth.
Take cuttings of winter-flowering chrysanthemums and carnations.

February
Ventilate when possible and gradually increase watering. Day length will increase. Maintain minimum temperature.
Sow bedding plants with long germination/growing periods, half-hardy annuals, sweet peas, begonia, calceolaria, salvia, schizanthus, and germinate in a propagating case.
Continue to take chrysanthemum cuttings.
Sow brassicas and onions for transplanting outdoors. Sow early bunching turnips, carrots, parsnips, beets, okra, tomatoes, cucumbers.
Plant tomato plants from middle of the month.
Begin re-potting of ferns and palms.
Bring in more bulbs for flowering.

March
Increase watering, ventilate well on sunny days and maintain a more humid atmosphere. Be alert for and combat insect pests such as aphids.
Sow sweet pepper, squash, half-hardy annuals, tomato, bedding plants, basil.
Transplant rooted cuttings taken in winter.
Repot orchids and other perennials as necessary.
Begin to take softwood cuttings.
Pot up tuberous begonias.

April
Pay attention to ventilation and watering as temperatures increase. Keep heating switched on, setting thermostat for minimum night temperature.
Sow cucumbers, squashes, pumpkins, dwarf French beans, runner beans for transplanting outdoors, primulas, half-hardy annuals such as stocks and zinnias, and *Campanula pyramidalis*.
Continue re-potting and potting on.
Move bulbs which have flowered to a frame. Move over-wintering pot plants outdoors into a sheltered position.
Transplant seedlings from seed sown earlier in the spring. Take further softwood cuttings.
Dust tomato flowers to encourage pollination.
Move half-hardy plants into a frame to harden off.

May
Water freely, shade as necessary in sunny weather and encourage a more humid atmosphere.
Sow cineraria, primula. Plant chrysanthemums and move outside. Pot on carnations, zonal pelargoniums, tuberous begonias, annuals raised from spring-sown seed. Feed all plants in active growth. Take precautions against insect pests.
Pinch out young fuchsias when 4–5 in high.
Remove cucumber laterals and all male flowers.
Tie in tomato plants and pinch out side shoots.

June
Turn off and overhaul heating system. Ventilate freely, shade whenever necessary and damp down and spray to raise humidity. Water as required, twice a day if necessary.
Sow calceolaria, *Primula malacoides*, zinnia, all for autumn and winter flowering.
Feed tomato plants and all other plants in growth. Pot on plants raised from seed as necessary.
Plant out bedding plants into their flowering positions in the open garden.
Plunge azaleas, hydrangeas and other pot plants which have finished flowering.
Cut back shoots of regal pelargoniums.

The year in a cool greenhouse 2

ensure that it only operates when the temperature falls below the pre-set level. The heater will raise the temperature, triggering the thermostat again and cutting off the system. Thermostats must be placed away from drafts and cold spots, where they will give an artificial reading.

Balance While the main stress of cold greenhouse management is on maintaining the winter minimum, thought must be given to the other components of greenhouse management. Shading, ventilation and humidity control are all crucial, especially in summer. Just as plants have a minimum temperature for healthy growth, so they have maximum levels of temperature which will harm them. Problems caused by high air temperatures are often magnified by failure to ensure adequate humidity. If there is not enough water vapor in the atmosphere, plants will transpire—give out water from their leaves into the air—too quickly. Increase

humidity by regular damping down and the installation of damp sand beds under benches.

While summer heat and winter cold have to be countered by active management, the most difficult times of the year for the running of the cold greenhouse can be spring and autumn. During these seasons the sun has power to quickly heat the greenhouse, while the nights are cool. Cold daytime temperatures can easily occur due to sudden weather changes. This combination can be particularly trying in the late winter and early spring. Sun heat is becoming more powerful, and the effect of the sun combined with artificial heating can quickly raise the temperature, often above the level required, unless ventilation is promptly given. Under these conditions automatic ventilators will begin to show their worth. A cold house will not suffer so much from this problem because it does not have the reservoir of artificially generated heat that a cool house has. More

sun heat is thus needed to raise the temperature to unwanted levels.

Growing plants

The following pages deal with the cultivation of ornamentals, including bedding plants which are covered in detail, and food crops. All the ornamentals and food crops covered in the preceding cold greenhouse section, such as annuals, tomatoes and salad crops, can be added to the list. The difference comes mainly in timing of sowing and cropping. Tomatoes, for instance, can be planted from mid-February onwards in a cool greenhouse, while in a cold house late April is the earliest possible date. Annuals will flower earlier in the spring in a cool house than in a cold one. Lettuce, radish and other salad crops can be sown in late summer and autumn for autumn and winter cropping.

Other plants Many more plants than those described in detail on the following pages can

be grown in a cool greenhouse. The plants chosen, especially those illustrated in the step-by-step sequences, are the most rewarding for the relatively inexperienced and/or those which illustrate a key growing principle. The information given can be adapted to cover the cultivation of many other plants.

There are other categories of plants of interest which are less popular but still worth considering if greenhouse space is available. For example, many shrubs can be grown in containers under glass and brought into flower earlier than outside. Examples are lilac, forsythia and hydrangea. Fruits such as citrus can be grown in tubs in cool greenhouse conditions. Most citrus trees will tolerate a winter minimum of 7°C/45°F, though the lime needs 10°C/50°F. Summer temperatures should be maintained at 13°–16°C/55°–61°F for successful cropping. Full details of the cultivation of warm temperate fruits are given in *Fruit* in this series.

July

Maintain a moist atmosphere and attend to watering. Ventilate well and shade as required. Sow sapiglossis and make a repeat sowing of *Primula malacoides* and calceolaria.
Take hydrangea cuttings.
Stake plants, especially annuals growing in pots, and train climbers.
Pot on pelargoniums reared from spring cuttings and plunge outdoors. Pot on carnations, and repot freesias.

August

Continue summer shading, watering and damping down regime. Watch for cool nights towards the end of the month as days shorten.
Sow annuals for spring flowering, cyclamen, cineraria.
Prick out calceolarias and other seedlings from earlier sowings.
Take cuttings of pelargoniums.
Pot on primulas, cinerarias.
Plant bulbs for winter and spring flowering, such as freesias, tulip, hyacinth, narcissi.
Feed chrysanthemums standing outdoors and water well.
Repair any structural damage to the greenhouse and repaint if necessary.

September

Reduce watering and damping down as temperatures drop.
Restart the heating system to check it and switch on if necessary towards the end of the month.
Check winter fuel supplies if necessary. Reduce shading.
Sow more annuals for spring flowering.
Pot up remaining bulbs.
Bring in azaleas, camellias, chrysanthemums and other pot plants that have spent the summer in the open.
Pot on cyclamen, cinerarias and primulas into final pots and move onto greenhouse shelves.
Take cuttings of bedding plants before they are discarded, and of coleus, heliotropes and fuchsias.

October

Switch on the heating system and set the thermostat to maintain a minimum night temperature of 4.5°C/40°F. Ventilate freely on warm days but exclude fog and damp. Reduce watering and remove shading completely.
Pot up the last of the bulbs.
Feed cyclamen, cinerarias, primulas and camellias.
If possible, remove all plants and fumigate the house against fungal diseases.
Scatter pellets to combat slugs.

November

Maintain minimum winter temperature as October and ventilate sparingly. Further reduce watering of all except plants in flower.
Pot on annuals. Keep in good light and give minimum water.
Bring in the first batch of bulbs for winter flowering.
Prune shrubs.
Sow lettuce.
Bring in fuchsias, begonias and hydrangeas and store under the staging. Keep almost dry.

December

Fit insulation to greenhouse sides if possible and stop up all drafts.
Cover the house with burlap or mats in very severe weather.
Protect tender plants with paper, polyethylene or burlap if severe frost is forecast. Cut watering to the minimum.
Ventilate a little when possible and run a fan heater to circulate the atmosphere.
Bring in more bulbs.
Box up seakale and witloof chicory for forcing.
Cut down chrysanthemums after they have flowered and start to take cuttings of soft growth.
Keep cineraria, cyclamen, primulas and other plants required for Christmas flowering in a warm part of the house. Water them with care, avoiding the foliage.
Clear debris, dead leaves and used pots from the greenhouse. Clean all pots, trays and propagating equipment.

Bedding plants 1

SOWING PLAN

JANUARY TO FEBRUARY
Antirrhinum; Begonia semper-
florens; Cineraria; Dianthus;
Matthiola; Papaver; Viola

FEBRUARY TO MARCH
Chrysanthemum carinatum;

Cosmos; Dahlia; Heliotropium;
Kochia; Salpiglossis

MARCH
Ageratum; Alyssum; Impatiens;
Lobelia; Lobularia; Nemesia;
Nicotiana

MARCH TO APRIL
Collistephus; Phlox; Portulaca;
Tagetes—French.

APRIL
Zinnia.

The cool greenhouse is an ideal place for raising summer bedding plants. Using the greenhouse in this way shortens the propagation period and, as long as plants are properly hardened off and precautions taken against disease, ensures the production of sturdy plants. The other advantages to the gardener of raising his own plants from seed compared with buying plants direct from the nursery are that he knows exactly what he is growing and that there is less risk of plants being damaged as they do not have to be transplanted from overcrowded seed flats.

Seed sowing

One of the most critical aspects of raising bedding plants from seed in the greenhouse is timing. As a general rule, the sequence of sowing is determined by the speed at which seeds germinate and by the growth rate of the developing seedlings. For this reason slow-growing species required for summer bedding are sown in February and March and a monthly sowing plan adopted according to the scheme shown above. Even with

the artificial heat provided by the cool greenhouse, development of seeds sown in the first two months of the year is slow because of low winter light intensity.

Seeds of bedding plants may be sown in flats or pans (dwarf pots). Fill the chosen containers with a good seed-growing mixture which should be damp. There is no need to avoid peat-based soils, with their low nutrient reserves, because the seeds will germinate relatively rapidly in the frost-free environment of the greenhouse. Once the containers are full, press down the soil with the fingers or a presser board to within $\frac{1}{4}$ in of the top, but be careful not to press too hard as this will restrict the drainage and tend to encourage damping off diseases and attack by sciarid flies.

The best method of sowing seed depends on the size of individual seeds. For small seeds such as those of *Begonia semperflorens*, mix the seeds with fine dry sand in the seed packet then sow them by broadcasting, keeping the hand close to the soil surface. Larger seeds can be broadcast in the same way, but

without the addition of sand. The larger seeds, such as those of zinnias—and small seeds that have been pelleted—are best planted singly by hand. Cover sown seed with soil but be careful not to make this covering layer too thick. Label the container clearly then water in the seeds with a dilute mixture of Captan or a copper-based fungicide to help prevent damping off disease. Use a rose on the watering can so that seeds are not dislodged from their planting positions by the water.

Germination

Even in a cool greenhouse, developing seeds, particularly those sown in mid-winter, will benefit from extra warmth. This is best provided by a propagating case. When using such a case, place the seed containers inside it and set the thermostat to 21°C/71°F. If a propagating case is not available, either take the seed containers indoors and put them in a warm place or cover them with a sheet of glass. A piece of newspaper may be placed on top of the glass as light is not

important until after germination.

As soon as the seeds germinate (this may take one to three weeks depending on temperature and the species) remove any covering and put the containers in a well lit place but be careful that they do not risk being scorched by strong sunlight. Water with dilute Captan to combat damping off and other seedling diseases. If possible maintain the temperature at 21°C/70°F to promote speedy development. The seedlings also need good ventilation and the greenhouse ventilators should be opened for at least an hour a day except in very severe weather conditions.

Pricking out

Seedlings should be pricked out as soon as they are large enough to handle. If left in their original containers they will become overcrowded and their roots will become so entangled that the gardener will be unable to avoid damaging them when they are removed. Prick out seedlings into individual pots or flats filled with John Innes No. 1 or a

Growing bedding plants from seed

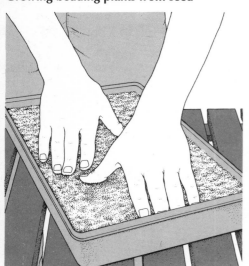

1 Fill a seed flat with seed-sowing soil. Firm the soil with the fingertips or a presser board to within $\frac{1}{2}$ in of the top.

2 Sow the seeds thinly. Small seeds can be mixed with fine dry sand and broadcast onto the soil to make sowing easier.

3 Sieve soil over medium-sized or large seeds so that they are just covered. Do not cover small seeds.

4 Water the seed flat with a dilute mixture of Captan or other fungicide to combat damping off and other diseases.

Bedding plants 2

similar potting soil, taking care to handle them by one leaf and between finger and thumb. Use a dibble to pry out the seedlings and to make a hole in the soil big enough to accommodate each plant. If seedlings are pricked out into flats, allow at least 1½ in between them each way to prevent overcrowding. Firm the soil round each seedling with the dibble, label and give another watering with dilute fungicide to guard against damping off.

Even in ideal conditions the seedlings will suffer some check to their growth after pricking out but careful handling and transplanting when the root system is small and unbranched will help to reduce this to a minimum. After pricking out the temperature can be reduced to 18°C/65°F but good ventilation is still essential to healthy seedling development. When seedlings are big enough and when there is no chance of frost, seedlings should be hardened off in a cold frame (see page 256) or by turning off the greenhouse heating system and gradually increasing the ventilation first by day and then at night.

Propagation

While most bedding plants are raised from seed, several important plants can be propagated by cuttings or division. Full details of these methods of propagation are given on pages 180–203.

Cuttings can be taken in autumn when the plants are lifted, or in spring from tubers kept dormant over the winter. Geraniums are one of many bedding plants that can be propagated by cuttings. Keep the cuttings at a minimum temperature of 4°C/40°F over winter, and water sparingly. Pot on as necessary into 4 or 5 in pots, harden off and plant out in the normal way.

Overwintering

Some bedding plants can be overwintered in a cool house for re-use the next season. Lift the plants in autumn and pot or box up. Cut back the foliage by about one-half, water very sparingly and ventilate freely to guard against gray mold. Plenty of light is necessary to avoid the production of drawn, weak growth. Plant out as normal in spring.

PEAT BLOCKS

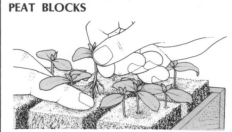

Larger seeds can be sown in peat blocks formed from damp peat-based soil with a blocking device, or in peat pots. Both have the advantage of being planted with the young plant in the flowering position. The seedlings are therefore not subject to the disturbance of pricking out. Sow 2–3 seeds in each block and water well. Provide the conditions described in the caption sequence below. When the seedlings have reached first true leaf stage, thin to the strongest per block.

PLANTING OUT

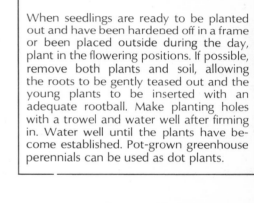

When seedlings are ready to be planted out and have been hardened off in a frame or been placed outside during the day, plant in the flowering positions. If possible, remove both plants and soil, allowing the roots to be gently teased out and the young plants to be inserted with an adequate rootball. Make planting holes with a trowel and water well after firming in. Water well until the plants have become established. Pot-grown greenhouse perennials can be used as dot plants.

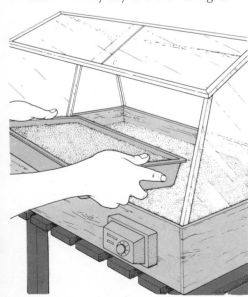

5 Place the flat in a propagating case at 21°C/70°F, or in a warm place indoors if a case is not available.

6 As soon as the first seedlings emerge, place the flat in good light. Keep the temperature at 21°C/70°F.

7 Spray seedlings with Captan or another dilute fungicide to combat damping off disease. Ensure that ventilation is adequate.

8 Prick out seedlings into flats, boxes or individual pots as soon as they are large enough to handle.

Ornamentals 1

The frost-free environment of the cool greenhouse is ideal for growing many popular ornamental plants including cyclamen, primulas, cinerarias and winter-flowering chrysanthemums.

Cyclamen

Greenhouse cyclamen are only slightly tender and may be grown successfully with the minimum of heat. They may be grown from seed or, much less frequently, from corms and with care will bloom regularly each autumn and winter for many years.

Raising from seed Although commercially it is possible to flower cyclamen from seed in 6–8 months it will normally take 12–14 months for seed-raised plants to reach flowering size. The seed should be sown between August and November to flower the following autumn and winter. Soak the seed for 12–24 hours in water to assist germination. Then sow thinly in containers filled and firmed to within $\frac{3}{8}-\frac{1}{2}$ in of the rim with John Innes seed compost or equivalent and cover with $\frac{1}{8}-\frac{1}{4}$ in of the same seed mix. Water and cover the container with a pane of glass. Place in a propagating case or on the greenhouse bench at 18°C/65°F. Keep moist. Germination is slow and sometimes erratic.

Pricking out Prick out the seedlings into small peat pots or flats of John Innes No. 1 compost when the first leaf is well developed. Keep them at 18°C/65°F for a few days before reducing the temperature to 15°C/60°F. When the seedlings have 3–4 leaves they will need to be potted on into $2\frac{1}{2}$–3 in pots again using John Innes No. 1 or equivalent. Be sure that the young corm is just proud of the surface of the mix. A second potting on, into $3\frac{1}{2}$–4 in pots of John Innes No. 2, is needed in April then finally into 5–6 in pots of John Innes No. 3 in May or early June.

A temperature of 10°–13°C/50°–55°F should be maintained and ample ventilation provided. Shading may be needed in summer to avoid leaf-scorch. Water carefully at all times preferably around the rim of the pot so that the corm is avoided. Feeding is usually unnecessary but a high-potash fertilizer may be given as the flower buds develop in late summer. Remove any odd blooms that appear before the main flush.

Care after flowering After cyclamen have flowered growing conditions should be maintained for at least 4–6 weeks before the leaves are allowed to die down by gradually withholding water. Then place plants in a light well-ventilated position in the greenhouse or plunge them in a frost-free frame. Keep them dry until July when they should be re-potted in John Innes No. 3 compost and brought into the greenhouse at 10°–13°C/50°–55°F. Water sparingly until the first leaves develop and then maintain an even watering regime while the plants are in growth.

Primulas

Tender primulas such as *P. malacoides*, *P. obconica* and *P. sinensis* bloom in the cool house during winter and early spring. They are usually treated as annuals.

Sowing seed Sow thinly in May or early June in containers filled and firmed to within $\frac{3}{8}$ in of the rim with seed-sowing mix or soil. The seed is very small and should not be covered with soil. Immerse the container in water to moisten the soil. Cover the container with a pane of glass and place it in a propagating case at 16°–18°C/60°–65°F.

Pricking out It is important to prick out the seedlings as soon as the first true leaf has developed as primula seedlings are very prone to damping off. Use small peat pots or trays of John Innes No. 1 compost. When the leaves begin to overlap in the flat (or the peat pots are filled with roots) the seedlings should be potted on into 3 in pots of John Innes No. 2 and in early autumn moved into 5 in pots of John Innes No. 2 or equivalent for flowering. Peat-based mixes can also be used.

Care of plants As flower buds form, a liquid feed may be given but is usually not required. Throughout their life primulas should be grown in light, cool, airy conditions at 7°–10°C/45°–50°F and during hot spells adequate ventilation and shading will be essential. Even watering is also important, preferably by immersion. If can watering is used apply water around the edge of the pots.

Chrysanthemums

Chrysanthemums for autumn and winter decoration in the greenhouse may be grown from seed or cuttings of named varieties.

Raising cyclamen from seed

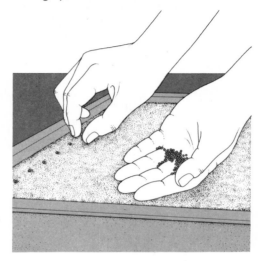

August. Sow the large seeds in flats or shallow pots of seed-sowing mix. Cover seeds with $\frac{1}{4}-\frac{1}{2}$ in of moist sieved peat. Place in propagating case at 18°C/64°F.

March–April. Pot on into 5 in pots of John Innes No. 1. Make sure that the embryo corm is just below the soil surface.

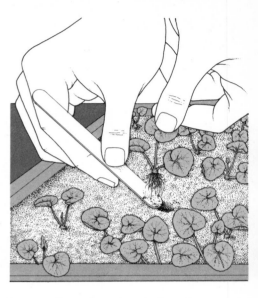

January. Transplant the seedlings into individual $2\frac{1}{2}$ in pots of John Innes No. 1 or equivalent. Keep moist and lower temperature to 15°3/61°F.

Summer. Keep the plants lightly shaded, well ventilated and moist in a greenhouse or better still in a frame from which the lights are removed in mild weather.

Ornamentals 2

Bush chrysanthemums Sow in February in John Innes seed compost and germinate at 16°C/60°F. The sowing technique is similar to that used for bedding plants (see page 250). Prick out the seedlings into seedboxes in John Innes No. 1 and pot on into 2½–3 in pots, using John Innes or an equivalent mix. At the 3-leaf stage pinch out the growing point. After potting on in late spring into 5 in pots of John Innes No. 2 move the plants to cold frame, and in June or July pot into John Innes No. 3 in 8 or 10 in pots to bloom. In late summer bring the plants into the greenhouse at a temperature of 7°–10°C/45°–50°F to flower. An occasional liquid feed may be needed while the plants are in the frames. Pinch back over-vigorous growths to maintain the neat rounded shape required.

Light, airy conditions and even watering are again the key to successful cultivation. The plants may be discarded after flowering and further stock raised from seed the following February or cuttings may be taken from particularly good plants using basal shoots as they develop during early winter.

Winter-flowering chrysanthemums

The late-flowering large-flowered florist's spray chrysanthemums are grown as pot plants outdoors during the summer and transferred to the greenhouse to flower in November and December at 7°–10°C/45°–50°F. There are many different types, varying considerably in color and form of flower, which may be obtained from specialist nurserymen in February or March as rooted cuttings; or cuttings may be rooted annually from existing plants.

Propagation Chrysanthemum stools, cut down after flowering, will produce new basal shoots that can be rooted at 7°–10°C/45°–50°F as softwood cuttings (see pages 196–197) in February or March.

Growing on Pot on the rooted cuttings into 3–3½ in pots using John Innes No. 2 compost and keep at 7°C/45°F. Give ample ventilation and light and keep the soil evenly moist. Higher temperatures will often result in soft, drawn growths. By late March or early April pot on the plants into 5 or 6 in pots of John Innes No. 3. Once established in these pots, harden them off in a cold frame, closing the

frame only in frosty or bad weather. In early June they will need transferring into their final 8 or 9 in pots again in No. 3 or an equivalent mix. Stand the pots outside in a sheltered but open site and stake the plants.

Training Naturally chrysanthemums form a single bud at the stem apex (the break bud). Normally this does not develop (or produces a poor flower) and a number of lateral shoots will develop beneath it. Each will produce terminal or "crown buds" that flower if left. Other lateral buds develop and their shoots form secondary crown buds.

In order to produce a small number of large blooms on each plant it is necessary to limit the number of shoots and flower buds by the process known as "staging". This involves removing the original break bud at an early stage of development, usually when the laterals below it are an inch or two long, and allowing each of the first crown buds to remain and eventually form large individual blooms by pinching out any small flower buds that form around them. This is disbudding. Usually six to eight blooms per plant are required (only 3 for exhibition) and in many varieties sufficient laterals are formed below the break bud for these to be produced without further stopping. Some varieties, however, may not produce more than 2 or 3 laterals (and hence first crown buds) so each lateral may need to be stopped to produce several further laterals which then flower.

The timing of stopping varies from variety to variety but normally begins in about mid-April, with the second stopping during June. During the late summer further laterals will develop and those should all be removed as soon as they can easily be handled. Similarly flower buds, other than the crown buds or secondary crown buds, should be removed as they appear if large blooms are required.

Flowering Bring the pots of chrysanthemums into the greenhouse in mid-September. They should be well-spaced and given light, well-ventilated conditions with a minimum temperature of 7°C/45°F. First crown buds bloom in November, the second a month later.

Care after flowering After flowering cut back the plants to about 2 ft. In January cut the old stems down to 2–3 in from soil level and begin the process of propagation again.

Winter-flowering chrysanthemums

1 February–March. Take cuttings of new growth from existing stools. Root in a propagating case. Pot the rooted cuttings into 3 in pots.

2 March–April. Pot on into 5 in pots of John Innes No. 3. Move the plants to a cold frame to harden off, closing the frame only in frosty or bad weather.

3 June. Transfer plants to 8 in pots and stand in a sheltered place outdoors and stake each plant. Fix stakes to a frame to prevent wind damage.

4 September. Bring the plants into the greenhouse and place in a well-lit spot. In November and December the plants will flower.

Fruits and vegetables 1

The cool greenhouse can be used to best effect in growing food crops if it is used to cultivate not only tomatoes, cucumbers and the other vegetable fruits described on pages 244–247 but also more tender vegetables such as okra. Melons and early strawberries are also good subjects for the cool house and so, if space allows, are peaches and nectarines which often fail to do well in the open.

Early strawberries

The cool house will enable the gardener to pick crops of strawberries in March or April.

Propagation In late June, peg down the runners of plants growing in the open garden into 3 in pots filled with John Innes No. 1 potting compost buried with their rims level with the soil surface. After four to six weeks, when the new plants are well established, sever them from the parents and place the pots on well-drained soil or in an open cold frame. Water them well and as plants grow pot them on into their final 6 in pots using John Innes No. 2 or an equivalent peat-based mix. Until September, liquid feed the plants once a week and water frequently.

Leave the plants undisturbed until November then bury the pots up to their rims in peat or well-drained soil to prevent frost from reaching their roots. Ideally, this should be done in a cold frame but a sheltered corner of the garden (not a frost pocket) will suffice if necessary. If there is any risk of frost damage, close the frame or cover the plants with straw.

Greenhouse cultivation In mid-December take the pots into the greenhouse and place them well apart on a sunny shelf to allow good air circulation and maximum light. For a fortnight keep the temperature just above freezing then raise it to 7°C/45°F. Do not be tempted to turn the heating up any higher as this will create too much foliage at the expense of fruiting capacity. When the flower trusses appear in February, raise the minimum temperature to 10°C/50°F and ventilate the house a little during the daytime if the greenhouse air temperature exceeds 21°C/70°F. At this stage plants will benefit if the house is damped down once a week and if they are given a high potash liquid feed twice a week.

When the flowers are open, increase the minimum temperature to 13°C/55°F but do not open the ventilators until the temperature reaches 24°C/75°F. As the flowers open, carry out a daily pollination routine, transferring pollen from flower to flower with a small paint brush. During this pollination period do not damp down the house as this may prevent fruit from forming. To obtain fewer, but larger fruit, remove the smallest flowers as soon as their petals have fallen off and leave eight to ten fruits on each plant.

Once fruit begins to set, resume the damping down routine and water the plants very well in sunny weather. Continue feeding until the fruits begin to turn pink in order to improve fruit flavor.

Melons

In the cool house, melons can be cultivated as described for the cold house on page 69 except that by maintaining a minimum springtime temperature of 21°C/70°C fruit will be produced much earlier. In the cool house melon seed can be planted in February and March to give earlier fruit in June and July respectively. Remember to damp down the house well except during pollination and when the fruits start to ripen.

Okra

Also known as gumbo and ladies' fingers, okra are unusual vegetable fruits particularly good for cooking in curries and other oriental dishes. They are not hard to grow but being tropical plants they need fairly high temperatures, particularly for germination and plant raising.

Raising from seed Sow seed thinly in a seed flat filled with moist soil mix or sow them singly in peat pots from February onwards. Cover the seeds with a thin layer of mix, water them in, then cover the pots or flats with a sheet of glass and one of newspaper. Turn the glass once a day and maintain a temperature of 18°–21°C/65°–70°F. The seeds will take from one to three weeks to germinate, depending on the temperature. As soon as they are big enough to handle, prick out the seedlings into 3 in peat or plastic pots filled with John Innes No. 1 potting compost.

Greenhouse cultivation In early spring, plant out okra direct into the greenhouse border soil or transplant them into 10 in pots of

Early strawberries

1 Mid-December Bring rooted plants in 6 in pots into the cool house. Make sure they are well spaced. Keep the temperature just above freezing. Liquid feed twice a week.

2 Two weeks later raise the temperature to 7°C/45°F. When flower trusses appear raise it to 10°C/50°F. Ventilate and damp down when the temperature exceeds 21°C/70°F.

3 When the flowers open stop damping down and increase the temperature to 13°C/55°F. Ventilate the house at 24°C/75°F. Pollinate the flowers daily with a brush.

4 When fruit has set resume damping down. Support fruit trusses with forked twigs inserted in the pots. Stop feeding when fruit begins to color.

Fruits and vegetables 2

John Innes No. 2 compost. Whichever method is chosen, plants should be provided with canes for support and placed 21–24 in apart in each direction. Throughout the growing season, water plants well and when they are 9–12 in high, pinch out the growing points to encourage a bushy habit and a good succession of flowers and fruit. Watch out for signs of whitefly and red spider mite.

Okra should be harvested when they are young and the seeds inside their pods still soft. Harvest between June and September.

Peaches

In a large greenhouse, especially a lean-to, it is possible to grow a fan-trained peach or nectarine. Both these fruits will crop more reliably in the cool house than in the garden. The best sort of peach to choose for a cool house is the common plum rootstock St Julien A which is semi-dwarfing and so more manageable.

Soil The border soil of the greenhouse can be used but should be enriched with plenty of organic matter before a peach is planted. Alternatively, the border soil may be re-placed with a preparation made from sods of fibrous chalky loam stacked for six months then mixed with one part of rubble to every ten parts of loam. A fortnight before planting in spring, mix in 8 oz of John Innes base fertilizer to every 2 gal bucketful of soil.

Care of plants A peach will need a minimum temperature of 7°C/45°F from late winter until fruit is formed. Only ventilate the house when the temperature rises above 18°C/65°F. Until the flowers open, damp down the house on sunny days and spray the foliage with clean water daily. In early summer, mulch plants well with rotted manure or garden compost and apply a liquid tomato feed every 10 days from bud burst to the start of fruit ripening.

When the flowers open hand pollinate them with a small paint brush and when fruitlets form thin them to about two per cluster when they are about ½ in long. Thin again at the 1 in stage to leave fruits evenly spaced 8–10 in apart.

Care after harvesting After the fruits have been picked, open the ventilators and leave them open until spring.

Okra

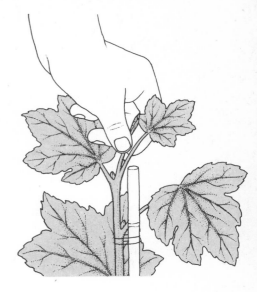

1 March Transplant young plants raised in heat direct into greenhouse soil or transfer them to 10 in pots. Space plants 21–24 in apart and provide canes for support.

2 Pinch out the growing points to encourage bushy growth and a good succession of fruits when plants are 9–12 in tall. Guard against pests.

FAN-TRAINED PEACH

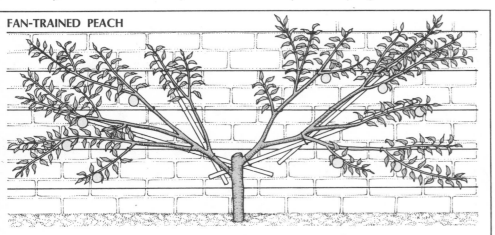

If space allows a fan-trained peach may be grown against the back wall of a lean-to greenhouse or under the roof of a double or single-span cool house. Ideally an area of 15 ft × 10 ft is needed. Plant the tree direct into greenhouse soil enriched with organic matter and provide wires 6 in apart for support. For early fruiting maintain a minimum temperature of 7°C/45°F from late winter until fruits are formed and ventilate only when the temperature exceeds 18°C/65°F.

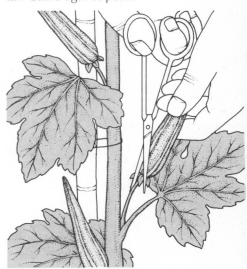

3 Through the growing period water plants regularly. If necessary spray against red spider mite using malathion or a similar low-persistence pesticide.

4 June onwards Cut young pods as soon as they are ready, using sharp scissors, to give a long cropping period. Remember that old pods are stringy and unpalatable.

Using frames 1

SOWING PLAN FOR FRAMES

FEBRUARY
Heated Broad beans, cauliflower, carrots, lettuce.
Unheated Radishes.

MARCH
Heated Beets, cauliflower, leeks, lettuce, spring onion.
Unheated Broad beans, cabbage, peas, radishes, turnips, rutabagas.

APRIL
Heated Celery, cucumber, runner beans.
Unheated Globe artichokes ("suckers"), beets, French beans, Brussels sprouts, cabbage, cauliflower, fennel, lettuce, parsley, peas.

MAY
Heated Celery, zucchini, tomatoes, eggplants, sweet peppers.
Unheated Runner beans, celeriac, cucumbers, squashes, corn, okra, melons.

A frame is a versatile piece of equipment which can be used as an extension of the greenhouse or on its own. A frame is particularly useful for a gardener without a greenhouse, especially if it can be heated, for given the restrictions in size, a heated frame can be used for most of the plants that can be grown in a greenhouse. Both heated and unheated frames can be used for raising new plants, including early vegetables; for extending the growing season; for hardening off greenhouse-grown plants before they are planted out in the garden; for overwintering plants such as chrysanthemums and for plunging potted bulbs that will later be taken indoors to bloom. The soil, mix or other growing medium placed in the frame will depend on the exact use to which the frame is put. The frame should be deep enough to accommodate the plants to be grown in it.

Siting

A frame can be placed abutting a greenhouse or on its own. If one wall of the frame is placed against the greenhouse wall the frame will benefit from improved insulation and reduced heat loss. Another advantage is that the heating system of the greenhouse can usually be extended to serve the frame. Place a frame that is to be used on its own in an open, sunny, easily accessible position that affords plenty of light and some shelter from high winds. Never place a frame in a corner of the garden known to be a frost pocket.

Heating

A cold frame, that is a frame with no form of heating, is less useful than a heated frame which will allow a wider range of plants to be grown. In a heated frame, early vegetables will be ready for cropping sooner and there is less chance of tender plants failing to survive the winter. A heating system for a frame works by heating the soil and/or the air. Soil heating can be provided by electric cables or, if the frame is abutting a heated greenhouse, by hot water pipes. The air in a frame can be heated by electric cables or hot water tubes placed round the walls. Whichever heating system is chosen it should always include an accurate thermostat to aid careful regulation of the growing conditions within the frame.

Insulation

To help conserve the heat built up in a frame during the day, the frame lights can be covered on cold nights with burlap sacking or a roll of old carpet. Place blocks of wood carefuly on top of the sacking or carpet to prevent it from blowing away. Alternatively, buy a special sheet with eyelet holes and tie it to wooden pegs placed in the soil. The sides of the frame can also be insulated by lining them with bales of straw encased in chicken wire.

Ventilation

Plants grown in heated and cold frames need good ventilation to encourage free air circulation. Poor ventilation increases air humidity within the frame and encourages the growth of disease-causing organisms. Make sure that the lights of the frame can be opened at several different levels and that they can easily be removed altogether. For ventilation the lights may be propped open with a block of wood, or a brick, or pushed back entirely off the frame and placed at an angle over the frame with one end on the ground, as long as they will not blow away. In very windy weather secure the lights with cord wound round cleats screwed to the frame wall, or by hooks and eyes.

Watering

To water the plants in a frame the lights can simply be lifted or removed. Always water plants with a rose fitted to the watering can or hose so that soil is not washed away from around plant roots. Semi-automatic watering with a perforated hose or capillary watering as used in the greenhouse (see pages 18–19) are also effective and time-saving. In the capillary system, water is supplied via a trickle irrigation line which ensures a slow, steady water supply to the growing medium in the frame. When the frame is not in use and in the summer, remove the lights so that the soil can get a good natural watering from the rain. This will also help to prevent a damaging build-up of mineral salts in the soil.

Growing early carrots in a heated frame

1 February Dig garden soil in the frame. Place heating cables in the frame and cover them with 6 in of good garden soil.

2 Rake in 2–3 oz of general fertilizer then water well. Close the frame.

3 A week later Sow seed in drills 4 in apart or broadcast at $\frac{1}{12}$ oz per square yard. Set thermostat to 18°C/65°F. Keep frame shut.

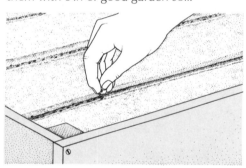

4 March As seedlings develop thin (if necessary) to 1–1$\frac{1}{2}$ in apart. Remove all thinnings. Water to firm. Replace lights.

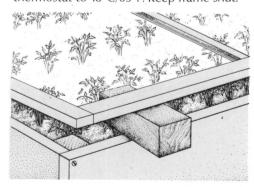

5 As weather warms open lights on sunny days but close them at night. Plants will now need more water.

6 April Remove lights completely when all chance of frost is past. Store lights in a safe place. Harvest carrots as needed.

Using frames 2

Light and shading

To ensure maximum entry of light, keep frame lights clean at all times and renovate and clean them in summer. As in the greenhouse, plants in a frame risk being scorched and badly damaged by hot sun. To prevent this, apply a shading compound to the inside of the frame lights as necessary, or place a sheet of muslin or small mesh plastic netting over the frame on hot, sunny days. The covering can be rolled back in cloudy weather.

Raising seed

Seed of all kinds can be sown in a heated or unheated frame in pots, boxes or flats or directly into prepared soil. Turn on the heating system, if there is one, for a day or two before sowing to warm the soil. Seeds of hardy plants can be sown in a heated frame as early as February, seeds of tender plants from late February to March. For an unheated frame, add on another month to six weeks in each case, and more if the spring is a cold one. Seedlings in pots or boxes are best placed in the frame on a 3 in layer of gravel or weathered ashes to allow good drainage or, if a capillary watering system is used, on a 2 in layer of coarse sand placed on a thick sheet of polyethylene. Note that seeds planted in pots or boxes will need more care in watering as they dry out more quickly than those planted direct into the soil. Seedlings of tender or half-hardy plants raised in a heated frame will also need hardening off before they are planted out into the garden.

Early crops in a heated frame

Carrots, radishes, lettuces, beets and spring onions are among the many vegetables that can be grown in a heated frame for early cropping and for eating when young and tender. Months of planting for heated frames are shown in the list above.

Soil Most early crops can be sown in the frame direct into good well-dug garden soil enriched with well-rotted manure, compost or peat, plus 2–3 oz of a general well-balanced fertilizer per square yard. If the garden top soil is very stony or shallow, it may be preferable to replace the top 1–1½ ft with new good-quality top soil or to replace the soil completely with good sterilized soil placed on a perforated polyethylene sheet placed in the frame. If necessary, make provision for any particular needs of the crop to be grown —lettuces for example do best in humus-rich soil while carrots prefer soil that has not been freshly manured.

Care of seedlings Freshly sown seed of most vegetable crops will germinate best at a temperature of 18°C/65°F so this is the ideal thermostat setting for seed planted in late winter or early spring. On cold nights, insulate the frame with burlap or similar material. The frame should be ventilated during the day as long as the weather is not very cold or windy. In bad weather ensure maximum entry of light by washing all debris off the lights regularly. As the weather warms the lights can be opened wider during the day and closed at night. Once all risk of frost is past and plants are well established, the lights can be removed altogether, cleaned and stored and the heating system turned off.

Crops in a cold frame

For vegetables, a cold frame provides similar protection to cloches (see page 259) but retains heat better and is cooled less by the wind. Vegetables sown in a cold frame will still crop earlier than those sown outdoors with no protection. Among the best crops for the cold frame are cucumbers, zucchinis, melons, smaller squashes and outdoor tomatoes. Cucumber and similar seeds are best pre-germinated at a temperature of 21°C/70°F before being planted in the cold frame in early May. Ventilate the frame as necessary during the day and close it down at night until plants are established then remove the lights in June.

For outdoor tomatoes, raise seeds in heat and plant them out in the cold frame in May or early June. Ventilate the frame as necessary but do not remove the lights completely until the plants are well established, by which time they will have probably outgrown the height of the frame. The lights can be replaced at the end of the season to help ripen the last fruits and combat frost.

Cuttings

Cuttings of all types can be grown in a frame. Use a heated frame for cuttings of tender

Hardening off in an unheated frame

1 Spring As air temperature rises, place boxes or pots of greenhouse-reared seedlings or cuttings in the frame.

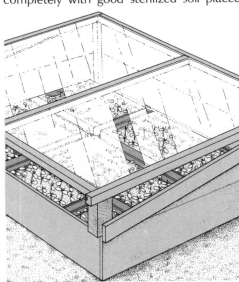

2 During first week (weather permitting) leave lights half open during the day for ventilation but close down each night.

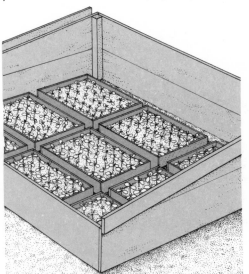

3 During second week leave lights open a little at night. Towards end of week remove lights completely except in windy weather.

4 In third week remove plants from the frame and plant in their permanent positions in the garden.

Using frames 3

plants such as fuchsias and pelargoniums taken in March (wait another six weeks for a cold frame) and dahlia cuttings taken in April. Softwood shrub cuttings can be planted in a cold frame in June, semi-hard ones in July and August. See pages 194–203 for details.

Hardening off
Many tender or half-hardy plants raised in the greenhouse need to be put through a "toughening-up" process called hardening off before they are planted out into the garden. A cold frame is ideal for this purpose. In spring, when there is no risk of tender or half-hardy plants being exposed to frost, once they are in their permanent positions in the garden, take pots or boxes of young plants from the greenhouse and place them in the frame. For one week leave the lights open during the day (as long as the weather is not cold or windy) but close them at night. During the second week, leave the lights open a little at night. Towards the end of the second week open the frame as wide as possible at night. In the third week the plants can be planted in their permanent positions in the garden.

Overwintering and storage
A frame can act as a useful protected storage site for plants during the winter and, at the same time, save valuable space in the greenhouse. A heated frame will be needed for tender plants such as pelargoniums and fuchsias which should be placed in the frame in September. In the same month, freesias can be potted up and placed in a heated frame. Outdoor chrysanthemums can be overwintered in an unheated frame after they have been cut back and boxed in a proprietary potting mix. The frame should be well ventilated except in very severe weather to help prevent diseases such as botrytis, which are encouraged by stagnant air.

Storage A cold frame can be employed to store dormant bulbs and tubers that are susceptible to frost damage. After lifting dahlia tubers, for example, pack them in boxes of dry peat before storing them in a heated frame. Store bulbs in a cold frame loosely packed in wooden boxes with plenty of room for air to circulate between them. Make sure the frame is well ventilated but guard against damp which can cause rot.

The plunge bed
A plunge bed is a bed of damp sand, peat or a mixture of gravel and weathered coal ashes 1ft deep into which pots are buried or plunged up to their rims. A plunge bed in a cold frame is useful for accommodating plants throughout the year. From spring onwards, as alpines finish flowering in the alpine house, transfer them to the plunge bed. Plunge the pots up to their rims and keep the bed damp but never let it become dry or waterlogged. The cool moist environment of the plunge bed will produce good strong growth. Similarly, pot-grown greenhouse plants can be plunged in summer, which will prevent them from drying out too quickly. During the summer there is no need to place the lights on the frame.

Bulb forcing In winter, use the plunge bed for forcing bulbs. Plant bulbs in pots, plunge them and cover the pots with a 3 in layer of peat. Place the lights over the frame, leaving them open a little for ventilation. After eight weeks the bulbs will have formed good root systems and can be taken indoors in succession for flowering.

OVERWINTERING

Heated and unheated frames are very useful for storing and protecting flowering plants in winter, so freeing valuable greenhouse space. Use a heated frame for tender plants such as pelargoniums. Lift plants from the garden in autumn, cut them back and plant in boxes before placing them in the frame. Similarly, make chrysanthemum "stools" by cutting back plants to within 4–6 in of the ground before boxing them up and placing them in an unheated frame. Ventilate well.

Plunging bulbs in an unheated frame

1 October Fill frame with a 1ft layer of sand, peat or a mixture of gravel and weathered coal ashes. Water and allow to settle.

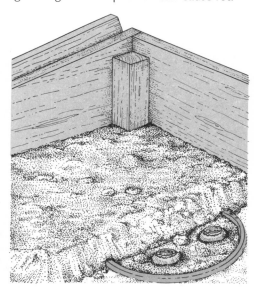

2 Plant hyacinth bulbs in pots then plunge up to their rims in the frame. Cover with a 3 in layer of peat to exclude light.

3 Place lights over frame to protect pots from heavy winter rainfall. Keep the frame well ventilated.

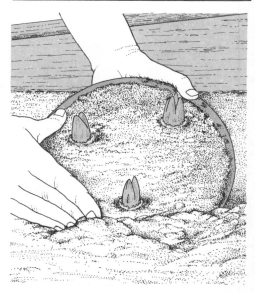

4 After eight weeks Remove pots from frame and take indoors in sequence for flowering.

Using cloches

YEARLY PLAN FOR CLOCHES

FEBRUARY
Sow Radishes.

MARCH
Sow Beets, broad beans, carrots, peas, spring onions, turnips.

APRIL
Sow Cabbage, cauliflower, Brussels sprouts, globe artichokes, French tarragon, parsley, sage. **Harvest** Lettuce.

MAY
Sow French beans, runner beans, celeriac, sweet corn. **Harvest** Lettuce, radishes.

JUNE
Harvest Beets, carrots, lettuce, turnips.

SEPTEMBER
Sow Lettuce. **Cover** Lettuce, land cress, watercress, harvested onions.

OCTOBER
Sow Spring lettuce. **Cover** Winter spinach, corn salad, herbs.

NOVEMBER AND DECEMBER
Harvest Lettuce.

Cloches provide plants with virtually the same protection as cold frames, except that they retain heat rather less well and that the air inside them is cooled more quickly by the wind. The advantage of cloches is that they are more mobile and versatile to use. Cloches can be employed in many ways—to warm the soil before seeds are sown; for raising seedlings, especially half-hardy annual bedding plants and vegetables to extend the growing season at each end of the year; to protect individual plants, particularly alpines, from cold and wet and to save blooms from splashing and spoiling by mud; to provide shelter from cold and wind and to ripen off onions and similar crops in poor weather. Cloches can also be used to spread the season of cut flowers. Rows of gladioli, for example, tend to flower at the same time, but if half is cloched, the cutting period is lengthened.

Using cloches
Cloches should be placed in an open position away from the shade of trees. Never put them in a very windy place where they will cool quickly and risk being damaged or blown over. Any cloches likely to be overturned by strong winds should have fittings to anchor them to the ground or should be secured with string tied to pegs placed in the ground. Leave plenty of room between rows of cloches for easy access and watering.

Ventilation
Ventilation is essential to prevent the build-up of stagnant, over-moist air that encourages disease. If single cloches are placed in rows, always leave a small gap between each one if the cloches have no built-in ventilation system such as adjustable top or sides. In the case of a polyethylene tunnel sides can be lifted and supported with a pot or wooden block. The gaps between the cloches can be increased if necessary to let in more air, but to avoid too much draft, and consequent heat loss, close the ends with purchased cloche ends or with a sheet of glass or thick plastic held in place with a wooden stake.

Soil preparation
Before placing cloches in position, prepare the soil for the plants or crop that is to be protected according to its specific needs and make sure that the same crop is not grown in the same soil two years running. Before sowing seed or planting out seedlings raised in a greenhouse or heated frame, put the cloches in position and leave them for two to three weeks to dry and warm the soil. A dressing of balanced fertilizer can be raked in before cloches are positioned.

Watering
Cloches need only be removed for watering if they are covering small seedlings which need a very even sprinkling of water. Otherwise, water can be applied to cloches from overhead with a watering can or hose if there is insufficient rain. The water runs down the sides of the cloches and is absorbed into the soil, reaching the roots of the plants which grow naturally towards sources of food and water. For long rows of cloches it is also possible to supply water via a sprinkler or irrigation tubing placed between the rows. On light soil make a shallow channel on the outside of each cloche in which water can easily collect and drain into the soil.

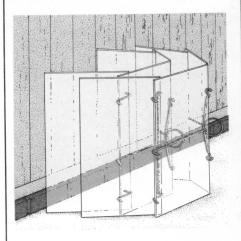

STORING CLOCHES

Store cloches not in use by stacking them on their ends in a sheltered corner of the garden where they will not get broken or blown over by strong winds.

Year-round uses for cloches

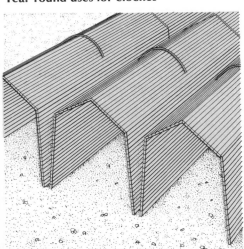

1 January Place cloches over soil prepared for seed sowing. Leave for 2–3 weeks to dry and warm soil. Do not close cloche ends.

2 Early spring Use cloches to protect newly sown seed and seedlings. Close cloche ends but ventilate well according to type.

3 Autumn In rainy weather place harvested onions under cloches to dry out before storage. Ventilate well. Leave ends open.

4 Winter Single cloches can be put over alpines such as cushion plants susceptible to rotting in wet soil.

Pests and diseases: fruit 1

STAGES OF BUD DEVELOPMENT

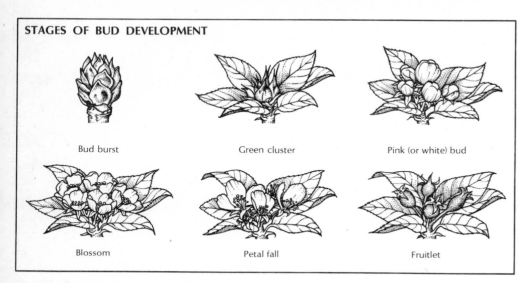

Bud burst

Green cluster

Pink (or white) bud

Blossom

Petal fall

Fruitlet

Correct cultivation and weed control help to prevent trouble with pests and diseases, although chemical control may be necessary.

Types of chemical control
Fungicides and pesticides prevent or help to control infection and infestation.

The various pesticides act in different ways. A contact spray such as derris affects the insect itself. Ovicides such as DNOC kill the eggs. These take effect on contact, so it is important to cover all plant surfaces. A third group, systemic insecticides such as formothion, dimethoate and menazon, are taken up through the roots and leaves of the plant into the sap. They are thus very effective against sap-sucking insects. Complete coverage is preferable but not essential because systemics can be applied as a root drench.

Most fungicides only check or prevent attacks so they should be applied before the disease appears. The new partly systemic fungicides such as benomyl are slightly absorbed into the plant's tissues only but are effective for a short period even after symptoms are visible. However, resistant strains of the fungus may develop if systemic fungicides are used too frequently.

Precautions
Always follow the manufacturer's instructions when mixing and applying chemicals. Wash hands and equipment after using chemicals. Do not use the fungicide and pesticide sprayer for weedkillers. Some chemicals must be treated with extra caution. Malathion, captan and thiram should not be used on fruit that is to be preserved. Captan, dinocap, thiram and zineb may irritate the eyes, nose and mouth; wear a mask and goggles if susceptible to allergic reactions. Do not use sulfur on sulfur-sensitive varieties. Do not use pesticides when the flowers are open because they kill bees and other pollinating insects.

DISEASES
American gooseberry mildew Affecting gooseberries and currants, it forms a white, powdery coating on young leaves, shoots and fruits, later turning brown and felted. The shoots may be distorted at the tips.
Treatment: Cut out and burn diseased shoots in late August or September. Spray with dinocap before flowering, repeating as necessary. Or spray with benomyl as the first flowers open, repeating two, four and six weeks later. Keep the bushes open by regular pruning and avoid excessive nitrogen feeding.
Apple canker It affects apples and pears. Sunken discolored patches appear on the bark, becoming extended ellipses surrounded by concentric rings of shrunken bark. White fungus spores are visible on the sunken bark in summer. The branch becomes swollen above the canker and it may die.
Treatment: Cut out and burn diseased branches and spurs. On branches without die-back, cut out and burn diseased tissue. Paint the wounds with canker paint. Spray with bordeaux mixture or liquid copper after harvest but before leaf-fall. Repeat when half the leaves have fallen and at bud burst.
Bacterial canker Round brown spots appear on the leaves of apricots, cherries, peaches, and plums, later developing into holes. There are elongated, flattened, oozing cankers on the branches. The buds do not develop the following spring or they produce small, yellow leaves which curl, wither and die. The branches also die back.
Treatment: Remove badly cankered branches and dead wood. Spray with bordeaux mixture in mid-August, and one and two months later.
Bitter pit It causes sunken pits on apple skins, brown flesh spots and bitter taste.
Treatment: Prevent by watering and mulching during dry weather. Spray with calcium nitrate at 1oz per 2gal of water in mid-June. Repeat ten days later. Ten days after that spray with 2oz calcium nitrate per 2gal and repeat at least three times at ten-day intervals.
Black knot Twigs of cherries, apricots and plums develop knotty, black excrescences.
Treatment: Remove twigs 4in below knots. Spray with lime-sulfur at bud burst.
Boron deficiency The pear fruits on most branches are distorted and have brown spots in the flesh. The leaves are small and misshapen. There is some die-back of shoots and the bark is roughened and pimply.
Treatment: Apply 1oz of borax mixed with sand per 20 sq yds.
Brown rot Affects apricots, cherries, peaches, plums, nectarines and to some extent other fruits. The fruits are brown with soft, decaying flesh, later becoming covered with concentric rings of grayish spores.
Treatment: The disease usually occurs in warm, humid weather. If humidity is high, spray with captan every three days during period of bloom and prior to harvest.
Cane blight It affects only raspberries. A dark area can be seen on the canes just above ground level. The canes become very brittle and the leaves wither.
Treatment: Cut back diseased canes to below soil level and burn. Disinfect tools. Spray new canes with bordeaux mixture.
Cane spot It affects raspberries, loganberries, hybrid berries and, rarely, blackberries. Small purple spots appear on the canes in May to June, later enlarging and turning white with a purple border and then splitting to form pits or small cankers. The tips of shoots may die back, leaves may be spotted and fruit distorted.
Treatment: Cut out and burn badly spotted canes in fall. Spray raspberries with liquid copper or thiram (but not on fruit for preserving) at bud burst and just before flowering. Or spray with benomyl at bud burst and repeat every two weeks until the end of flowering. Spray loganberries with bordeaux mixture, liquid copper or thiram (but not on fruit for preserving) just before flowering and when the fruit sets.
Cedar-apple rust This disease occurs only in areas with red cedars. Leaves of apples, crabapples, pears and quinces look rusty and distorted.
Treatment: Spray apples, and other similar fruit, in mid-spring with ferbam.
Chlorosis All trees may be affected if unable to take up sufficient iron from soil. Leaves turn yellow between the veins.
Treatment: Apply iron chelates to the soil.
Coral spot Red currants are very susceptible, but other currants and figs are also affected. The branches die back and coral red pustules appear on the dead shoots.
Treatment: Cut out affected branches several inches below the diseased tissues. Paint the wounds. Burn infected shoots and any other woody debris in the garden.
Crown gall A walnut-size gall can be seen at ground level on cane fruits or there is a chain of small galls higher up.
Treatment: Destroy diseased canes.
Die-back The shoots and branches die back. It is usually caused by fungi but occasionally by adverse cultural conditions.
Treatment: Cut back all dead wood to healthy tissue and paint the wounds. Check that feeding, watering and mulching are adequate.
Fireblight Affects pears and occasionally

Pests and diseases: fruit 2

apples. The shoots die back and the leaves become brown and withered. Cankers at the base of the diseased tissue ooze in spring.
Treatment: Do not over-fertilize trees, because this encourages strong growth which, in turn, encourages disease. Spraying several times during bloom with bordeaux mixture or copper may help. Cut out and burn diseased wood 6 in or more below blighted area.

Gray mold (*Botrytis cinerea*) Strawberries, cane fruits, currants and grapes are among the many fruits affected. The berries rot and are covered with gray-brown fluff.
Treatment: Remove and destroy infected fruits if possible. Spray with benomyl as soon as the flowers open, repeating two, four and six weeks later. Do not use on strawberries under glass or polyethylene.

Greasy spot It causes small oily brown spots on leaves of citrus trees.
Treatment: Spray with copper fungicides in the summer.

Gummosis Bark near the graft on citrus trees decays and gum flows from the infected areas on the trunk.
Treatment: This fungus disease is best controlled by proper planting and care of citrus. If trouble starts, check whether decayed bark extends more than half way around the trunk. If it does, destroy the tree. If it does not extend more than half way around the trunk, remove the decayed bark and a little of the adjacent live bark and disinfect the wound with 1 teaspoon of potassium permanganate in 1 pint of water. Cover the wound with tree paint when it heals.

Honey fungus It affects all fruit crops. White, fan-shaped patches of fungus appear beneath the bark on roots and on the trunk just above ground level. There are blackish growths on the roots and honey-colored toadstools grow at the base of the tree in the fall. Sudden death of the plant may occur.
Treatment: Dig out affected plants with as many roots as possible and burn them. Sterilize the soil with a two per cent solution of formaldehyde at 5 gal per square yard, or use a phenolic compound.

Leaf blotch Strawberries are affected by several diseases that cause browning of the leaves or dark spots that may be surrounded by various colors on leaves and stems. The

leaves die and the fruit often rots.
Treatment: Remove and burn affected leaves. Spray or dust with copper in the early fall and after bloom in the spring. Make several spring treatments if weather is wet.

Leaf spot of currants and gooseberries Dark brown spots can be seen on the leaves, later coalescing and turning the leaves brown. Premature leaf-fall results.
Treatment: Collect and burn all diseased leaves. Spray with zineb or thiram after flowering, repeating every 10–14 days, as necessary. Or spray with thiophanate-methyl as the flowers open, repeating two, four and six weeks later. Feed the bushes well to help overcome the disease.

Magnesium deficiency Orange, red or brown bands develop between the leaf veins, especially of apples, citrus fruits, grapes and raspberries.
Treatment: Spray at petal fall, or when the trouble shows, with magnesium sulfate at 8 oz per $2\frac{1}{2}$ gal of water. Repeat twice at 14-day intervals.

Melanose Leaves, fruits and shoots on citrus trees develop rough, irregular spots.
Treatment: Remove and burn infected parts. About a week after fruit set, spray trees with a neutral copper fungicide and wettable sulfur.

Peach leaf curl Reddish blisters appear on the leaves. Later, the leaves swell and have a powdery white covering of spores. Premature leaf-fall results.
Treatment: Spray with bordeaux mixture or liquid copper in January or February. Repeat 10–14 days later and just before leaf-fall.

Powdery mildew Apple, grape, melon, peach and quince are affected. A white powdery coating of fungus spores appears on emerging shoots and young leaves. Apple and pear shoots are stunted, the fruits fail to set or develop brown patches, and the leaves fall. The skins of grapes become discolored and shrivel and split.
Treatment: Remove silvered shoots at pruning. Cut off infected shoots of apples, peaches and quinces in spring and summer. Spray apples and quinces with dinocap at the pink bud stage. Repeat every 7–14 days until mid-July. Spray grapes with dinocap at first symptoms, repeating two, four and six weeks

later. For melons, spray with benomyl or dino-cap at first symptoms. Repeat every two weeks, as necessary. On peaches use a sulfur fungicide at first symptoms, repeating every two weeks as necessary.

Quince leaf blight Dark red irregular spots appear on leaves, later becoming blackish. The leaves may turn brown or yellow and fall prematurely and the fruit may be spotted and deformed. Shoot tips die back.
Treatment: Rake up and burn fallen leaves. Cut out dead shoots in winter. Spray with bordeaux mixture when leaves are fully developed, and in summer, if necessary.

Raspberry virus diseases These are very troublesome; loganberries, blackberries susceptible to viruses and related organisms, and other cane fruits may also be affected. Yellow blotching or mottling is visible on the leaves. Growth is poor and the crop reduced.
Treatment: Remove and burn all affected plants at the same time. Plant new canes certified as healthy in a new site 50 ft away or change the soil on the old site to a depth of $1\frac{1}{2}$ ft.

Reversion This affects only black currants and is spread by the big bud mite. Mature leaves on the basal shoots are narrow with fewer than five pairs of veins on each main lobe. The flowers are bright magenta-colored and there is a reduced fruit yield.
Treatment: Control big bud mite (see page 262). Destroy all diseased bushes at the same time. Plant new certified bushes on a fresh site.

Scab Affects apples, pears, peaches, pecans and citrus fruits. Brown or black scabs are visible on the fruits which are sometimes mis-shapen and cracked. Olive-green blotches develop on the leaves and they fall prematurely. There is a general loss of vigor and a reduced crop. Pimples on the young shoots later burst the bark as cracks or scabs.
Treatment: Rake up and burn all leaves in fall. Cut out cracked and scabby shoots.

Shothole Affects cherries, peaches and nectarines, and plums causing brown spots on leaves which later become holes. Only weak trees are affected.
Treatment: Proper feeding should prevent a recurrence but, if not, spray with copper fungicide at half strength in summer and at full strength just before leaf-fall.

Silver leaf It can affect most tree fruits, currants and gooseberries, but it is most troublesome on plums, appearing as silvering leaves which may turn brown. There is progressive die-back of branches and a purplish fungus grows on the dead wood, later turning white or brown. Inner tissues are stained brown or purple.
Treatment: If there is fungus on the trunk, destroy the tree. Otherwise, cut back dead branches to 6 in behind the staining of inner tissues. Paint the wounds. Sterilize all tools after use on diseased trees.

Split stone Affects peaches and nectarines. Fruits crack at the stalk end producing a hole through which earwigs can enter. The stone is split and the kernel (if formed) rots.
Treatment: Hand pollinate the flowers. Lime the soil if necessary. Water when required.

Spur blight This affects raspberries and sometimes loganberries. Dark purple blotches appear around the nodes on canes. They later enlarge, turn silver and become covered with minute black dots. Buds wither and die or produce shoots which die back in spring.
Treatment: Cut out and burn diseased canes. Spray with benomyl, dichlofluanid, thiram or captan when the new canes are a few inches high. Repeat two, four and six weeks later. Or spray with bordeaux mixture or liquid copper at bud burst, repeating when the flower tips are just showing white.

Strawberry mildew Purple patches are visible on leaves, which curl upwards. Grayish fungal spores develop on the undersides and spread to flowers and berries.
Treatment: Dust with sulfur or spray with dinocap just before flowering. Repeat every 10–14 days until two weeks before harvest. Or spray with benomyl just after flowering, repeating two and four weeks later. After harvest, cut off old leaves and spray with fungicide.

Strawberry virus diseases Various diseases cause stunting or death. The symptoms are most obvious from April to September. The leaves become dwarfed and puckered with yellow edges and yellow or purple mottling. A virus-related organism causes old leaves to turn red and young leaves yellow. The flowers have green petals and the fruits fail to ripen. Eventually the plant dies.

Pests and diseases: fruit 3

Treatment: Destroy all affected plants at the same time. Do not take runners. Plant disease-resistant strawberries in a fresh site or change the soil on the old site to a depth of 1ft × 1½ ft wide.

Wilt Several wilts affect melons. Lower leaves turn yellow and wilt and then the whole plant wilts and collapses.

Treatment: Destroy diseased plants and sterilize the soil. Replant with disease-resistant varieties.

PESTS

Aphids (Greenfly) Aphids suck sap from the leaves and shoots of most tree, bush, cane and other soft fruits, causing leaf curling and distortion, reddish discoloration, stunted growth and black sooty mold. They spread virus diseases.

Treatment: Spray with miscible oil in late winter (but not strawberries) to kill over-wintering eggs. Use a systemic insecticide, such as formothion, in the spring if aphids are present, repeating as necessary.

Apple curculio A brown beetle with humped back that makes puncture holes in apples, cherries, pears and quinces. The mis-shapen fruit falls.

Treatment: Apply a general-purpose fruit spray at two-week intervals throughout the growing season.

Apple maggot White larvae tunnel into apples, cherries, blueberries.

Treatment: Spray on a regular schedule with a general-purpose fruit spray.

Apple sawfly Caterpillars tunnel into the fruitlets, causing them to fall in June. A ribbon-like scar forms on the remaining fruits.

Treatment: Spray with lindare, dimethoate or fenitrothion one week after petal fall. Pick up and burn infested fruitlets.

Big bud mite A pest of black currants. It lives inside buds, making them swollen and rounded (instead of narrow and pointed) and they fail to develop in spring. The mites spread reversion disease (see page 261).

Treatment: Pick off and burn big buds during the winter. Spray with benomyl at the first open flower and again two and four weeks later. Destroy badly infested bushes and re-plant with virus-free stock on a fresh site.

Cankerworms These inchworms, or measur-ing worms, are seen looping and hanging from long threads on many kinds of tree fruits. If present in numbers, they can defoliate the trees rapidly.

Treatment: Apply a general-purpose fruit spray on a regular schedule.

Caspid bugs Affect currants, gooseberries and apples. Capsids suck sap from shoot tips, leaves and fruits. Leaves at the shoot tips develop with tattered holes. Mature apple fruits have corky scabs or bumps on the skin.

Treatment: Spray with a systemic insecticide such as formothion shortly after flowering has finished.

Caterpillars Caterpillars of various kinds feed in the spring, causing damaged and ragged buds, leaves and blossoms. Tent caterpillars are particularly troublesome on cherries and apples in spring and also in the fall.

Treatment: Spray with fenitrothion or tri-chlorphon as the young leaves appear. Place a sticky greaseband around the trunk to trap emerging wingless female winter moths. Keep bands sticky and in position until late March. Do not burn nests, as this damages the tree.

Codling moth Caterpillars of small gray-brown moths tunnel into the mature fruit of apples and English walnuts.

Treatment: Spray with fenitrothion in mid-June, repeating three weeks later. A regular spray schedule with a general-purpose fruit spray is also effective.

Gooseberry sawfly These caterpillars are up to 1in long, creamy-green with black dots. They can completely defoliate gooseberry and red currant plants.

Treatment: Spray with derris or malathion as soon as caterpillars are seen, repeating as necessary from late April onwards.

Japanese beetles Handsome, metallic-green beetles with coppery wings that feast on grape leaves and may attack other fruits.

Treatment: Many of the beetles can be picked off by hand into a can of kerosene. But, for general control, spray with carbaryl.

Mealy bugs Sap-feeding pests of apples, citrus fruits, grapes and other fruits. The small white-pink insects can be seen in the leaf axils covered with a white fluffy wax.

Treatment: Control by spraying with mala-thion 2 or 3 times at 2 week intervals.

Nematodes A microscopic soil insect that attacks citrus tree roots, causing a general malaise of the trees.

Treatment: Fumigate the soil with SMDC or other fumigant.

Oriental fruit moth A gray and brown moth with pink larvae that attacks leaves and twig tips on peaches and bores into the fruit through the stems. They also attack quinces and other deciduous fruits.

Treatment: Spray regularly with a general-purpose fruit spray.

Peach tree borer This yellow caterpillar bores into the trunks of peaches and related stone fruits, leaving masses of gum oozing from the holes they make.

Treatment: Fumigate the soil around the trees with para-dichlorobenzene in the fall. Spray endosulfan on the trunks and branches when the buds start to open in the spring.

Plum curculio Similar to apple curculio and treated in the same way.

Plum sawfly Its grubs tunnel into the young fruits and cause them to fall early.

Treatment: Spray with fenitrothion or di-methoate at 7–10 days after petal fall.

Raspberry beetle The maggot-like larvae damage the ripening fruits of raspberry, blackberry, loganberry and similar fruits.

Treatment: Prevent damage by spraying at dusk with derris or malathion on the raspberry when first pink fruit is seen; on the logan-berry when flowering is almost over; and on the blackberry when flowering starts.

Red spider mite A tiny, sap-feeding pest of apples, plums and many other fruits. It causes a yellowish mottling of the leaves which can dry up and fall early.

Treatment: Apply a winter wash in February to control over-wintering eggs. Check the mite with a dinocap spray or use a systemic insec-ticide such as dimethoate or formothion in summer if it persists. Give two or three applications at 7–10 day intervals.

Scale insects These are sap-feeding pests with shell-like coverings which are attached to the bark. The various kinds attack fruits such as apples, peaches and pears.

Treatment: Control with a dormant oil spray in late winter. Apply malathion in late May and late June.

Slugs These damage fruits on strawberries.

Treatment: Scatter metaldehyde baits among the plants. Keep the garden clear and tidy in winter to reduce numbers.

Vine weevil Grubs feed on the roots of grapes and strawberries, sometimes destroy-ing the plants. The adult beetles eat irregular-shaped notches from the leaf margins at night, but this is less serious.

Treatment: Drench the root area with lindare.

Wasps These feed on the ripe fruit of apples, pears, plums and grapes.

Treatment: Enclose fruit trusses in bags made from muslin or old nylon stockings. Destroy wasp nests by placing carbaryl dust in the entrance at dusk.

Woolly aphid This aphid sucks sap from cracks in the bark and young shoots of apples. The colonies can be recognized by their white fluffy waxy coating.

Treatment: Spray or paint the colonies with a systemic insecticide such as formothion or dimethoate when the aphid appears in late May to June.

ANIMAL PESTS

Birds There are a number of methods of protecting food crops from damage or des-truction by birds. Such methods include bags and sleeving, collars, cotton as a deterrent, fruit cages and netting.

Mice Mice eat the bark on trunks and roots of fruit trees, and if they succeed in girdling a trunk, the tree dies.

Treatment: Keep grass cut around trunks and pull mulches away from them. Surround trunks with $\frac{1}{4}$ in wire mesh that extends about 4 in below ground and 20 in above.

Rabbits Like mice, they eat tree bark and may kill trees by girdling.

Treatment: Use traps to catch rabbits. En-close trunks in wire mesh.

Squirrels If other food is scarce, squirrels eat the fruits of peaches, pears and apples, even while these are still green.

Treatment: Trapping.

Deer These animals can be pests when they strip apples off trees in the fall. In winter, they injure many different trees by nibbling on tender shoots and by rubbing their antlers on the trunks.

Treatment: Repellents sprayed on trees in winter are reasonably effective, but they can-not be used during summer and fall.

Pests and diseases: vegetables 1

Strong, healthy plants are less susceptible to disease and better able to withstand damage from pests. However, despite correct cultivation, vigilant weed control, crop rotation and the increasing availability of disease-resistant varieties, damage due to pests and diseases occurs even in the most carefully managed vegetable gardens. It is therefore important to be able to make a rapid and accurate diagnosis of each problem so that the right action, often involving the use of chemicals, can be taken as soon as possible.

The use of chemicals

Always follow the manufacturer's instructions precisely, especially concerning dilution, the time of application and the period which must elapse between the final application and harvesting. Always store chemicals, sealed and labeled, out of the reach of children, pets and wild animals. Never transfer them to soft drinks bottles. Do not spray on windy days and do not allow spray to drift on to other crops or neighboring gardens, ponds, rivers, ditches or water sources. Never use containers previously used for weedkillers when mixing or applying other sprays and do not mix up more material than is required because it is difficult to dispose of the excess safely. Wash hands and all equipment thoroughly after spraying.

Some chemicals must be treated with extra caution. For example, calomel dust is poisonous and protective gloves should be worn. Captan, dinocap, maneb, thiram and zineb may irritate skin, eyes, nose and mouth: wear gloves, mask and goggles if susceptible to allergic reactions.

Not all insects and animals in the garden are harmful to vegetables and some are beneficial. They can be killed by the chemicals used to control pests so never use pesticides indiscriminately or excessively.

Types of pesticides and fungicides

Fungicides are used to prevent infections, and pesticides to treat infestations. There are various kinds of pesticides and they act in different ways. Contact types such as derris affect the insect itself and it is important to cover all the plant's surfaces for maximum kill. They remain effective for a relatively short period after application. Systemic types such as formothion and dimethoate are absorbed into the plant and spread through the sap. They are very effective against sap-sucking insects. Complete coverage of the plant is not essential and most systemics can be applied as a root drench. Most fungicides only check or prevent disease and should therefore be applied before signs of disease are seen. A few partially systemic fungicides such as benomyl are now available. These are absorbed slightly into the plant's tissues and are effective for a short period even after disease symptoms are visible.

Methods of application Chemicals are available as dusts, sprays, pastes, pellets, wettable powders and aerosols. Not all chemicals are in all forms, however, and not all forms of a chemical are effective against the same range of pests or diseases.

Most of the materials are listed in this book according to their active chemical ingredient and not by their trade name. Use products that contain the appropriate active ingredient which is given on the label or in the instructions issued by the manufacturer.

DISEASES

In the following section the main diseases are briefly described and appropriate control methods are recommended.

Bacterial blight is a seed-borne bacterial disease which appears as spots on the leaves of beans. The spots are surrounded by a light-colored ring or halo. There is no adequate control and the plants should be burnt once the crop has been picked.

Blackleg of potatoes is caused by the bacterium *Erwinia carotovora* var. *atroseptica*. Early in the season the foliage of an affected plant turns yellow and the shoots collapse because of blackening and rotting of the stem bases, although occasionally one or two healthy stems develop. The plant may die before any tubers form but any which have already developed show a brown or gray slimy rot inside starting at the heel end. Destroy affected plants. If severely infected tubers are stored they will decay, but those only slightly infected may show no symptoms and, if planted, will introduce the infection the following season.

Chocolate spot disease (a form of botrytis) causes discoloration on the leaves and stems of broad beans and can seriously affect over-wintered crops. Plants grown in acid soils or which have become soft through excessive applications of nitrogenous fertilizers are more susceptible to attack. Sowing the seeds thinly, applications of potash at $\frac{1}{2}$ oz per square yard before sowing and the maintenance of a pH of 6.5–7.0 will cut down the likelihood of infection. Where the disease is endemic spray the young foliage with a copper fungicide before any symptoms are seen.

Club-root distorts the roots and badly affects the growth of all brassicas. The disease is more prevalent in acid soils so where necessary raise the pH to 6.5–7.5 by applying limestone at 14 oz per square yard and maintain the pH level with smaller dressings as required in subsequent years. Four per cent calomel dust raked into the soil before sowing at $1\frac{1}{2}$ oz per square yard helps to control club-root, and also have some combative function against cabbage maggot (see page 265). Seedlings may also be dipped in calomel paste or a solution of benomyl to protect them from attack. In soils where club-root of brassicas is a major problem sterilization with SMDC (Vapam) or DMTT (Mylone) may be needed.

Common scab of potatoes occurs most frequently in dry soils lacking in humus and is also prevalent on alkaline soils. A soil pH of 5.0–6.0 and improvement of the soil humus content will cut down the incidence of the disease. Potatoes should also be kept well watered, particularly during dry spells. No available chemical control measures are effective against it.

Damping off diseases of seedlings are encouraged by overcrowded, stagnant conditions and the use of garden soil rather than sterilized soils or compost for raising seedlings under glass. Affected seedlings rot and collapse at ground level. Thin sowing in sterilized soil will cut down the incidence of damping off. Slight attacks may be checked by watering with captan or zineb after removing dead seedlings.

Downy mildews may affect lettuce, onions, spinach and young brassicas. Thin sowing and early thinning of seedlings will cut down incidence of these mildews but if seedlings are attacked, remove the affected leaves and spray with zineb. Bordeaux mixture on brassicas, onions and spinach and thiram on lettuce are also effective.

Foot and root rot is caused by several different fungi which kill the roots and bases of the stems of young plants. A seed dressing of captan may help to avoid this trouble but at the first signs of this disease, water the crop with a solution of captan or zineb. Mound sterile compost around the bases of affected tomatoes. Burn badly affected plants.

Gray mold (*Botrytis cinerea*) may affect most vegetables at some stage in their lives. It is encouraged by overcrowded, stagnant conditions and affected stems, leaves or fruits rapidly rot and become covered with a gray-brown fungal growth. To cut down attacks sow seeds thinly and keep seedlings and plants well spaced. Provide good ventilation under glass and make sure that dead or dying material is removed and burnt. Terraclor or dicloran (both only available in commercial packs) raked into the soil prior to sowing or planting helps to protect lettuces. Spray over-wintering plants with thiram.

Leaf spots Several fungal diseases (antracnose is among the best known) cause spots on vegetable leaves and on fruits. The spots vary in color and, often, have pronounced centers. Brassicas, spinach beet and beets are among those crops susceptible to leaf-spot fungi, which usually affect older leaves. Affected tissue sometimes fall away, leaving holes. Leaf spots are most troublesome in wet seasons, particularly among overcrowded plants and on brassicas grown too soft as a result of heavy dressings of nitrogenous fertilizers. Burn infected parts, and spray with zineb or maneb at the first sign of infection.

Neck rot fungus (*Botrytis allii*) can cause considerable loss of stored onions. A gray moldy growth develops on or near the neck of an affected bulb, which subsequently becomes soft and rotten. Later, large black resting bodies of the fungus develop on the rotting tissues. Store only hard, well-dried bulbs in a cool, dry place where there is free circulation of air around them. Examine bulbs frequently and remove rotting onions as they are seen. The disease can be seed-borne, therefore buy good quality seed which has been treated

Pests and diseases: vegetables 2

against neck rot, or sets from a reputable grower, and dust seeds and sets with dry benomyl before sowing or planting.

Parsnip canker causes rotting of the shoulder tissues of parsnips. There are no satisfactory control measures although the incidence of the disease can be reduced by growing parsnips on a fresh site each year in deep well-worked soil of pH 5.5–7.0. Some varieties are resistant to parsnip canker.

Potato blight is a serious disease of potatoes and is also liable to infect tomatoes. Foliage, stems and tubers of potatoes can be affected and destroyed. Deep planting of healthy tubers in drills at least 5 in deep and timely hilling up minimize infection. Main crop potatoes should also be sprayed from July onwards with maneb, zineb or bordeaux mixture to control the disease. Cut off and remove the stems before lifting. A few varieties are resistant to potato blight and can be grown in areas where this disease is prevalent. Potato blight can be controlled on tomatoes by spraying each season with one of the chemicals recommended for potatoes, as soon as the tops have been pinched out of most of the plants in midsummer. In cool wet seasons the spray should be repeated every 2–3 weeks.

Powdery mildews occur on squashes, cucumbers and some other vegetable crops, particularly if they become dry at the roots. The leaves and stems become covered with a white powdery coating. Control by spraying with benomyl or dinocap as soon as the first symptoms appear, and repeat if necessary.

Sclerotinia disease can attack the roots or stem bases of several vegetables including carrots, cucumbers, Jerusalem artichokes and roots or tubers in storage. Any infected plants must be burnt to avoid further soil contamination from the large resting bodies that form if diseased plants are allowed to remain. There is no practical chemical control. Good hygiene and rotation of affected crops are the only practical methods of control.

Smut is characterized by large, gray and black fungus growths on corn ears and other parts of the plant. Cut off and burn the infected parts. Rotate crops annually.

Violet root rot of asparagus is caused by the soil-borne fungus, *Helicobasidium pur-*

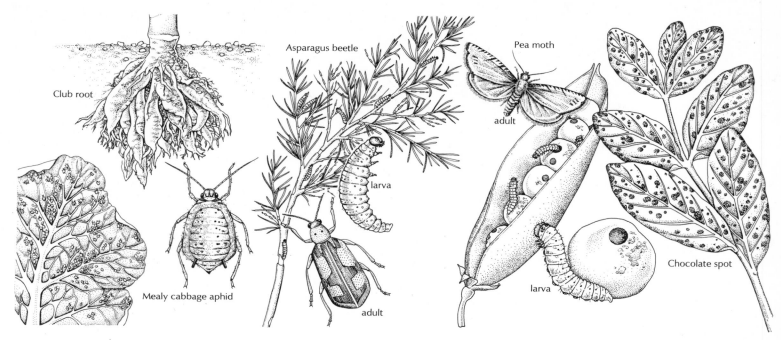

Club root

Mealy cabbage aphid

Asparagus beetle

larva

adult

Pea moth

adult

larva

Chocolate spot

pureum, which kills the crown and roots. It grows on them as violet web-like strands. Small round masses of fungal threads may also appear. With the death of the roots the top growth turns yellow and dies, and a gap develops in the asparagus bed as the disease gradually spreads outward. Where only slight infection has occurred, isolate the diseased area by sinking sheets of thick polyethylene into the soil to form a vertical cylinder to a depth of 12 in. In severe cases abandon the infected bed.

Viruses causing leaf mottling and distortion and often stunting of the plants can affect squashes in particular, celery, cucumbers, tomatoes and several other vegetables. They are spread by aphids or eelworms and so control of these pests and removal of weeds that may act as hosts for both the viruses and their vectors is important. There is no cure for virus-affected plants, which should be burnt once the trouble has been diagnosed. Always wash hands and tools after handling virus-infected plants.

White rot of onions appears as a fluffy white growth at the bases of onions and quickly affects and kills the foliage. Affected plants should be burnt as soon as the disease is seen. Control may be obtained by applying four per cent calomel dust or benomyl to the drills prior to sowing, or spraying with the recommended rate of benomyl when the plants are approximately 7–8 in tall.

Wilt Fusarium wilt occurs in hot weather; verticillium wilt occurs in cool weather. Both diseases cause wilting, yellowing and death of tomatoes, peppers and other vegetables. Control is to plant resistant varieties.

PESTS

In the following section the main pests are briefly described and appropriate control methods are recommended.

Aphids (greenfly and blackfly) will infest most vegetable crops. Apart from the damage caused by the aphids themselves, they are carriers of virus diseases and vegetables should be checked regularly for their presence. Infestations should be dealt with at an early stage by spraying with dimethoate, derris or malathion. If the plants are to be harvested within one week of applying the

spray use derris. Cucurbits are also best sprayed with derris or a pyrethroid compound to avoid damage.

Root aphids may also be troublesome on beans, lettuce and artichokes. Attacks are not usually noticed until the plants are infested. A malathion drench may check heavy infestations but soil treatment with diazinon granules prior to sowing or planting should prevent attack. Some lettuce varieties are resistant to root aphids.

Asparagus beetle Small yellow and black beetles and their gray-black grubs can defoliate the plants during the summer. Control by spraying with derris or lindane as soon as these pests are seen. Rotenone, malathion and carbaryl also are recommended chemicals for the control of asparagus beetle.

Bean seed fly maggots can prevent germination of all types of bean seed and they can also damage onions. Damage usually occurs in cold, wet seasons when germination is slow. The use of cloches to warm the soil early in the year encourages germination and cuts down attacks. Treating the seed row with diazinon gives some protection.

Pests and diseases: vegetables 3

Birds Damage to vegetable crops by birds, can occur throughout the year. Scaring devices and bird repellent sprays are of limited value in deterring birds. In some instances they may be effective for short periods, but where birds are a persistent problem some form of cage or netting is essential to produce worthwhile crops.

Cabbage maggots (*Hylemya brassica*) can devastate many brassica seedlings and young plants. The seed rows and transplanting sites should be treated with diazinon prior to sowing or planting. Attacks on established plants can be checked with trichlorphon.

Cabbage worms Several green worms riddle the leaves of cabbages, broccoli, cauliflower and related plants with holes. Regular weekly dusting with rotenone from the time the worms first appear in the spring gives control.

Carrot rust fly (*Psila rosae*) is one of the most damaging pests of carrots and also attacks parsley, parsnip and celery. Growth is stunted and secondary rots may develop in the damaged carrots. Careful spacing of pelleted seed or very thin sowing to cut down the need to thin carrots will help to minimize damage because the female carrot rust flies are strongly attracted by the aroma of carrot foliage bruised when thinning. Sowings made after the end of May normally miss the first generation of maggots but carrot rust fly is such a widespread pest that treatment of the seed drills with diazinon is advisable to give protection for 6–8 weeks. Carrots that are not to be lifted until fall should also be sprayed with trichlorphon in late August.

Caterpillars are troublesome on cabbages and should be controlled before they penetrate the hearts, where they are difficult to reach. Hand picking with a small number of plants or treatment with carbaryl, lindane, fenitrothion or trichlorphon is effective.

Celery leaf miner lives in the leaves of celery, parsnip and some herbs. Heavy attacks can be controlled by spraying with trichlorphon or dimethoate. Light infestations of celery leaf miner can be overcome by hand picking and burning affected leaves.

Colorado potato beetles are wide beetles with yellow and black stripes and black spots on the head. They lay clusters of orange eggs, from which red grubs emerge in the spring.

Both the larvae and adults feed on the leaves of potatoes, tomatoes, eggplants and peppers. Spray, or dust, with carbaryl.

Corn earworms are 2-in caterpillars with a yellow head and several body colors. They eat the silks and top kernels of corn, and also attack tomatoes and lima beans. Dusting or spraying with carbaryl when the silks start to appear usually controls them, but a repeat application may be necessary.

Cucumber beetles are of two kinds: one with black spots on a yellow background; the other with black stripes on yellow. Both eat the leaves of cucumbers and all related vegetables, and the grubs attack the stems. Dust young plants frequently with rotenone.

Cutworms are large, smooth, fat, soil-dwelling caterpillars, most often brown in color. They chew through the stems of cabbages and related vegetables, tomatoes and other seedling plants. Loosely wrap the stems of plants when set out with aluminum foil or kraft paper. The collars should extend from just below the soil to 4 in above.

Deer, rabbits, raccoons and woodchucks do extensive damage to suburban and country gardens. Repellents are not effective, and should not be applied to vegetables anyway. Control deer by erecting 8 ft high mesh fences around the garden. Rabbits can be controlled by fences that are buried 6 in below ground and extend 2 ft above ground. Trapping is the best control for raccoons and woodchucks.

Eelworms attack mainly members of the onion family but can also damage carrots, parsnips and beans. They are microscopic, worm-like creatures that live inside the stem and leaves. They cause the tissues to become soft and swollen, and infested plants usually rot off and die. There are no chemical controls available to amateur gardeners and infested plants should be burnt. Host plants, which include some weeds, should not be grown in ground infested by onion eelworms for at least two years.

European corn borers are whitish, 1-in caterpillars that eat corn tassels and tunnel into the ears. They may attack beans, too. Spray or dust with carbaryl when tassels appear and four times thereafter at five-day intervals.

Flea beetles Heavy infestation of these tiny

beetles, which eat small holes in the leaves of brassica seedlings, can be controlled with derris or lindane. Damage seldom occurs once the plants have developed beyond the seedling stage.

Gophers are burrowing rodents that eat roots, tubers and underground stems. They can be controlled by the use of traps and poisoned baits in the runs.

Hornworms are enormous green caterpillars that feed on tomato plants and, to some extend, on peppers, potatoes and eggplants. They are not easily seen, despite their large size, but partly eaten leaves are an indication that they are present. Look for them at night with a flashlight and pick them off by hand.

Leafhoppers are small, hopping insects that feed on beans, carrots, cucumbers, melons and potatoes. They stunt the plants and cause leaves to turn brown. Spraying with carbaryl or methoxychlor at weekly intervals controls them effectively.

Mexican bean beetles have yellow and black stripes and lay clusters of yellow eggs under bean leaves. Yellow grubs emerge from the eggs to feed on the foliage. Dust the undersides of beans with rotenone or carbaryl.

Mice In rural areas, mice can be troublesome, eating peas, beans and corn seeds. Chemical deterrents are seldom effective. Covering seeds with holly or other spiky leaves, or dipping seeds in kerosene and dusting them with alum prior to sowing may deter mice, but persistent trapping is the only long-term solution. Traps should be covered to prevent birds and pets being harmed.

Moles can be a considerable nuisance. Trapping in the runs is the only effective method of control.

Nematodes are microscopic soil insects that cause general sickness of many vegetables. Plants are stunted; leaves turn yellow; warty growths appear on roots and stems. Rotate crops annually wherever the insects are present. If they are a serious problem, fumigate the soil before planting. Growing marigold in the vegetable garden also helps.

Onion maggot (*Hylemya antiqua*) attacks all members of the onion family. Young plants may be killed by the maggots, and the bulbs of older onions are tunneled and made useless for consumption. Soil treatment with

diazinon or chlorpyrifos granules when sowing or planting will control this pest during the vulnerable early stages.

Pea and bean weevils feed by eating notches from the leaf margins of pea and broad bean plants. Control measures, using HCH are necessary only if seedlings are being attacked.

Pea moth caterpillars badly damage peas, eating the green peas and spoiling the crop, particularly of late-maturing varieties. Early-maturing crops usually escape damage because they flower before the pea moth lays its eggs. Peas that flower between mid-June and mid-August should be sprayed with fenitrothion 7–10 days after flowering starts.

Slugs, snails, woodlice and millipedes can destroy seedlings and attack many developing vegetable crops. Slugs can be controlled by using metaldehyde pellets along the rows. Lindane controls woodlice and millipedes.

Squash bugs are dark-brown insects which are also known as stink bugs because they have a bad smell when crushed. By sucking the sap of squashes and related plants, they cause leaves to wilt and die. Spray with carbaryl or malathion at the first appearance of the bugs and later when you find brown egg masses on the undersides of the leaves.

Squash vine borers are 1-in white caterpillars with brown heads that tunnel through the stems of squashes and related plants. The parents are red and orange, wasplike moths. Apply carbaryl or methoxychlor to 8 in plants and repeat at weekly intervals for a month.

Whitefly Brassicas, cucurbits, tomatoes and other vegetables are attacked by various whitefly species that may cause a black deposit of sooty mold on the leaves. Cabbage whitefly is a distinct species from the glasshouse whitefly that affects tomatoes and cucurbits, but both may be controlled by three or four sprays with pyrethroid compounds at seven day intervals. Under glass biological control with the wasp *Encarsia formosa* avoids the problems of pesticide residues and resistance.

Wireworms may occur in large numbers in grassland or weed infested areas. They attack the roots of a wide variety of vegetables and may seriously affect the quality of crops such as potatoes. Soil dressings of diazinon at planting or sowing will control infestations.

Glossary

Abort Failure to develop properly; usually refers to flowers or their parts.
Acid Describes soil with a pH of below 7.
Adventitious buds Growth buds that arise without any direct relation to the leaves, usually in response to a wound.
Adventitious roots Roots that develop from stems.
Aeration The process of spiking a lawn in order to allow air into the soil and relieve compaction.
Alkaline Describes soil with a pH over 7.
Annual A plant that completes its life-cycle within one growing season.
Anthers The pollen-producing structures at the apices of the stamens of a flower.
Anti-desiccant Chemicals used as a spray to reduce water loss when transplanting trees and shrubs in the dormant season. Especially useful with evergreens and conifers.
Apex The tip of a stem, hence apical bud, the uppermost bud on the stem, and apical shoot, the uppermost stem on a system of branches.
Apical bud The bud on a shoot.
Apical dominance Used of a terminal or apical bud which inhibits the growth of lateral buds and grows more rapidly than they do.
Axil The upper angle between a leaf, or leaf-stalk, and the stem from which it grows.
Bacterial Parasitic or saprophytic single-celled micro-organisms. Many are beneficial but some cause diseases.
Bark-ringing The removal of a ring of bark from the trunk of an unfruitful tree to check shoot growth.
Bare-root plant A plant lifted from the open ground (as opposed to a container-grown plant).
Bare rootstock Rootstock lifted from the open ground to be used for bench grafting.
Base dressing Fertilizer applied immediately before sowing or planting.
Bedding plant A plant used for temporary garden display.
Bench grafting Grafting on to a rootstock that is movable—that is, a pot-grown or a bare rootstock.
Biennial A plant that completes its life-cycle over two growing seasons.
Biennial bearer A tree bearing a good crop of blossom or fruit only in alternate years.
Blanching The exclusion of light from a plant to whiten the shoots.
Blindness A condition in which a shoot or bud fails to develop fully and aborts.
Bloom Either a blossom, or a natural white powdery or waxy sheen on many fruits and leaves, or an abnormal white powdery coating of fungus on galled leaves.
Bolting Producing flowers and seed prematurely.
Bonemeal Bones ground to a powder and used as a fertilizer.
Bottom heat The warmth, normally provided artificially, from under the compost in, for example, a propagator.
Bract A modified, usually reduced, leaf that grows just below the flowerhead.
Branched head A branch system on a tree in which there is no central leader shoot.
Brassica The cabbage, cauliflower and turnip genus of the Cruciferae.
Break The development of lateral shoots as a result of pruning a shoot to an auxillary bud.
Breastwood Shoots growing forward from plants trained against support structures.
Broadcast To distribute seed evenly over the entire seedbed, as opposed to sowing in rows.
Bud The embryo shoot, flower or flower cluster, hence growth bud, flower bud.
Budding A method of grafting using a single growth bud rather than part of a stem with several buds.
Bulb An underground storage organ that consists of layers of swollen fleshy leaves or leaf bases, which enclose the following year's growth buds.
Bud burst The period at the end of the dormant season when new buds begin to swell and produce leaves or flowers.
Bulbil A small bulb, formed in the leaf axil on a stem or in the inflorescence.
Bulblet Very small bulbs that develop below ground on some bulbs.
Bush tree A tree pruned to give a dwarf form with about 2–2½ft of clear stem.
Bushel An Imperial measure of volume equal to 1.28 cu ft; for example, the amount of compost that will fit into a box 22 in × 10 in × 10 in without compacting.
Calyx The outer whorl of a flower, consisting of sepals which may be free to the base or partially joined, as in tomato flowers.
Canker A sharply defined diseased area on a woody stem, which often has malformed bark.
Cap A hard crust on the soil surface.
Capillarity The process by which water will rise above its normal level.
Carpeting plant A plant whose stems take root as they spread; also known as a carpeter.
Catch crop A rapidly maturing crop grown between harvesting one vegetable and sowing or planting the next on the same ground.
Central leader The central, vertical, dominant stem of a tree.
Chard The young stems of salsify, seakale, beet or globe artichokes.
Chelated Describes a special formulation of plant nutrients, which will remain available in alkaline soils.
Chestnut compound A fungicide made up of 2 parts by weight fine copper sulphate and 11 parts by weight ammonium carbonate. Store for a few days before using at the rate of 1 oz to 2 gallons of water to prevent damping off in seedlings.
Chitting The germination or sprouting of seed prior to sowing.
Chlorophyll The green pigment present in most plants, by means of which they manufacture carbohydrates.
Climber A plant that climbs by clinging to objects by means of twining stems with hooks or tendrils, or more generally, any long-stemmed plant trained upwards.
Clone A plant propagated sexually, with identical characteristics to its parent.
Clump plant A deciduous plant that grows in spring from clusters of buds or an over-wintering rosette at the top of a rootstock.
Compost, garden Rotted organic matter used as an addition to or substitute for manure.
Compost seed and potting Mixtures of organic and inorganic materials, such as peat, sand, and loam, used for growing seeds, cuttings and pot plants.
Compound fertilizer One which contains all three major constituents needed for healthy growth, ie nitrogen, phosphorus and potassium.
Conifer A plant that bears its seeds in cones.
Contact insecticide An insecticide that kills pests by direct contact.
Contractile roots Roots of bulbs and corms that contract in length, thereby pulling the organ deeper into the soil.
Copper naphthenate A liquid timber preservative which is harmless to plants once it is dry, unlike creosote.
Coppicing The regular pruning of a tree or shrub close to ground level resulting in the production of a quantity of vigorous basal shoots.
Cordon A normally branched tree or shrub restricted by spur pruning to a single-stem.
Corm A solid, swollen stem-base, resembling a bulb, that acts as a storage organ.
Cotyledon A seed leaf; usually the first to emerge above ground on germination.
Crocking The use of small pieces of clay flower pot placed concave-side down in a pot or container over the drainage hole to facilitate drainage.
Crown Either the basal part of an herbaceous perennial plant from which roots and shoots grow, or the main branch system of a tree.
Cultivar *see* Variety.
Cultivator A tool used to break up the soil surface to improve its texture. A rotary cultivator, or rotavator, has revolving tines or blades and is power-driven.
Current year's growth/wood The shoots which have grown from buds during the present growing season.
Cutting A separated piece of stem, root, or leaf taken in order to propagate a new plant.
Deciduous Describes a plant that loses all its leaves at the end of the growing season.
Dead-head To prune the spent flowers or the unripe seedpods from a plant.
Dibber A tool that is pushed into the soil to make a hole in which to plant a seedling, cutting or small plant.
Dicotyledon A flowering plant that produces two seed leaves at germination.
Die-back The death of branches or shoots, beginning at their tips and spreading back towards the trunk or stem.
Disbudding The removal of surplus buds or shoots that are just beginning growth.
Dot plant Bedding plant used to give height or contrast to carpet plant arrangements.
Double leader Two shoots competing as leaders on a tree, each trying to assert apical dominance.
Dressing A material such as organic matter, fertilizer, sand or lime that is incorporated into the soil. A top dressing is applied to the surface only, without being dug in.
Dribble bar A sealed, perforated tube attached to a watering can spout that enables weedkiller or other liquid to be dribbled on to the plants or soil.
Drills Straight furrows, narrow and shallow, in which seeds are sown.
Dwarf pyramid A tree pruned to form a pyramid-shaped central-leader tree about 7 ft high.
Earth up Mounding earth around the base and stems of a plant.
Epiphyte (epiphytic) A plant that grows on another but gets no nourishment from it; e.g. an orchid growing on a branch of a tree. Other examples are lichens, mosses and some ferns.
Espalier A tree trained with a vertical main stem and tiers of horizontal branches.
Etiolation The blanching of a stem caused by the exclusion of light.
Evergreen A plant that retains its foliage for more than one year.
Eye Used to describe a growth bud, particularly of roses and vines.
F_1 hybrid A plant that is the result of a cross between two parent strains, usually with the best features of each. It does not breed true in further generations.
Fallowing Allowing land to remain uncropped for a period.
Family A group of related genera. For example, the genera *Poa* (meadow grass), *Festuca* (fescue) and *Agrostis* (bent) all belong to the family of grasses, Graminea.
Fan A shrub or tree in which the main branches are trained like the ribs of a fan against a wall, fence or other support system.
Fertilizer Material that provides plant food. It can be organic, i.e. derived from decayed plant or animal matter, or inorganic, i.e. made from chemicals.
Flowers of sulfur Pure yellow sulfur in finely powdered form, used to correct the pH of alkaline soils.
Flushes Irregular successive crops of flowers and fruit, as on perpetual strawberries.
Foliar feed A liquid fertilizer sprayed on to, and partially absorbed through, the leaves.
Foot The base of the main stem of an herbaceous plant.
Forcing The hastening of growth by providing warmth and/or excluding light.
Firable Describes a fine, crumbly soil with no hard or wet lumps.
Fritted trace elements A special formulation of plant nutrients, which will remain available to plants in alkaline soils.
Frost-lifting The loosening and lifting of plants in the soil after hard frost.
Fungicides A substance used for controlling diseases caused by fungi and some bacteria.
Fungus Any member of a group of non-flowering plants that, since they have no green colouring (chlorophyll), cannot manufacture their own food. Therefore, they are incapable of surviving independently and live on either another living organism or on decaying organic matter.
Gall An abnormal outgrowth of plant tissue.
Genus (plural genera) A group of allied species in botanical classification.
Germination The development of a seed into a seedling.
Grafting Propagation by uniting a shoot or single bud of one plant—the scion—with the root system and stem of another—the stock or root stock.
Growth bud A bud that gives rise to a shoot.
Growing point The extreme tip of roots or shoots.
Habit The natural mode of growth of a plant.
Half-hardy A plant unable to survive the winter unprotected but not needing all-year-round greenhouse protection.
Half-standard A tree grown with 3–4 ft of clear stem.
Harden off To acclimatize plants raised in warm conditions to colder conditions.
Hardy Describes a plant capable of surviving the winter in the open without protection.
Heeling in The storing of plant material, upright or inclined, in a trench which is then filled in with soil and firmed.
Herbaceous perennial *See* Perennial.

Glossary

Herbicide Synonym for weedkiller.

Hormone weedkiller Chemicals which, when applied to weeds, affect their growth, often causing the stems to extend rapidly before the plant collapses and dies.

Host A plant that harbours, or is capable of harbouring, a parasite.

Humidity The amount of water vapour in the atmosphere. Relative humidity is the amount of water in the atmosphere, relative to it being saturated, at a particular temperature. (Warm air will hold more water than cool air.)

Humus Fertile, organic matter that is in an advanced stage of decay.

Hybrid A plant produced by the cross fertilization of two species or variants of a species.

Incipient roots Roots that develop from stems; they frequently abort.

Inflorescence The part of a plant that bears the flowers.

Insecticides A substances used to kill injurious insects and some other pests.

John Innes Compounds Standard soil mixes that can be easily reproduced to give good results. Developed at the John Innes Horticultural Institute in 1939. Revolutionized the growing of plants in pots.

Lanceolate Describes a leaf that is much longer than it is wide, and is shaped like the head of a lance.

Larva The active immature stage of some insects. The larva of a butterfly, moth or sawfly is known as a caterpillar, a beetle or weevil larva as a grub, and a fly larva as a maggot.

Lateral A side growth that develops at an angle from the main stem of a tree.

Layering Propagating by inducing shoots to form roots while they are still attached to the parent plant.

Leader shoot The shoot that is dominating growth in a stem system, and is usually uppermost.

Leaching The removal of soluble minerals from the soil by water draining through it.

Leaf Axil See Axil.

Leaf-mould Well rotted leaves, which can be used as a mulch or added to the soil to improve its texture.

Leaf-fall The period when deciduous plants begin to shed their leaves.

Light The glass or plastic covering of a cold frame.

Lime A compound that contains calcium and/or magnesium, added to the soil to reduce acidity.

Line out To plant out young plants or cuttings in temporary positions.

Loam A fertile soil with balanced proportions of clay, sand and humus.

Long Tom A pot about half as deep again as a normal pot.

Maiden A one-year-old tree or shrub.

Manure Bulky material of animal origin added to soil to improve its structure and fertility.

Mature A plant that can produce flowers and, hence, reproduce sexually.

Mechanical digger See Cultivator.

Microclimate The climatic conditions in a particular small area.

Micro-organisms A microscopic animal or plant organism that can cause plant disease. Micro-organisms are beneficial when decomposing plant and animal residue to form humus.

Mole plough A plough pulled through the soil to form a drainage tunnel. Used on clay soils.

Monocotyledon A flowering plant that produces only one seed leaf.

Mosaic A patchy variation of normal green colour; usually a symptom of virus disease.

Mound layering An alternative term for stooling.

Mulch A top dressing of organic or inorganic matter, applied to the soil around a plant.

Mutant or Sport A plant that differs genetically from the typical growth of the plant that produced it.

Naturalized Describes plants grown in natural surroundings where they increase of their own accord and need little maintenance. Also plants established in an area, although they are not native to it.

Nitrate A nitrogen-containing fertilizer that can be natural, such as potassium or sodium, or synthetic, such as calcium nitrate.

Nymph The active, immature stage of some insects and mites.

Offsets Small bulbs produced at the base of the parent bulb; also a young plant developing laterally on the stem close to the parent.

Organic matter Matter consisting of, or derived from, living organisms. Examples include farmyard manure and leaf-mould.

Ornamental A plant grown for its decorative qualities.

Over-winter Refers to the means by which an organism survives winter conditions.

Pan A hard layer of soil beneath the surface.

Parasite An organism that lives on, and takes part or all of its food from, a host plant; usually to the detriment of the latter.

Pelleted seeds Small seeds coated to make them easier to handle for space sowing.

Perennial A plant that lives for more than three seasons.

Perlite A natural, sterile, granular medium derived from volcanic rock. Used as a rooting medium and an ingredient of potting and seed-sowing composts.

Pesticides A chemical used to kill pests; also generally for chemicals used to control pests and diseases.

Petiole The stalk of a leaf.

pH The degree of acidity or alkalinity. Below 7 on the pH scale is acid, above it is alkaline.

Phosphatic fertilizer Fertilizer with a high proportion of phosphorus.

Photosynthesis The process by which a green plant is able to make carbohydrates from water and carbon dioxide, using light as an energy source and chlorophyll as the catalyst.

Pinching (or Stopping) The removal of the growing tip of a shoot.

Planting mark The slight change in colour on the stem of a bare-root plant, indicating the depth at which it was formerly planted.

Plunge outside To bury container-grown plants up to the pot rims in ash, peat or sand bed to protect the roots from frost in winter.

Pollination The transference of pollen from the male to the female parts of a flower.

Pot-bound The condition reached by a pot plant when its roots have filled the pot and exhausted the available nutrients.

Potash (K_2O) Also called sulphate of potash. Essential for plant growth. Present in all balanced fertilizers.

Presser board A piece of flat wood with a handle used to firm and level compost.

Pricking out The transplanting and spacing out of seedlings.

Propagation The production of a new plant from an existing one, either sexually by seeds or asexually, for example by cuttings.

Proteins Organic nitrogenous compounds synthesized by plants from simple substances. An essential component of living cells.

Quicklime chalk or limestone which has been burnt in a kiln. It is caustic and will burn foliage and skin, so the milder hydrated lime is usually employed in correcting soil acidity.

Rambler Roses producing long, flexible basal canes, trained on walls, fences and screens.

Reaction The degree of acidity or alkalinity in soil or compost. Reaction is measured on the pH scale.

Recurrent flowering The production of several crops of flowers during one season more or less in succession.

Regulatory pruning Pruning to remove crossing, crowded and weak shoots and branches.

Relative Humidity See Humidity.

Renewal pruning Pruning to maintain a constant supply of young shoots.

Repotting Replacing of some of the compost around the roots of a pot-grown plant with fresh compost.

Resistant Describes a plant that is able to overcome completely or partially the effect of a parasitic organism or disorder. It also describes a pest or disease that is no longer controllable by a particular chemical.

Rhizome A creeping horizontal underground stem that acts as a storage organ.

Rhizomorph A root-like mass of fungal threads, by means of which certain fungi spread through the soil.

Riddle To sieve soil, compost or leaf-mould.

Ring culture A method of growing plants in bottomless pots known as rings. Nutrients are absorbed by the roots of the plant from the compost in the ring and water is taken up from the sand or pebbles on which the ring stands.

Ring pattern Circular areas of chlorosis, the centre of each remaining green. It is a symptom of some virus diseases.

Rod The main, woody stem of a vine.

Rootball The soil or compost ball formed among and around the roots of a plant.

Root cutting A piece of the root of a plant used for propagation.

Root-pruning Severing some or all of the main roots of a tree to reduce vigour.

Rooted tips The shoot tips of plants such as blackberries that have been buried in the soil and taken root to form a new plant.

Rootstock See Grafting.

Rose (spray head) The watering can or hose attachment producing a fine spray.

Rossette A small cluster of overlapping leaves, often close to ground level.

Rotavator See Cultivator.

Runner A rooting stem that grows along the surface of the soil, as in strawberries.

Run-off When spraying, the point at which a plant becomes saturated, and further liquid runs off on to the surrounding area.

Sap The fluid in living plants that transports nutrients to various parts of the plant.

Scab A roughened, crust-like, diseased area.

Scarifying The process of vigorously raking a lawn in order to remove thatch.

Scion See Grafting.

Scramblers Climbing plants that do not twine or bear tendrils, clambering up by pushing through surrounding trees and shrubs, e.g. the so-called climbing roses.

Seedcoat The tough, protective layer around a seed.

Seed dressing A fine powder applied to seeds before sowing to protect them from pests or diseases.

Seed drill A machine for sowing at regular intervals in rows.

Seedheads Faded flowerheads that have been successfully fertilized and contain seeds.

Seed leaf (syn. cotyledon) The first leaf or leaves produced by germinated seed.

Self-sterile Describes a plant whose pollen cannot fertilize its own female parts.

Semi-evergreen Describes a plant intermediate between evergreen and deciduous. It bears foliage throughout the year, but loses some leaves during the winter.

Sepal The outermost, leaf-like structures of a flower.

Sets Whole or part bulbs or tubers used for propagation.

Shrub A perennial plant with persistent woody stems branching from the base. If only the lower parts of the branches are woody and the upper shoots are soft and usually die in winter, it is known as a sub-shrub.

Silt Very fine soil formed from clay.

Snag A short stump of a branch left after incorrect pruning.

Soil profile Used to describe a cross-section of soil from surface to bed-rock, showing layers such as sub-soil, top-soil.

Species A group of closely related organisms within a genus. Abbreviations: sp. (singular) or spp. (plural).

Spit The depth of a normal digging spade, roughly equal to 10 in.

Spore A reproductive body of a fungus.

Sport See Mutant.

Spot-treat To treat a small defined area or a particular plant, usually with weedkiller, fungicide or pesticide.

Spreader A substance added to a spray to assist its even distribution over the target.

Spur A slow-growing short branch system that usually carries clusters of flower buds.

Stamen The male reproductive organ of a flower, comprising a stalk with an anther.

Standard A tree or shrub grown with 5–7 ft of clear stem.

Station sowing The individual sowing of seeds at a predetermined spacing in the site in which they will grow until pricking out or harvesting.

Stock See Grafting.

Stool The base of a plant, such as a cane fruit, that produces new shoots.

Stopping See Pinching.

Strain A distinct group within a species of fungus or eelworm.

Strike To take root, usually of cuttings.

Strike off To remove excess compost above the rim of a pot or seed tray.

Sub-lateral A side-shoot growing from a lateral shoot.

Sub-shrub See Shrub.

Sub-soil See Top-soil.

Sub-species A category intermediate between a variety and a species.

Succulent A condition in certain plants that has de-

267

Glossary/Acknowledgements

veloped as a response to a lack of readily available fresh water. A succulent plant is capable of storing relatively large quantities of water.

Sucker A shoot growing from a stem or root at or below ground level.

Suckering plant A plant that spreads by means of underground shoots, suckers or stolons.

Sump Syn. for soakaway.

Syn. Abbreviation for synonym.

Systemic fungicide or insecticide A chemical which permeates a plant's sap stream and kills biting or sucking insects.

Tap root The primary vertical root of a plant; also any strong-growing vertical root.

Terminal bud, shoot, flower The uppermost, usually central, growth on a stem. (*See* Apex.)

Thatch On a lawn, a layer of dead or living organic matter, along with debris, found between the roots and foliage of the grass.

Thin To reduce the number of seedlings, buds, flowers, fruitlets or branches.

Tilth A fine crumbly surface layer of soil. It is produced by weathering or careful cultivation.

Tine The prong of a fork, rake or other tool.

Tolerant Describes either a plant that can live despite infection by a parasitic organism, or a fungus that is unaffected by applications of a certain fungicide.

Top dressing *See* Dressing.

Top-soil The upper layer of dark fertile soil in which plants grow. Below this lies the sub-soil, which is lighter in colour, lacks organic matter and is often low in nutrients.

Transpiration The continual loss of water vapour from leaves and stems.

Trace elements Food materials required by plants only in very small amounts.

True leaves Leaves typical of the mature plant as opposed to simpler seed leaves.

Truss A cluster of flowers or fruit.

Tuber A swollen underground stem or root that acts as a storage organ and from which new plants or tubers may develop.

Turgid Plant material that contains its full complement of water and is not therefore under stress.

Union The junction between rootstock and scion or between two scions grafted together.

Var Abbreviation for the botanical classification *varietas* (variety); it refers only to naturally occurring varieties.

Variegated Describes leaves with coloured markings, usually white or cream, due to an absence of chlorophyll.

Variety A distinct variant of a species; it may be a cultivated form (a cultivar) or occur naturally (varietas).

Vegetative growth Leaf and stem growth as opposed to flowers or fruit.

Vermiculite A sterile medium made from expanded mica. It is light, clean and moisture retentive and is used in seed, cutting and potting composts.

Virus Disease-causing organism, not visible to the naked eye, that may live in plants and less often in the soil.

Watering-in To water around the stem of a newly transplanted plant to settle soil around the roots.

Water shoot A vigorous, sappy shoot growing from an adventitious or dormant bud.

Water stress A variable condition of wilting in which plant material is losing water faster than it can take it up.

Water table The level in the soil below which the soil is saturated by ground water.

Weedkiller, contact action A weedkiller that kills only those green parts of plants with which it comes into contact.

Weedkiller, residual A weedkiller that acts through the soil and remains effective for a period ranging from a few weeks (short-term residual weedkillers) to several months (long-term residual weedkillers).

Weedkiller, selective A weedkiller that kills only certain types of plant, leaving others unharmed.

Weedkiller, translocated A weedkiller that is absorbed through the leaves and stems and is rapidly carried via the sap-stream to kill the whole plant.

Wetting agent A chemical added to a liquid that is to be sprayed, in order to improve the spray's adherence to a plant.

Wind-rock The loosening of a plant's root system by strong winds.

The Royal Horticultural Society and Publishers can accept no liability either for failure to control pests, diseases or weeds by any crop protection methods or for any consequences of their use. We specifically draw our readers' attention to the necessity of carefully reading and accurately following the manufacturer's instructions on any product.

Acknowledgements

Some of the artwork in this book has been based on photographs specially commissioned from the Harry Smith Horticultural Photographic Collection.

The publishers also wish to thank the many companies, academic institutions, public bodies and individuals who supplied illustration references.

Artists

Arka Cartographic Ltd, Nick Bartlett, Janet Blakeley, Lindsay Blow, Linda Broad, Paul Buckle, Ray Burrows, Charles Chambers, Harry Chlow, Pamela Dowson, Chris Forsey, Tony Graham, William Giles, Vana Haggerty, Eric Howley, Roger Hughes, Edwina Keene, Roman Kowalczyk, Terri Lawlor, Alan Male, Sandra Pond, Ed Roberts, Colin Salmon, Mike Saunders, Anne Savage, Bob Scott, Paul Stafford, Ralph Stobart, Stonecastle Graphics, Rod Stutterby, Cynthia Swaby, Lorna Turpin, Venner Artists, West One Arts, Alan White and John Woodcock.

Index

Almonds, cultivation 136
   fan-trained tree 136–7, 138–9, 255
   frost protection 137
   harvesting and storage 138
   in cold greenhouses 243
   in cool greenhouses 255
   pests and diseases 138
   planting 137
   pollination nature 114
   propagation 138
   pruning after harvesting 138
   pruning and training 136
   thinning 138
   varieties 139
Anemones, varieties suitable for root
   cuttings 180
Angelica 86
Apples, biennial bearing 129
   central leader tree 120
   cultivation 127
   grassing down orchard 128, 129
   harvesting and storing 128
   maypoling 128
   overcrowded spur systems 122
   pests and diseases 128–9
   planting and staking 116, 125
   planting and training oblique cordons 121
   pollination nature 114
   propagation 129
   protection from wasps and birds 128
   pruning 118–25 passim
   restricted tree forms 117
      cordon 117, 121–2, 125–6
      dwarf pyramid 117, 125–6
      espalier 123–4
   rootstocks 116, 121, 123, 125
   selecting tree 118, 121, 123
   selecting tree form 117
   site 116
   soil 116
   soil preparation and planting 116, 118, 120, 123
   spacing 121, 123, 125
   structure of blossom 114
   support system 121, 123
   thinning 128
   trees in open 117, 118
   varieties 116, 117, 118, 119
Apricots 140
   cultivation 140
   harvesting 140
   in cold greenhouses 243
   pests and diseases 140
   pollination nature 114
   varieties 140
Asparagus 50–1, 185
   aftercare 51
   cultivation 50–1
   harvesting 51
   pests and diseases 51
   sowing 50
   varieties 50
Asparagus peas 60, 61
   cultivation and harvesting 61
Azaleas, evergreen 242

Basic tools 20–1
Basil 86
Beans, see Broad, Bush, Lima, and Runner beans
Bedding plants in cool greenhouses 250–1
   germination 250
   growing from seed 250–1
   overwintering 251
   picking out 250–1
   planting out 251
   propagation 251
   seed sowing 250
   sowing plan 250
   use of peat blocks 251
Beets, cultivation 72
   globular 72
   harvesting 72
   long 72
Black currants 101–2
   cultivation 101, 102
   early 101
   frost and bird protection 101
   harvesting 101
   late 102
   mid-season 101
   pests and diseases 101
   pollination 101
   propagation 101
Blackberries 99–100
   cultivation 99, 100
   harvesting 99
   pests and diseases 99
   pollination 99
   propagation 99
Blueberries 107–8
   cultivation 107–8
   harvesting and storing 108
   high bush 107
   pests and diseases 108
   varieties 107
Borage 87
Boysenberries 99
Brassica growing 38
   permanent (planting) bed 38
   seedbed 38
   transplanting 38
Brassicas, pests and diseases 45
Broad beans, autumn-sown 59
   cultivation 58–9
   harvesting 59
   pests and diseases 59
   single and double rows 58–9
   varieties 58
Broccoli, harvesting 46
   pests and diseases 46
   winter 44
Broom pruning 220
Brussels sprouts 42–3
   aftercare 43
   conventional 42, 43
   cultivation 42–3
   harvesting 43
   hybrids 42, 43
Bush beans, cultivation 54–5
   harvesting 55

   pests and diseases 55
   support systems 55
   varieties 54

Cabbages 39–41
   Chinese 39, 41
   harvesting 39, 41
   red 39, 41
   Savoys 39
   spring 39, 40
   storing 41
   storing varieties 39
   summer 39
   summer/fall varieties 39
   types 39
   winter 39, 41
Calamondrin, see Citrus fruits
Camellias 241
Carrots 68
   cultivation 68
   growing in heated frame 256
   harvesting 68
   pests and diseases 68
Cauliflowers 44–5
   autumn 44
   cultivation 44–5
   Purple Head 44, 46
   summer 44–5
Ceanothus pruning 234
Celery, cultivation 52
   harvesting 52
   pests and diseases 52
   self-blanching 52
   trench varieties 52
Chaenomeles pruning 235
Chayote or mirliton, see Squashes
Cherries, see Duke, Sour, and Sweet cherries
Chicory, witloof 247
Chives 87
Chrysanthemums 252–3
   bush 253
   winter-flowering 253
Citrus fruits 142–3
   cultivation 142–3
   frost protection 143
   harvesting 143
   pests and diseases 143
   tree selection 142
Clematis 228
   pruning 229–31
Climbing and wall plants 228
   training and pruning 228
Cloche use 259
   soil preparation 259
   storing cloches 259
   ventilation 259
   watering 259
   yearly plan 259
Collards 47
Corn 62, 257
   cultivation 62
   F₁ hybrids 62
   harvesting 62
Cornus alba pruning 225

Cotinus coggygria pruning 224
Crabapple pollination 114
Cranberries, cultivation 108
   harvesting and storing 108
   preparing cranberry bed 108
   varieties 108
Crop rotation 34
   catch cropping 34
   grouping crops 34
   intercropping 34
Cucumbers 77
   cultivation 77
   harvesting 77
   in cold greenhouses 247
   pests and diseases 77
Cultivation techniques 22–5
   blanching 22–3
   disbudding 24
   feeding 24–5
   forcing 23
   hilling or earthing up 22
   hoeing 22
   mulching 25
   pollination 24, 25
   pinching 24, 25
   ring culture 23
   thinning 24, 25
Cyclamen 252

Dewberries 99
Digging 16–17
   no-dig gardening 17
Dill 87
Drainage 9, 10–11
Duke cherries 133–4
   cultivation 133
   harvesting 134
   pests and diseases 134
   pollination 134
   propagation 134
   protection against frost and birds 134
   pruning 133–4
   varieties 134

Eggplants 85
   cultivation and harvesting 85
   in cold greenhouses 247
   pests and diseases 85

Fennel 87
Fertilizers 13, 176
Frame use 256–8
   crops in cold frame 257
   cuttings 257–8
   early crops in heated frame 256, 257
   hardening off 257, 258
   heating 256
   light and shading 257
   overwintering and storage 258
   plunge bed 258
   raising seed 257
   siting 256
   ventilation 256
   watering 256

Index

Fruit planning 90–1
  aspect 90–1
  buying plants 91
  fruit against walls and fences 90
  planning small garden 91
  spacing 90
  tree forms 90
  wiring walls and fences 91
  yield 90
Fruit tree planting, against wall 115
  heeling in 115
  preparation 115
  staking 115
  time to plant 115
Fruits, in cold greenhouses 243
  in cool greenhouses 254, 255
  soft 92
  tree 113
Fuchsias 242

Garden compost 14–15
  building heap 14, 15
  compost bins 14, 15
  compostable materials 14–15
  green manure 13, 15
  leaf-mold 15
  making 14
  using 15
Garden peas 60–1
  cultivation 60–1
  harvesting 61
  pests and diseases 61
Garlic 66
Gooseberries 105–6
  cultivation 105–6
  pests and diseases 106
  propagation 106
  protection against frost and birds 106
  pruning 106
  thinning and harvesting 106
  types 105
  varieties 105
  weed control 106
Grapefruit, see Citrus fruits
Grapes 109–11
  American bunch grapes 109–10
  cultivation 109, 110, 111
  harvesting 111
  in cold greenhouses 243
  maintenance 109
  Muscadine grapes 110–11
  pests and diseases 111
  soil suitable for 109
  staking and planting 109
  thinning 111
  training and pruning 109
  training systems 109–10, 111
  varieties 109, 110, 111
  Vinifera grapes 111
Greenhouse growing 173, 236
  cleaning greenhouse 236–7
  cold greenhouse 238–47
    conditions and choice of plants 238–9
    flowering plants from seed 239

fruits 243
  ornamentals 240–2
  plants for 239
  tomatoes 244–5
  vegetables and salads 246–7
  year in 238–9
cool greenhouse 248–55
  bedding plants 250–1
  fruits and vegetables 254–5
  growing plants 249
  management 248–9
  ornamentals 252–3
  year in 248–9
environmental control 173
pest and disease control 237
Ground cover 163–9
  maintenance 165
    fertilizer use 165
    propagation 165
    pruning 165
    weed control 165
  planting and spacing 164
    planting distances 164
    planting method 164
    when to plant 164
  preparing site 163
    improving soil 163
    planning 163
    weeding 163
  problem sites, with plants for 166–70
    bulbs in 170
    exposed coastal gardens 169–70
    exposed inland gardens 170
    hot and dry 167–8
    large areas 169
    moist 166–7
    rose beds in 170
    shaded 166
    slopes and banks 168–9
Growing under glass 236–58
  bedding plants 250–1
  daily routine 236
  fruits 243, 254, 255
  hygiene 236–7
  ornamentals 240–2, 252–3
  pest and disease control 237
  tomatoes 244–5
  using frames 256–8
  vegetables and salads 246–7, 254, 255

Heather pruning 227
Heathland fruits 107–8
Hedges, aftercare 32
  clipping and pruning 33
  hedging plants 33
  planting 32
  pruning 32
  screens and windbreaks 33
Herbaceous plants, division of 188–9
  suitable for taking root cuttings 180
Herbs 86–9
  in cold greenhouses 246
  propagating 86
Hoe 20–1, 22

Honeysuckle pruning 234
Hydrangea pruning 220

Ivy 228

Japanese maple pruning 218

Kale, cultivation 47
  curly 47
  harvesting 47
  plain 47
Kerria pruning 220
Kumquat, see Citrus fruits

Lavender pruning 227
Lawn grasses 150–1
  cool-season· 150
  extreme-season 151
  hardest-wearing 151
  most tolerant of close mowing 151
  warm-season 150–1
Lawn growing from plugs 152
Lawn growing from seed 156
  advantages and disadvantages 156
  after germination 156
  damping-off diseases 156
  first season of growth 156
  sowing 156
  when to sow 156
Lawn growing from sod 153–5
  advantages and disadvantages 152
  before and after laying 153
  buying sod 153
  laying 153, 154–5
  seedling sod 155
  trimming sod 153
  when to sod 153
Lawn growing from sprigs 152
Lawn month-by-month guide 158
Lawn moss control 162
  mosskillers 162
Lawn mowing 159–60
  composting mowings 159
  frequency 159
  height of cut 159
  method 160
  problems 160
  producing banded finish 160
  removing mowings 159
  retarding growth 160
  seasonal guide 160
Lawn site preparation 146–9
  clearing site 146
  digging 146
  draining 149
  final preparation 147
  firming soil 149
  grading 146, 147
  levelling 146, 148
  pre-sowing fertilizer 147
  soil pH 146–7
  terracing 149
Lawn weed control 157, 161
  annual broad-leaved weeds 157

grass weeds 157
  in new lawns 157
  newly laid turf and 157
  perennial weeds 157
  spot-treating 161
  weedkillers 161
Leeks 67
  harvesting 67
  pests and diseases 67
  planting on flat 67
  sowing and planting 67
Lemon, see Citrus fruits
Lettuces 35–7
  cultivation 35, 37
  in cold greenhouses 246
  pests and diseases 36
  protected 36
  spacing 35–6
  types 35, 36
  varieties 35
Lilies, bulblet- and bulbil-producing 187
Lima beans 59
Lime, see Citrus fruits
Loganberries 99

Mandarin, see Citrus fruits
Marjoram 88
Marrows, see Squashes
Melons 112
  cultivation and harvesting 112
  in cold greenhouses 243
  in cool greenhouses 254
  in open 112
  pests and diseases 112
  under clothes 112
  varieties 112
Mint 88, 185
Moss control 162
Moving and storing plants 27
  moving trees and shrubs 27
Mustard and cress 246

Nectarines, cultivation 136
  fan-trained tree 136–7, 138–9, 225
  frost protection 137
  harvesting 138
  in cold greenhouses 243
  in cool greenhouses 255
  pests and diseases 138
  planting 137
  pollination nature 114
  propagation 138
  pruning after harvesting 138
  pruning and training 136
  thinning 138
  varieties 137–9

Okra 254–5
Onions 63–5
  autumn-sown 63, 64
  cultivation 63
  growing from sets 63–4
  onion sets 63, 65
  pests and diseases 64

Index

pickling 63
potato onion 64
ripening and storage 65
spring 64, 65
spring-sown 63, 64
transplanted 64
tree onion 64
Orange, see Citrus fruits
Ornamentals 240—2
in cold greenhouses 240—2
biennials 240
bulbs 240—1
growing annuals from seed 240
in cool greenhouses 252—3

Parsley 88
Parsnips 69
cultivation and harvesting 69
exhibition vegetables 69
pests and diseases 69
Passion fruit, harvesting and storage 141
outdoor cultivation 141
pests and diseases 141
pollination 141
Patty pans, see Squashes
Peaches, cultivation 136
fan-trained tree 136—7, 138—9, 255
frost protection 137
harvesting 138
in cold greenhouse 243
in cool greenhouse 255
pests and diseases 138
planting 137
pollination nature 114
propagation 138
pruning after harvesting 138
pruning and training 136
thinning 138
varieties 137—9
Pears, biennial bearing 129
central leader tree 120
cultivation 127
grassing down orchard 128, 129
harvesting and storing 128
maypoling 128
overcrowded spur systems 122
pests and diseases 129
planting and staking 116, 125
planting and training oblique cordons 121
pollination nature 114
propagation 129
protection from wasps and birds 128
pruning 118—25 passim
restricted tree forms 117
cordon 117, 121—2, 125—6
dwarf pyramid 117, 125—6
espalier 123—4
rootstocks 117, 120, 121
selecting tree 118, 121, 123
selecting tree form 117
site 116
soil preparation and planting 116, 118, 120, 123
spacing 121, 123, 125

support system 121, 123
thinning 128
trees in open 117, 118
varieties 116—19 passim
Pecans, cultivation 144
harvesting 144
pests and diseases 144
varieties 144
Peas, see Asparagus peas and Garden peas
Pelargoniums 242
Peppers 84
cultivation and harvesting 84
hot 84
pests and diseases 84
sweet 84, 247
Perovskia pruning 222
creating framework 222
Pests and diseases 260—5
chemical control 260, 263
precautions 260
fruit diseases 260—2
fruit pests 262
pesticides and fungicides 263
vegetable diseases 263
vegetable pests 264—5
see also under Growing under glass, Lawn weed control, and various fruit and vegetable entries
Physalis, cultivation and harvesting 145
pests and diseases 145
Plant placing 28—9
Plant protection 26
Plums 130—2
beach plums 132
classification 130
cultivation 130—1
European 130
feeding and watering 131
harvesting and storing 132
Japanese 130, 131
native 130, 132
pests and diseases 132
plum fan 132
pollination 114, 130
propagation 132
protection against birds 132
pruning 131
pyramid plums 131
sandcherry-plum hybrids 132
supporting the branches 132
thinning fruits 131—2
Pollarding 225
Pollination, fruit tree specifics 114
groups 114
hand 114
incompatibility groups 114
ineffective pollinators 114
Popcorn 62
Potatoes 74—6
cultivation 74, 75
early varieties 74
growing in pots 76
growing under black polyethylene 76
harvesting 74—5
main crop varieties 74

non-cultivation system for 76
out-of-season 76
pests and diseases 75
sprouting 76
tuber 184
Primulas 252
Propagation, bulblets and bulbils 187
composts 174
sieving peat 174
corms 186
cormels 186
developing seed 178—9
germination 178
hardening off 179
pricking out 178—9
seed leaves 178
division 188—9
herbaceous plants with fibrous crowns 188
herbaceous plants with fleshy crowns 188
Irishman's cuttings 189
naturally dividing alpines 189
semiwoody herbaceous plants 189
environmental control 173
cold frames 173
greenhouses 173
mist propagation units 173
polyethylene tents and tunnels 173
propagators 173
fertilizers 176
foliar embryos 201
establishing naturally produced plantlets 201
stimulating plantlet development 201
where development can take place 201
grafting 202—3
whip-and-tongue 202, 203
greenwood cuttings 178
layering 191
simple 191—2
tip 193
ways to guide stem 191
leaf petiole cuttings 200
making stem cuttings 194—5
heel 195
leaf bud 194
mallet 195
offsets 190
rhizomes 185
root cuttings 180—2
aftercare 182
obtaining cutting material 181
planting 182
preparing plant 180—1
recognizing top 181
size 181
taking 181
treatment 182
when to take 180
rooting hormones 175
runners 174
semiripe wood cuttings 199
softwood cuttings 196—7
sowing in containers 177
tools and equipment 172

tuberous roots 183
tubers 184
tubercles 184
wounding 175
Pruning 204—35
ceanothus 234
chaenomeles 234
clematis 229—31
climbing and wall plants 228
honeysuckle 234
pyracantha 234
roses 204—15
shrubs 216—27
wisteria 232—3
see also under various flower, fruit, and shrub entries
Pumpkins 80, 82
cultivation 82
harvesting 82
pests and diseases 82
Pyracantha pruning 235

Quinces, pollination nature 114

Radishes 73
Rake 20, 21
Raspberries 96—8
cultivation 96, 98
ever-bearing 97, 98
feeding and watering 97
harvesting 97
initial pruning 97
pests and diseases 98
propagation 97
pruning and training 97
Scandinavian fence system for 97
selecting healthy plants 98
standard varieties 96
support systems 97
supporting the canes 96—7
Red and white currents 103—4
cultivation 103
frost and bird protection 104
harvesting 104
pests and diseases 104
pollination 104
propagation 104
pruning 103
varieties 103
weed control 104
Rhubarb 53
cultivation 53
forcing 53
harvesting 53
main crop varieties 53
pests and diseases 53
Rock gardens 30—1
construction 30—1
maintenance 31
planting 31
scree beds 31
types 30
Rose pruning 204—15
autumn 205

Index

blind shoots 205
climbers and ramblers 208—11
  horizontal training 211
  vigorous climbers 211
exhibition 205
floribundas 205, 207
hybrid perpetuals 206
hybrid teas 205, 206
species and shrub roses 212—14
standard roses 215
  weeping standards 215
suckers 204
summer 205
winter 205
Rosemary 89
Rubus cockburnianus pruning 225
Runner beans 56—7
  cultivation 56—7
  early crops 56
  harvesting 57
  pests and diseases 57
  pinched beans 57
  support systems 56—7
  varieties 56
Rutabagas 70, 71
  cultivation 70
  pests and diseases 70
  shoots as greens 71

Sage 89
Salads, in cool greenhouses 246—7
  leaf crops 246
  pods 246—7
    raising seed 247
    root crops and bulbs 246
    vegetable fruits 247
Satsuma, *see* Citrus fruits
Scallions, *see* Onions, spring
Seakale 246
Shaddock, *see* Citrus fruits
Shallots 66
  cultivation and harvesting 66
Shrub pruning 216—27
  deciduous 218—25
    pollarding 225
  evergreen 226—7
    dead-heading 226
    training 226
Soft fruits 92
  clearing site 92
  planting 92
  protection against birds 92
  suitable site for 92
Soil 8—9, 12—13
  acidity and alkalinity 8
  adding organics 9
  drainage 9
  formation 8
  humus 8
  improving 12—13
  life in 8
  nutrients in 9
  panning 9
  profile 8

sandy 8
testing 8
types 8
water cycle 9
weather's effect on 7
Sour cherries 135
  cultivation 135
  pollination nature 114
  pruning 135
  varieties 135
  see Sweet cherries for feeding, watering,
    protection, thinning, harvesting, propagation,
    and pests and diseases
Southern peas 83
  cultivation and harvesting 83
  pest and diseases 83
Spinach 48—9
  cultivation 48—9
  fall 48
  harvesting 49
  New Zealand 48
  pests and diseases 49
  summer 48
  Swiss chard 48, 49
  varieties 48
  winter 48
Squashes 80—2
  chayote or mirliton 80, 81
  cultivation 80, 81, 82
  custard marrow 80
  harvesting 80, 81, 82
  marrow 80
  patty pans 80
  pests and diseases 80, 82
  pumpkin, *see* separate entry
  varieties 80
  winter squash 82
  yellow squash 80
  zucchini 80
Strawberries 93—5
  Alpine 95
  cultivation 93—4, 95
  ever-bearing 95
  harvesting 94, 95
  in cold greenhouses 243
  in cool greenhouses 254
  June-bearing 93
  late 94
  mid-season 93—4
  propagation 94, 95
  standard 93
  varieties 94
  winter protection 94
  work at end of season 94
Subshrubs, suitable for taking root cuttings 180
Swedes, *see* Rutabagas
Sweet bay 89
Sweet cherries 133—4
  cultivation 133
  harvesting 134
  pests and diseases 134
  pollination 114, 134
  propagation 134
  protection against frost and birds 134

pruning 133—4
varieties 133
Sweet potatoes 83
  cultivation and harvesting 83
  pests and diseases 83

Tangelo, *see* Citrus fruits
Tangerine, *see* Citrus fruits
Tarragon 88
Thyme 89
Tomatoes 78—9
  dwarf varieties 79
  harvesting 79
  in cold greenhouses 244—5
    harvesting 245
    pests and diseases 245
    planting 244
    pollination and fruit setting 245
    raising plants 244
    stopping 245
    support 245
    training systems 245
    trimming and de-leafing 245
    watering and feeding 244—5
  pests and diseases 79
  raising plants 78—9
Tree fruits 113
  choice of site 113
  fruit under glass 113
  pollination 113
  protection against birds 113
  pruning and training 113
  rootstocks 113
  storage 113
  wall- and fence-trained trees 113
Trees, suitable for taking root cuttings 180
Trowel 21
Turnips 70, 71
  cultivation 70
  early bunching 70
  main crop 70—1
  pests and diseases 70
  tops as spring greens 71

Vegetables, in cold greenhouses 246—7
    leaf crops 246
    pods 246—7
    raising seed 247
    root crops and bulbs 246
    vegetable fruits
  in cool greenhouses 254, 255
  see also individual entries

Watering 18—19
  growing plants 18, 19
  plants on susceptible sites 18, 19
  techniques 18—19
  timing 18
  use of natural sources 19
Watermelons 83
Weather and climate 6—7
  effect of altitude 7
  effect on soil 7
  frost 7

hardiness of plants and 6
major factors 6
microclimate 6, 7
rainfall 7
record-keeping 7
sun and shade 6—7
sun angles 6
urban heat 7
wind 7
windbreaks 6
zones of hardiness 6
Weed control 171
  annual weeds 171
  chemical use 171
  digging 171
  ground cover 165
  hoeing 171
  lawns 157, 161
  moss control 162
  mulching 171
  perennial weeds 171
Wheelbarrow 21
White currants, *see* Red and white currants
Winter endive 246, 257
Wisteria pruning 232—3

Yams, *see* Sweet potatoes
Youngberries 99

Zucchini, *see* Squashes